REAL TEXTS
READING AND WRITING ACROSS THE DISCIPLINES

Dean Ward
Calvin College

Elizabeth Vander Lei
Calvin College

With contributions by
William J. Vande Kopple

Longman

Boston   Columbus   Indianapolis   New York   San Francisco   Upper Saddle River
Amsterdam   Cape Town   Dubai   London   Madrid   Milan   Munich   Paris   Montreal
Toronto   Delhi   Mexico City   São Paulo   Sydney   Hong Kong   Seoul   Singapore   Taipei   Tokyo

Executive Editor: Lynn M. Huddon
Senior Marketing Manager: Sandra McGuire
Senior Supplements Editor: Donna Campion
Production Manager: Denise Phillip
Project Coordination, Text Design, and Electronic Page Makeup: Laserwords Maine
Cover Design Manager: Wendy Ann Fredericks
Cover Designer: Nancy Sacks
Cover Photos: *lower right photo:* © iStockphoto; all other photos © Fotalia
Photo Researcher: Poyee Oster
Senior Manufacturing Buyer: Roy Pickering
Printer and Binder: R. R. Donnelley & Sons/Harrisonburg
Cover Printer: R. R. Donnelley & Sons/Harrisonburg

Library of Congress Cataloging-in-Publication Data

Ward, Dean.
   Real texts : reading and writing across the disciplines / Dean Ward,
Elizabeth Vander Lei; With contributions by William J. Vande Kopple. —
2nd ed.
      p. cm.
   Includes index.
   ISBN-13: 978-0-205-02069-0
   ISBN-10:   0-205-02069-0
   1. English language—Rhetoric—Problems, exercises, etc. 2. Report
writing—Problems, exercises, etc. 3. Interdisciplinary approach in
education. I. VanderLei, Elizabeth. II. Vande Kopple, William J. III. Title.

PE1408.W3213 2011
808'.0427—dc22
                                                    2010053117

Longman
is an imprint of

www.pearsonhighered.com

1 2 3 4 5 6 7 8 9 10—DOH—14 13 12 11
ISBN-13: 978-0-205-02069-0
ISBN-10: 0-205-02069-0

Why Do You Need This Edition?

If you're wondering why you should buy this new edition of *Real Texts*, here are a few great reasons!

- Twenty new readings offer contemporary and accessible models of writing in various disciplines, addressing current issues such as the intellectual and physical effects of video gaming, crisis management in the Obama administration, democracy and education, and more.

- Chapter 1 now provides specific reading strategies that you can use to improve your ability to read college-level texts efficiently and effectively.

- Chapter 2 also provides concrete writing strategies that you can use to overcome writer's block, to make your point more clearly and persuasively, and to organize and present your work. It also includes a new sample student paper that's annotated to highlight important writing strategies that you can use when doing your own writing in different college courses.

- Chapters 3–13 give you opportunities to see how writers work in a range of different academic disciplines. Each chapter focuses on one discipline and one particular writing "lesson" or strategy. Annotated student and professional readings in each chapter and a range of different kind of assignments help you adapt the disciplinary strategies that you learn in each chapter to your own writing.

- A new Chapter 10 on Media Studies introduces the increasingly important skill of analyzing visual images and conveying your analysis to others.

- A new appendix, Citing Sources and Avoiding Plagiarism, helps you understand when and why you should document the sources that you use in your writing and also shows you how and why to avoid plagiarizing the work of others.

CONTENTS

ALTERNATE CONTENTS—BY DISCIPLINARY GROUPS

READING AND WRITING IN THE PROFESSIONS

PREFACE

We believe that every academic discipline produces effective writing. Students who study effective texts from a variety of academic disciplines can use the distinctive rhetorical strategies that make these texts effective—both in school and on the job.

WHAT'S NEW IN THE SECOND EDITION?

- Twenty of the almost 50 readings in the text are new to this edition. The new readings enhance the coherence of each chapter's topic, they focus on areas of student interest, and they offer greater accessibility to writing in disciplines that can be challenging to students.

  Support for the readings (introductions, annotations, and reading response questions) has also been extensively revised to increase students' comprehension.

- The introductory chapters in Part One have been completely rethought and reorganized. Chapter 1 introduces students to "Rhetorical Reading" by providing a handy chart of Key Rhetorical Concepts, an expanded set of reading strategies that correspond to those concepts, an article about the reading habits of college students, and a writing assignment that asks students to try out these concepts and strategies. Chapter 2 introduces students to "Rhetorical Writing" by providing an expanded set of composing strategies that correspond to the Key Rhetorical Concepts, an essay by a student in a first-year writing course, and a writing assignment that asks students to explore their expertise as an academic writer.

- In Part Two, the opening of each discipline-specific chapter has also been completely revised. Now, Chapters 3 through 13 open with an exercise that draws students into the dance of the discipline. These exercises allow students to experience the rhetorical strategies practiced in each discipline and prepare them for each chapter's portable rhetorical lesson.

The sections on Portable Rhetorical Lessons all have been completely rewritten and reformatted to help students better understand how the lessons are practiced in the disciplines and how they can apply the lessons in their own writing.

Each chapter also explains how the chapter's Portable Rhetorical Lesson is connected to the Key Rhetorical Concepts described in Chapters 1 and 2.

- Chapter 10: A new chapter on Media Studies gives students and faculty the opportunity to learn strategies for analyzing images.

- The Appendix, "Citing and Documenting Sources: Avoiding Plagiarism," explains the basic elements of all citation and documentation styles and encourages students to credit sources as a way for joining academic conversations rather than simply avoiding plagiarism. The student-written essays in Chapters 2 and 5 present, respectively, examples of papers formatted in MLA and APA style.

WHAT HAS STAYED THE SAME?

Principles

Real Texts.   This book contains real academic, professional, and public texts—what professors, students, and professionals write every day. Reading these selections, students learn how writers from a variety of disciplines and professions use writing effectively.

Best Practices.   This book affirms that good writing happens in all academic disciplines, and that the "best practices" of these disciplines provide important rhetorical lessons for all writers. As students observe these best practices, they expand their ability to read effectively. When students enact these practices in their own writing, they follow the Aristotelian advice to seek "*all* available means of persuasion."

Writing Creates Change.   Professional writing recognizes and solves problems. Unfortunately, students rarely write with the hope that their writing somehow matters outside the classroom. Without that belief, students are not motivated to improve their writing. These real-world readings encourage students to develop their own rhetorical skills by persuading them that writing makes a difference.

Rhetoric as Course Content.   These readings showcase particular rhetorical lessons from the academic disciplines that students are likely to encounter as undergraduates. Topics of individual chapters range across classic and contemporary issues, but the book is really *about* the rhetorical choices demonstrated in the readings.

Realities

This book asks its readers to acknowledge several realities:

- **Students' daily rhetorical experience is broader than that of their instructors.**   Regardless of their major, college students read and write in a variety of academic disciplines. Although professors typically engage a small set of closely related issues and write in a few familiar genres, students must learn to read and write about a variety of academic topics in many genres.

- **College-level reading and writing is difficult.**   Professors do most of their thinking and writing within disciplinary boundaries, and they write to other professionals within those boundaries. All readers and writers find it challenging to enter a closely-knit discourse community that shares a way of studying the world and writing about their research.

- **To write efficiently and effectively, students must learn how to transfer rhetorical strategies into new writing situations.**   To do so, students need to be (1) aware of the rhetorical strategies they already possess, (2) trained to analyze new rhetorical strategies they encounter as they read in the disciplines, and (3) able to adapt and apply the rhetorical strategies they learn to fit the rhetorical challenges they will face. When we use the phrase *portable rhetorical lesson*, we are advocating the practice of adapting, not merely imitating, rhetorical strategies from one situation to meet the needs of another.

- **Reading and writing are collaborative activities.**   Writing teachers are well prepared to help students learn how to read and write better, but they cannot possibly know "best practices" from all academic disciplines. For this information, teachers can rely on experts and students who have contributed to this book; students can contribute what they've learned when writing in other disciplines.

FEATURES

The Two Main Parts of the Book

Part One: Rhetorical Reading and Writing offers two chapters that introduce students to the Key Rhetorical Concepts that writers in all disciplines and professions rely on when reading (Chapter 1) and writing (Chapter 2). These chapters prepare students to better understand the rhetorical lessons in subsequent chapters. These chapters also provide practical advice to student readers and writers in an easy-to-find format that encourages students to return to these chapters throughout a course.

    Part Two: Reading and Writing Across the Disciplines (Chapters 3 through 13) offers students a chance to observe and practice important rhetorical lessons from writers who specialize in a particular academic discipline. The disciplines range from media studies to marketing to biotechnology. Because these rhetorical lessons are examples of how writers' respond to specific disciplinary challenges through Key Rhetorical Concepts, students have opportunity to deepen their understanding of the Key Rhetorical Concepts introduced in Part One, even as they experience how writers and readers adapt them to fit the needs and opportunities of a given rhetorical situation. Three writing assignments at the end of each chapter also give students the chance to put the Key Rhetorical Concepts and the Portable Rhetorical Lessons to work in their own writing.

The Parts of Each Chapter

Each chapter in Part Two contains the following:

Opening Assignment and Portable Rhetorical Lesson*	• A short reading and writing assignment that introduces students to the topic of the readings in the chapter and the Portable Rhetorical Lesson. These assignments lead directly into a section on the chapter's Portable Rhetorical Lesson.
Writing in the Discipline	• Published writing in the discipline, selected, introduced, and annotated by an expert in the discipline. "Reading Tips" on how to read in the genre. An essay, "Notes on Grammar, Style, and Rhetoric," that focuses on a distinctive linguistic feature of the reading.
Student Writing	• A sample of student writing in the discipline, introduced and annotated by the student.
Public Writing	• Published writing by an expert in the discipline for a general audience.
More Writing	• Additional example of writing in the discipline. In chapters with a difficult first reading, this fourth reading is more accessible.
Assignments	• Reading response questions after each reading. A set of writing assignments at the end of each chapter asking students to apply the portable rhetorical lesson, make connections across disciplines, or conduct research.

*The team that assembled the readings and emphases for this book shortened "portable rhetorical lesson" to PRL, pronouncing it *pearl*. You and your class can decide if the acronym is convenient or corny.

Organization of Chapters and Flexibility in Assigning Readings.   Chapters 3 to 13 in Part Two are arranged to follow fairly typical patterns of topics in composition courses, moving, for example, from addressing audience to expressing main points to using research and evidence. At the same time, the Portable Rhetorical Lessons gradually increase in complexity and challenge.

However, the introductions to each chapter and each reading allow an instructor to use the readings in any order. Furthermore, teachers can combine readings from a variety of chapters to offer lessons that apply directly to a particular writing assignment. Consider, for example, readings that would help students who are writing a research paper. When writing about research, students must summarize published research; summary is the focus of Chapter 11: "Chemistry." They must decide whether it is appropriate to include personal observation; Chapter 7: "Nursing," teaches that lesson. And they must cite and document sources effectively, a lesson that Chapter 8: "Political Science," teaches well. Similar lessons are available for any writing assignment.

A Note on Titles and Citation Styles

You will see that the titles in this book vary in punctuation and that the citations and lists of references appear in various styles. Our guiding principle was to retain the style of the original publications and student papers. Honoring the originals in this way provides another lesson in the reality of rich disciplinary variety.

RESOURCES FOR INSTRUCTORS AND STUDENTS

The **Instructor's Manual** offers practical—and sometimes playful—advice on using Real Texts in a composition course. The Manual begins with advice on ways to apply the "Principles" section of this preface to create coherence and unity in a course. The Manual's chapters then parallel those of the book, discussing main opportunities and challenges, portable rhetorical lessons, preparations for reading, exercises, reading response questions, in-class activities, and major assignments.

mycomplab   **MyCompLab** is an eminently flexible application that empowers student writers and teachers by integrating a composing space and assessment tools with multimedia tutorials, services (such as online tutoring), and exercises for writing, grammar, and research. Students can use MyCompLab on their own, benefiting from self-paced diagnostics and a personal study plan that recommends the instruction and practice each student needs to improve his or her writing skills. Teachers can recommend it to students for self-study, set up courses to track student progress, or leverage the power of administrative features to be more effective and save time. The assignment builder and commenting tools, developed specifically for use in writing courses, bring instructors closer to their student writers, make managing assignments and evaluating papers more efficient, and put powerful assessment within reach. Students receive feedback within the context of their own writing, which encourages critical thinking and revision and helps them to develop skills based on their individual needs. Learn more at www.mycomplab.com http://www.mycomplab.com.

Pearson Longman offers a wide array of other supplementary materials perfect for use in first-year composition courses as well as more advanced settings, some available at no additional cost when packaged with a Pearson text, and some available at a deep discount. Please contact your local Pearson Arts and Sciences sales consultant to find out more.

ACKNOWLEDGMENTS

The editorial team: From our earliest conversations about this book, we realized that we would depend on the help of a cross-disciplinary team of faculty members, professionals, and students. The faculty and professionals developed the principles and assembled and introduced most of the readings for the book. They patiently explained their disciplinary rhetorical traditions to us, to the students on the team, and to students who will read the book. We are deeply grateful for all they gave to this book and all they have taught us. It is their expertise and passion for student writing that invigorates every page of this book. Their names appear in the chapters to which they have contributed.

Student partners collaborated with each member of the faculty and professional team. In our early meetings, the student authors sat elbow-to-elbow with professors around the conference table. They contributed ideas, challenged our assumptions, and taught us much about what motivates student writers. And, of course, their own writing shapes every chapter. Most of these students have graduated now; they continue to improve the world through their words, and we thank them. Their names appear with their contributions in the text. An individual who played a critical role in this book is William J. Vande Kopple, author of the "Notes on Grammar, Style, and Rhetoric." His ability to discern telling linguistic habits in the disciplines allowed us to link large-scale and sentence-level rhetorical practices. The "Notes" thereby model a positive attitude toward learning about writing from all writing traditions—a lesson that sits at the heart of this book.

Our initial research was supported by a grant from the Calvin Center for Christian Scholarship, and we are very grateful for their generous support of cross-disciplinary collaboration.

Special thanks go to Mandy Suhr-Systema, who, as an undergraduate McGregor Fellow, quickly grasped complex ideas and brought both insight and passion to the project. She helped us shape the idea of a "portable rhetorical lesson" into something that we could hope to be able to teach to others, and she was instrumental in refining the portable rhetorical lesson in each chapter.

The students who have populated our classes also deserve our thanks. They suffered through rough drafts with kindness and equanimity, and they offered many suggestions that have greatly improved this textbook.

We relied heavily on the competence and goodwill of the administrative staff in the Provost's office and the Department of English at Calvin College, especially Becky Moon. Without their help, we would not have completed this project. Calvin College's work-study students (notably, William Overbeeke) supplied frequent technical help.

Throughout the project we have been ably assisted by the professors who make up the advisory board for Calvin College's Academic Writing Program, in particular, codirectors Karen Saupe and Kathi Groenendyk. Colleagues in the English Department tested chapters for us and provided helpful feedback. Many in the department have contributed ideas, scholarly references, or pedagogical strategies. We pay special homage to E. Shelley Reid, who has been a good friend and a wise advisor throughout this project.

And, of course, the folks at Longman have been terrific. Our thanks to Ginny Blanford, who helped with our planning for the second edition. Lynn Huddon at Longman deserves our deep and abiding gratitude for taking on—and staying with—this project. As our primary editor, Lynn asked the right questions and pressed us, Thoreau-like, to simplify, simplify, simplify. She helped us develop our ideas into a textbook that teachers and students can use. Rebecca Gilpin offered welcome and able hands in the Longman office. The production team was efficient and humane; we thank them all, especially those with whom we had frequent contact: Denise Phillip, Jenny Bevington, Poyee Oster, Bruce Hobart, and Teresa Ward. The readers who carefully reviewed the first edition of this book offered encouragement, ideas, strategies, and even language and helped in innumerable ways. Thank you all, including: Anne Balay, Indiana University Northwest; Susan M. Lang, Texas Tech University; Gary A. Negin, California State University; Angelia Northrip-Rivera, Missouri State University; David Ryan, University of San Francisco; and Claudia Skutar, University of Cincinnati.

To our families, we owe a debt of gratitude that stretches the capacity of words. Thank you.

Dean Ward
Elizabeth Vander Lei

PART ONE

RHETORICAL READING
AND WRITING

Part One sets the foundation for this book's study of rhetoric in the disciplines. Part Two takes you into the worlds of several very different disciplines, in which you will sometimes feel like you've entered foreign territory. Part One makes all that exploration possible by focusing on a small set of "Key Rhetorical Concepts"; a chart of these concepts appears in Chapter 1 (pages 4–5).

After introducing and explaining the key concepts, Chapters 1 and 2 apply those concepts, giving you specific reading strategies in Chapter 1 and writing strategies in Chapter 2.

To illustrate the application of the key concepts to reading and writing, Chapters 1 and 2 show you how the concepts function in a piece of writing that you might read for a college writing class (Chapter 1) and a piece of writing that you might compose for a college writing class (Chapter 2).

Part One also establishes—in concrete contexts—the principle that we introduce in the book's title and Preface: the realities of reading and writing. Those realities are sometimes frustrating, sometimes surprising, and always challenging. Thus the work of Part One gives you a stable foundation from which to explore the realities of reading and writing in the disciplines.

READING RHETORICALLY

On her award-winning blog "indexed" (www.thisisindexed.com), Jessica Hagy uploads charts and graphs that she has hand-drawn on index cards. Hagy's sketches are popular because they provide readers with a new perspective—sometimes funny, sometimes depressing—on some aspect of modern American culture. Here are two that focus on college students:

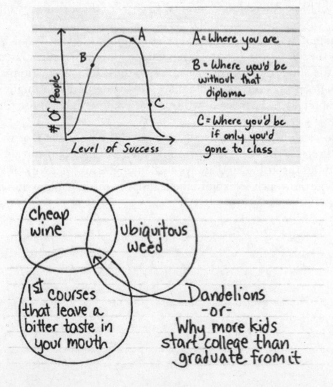

- Jessica Hagy's drawings depend on her ability to capture experiences, knowledge, or beliefs that she and her readers share. What common stereotypes of college students does Jessica Hagy rely on in both of these drawings?

- In these two drawings, Hagy describes college students in somewhat different terms. How would you describe the difference between her description of college students in the first drawing and in the second drawing? Based on your experience in college so far, would you say that Hagy has accurately described students? What is inaccurate?

- What is Hagy claiming about the importance of college classes? Based on your experience, list reasons and evidence that support her claim as well as reasons and evidence that contradict or complicate her claim.

Like Jessica Hagy, we believe that college courses can help you develop the skills you need to succeed in life—in your career, sure, but also as a thinker, reader, and writer who is prepared for the challenges of your world. Each of the readings in this book demonstrates strategies that writers use in different disciplines to communicate effectively. If you read with an eye for the choices that the writer has made, you will better understand what you read, and you will discover strategies that you can use in your own writing. Furthermore, we believe that you can adapt the rhetorical strategies that you learn when reading to fit the rhetorical challenges you will face. So we call these strategies "portable rhetorical lessons," in the hope that you will take these lessons with you wherever you go.

Before we send you into the whirl of new and different kinds of writing and the rhetorical lessons you will find in this book, we offer you some grounding—a way to manage all that complexity. We focus on "Key Rhetorical Concepts," concepts that readers and writers encounter in every discipline and in every type of writing.

WHAT ARE KEY RHETORICAL CONCEPTS?

We begin with the most basic of ideas: readers and writers communicate with each other via some kind of text. As a student, you encounter writers through their texts every day. You read texts that are electronic (a blog) and print (a magazine); formal (a syllabus) and informal (a Facebook update); academic (a textbook); and personal (a text message from a friend), but they are all written texts. When you read what someone you can talk to has written, you and the writer can negotiate the meaning. If, for example, you don't understand how your professor has scheduled the reading assignments for a course, you might ask for clarification: "Are the readings due on the date they appear or the next class period?" Or, if you were caught unprepared for a quiz on the reading, you might negotiate differently: "But the syllabus makes it look like that reading is due next class period!"

When it comes to your reading assignments, however, you don't have easy access to the writer. You are on your own to understand what the writer has written and how to make use of what you've read. Textbooks are written with student readers in mind; you can expect textbook authors to define technical terms and to provide explanations that will make sense to most readers. And yet, in advanced courses, and certainly for research papers, your professors will expect you to read what professors and professionals are writing about your subject. You are likely to find the reading much more challenging for several reasons: academic writers typically write to other professionals in their research area, not students. Because professors have devoted their professional lives to learning and using the language and methods of their discipline, they expect their readers to understand complicated terms, concepts, and methods. Even when professors from different disciplines tackle aspects of the same real-world problem, they write in different ways, ways that are expected by other professionals in their field.

Your experience with academic research is quite different. Regardless of your major, as an undergraduate you read and write in a variety of academic disciplines. You may spend as little as a few weeks reading and writing about an academic topic; at most, you will spend only a couple of semesters reading and writing about a given topic in your major. Consequently, it should come as a surprise to no one—not you or your professors— that writing in college will prove difficult. But if Jessica Hagy is right that your future success depends less on your getting a diploma and more on your learning from the intellectual challenges of your course work, you should find that your hard work pays off in the end.

Learning how to make effective choices about what to say and how to say it— rhetorical choices—has drawn students to study rhetoric for thousands of years. Outside colleges and universities people sometimes use the term *rhetoric* to describe an unethical use of language, such as "empty rhetoric." But you will find us and your instructor talking about rhetoric in positive terms, as strategies for effective reading and writing. In fact, Aristotle describes rhetoric as the process of discovering "all available means of persuasion." If you learn to think about reading and writing as processes of discovering different strategies, you will increase the number of choices, or "means," available to you. If you develop the habit of analyzing the rhetorical strategies represented in what you read, you will continue to develop your own set rhetorical options long after you earn that diploma.

In this chapter, we introduce you to seven Key Rhetorical Concepts, basic rhetorical features of all texts. To give you an overview, we provide the following chart.

Key Rhetorical Concepts

Key Concepts	Associated Concepts	Typical Questions All Writers Must Answer
Purpose	**Problem & solution**	What problem do I hope to solve by writing?
	Question & answer	What question do I answer in my writing?
	Effect	What effect do I hope to have on my audience?
Point	**Focus**	What is the main issue I'm focusing on?
	Scope	What are the boundaries that limit my topic?
	Thesis, hypothesis, recommendations	Do I express my point in a thesis, hypothesis, or recommendations?

(*Continued*)

Key Rhetorical Concepts

Key Concepts	Associated Concepts	Typical Questions All Writers Must Answer
Author	**Expertise**	How do I establish my credibility?
	Assumptions & values	What assumptions and values shape my work on this topic?
	Role	What version of myself do I present to my audience?
Audience	**Needs**	What do my readers need that I can provide?
	Expertise	What knowledge or skill does my audience already have?
	Relationship	What is my relationship to my audience?
Research and Evidence	**Research methods**	What research methods are expected and accepted in my discipline?
	Evidence	Have I presented enough of the right kinds of evidence?
	Research framework	What previously published research demonstrates the significance of my problem and reliability of my methods?
Organization	**Order of parts**	What's the best way to arrange the parts?
	Organizational map	How do I map out the parts? What signposts do I provide for my audience?
	Patterns	How do I use visual and verbal patterns to help my audience understand my point?
Presentation	**Verbal style**	What verbal style does my audience expect, and what style is consistent with my persona and goals?
	Visual design	What visual design elements (headings, white space, boldface, fonts, etc.) best serve my audience?
	Graphic elements	What graphic elements (tables, charts, photos, diagrams, etc.) will help the audience understand better?

Although you are likely to find a chart like this useful for remembering key rhetorical concepts, be aware of two limitations: (1) rhetorical concepts never operate independently. They always depend on and respond to other rhetorical pressures and to the specifics of the situation. (2) Rhetoric includes many more concepts than the seven listed here. In the following chapters, you will encounter rhetorical strategies that writers in specific academic disciplines have developed. Although these strategies have been shaped by specifics of their rhetorical context, they are strategies that you can adapt to other situations as well. Because you can take these strategies with you, wherever your reading and writing takes you, we call these concepts portable rhetorical lessons (PRLs).

RHETORICAL READING

When reading is most pleasurable for me, it is like a fishing trip to a large and complex lake, a lake with numerous bays and inlets, seemingly endless islands and channels, and creek channels braiding their way from the main lake through thick marshes to ponds where great blue herons hold one-legged poses among the reeds. I always fish such lakes with a deep, almost clenching, excitement, the excitement of being on water that might yield to me creatures more wondrous than any I have ever wrested from the dark before. But I never go without some apprehension, too, for on such lakes it is possible to become disoriented, even lost for a time. I like the excitement and apprehension: the emotions of a quest.

William J. Vande Kopple

Few students approach the reading required in school with the sense of excitement that Vande Kopple describes, but his metaphor of reading as fishing emphasizes a sense of adventure and exploration that characterizes how most professors read research in their area of specialization. We challenge you, too, to think about reading as an exploration: for new knowledge, for effective methods, for reasons and evidence to support a recommendation. Certainly some of the readings in this book will take you into new territory beyond your usual range of interest or experience. Although we provide some help in the form of marginal explanations, we have not simplified the vocabulary, the sentence structure, or the concepts. To get the most out of these readings you will need to read like Vande Kopple fishes—intending to make the most of it. To help you do so, we offer the following advice:

- Analyze the terrain: Skim the reading before you set your homework schedule so you can get a sense of the difficulty and estimate how much time you will need to complete the work. To make a good estimate, you should first inventory your biorhythms and study habits. When are you most able to concentrate on what you're reading?

- Use equipment to enhance your performance: Use a highlighter or sticky notes to flag important information. Use the margins to record summaries of paragraphs and your responses to what you are reading. If the reading appears to be difficult, alter your environment to enhance your ability to concentrate.

- Take frequent breaks: Break up your reading to keep your mind fresh. Divide your reading into either chunks of time or chunks of text, and give yourself a break after you finish each section.

- Go with a group: Read in a team. Readers in professional settings often read as part of a group, dividing up the reading among several people. If your instructor allows it, read like professionals do. Because your instructor will hold you responsible for the entire reading, though, be sure that you organize your team so that everyone understands the reading completely. As you read with others, observe the reading strategies that others find useful. What strategies might work for you?

- Follow the leader: Consider your instructors as model readers. Listen carefully to how they talk about texts, what they focus on, the other texts they refer to, and how they apply the text to the course. When you read, are you focusing on what your instructors value?

- Document your experiences. Most professionals keep detailed records of their work. Sometimes they share what they've recorded with team members; other times, they use the information themselves, as a way to brainstorm ideas, record information, or sketch out a plan. Often, writing teachers will ask students to record their work in a reading journal or on a research blog. Although each teacher will frame up the task in a particular way, most teachers will require three kinds of information:

1. The bibliographic information of what you've read, formatted in the citation style used by scholars in the discipline (see Appendix A).
2. A summary that includes the following: (a) a description of the topic, the research methods, results, and conclusions; (b) a list of what you might find useful in your own writing (quotes, examples, data, illustrations, etc.); and (c) items from the reading's bibliography that relate to your topic.
3. An evaluation that includes your assessment of the value of what you read. What is useful? What are the limitations of this reading for your own work? What rhetorical strategies could you use in your own writing? What about this reading would you hope to avoid in your own writing?

USING THE KEY RHETORICAL CONCEPTS TO READ BETTER

1. Reading to Understand the Purpose

Before you begin reading, determine your reasons for reading, and let that purpose shape how you read. For example, if you are looking for something particular—such as evidence to support a claim or details about a research method—skim until you find what you need; if you are reading to understand a complex issue, however, read more slowly, connecting ideas to each other and to your experience in the world. Remember: your purposes for reading do not always match an author's purposes for writing; if they do not match, you will likely have to work harder. Generally speaking, however, if you stay aware of an author's purpose, you'll be a more efficient reader.

Three of the most common academic purposes for writing are analyzing, reporting, and recommending. These purposes are closely related to one another, and writers will have different purposes for different parts of their texts. If you look for these key words and the intellectual work they usually cover, you may find it easier to determine an author's main purpose for writing.

When analyzing, an author breaks it into the parts that make it up and focuses on the relationships of the parts to the whole or the relationships between those parts. Similar intellectual work is describing (focusing on important features), comparing (focusing on similarities), contrasting (focusing on differences), and making analogies/noting resemblances (focusing on similarities between seemingly dissimilar things).

When reporting, an author gathers information and presents it to readers in a form that is clear, accessible, and useful. Similar intellectual work is classifying (categorizing pieces of information), defining (focusing on the meaning of something), narrating (focusing on the history of something), and presenting a problem that deserves investigation and a solution to a problem.

When recommending, an author makes a case for actions that the reader should take. Similar intellectual work is considering causes or effects of an action, focusing on a process (breaking a complex action into a series of steps), evaluating (using criteria to determine the value or quality of something), promoting best practices (arguing that one approach is better than alternatives), and setting policy (arguing for one way of doing something).

Reading Strategy 1: Interpret key terms.   As you read, you are likely to encounter two types of key terms, both of which you will need to interpret to read effectively. The first type is words that refer to specific concepts, events, or things associated with a particular topic. You will more fully understand what you're reading if you take the time to look up the definition of these terms and then revise that definition to account for particular meanings that key terms take on when associated with the topic. The second type of key terms will help you determine what a writer was hoping to accomplish in different parts of the text. These key terms are the verbs that writers use to communicate their purposes. You will find writers using some verbs (like "discuss") to communicate any purpose and other verbs in discipline-specific ways. Keep a list of a writer's verbs and see what they can tell you about the writer's purpose. Here is a rough guide of verbs that are commonly associated with each purpose:

> Analysis: breakdown, discuss, dissect, examine, investigate
>
> Report: clarify, discuss, detail, distill, explain, inform, interpret, record, recount, review, summarize
>
> Recommend: advise, advocate, caution, critique, direct, discuss, instruct, prescribe, promote, propose, suggest, warn

Related PRLs.   The Key Rhetorical Concept of **purpose** is highlighted through the Portable Rhetorical Lesson sections in Chapter 11, "Chemistry," and Chapter 13, "Marketing."

2. Reading to Understand the Main Point

A writer's *point* is the main thing she has to say about the topic. Most academic writers state their main point clearly, but others may choose to make their point more subtly, allowing readers to develop their own ideas about the main emphasis of the writing. Most students are familiar with a point in the form of a thesis, but writers may also frame their main point as a hypothesis or a set of recommendations. Typically, writers introduce their main point through a description of the problem that they are attempting to solve; often they use a research question to focus the reader's attention on the particular aspect of the problem that they will address in their writing. Their point—thesis, hypothesis, or recommendation—is the writer's answer to that question (and, consequently, the solution to the problem).

If you can identify the problem that the writer is trying to solve, you will be able to understand what point the writer is trying to communicate.

Reading Strategy 2: Cross-examine the point.   Writers communicate their point by addressing a series of smaller points throughout their writing. As they do so, they emphasize some more than others, even sometimes drawing the reader's attention away from the main point that they state in their thesis, hypothesis, or recommendations. To determine the main point of what you're reading, and whether the writer's emphasis matches the stated main point, analyze the tensions between the problem(s) that the writer identifies, the solution(s) that she offers. Here are strategies you can use to increase your understanding of a writer's main point.

- Analyze the relationship between the problem and the question: Describe the problem that the writer identifies and the research question that the writer provides. What parts of the problem does the question leave out? What aspects of the problem does the question focus on? Write out a research question that more accurately accounts for the problem. Write a description of the problem that better fits the scope of the research question.

- Check the writer's question against the conclusion. Sometimes writers use a series of questions to introduce their writing; this strategy can make it difficult for readers to determine which research question is most central to the writer's main point. To determine which research question is most important, compare each question to the writer's main point in the conclusion, noting which question best fits what the writer focuses on at the end of the writing.

- Find the writer's main point. Writers often include a succinct statement of their main point at the beginning of their writing (in the abstract or introduction). Frequently, they restate that main point at the end of a literature review, at the beginning of the discussion section, and under a header that marks recommendations.

- Track the writer's emphasis. Read the introduction. On the top of a blank document, write out the problem the writer has identified in one sentence. Now turn that sentence into a question (if the writer provides a research question in the introduction, just write out that question). Read the next three paragraphs. Beneath your original sentence and question, write a new description of the problem and a new formulation of the research question to account for what you read. Continue this process of revising and refining until you are finished reading, paying special attention to how the writer describes the problem in her conclusion.

- Check the solution against the problem. List the features of the problem as precisely as you can. Apply the solution to these features, noting which features of the problem the solution targets and which it misses.

Related PRLs.   The Key Rhetorical Concept of **point** is highlighted through the Portable Rhetorical Lesson sections in Chapter 4, "Religious Studies"; Chapter 5, "Sociology"; and Chapter 6, "Biotechnology."

3. Reading to Understand the Author

Throughout their careers, most professionals and professors write about a handful of topics, topics that they have expertise in. As experts, they should know the history of research on the topic—which problems have captured the attention of researchers in the past, which aspects of the problem researchers are currently working on, and which aspects should be the focus of future research. When you read with the author in mind, you assess the trustworthiness of the author: the author's expertise, the values the author holds, and the strategies the author uses to persuade you to accept those values. As you read, keep in mind that although in general you can presume that anything published by an academic journal or press has been reviewed by other specialists, sloppy methods, bad logic, and bad writing still get published. This is, of course, even truer of texts that experts have not reviewed.

What an author believes about the world—the assumptions he makes about how the world works and what is important—will shape all aspects of the text. You should analyze what an author values and how he seeks your assent to those values: Does he leave important or controversial assumptions unstated, presuming that you'll agree? Or does the author identify those assumptions and give you reasons to accept them? Evaluating an author's expertise, assumptions, and values will help you determine whether to trust him as you read and whether to rely on his writing as a reference in your own text.

Reading Strategy 3: Background-check the author.

- Develop a professional profile of the author, based on what you can infer from the text (including the bibliography). How much does the author know about the topic? How does he demonstrate that knowledge?
- Seek confirmation of the author's expertise. Does the author have an advanced degree or hold a job in this area of research?
- Develop an intellectual profile of the writer. What does the writer most highly value? What assumptions does the writer make about the world? Which values and assumptions do you and the writer share? Is the writer aware of and forthright about his values and assumptions, comparing them openly to those that differ?

If you will be relying heavily on an author's research, explore the author's professional standing. Do other scholars in the field value this author's work? Do they refer to it in their own research? How transparent is he about his research methods? Are the author's methods consistent with those used by other scholars in the field?

Related PRLs.   The Key Rhetorical Concept of **author** is highlighted through the Portable Rhetorical Lesson sections in Chapter 3, "Speech Communication"; Chapter 8, "International Relations"; and Chapter 12, "English Education."

4. Reading to Understand Audience

Professionals and professors usually write to researchers like themselves, people with expertise and background knowledge on the topic. You, on the other hand, are not likely to be an expert yet on any of the topics you read about. This difference between you and the audience that these writers are imagining as they write can cause you big headaches unless you read well and wisely. To read well, you need to tap into what you already know and supplement that with additional information. To read wisely, you should assess how well the writer works with readers to build knowledge and understanding. Sometimes, the difficulty that you experience reading a text is rooted in your own knowledge and expertise. Other times, the difficulty is rooted in the author's attitudes toward the audience. For a variety of reasons, authors can make things unnecessarily complicated or they can oversimplify things for readers. If an author does not respect you as a reader, you may decide that the author's writing is not worth your time reading.

Reading Strategy 4: Define your relationship with the author.

- Expand your knowledge. Before you start reading, read some general information about the topic from Web sites like Answers.com or Wikipedia.
- Remind yourself of what you've already learned or experienced. Spend five minutes free-writing narratives of your experiences with the subject matter. If you can't tell any stories from your own experience, write about the experiences of family and friends. After you have written continuously for five minutes, take a break. Reread what you've written, and create a list of what you know about the topic.
- Assess what the author believes about you. What knowledge or expertise does the author presume that you have? What assumptions about the world does the author imagine that you hold?
- Assess how the author respects you. What freedoms does the author allow you in reading for your own purposes, drawing your own conclusions from the evidence? How carefully does the author identify and justify her assumptions so that you can choose to agree or disagree with them?
- Assess the demands that the author puts on you. What does the author ask of you? What resources does the author provide you for doing that work?

Related PRLs.   The Key Rhetorical Concept of **audience** is highlighted through the Portable Rhetorical Lesson sections in Chapter 3, "Speech Communication"; Chapter 6, "Biotechnology"; and Chapter 7, "Nursing."

5. Reading for Research Methods and Evidence

Because evidence is only as good as the method that produced it, good readers decide if they can trust a writer's research methods before they allow themselves to be convinced by the evidence. Different rhetorical situations require different methods for gathering evidence, types of evidence, amounts of evidence, and ways of presenting evidence. Therefore, most academic writers include a section that lays out the research framework for the methods they use in their study. This research framework, sometimes called a literature review, summarizes the previous research on a topic that influenced the writer's choice of methods. In the natural and social sciences, writers must persuade readers that the evidence is objective and reliable. Consequently, writers in these fields typically include a section labeled

"Methods" that details the researchers' exact procedures so that other researchers can test the results by duplicating the study. In the humanities, on the other hand, researchers typically do not draw attention to their methods in a particular section of their writing. Common research methods are critiquing, extending, or applying previous research.

Regardless of the discipline, academic research relies on both primary and secondary evidence. Primary evidence is evidence that the writer has collected herself. In the social sciences and natural sciences, primary research could include lab results and observations of the natural world or parts of human society. In the humanities, primary evidence comes from the literary or cultural artifact being examined, such as a novel, painting, or movie. The writer's personal experience constitutes another common form of primary evidence in the humanities. Secondary evidence is the research that was conducted by other writers.

Reading Strategy 5: Narrate the research method.

- Dramatize the research methods. Describe the research method as actions taken by characters in a play, noting which character did each action, where the characters performed each action, who else was present, and the instruments that characters used for each action. Describe each character's motivation: What propelled the characters to act as they did?

- Create a backstory for the research method: What parts of the research method are borrowed from the research methods of other studies? What parts of the research method are untested by others?

- Put the research method in the witness box: How does the research method testify to the validity and reliability of the evidence? How does the research method raise doubt about the validity or reliability of the evidence?

- Put the evidence in the witness box: How much evidence has the writer provided? Is it sufficient? Which points does the evidence corroborate? Which points require additional evidence? How much has the writer tampered with the evidence (summarizing, paraphrasing, graphic representation) when presenting it?

Related PRLs.   The Key Rhetorical Concept of **research methods and evidence** is highlighted through the Portable Rhetorical Lesson sections in Chapter 5, "Sociology"; Chapter 7, "Nursing"; and Chapter 8, "Political Science."

6. Reading to Understand Organization

A good organization acts like a compass for readers, helping them know where they are headed and keeping them from feeling lost. Organizational patterns orient readers in a variety of ways; they can recreate the familiarity of walking a well-known path, or they can play with a reader by offering suspense and surprise. The way an author organizes an entire text depends heavily on the reader's expectations and on requirements of the genre and discipline. In general, writers begin by giving the reader a reason to read and enough background information to read well. They also establish the problem they are addressing, their research question, and their point. Look for these features in an abstract (if applicable) and the introduction.

Authors typically end a text by recommending what the reader should do with what they've just read. In the humanities, many academic writers describe the organization of a text in a sentence-long summary of the essay's main points, called an "organizational statement" or a "thesis map." In some disciplines, writers rely on headers to signpost their organization for readers. Regardless of discipline, most writers use topic sentences—the first sentence of each paragraph—to signal not only the main point of the paragraph but also the relationship of the point to the writer's main point and to the points that precede and follow it.

Reading Strategy 6: Map the trail.

- As you read, jot in the margins of your book the point of each paragraph. When you are finished, use what you've jotted to create an outline of the reading. To do this, you will have to think hard about hierarchical relationships within the text, asking yourself questions like, "Why did the author create a new paragraph at this point?" "Is this a new point?" "Is this a subpoint?" "An example?"

- Summarize the reading in three to five sentences, emphasizing the writer's key points. Compare your summary to the summary of the text's main points that the writer provides in an organizational map, a series of headers, or a sequence of topic sentences. If your summary differs from the organization that the writer provides, evaluate the cause of the difference. Do you have different reasons for reading than the writer may have presumed? Does the writer's organization help or hinder the reader's understanding of the main point?

- Describe the kind of path that the organization lays out for the reader: Is it a city sidewalk, a clearly marked trail through a forest, or a free-form mountain climb? What percentage of the organizing work has the writer left for the reader to do? What is the effect of doing this organizing work on your reading? Does it make you more attentive? Does it offer moments of discovery and delight? Does it leave you confused and frustrated?

- Given the writer's academic discipline, how typical is the organization? What kind of reading does this type of organization encourage—skimming, reading only some parts, or reading straight from start to finish?

Related PRLs.   The Key Rhetorical Concept of **organization** is highlighted through the Portable Rhetorical Lesson sections in Chapter 4, "Religious Studies"; Chapter 11, "Chemistry"; and Chapter 12, "English Education."

7. Reading to Understand Presentation

Most writers focus on the presentation of their text to enhance four features: clarity, efficiency, beauty, and emotional appeal. The word *presentation* implies handing over, or introducing a text to a reader, and presentation does take advantage of opportunities to make a first impression. But the presentation of words and images is much more than a pleasant face at the door. How a writer presents words and images can serve as a vehicle for achieving other rhetorical goals. Verbal style, for example, can create the impression of an author as a credible expert, it can convey the sound of emphatic speech so a reader knows what are the more important points, or it can grab an audience's attention and clarify and idea with a memorable metaphor. Visual presentation can clarify a point with an illustration or photograph, it can make reading efficient by making evidence accessible (for example, in a table or graph), or it can signpost an organizational map with features like headings.

Beyond serving other rhetorical goals, the presentation of words and images achieves its own goals. An author's verbal style can encourage a reader to share a writer's sense of comfort or urgency. And images carry meaning in ways beyond what can be translated into words. Readers respond to the various messages of images much faster than they respond to words, and readers remember images more easily than they remember words.

Reading Strategy 7: Look and listen.

Visual Presentation.   All texts are visual; modern texts, thanks to desktop publishing capacity and Web-based writing, can be highly visual. Several techniques of assessing visual elements of a text will improve your reading. To begin, scan the whole reading, looking for all visual choices that the author made; make note of the features that most strongly catch your eye. Then locate and assess the purpose of visual elements in five different categories:

- Location signs. These visual elements tell you where you are in the text, reminding you of the organization. They include headings (especially familiar headings like "Methods" and "Results" in scientific texts), numbers that identify a sequence of parts, and headers or footers on each page (at the top of each page of this book, for example, is either the chapter title or a descriptor of the part of the chapter you're reading).
- Signs of importance. Keep an eye out for how writers denote the special importance of certain parts (and use a highlighter pen to mark theses parts). Note *key words* highlighted with italics or boldface. Mark *lists*—whether numbered or bullet-pointed. Mark the contents that are placed in a *textbox;* they can offer supplementary information or summaries of key ideas. Mark any items presented in large or eye-catching *fonts*.
- Signs of difference. When the font or size of the font changes, the author is signaling that the section identified by the change is different from the regular text. Pay attention to those signs.
- Visual information. Pay especially close attention to the visual elements that present essential information in accessible and efficient forms. These visual elements include tables, various kinds of graphs, diagrams, illustrations, photographs, and (in electronic texts) video. Look, for example at the side-by-side graphs on page 268 of the Biology chapter; they are the heart of that reading.
- Decoration. Sometimes writers use visual effects just because they look cool. Good readers distinguish between decoration and purposeful use of visual effects.

Verbal Presentation.   When most people think of an author's "style," they think of the author's distinctive "voice" or presence in a text, and certainly this is one aspect of style.

Sometimes people describe style as if it is a separate, added feature of writing—as frosting is to a cake, and sometimes this is the case. But style is more than either of these; an author's stylistic choices profoundly affect the reader's experience. As you read to analyze an author's style, begin with the following general questions:

- How would you describe the author's style? Authoritative? Arrogant? Playful? Exactly what verbal features create a certain style? Why does the author choose her style? Does it seem that the style results from habit, a wish to be consistent with the style of others in the field, a desire to present a certain personality to the reader, an attempt to appeal to the reader's emotions?
- What effect does the author's style have on the readability of the text? Does the author's style enhance your ability to understand and agree with the author's point?
- How do relatively small deviations from formal, conventional style (contractions, slang, sentence fragments) shape your responses to a text and its author?
- How does the author's style focus your attention in the text? What does the author's style emphasize? What does it de-emphasize?

Related PRLs.   The Key Rhetorical Concept of **presentation** is highlighted through the Portable Rhetorical Lesson sections in Chapter 9, "Biology"; Chapter 10, "Media Studies"; and Chapter 13, "Marketing."

The Reading Strategies

1. Interpret key terms: Build definitions for important terms in the text and interpret the writer's verbs to determine the writer's purpose.
2. Cross-examine the point: Find the writer's main point and analyze the relationship between (a) that point and the problem that the writer addresses and (b) that point and the subpoints.
3. Background-check the author: Evaluate the writer's expertise, assumptions, and values.
4. Define your relationship with the author: Prepare yourself to be a competent reader and analyze how the writer views you.
5. Narrate the research method: Tell the story of how the writer gathered evidence. Research the history of that method for gathering evidence.
6. Map the trail: Track the order of the writer's points and evidence.
7. Look and listen: Analyze how the writer presented the text to you.

A MODEL FOR READING RHETORICALLY

The article that appears next was written by two college writing teachers, David Jolliffe and Allison Harl, and it appeared in an academic journal read by college writing teachers. This article provides you with two opportunities: first, it gives you a chance to identify the seven

Key Rhetorical Concepts in action. Second, it helps you better understand your own reading habits and those of other college students.

Jolliffe and Harl present their research as a social scientist might—they describe a social problem; they carefully detail their case-study methodology; they present their results in quotes, numeric summaries, and three case studies (this excerpt includes only one of those); they discuss these results; and they make recommendations to other teachers of writing.

Jolliffe and Harl paid students to log all the minutes they spent reading, not only their homework reading but also the reading they did for work, pleasure, and social purposes. Based on their data, Jolliffe and Harl and make this main point: "We discovered students who were extremely engaged with their reading, but not with the reading that their classes required."

David Jolliffe is a professor of English and Curriculum and Instruction at the University of Arkansas. He has won acclaim for his practical and well-researched publications on the teaching of college writing. At the time of this study Allison Harl was a graduate student at the University of Arkansas, where she now teaches.

Texts of Our Institutional Lives: Studying the "Reading Transition" from High School to College: What Are Our Students Reading and Why?

David A. Jolliffe and Allison Harl

College English, Volume 70, Number 6, July 2008

. . . If the scuttlebutt about reading is true, the Visigoths are at the door. An array of national surveys and studies suggests that neither high school nor college students spend much time preparing for class, the central activity of which we presume to be reading assigned articles, chapters, and books. . . . The water-cooler conversation in English departments and indeed throughout the university seems to confirm the reports and corroborate the end-of-reading treatises and memoirs: legions of students apparently come to class ill prepared, not having done the assigned reading at all or having given it only cursory attention. Professors admit that students can actually pass exams if they come to the lectures and take (or buy) good notes, whether or not they have read the assigned material. In short, careful reading seems have become a smaller blip on the higher educational radar screen or dropped off it altogether.

Despite the attention paid to student reading in the national surveys, relatively little scholarship has examined empirically what, how,

Purpose: Jolliffe and Harl introduce the problem.

Purpose: They narrow the focus of the problem to a lack of academic scholarship on (1) reading practices and (2) students' ability to transition from high school to college. This excerpt focuses on the first of these two problems.

and whether college students actually do read and how reading thus figures in the transition from high school to college. We set out to address this knowledge gap in a local way during a recent fall semester at our institution, the University of Arkansas. We wanted to know how our first-year students taking college composition, a course in which students mostly write about their reading, perceived and effected the transition from high school to college as readers. Therefore, we studied the reading habits and practices of twenty-one first-year composition students during the first two weeks of October, at which time they were in their sixth and seventh weeks of a fifteen-week semester. In some ways, our study provides a remarkably accurate local representation of the data about student reading as reported in the national surveys: first-year students at the University of Arkansas spend just about the same amount of time reading and preparing for class as students at other research universities—probably not as much time as their instructors and institutional administrators think they should. In other ways, however, our study offers insights into the reading environments of first-year college students that neither the national surveys nor the status-quo chatter hints at. We found students who were actively involved in their own programs of reading aimed at values clarification, personal enrichment, and career preparation. In short, we discovered students who were extremely engaged with their reading, but not with the reading that their classes required. . . .

Purpose: The authors turn the problem into a specific research question.

Point: The authors state their main point at the end of their introduction.

What Do We Know About Reading? High School, College, and the Transition

Any faculty member who wonders how and whether students prepare for class can probably find sources of consternation and concern in two national surveys. Since its inception in 1999, the National Survey of Student Engagement (NSSE), directed by George Kuh at Indiana University, has provided valuable data to college and university administrators and faculties about first-year and senior-year students' practices and beliefs as related to the survey organization's five "national benchmarks of effective educational practice": "level of academic challenge, active and collaborative learning, student-faculty interaction, enriching educational experiences, and supportive campus environments" (12). . . .

Audience: Although they can presume that most readers will recognize the NSSE acronym, Jolliffe and Harl provide background information that their readers are not as likely to know.

Under the traditional rule of thumb of two hours' preparation time for every one hour in class, the average full-time student should be devoting 24 hours per week to studying, reading, writing, and so on. However, in the 2005 NSSE, taken by about 130,000 first-year students and a similar number of seniors from 523 colleges and universities, 66 percent of first-year students and 64 percent of seniors at all participating colleges and universities reported spending fewer than sixteen hours during a typical seven-day week preparing for class—"studying, reading, writing, doing homework or lab work, analyzing data, rehearsing, and other academic activities."[2] . . .

The NSSE and HSSSE data find an ominous counterpart in a study reported by Alvin Sanoff in 2006. Nearly 800 high school teachers and about 1,100 college faculty members were surveyed to determine their perceptions of how well students were prepared for college in reading, writing, science, mathematics, and oral communication, as well as in more attitudinal domains such as "motivation to work hard," "study habits," and "ability to seek and use support services." Only one-quarter of high school teachers and one-tenth of college faculty members thought that entering first-year students were "very well prepared" to read and understand difficult materials. . . .

Although the NSSE . . . stud[y] provide[s] fodder for the perception that college-bound and college students can't and/or don't read extensively, critically, or even sufficiently, the surveys and reports did not provide us with a rich enough perspective as we planned how to engage in conversations with our institution's faculty members about designing, adjusting, and delivering reading-based composition and general-education curricula to our students. Very few scholars have actually investigated the quality or quantity of college students' reading.[4] We wanted to know more about the reading lives of our students.

Purpose: Jolliffe and Harl re-state their purpose for studying the reading habits of University of Arkansas students.

How We Studied Student Reading

Organization: The authors communicate the organization of their essay to the reader through headers. This heading stands in for the more formal "Methods."

In that semester, we randomly selected twenty-one full-time freshmen from a volunteer pool of about one hundred students and paid the participants to complete three tasks. First, they filled out a questionnaire about their perceptions of their own reading abilities and habits in high school and college. . . .

The second task required them to keep a reading journal for two consecutive weeks. We asked them to write for at least thirty minutes daily, describing in detail everything they read that day, and to produce at least ten full entries over the two weeks. For each entry, we asked the students to provide the title and author and the number of pages of each reading, indicating whether each text was read for a class, for a job, or for their interest or pleasure. Additionally, we asked students to indicate approximately how many minutes they spent reading during each day. Finally, we asked participants to focus specifically on *one* of the texts they read for each day and write about that text, responding to a series of questions. These questions were divided into five major categories: 1.) Focusing on One Specific Text, 2.) Reading Critically 3.) Drawing Relationships: Text to Self, 4.) Drawing Relationships: Text to Text, and 5.) Drawing Relationships: Text to World.[5] . . .

For the third task in the study, students participated in an exit interview, in which they provided a think-aloud protocol about a self-selected 250-word portion of a textbook that they were currently reading for one of their classes. In the remainder of this article, after a brief comment on data from the intake questionnaires, we focus on what the students' reading journals taught us. . . .

What We Learned from the Journals, Part I: Toeing the NSSE Line

Author: Jolliffe and Harl present themselves as humble researchers by emphasizing what they learned.

. . . Above all else, the journals offered a considerably richer picture of the students' reading lives than we had anticipated—the journals turned out to be a bountiful data source. One could certainly drop into them like an anthropologist and find several aspects of the late-adolescent reading culture that are worthy of note and, from an educationally conservative viewpoint, perplexing. For example,

Presentation: Jolliffe and Harl use bullet points to efficiently communicate these findings that they expect will interest their readers, even though they are incidental to the research question.

- All of the students spent lots of time reading online documents.
- A substantial majority of them read their Facebook sites almost daily, sometimes for extended periods.
- Most of them read while doing something else: listening to music, checking emails and sending instant messages, watching television, and so on.

But, as fascinated as we were by the minutiae of the students' rituals, we wanted to look for bigger patterns in the journals. Initially, we simply wanted to see how our first-year students stacked up against the national numbers reported in the NSSE.

Research and Evidence: Jolliffe and Harl carefully describe their methods of gathering evidence and analyzing that evidence.

For each journal entry, we asked the participants not only to list everything they read during the course of each day but also to estimate the amount of time they had spent reading each item. All of the participants provided at least ten full entries, but only half of them were faithful recorders of texts and time. As we made a first pass through the journals of these accurate respondents, we tried to categorize the texts that they read as either "academic"—that is, texts that they read for their courses— or "nonacademic"—that is, texts that they read for pleasure, leisure, personal interest, or work. Given our interest in technologically mediated writing, moreover, we found it interesting to subdivide the "nonacademic" category into "nonacademic/technological"—reading done on a computer screen—and "nonacademic/nontechnological." The students who were faithful recorders of their texts and time spent an average of 1 hour and 24 minutes per day on academic reading, some of which—a surprisingly small proportion—was done using technology. The faithful recorders devoted an average of 54 minutes a day to nonacademic reading involving technology—Facebook profiles, emails, instant messages,

Internet sites, and so on. They spent an average of 25 minutes per day on nonacademic reading that did not involve technology—magazines, books, newspapers, and so on. Thus, the faithful, categorizing respondents reported spending an average of 2 hours and 43 minutes per day on all types of reading, almost evenly divided between academic and nonacademic reading.[7]

Research and Evidence: The authors provide their general findings here.

If we assume, however, that the faithfully categorizing respondents and the summative respondents were devoting roughly the same proportion of time to academic and nonacademic reading, their reports place these University of Arkansas first-year students right smack in the middle of that 66 percent of first-year students in the NSSE who spent fewer than 16 hours per week "preparing for class."[8]

What We Learned from the Journals, Part II: Hints of a Reading Life

. . . .

Considering that all of the participants in the study were full-time students one might expect the reading that they were doing for their courses to occupy the top position in their list of intellectual priorities. Moreover, considering that the participants had reported spending 84 percent of their reading time during the first six weeks of the semester occupied with academic reading, one might expect that their nonacademic reading was done primarily for rest and relaxation.

The journal entries do not support these presumptions. Like the students in the Stanford Study of Writing, who reported having actively "performative" writing lives that transcended the writing they must do for courses (Fishman et al.), many of the students in our study described having regular, steady, full reading lives in which they engaged with a wide variety of texts for reasons both academic and nonacademic. We encountered students who, during the two-week period, were reading novels (examples: *The Fellowship of the Ring, A Handmaid's Tale,* and *Angels and Demons*), nonfiction books (*Guns, Germs, and Steel* and *Under the Banner of Heaven*), magazines (*Seventeen* and *Cosmopolitan* were favorites among the females; exercise and hunting magazines prevailed among the males), and newspapers (both the campus paper and the statewide one) for personal interest and pleasure. We found students, perhaps because of our prompting, drawing solid connections between the texts that they were reading and their emerging sense of themselves as adults in the world. One student unpacked her connection to a magazine article about the untimely death of young woman who had had an unresolved argument with her father; the journal entry described the student's own estrangement from her father following her parents' divorce. Another student noted that she connected to *The Diary of Anne Frank* because, as a Jew, she had experienced racial slurs

Audience: The authors summarize this evidence, providing examples that help readers understand and remember what they have read.

herself. A third student described her memory of training a puppy to help her connect to part of her psychology textbook about behavioral conditioning. A fourth student explained his connection between Plato's *Republic* and Marxist governments: "Karl Marx and socialist and communist societies tried to use many of Plato's ideas in their writings and governments, but they all consistently failed, while democracy thrived and continues to spread today."

The following three brief case studies offer slightly more extended profiles of students who defy the status-quo thinking that portrays first-year college students as incapable of and uninterested in reading. Angela, Pauline, and Corey have come to college as readers of texts that speak to their own exigencies and interests. . . .

In this excerpt we include paragraphs only about Corey.

Corey Essene was enrolled in the College of Arts and Sciences Honors Program at the time of our study, and, as such, was the type of student that one might expect to take his class preparation very seriously. A superficial reading of his journal entries might lead one to question that expectation. In short, Corey seemed to blow off his required reading. On the other hand, however, his journal entries show a young man devoted to reading fantasy fiction and learning French—not so much to do well in his French class, but instead to communicate with a friend he met while traveling the previous summer and to fulfill his goal of getting a job working in the American Embassy in Paris.

Corey's first journal entry was one of only two in which he had anything substantial—or positive—to say about his assigned reading. He described his admittedly superficial reading of an essay, "The Genocidal Killer in the Mirror," simply because he and some classmates in his Honors Composition class had to meet and collectively come up with a thesis statement for an essay about it. In his next entry, however, he focused at some length on a chapter entitled "Celbedeil" in a book called *Eldest* by Christopher Paolini, which he chose to spend thirty minutes reading "to break the monotony of studying and doing homework for all of my classes." *Eldest* is clearly mainstream fantasy, the second book in a trilogy, Corey reported: "It's a story about dragons in a mythical setting. It is kind of like books I have read including Tolkien's books because it has many of the same mythical races and similar settings." Corey offered a connection-filled thought to conclude this entry: "This really relates to the real world because this symbolizes bigotry that still exists across the planet. I think that because I am aware of bigotry in society that I was able to see Paolini's throw back and symbology [sic] of these ancient grudges and beliefs. This text basically reaffirmed my passion against the ignorance of bigotry, whether it be in fiction novels, or real life and history." . . .

In his next-to-last entry, Corey returned to some assigned reading, this time for his Fundamentals of Communication class: "The text was the basic dry, boring textbook type text, but it was highly informative. I read it in about an hour. This relates to me because I know it will help me give my assigned speech and later speeches I am to give throughout my college career and life."

We don't want to argue that Angela, Pauline, and Corey are necessarily representative of any particular population, but they do evince a strong interest in personal reading, something that status-quo thinking would assert that college students lack. Angela, Pauline, and Corey engage thoughtfully with texts; however, most of the texts that they value and connect with are not those assigned in their courses.

Rethinking Reading in College Courses

. . . So what did we learn about these kinds of students by reading their journals? . . .

First of all, our students were reading, but they were not reading studiously, either in terms of the texts they were engaging with or the manner in which they read them. Like the high school boys whose literate practices Michael Smith and Jeffrey Wilhelm describe in *Reading Don't Fix No Chevys*, the University of Arkansas students often manifested a passion for reading that was not connected to their courses. Instead, they saw the reading that they had to do for school as uninspiring, dull, and painfully required. Here was Angela's response to her sociology text: "I completely agree" with it and it "raises no questions." Corey assessed his Fundamentals of Communication reading as being self-evident, and said that he rapidly perused "The Genocidal Killer in the Mirror" just in order to generate a thesis about it. Although Angela's and Corey's responses to school-based reading, typical of those of many of the participants, were rather neutrally dismissive, other students were more adamantly critical. One student, Jennifer Respighi, described how she took only five minutes to read a sample biology lab report "because it was so boring." Another student, Katherine Quick, characterized her psychology textbook as "a brutally boring overwad" and wrote that she skipped sections "because there was no reason to read a bunch of bullshit." A third student, Walter Hope, simply opined that "my chemistry book sucks."

Many of the participants clearly rushed through their required reading simply to get it done and then move on to reading that they found more engaging. In the journals, we found daily reading schedules such as the following:

- Andrea Less, Day 5: 30 minutes reading an article for an English assignment, 20 minutes reading email and eBay ads.
- Kathy Gravette, Day 1: 30 minutes total for reading an English assignment and the essay it required her to read, plus her art

> Audience: Jolliffe and Harl's examples help the reader remember the point.

assignment, and *Cosmopolitan* magazine; Day 5: 30 minutes total for reading her English assignment ("It was difficult to read") plus *Cosmopolitan* and the newspaper.

- Fred Borg, Day 1: 45 minutes reading a selection from Descartes's *First Meditation, during* a lecture in a math class; Day 3: 20 minutes reading an essay for English.
- Tony Richardson, Day 2: 30 minutes reading an essay for English; Day 5: 96 minutes reading *The Boater's Handbook*.

In many of these reports, we would be hard pressed to find reading experiences that we would characterize as focused and contemplative.

Second, although the students generally showed some ability to draw the three types of connections that we urged them to create with our leading questions, their reported connections were not evenly distributed among the three categories. Our students seemed quite capable of making text-to-self connections—Lindsey James, for example, related her response to an article about cults to her own religious upbringing—and text-to-world connections—recall Angela's repeated connections between texts that she was reading and campus/ community/world events. But it was the rare student who, like Pauline, would draw connections between and among texts that she was reading for her classes, or like William Hope, who described the connections that he drew between *Helter Skelter* and *Under the Banner of Heaven,* two books that he read for his own pleasure and interest.

Third, students are motivated by and engaged with reading, but the texts that they interact with most enthusiastically are technologically based. In addition, students have become proficient in the art of multitasking as they navigate in and out of electronic media. Virtually all of the students indicate in their journals that they spend a substantial amount of time reading online. . . . The majority of their time reading for pleasure is spent reading and writing emails, instant messaging, or creating and perusing Facebook and MySpace profiles. . . . As a result of the amount of time that students spend with electronic media, their reading practices and habits have shifted with influence of these technologies. Their journal entries consistently refer to the myriad ways in which they multitask as they read. For instance, many students email and instant message their friends while surfing the Internet and reading texts on the computer. Many watch television, listen to music, or talk on their cell phones as they read their textbooks.

Given that our students seem to engage with some types of reading, what did we suggest that faculty members the University of Arkansas do to help their students engage more fully with, and read more critically, the material that they need to read for their classes? . . .

> Organization: Jolliffe and Harl shift their focus to another research question. This focuses their readers' attention to teaching. In this way, they introduce their recommendations.

Point: Jolliffe and Harl use past tense to emphasize the limited scope of their study. Because they studied only University of Arkansas students, they describe the recommendations they made to faculty on their own campus.

First, we argued that faculty members need to teach students explicitly how to draw the kinds of connections that lead to engaged reading, particularly text-to-world and text-to-text connections. It's not that we think text-to-self connections are not important. We do think, however, that, as valuable as these kinds of personal connections are for initiating engaged reading, students ultimately need to be stretched beyond the boundaries of their own personal reactions. As Wayne Booth contended in *Modern Dogma and the Rhetoric of Assent,* one major function of college is to drag students "kicking and screaming, out of infantile solipsism into adult membership in an inquiring community" (13). As they read, students need to be walked through demonstrations of mature, committed, adult readers who draw connections to the world around them, both historical and current, and to other texts. . . .

Second, we suggested that faculty members and administrators need to create curriculums, co-curriculums, and extra-curriculums that invite students to engage in their reading and to connect texts that they read to their lives, their worlds, and other texts. Certainly, learning-community programs—in which students are taking two or three courses together, focusing on a common theme—foster this kind of curricular connectivity, as do service-learning and community-outreach programs, in which students accomplish necessary and useful projects that reflect principles and ideas from their reading. . . .

Third, we urged faculty members to look for ways to incorporate more technology into their reading assignments. It is becoming common knowledge that students engage effectively with reading done in interactive electronic contexts. For example, Gail E. Hawisher and her colleagues point out that all students have different "cultural ecologies" and therefore experience different "technological gateways" for acquiring and developing literacy, but many students have developed literacies in electronic contexts that instructors overlook or ignore. "As a result," according to Hawisher et al., "we fail to build on the literacies students already have" (676). We suggested that faculty members could enhance student learning through better engagement with reading by incorporating assignments that achieved two primary goals:

- They would provide students with opportunities to interact with electronic hyperlinked texts.
- They would engage student readers through reflection in electronic public spheres.

. . . . .

Although our study was most useful for motivating and shaping discussions at our own institution, we see merit in faculty members and administrators conducting similar studies on their own campuses; reporting the results to groups of students, instructors, and administrators; and discussing the implications of the results for teaching and learning on the campus. Indeed, we would urge any college or university serious about improving undergraduate composition and general education to examine student reading on its own campus. . . .

There's no need for any college or university to be apologetic about looking at students' reading habits and practices. The transition from high school to college must entail a transition to different types of reading, different amounts of reading, and different approaches to success with reading. If we intend to continue basing assignments, syllabi, and entire academic programs on student reading, then we need to know more about it.

Notes

2. The responses about the "number of assigned textbooks, books, or book-length packs of course readings" that students reported reading are also instructive: 64 percent of first-year students and 56 percent of seniors reported reading ten or fewer textbooks, books, or course packs during the academic year (38).

4. [In this footnote Jolliffe and Harl summarize five previous studies of students' reading habits.]

5. The "drawing-relationships" questions were motivated by the types of connections that Ellin Keene Oliver and Susan Zimmerman teach students to draw in *Mosaic of Thought: Teaching Comprehension in a Reader's Workshop,* a widely used resource for teacher-development programs in high schools.

7. Over a seven-day week, therefore, these students devoted about 19 hours per week to reading— in other words, somewhat more than they had reported on their intake questionnaires, perhaps because the act of listing *everything* that they read during a day turned "reading" into a larger activity for these students. In contrast, the students who did not record how much time they spent reading each item, but simply provided a total number of minutes of reading per day, reported spending an average of 1 hour and 41 minutes daily on all types of reading, or about 11.8 hours per week—a bit less than they had reported on their intake questionnaires.

8. The largest subgroup within that 66 percent is the students who reported spending 6 to 10 hours per week preparing for class—27 percent. Because the participants in our study included *everything* that they read in their daily tallies, we think it's safe to assume that the amount of time that they spent on reading *in preparation for class* probably lies within this 6- to-10-hours-per-week category.

9. By agreement with the participants, all names have been changed to pseudonyms.

Works Cited [We include only those works that are cited in the excerpt.]

Booth, Wayne. *Modern Dogma and the Rhetoric of Assent.* Chicago: U of Chicago P, 1974.

Fishman, Jenn, Andrea Lunsford, Beth McGregor, and Mark Otuteye. "Performing Writing, Performing Literacy." *CCC* 57 (2006): 224–52.

Hawisher, Gail E., Cynthia L. Selfe, Brittney Moraski, and Melissa Pearson. "Becoming Literate in the Information Age: Cultural Ecologies and the Literacies of Technology." *CCC* 55 (2004): 642–92.

National Survey of Student Engagement. *Exploring Different Dimensions of Student Engagement: 2005 Annual Survey Results.* 15 Dec. 2007 http://nsse.iub.edu/pdf/NSSE_2005_annual_report.pdf.

Oliver, Ellin Keene, and Susan Zimmerman. *Mosaic of Thought: Teaching Comprehension in a Reader's Workshop.* Portsmouth, NH: Heinemann, 1997.

Sanoff, Alvin P. "What Professors and Teachers Think: A Perception Gap over Students' Preparation." *Chronicle of Higher Education* 10 Mar. 2006. 15 Dec. 2007 http://chronicle.com/free/v52/i27/27b0091.htm.

Smith, Michael W., and Jeffrey Wilhelm. *Reading Don't Fix No Chevys: Literacy in the Lives of Young Men.* Portsmouth, NH: Heinemann, 2002.

Reading Responses

1. How do your reading habits and attitudes about reading compare to those of the students Jolliffe and Harl studied? Make two lists: one for the habits and attitudes that are familiar to you and one for those that are not.

2. Speculate on the reasons that students dislike the reading they do for classes. Include reasons that focus on students' interests, abilities, and attitudes; on the nature of the texts they read; and on the way that teachers use readings in courses.

3. How might Jolliffe and Harl's study been affected by their status as faculty members? If a student were to conduct this research, for example, how might the results have been affected? What recommendations might a student researcher make?

WRITING ASSIGNMENT

Who knows more about the way students read than students themselves? Your task for this assignment is to gather evidence about one of the three subjects that Jolliffe and Harl mention but do not discuss in-depth:

- All the students spent lots of time reading online documents.
- A substantial majority of them read their Facebook sites almost daily, sometimes for extended periods.
- Most of them read while doing something else: listening to music, checking emails and sending instant messages, watching television, and so on.

Create a set of interview questions about one of these three topics, testing them out on a classmate and revising them before using them with your research subjects. Interview at least five students. Report your findings in two ways: (1) a sketch like the ones that Jessica Hagy creates and (2) a short report that includes the following:

- A description of a problem and a research question
- A main point that answers that research question
- A description of your methods (include a copy of your interview questions and your raw data each as an appendix)
- A presentation of your results
- A set of recommendations for further student research on your topic

WRITING RHETORICALLY

When Mike's writing teacher asked students to visually represent their experience researching and writing in English 101, he drew this:

Mike, first-year student

Most writers, student as well as professional, can empathize with Mike. We have all faced writing tasks that make us want to take a nap.

On the other hand, most writers have also experienced the thrill of working on an interesting, challenging writing task, which Andrea describes in this metaphor:

> For me, writing essays in college is like going on a week-long mountain-biking trip with my church. I know how to ride a bike; I do it for fun all the time. I've done some mountain-biking before, so I remember what it's like to ride trails, to pedal fast and hard to get to the day's destination. But as soon as I get on that bike, I know that I haven't trained enough and that this day is going to be long and tiring. I encounter turns, rocks, sandpits, and hills that challenge my intelligence, my reflexes, and my strength. My body tries to rush into shape all at once, making my muscles and lungs burn. Before noon, I'm worn out—I just want to sleep, eat, and cry. When the group takes a break, I collapse beside my bike until I have to get back on the rocky, bruising trail. Finally, at the end of the day, a shimmering lake greets my sweaty face, my quickly stiffening muscles, and my sore backside. I plunge into the freezing, refreshing water, enjoying the fact that I'm done for the day, even though I know I have to get back on my bike again tomorrow.
>
> *Andrea, first year student*

In this third metaphor for writing, Marty draws the reader's attention to the relationship between the student-writer and the professor-reader:

> Writing is like being flogged in a dungeon. It is like this because we're being held prisoner here at school, and we are tortured with writing assignments. Writing is like being flogged because it is a painful process that can go on for hours, and you just wish that you would die. It is also like being flogged because weeks later you get your grade, and seeing it, like seeing scars on your body, reminds you of a past painful experience.
>
> *Marty, first-year student*

- Reflect on the writing you have done in response to school assignments. At the top of your paper, jot down two particular experiences: the time when you were most successful as a writer in school and the time that you were least successful. Write a metaphor for one of them. Draw an image that represents the other.
- Choose one of those experiences, and dramatize it. Who or what is the hero? Who or what is the villain? What is the setting? How does the plot unfold?

RHETORICAL WRITING

In their representations of writing in college, Mike, Andrea, and Marty describe feelings that most writers experience: Writing can be boring or overwhelming; it can challenge you to work hard and provide a feeling of deep satisfaction. It can also leave you feeling as if you have little control because if you want to earn academic credit, you have to complete the task the teacher assigns.

Professors and other professionals will tell you that the writing they do is often constrained in exactly these ways. Although writing in professional settings sometimes feels like the adventure that Andrea describes, it can also feel like drudgery or a flogging.

Writing is painful when the task is either too simple or too complex. Simplistic tasks bore writers, and when writers are bored, bad things happen: They put off the work; they allocate little time for the task; they make sloppy errors in grammar and thinking. Complex tasks overwhelm students by requiring them to try too many new things, to write about topics that are too vast, or to write to audiences they find intimidating. When writers feel overchallenged, bad things happen, too: Writers become anxious, so they write hurriedly, or they procrastinate, or they get a bad case of writer's block and don't write at all. Pretty much, writers have the same response to tasks that are either overly simplistic or overly complex: they do what Mike represents in his drawing—they avoid writing. We call this response "doing a Bartleby," after the title character in a Herman Melville short story, who politely refuses to work, saying, "I would prefer not to." All writers feel the pull of the Bartleby response; effective writers have developed strategies for countering that feeling.

Although you may think that you have little control over the writing assignments that professors hand out, you can shape the rhetorical situation—your relationship with your reader or the scope of your topic—to manage the complexity of the writing task. Experienced writers have developed composing strategies that help them control their writing tasks. See if these strategies can work for you:

Keep good records. Most professional writers consider "writing" to include all stages of a project, from when they realize that a problem exists, through their research on that problem, to final negotiations about document design with the publisher. These writers track their ideas and developing sense of purpose by means of a personalized system for recording resources, ideas, evidence, and citations. Follow the habits of professional writers by systematically documenting all aspects of your work. If you do, you'll have plenty of information and ideas to work from when it comes time to put words on a page.

Manage the challenge. Because professors engage in complex research problems themselves, they value—and reward—writing that tackles challenging tasks more highly than they reward writing that addresses simple problems. In this way, they grade writing the way judges score diving: They calculate the final score by multiplying the difficulty of the dive by how well the diver completed it. Neither a really complicated dive done badly nor a perfectly executed swan dive will win Olympic gold. Throughout your composing process, constantly monitor the complexity of the task that you have set for yourself so that you take on as much challenge as possible without overwhelming yourself. Adjust the scope of the problem, the type and amount of evidence you provide, and the sophistication of your presentation.

Consult your editor. When most people think of a "writer," they imagine a creative writer who works alone, fitting words to imagination. Most writing, however, is much more collaborative than that; writers negotiate all aspects of their writing—from scope and definition of the problem to the best formulation of results and recommendations— with others, such as coauthors and editors. Consider treating your professor as you would a coauthor or an editor: Meet with your professor to clarify your understanding of the task, or to sanity-check your approach to completing the task. Ask your professor for help when you are confused or frustrated, and get feedback on rough drafts.

Accept recursivity and revision.   Too often, writing is described as a linear process—a writer chooses a topic, researches, outlines, drafts, and edits. Professional writers expect to encounter (and even invite) revision throughout their composing process. They're not surprised when creating an outline shows them additional topics they need to research or when putting words on the page gives them new insight into their main point, insight that they may need to research before they can use it in their writing. Expect your composing to be more like a rollercoaster of loops and turns than a highway. Jot down revision ideas as they come to you, and follow up on them. In other words, revise.

Seek out new strategies for writing.   Some students may have learned one "right" way to write. That instruction is not likely to have worked for everyone in the class because people compose in a variety of ways. In fact, the strategies that writers find useful are likely to change over their lifetime. Writers who need to complete a great deal of research, thinking, and planning before they begin drafting are sometimes called "think-write" writers. Writers who compose by writing multiple drafts are sometimes called "write-rewrite" writers. Both types of writers can be highly effective if they are aware of the strategies that currently work for them yet remain open to trying new strategies when they face more complex challenges.

Get moving and stay moving.   It's common to hear students describe writing as an activity that requires inspiration: they think writing should "flow" out of them, and they complain of writer's block when it doesn't. If you think of writing as a recursive process, you will see writer's block not as a stop sign but as a sign that detours you to rethink your logic or to research an underdeveloped idea. If you find yourself with writer's block, try strategies that other writers find useful. If you are a think-write writer, for example, you might discover that writing a two-minute draft about some aspect of the project, the reasoning behind the organization, for example, loosens your thinking. If you are a write-rewrite writer, on the other hand, you might sketch a family tree of ideas as a way to see the relationships among ideas.

These general strategies for taking control of your writing—for writing rhetorically—will help you write more efficiently and more effectively.

If you also use the Key Rhetorical Concepts to analyze the rhetorical situation of your writing, you will discover additional strategies for writing well.

USING THE KEY RHETORICAL CONCEPTS TO HELP YOU WRITE BETTER

1. Writing for a Purpose

Everyone hates to write when the writing seems like a waste of time and effort. If you take the time to figure out your purpose for writing, you will be more likely to resist the urge to "do a Bartleby." To determine your own purpose for writing, consider the effect you hope to have on yourself, your reader, or the world. Why are you writing? To understand something or someone else better? To find and organize information about a topic? To persuade your reader to believe a certain way? If you can connect your purpose for writing to what you're passionate about, you're more likely to write effectively.

Most writers describe their purpose for writing at the beginning of their text, often in the abstract or introduction, by describing the problem that their writing addresses. Depending on the discipline, this description will take the form of a research problem statement or a research question. A well-defined research problem is characterized by these features:

- Specificity: It details who, when, where, and how.
- Significance: It shows the importance of studying the problem.
- Timeliness: It explains the urgency of solving the problem.
- Focus: It targets particular aspects of the problem.
- Feasibility: It can be adequately addressed in the number of pages you have or with the resources available to you..

Composing Strategy 1: Write about what you care about.

- If the writing assignment allows you the freedom to select your own topic, choose a topic that will motivate you to research and write, even during the times when the work is difficult. Choose a topic that
    a. Makes use of what you already know from previous coursework or life experiences
    b. Builds knowledge or understanding that you can use later
    c. Gives you a chance to learn something that you want to know—piques your curiosity
    d. Prepares you to take advantage of future opportunities
    e. Does something good for the world

- If the writing assignment requires you to write about a particular topic, explore the kinds of problems associated with that topic and focus on a problem that is of particular interest to you. If, for example, the assigned topic is your college's plan to eliminate food trays from dining halls, brainstorm a variety of associated problems such as the budgetary consequences of students taking more food than they can consume; physiological effects of overeating; psychological consequences of taking repeated trips for second helpings; or environmental damage from food waste.

- Remembering that not all topics are equally good, test-drive a few topics before you make your final decision. Do a little research to confirm that academic researchers are currently researching problems related to the topic. Make a list of the problems that researchers are currently writing about. Which problems do you know something about? Which do you care about? Read a little of what these researchers are writing to ensure that you can understand what academic researchers have to say about the topic.

2. Writing to Make a Point

Writers use three primary strategies to convey their main point: thesis statements, hypotheses, and recommendations. Any of these strategies can describe a solution to a research problem that is the purpose for writing.

A thesis statement provides a succinct answer to the writer's research question. Good thesis statements contain an element of risk for the writer in that they challenge the writer to state what she believes and they open her to counterarguments from her readers. Good thesis statements contain an element of risk for the reader, too, in that they surprise the reader with an unexpected or challenging answer to a problem, they stretch the reader's thinking with counterclaims and alternatives, and they free the reader to decide for himself whether or not he agrees with the writer's thesis.

Hypotheses are also commonly used in academic writing to provide a provisional, testable answer to a research problem or a tentative explanation for observations. The writer uses the results of the tests to determine whether the hypothesis is valid or invalid. If the results do not support the hypothesis, writers may analyze them to see if they provide insight into an improved hypothesis.

In professional disciplines such as engineering, nursing, or business, writers usually make their point through a list of recommendations. Effective recommendations describe a limited number of actions that will likely solve the problem that the writer has described. The writer should be as specific as possible about who should enact the recommendations and what actions those people should take. The writer must provide reasoning and evidence to support his recommendations. Often writers will provide a set of benchmarks for others to test how well the recommendations solved the problem.

Composing Strategy 2: Draft a working description of your research problem and point.

- Create a brief history of research problems or research questions about your topic. Jot down one-sentence descriptions of the research problems and questions that you come across. Plot them on a timeline so that you can trace the evolution of the problems that researchers have tackled. Look for commonalities—what problems have remained constant across time? What are the most current problems that researchers are studying? Which current problem could you take on?

- As you begin work on a writing assignment, draft a one-sentence working description of the research problem and a one-sentence statement of your point. As you learn more about the topic, refine your working description of the problem and your point. Once you are satisfied with your description, analyze the relationship between the problem and your point. Make adjustments so that your point directly answers the problem you identify.

3. Writing as an Effective Author

When you write, you present a version of yourself to readers, and readers will be more likely to agree with you if you present a version that is self-controlled, trustworthy, informed, perceptive, and caring. You convey this version of yourself through all aspects of your writing. For example, if you turn in an essay that follows all the nitty-gritty rules of MLA style, you have demonstrated that you have the self-control to follow rules. And a reader is likely to assume that you paid attention to other, more important details. More significantly, if you carefully describe how your assumptions about human nature influence your reasoning about a social problem, readers will be more willing to listen to your argument, even if they do not share your assumptions.

One way writers can foster this trust is by commanding expertise. Writers depend, especially in critical spots, on the expertise of others—on information, ideas, or recommendations of researchers who are recognized as experts in the field. Writers also draw on personal experiences or specialized knowledge expertise that they developed in their academic major, on a job, or through public service.

Composing Strategy 3: Take on a role.   All writers present a version of themselves to their readers. If you want to enhance your credibility, present a version that your readers recognize and value, such as these common personas for student writers:

- Writer as intellectual sleuth. Acting as a detective, the writer hunts down hard-to-find or hard-to-understand information. The writer presents that information to answer a question or challenge a common understanding of a problem.

- Writer as matchmaker. Acting as a dating service, the writer brings in theories, methods, or evidence from one academic discipline or subject area to address a problem in another.

- Writer as critic. Acting as an analyst, the writer closely examines particular features of a problem. The writer uses evidence from that examination to explain the function or the importance of those features to the overall problem. The writer may offer recommendations for solving the problem based on that analysis.

- Writer as talk-show guest. Acting as someone with specialized knowledge or experience, the writer describes personal experiences or relies on expertise to provide readers with insights about the nature or importance of a problem.

4. Writing to Establish a Relationship with an Audience

Writers sometimes know specifically who will be reading what they write; sometimes they know characteristics but not specifics; and other times, they know nothing at all. Regardless of what writers know about their readers, they have to decide how much they will accommodate their readers' needs and interests as they write. As a writer, you can look to your purpose for writing as a sure guide in your thinking about how much you should consider your readers. If you're writing a quick free-write to stimulate your own thinking, for example, you're not likely to think about audience at all. If, on the other hand, you're writing an essay for a scholarship application, you're likely to pay close attention to your audience's interests by providing reasons and evidence that you meet the selection criteria.

As a student writer, you can establish a positive relationship with professor-readers by meeting their needs. As busy people, professors want to understand your main point quickly and with certainty. As professionals in a particular academic discipline, professors want to believe that you that you write as an apprentice in their field, learning about your subject matter, and are respectful of the conventions used by scholars. As teachers, professors want to believe that you found the assignment interesting and that you worked hard on it.

To establish an effective relationship with your audience, you must give them "reader-based prose," writing that takes into account the needs and interests of the reader, rather than "writer-based prose," writing that makes sense to the author alone. All writers sometimes slip into "writer-based prose," especially when they face new or complex writing tasks. Effective writers revise their writer-based prose into reader-based prose that makes sense to readers, too.

Composing Strategy 4: Be a good host.   Revising with an eye to providing a good experience for your reader is like being a good party host.

- Make introductions. Explain important background information before you refer to it in your writing. Define technical terms. If you are unsure about your readers' level of knowledge, direct the readers to sources of additional information. Avoid talking down to your readers by explaining what they are likely to know already.
- Accommodate your readers' assumptions. You can assume that your readers share assumptions about how the physical world works; you can be less sure that your readers share your assumptions about such things as politics, religion, or social policy. You can accommodate your readers' assumptions without compromising your own by identifying the assumptions that guide your thinking.
- Recognize your readers' experience. Because of differences in age, gender, race, economic class, or geography, your readers will have had different life experiences than you. Allude to shared knowledge or experiences when you are fairly certain that your readers will recognize them. If you are uncertain, provide an example or background information.
- Respect your readers' needs and expectations. Readers hope to use what they've read. Unless you have good reason to do otherwise, write so that readers can find information quickly and understand it thoroughly.
- Acknowledge your readers' abilities. All readers do not read with the same skill, ease, or pleasure. At complex or crucial parts of your writing, accommodate readers by using simpler sentence structures, repeating information, or providing an example.

5. Writing about Research Methods and Evidence

Whether or not they state their methods explicitly, writers become credible to readers when (a) they use reliable research methods to find and evaluate ideas and information and (b) they provide a sufficient amount of the kind of evidence that readers respect. Often a writing assignment will give you clues about the kind of research methods and the types of evidence that the professor expects. If it does not, or if you are writing without the guidance of an assignment, analyze the research methods and evidence used by others writing on the same topic.

Research methods.   Because the quality of evidence is determined by the research methods, most researchers use methods that are widely accepted by researchers in their discipline. And they make sure that they communicate their methods to readers, either in a separate "Methods" section or in the way that they present their evidence.

Different disciplines use methods that best produce the kinds of evidence they study. The natural sciences prefer experiments that record what happens in a controlled setting. Social scientists use experiments in which they control what they observe about human social interactions, but they also use surveys, focus groups, and case studies to produce reliable and useful evidence. In the humanities researchers analyze primary documents: Historians look at records such as letters or newspapers, literary critics and philosophers study original texts. Theory also determines methods in the humanities. A literary critic who believes in the theory that we cannot understand literature apart from its historical context, for example, will study historical context; a psychoanalytic critic's method, on the other hand, will focus on the psychological evidence in characters' thoughts and actions.

All methods, however, serve the purpose of uncovering evidence—the concrete witness without which writers cannot hope to be persuasive.

Evidence.   Writers in different disciplines use different types of evidence. Primary evidence is original source material or raw data that the researcher is analyzing. For example, in literary research primary evidence is the literary texts; in history it is the old newspapers, diaries, or archeological artifacts; in sociology it is the actual social interactions. Secondary evidence is what other researchers have written about the primary evidence. In literary research and historical study, secondary evidence would be the interpretations or theories of other scholars; in sociology or natural sciences, it would be theories, methods, or results from the research of other scholars. In your own writing, use a ratio of primary and secondary evidence that is appropriate to your topic and discipline.

Because evidence originates in a particular time and place, it reflects the knowledge and ways of thinking of that time period. In some disciplines (like literary studies, for example), the age of the primary evidence does not matter; writers can even use secondary evidence that is old but important to support an argument. In other disciplines (biology, for example), the age of primary evidence might matter; the age of secondary evidence is likely to matter a great deal, as scientists rely most heavily on the results of the most up-to-date research methods.

Some common types of evidence include statistics, facts, experimental results, examples, anecdotes, quotations, expert opinions, interviews, and personal experience. Once you have decided on the kind of evidence you will use, you need to determine how you will present it. To demonstrate that they researched thoroughly, writers sometimes provide only a citation for other research. Use this strategy when the research provides background or additional information rather than information that is key to answering your research question.

Writers present evidence in a variety of ways. They use tables and graphs for numeric information; pictures and graphics for visual information. For verbal information, writers use the following strategies:

- *Quotation.*   When you quote evidence, you invite the original author—his words, sentence structures, and ideas—into the room with you and your reader. Because you do not control the focus of the quoted author's words and ideas, readers may be inclined to trust quotations more than summary or paraphrase, so quotations work well for evidence that is cutting edge, surprising, or controversial.

- *Paraphrase.*   When you paraphrase, you restate an author's words in about the same number of your own words. Paraphrase when you want to fit the tone or sentence structure of evidence to your own writing. Also paraphrase to better fit evidence into your own focus—without misrepresenting the intent of the original author.

- *Summary.*   When you summarize, you present the main ideas of a source in a shorter version, using your own words. Effective summaries balance between emphasizing the most the relevant evidence from the source and accurately portraying the original point of the source. You can summarize evidence visually (in tables, graphs, or images) or verbally.

- *Synthesis.*   When you synthesize, you help the reader understand the topical and logical connections among two or more pieces of evidence. Synthesize to blend evidence from a variety of sources. Researchers also synthesize to represent the history of thinking about a topic in a research review, literature review, or a theoretical framework section of an academic essay.

Finally, you must credit the source of the evidence in the citation style preferred by the discipline of your topic. Someone—either a person or group—claims intellectual property rights to most information. If you fail to acknowledge the ideas, data, or words of others, either mistakenly or intentionally, you risk being accused of intellectual dishonesty—plagiarism. (See the appendix on citing sources and plagiarism at the end of this book.)

Composing Strategy 5: Make friends.   Finding enough useful evidence causes writers big headaches. Most student writers underestimate the amount of time it will take them to track down the information they need, and few students are expert at using library databases to access the full range of information on their topic. Because undergraduate students write in a variety of disciplines and because library databases are constantly adding features, your best strategy is to look for help from experts.

- Work with a research librarian from the very beginning. At most academic libraries you will find research librarians who are available to help students use the library's research databases. These librarians will advise you on the most useful databases for your topic and the best strategies for using those databases. Furthermore, these librarians are expert researchers; you can learn excellent research strategies by watching them in action.

- Mine the bibliographies of the research you read. See what research other authors have used; find and skim that research to determine if it might be useful to you.

- Use a citation generator to create a citation for a source as soon as you have determined that it might be useful. Citation generators will produce citations in all the commonly used citation styles. The citation it generates, however, is only as accurate as the information that you provide. If you create the citation while you are accessing the source, you can more easily find all the required information.

- Keep a working bibliography of all the sources that you have reviewed in the citation style that you will be required to use. If you categorize the sources, you will be able to see how you could narrow your topic. You can easily create a list of works cited by copying the citations of the sources that you actually used in your essay from your working bibliography.

6. Organizing Your Writing

Sometimes writers have little choice about how they organize their writing. For example, most scientific reports follow a commonly used format: Introduction, Methods and Materials, Results, Discussion (the IMRAD format). Many business reports start with an executive summary and then move into an analysis of a business problem, a description of a way to solve that problem including associated costs, and a list of recommendations that the business should enact.

Even when it seems that you have a great deal of freedom to develop your own organizational plan, you must use a plan that makes sense to readers. Readers need to understand a problem before they will be interested in its solution; they expect to understand general concepts before they learn about specific ones; they expect to read how current research grows out of earlier research and how proposed solutions avoid the weaknesses of earlier ones. When you have freedom to organize your text, consider how you will divide your text into parts; how you will arrange those parts (both ordering the parts and creating hierarchies among ideas), and what repetitions, patterns, and transitions you can use to help readers understand the relationships among the parts.

Composing Strategy 6: Follow models.   If you analyze other texts on your topic to identify effective organizational patterns, you are likely to save time and write in ways that your reader understands and respects.

- Outline four or five pieces of writing on your topic. Note how the writers introduce the problem and communicate their solution to the problem. Where do they present background information like a literature review or research framework? How do they order their main points? What conventions of the discipline do they seem to be following?

- Create a web of the ideas that a writer includes in the text. Put the writer's main point in the center of the web, the subpoints in nodes that radiate from that center, and evidence and reasoning radiating out of those nodes. Analyze the relationship between the writer's ideas and how those ideas are ordered in the text. What logic did the writer use in ordering the presentation of those ideas to the reader?

- Track your experience as a reader. As you read texts, circle the devices that writers use to help you navigate through their texts, paying attention to headings, key words, and visual features of the texts.

7. Presenting Your Writing

When writers make choices about how they will present their writing to their readers, they must consider the visual design and the verbal style of their prose.

Visual design.   If we were to show you a few pages from published papers in several different disciplines—even if we held them far enough away that you could not read the words, you would immediately notice different visual features. Disciplines have strong traditions for the visual design of texts. In academic disciplines such as English and philosophy, the implicit message is that visuals are less important than the words, growing ideas, and layered complexity that the reader experiences by reading a text word-by-word, from beginning to end. Writers who rely mainly on words think of images as ways to illustrate what they write verbally. In business, on the other hand, writers rely on images as efficient and powerful ways to communicate information and convince people to take action. Those who depend on images know that images communicate on their own.

Visual design sharpens focus and clarifies organization through features such as headings, headers, and white space. It illustrates key ideas with photos and diagrams. It highlights individual words and sentences through features such as italics, boldface, and bullet points. Writers use visual design to show relationships and processes through figures and drawings. And they present numeric information efficiently through tables and graphs that are anchored to the rest of the text by verbal descriptions and references.

Prose style.   Although some writers think of style as an unchangeable feature of writers—like the size of their feet—most teachers of writing think about style as something that writers can control by choosing words, constructing sentences, and developing verbal images. Writers adapt their prose style, just as they do all other aspects of their writing, to respond to the opportunities and challenges of the topic and the audience. In some contexts, writers and readers enjoy playful prose filled with complexity, surprise, and delight. In other contexts, writers and readers appreciate clear prose that is efficient and unambiguous.

Composing Strategy 7: Storyboard the reader's experience of your text. Visual design and prose style are intertwined with each other and with other features of your text. You may find it helpful to borrow a composing strategy from cartoonists and screenwriters: storyboarding. Create a series of panels that represent the reader's experience of your text. Fill each panel with quick sketches of visuals and words to help you decide (1) what you will represent visually and what you will represent with words, and (2) how the visuals and the words will cooperate to convey your meaning to the reader.

- When you are organizing your ideas, create a series of panels, one for each of your points, to represent the reader's experience of your text. Consider which points may need to be broken into smaller points, how best to order your points, and how to help the reader move from one point to the next.

- When you find yourself struggling to put your ideas into sentences, storyboard the sentence (you may need to think metaphorically to put your ideas into a storyboard). List who or what is doing something, what they are doing, and the consequences of that action. Next, sketch out that scene in a series of panels.

- Finally, move from storyboard to words. Start with a simple sentence structure: Put one of the doers in the subject position of your sentence, one of the actions in the verb position, and someone or something that gets altered in the object position. After you create a few simple sentences, try joining them together with the words *because, if, although,* and *therefore.* The resulting complex sentence structures may help you better understand the complex relationships within your topic.

The Composing Strategies

1. Write about what you care about: Choose a topic that builds on your knowledge or expertise and piques your curiosity.

2. Draft a working description of your research problem and point: Revise your description of the research problem and point as your understanding of the topic develops.

3. Take on a role: Present a version of yourself that the reader recognizes and values.

4. Be a good host: Provide the best experience possible for your reader.

5. Make friends: Seek help at all stages of your composing process.

6. Follow models: Try out effective organizing strategies from what you have read on the topic.

7. Storyboard the reader's experience of your text: Test out how to use visual and verbal strategies for presenting your text to the reader.

A MODEL FOR WRITING RHETORICALLY

Of course, there are as many ways of using these Key Rhetorical Concepts as there are people writing. As you write, keep assessing your composing strategies—identify which are helping you and which are holding you back. Double-check your work against the chart of Key Rhetorical Concepts—take the time to ensure that you are paying attention to all aspects of your rhetorical situation. As you talk to others who write, consider whether their approaches to writing tasks might work for you. To get started, read what student Abby DeCook has to say about her essay, "Just as Human."

The Assignment.   I wrote this essay in response to my very first English 101 essay assignment—one of those assignments in which you get your creative juices flowing and introduce yourself as a writer to your professor. All the students in my honors section were also enrolled in the same honors biology class, and our professors tried to coordinate the material in the courses. So for this introductory writing assignment, my English professor asked us to describe an encounter with science that had strongly influenced us in some way.

My Composing Process.   The open-ended nature of this assignment seemed great at first and then very frustrating. The great part was that I came up with the topic for my essay almost immediately. A few years ago, I had gone on a medical missions trip to Bangladesh with my friend Kristine and my dad; I jumped at the opportunity to write about one part of that trip—watching my dad perform surgery. There's something both earthy and surreal about surgery in developing countries. It's weird enough to see somebody's insides pulled out, repaired, and tucked back in, but it's more bizarre still to see that happen outside the clinically sterile environment that Americans expect in hospitals.

I called up my dad to pick his brain about some of the specifics of the event that I'd forgotten, and badgered my patient roommate to read over sections for me. Pretty soon I was satisfied with the descriptive part of the essay.

When I got to the second part of my essay, I really struggled with what to say about why the experience had been so meaningful for me. I had a lot of different thoughts and emotions about that event, and I didn't have space to talk about all of them, so I had to edit and rewrite many, many times to come up with something relatively concise. I don't think there was ever a moment when I consciously chose exactly what I wanted to say at the end of the essay—rather, I sort of sifted and resifted through my thoughts by arduously drafting, editing, redrafting, reediting, and then discussing my writer's block with other people when I got stuck.

Writing in College.   Probably the most useful thing you can do in college writing classes is make multiple drafts. It might seem easier to just write the first draft really carefully, spell-check it, and turn it in, but that approach just doesn't hold up for most college writing assignments because your first idea about how to approach the assignment isn't usually your best idea. To really get a handle on your topic, try writing a first draft where you just scribble down all of your thoughts and ideas about the subject, and then pick through those ideas until you find something you like. If I had stuck with my first draft version of this essay, it would have been extremely long and convoluted, with too much description and too little purpose. By making two, three, and eventually four drafts, I was able to get a much clearer sense of what I wanted to talk about and how to express it most effectively to my professor.

[Abby DeCook is studying pre-Veterinary Zoology with the intention of becoming a veterinarian. She visited Bangladesh in 2008.]

[This student essay follows MLA guidelines for formatting and documentation.]

Just as Human

Abby DeCook

[1] Purpose: Because my purpose for writing is to emphasize this boy's humanity, I focused the reader's attention on him and the poor condition of the operating room.

[1] The boy's fear was palpable, as conspicuous as the shabby medical equipment cluttering the surgery room. He was, as my dad explained, about twelve years old, and a member of a tribal group from the Chittagong hill tracts of Bangladesh. He had probably never been inside a hospital before, and now he was lying exposed on a surgical bed, [2] panting and quivering like a trapped cat. My friend Kristine and I felt edgy and uncomfortable, decked out in musty smelling hand-me-down hospital scrubs that we had to wear in the operating room. What made me more uncomfortable than the clothing, however, was the desperate look on the boy's face. His dark, almond-shaped eyes seemed close to tears as they darted around the room.

[2] Audience: I compared the boy to an animal to encourage my reader to wonder if I saw this boy as a human being equal to me.

[3] In the back of my mind, I reconsidered how much I really wanted to be on this trip at all. I was visiting Bangladesh with my dad and Kristine, on a trip that would be educational for Kristine and me and service-based for my dad. His parents had been missionary doctors in this very hospital, in the country that they had known as East Pakistan.

[3] Organization: I used this flashback to give my reader some background information as well as hint at my purpose with the word "educational."

Now a surgeon himself, my dad had come back to volunteer for a few weeks. Kristine and I had both been eager to come along and see the country, which was already proving to be more drastically different from home than we could have imagined.

[4] Author: I wanted to present my dad as someone who had a deep understanding of the problem. This photo emphasizes his experience in Bangladesh.

[4] My dad is the boy in the upper left.

The boy was here for a decidedly more unpleasant reason. He had an enormous stone in his bladder, visible on the X-ray displayed on the far wall of the surgical room (it's the thing that looks like a lima bean, in the middle of the pelvis).

[5]
Presentation:
This image
shows the size
of the stone
better than my
words can.

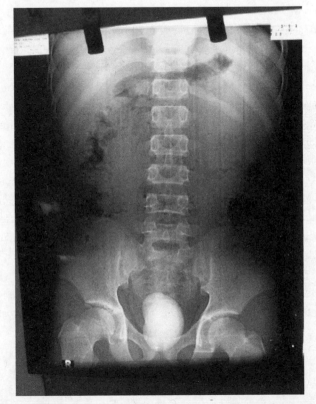

[5] DeCook

[6] Research
and evidence:
The assignment
did not require
us to use
secondary
research, but I
wanted to add
this information
to prepare my
reader for my
main point at
the end, so I
included it.

[6] The resident doctor explained to us that the stone had been in his system for the past seven or eight years of his life; only excruciating pain and his inability to urinate had finally brought him to a hospital. While Bangladesh is the eighth most populated country in the world (U.N. 44), the tribal people who reside in its hill tracts are still almost completely cut off from the outside world—and this isolation extends to medical care. Of all the health care visits made in rural Bangladesh, only 17% are made to

doctors and paramedics, while over 70% are made to untrained "village doctors." Usually only severe, enduring, or life-threatening conditions are considered worth an arduous trip to a hospital (Alam 127). It had taken nearly an entire lifetime of pain to get this boy where he was now, in an operating room at Memorial Christian Hospital.

One of the several cloth-masked assistants hovering around the surgical table swabbed the boy's lower stomach with a wad of cotton, damp with sterilizing alcohol. [7] I cringed empathetically when the doctor inserted a needle and a tube into the boy's wrist, then felt my body unclench when the anesthetic began to flow and his eyes fluttered shut. My dad cheerfully snapped on latex gloves, cracking jokes as he went along. I wasn't sure if his quips made me more confident or less in his abilities as a surgeon.

[7] Author: I wanted to show myself changing as a result of this experience by becoming more connected to the boy's suffering.

He then took a good-size scalpel from the tray next to the surgical bed and began to cut delicately through the thin layers of tissue.

"This guy's skinny, so this part will go quick," he commented. "It usually goes a lot slower on fat people."

He followed the incisions of the scalpel with an odd electrical tool that buzzed and caused the flesh it came into contact with to sizzle and let out little wisps of steam. This treatment, he explained, stopped the patient from bleeding too much. This particular patient couldn't afford to bleed—due to a nutritionally poor, vegetable-based diet, he was severely anemic, and any significant blood loss could be fatal (DeCook).

After a relatively short time, my dad pulled the flesh back slightly from a pearly-purple bladder. "And THAT," he said, poking at what appeared to be something distinctly un-fleshy underneath. "Is the stone. Hey, looks like we got it."

"You thought you wouldn't?" Kristine and I said almost simultaneously, only half joking.

"Well, I've never actually done this surgery before. Normally you'd want a urologist for this, but if you know the anatomy this is a pretty straightforward procedure," he explained, slicing through the bladder and spreading it apart with a medieval looking pair of pliers. "Now, we just have to hope that the stone fits through the incision . . ."

He grasped the stone with latex-gloved fingers and pulled it free from the impossibly tiny opening. It was lumpy and gray, asymmetric and nearly the size of a baseball.

My father deposited it into a metal dish on the side of the surgery table with a ceramic clinking sound.

"Can I take a picture?" Kristine enquired.

"Sure," agreed my dad. "Do you want me to pose with it? Or maybe we can lay the scalpel next to it for scale?"

The two of them composed pictures of the grisly medical souvenir for a couple of minutes before my dad decided that it was time to stitch the kid up before the anesthetic wore off.

As he stitched, the boy started to twitch and moan, flinging his head to one side. I gasped, worrying that he was somehow waking up mid-surgery. He wasn't, as the other doctor present explained. It was just a side effect of the anesthetic. To knock him out, they had used Ketamine—a chemical relative of LSD that is mostly discontinued as a human anesthetic (though it is still commonly used in veterinary medicine) in the U.S. as it caused people to have vivid nightmares during their surgeries (Ketamine). They had also dosed him with Valium, an amnesiac, so he would be unable to remember whatever frightening dream he was having (DeCook). Still, I felt a weird twinge of privileged guilt knowing that someone just as human as myself was being treated with a drug that wouldn't be considered good enough for people who happen to live in a developed nation.

The uncomfortable wrench only grew worse as he was wheeled away to the recovery room. [9] I began to really appreciate the overwhelming

[8] Presentation: This image creates mixed feelings for the reader, exactly the kind of feelings I experienced while observing surgery. On the one hand, the reader can't help but appreciate the beauty of the photo's color and composition; on the other hand, the reader feels a twinge of guilt at finding pleasure in the image of something that could have killed the boy.

[9] Purpose: Here, I direct my reader's attention toward the main problem that I'm writing about. I start by listing my assumptions about easy access to high-quality medical care.

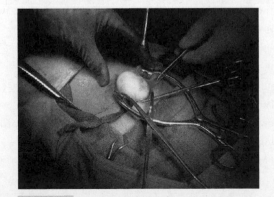

[8] DeCook

difference between how life is valued, more or less, in our own country and the developing world. If I ever developed a bladder stone, I would have undoubtedly had it treated as soon as any symptoms began to show. I would consider this my right, in fact. I would not have had to live with agonizing discomfort for seven years, I would not have had to walk several days to get to a hospital, I would not have been treated with an anesthetic that is used on horses, and I would not have had to recover in a room packed with other sick people. [10] The worth of our lives in the eyes of the world came down to a simple equation of geography and economics.

> [10] Point: Here is the main problem that I want my reader to think about.

And yet—despite those formidable odds, that boy recovered. We would have been foolish, I think, to congratulate ourselves and our foreign equipment and skills too much for that. America in particular is very fond of swooping into developing countries handing out gifts and services like [11] some tremendously misguided Santa Claus. We churn out solutions at lightning speed before we even understand the problem, and then shake our heads in bewilderment when our wonderful antibiotics foster drug-resistant bacteria, our vaccine needles spread HIV, and our cash donations find their way into dictators' Swiss bank accounts. We wonder why we tried to help in the first place.

> [11] Presentation: I think that this verbal image communicates my point effectively.

But yet—that boy recovered. For him, for all of us, it was worth it. In the moments when we can put aside our foreign smugness, and become just one person helping another—those are the times when we become most human. [12] Whether we live next-door or half a globe apart, people need to help and be helped by one another. Much as we might like to preen and congratulate ourselves for giving our valuable help to the needy, we can't change the uncomfortable truth—there is no essential difference between Us and Them. [13] They might be the ones in crisis right now, but we are just as human, just as needy, just as potentially desperate.

> [12] Point: Finally I state my point in a single sentence: humans—those who need help and those who are helping—should recognize how we depend on each other.

> [13] Organization: I organized my text so that my reader would experience my main point as I did: first through experience, then by thinking through arguments and counterarguments. For this reason, I delayed stating my point until near the end of my essay.

I'll never know that boy's name. I don't think any of us ever did—he came from some mysterious place in the jungle and returned there as inconspicuously as he arrived. I'll never forget him, though. His look of pained terror on the hospital bed is still clear in my mind, but clearer still is the tremendous relief of knowing that he would be all right—that we could help him be all right. He'll never know who I am, but in an anonymous and yet strangely personal way, he gave more to me than I could ever have given to him.

Just as Human 6

Works Cited

Alam, Nurul, Jeroen van Ginneken, and Ian Timaeus. "Determinants of Perceived Morbidity and Use of Health Services by Children Less Than 15 Years Old in Rural Bangladesh." Maternal and Child Health Journal 13 (2009): 119–129. Web. 9 July 2010.

DeCook, Daniel. Personal Interview. 16 Sept. 2009.

—. Photograph. 8 July 2010.

"Ketamine." Encyclopædia Britannica. Encyclopædia Britannica Online. Encyclopædia Britannica, 2010. Web. 9 July 2010 http://search.eb.com/eb/article-9474649>.

United Nations, Department of Economic and Social Affairs Population Division

"World Population Prospects: The 2008 Revision Highlights," 2009. 10 July, 2010.

Reading Responses

1. Abby DeCook delays stating her main point in a single sentence until near the end of her essay. In what ways is that an effective rhetorical choice? In what ways is she taking a risk?

2. Use three different means to chart the organization of DeCook's essay: an outline, a sentence summary of each paragraph, and a drawing of the "path" of the essay, with topics placed as locations on the path that she comes across, leaves, and then returns to. Which method do you find most useful for describing the organization of this essay?

3. DeCook does not include a photograph of the boy who endured the operation nor a picture of herself. What effect does that have on her essay?

WRITING ASSIGNMENT

When choosing which academic discipline to major in, most students rely on their skills, aptitudes, and previous experiences to guide them to work that they will enjoy. When students choose topics for research in the same way, they are likely to find the work more interesting and more rewarding. Your task for this assignment is to tell a story about a personal experience with the academic discipline that you hope to major in or with a topic for a major writing project. To begin, free-write about a few experiences in which you demonstrated skill in or curiosity about the discipline or topic. Choose one or two of your free-writes to explore more fully: what events in your life led up to the moment you describe? Who influenced your actions or shaped your thinking? What meaning does the experience have for you? Examine what you have written to determine how you could use primary research (interviews, photographs, etc.) and secondary research (definitions, background information) to enhance your own understanding and the reader's experience of your writing. As you draft, begin with a working draft of your research problem and your point. Continue to refine these as you draft your essay. Be sure to cite your use of primary and secondary sources.

PART TWO

READING AND WRITING ACROSS THE DISCIPLINES

In Part Two you will read the work of professionals and students in eleven different disciplines. The chapters in Part Two will not teach you how to write in these eleven disciplines. Rather, our hope is that your reading and rhetorical study of published and student writing in these disciplines will habituate you to look for lessons in everything you read, lessons that you can take with you to make you a more adaptive, inventive writer.

To make it possible for you to build the habits that will allow you to continue to become a more effective writer by reading rhetorically, we focus on one "portable rhetorical lesson" in each chapter. These are lessons that you can apply in your writing, whatever your discipline or eventual profession. The special rhetorical demands of each different discipline incite writers to devise strategies to meet the demands, to solve the problems. Scientists, for example, learn ways to present lots of data efficiently, speechwriters learn how to write for audiences, marketers learn to use images, and so on.

To maximize the habit of reading to discover a discipline's rhetorical expertise, we present writing that experts compose for one another, writing that students compose as they learn the practices of a discipline, and writing that experts compose for a public audience. And we help you to see how the portable rhetorical lesson of each chapter informs each different writing sample.

We hope that learning good habits as a rhetorical reader and writer in a world of many different disciplinary specializations will enable you to tackle all the rhetorical challenges that you will someday face.

SPEECH COMMUNICATION: ANALYZING AUDIENCES

June 2, 2010. Armando Galarraga was in his first baseball season as a pitcher for the Detroit Tigers. As he racked up inning after inning of perfect pitching, people began to alert their friends, and ESPN cut away from its usual programming to cover the end of the game. Few players had ever pitched a perfect game—only twenty in professional baseball at that time. An easy throw to first base looked to be the final play. It was obvious to everyone watching that the runner was out, that Galarraga had pitched the twenty-first perfect game in baseball history. And then the umpire, Jim Joyce, called the runner safe, ending Galarraga's bid for a perfect game. As viewers watched replays that confirmed the umpire's error, they got angry.

After the game, Joyce watched a replay of the play. And then he amazed everyone: in a postgame news conference he admitted his mistake. "No, I did not get the call correct. . . . I missed the damn call. I missed it. . . . There's nobody that feels worse than I do. I take pride in this job . . . and I took a perfect game away from that kid over there who worked his ass off all night. This is probably the most important call in my career, and I missed it." Joyce later apologized in person to Galarraga.

And then Jim Joyce had a chance to be amazed himself. From across the nation, he heard praise for his apology, some calling it the perfect response to human imperfection.

- Have you ever had to apologize in public? If you had to craft a public apology, what would you be sure to include?
- Reread Joyce's words above (you can hear the full six minutes of the news conference at http://www.youtube.com/watch?v=5P1oMy4WIf0). He admits that he made a mistake, but does he ever apologize? What is the difference between admitting to a mistake and apologizing for that mistake? Does that difference matter? What made Joyce's words effective for most people?

PORTABLE RHETORICAL LESSON: WRITING FOR MULTIPLE AUDIENCES

The exercise of thinking about apologies poses a straightforward challenge: How do you respond—in words—when people you can't ignore blame you for mistakes that may or may not be your fault? You always write for an audience and try to establish a positive relationship between yourself and your readers or listeners; a crisis management situation dramatizes the need to pay careful attention to that relationship.

Two rhetorical concepts jump to attention as you imagine facing the challenge of responding to blame and managing a crisis: **audience** and **author.** Audience: Who are the people to whom you need to aim your apology? If the audience is a single person, someone you know well, you can more easily judge what you need to say. If your audience is public, less predictable, made up of people of different opinions, keeping the audience on your side becomes much harder. Author: What are your character and values—and are they consistent with the image of yourself (the persona) you need to communicate? And what's your motivation for communicating? Why do you care about what your audience thinks and does?

Any situation in which you have to keep a crisis from blowing up is difficult, but the readings in this chapter give you a chance to see writers responding to audiences at a much harder level—thus giving you the chapter's **Portable Rhetorical Lesson** of analyzing and writing for multiple audiences. Presidents Obama, Clinton, and Bush (whose speeches you either read or read analyses of in this chapter) each faced public relations nightmares—national crises for which they were being blamed. And their audiences were as varied as is possible: supporters, opponents, people whose health and livelihood would be directly affected by the presidents' words, people across the globe who would pass judgment.

To influence audiences, and to do so in the high-stakes situation of restoring the public faith, a speaker must carefully analyze those different audiences, studying their:

- Background (age? gender? class?)
- Attitudes and assumptions (beliefs? opinions? concerns?)
- Knowledge (expertise? common knowledge?)
- Needs from and expectations of the speaker

Beyond those basic elements of audience analysis, consider how you might encourage your readers to be receptive to your ideas, to remember what you wrote, and to be willing to consider new options.

In a future profession, you may need to address multiple audiences about crisis situations using means like those used by the presidents in this chapter. Even as a student, though, you face multiple audiences. You write for different teachers—in different disciplines, with different expectations and ways of grading. Many schools use teams of teachers (some of whom you may not know) to grade essays or written portfolios. And you will probably make presentations to your classmates, some of whom you won't know and who think very differently than you.

In these situations:

- Gauge the controversy of your topic for your audience (the more controversial your topic for your audience, the more careful you will have to be—something like presidents in crisis-management mode).
- Study the grading criteria for the assignment. They should help you determine what the teacher expects and considers most important; if your teacher doesn't supply criteria, ask for them. Do *not* assume that each teacher wants the same thing.
- Get audience feedback (that is, talk with your teacher about papers and presentations as you are working on them and after they are graded).

These strategies are all versions of the audience analysis that presidents and other professionals conduct as they seek to satisfy their audiences.

WRITING IN THE DISCIPLINE

INTRODUCTION

by Kathi Groenendyk, Professor of Rhetoric

Scholars studying communication and rhetoric examine a range of texts—presidential speeches, popular television shows, newspapers, and propaganda posters, to name a few. What's in common? Communication scholars try to understand how the person creating the message (the rhetor) communicates certain meanings to an audience in a particular situation. Some of the most interesting studies examine the multiple audiences a rhetor may face and how speaking to that audience may actually *change* the audience's perception of the situation.

Political communication scholars (as well as news commentators) frequently note the strong political divisions in our country: politicians face an almost impossible task of presenting policy plans or uniting citizens on a certain issue. If the politician identifies too narrow an audience, she will, most likely, be speaking only to those who already agree with her. If she thinks of too broad an audience, her speech will be vague and will not be emotionally moving or persuasive. The politician, then, needs to both engage her critics and energize her supporters.

Communication theorists have developed various definitions of "audience" to help achieve this goal. Instead of only thinking of "audience" as those people who are sitting in front of the podium, the speaker can consider the "universal" audience—the speaker imagines what a rational group would want to know and what questions they would ask. When the speaker prepares his speech, he critiques his speech with this audience in mind. This will help the speaker avoid regional biases and help him think carefully about competing arguments. In political settings, the speaker also will benefit from thinking of his audience as those who are able to act to change the situation, for example, when a politician is looking for support on a piece of legislation. If the politician considers what is important to this audience—the one who can act to make a change—the politician can determine which information and emotional appeals should be in the speech.

With the Gulf of Mexico oil spill, President Barak Obama had to respond to a complex situation: an increasingly harmful oil spill that defied the usual technological solutions as well as growing public criticism first of BP and then of the presidential administration. The Deepwater Horizon oil rig, operated for the oil company BP, sank into the Gulf on April 20, 2010, killing eleven workers. With the collapse of the rig, oil from the well flowed directly into the waters, with scientists and BP officials debating the actual amount of oil gushing from the well. Throughout May, BP engineers and various outside experts (including even Hollywood connections—James Cameron and Kevin Costner) consulted about the best means to stop the flow. On May 28, with oil still flowing, President Obama spoke at a press conference, which was televised and reprinted in various news sources.

Who was Obama's audience? Gulf coast residents, local politicians, BP executives, and the larger American public (many of whom were distrustful of governmental bureaucracies) were a few of the audiences Obama faced, and these groups held different values and goals. Obama had to acknowledge the criticism he was facing yet change the audience's perception of his administration (that they were doing little to solve the problem) and of the crisis (that it could be fixed quickly). Obama's remarks, then, are a blend of rational explanations of current and proposed actions and appeals to shared values with Gulf coast residents and the "regular folks" of the American public. These elements make it more likely that his audiences will take action helping the effected environment, holding BP accountable, and supporting new legislation to prevent future disasters.

✓ Reading Tips

Read President Obama's speech just as you would *listen* to a speech—straight through, at a normal speaking pace. Pay attention to the main ideas and language choices to imagine how the president was writing for his audiences.

- Try to imagine how President Obama would have delivered the speech: Where would he pause, when would his voice get softer or stronger?
- Track your emotions and thoughts as you read, and mark places where you think the speech is more or less persuasive.
- Identify places in the speech that seem intended to appeal to a particular segment of the audience.

Remarks by the President after Briefing on BP Oil Spill, May 28, 2010

President Barack Obama

The White House, Office of the Press Secretary May 28, 2010

U.S. Coast Guard Station Grande Isle, Grande Isle, Louisiana

> In most speeches, the speaker usually attempts to build identification with the audience—create a bond with the audience and establish the common interests. Other speakers often try to capture the audience's attention with the beginning comments. Obama takes a different approach: he provides a "news update" on the latest spill conditions. He summarizes the situation—the crisis—to which this speech responds.

Good afternoon, everybody. I know it's a little warm out here so want to get started. I've just had a meeting with these governors, members of Congress, local officials, as well as Admiral Thad Allen, the National Incident Commander in charge of response efforts to the BP oil spill. Admiral Allen gave us an update, the latest information on both the efforts to plug the well, as well as giving us an update on arrangements and coordination that's being made with respect to mitigating this damage that's been done.

He updated us on these latest efforts to stop the leak, mitigate the damage to the great beaches of the Gulf coast, and I had the chance to visit with—Charlotte—a beach like Port Fourchon that gives you a sense of what extraordinary efforts are being made at the local level, but also the damage that we're already starting to see as a consequence of this spill.

> In this third paragraph, Obama builds his ethos (credibility), summarizing the actions the administration wants to take.

Now, our mission remains the same as it has since this disaster began, since the day I visited Louisiana nearly four weeks ago: We want to stop the leak; we want to contain and clean up the oil; and we want to help the people of this region return to their lives and their livelihoods as soon as possible.

And our response treats this event for what it is: It's an assault on our shores, on our people, on the regional economy, and on communities like this one. This isn't just a mess that we've got to mop up. People are watching their livelihoods wash up on the beach. Parents are worried about the implications for their children's health. Every resident of this community has watched this nightmare threaten the dreams that they've worked so hard to build. And they want it made right, and they want to make it right now.

> When Obama gave these remarks, certain American audiences were questioning the administration's efforts. Obama acknowledges those concerns in an effort to build common ground with the audience.

I just had a chance to listen to Mayor David Carmadelle of Grande Isle, our host here, telling us heartbreaking stories about fishermen who are trying to figure out where the next paycheck is going to come from, how are they going to pay a mortgage or a note on their boat. And he is having to dig into his pocket at this point to make sure that some of them are able to deal with the economic impact. So this is something that has to be dealt with immediately, not sometime later. And that's everybody's driving focus—everybody who is standing behind me. This is our highest priority and it deserves a response that is equal to the task.

Obama states what work has already been done as a way to answer the administration's critics. Obama seems to imply that his audience does not know the complete situation; his administration has begun work.

That's why this has already been the largest cleanup effort in U.S. history. On the day this disaster began, even as we launched a search and rescue effort for workers on the drilling rig, we were already staging equipment in the event of a larger-scale spill. By the time we discovered the third breach, a week after the Deepwater Horizon platform sank, we had already stationed more than 70 vessels and hundreds of thousands of feet of protective boom on site.

Today, there are more than 20,000 people in the region working around the clock to contain and clean up this spill. We've activated about 1,400 members of the National Guard across four states. Nearly 1,400 vessels are aiding in the containment and cleanup effort. And we deployed more than 3 million feet of hard and sorbent boom, including an additional 100,000 just yesterday for these parishes in Louisiana that face the greatest threat.

In most environmental disasters, the American public believes that technology will solve the problem. Obama implicitly refers to that belief.

Now, I've made clear to Admiral Allen and I did so again today that he should get whatever he needs to deal with this crisis. Whatever he needs, he will get. . . .

We have ordered BP to pay economic injury claims, and we will make sure they deliver. And the parish presidents and governors here in Louisiana were already giving us some sense of some of the bureaucratic problems that we're going to have to cut through, but we are going to cut through them. And for those who are in economic distress, if you've already filed a claim and you're not satisfied with the resolution, then whitehouse.gov will point you in the right direction.

Obama makes a populist claim: much like most of his audience, Obama blames a giant corporation and governmental bureaucracy, which means that Obama does not see himself as part of that bureaucracy.

As I said yesterday, the Small Business Administration has stepped in to help businesses by approving loans, but also as important, allowing many to defer existing loan payments. A lot of folks are still loaded up with loans that they had from Katrina and other natural disasters down here, so they may need some additional help.

If you're a small business owner and you weren't aware of some of the programs that have been put in place or haven't participated, then, again, the White House website will connect you to the resources you need. And we are making sure that all the parish presidents know, and folks like the mayor, other local officials are going to be aware of how they can get immediate help from us.

What's more, we've stationed doctors and scientists across the five Gulf States to look out for people's health and then to monitor any ill effects felt by cleanup workers and local residents. And we've begun setting up a system to track these efforts—excuse me, to track these effects—and ensure folks get the care that they need. And we've told BP that we expect them to pay for that, too.

As I've said before, BP is the responsible party for this disaster. What that means is they're legally responsible for stopping the leak and they're financially responsible for the enormous damage that they've created. And we're going to hold them accountable, along with any other party responsible for the initial explosion and loss of life on that platform.

But as I said yesterday, and as I repeated in the meeting that we just left, I ultimately take responsibility for solving this crisis. I'm the President and the buck stops with me. So I give the people of this community and the entire Gulf my word that we're going to hold ourselves accountable to do whatever it takes for as long as it takes to stop this catastrophe, to defend our natural resources, to repair the damage, and to keep this region on its feet. Justice will be done for those whose lives have been upended by this disaster, for the families of those whose lives have been lost—that is a solemn pledge that I am making.

I think I can speak for anybody here, and for anybody who has been involved in the response and the cleanup effort, and for most Americans, when I say that I would gladly do whatever it takes to end this disaster today. But I want to also repeat something that I said to the group as a whole while we were meeting. This is a manmade catastrophe that's still evolving and we face a long-term recovery and restoration effort.

America has never experienced an event like this before. And that means that as we respond to it, not every judgment we make is going to be right the first time out. Sometimes, there are going to be disagreements between experts, or between federal and state and local officials, or among state officials, or between states, about what the most effective measures will be.

Sometimes, there are going to be risks and unintended consequences associated with a particular mitigation strategy that we consider. In other words, there are going to be a lot of judgment calls involved here. There are not going to be silver bullets or a lot of perfect answers for some of the challenges that we face.

Understandably, the feelings of frustration and anger, the sense that any response is inadequate—we expect that frustration and anger to continue until we actually solve this problem. But in the meantime, we've got to make sure that everybody is working in concert, that everybody is moving in the same direction. And I want everybody to know that everybody here—at every level—is working night and day to end this crisis. We're considering every single idea out there, especially from folks who know these communities best. . . .

The bottom line is this: Every decision we make is based on a single criterion—what's going to best protect and make whole the people and the ecosystems of the Gulf.

And I want to thank everybody in this region who's rolled up their sleeves and pitched in to help—from the National Guard putting their experience to the task, to the local officials and every citizen who loves

---

In this situation, the administration has little control—they cannot control the oil spill into the waters, they cannot control the technology being used, and they have to assert control over BP. Obama, by saying "the buck stops here," implies that his administration is responsible, and therefore capable of finding a solution. Obama is changing the audience's perception of the situation (crisis). Using these words will also remind some American citizens of President Truman, who many now view favorably. Obama is borrowing ethos, then, from Truman.

Obama attempts to caution his audience against expecting a quick fix. This is an important element when many Americans want immediate results.

this area and calls it home, every American who's traveled to the region to lend a hand. If any American is looking for ways to volunteer and help, then we've put links to that information on our website, as well—that's whitehouse.gov. . . .

To the people of the Gulf Coast: I know that you've weathered your fair share of trials and tragedy. I know there have been times where you've wondered if you were being asked to face them alone. I am here to tell you that you're not alone. You will not be abandoned. You will not be left behind. The cameras at some point may leave; the media may get tired of the story; but we will not. We are on your side and we will see this through. We're going to keep at this every day until the leak has stopped, until this coastline is clean, and your communities are made whole again. That's my promise to you. And that is a promise on behalf of a nation. It is one that we will keep.

> In this paragraph Obama is appealing to the audience's emotions (pathos) and refers to shared values. This is a memorable ending to his remarks and makes his earlier statements about cleanup strategy less impersonal.

And I will make one last point—and I said this to every leader who is here: If something is not going right down here, then they need to talk to Thad Allen. And if they're not getting satisfaction from Thad Allen, then they can talk to me. There's nobody here who can't get in touch with me directly if there is an idea, a suggestion, or a logjam that needs to be dealt with.

> Obama ends with a call to action and stresses his personal connection.

So we're in this together. And it's going to be a difficult time, and obviously the folks down here are going to be feeling the brunt of it, but we're going to make sure that we're doing everything we can to get this solved as quickly as possible.

And I want to again thank everybody here for the extraordinary work that they're putting in. You shouldn't underestimate how hard these folks are working, day in, day out, on behalf of their constituencies.

So thank you very much. Thank you, everybody.

Reading Responses

1. List the actions that President Obama draws his audience's attention to in his speech. How does this emphasis on action affect different audiences for Obama's speech? Concentrate on Gulf Coast residents, local politicians, Americans who know only a little about the crisis, and political pundits who were criticizing the president.

2. Imagine a different speech, one in which Obama admitted that the federal government had acted too slowly and apologized for this slow response. What effect would such a speech have on some of the audiences for Obama's speech? In your answer, concentrate on Democrats running for reelection, BP oil executives, and the engineers who were working to stop the oil spill.

3. Who do you think was Obama's primary audience? Give evidence from the speech and reasons to support your answer.

NOTES ON GRAMMAR, STYLE, AND RHETORIC:
SENTENCE SUBJECTS

One part of the sentence that writers and speakers should pay special attention to is the subject. The subject names who or what acts, experiences something, is described, is identified further, or is acted upon.

Examining the sentence subjects in a speech or written text can reveal much about what the speaker or writer is most concerned to focus on. You might guess that he would focus on BP and how this corporation must stop the spill and pay for the damages, or on the extent of the damage of the oil spill to the environment, or on the economic toll that the oil spill was taking on people along the Gulf Coast. And President Obama does focus some attention on all of these topics. But he mainly uses sentence subjects to focus attention on himself and those under his command in the battle against the oil spill.

Not including the introductory "Good morning, everybody" and the closing "So thank you very much. Thank you everybody," there are one hundred independent clauses in the president's selected remarks. Among those one hundred independent clauses, twenty-six have as their subject the pronoun *we* (sometimes included in the contracted forms *we've* or *we're*). And there are as many as ten additional independent-clause subjects that connect closely to the people whom the *we* refers to (these are phrases such as *our mission* and *our response*).

Toward the end of his remarks, the president uses one *we* to refer to all the people of the United States. And he uses another *we* apparently to refer to himself and the people of the Gulf Coast. But overwhelmingly these *we's* refer to himself and the people that he as president can bring into the fight against the oil. It is easy to sense while reading these remarks that these *we's* refer to a great many people. These people have will and determination, expertise, and vast resources. And they are all under the president's command.

Beyond the sentence subjects in which *we* or some closely related term appears, there are nineteen sentence subjects in which the pronoun *I* appears. If you bring the twenty-six appearances of *we* together with the roughly ten appearances of phrases closely related to *we*, and then if you add to that number the nineteen appearances of *I*, you find that over half of the sentence subjects in this speech refer to the president or to people under his command. On the basis of those figures, it is possible to argue that this speech is mainly about the president's response to the oil-spill disaster.

Why might President Obama have decided to craft so many of his sentences in this way? At the time immediately preceding President Obama's remarks, some people were starting to write and say things about him that were similar to the things written and said about President Bush after Hurricane Katrina. And no politician could overlook the devastating effects if he or she were to come to be perceived as a slow responder to a crisis and as uncaring about some of his constituents. Thus it could be argued that President Obama crafted his remarks to present himself as very much in charge. Further, he works to show that he cares about the health and well-being of the residents of the Gulf states. As Obama says and implies, he is the president; the buck stops with him. This is the message he seems most intent on conveying.

This strategy does not come without some risks. By insisting that he is in charge, that he is responsible, President Obama sets himself up to take the brunt of blame if efforts to stop the flow of oil and to clean up the mess that the oil has made do not go well or take longer than people expect or allow.

Of course, he works hard in his speech to counter current and possible future criticism. He stresses how complex the problems are, he points out that intelligent people might not agree on possible solutions, and he notes that there might be unintended consequences of some relief efforts. But through it all President Obama and his speechwriters chose sentence subjects that kept listeners' attention fixed on the president and the people he commands. At the time and place of his remarks, his choice to focus so much attention on himself and the forces he could muster looks like rhetorical and political wisdom.

In Your Own Writing . . .

- Decide what you want your readers to focus on, and then refer to that in the subject position of your sentences.
- Consider gradually adjusting the subjects of your sentences to introduce your readers to ideas that they might otherwise oppose.
- Put information at or near the end of your sentence (in the predicate) that will shape your readers' attitude toward what you've chosen for the subjects of your sentences.

STUDENT WRITING

INTRODUCTION

by Laura McGiness,
communication arts and sciences major

The Assignment.   In a class called "American Voices," we devoted the entire semester to studying and discussing speeches throughout American history. The final assignment asked us to critically interpret an American rhetorical text by using analytical tools we had learned in class. We had to identify a significant issue or set of issues related to the text's rhetoric that we would like to explore, develop a central claim for our papers about these issues, and support our theses with a logical and clear argument. We could focus on a variety of issues, such as these: What is the meaning of the text, and how is it revealed? How does the structure of the text relate to its message? What narratives or myths are developed in the speech, and how do they relate to cultural ideals?

The Content.   Because understanding the audience is an integral part of effective public speaking, my analysis focused on strategies that President Bill Clinton used to reach a diverse audience in his public address at the Presidential Prayer Breakfast in September of 1998, when he apologized for his affair with White House intern Monica Lewinsky. Particularly, I explored how Clinton fit the content of his speech within the genre of a personal apology and how this allowed him to present a likeable persona that could appeal to both his immediate audience of clergymen and his broader audience of the American public. I also wrote about the way that the historical context and audience's values affected Clinton's potential for rhetorical success in this speech.

Learning to Write in Speech Communication.   Oratory is only considered effective communication when the speaker, audience, and text interact; therefore, communications students must appreciate these important relationships. To successfully communicate, speakers must suit both the content and style of the speech to their audience. They must speak about a pertinent topic that the audience can understand and deliver the speech in a way that makes the audience willing to listen. Likewise, if the content and style of the speech are appropriate but speakers damage their credibility (either before or during the speech), they are not likely to persuade the audience.

Therefore, good public speakers intentionally choose various rhetorical strategies to persuade their audiences, and writers in the communications discipline must be able to identify these strategies. But analyzing oratory goes beyond simple identification. When I analyzed Clinton's speech, I had to explain how and why his rhetorical strategies either worked or didn't work; I also had to speculate about why Clinton may have chosen particular strategies in his speech. I considered a variety of issues related to my speech text before deciding on my central claim. I asked myself some questions: What is the purpose of the speech and how is that revealed? What is the structure of the text and how does that relate to its message? How does the speaker relate to his audience? I then had to decide which topics would most effectively support my main point and how I could best explain these ideas in my paper. After that analysis, I was able to develop a clear central claim and support that thesis with logical evidence.

Apologizing to Friends, Enemies, and Everyone in Between: Analyzing Clinton's Rhetoric

Laura McGiness

> I intentionally began with an anecdote that my readers could relate to, but I tried to present it in such a way that focused readers on the nature of an audience.

We all get plenty of practice apologizing for our mistakes. And the more we apologize, the more we appreciate how our audience influences the way we ask for forgiveness. For instance, an apology for being late would sound different if I were speaking to my boss as opposed to one of my friends. When we know what our audience expects to hear, we can adjust our apology accordingly. However, apologizing to a group of people rather than an individual suddenly makes the task much more challenging. When President Bill Clinton spoke at the Presidential Prayer Breakfast on September 11, 1998, at the height of the Monica Lewinsky sex scandal, he faced the daunting task of crafting an apology that would be appropriate and meaningful to multiple audiences: the clergymen in attendance at the prayer breakfast, who heard it live, and the American public, who would hear it broadcasted later. In an attempt to influence his immediate and wide-ranging audiences, Clinton suited both his content and style to the genre of what rhetoricians call a "personal apologia," which offered him the greatest potential for rhetorical success.

> The thesis must focus on one or several specific aspects of the speech. I decided to explore the genre of a personal apologia because I believe it enabled Clinton to meet certain rhetorical goals that he otherwise would not have been able to accomplish.

In this "Prayer Breakfast Speech" Clinton appears to have learned from his previous failed apology only a few weeks earlier in August of 1998. That nationally-televised speech, nicknamed the "Map Room Speech," took the form of "forensic self-defense," which argues that (1) the president had kept the oath of office, (2) the accusers had undermined the Constitution, and (3) the president is responsible to the people and the Constitution, not to the Congressional accusers (Campbell and Jamieson). As a forensic self-defense, his August apology sounded insincere. Many Americans found the formal language and distant style inconsistent with the highly personal nature of his situation. Moreover, the fact that Clinton spoke into a television camera rather than directly addressing a live audience contributed to the impersonal tone of this speech. His decision to begin a speech about such a delicate moral decision with information about his grand jury indictment seemed devoid of true emotion. He focused a large part of his content on legal issues related to the investigation, which further degraded the personal manner of this speech. Clinton ended by actually rebuking his audience, a tactic that many Americans would not have expected. In fact, Clinton even portrayed himself as the victim of ruthless privacy invasion, a rhetorical move that did not help him establish a desirable ethos throughout the speech. By the end of the speech, Clinton seemed to be saying that his audience should apologize to him, an understandably awkward situation considering the fact that this speech was supposed to be Clinton's apology to them. Self-defense, at this point, was futile. His supporters did not need to hear an apology because they already approved of his leadership despite his moral weaknesses. His enemies used the speech to further accuse Clinton of placing blame on external factors outside his control rather than taking personal responsibility for the situation. The nature of his speech as a self-defense rather than an apology likely left many moderate Americans still wondering about the authenticity of Clinton's remorse. His personal apologia at the Prayer Breakfast, on the other hand, provided him with the tools necessary to develop a persona that proved more rhetorically effective for his diverse audiences.

Campbell and Jamieson point out the various factors that comprise a personal apologia: (1) a shift in focus from the accuser to the defender, (2) a favorable presentation of the defender's personal character, (3) a personal tone, (4) an argument that the actions do not merit impeachment, and (5) an argument that the actions do not call executive leadership into question. Given that Clinton delivered this speech at a prayer breakfast, his decision to share a personal apologia was an appropriate strategy. The apology's personal nature and emphasis allow Clinton to display a greater degree of sincerity and humility, values that the clergymen in his audience would have anticipated and appreciated. These qualities also enable Clinton to discuss his personal journey of repentance—again, another ideal highly esteemed among his audience members. Furthermore, the very fact that a live audience is listening to his address strengthens the personal nature of his speech. The personal apologia also proves effective for Clinton's broader audience of the American people. Clinton often referred to religious themes in his speech, a tactic that could have alienated some members of his more broad audience. However, once again, the personal nature of the apology, and the humble persona that it allowed Clinton to embody,

---

Sidebar annotations:

The element of surprise, whether or not it helps a speaker, always gains audience attention. Therefore, it is worth exploring how this surprising element of Clinton's speech ultimately worked against him in this situation.

Because we know that Clinton was trying to appeal to a very broad audience, it helps to examine particular parts of that audience. Knowing how specific groups of Americans might have reacted to this speech furthers our understanding of the speech's purpose and overall effect.

Here I refer directly to a text we read in class so that my professor can see that I am fulfilling the requirement to analyze a speech using the knowledge I gained in the class.

enabled his message to resonate with many Americans. Most people appreciate a humble and repentant spirit in a sincere apology.

Contrasting the defiant nature of his Map Room Speech, Clinton focuses attention away from his accusers and instead directs it toward himself: "First, I want to say to all of you that, as you might imagine, I have been on quite a journey these last few weeks." When he does address his enemies, he approaches their accusations in a gracious and humble manner by paradoxically noting that the invasion of his privacy, although a painful experience, may ultimately produce a stronger man and country. Therefore, instead of attacking his opponents, he smartly uses their accusations to further strengthen his personal appeal. He employs a classic and effective rhetorical strategy by establishing common ground with and goodwill towards his critics: he mentions near the beginning that he agrees with their criticisms of his past apologies ("I agree with those who have said . . . I was not contrite enough"). Furthermore, he fashions various aspects of his content in such a way that could particularly resonate with his immediate audience. When he states, " . . . hope that with a broken spirit and a still strong heart I can be used for greater good," he suggests the principles of grace and mercy. The clergymen in attendance would have predominantly valued these ideals and appreciated Clinton's intention to use the lessons learned through this ordeal for "greater good" in the future.

Since Clinton's moral failures had resulted in legal action against him, he naturally needed to address this issue in his speech. However, his previous speech met with disastrous results when he focused too heavily on this particular aspect. In his Prayer Breakfast speech, however, Clinton wisely establishes the point that his actions did not merit impeachment, "I will instruct my lawyers to mount a vigorous defense, using all available appropriate arguments," and then he quickly moves on to the spiritual implications of his actions. Obviously, his immediate audience would find this emphasis appropriate, and it also helps further establish his ethos among his audience of the American public. Additionally, Clinton suggests that his mistakes have not permanently damaged his leadership abilities by noting his continuing goals for leading America ("I will intensify my efforts to lead our country and the world toward peace and freedom"). He builds on this idea with a touching story about a little Florida boy who told President Clinton that he wanted to grow up to be the President. By mentioning that children can still look up to him as a role model, not necessarily because of his moral actions but because of his repentance and ability to learn from mistakes, Clinton effectively points out, albeit indirectly, that he is still a legitimate leader. Granted, some members of his audience would disagree with this point; nevertheless, Clinton includes this argument to strengthen his credibility among audience members who are willing to support his leadership.

With background established, here's where I begin my analysis of the speech.

This is an example of when I speculate about why Clinton crafted his speech as he did.

Clinton indirectly suggests rather than explicitly states his legal innocence. Depending on how one views Clinton's personal character and intentions, it could either help or hinder his credibility at this point in the speech.

It is very important that Clinton makes this distinction about his position as a role model, considering that his immediate audience valued moral uprightness. If he had simply said that children should grow up to be like him, without distinguishing which aspects of his character were worth imitating, his audience could have been offended.

Since a personal apologia, by its very nature, must be sincere, Clinton's stylistic choices prove equally as important as his content. Mending broken trust is a nearly impossible task. We often find it difficult to forgive others based solely on their words. While the apology may sound good, how can we be sure that this individual isn't still lying to us? Therefore, however convincing the content of Clinton's personal apologia, it would have been a complete loss without a convincing presentation of the content. In other words, Clinton's language delivery was necessary to the effectiveness of his message. His style both reiterated and enabled his content. Primarily, his decision to write the speech himself signified the profound personal nature of this speech. His continual use of the personal pronoun *I* emphasizes this point. Very early in the speech Clinton admits uncertainty regarding his personal message: "I may not be quite as easy with my words today as I have been in years past." Although that admission violates a basic guideline of public speaking, it works in this situation to further demonstrate the authenticity of his apology and develop his humble persona.

Sensitive to his immediate audience, Clinton often speaks in religious terms. Toward the beginning of his address, he invokes clerical vocabulary by using phrases such as "repentance," "a broken spirit," and "forgiveness." All of these phrases helped him build his credibility with his immediate audience. Acknowledging the fact that repentance takes time, Clinton asks for prayer in helping him and the country move forward; naturally, the religious leaders in his audience would have appreciated his request for God's help in healing the emotional scars of this experience. Clinton further reaches out to his immediate audience by quoting a passage from the Yom Kippur liturgy, appealing to the Jewish members of his audience. Finally, Clinton ends his speech by combining phrases from the Prayer of Saint Francis and the Bible, leaving his religiously-minded immediate audience with spiritual themes.

On a more general level, the speech's simple and direct style helps Clinton's overall message. Whereas a more formal and polished speaking style normally befits a president, the highly personal nature of this speech demanded that Clinton present himself in the most genuine way possible. Therefore, he strategically avoids using complicated words or phrases and instead delivers his speech in a way that emphasizes his humanity. When he confesses, "I don't think there is a fancy way to say that I have sinned," it sounds like a heartfelt apology.

At this point, an important rhetorical situation appears. Although the speech itself displays many rhetorical strengths, the context in which Clinton delivered it also proves fundamentally significant. His humility and remorse appear genuine in this speech, which strengthens his credibility with the audience; however, one cannot forget that he had already

> Rhetoric never occurs in a vacuum; the historical, social, and political context in which a speech is delivered always affects the speech itself and the audience's response in some way. This speech is a somewhat extreme example of the context's effect on an audience.

As Clinton spoke to multiple audiences, I wrote this paper for multiple audiences: my professor and students who would read this textbook. Knowing that some students may read this paper with little to no understanding of communication theory, I explained this idea in a more detailed manner than I may have if I was only writing for my professor.

severely damaged his credibility before the speech took place. By the time he delivered this address, his audience had been following this sad saga for nearly nine months and had likely already judged his behavior and personal character. Naturally, some members of both audiences were hesitant to forgive Clinton or were downright opposed to accepting his apology from the onset. No matter how effectively he presented his personal character in this speech, his audience's diversity made it nearly impossible for him to completely repair his reputation and trustworthiness in a single rhetorical act. This demonstrates the important rhetorical phenomenon of the audience: speakers do not simply act upon passive audience members nor persuade by injecting them with information or arguments. Audience members use their own perceptions and beliefs to critically interpret all speeches within their contexts. Clinton's personal apologia is an extreme example of the context retaining just as much rhetorical influence as the speech itself.

Because we can't get inside the head of each audience member, it is ultimately impossible to finally assess the overall "effectiveness" of the speech, because individuals interpreted its message differently. Therefore, the concluding paragraph provides me with a place to merely speculate why Clinton chose certain rhetorical strategies and how those choices most likely affected his audience members.

Given the context, the speech itself contained appropriate content and a meaningful delivery style that allowed Clinton to develop the most appealing persona possible. Though we cannot measure the overall effect of this speech, his intentional rhetorical choices strengthened the impact of his personal apologia. Where this speech lacked the formality and finesse of typical presidential addresses, it contained vulnerable and humble pleas for forgiveness. In so doing, Clinton made the most of a challenging rhetorical situation.

Work Cited

Campbell, Karlyn Kohrs and Kathleen Hall Jamieson. *Deeds Done in Words: Presidential Rhetoric and the Genres of Governance*. Chicago: The University of Chicago Press, 1994. 127–43.

Reading Responses

1. Which two parts of McGiness's analysis do you find most persuasive? For each part, list the features that McGiness uses to persuade you.

2. In her introduction, McGiness describes how her own feelings about Clinton's actions shaped her analysis of his speech and her claim about that speech. Note places in her essay that seem affected by McGiness's feelings. For each place, describe how you see her feelings shaping the essay.

3. When she presents her analysis of Clinton's speech, McGiness focuses first on the content of the speech and then on the style. Analyze the style of McGiness's essay, paying special attention to her word choice, her sentence structures, and her sentence subjects. What changes would you recommend if she were delivering the paper as an oral presentation?

PUBLIC WRITING

INTRODUCTION

Place yourself in President Bush's position soon after Hurricane Katrina devastated New Orleans and other parts of the Gulf Coast: A growing number of citizens angrily accuse the administration of incompetence in providing relief to the disaster area and injustice toward New Orleans' poor black population. The number of critical voices grows. President Bush and his administration decide that he must speak to the nation, but should he apologize for the poor disaster preparation and relief? How does a speaker face a skeptical—maybe even hostile—audience?

In this speech, President Bush tries to gain the audience's trust, acknowledging the victims' desperation ("grieving for the dead, and looking for meaning in a tragedy that seems so blind and random") and their bravery ("a powerful American determination to clear the ruins and build better than before"). He also appeals to a "united country," which both names his ideal audience and challenges his audience to become united. In his seventh paragraph, Bush also lists the recovery that has happened (electric power and river shipments restored, levee breaks repaired, among others), and then outlines his plan for further action.

Bush does not acknowledge responsibility for the poor response until much later in the speech, yet he does not apologize. He states, "I, as President, am responsible for the problem, and for the solution." He does not let the audience doubt his position of authority, nor does he cast himself as weak. But he does not apologize until he has fully described the action that federal agencies are currently planning, and then only implicitly.

Did President Bush make the right choices when he addressed an upset nation? The day after his speech, the *New York Times* reported that evacuees, Governor Kathleen Babineaux Blanco (Democrat), and Senator Mary L. Landrieu (Democrat) responded positively, with Landrieu claiming that the ideas were "innovative and bold." President Bush's head speech writer, Michael Gerson, has said that he took special pride in this speech because it addressed issues of race and poverty. As time passes, historians and other critics will judge Bush's ability to reframe his work after this natural disaster.

Post-Katrina Speech from Jackson Square, New Orleans, September 15, 2005

President George W. Bush

Good evening. I'm speaking to you from the city of New Orleans—nearly empty, still partly under water, and waiting for life and hope to return. Eastward from Lake Pontchartrain, across the Mississippi coast, to Alabama into Florida, millions of lives were changed in a day by a cruel and wasteful storm.

In the aftermath, we have seen fellow citizens left stunned and uprooted, searching for loved ones, and grieving for the dead, and looking for meaning in a tragedy that seems so blind and random. We've also witnessed the kind of desperation no citizen of this great and generous nation should ever have to know—fellow Americans calling out for food and water, vulnerable people left at the mercy of criminals who had no mercy, and the bodies of the dead lying uncovered and untended in the street.

These days of sorrow and outrage have also been marked by acts of courage and kindness that make all Americans proud. Coast Guard and other personnel rescued tens of thousands of people from flooded neighborhoods. Religious congregations and families have welcomed strangers as brothers and sisters and neighbors. In the community of Chalmette, when two men tried to break into a home, the owner invited them to stay—and took in 15 other people who had no place to go. At Tulane Hospital for Children, doctors and nurses did not eat for days so patients could have food, and eventually carried the patients on their backs up eight flights of stairs to helicopters.

Many first responders were victims themselves, wounded healers, with a sense of duty greater than their own suffering. When I met Steve Scott of the Biloxi Fire Department, he and his colleagues were conducting a house-to-house search for survivors. Steve told me this: "I lost my house and I lost my cars, but I still got my family . . . and I still got my spirit."

Across the Gulf Coast, among people who have lost much, and suffered much, and given to the limit of their power, we are seeing that same spirit—a core of strength that survives all hurt, a faith in God no storm can take away, and a powerful American determination to clear the ruins and build better than before.

Tonight so many victims of the hurricane and the flood are far from home and friends and familiar things. You need to know that our whole nation cares about you, and in the journey ahead you're not alone. To all who carry a burden of loss, I extend the deepest sympathy of our country. To every person who has served and sacrificed in this emergency, I offer the gratitude of our country. And tonight I also offer this pledge of the American people: Throughout the area hit by the hurricane, we will do what it takes, we will stay as long as it takes, to help citizens rebuild their communities and their lives. And all who question the future of the Crescent City need to know there is no way to imagine America without New Orleans, and this great city will rise again.

The work of rescue is largely finished; the work of recovery is moving forward. In nearly all of Mississippi, electric power has been restored. Trade is starting to return to the Port of New Orleans, and agricultural shipments are moving down the Mississippi River. All major gasoline pipelines are now in operation, preventing the supply disruptions that many feared. The breaks in the levees have been closed, the pumps are running, and the water here in New Orleans is receding by the hour. Environmental officials are on the ground, taking water samples, identifying and dealing with hazardous debris, and working to get drinking water and waste water treatment systems operating again. And some very sad duties are being carried out by professionals who gather the dead, treat them with respect, and prepare them for their rest.

In the task of recovery and rebuilding, some of the hardest work is still ahead, and it will require the creative skill and generosity of a united country.

Our first commitment is to meet the immediate needs of those who had to flee their homes and leave all their possessions behind. For these Americans, every night brings uncertainty, every day requires new courage, and in the months to come will bring more than their fair share of struggles.

The Department of Homeland Security is registering evacuees who are now in shelters and churches, or private homes, whether in the Gulf region or far away. I have signed an order providing immediate assistance to people from the disaster area. As of today, more than 500,000 evacuee families have gotten emergency help to pay for food, clothing, and other essentials. Evacuees who have not yet registered should contact FEMA or the Red Cross. We need to know who you are, because many of you will be eligible for broader assistance in the future. Many families were separated during the evacuation, and we are working to help you reunite. Please call this number: 1–877–568–3317—that's 1–877–568–3317—and we will work to bring your family back together, and pay for your travel to reach them.

In addition, we're taking steps to ensure that evacuees do not have to travel great distances or navigate bureaucracies to get the benefits that are there for them. The Department of Health and Human Services has sent more than 1,500 health professionals, along with over 50 tons of medical supplies—including vaccines and antibiotics and medicines for people with chronic conditions such as diabetes. The Social Security Administration is delivering checks. The Department of Labor is helping displaced persons apply for temporary jobs and unemployment benefits. And the Postal Service is registering new addresses so that people can get their mail.

To carry out the first stages of the relief effort and begin rebuilding at once, I have asked for, and the Congress has provided, more than $60 billion. This is an unprecedented response to an unprecedented crisis, which demonstrates the compassion and resolve of our nation.

Our second commitment is to help the citizens of the Gulf Coast to overcome this disaster, put their lives back together, and rebuild their communities. Along this coast, for mile after mile, the wind and water swept the land clean. In Mississippi, many thousands of houses were damaged or destroyed. In New Orleans and surrounding parishes, more than a quarter-million houses are no longer safe to live in. Hundreds of thousands of people from across this region will need to find longer-term housing.

Our goal is to get people out of the shelters by the middle of October. So we're providing direct assistance to evacuees that allows them to rent apartments, and many already are moving into places of their own. A number of states have taken in evacuees and shown them great compassion—admitting children to school, and providing health care. So I will work with the Congress to ensure that states are reimbursed for these extra expenses.

In the disaster area, and in cities that have received huge numbers of displaced people, we're beginning to bring in mobile homes and trailers for temporary use. To relieve the burden on local health care facilities in the region, we're sending extra doctors and nurses to these areas. We're also providing money that can be used to cover overtime pay for police and fire departments while the cities and towns rebuild.

Near New Orleans, and Biloxi, and other cities, housing is urgently needed for police and firefighters, other service providers, and the many workers who are going to rebuild these cities. Right now, many are sleeping on ships we have brought to the Port of New Orleans—and more ships are on their way to the region. And we'll provide mobile homes, and supply them with basic services, as close to construction areas as possible, so the rebuilding process can go forward as quickly as possible.

And the federal government will undertake a close partnership with the states of Louisiana and Mississippi, the city of New Orleans, and other Gulf Coast cities, so they can rebuild in a sensible, well-planned way. Federal funds will cover the great majority of the costs of repairing public infrastructure in the disaster zone, from roads and bridges to schools and water systems. Our goal is to get the work done quickly. And taxpayers expect this work to be done honestly and wisely—so we'll have a team of inspectors general reviewing all expenditures.

In the rebuilding process, there will be many important decisions and many details to resolve, yet we're moving forward according to some clear principles. The federal government will be fully engaged in the mission, but Governor Barbour, Governor Blanco, Mayor Nagin, and other state and local leaders will have the primary role in planning for their own future. Clearly, communities will need to move decisively to change zoning laws and building codes, in order to avoid a repeat of what we've seen. And in the work of rebuilding, as many jobs as possible should go to the men and women who live in Louisiana, Mississippi, and Alabama.

Our third commitment is this: When communities are rebuilt, they must be even better and stronger than before the storm. Within the Gulf region are some of the most beautiful and historic places in America. As all of us saw on television, there's also some deep, persistent poverty in this region, as well. That poverty has roots in a history of racial discrimination, which cut off generations from the opportunity of America. We have a duty to confront this poverty with bold action. So let us restore all that we have cherished from yesterday, and let us rise above the legacy of inequality. When the streets are rebuilt, there should be many new businesses, including minority-owned businesses, along those streets. When the houses are rebuilt, more families should own, not rent, those houses. When the regional economy revives, local people should be prepared for the jobs being created.

Americans want the Gulf Coast not just to survive, but to thrive; not just to cope, but to overcome. We want evacuees to come home, for the best of reasons—because they have a real chance at a better life in a place they love.

When one resident of this city who lost his home was asked by a reporter if he would relocate, he said, "Naw, I will rebuild—but I will build higher." That is our vision for the future, in this city and beyond: We'll not just rebuild, we'll build higher and better. To meet this goal, I will listen to good ideas from Congress, and state and local officials, and the private sector. I believe we should start with three initiatives that the Congress should pass.

Tonight I propose the creation of a Gulf Opportunity Zone, encompassing the region of the disaster in Louisiana and Mississippi and Alabama. Within this zone, we should provide immediate incentives for job-creating investment, tax relief for small businesses, incentives to companies that create jobs, and loans and loan guarantees for small businesses, including minority-owned enterprises, to get them up and running again. It is entrepreneurship that creates jobs and opportunity; it is entrepreneurship that helps break the cycle of poverty; and we will take the side of entrepreneurs as they lead the economic revival of the Gulf region.

I propose the creation of Worker Recovery Accounts to help those evacuees who need extra help finding work. Under this plan, the federal government would provide accounts of up to $5,000, which these evacuees could draw upon for job training and education to help them get a good job, and for child care expenses during their job search.

And to help lower-income citizens in the hurricane region build new and better lives, I also propose that Congress pass an Urban Homesteading Act. Under this approach, we will identify property in the region owned by the federal government, and provide building sites to low-income citizens free of charge, through a lottery. In return, they would pledge to build on the lot, with either a mortgage or help from a charitable organization like Habitat for Humanity. Home ownership is one of the great strengths of any community, and it must be a central part of our vision for the revival of this region.

In the long run, the New Orleans area has a particular challenge, because much of the city lies below sea level. The people who call it home need to have reassurance that their lives will be safer in the years to come. Protecting a city that sits lower than the water around it is not easy, but it can, and has been done. City and parish officials in New Orleans, and state officials in Louisiana will have a large part in the engineering decisions to come. And the Army Corps of Engineers will work at their side to make the flood protection system stronger than it has ever been.

The work that has begun in the Gulf Coast region will be one of the largest reconstruction efforts the world has ever seen. When that job is done, all Americans will have something to be very proud of—and all Americans are needed in this common effort. It is the armies of compassion—charities and houses of worship, and idealistic men and women—that give our reconstruction effort its humanity. They offer to those who hurt a friendly face, an arm around the shoulder, and the reassurance that in hard times, they can count on someone who cares. By land, by sea, and by air, good people wanting to make a difference deployed to the Gulf Coast, and they've been working around the clock ever since.

The cash needed to support the armies of compassion is great, and Americans have given generously. For example, the private fundraising effort led by former Presidents Bush and Clinton has already received pledges of more than $100 million. Some of that money is going to the Governors to be used for immediate needs within their states. A portion will also be sent to local houses of worship to help reimburse them for the expense of helping others. This evening the need is still urgent, and I ask the American people to continue donating to the Salvation Army, the Red Cross, other good charities, and religious congregations in the region.

It's also essential for the many organizations of our country to reach out to your fellow citizens in the Gulf area. So I've asked USA Freedom Corps to create an information clearinghouse, available at usafreedomcorps.gov, so that families anywhere in the country can find opportunities to help families in the region, or a school can support a school. And I challenge existing organizations—churches, and Scout troops, or labor union locals to get in touch with their counterparts in Mississippi, Louisiana, or Alabama, and learn what they can do to help. In this great national enterprise, important work can be done by everyone, and everyone should find their role and do their part.

The government of this nation will do its part, as well. Our cities must have clear and up-to-date plans for responding to natural disasters, and disease outbreaks, or a terrorist attack, for evacuating large numbers of people in an emergency, and for providing the food and water and security they would need. In a time of terror threats and weapons of mass destruction, the danger to our citizens reaches much wider than a fault line or a flood plain. I consider detailed emergency planning to be a national security priority, and therefore, I've ordered the Department of Homeland Security to undertake an immediate review, in cooperation with local counterparts, of emergency plans in every major city in America.

I also want to know all the facts about the government response to Hurricane Katrina. The storm involved a massive flood, a major supply and security operation, and an evacuation order affecting more than a million people. It was not a normal hurricane—and the normal disaster relief system was not equal to it. Many of the men and women of the Coast Guard, the Federal Emergency Management Agency, the United States military, the National Guard, Homeland Security, and state and local governments performed skillfully under the worst conditions. Yet the system, at every level of government, was not well-coordinated, and was overwhelmed in the first few days. It is now clear that a challenge on this scale requires greater federal authority and a broader role for the armed forces—the institution of our government most capable of massive logistical operations on a moment's notice.

Four years after the frightening experience of September the 11th, Americans have every right to expect a more effective response in a time of emergency. When the federal government fails to meet such an obligation, I, as President, am responsible for the problem, and for the solution. So I've ordered every Cabinet Secretary to participate in a comprehensive review of the government response to the hurricane. This government will learn the lessons of Hurricane Katrina. We're going to review every action and make necessary changes, so that we are better prepared for any challenge of nature, or act of evil men, that could threaten our people.

The United States Congress also has an important oversight function to perform. Congress is preparing an investigation, and I will work with members of both parties to make sure this effort is thorough.

In the life of this nation, we have often been reminded that nature is an awesome force, and that all life is fragile. We're the heirs of men and women who lived through those first terrible winters at Jamestown and Plymouth, who rebuilt Chicago after a great fire, and San Francisco after a great earthquake, who reclaimed the prairie from the Dust Bowl of the 1930s. Every time, the people of this land have come back from fire, flood, and storm to build anew—and to build better than what we had before. Americans have never left our destiny to the whims of nature—and we will not start now.

These trials have also reminded us that we are often stronger than we know—with the help of grace and one another. They remind us of a hope beyond all pain and death, a God who welcomes the lost to a house not made with hands. And they remind us that we're tied together in this life, in this nation—and that the despair of any touches us all.

I know that when you sit on the steps of a porch where a home once stood, or sleep on a cot in a crowded shelter, it is hard to imagine a bright future. But that future will come. The streets of Biloxi and Gulfport will again be filled with lovely homes and the sound of children playing. The churches of Alabama will have their broken steeples mended and their congregations whole. And here in New Orleans, the street cars will once again rumble down St. Charles, and the passionate soul of a great city will return.

In this place, there's a custom for the funerals of jazz musicians. The funeral procession parades slowly through the streets, followed by a band playing a mournful dirge as it moves to the cemetery. Once the casket has been laid in place, the band breaks into a joyful "second line"—symbolizing the triumph of the spirit over death. Tonight the Gulf Coast is still coming through the dirge—yet we will live to see the second line.

Thank you, and may God bless America.

Reading Responses

1. President Bush ends his speech with an image of New Orleans funeral bands playing first sad music and then joyful. List the "sad" sections of this speech and then the "joyful" ones. How do they relate to each other?

2. Prior to this speech, many had criticized the federal government for responding too slowly to the needs of the victims of Hurricane Katrina. Note the places where President Bush responds to those criticisms. How would you describe his responses? How are they like/unlike an apology?

3. President Bush devotes much of his speech to listing the actions of specific federal agencies. How do you think employees of those agencies responded? How did those who were affected by the hurricane respond? How do you think President Bush hoped Americans in general would respond?

MORE WRITING IN SPEECH COMMUNICATION

INTRODUCTION

You've now read a speech by President Obama on the Gulf oil spill (which some have called "Obama's Katrina"), and you've read a speech that President George W. Bush delivered in the wake of Katrina. The following essay analyzes the rhetoric that then-Senator Obama used in 2005 in public comments about President Bush's handling of the Katrina crisis.

The authors of the essay were both professors of communication when they wrote the essay that follows (Waymer is at Virginia Tech, and Heath is now retired from the University of Houston). They did not know, of course, that Senator Obama would go on to become president and have his own environmental crisis to deal with. The focus of Waymer and Heath's argument is on the ways that two senators—Obama and Landrieu (Louisiana)— effectively used rhetoric that drew into the public conversation the voices of those groups who were most affected by Hurricane Katrina but who had the least power to do anything. Waymer and Heath care less about the two senators than they do about how politicians can affect ideas and actions when dealing with crises like Katrina.

The excerpt from the essay gives you the main points of Waymer and Heath's argument (summarized in the Abstract), as it is supported by examples of Senator Obama's public comments. (We deleted the sections on Senator Landrieu's rhetoric.)

Emergent Agents: The Forgotten Publics in Crisis Communication and Issue Management Research

Damion Waymer and Robert L. Heath

Journal of Applied Communication Research, Vol. 35. 1, February 2007, pp. 88–108

[Abstract] *Crisis communication research rarely highlights the voices of marginalized publics or their advocates whose interests are affected by crisis situations. We take a different approach by using a response to a natural disaster to expand our theorizing about crisis situations beyond those that hurt the bottom line. Using official statements from Senators Landrieu and Obama about events surrounding Hurricane Katrina as texts for analysis, we demonstrate how they used transcendence, rhetorically, and appropriated the Bush administration's key term—security—to garner more support for their positions, Katrina sufferers, and relief efforts. Implications of this strategy serve to broaden crisis communication theorizing, and to provide insights into ways to strengthen the quality of crisis emergency response planning and response protocols.*

Keywords: Crisis Communication; Hurricane Katrina; Emergent Agents; Transcendence; Issues Management; Public Relations; Security. . . . .

Displaying Transcendence During a Crisis: A Means of Combating the Narratives of Continuity and Control

. . . In times of crisis, organizations use public relations tools, such as press conferences, press releases, and other forms of mediated communication, as the primary means to reach the goal of minimizing or reversing damage to relationships. They also make statements to enact control in the face of uncertainty and to frame crisis events by demonstrating that they influence their destinies (Heath, 1997). Although the narrative frame of an organization's being in control of its destiny is the one we often hear in crisis situations, there are other frames, at times competing ones, that support or circumvent a responsible party's story.

The very nature of crisis situations provides publics with the opportunity to challenge the frame that the organization is, in fact, in control of its destiny. Crises can provide individuals and publics that are not directly affected by a crisis situation with a platform from which to speak, and can possibly empower otherwise marginalized stakeholders and publics by equipping them with negotiation tools to enter into a dialogue. . . .

Through analysis of discourse of this sort, we believe that we can demonstrate how, in crisis planning and response, key voices not ordinarily considered can be heard, and why they need to be. If not, they might be heard at some other point; or they might be totally ignored to the detriment of developing a full and honest sense of the crisis into public scrutiny. These voices help frame the crisis, the quality of response to it, and the lessons learned that can mitigate future crises of similar kinds. If the voices are not heard during the crisis, they are likely to be stronger and more condemning after the fact. This realization can inform and enhance crisis communication research and best practices while also strengthening the quality of emergency response planning and response protocols.

Below, we turn to Senators Landrieu and Obama, who sagely displayed transcendence and featured "security" in such a manner that the term resonated with public sentiments about the government's responsibility to its citizens. More specifically, Senator Obama took advantage of the outpouring of public sympathy for those affected by Hurricane Katrina and the floods by stretching the favored term "security" to make these events a matter of national concern just like the Bush administration did for 9/11 (which could have remained regional, New York and Pentagon problems) and for the Iraq war (which could have been regarded as a regionalized, overseas skirmish). By using the rhetoric of security—just as had been done in the two previous instances before Katrina—Obama appropriated the technique of the Bush administration to transcend the discourse of Katrina from a regional, localized concern to a national concern.

According to Hearit (1997), to transcend means to "go beyond" or "cross over"; moreover, in the terms of external "organizational communication, transcendence is a form of symbolic action whereby a corporation [or other organization] redefines its acts so that they are viewed from a larger context, one that customarily features an ethical dimension" (pp. 219–220). Hearit's (1997) use of transcendence featured the organization's point of view rather than that of the victims; however, in the current case, transcendence was used by emergent agents on behalf of marginalized stakeholders. Senators Landrieu and Obama refused to allow for the events surrounding Katrina to stop at the level of race or class, which could be perceived as intolerable. Instead they found a way to remedy the problem by appealing to a broader, unifying concept of security. This strategy was a clever form of rhetorical invention, as few U.S. citizens would question the ethicality of ensuring the safety and security of all citizens. Moreover, since at least 9/11, and including the 2004 campaign that launched Obama into national prominence, the term "security" has been the hallmark of the Bush administration.

Stretching the Rhetoric of National Security

Senators Landrieu and Obama used the rhetorical invention of transcendence based on the term "security" to interpret and criticize the planning and preparation for and response of government agencies to the Hurricane Katrina crisis. . . .

Although we cannot attribute motives with complete accuracy, by closely analyzing the rhetorical strategies the Senators employed, we can develop useful insights into the meaning of and possible motivation for their statements, as well as the meaning and motivations that these statements might have induced in others. Undeniably, Hurricane Katrina shed light on the important issues of race and class; however, the Senators responded to this national disaster through transcendence; in doing so, they cleverly appropriated the administration's favored term, "security," along the way. The Senators used the term in the following ways: (1) security is national, not bi-partisan; (2) security must do more than plan for the "haves and cans"—it must also encompass planning for the "have nots," the "have nothings," and the "can'ts"; (3) security additionally must strike a strategic balance between, as opposed to a bifurcation of, free market solutions and government intervention as viable ways to address this crisis situation; (4) security further entails making such organizations as FEMA more reflective and responsible, as well as creating oversight and appointing a CFO to assure responsiveness to the issues and needs instead of profit maximization for those who might seek to profit unjustly from the crisis; and (5) finally, security involves being accountable to all citizens, especially those who are most vulnerable.

Throughout our analysis, we further develop these five notions and demonstrate how the Senators used them rhetorically to transcend the dividing lines of race and class. We have collapsed these five notions into three overarching themes. Thus, we have separated the Senators' remarks into three parts: (1) "We failed our citizens so badly"; (2) "Ineptitude is colorblind"; and (3) "We need to be pragmatic instead of ideological."

We Failed Our Citizens So Badly . . . Senator Obama's argument is . . . clear; we failed as a nation (and are failing in other ways, such as energy policy) to make our nation—especially its most vulnerable citizens—secure. When emergency response and crisis prevention measures in times of natural disasters seem predicated on an "SUV" (sports utility vehicle) evacuation model instead of one that acknowledges a non-SUV population, a lack of national security is present. Senator Obama (2005c) illustrated this point in stating:

> [W]hat must be said is that whoever was in charge of planning and preparing for the worst case scenario appeared to assume that every American has the capacity to load up their family in an SUV, fill it up with $100 worth of gasoline, stick some bottled water in the trunk, and use a credit card to check in to a hotel on safe ground. (para. 11)

This clearly was not the case in New Orleans, where the overwhelming majority of the citizens who were left behind did not have such means. . . .

Obama (2005c), in addition to asking, "How we could have failed our fellow citizens so badly?" evoked the memory of 9/11 to show the unity of the nation, as well as to show the nation that by failing to plan adequately for and evacuate citizens of New Orleans the nation was vulnerable to both natural and terrorists attacks:

> One of the heartening things about this crisis has been the degree to which the outrage has come from across the political spectrum; across races; across income. The degree to which the American people sense that we can and must do better, and a recognition that if we cannot cope with a crisis that has been predicted for decades—a crisis in which we're given four or five days notice—how can we ever hope to respond to a serious terrorist attack in a major American city in which there is no notice, and in which the death toll and panic and disruptions may be far greater? (para. 9)

Obama sagely made the connection between preparing for a natural disaster and preparing for a terrorist attack by using a trifecta of invocations of "national security": (1) The Bush administration deemed 9/11 a matter of national security; (2) The Bush administration deemed the situation in Iraq a matter of national security; and (3) Senator Obama deemed Hurricane Katrina a matter of national security. Although Mayor Nagin made this point well in his public statements, this point did not seem to be widely accepted until Senator Obama connected the pieces of this trifecta and articulated them. Therefore, if preparation for a natural disaster is on a par with terrorism, then it is a matter of national security; failure to prepare adequately constitutes a national crisis. Thus Obama, by showing us the interconnectedness of the failings in the Katrina crisis and the failings of 9/11, as well as the threats associated with both, forces us to give serious thought to his question: "How we will prevent such a failure from ever occurring again?"(para. 8).

Ineptitude is Colorblind   Obama (2005c) noted:

> There's been much attention in the press about the fact that those who were left behind in New Orleans were disproportionately poor and African American. I've said publicly that I do not subscribe to the notion that the painfully slow response of FEMA and the Department of Homeland Security was racially-based. The ineptitude was colorblind. (para. 10)

The crisis situation that Katrina created was not an issue of race, but rather one of neglect and disparity in income and opportunities. The Senator further illustrated this point in stating:

> [It] is the deeper shame of this past week—that it has taken a crisis like this one to awaken us to the great divide that continues to fester in our midst. That's what all Americans are truly ashamed about, and the fact that we're ashamed about it is a good sign. (para. 13)

The Senator, in taking the position that the issue was not a racial issue and reassuring the audience that all Americans were ashamed by what they had witnessed, was able to transcend local white-versus-black conflicts and position the crisis as a national concern and, in doing so, brought the interconnectedness of society to the fore. In this society, like all others, we need, rely on, and are dependent on one another for survival; however, the Senator reminds his audience that U.S. citizens have neglected this all-important precept:

> And so I hope that out of this crisis we all begin to reflect—Democrat and
> Republican—on not only our individual responsibilities to ourselves and
> our families, but to our mutual responsibilities to our fellow Americans.
> I hope we realize that the people of New Orleans weren't just abandoned
> during the Hurricane. They were abandoned long ago—to murder and
> mayhem in their streets; to substandard schools; to dilapidated housing;
> to inadequate health care; to a pervasive sense of hopelessness. (Obama,
> 2005c, para. 12)

By framing this issue as a threat to national security, the Senator was able to span partisan lines.

Usually, during the onset of wars and times of domestic discord, such as terrorist attacks, the nation is united. There is no time for bi-partisan politics. Only after a situation has lingered do bi-partisan politics begin to enter the discussion. In framing the Katrina crisis as a threat to national security, Obama likens it to other non-partisan concerns. In short, this crisis spans party lines and political orientation.

Senator Obama exhibited non-partisanship, both in terms of what he said in his public utterances and in his actions. He openly spoke about his association with Presidents Clinton and Bush, Sr., as well as joint sponsorship of federal legislation. He used these associations and the transcendent security frame to induce unity among U.S. citizens as it pertained to this national crisis. As the Senator stated, "Indeed, if there's any bright light that has come out of this disaster, it's the degree to which ordinary Americans have responded with speed and determination even as their government has responded with unconscionable ineptitude" (Obama, 2005c, para. 7).

Obama (2005c) acknowledged that ineptitude is colorblind, but he refused to dismiss it. In fact, he brings it to the fore in noting its unacceptability: "We're gonna have to do some hard thinking about how we could have failed our fellow citizens so badly, and how we will prevent such a failure from ever occurring again" (para. 8). . . .

We Need to be Pragmatic Instead of Ideological.   The Senators, through discourse, established the following: being ideological about Katrina largely contributed to this crisis situation. . . .

Senator Obama (2005b) stated that, in recent times, the Democratic Party has often been considered one that looks "for government for the first answer to every problem," whereas the Republican Party has often been seen as preferring to rely on free market forces as solutions to crisis; he quickly tried to move away from the philosophical differences and became pragmatic: "I think that what we are going to have to figure out is how do we do both and as opposed to either/or" (para. 5).

Senator Obama furthered his point through the following example:

> All of us recognize that jobs are the best anti-poverty program and . . . we
> should ask the market to create those jobs and create the framework in
> which entrepreneurship and business development can occur . . . [; how-
> ever,] we also have to recognize that there are communities that may not
> have access to capital and they may need government to help initially seed
> their entrepreneurial efforts. (para. 5)

The Senator (2005a) concluded his comments by observing that ideally everyone would recognize that individuals "have to take responsibility and that the market solution, where possible, is potentially the more efficient and preferable one, but also recognizing government has a role. That's the kind of practical, common sense, pragmatic America that I think works best" (para. 5).

Part of ensuring security is to be sure that individuals and organizations do not misappropriate or mismanage funds that are intended to help those in need. The Senator recognized that there would be individuals and organizations attempting to profit from the crisis. In two of his presentations, he drew attention to "no-bid" and "cost-plus" contracts that the government used in Iraq (Obama, 2005a, 2005b). He did not want the funds allotted for the Katrina recovery efforts to be squandered. Thus, the Senator paired up with Republican Senator Tom Coburn to "create a Chief Financial Officer (CFO) to oversee all expenditures associated with the Hurricane Katrina relief and reconstruction effort" (Obama, 2005a, para. 4).

In this bill, the Senators specifically laid out the details concerning the duties of the CFO. The bill required the President to appoint this officer, this appointment had to be confirmed by the Senate, and this officer was to oversee and manage any agency using federal funds for the Hurricane Katrina relief effort. In addition, he or she was to oversee the dispersing of the funds to determine whether the people most in need were receiving the aid and to determine whether companies that hired local workers were receiving the funds. Ultimately, the Senator was prodding the federal government and federal agencies to be reflective, responsible, and above all accountable. This is evident in the following comment: "As we look towards the massive Gulf Coast rebuilding efforts ahead, we must demand accountability over how the billions of dollars we've given to FEMA are spent" (Obama, 2005a, para. 5). In his rhetoric, however, Senator Obama was holding the federal government and agencies accountable for a great deal more.

Conclusion

Hearit (1997) has suggested that successful use of a transcendent strategy requires two components: redefinition and an appeal to higher values. The Senators, by redefining what Mayor Ray Nagin, Kanye West, and others deemed issues of race and class and positioning the events surrounding Hurricane Katrina more broadly as relating to a national security promise that was going unfulfilled, were successful in garnering more support for their positions and Katrina sufferers. By stretching the rhetoric of security, the Senators were able to equate preparation for a national disaster with preparation for a terrorist attack. They also emphasized that both are matters of national security, and failure to prepare adequately for a natural disaster—just as failure to prepare for terrorist attacks—as grounds for a national crisis. . . .

Senators Landrieu and Obama's comments, as well as the positioning and the accuracy of their positions, helped give other alternative frames power that probably forced government agencies into positions they would have preferred to avoid. We believe, for instance, that the Senators' voices helped to secure more financial assistance for Katrina victims and restoration efforts from the Bush administration. Simply put, the Senators' discourse and actions help us to explain how during a crisis an alternative frame can emerge and acquire legitimacy when expressed in ways that give voice to a group that otherwise is likely to be marginalized by the crisis—and is silent because it is marginalized. In this case, transcending issues of race and class by using the Bush administration's key term of "security" enabled the Senators to add strength and credibility to their positions, as well as empower other marginalized publics' frames. . . .

References

[We include only the references cited in the excerpted portion of the article.]

Hearit, K. M. (1997). On the use of transcendence as an apologia strategy: The case of Johnson controls and its fetal protection policy. *Public Relations Review, 23*, 217–231.

Heath, R. L. (1997). *Strategic issues management: Organizations and public policy challenges.* Thousand Oaks, CA: Sage.

Obama, B. (2005a, September 14). *Obama, Coburn to introduce Hurricane Katrina oversight legislation.* Retrieved January 5, 2006, from http://obama.senate.gov/press/050914-obama_coburn_to_introduce_hurricane_katrina_oversight_legislation/index.html

Obama, B. (2005b, September 21). *Poverty in America and opposing photo ID requirement for voting.* Retrieved January 5, 2006 from, http://obama.senate.gov/podcast/050921-poverty_in_america_and_opposing_a_photo_id_requirement_for_voting/index.html

Obama, B. (2005c, September 6). *Statement of Senator Barack Obama on Hurricane Katrina relief efforts.* Retrieved January 5, 2006, from http://obama.senate.gov/statement/050906-statement_of_senator_barack_obama_on_hurricane_katrina_relief_efforts/index.html

Reading Responses

1. Use the examples from this essay to compare Barack Obama's rhetoric in 2005, when he was a U.S. senator, to his BP Oil Spill remarks. How have his appeals to multiple audiences changed? How have they remained the same?

2. What evidence from Waymer and Heath's essay would support an argument that a president must appeal to more audiences than a senator must? What evidence would support an argument that senators and presidents have similar audiences?

3. Summarize Waymer and Heath's argument that Senator Obama used rhetoric of "transcendence" effectively. Identify evidence that President Obama used "transcendence" and "security" to appeal to his audiences in his BP Oil Spill remarks.

WRITING ASSIGNMENTS

Assignment 1

On February 24, 2009, President Obama delivered his first State of the Union address, and, as is common practice, a spokesperson for the opposing political party responded to the president's speech in nationally televised remarks. The Republican Party selected Louisiana

Governor Bobby Jindal to complete this task. It seemed like a wise selection: Governor Jindal enjoyed enormous voter approval and seemed destined for future political success, perhaps even a run for the presidency himself. But Jindal's speech, entitled "Americans Can Do Anything," was criticized as ineffective by political analysts and even members of the Republican Party (you can find text of the speech at http://www.gov.louisiana.gov/index.cfm?md=newsroom &tmp=detail&catID=3&articleID=1032. Search online to watch video of the speech). In the days after that speech, it was difficult to imagine that Bobby Jindal could ever overcome that bad performance and regain the trust of his political party.

Your task for this assignment is to write a speech that Governor Jindal could give that would help him put to rest lingering doubts about his potential for national political leadership. Decide whether Jindal should apologize, defend his performance, or combine apology with defense. Determine how specific you will be about the weaknesses of Jindal's performance and how directly you will address the criticism he earned for that speech. Craft a speech that will address multiple audiences—political analysts, members of the Republican Party, and Americans who may some day decide about voting Jindal into a national office.

Assignment 2

Although few of us will ever speak before an international audience as President Obama did, academics regularly defend their ideas from critique. They do so in "exchange" sections of major research journals, before governmental bodies, and in subsequent articles that they publish. Your task for this assignment is to analyze how academics in an academic discipline (perhaps your major) respond to the critique of others. Interview a professor to determine where critique occurs in her academic discipline. Locate an exchange between two or more authors in which they critique the work of others. Analyze that exchange to determine how authors describe not only the ideas they are critiquing but also how they address the authors of those ideas. If the original author has a chance to respond, how does that author respond to the critique?

As you begin drafting, consider who would be interested in your findings and what they could do with the information that you provide. How comfortable are you with the uses to which others might put your research? What uses would you like to encourage, and how can you encourage readers to do those? What uses would you like to discourage, and how can you discourage readers from doing those?

Assignment 3

Nearly every college and university has a policy on plagiarism. In fact, the National Council of Writing Program Administrators has drafted a position statement on plagiarism found online at http://wpacouncil.org/node/9. These policies usually include a description of plagiarism and the consequences that result when students plagiarize.

Your task for this assignment is to collect data and write a report that either justifies your school's plagiarism policy or suggests future revisions to the policy. To begin, determine the kind of information you want to gather about plagiarism at your institution and how you will gather that information. Are you interested in how students think about plagiarism? How much and what kinds of plagiarism occur? How teachers detect plagiarism? How they train students to avoid plagiarism? How attitudes about plagiarism at your school fit with those nationwide?

As you begin drafting, consider the audiences of your report carefully. If you justify the policy, your primary audience will be students. But others will be interested, too: teachers and administrators rely on documents such as yours as they talk about plagiarism with students. If you recommend revisions to the plagiarism policy, your primary audience will be school administrators who must approve such changes, but you can expect that teachers and students will read the document carefully, too. Decide on the central message of the report, its organization, and its tone. Determine the type and amount of evidence you will include in the report and how you will present that evidence.

4

RELIGION AND SOCIETY: ANALYZING CULTURAL ASSUMPTIONS

The Pledge of Allegiance has been a part of American culture since 1892; in 1942, Congress formally adopted a version of the pledge that read: "I pledge allegiance to the flag of the United States of America and to the Republic for which it stands, one Nation indivisible, with liberty and justice for all." That's right, no "under God." Congress added those two words in 1954. In 2004, Michael Newdow argued before the Supreme Court that the words "under God" are unconstitutional because they discriminate against people who do not believe in a god. Newdow claimed, "There's a principle here, and I'm hoping the court will uphold this principle so that we can finally go back and have every American want to stand up, face the flag, place their hand over their heart and pledge to one nation, indivisible, not divided by religion, with liberty and justice for all."*

In his claim, Newdow argues that removing the words "under God" will improve national unity. This is a controversial claim, one that depends on what Americans understand the words "under God" to mean. Whereas Newdow argues that they refer to a particular religious god, others would describe these words as "civil religion" or "ceremonial deism," a distinctive feature of American culture rather than a religious reference.

- What is the purpose of a Pledge of Allegiance? Why do people recite it? Do the words "under God" make it less useful? More useful? Explain your reasoning.

- Do you agree with Newdow's claim? Write out a version of his claim that you would find more persuasive. Include reasons that would support your claim and any evidence you can think of.

*Linda Greenhouse, "Atheist Presents Case for Taking God from Pledge," *New York Times On the Web*, March 25, 2004.

PORTABLE RHETORICAL LESSON: WRITING EFFECTIVE THESIS STATEMENTS

The problem that Newdow faced when he argued before the Supreme Court is that he could not ground his point in scientific data; he had to try to *persuade* the court—arranging a logical argument that supported a single thesis.

When you write your own thesis-driven arguments, you will likely focus particularly on your thesis, which is the main **point** that you will argue for, and your **organization.** As Newdow probably did, you will start with a general idea of what your thesis will be, collect your best logical arguments and supporting evidence, and try out different organizational strategies until you find a logical arrangement that best supports your point. In working through different options for organizing and choosing the most logical sequence to march readers toward the thesis, you will refine and clarify your thesis.

The concepts of thesis and organization are commonly taught in writing classes, so you have probably encountered these general rhetorical concepts. In this chapter, however, we use the readings to demonstrate the **Portable Rhetorical Lesson:** how to write effective thesis statements for college-level courses.

An effective thesis does the following:

- Responds to a problem or question: Across disciplines, it is common for researchers to begin writing by describing the research problem that they will attempt to solve, often framing the problem as a research question. A thesis is a succinct statement of an answer to such a question. Consider, for example, this thesis: "Summer vacation travel has driven up gas prices 10 percent in the past month." Behind that thesis lies the implied question: "What has caused gas prices to jump 10 percent this past month?" But this thesis could be more interesting if it responded to a more complex research question.

- Accounts for the complexities of a research problem or question: In college, professors and students study complex problems, ones that are not likely solved once and for all in a single essay. Typically, a thesis acknowledges at least some of the complexities of the problem and identifies people who might disagree with the thesis. This example acknowledges one complexity: "While gasoline prices generally correspond to the cost of crude oil, state legislators can limit price increases by regulating regional supply and demand pressures."

- Focuses on a limited aspect of the problem: Because college-level research problems are complex, a college-level thesis isolates a limited part of the topic for in-depth study. "Although several factors affect the price that consumers pay for gasoline, the price of crude oil set by OPEC countries is the most significant."

- Takes risks: A risky thesis is one that a reasonable, informed reader might disagree with. Often this disagreement will center on key assumptions that the author makes about the nature or the significance of the problem: the value or the workability of the solution, or the nature of human beings or the world. A good thesis takes on this risk by openly expressing the assumptions that undergird the author's claim.

"Although OPEC prices for crude oil are the most significant factor in the price of gasoline, the United States should attempt to control prices by increasing production of alternative fuels." In this thesis, the writer assumes that the federal government can and should control the price of commodities. Some readers would vehemently oppose that assumption; the thesis is effective because it asks readers to understand and reconsider the author's and their own assumptions.

The fourth bullet point in the preceding list mentions the need to clarify the assumptions imbedded in thesis statements. Sometimes your assumptions are shared by most readers. For example, in the first reading of this chapter Robert Bellah employs the unstated assumption that history teaches valuable lessons—most people assume that, so it doesn't require an explicit statement. But a second of Bellah's unstated assumptions about his topic is that civic use of religion is an acceptable topic for scholarly analysis. This assumption is more controversial (though probably less so when Bellah was writing in 1967), and Bellah may have improved his argument by stating that assumption and providing reasons for his readers to accept it.

If you tackle a research question that is complex enough to demand college-level thinking, writing an effective thesis will be very difficult. Observe the features of effective thesis statements and emulate the models in this chapter's readings.

WRITING IN THE DISCIPLINE

INTRODUCTION

by Richard Plantinga,
Professor of Religion

It may make you uncomfortable to discuss religious aspects of human culture, but it is almost impossible to avoid the topic when examining American society. To understand the place of religion in American culture, we must bear in mind that the founders of the United States envisioned it as a new, better world. Many of them believed that the young republic was chosen by God to be a blessing to the world (analogous to Israel as the "chosen people" depicted in the Hebrew Bible). Despite this belief, the founders wanted to avoid the problems that national religions had caused in Europe. America's founders recalled problems of Europe's national churches (the Anglican Church in England, the Presbyterian Church in Scotland, etc.). They were also unhappily aware of the restrictions on religious freedom that nations imposed on citizens who professed a faith different from the one sanctioned by the state. As a result, when they crafted the Constitution of the United States (1787), they disallowed a national religion. The First Amendment of the Constitution declares: "Congress shall make no law respecting an establishment of religion, or prohibiting the free exercise thereof."

Even though the United States has never had a national religion, religion has always played an important role in national life. Describing how religion functions in American society has been an ongoing interest of Robert Bellah (born in 1927), retired professor of sociology at the University of California at Berkeley. His well-known and much-cited essay on the subject, "Civil Religion in America," was first published in 1967. To fully appreciate

Bellah's argument, you must remember the time in which he wrote. In 1960, the country had elected a young, charismatic, Catholic president, who articulated a vision embraced by many, especially the young. On November 22, 1963, a shocked nation learned that President John Fitzgerald Kennedy had been assassinated in Dallas, Texas. He left to his successor, President Lyndon Baines Johnson, an escalating conflict in Vietnam as well as an unfinished agenda for addressing social inequalities like poverty and racism. As Johnson sought to win the war in Vietnam, he simultaneously attempted to build a "Great Society" at home. In this "Great Society," civil rights would flourish and poverty would be eradicated. In this tumultuous decade Robert Bellah wrote his essay.

In "Civil Religion in America," Bellah tries to accomplish three things. First, he catalogs the features of civil religion by analyzing how government officials use religion in speeches and documents. Second, he looks for historical reasons for the nature of civil religion in the United States—the historical events or philosophies that shaped it. Finally, Bellah speculates how civil religion might change in the future and what future influences it might have.

The structure of "Civil Religion in America" is typical for a thesis-based essay except for the opening abstract. Bellah begins the body of the essay by using an example—President Kennedy's inaugural address—to pose questions about the generic references to "God" in presidential addresses and government documents like the Declaration of Independence. The rest of the essay answers the questions he poses in his research question. At the end of his introduction, Bellah explains the importance of the topic: "These questions are worth pursuing because they raise the issue of how civil religion relates to the political society on the one hand and to private religious organization on the other" (page 85). Following this justification, Bellah states his thesis: "there actually exists alongside of and rather clearly differentiated from the churches an elaborate and well-institutionalized civil religion in America" (83). He provides specifics about his thesis by noting that "[t]his public religious dimension is expressed in a set of beliefs, symbols, and rituals that I am calling the American civil religion" (85).

In this provocative and still relevant essay, Bellah makes some key assumptions about religion—and assumptions are always debatable. His definition of religion—"a collection of beliefs, symbols, and rituals with respect to sacred things and institutionalized in a collectivity" (88)—affirms the definition proposed by Émile Durkheim, the father of sociology. Like Durkheim, Bellah holds that religion is more than just private beliefs. Rather, Bellah and Durkheim argued that religion is a part of culture, too; and they believed that a "civil" religion expresses the key beliefs and practices that bind a society together.

✓ Reading Tips

1. Locate the thesis statement and write it down (it's the last sentence of Bellah's "abstract"). After each section, jot down what you think the section contributes to the thesis. When you are finished, you will have an outline of an academic argument that you can use in class discussions and for quick reviews.

2. Write down the four headings and start to work out what pattern they reveal. Headings in the humanities are not as straightforward as headings in science writing, but they do give important clues about the author's point and organization. For example, note that three of Bellah's four headings refer to an historical period: he's making an argument based on history.

3. Read, do not scan, individual sections of the essay. Like other writers in the humanities, Bellah assumes that readers will attend to each sentence and each paragraph.

4. Assess whether all the parts have added up to an argument that you find clear and reasonable. Make notes on the reasons and evidence that convince you and those you find unconvincing.

Civil Religion in America
Robert N. Bellah

Daedalus, Journal of the American Academy of Arts and Sciences, Winter 1967.

[Abstract]

An abstract is only occasionally used in essays in the humanities. This opening paragraph differs from a scientific abstract in that it does not summarize the essay. Rather, it states the essay's thesis.

While some have argued that Christianity is the national faith, and others that church and synagogue celebrate only the generalized religion of "the American Way of Life," few have realized that there actually exists alongside of and rather clearly differentiated from the churches an elaborate and well-institutionalized civil religion in America. This article argues not only that there is such a thing, but also that this religion—or perhaps better, this religious dimension—has its own seriousness and integrity and requires the same care in understanding that any other religion does.[1]

The Kennedy Inaugural

By starting with Kennedy, just four years after his assassination and when Americans cherished his memory, Bellah puts himself at an immediate advantage with his readers.

Kennedy's inaugural address of 20 January 1961 serves as an example and a clue with which to introduce this complex subject. That address began:

We observe today not a victory of party but a celebration of freedom—symbolizing an end as well as a beginning—signifying renewal as well as change. For I have sworn before you and Almighty God the same solemn oath our forebears prescribed nearly a century and three quarters ago.

The world is very different now. For man holds in his mortal hands the power to abolish all forms of human poverty and to abolish all forms of human life. And yet the same revolutionary beliefs for which our forebears fought are still at issue around the globe—the belief that the rights of man come not from the generosity of the state but from the hand of God.

And it concluded:

Finally, whether you are citizens of America or of the world, ask of us the same high standards of strength and sacrifice that we shall ask of you. With a good conscience our only sure reward, with history the final judge of our deeds, let us go forth to lead the land we love, asking His blessing and His help, but knowing that here on earth God's work must truly be our own.

> Bellah presents himself as reasonable, open to different opinions—a good strategy to use at the beginning of a very opinionated essay.

These are the three places in this brief address in which Kennedy mentioned the name of God. If we could understand why he mentioned God, the way in which he did it, and what he meant to say in those three references, we would understand much about American civil religion. But this is not a simple or obvious task, and American students of religion would probably differ widely in their interpretation of these passages.

> In the 1960s, many scholars assumed that the nation was becoming increasingly secular. Many now disagree with that assumption. America seems to be diversely religiously engaged.

Let us consider first the placing of the three references. They occur in the two opening paragraphs and in the closing paragraph, thus providing a sort of frame for more concrete remarks that form the middle part of the speech. Looking beyond this particular speech, we would find that similar references to God are almost invariably to be found in the pronouncements of American presidents on solemn occasions, though usually not in the working messages that the president sends to Congress on various concrete issues. How, then, are we to interpret this placing of references to God?

> In this paragraph Bellah justifies what he has presented and pauses for reflection. The pause helps the reader move from focusing on the past to the present, and then from the present to the future.

It might be argued that the passages quoted reveal the essentially irrelevant role of religion in the very secular society that is America. The placing of the references in this speech as well as in public life generally indicates that religion has "only a ceremonial significance"; it gets only a sentimental nod that serves largely to placate the more unenlightened members of the community before a discussion of the really serious business with which religion has nothing whatever to do. A cynical observer might even say that an American president has to mention God or risk losing votes. A semblance of piety is merely one of the unwritten qualifications for the office, a bit more traditional than but not essentially different from the present-day requirement of a pleasing television personality.

But we know enough about the function of ceremonial and ritual in various societies to make us suspicious of dismissing something as unimportant because it is "only a ritual." What people say on solemn occasions need not be taken at face value, but it is often indicative of deep-seated values and commitments that are not made explicit in the course of everyday life. Following this line of argument, it is worth considering whether the very special placing of the references to God in Kennedy's address may not reveal something rather important and serious about religion in American life.

It might be countered that the very way in which Kennedy made his references reveals the essentially vestigial place of religion today. He did not refer to any religion in particular. He did not refer to Jesus Christ, or to Moses, or to the Christian church; certainly he did not refer to the Catholic Church. In fact, his only reference was to the concept of God, a word that almost all Americans can accept but that means so many different things to so many different people that it is almost an empty sign. Is this not just another indication that in America religion is considered vaguely to be a good thing, but that people care so little about it that it has lost any content whatever? Isn't Eisenhower reported to have said "Our government makes no sense unless it is founded in a deeply felt religious faith—and I don't care what it is,"[2] and isn't that a complete negation of any real religion?

These questions are worth pursuing because they raise the issue of how civil religion relates to the political society, on the one hand, and to private religious organization, on the other. President Kennedy was a Christian, more specifically a Catholic Christian. Thus his general references to God do not mean that he lacked a specific religious commitment. But why, then, did he not include some remark to the effect that Christ is the Lord of the world or some indication of respect for the Catholic Church? He did not because these are matters of his own private religious belief and of his own particular church; they are not matters relevant in any direct way to the conduct of his public office. Others with different religious views and commitments to different churches or denominations are equally qualified participants in the political process. The principle of separation of church and state guarantees the freedom of religious belief and association, but at the same time clearly segregates the religious sphere, which is considered to be essentially private, from the political one.

Considering the separation of church and state, how is a president justified in using the word *God* at all? The answer is that the separation of church and state has not denied the political realm a religious dimension. Although matters of personal religious belief, worship, and association are considered to be strictly private affairs, there are, at the same time, certain common elements of religious orientation that the great majority of Americans share. These have played a crucial role in the development of American institutions and still provide a religious dimension for the whole fabric of American life, including the political sphere. This public religious dimension is expressed in a set of beliefs, symbols, and rituals that I am calling the American civil religion. The inauguration of a president is an important ceremonial event in this religion. It reaffirms,

---

Bellah makes a key point here with respect to his argument. In civil religion, references are not to specific religions (e.g., Methodism) but to a general idea of "God."

This is a key issue, namely, the relation between the private and public dimensions in religion. Civil religion is public. Toward the end of the paragraph, Bellah indicates why the private–public matter is so important: The United States was founded on the principle of the separation of church (private) and state (public), as indicated in the First Amendment to the Constitution, but civil religion extends beyond the private sphere.

Through most of this paragraph Bellah is restating his thesis and then listing the features of civil religion. In a long essay, it usually helps to remind your readers of your thesis to keep their attention focused on it.

among other things, the religious legitimation of the highest political authority.

Let us look more closely at what Kennedy actually said. First, he said, "I have sworn before you and Almighty God the same solemn oath our forebears prescribed nearly a century and three quarters ago." The oath is the oath of office, including the acceptance of the obligation to uphold the Constitution. He swears it before the people (you) and God. Beyond the Constitution, then, the president's obligation extends not only to the people but to God. In American political theory, sovereignty rests, of course, with the people, but implicitly, and often explicitly, the ultimate sovereignty has been attributed to God. This is the meaning of the motto, "In God we trust," as well as the inclusion of the phrase "under God" in the pledge to the flag. What difference does it make that sovereignty belongs to God? Though the will of the people as expressed in the majority vote is carefully institutionalized as the operative source of political authority, it is deprived of an ultimate significance. The will of the people is not itself the criterion of right and wrong. There is a higher criterion in terms of which this will can be judged; it is possible that the people may be wrong. The president's obligation extends to the higher criterion.

When Kennedy says that "the rights of man come not from the generosity of the state but from the hand of God," he is stressing this point again. It does not matter whether the state is the expression of the will of an autocratic monarch or of the "people"; the rights of man are more basic than any political structure and provide a point of revolutionary leverage from which any state structure may be radically altered. That is the basis for his reassertion of the revolutionary significance of America.

But the religious dimension of political life as recognized by Kennedy not only provides a grounding for the rights of man that makes any form of political absolutism illegitimate, it also provides a transcendent goal for the political process. This is implied in his final words that "here on earth God's work must truly be our own." What he means here is, I think, more clearly spelled out in a previous paragraph, the wording of which, incidentally, has a distinctly Biblical ring:

Now the trumpet summons us again—not as a call to bear arms, though arms we need—not as a call to battle, though embattled we are—but a call to bear the burden of a long twilight struggle, year in and year out, "rejoicing in hope, patient in tribulation"—a struggle against the common enemies of man: tyranny, poverty, disease and war itself.

The whole address can be understood as only the most recent statement of a theme that lies very deep in the American tradition, namely the obligation, both collective and individual, to carry out God's will on

> self-governing, or having the right to self-government

> "Absolutism" is a conception of government that democracy rejects. It refers to the idea that kings have absolute rule over their subjects. Their power to rule in this fashion they understood to come from God, whom they represent.

earth. This was the motivating spirit of those who founded America, and it has been present in every generation since. Just below the surface throughout Kennedy's inaugural address, it becomes explicit in the closing statement that God's work must be our own. That this very activist and noncontemplative conception of the fundamental religious obligation, which has been historically associated with the Protestant position, should be enunciated so clearly in the first major statement of the first Catholic president seems to underline how deeply established it is in the American outlook. Let us now consider the form and history of the civil religious tradition in which Kennedy was speaking.

The Idea of a Civil Religion

After the first section, which introduces the idea of civil religion by analyzing the Kennedy inaugural, Bellah in this section seeks to provide historical background and the basic point of his argument.

The phrase *civil religion* is, of course, Rousseau's. In Chapter 8, Book 4 of *The Social Contract,* he outlines the simple dogmas of the civil religion: the existence of God, the life to come, the reward of virtue and the punishment of vice, and the exclusion of religious intolerance. All other religious opinions are outside the cognizance of the state and may be freely held by citizens. While the phrase *civil religion* was not used, to the best of my knowledge, by the founding fathers, and I am certainly not arguing for the particular influence of Rousseau, it is clear that similar ideas, as part of the cultural climate of the late eighteenth century, were to be found among the Americans. . . .

Jean-Jacques Rousseau was a Swiss thinker who lived from 1712 to 1778. Writers in the humanities often ground their claims in particular philosophical theories.

Kennedy's inaugural pointed to the religious aspect of the Declaration of Independence, and it might be well to look at that document a bit more closely. There are four references to God. The first speaks of the "Laws of Nature and of Nature's God," which entitle any people to be independent. The second is the famous statement that all men "are endowed by their Creator with certain inalienable Rights." Here Jefferson is locating the fundamental legitimacy of the new nation in a conception of "higher law" that is itself based on both classical natural law and Biblical religion. The third is an appeal to "the Supreme Judge of the world for the rectitude of our intentions," and the last indicates "a firm reliance on the protection of divine Providence." In these last two references, a Biblical God of history who stands in judgment over the world is indicated. . . .

The words and acts of the founding fathers, especially the first few presidents, shaped the form and tone of the civil religion as it has been maintained ever since. Though much is selectively derived from Christianity, this religion is clearly not itself Christianity. For one thing, neither Washington nor Adams nor Jefferson mentions Christ in his inaugural address; nor do any of the subsequent presidents, although not one of them fails to mention God.[3] The God of the civil religion is not only rather "unitarian," he is also on the austere side, much more related to order, law, and right than to salvation and love. Even though

"Unitarian" is a reference to a concept of God as simply one, not the Trinitarian God of traditional Christianity.

Deism (from the Latin term for God, "*deus*") is a seventeenth- and eighteenth-century position that declares general belief in God and an afterlife. The beliefs in deism fit the beliefs in civil religion quite closely.

This conception of religion is adapted from the French sociologist Émile Durkheim (1858–1917). See Bellah's first endnote, where he shows his dependence on this early twentieth-century source.

"Sectarian" is the adjectival form of the word *sect,* meaning party, group, or faction.

A magistrate is a government representative empowered to administer the law, such as a judge or a president.

In this next section, Bellah demonstrates the origins and development of the American civil religion in the Revolutionary War against Britain and in the American Civil War.

he is somewhat deist in cast, he is by no means simply a watchmaker God. He is actively interested and involved in history, with a special concern for America. Here the analogy has much less to do with natural law than with ancient Israel; the equation of America with Israel in the idea of the "American Israel" is not infrequent. . . .[4]

What we have, then, from the earliest years of the republic is a collection of beliefs, symbols, and rituals with respect to sacred things and institutionalized in a collectivity. This religion—there seems no other word for it—while not antithetical to and indeed sharing much in common with Christianity, was neither sectarian nor in any specific sense Christian. At a time when the society was overwhelmingly Christian, it seems unlikely that this lack of Christian reference was meant to spare the feelings of the tiny non-Christian minority. Rather, the civil religion expressed what those who set the precedents felt was appropriate under the circumstances. It reflected their private as well as public views. Nor was the civil religion simply "religion in general." While generality was undoubtedly seen as a virtue by some, . . . the civil religion was specific enough when it came to the topic of America. Precisely because of this specificity, the civil religion was saved from empty formalism and served as a genuine vehicle of national religious self-understanding.

But the civil religion was not, in the minds of Franklin, Washington, Jefferson, or other leaders, with the exception of a few radicals like Tom Paine, ever felt to be a substitute for Christianity. There was an implicit but quite clear division of function between the civil religion and Christianity. Under the doctrine of religious liberty, an exceptionally wide sphere of personal piety and voluntary social action was left to the churches. But the churches were neither to control the state nor to be controlled by it. The national magistrate, whatever his private religious views, operates under the rubrics of the civil religion as long as he is in his official capacity, as we have already seen in the case of Kennedy. This accommodation was undoubtedly the product of a particular historical moment and of a cultural background dominated by Protestantism of several varieties and by the Enlightenment, but it has survived despite subsequent changes in the cultural and religious climate.

Civil War and Civil Religion

Until the Civil War, the American civil religion focused above all on the event of the Revolution, which was seen as the final act of the Exodus from the old lands across the waters. The Declaration of Independence and the Constitution were the sacred scriptures and Washington the divinely appointed Moses who led his people out of the hands of tyranny. The Civil War, which Sidney Mead calls "the center of American history,"[5] was the second great event that involved the national self-understanding so deeply as to require expression in civil religion. . . .

The Civil War raised the deepest questions of national meaning. The man who not only formulated but in his own person embodied its meaning for Americans was Abraham Lincoln. For him the issue was not in the first instance slavery but "whether that nation, or any nation so conceived, and so dedicated, can long endure.". . .

The phrases of Jefferson constantly echo in Lincoln's speeches. His task was, first of all, to save the Union—not for America alone but for the meaning of America to the whole world so unforgettably etched in the last phrase of the Gettysburg Address.

But inevitably the issue of slavery as the deeper cause of the conflict had to be faced. In the second inaugural, Lincoln related slavery and the war in an ultimate perspective:

If we shall suppose that American slavery is one of those offenses which, in the providence of God, must needs come, but which, having continued through His appointed time, He now wills to remove, and that He gives to both North and South this terrible war as the woe due to those by whom the offense came, shall we discern therein any departure from those divine attributes which the believers in a living God always ascribe to Him? Fondly do we hope, fervently do we pray, that this mighty scourge of war may speedily pass away. Yet, if God wills that it continue until all the wealth piled by the bondsman's two hundred and fifty years of unrequited toil shall be sunk, and until every drop of blood drawn with the lash shall be paid by another drawn with the sword, as was said three thousand years ago, so still it must be said "the judgements of the Lord are true and righteous altogether."

But he closes on a note if not of redemption then of reconciliation—"With malice toward none, with charity for all."

With the Civil War, a new theme of death, sacrifice, and rebirth enters the new civil religion. It is symbolized in the life and death of Lincoln. Nowhere is it stated more vividly than in the Gettysburg Address, itself part of the Lincolnian "New Testament" among the civil scriptures. Robert Lowell has recently pointed out the "insistent use of birth images" in this speech explicitly devoted to "these honored dead": "brought forth," "conceived," "created," "a new birth of freedom." He goes on to say:

The Gettysburg Address is a symbolic and sacramental act. Its verbal quality is resonance combined with a logical, matter of fact, prosaic brevity. . . . In his words, Lincoln symbolically died, just as the Union soldiers really died—and as he himself was soon really to die. By his words, he gave the field of battle a symbolic significance that it has lacked. For us and our country, he left Jefferson's ideals of freedom and equality joined to the Christian sacrificial act of death and rebirth. I believe this is the meaning that goes beyond sect or religion and beyond peace and war, and is now part of our lives as a challenge, obstacle and hope.[6]

Lowell is certainly right in pointing out the Christian quality of the symbolism here, but he is also right in quickly disavowing any sectarian implication. The earlier symbolism of the civil religion had been Hebraic without being in any specific sense Jewish. The Gettysburg symbolism (". . . those who here gave their lives, that that nation might live") is Christian without having anything to do with the Christian church. . . .

The Civil Religion Today

In reifying and giving a name to something that, though pervasive enough when you look at it, has gone on only semiconsciously, there is risk of severely distorting the data. But the reification and the naming have already begun. The religious critics of "religion in general," or of the "religion of the 'American Way of Life,'" or of "American Shinto" have really been talking about the civil religion. As usual in religious polemic, they take as criteria the best in their own religious tradition and as typical the worst in the tradition of the civil religion. Against these critics, I would argue that the civil religion at its best is a genuine apprehension of universal and transcendent religious reality as seen in or, one could almost say, as revealed through the experience of the American people. Like all religions, it has suffered various deformations and demonic distortions. At its best, it has neither been so general that it has lacked incisive relevance to the American scene nor so particular that it has placed American society above universal human values. . . .

With respect to America's role in the world, the dangers of distortion are greater and the built-in safeguards of the tradition weaker. The theme of the American Israel was used, almost from the beginning, as a justification for the shameful treatment of the Indians so characteristic of our history. It can be overtly or implicitly linked to the ideal of manifest destiny that has been used to legitimate several adventures in imperialism since the early nineteenth century. Never has the danger been greater than today. The issue is not so much one of imperial expansion, of which we are accused, as of the tendency to assimilate all governments or parties in the world that support our immediate policies or call upon our help by invoking the notion of free institutions and democratic values. Those nations that are for the moment "on our side" become "the free world." A repressive and unstable military dictatorship in South Vietnam becomes "the free people of South Vietnam and their government." It is then part of the

---

The term *reification* comes from the Latin term for "thing" (*res*). To reify, therefore, is to bring something into being through speaking.

A key equation in the civil religion is the identification of the ancient nation of Israel with the United States. Just as Israel was to bring goodness and hope to the ancient world, so America saw itself as being charged with bringing virtues to the new world.

"Manifest destiny" is the idea that America was destined to possess much of the continent of North America, "from sea to shining sea."

role of America as the New Jerusalem and "the last hope of earth" to defend such governments with treasure and eventually with blood. When our soldiers are actually dying, it becomes possible to consecrate the struggle further by invoking the great theme of sacrifice. For the majority of the American people who are unable to judge whether the people in South Vietnam (or wherever) are "free like us," such arguments are convincing. Fortunately President Johnson has been less ready to assert that "God has favored our undertaking" in the case of Vietnam than with respect to civil rights. But others are not so hesitant. The civil religion has exercised long-term pressure for the humane solution of our greatest domestic problem, the treatment of the Negro American. It remains to be seen how relevant it can become for our role in the world at large, and whether we can effectually stand for "the revolutionary beliefs for which our forebears fought," in John F. Kennedy's words.

The civil religion is obviously involved in the most pressing moral and political issues of the day. But it is also caught in another kind of crisis, theoretical and theological, of which it is at the moment largely unaware. "God" has clearly been a central symbol in the civil religion from the beginning and remains so today. This symbol is just as central to the civil religion as it is to Judaism or Christianity. In the late eighteenth century this posed no problem; even Tom Paine, contrary to his detractors, was not an atheist. From left to right and regardless of church or sect, all could accept the idea of God. But today, as even *Time* has recognized, the meaning of the word *God* is by no means so clear or so obvious. There is no formal creed in the civil religion. We have had a Catholic President; it is conceivable that we could have a Jewish one. But could we have an agnostic president? Could a man with conscientious scruples about using the word *God* the way Kennedy and Johnson have used it be elected chief magistrate of our country? If the whole God symbolism requires reformulation, there will be obvious consequences for the civil religion, consequences perhaps of liberal alienation and of fundamentalist ossification that have not so far been prominent in this realm. The civil religion has been a point of articulation between the profoundest commitments of Western religious and philosophical tradition and the common beliefs of ordinary Americans. It is not too soon to consider how the deepening theological crisis may affect the future of this articulation. . . .

Behind the civil religion at every point lie Biblical archetypes: Exodus, Chosen People, Promised Land, New Jerusalem, Sacrificial Death and Rebirth. But it is also genuinely American and genuinely new. It has its own prophets and its own martyrs, its own sacred events and sacred places, its own solemn rituals and symbols. It is concerned

By mentioning "liberal alienation" and "fundamentalist ossification" in the same sentence with "God symbolism," Bellah seems to have in mind two opposite tendencies of religious groups. Liberals, he suggests, find the traditional idea of God troubling; fundamentalists define God in particular ways that suit their group's religious beliefs.

that America be a society as perfectly in accord with the will of God as men can make it, and a light to all nations.

It has often been used and is being used today as a cloak for petty interests and ugly passions. It is in need—as any living faith—of continual reformation, of being measured by universal standards. But it is not evident that it is incapable of growth and new insight.

It does not make any decisions for us. It does not remove us from moral ambiguity, from being, in Lincoln's fine phrase, an "almost chosen people." But it is a heritage of moral and religious experience from which we still have much to learn as we formulate the decisions that lie ahead.

> Bellah ends the piece by reiterating his point about the ongoing relevance of civil religion. In a "post-9/11" world his point is indeed suggestive.

References

1. Why something so obvious should have escaped serious analytical attention is itself an interesting problem. Part of the reason is probably the controversial nature of the subject. From the earliest years of the nineteenth century, conservative religious and political groups have argued that Christianity is, in fact, the national religion. Some of them from time to time and as recently as the 1950s proposed constitutional amendments that would explicitly recognize the sovereignty of Christ. In defending the doctrine of separation of church and state, opponents of such groups have denied that the national polity has, intrinsically, anything to do with religion at all. The moderates on this issue have insisted that the American state has taken a permissive and indeed supportive attitude toward religious groups (tax exemptions, et cetera), thus favoring religion but still missing the positive institutionalization with which I am concerned. But part of the reason this issue has been left in obscurity is certainly due to the peculiarly Western concept of "religion" as denoting a single type of collectivity of which an individual can be a member of one and only one at a time. The Durkheimian notion that every group has a religious dimension, which would be seen as obvious in southern or eastern Asia, is foreign to us. This obscures the recognition of such dimensions in our society.

2. Dwight D. Eisenhower, in Will Herberg, *Protestant-Catholic-Jew* (Garden City, N.Y.: Doubleday & Co., 1955), 97.

3. God is mentioned or referred to in all inaugural addresses but Washington's second, which is a very brief (two paragraphs) and perfunctory acknowledgement. It is not without interest that the actual word "God" does not appear until Monroe's second inaugural, March 5, 1821. In his first inaugural, Washington refers to God as "that Almighty Being who rules the universe," "Great Author of every public and private good," "Invisible Hand," and "benign Parent of the Human Race." John Adams refers to God as "Providence," "Being who is supreme over all," "Patron of Order," "Fountain of Justice," and "Protector in all ages of the world of virtuous liberty." Jefferson speaks of "that Infinite Power which rules the destinies of the universe," and "that Being in whose hands we are." Madison speaks of "that Almighty Being whose power regulates the destiny of nations," and "Heaven." Monroe uses "Providence" and "the Almighty" in his first inaugural and finally "Almighty God" in his second. See *Inaugural Addresses of the Presidents of the United States from George Washington 1789 to Harry S. Truman 1949*, 82d Congress, 2d Session, House Document No. 540, 1952.

4. For example, Abiel Abbot, pastor of the First Church in Haverhill, Massachusetts, delivered a Thanksgiving sermon in 1799, *Traits of Resemblance in the People of the*

United States of America to Ancient Israel, in which he said, "It has been often remarked that the people of the United States come nearer to a parallel with Ancient Israel, than any other nation upon the globe. Hence 'Our American Israel' is a term frequently used; and common consent allows it apt and proper." In Hans Kohn, *The Idea of Nationalism* (New York: Macmillan Co., 1961), 665.

5. Sidney E. Mead, *The Lively Experiment* (New York: Harper & Row, 1963), 12.

6. Robert Lowell, "On the Gettysburg Address" in Allan Nevins, ed., *Lincoln and the Gettysburg Address* (Urbana, Ill.: Univ. of Ill. Press, 1964), 88–89.

Reading Responses

1. Many scholars in religious studies still use Bellah's essay in their research. List the claims that Bellah makes that you believe are still true about America. List Bellah's claims that you find outdated or untrue about America.

2. In his article, Bellah justifies the kind of evidence he uses to support his theory by claiming that "what people say on solemn occasions need not be taken at face value, but it is often indicative of deep-seated values and commitments that are not made explicit in everyday life." Do you agree with Bellah? Has Bellah provided enough evidence to persuade you? List three other kinds of evidence that you would find equally or even more persuasive.

3. Bellah calls the religious dimension of Americans' public discourse a "civic religion." Some might see these terms to be mutually exclusive. Do you? In your answer, provide definitions and examples of what is "civic" and "religious" to support your claim.

NOTES ON GRAMMAR, STYLE, AND RHETORIC:
FIRST-PERSON PRONOUNS

Nearly every time students receive a writing assignment, one or two will linger after class to ask questions. And it seems that one question is always something like this: "In this next essay, may I use the word *I?* All of my high-school teachers told me not to, but I'm the one doing the writing, so why shouldn't I be up front about that fact and use *I* when it feels natural?"

Robert N. Bellah uses first-person pronouns in "Civil Religion in America," and his essay can help us answer that question. Even though his essay is an extended piece of formal academic prose, he often uses the pronoun *I.* For example, he uses this pronoun when he clarifies his use of terms: "This public religious dimension is expressed in a set of beliefs, symbols, and rituals that I am calling American civil religion" (85). Further, he uses *I* to indicate how he personally reacts to others' claims that bear on his case: "Against these critics, I would argue that the civil religion at its best is a genuine apprehension of universal and transcendant religious reality . . ." (90).

But Bellah's pronouns get even more intriguing when he shifts from the first-person singular *I* to the first-person plurals *we* and *us.* With these plural pronouns, he invites readers to take on a certain role. But soon after that, he proceeds as if he can assume that they have accepted his invitation.

What role does he initially invite readers to accept? He uses *we* to invite readers to become coexplorers with him of the phenomenon he calls American civil religion: "If we could understand why he [President Kennedy] mentioned God, the way in which he did, and what he meant to say in those three references [to God], we would understand much about American civil religion" (84).

Soon after he issues this invitation, however, it becomes clear that Bellah assumes that readers have accepted the role of coexplorers because at several points where he uses some kind of transition marker, he refers both to his readers and to himself. In the paragraph immediately following his opening invitation, he announces his opening exploratory move: "Let us consider first the placing of the three references [to God]" (84). After he examines the issue of Kennedy's referring to God, he pauses and directs his readers: "Let us look more closely at what Kennedy actually said" (86). And when he thinks that readers need a reminder about the ground that they and he have already covered, he again uses a first-person plural pronoun: "The national magistrate . . . operates under the rubrics of the civil religion . . . , as we have already seen in the case of Kennedy" (88).

As Bellah moves along, he shows with his use of *we* and *us* that he is making other striking assumptions. For example, he writes as if he can assume what his readers know: "But we know enough about the function of ceremonial and ritual in various societies to make us suspicious of dismissing something as unimportant because it is 'only a ritual'" (84).

Furthermore, toward the end of his essay Bellah's use of *we* and *us* leads to something even more striking: He assumes that his readers not only are exploring American's civil religion but also are participating in it. He is, one suspects, trying to clinch his case for the existence of an American civil religion by leading his readers to admit that they see the civil religion in themselves. This may be the best explanation of Bellah's use of sentences such as his concluding one: "But it [the civil religion] is a heritage of moral and religious experience from which we still have much to learn as we formulate the decisions that lie ahead" (92).

With all these uses of *we* and *us,* then, Bellah is attempting something extraordinary. These pronouns reflect his attempt to unite readers with him in what he presents as a clear and companionable exploration of a significant subject. Beyond that, what better way is there to persuade readers that a social movement exists than to have them recognize that they themselves already believe in it and contribute to it?

If in your own writing you could use *we* and *us* in ways that move readers to accept the roles you are suggesting for them, you would experience a remarkable degree of rhetorical power. But before imitating Bellah's use of first-person pronouns, you must remember several things. First, when Bellah wrote this essay, he already had more impressive credentials as an author than many of us might ever have. Second, he had a long essay with which to build a relationship with his readers. And third, most of his original readers probably had some connection to the United States and the civil religion he sees there.

In this light, consider what would happen if his readers did not share the assumptions signaled by Bellah's uses of *we* and *us.* That, of course, is not likely to happen as he marks the way for his readers, using expressions such as "Let us consider first." But it could very well happen as he signals assumptions about what readers know. And it could happen even more easily with his assumption that readers represent and enact America's civil religion. Just imagine how non-U. S. citizens who despise aspects of U.S. culture and foreign policy would react to the assumption that they have much to learn from American civil religion to "formulate the decisions that lie ahead" (92). With such readers, Bellah's use of *we* and *us* would fail: They would probably deny all his claims and be angry that he had ever made them. The tactic of using *we* and *us,* therefore, is one that in some situations can have great rhetorical power and in others can lead to rhetorical ruin.

In Your Own Writing . . .

Before using any first-person singular or plural pronouns in one of your own essays, you must be able to answer "yes" to both of these questions:

- First, will it likely seem logical and natural to your readers for you to signal your personal role in carrying out various tasks associated with the essay (such as providing guideposts to the essay's structure and detailing what you mean by certain phrases)?
- Second, will the roles that you suggest for your readers be roles that they could conceivably agree to take on?

STUDENT WRITING

INTRODUCTION

by Philip Park, religious studies major

The Assignment.   I was told to write a thesis-driven term paper, about 6,000 words long, for a class called Introduction to the Study of Religion. The assignment required that "the paper must argue a thesis clearly and consistently, based on the research done and the evidence presented."

The Content.   Peter Berger was a sociologist who studied religion. I read two books by him and realized that between writing the first and the second he'd changed his ideas about research methods. The first book argued that only observable evidence could be used to explain religion. In the second book Berger speculates that observable characteristics in human beings may tell us about a supernatural reality that lies beyond our physical one. I wondered why Berger would abandon his previous commitment to observable evidence and how he could use observable evidence to talk about what we cannot observe. Answering these questions became the purpose of my paper.

Learning to Write in the Humanities.   I first discovered that researchers in the humanities argue about scholarly assumptions when I was assigned to read Charlotte Allen's article, "Is Nothing Sacred?" Allen notes that most scholars of religious studies attempt to conduct their research without assuming that a sacred or transcendent aspect of reality actually exists; if scholars assumed the existence of a sacred element, readers would dismiss their research as nonacademic. Because they assume that any transcendent aspect of reality is off-limits for researchers, scholars use only objective evidence to support their claims.

For that same class, I read Berger's "classic," *The Sacred Canopy: Elements of a Sociological Theory of Religion*. In it, he theorizes that religion is constructed largely by society; in his appendix he emphasizes that his sociological theories are based exclusively on observable evidence and that, consequently, he is making no claims regarding theological truth. Berger reasons that he is committed to studying only that which is observable because he is engaged in "an enterprise of sociological theorizing." In this way I learned that the assumptions a humanities writer chooses affects the type of evidence he uses.

While reading books by Berger and scholarship about him, I began to form an opinion about Berger's mixture of theology and sociology and its relation to the controversy over acceptable methods of research. This opinion gradually became my thesis statement, the main argument of my paper. I say "gradually" because it was only through researching primary sources (works by Berger) and secondary sources (works about Berger) that I developed a specific thesis. First, I carefully examined the evidence that supported as well as contradicted my thesis. For instance, if someone disagreed about what I had to say about Berger, could I make a counterargument? What evidence could I use?

Once I gathered what I thought was a sufficient amount of evidence, I began writing the paper. I first introduced the reader to the context and the problem that my thesis responded to. In this case, I introduce religious studies by briefly describing its beginnings. Then, of course, I describe the problem: how two groups argue about the method for studying religion. After the introduction, I present evidence and argumentation that I hope will convince my reader.

Because I argue in my thesis for the value of a nonscientific approach, I begin by describing Berger's two books to show the weaknesses of an exclusively scientific approach. I also claim that theological speculation like Berger's can provide important knowledge about religion. In my presentation and analysis of the scholarly criticism of Berger's nonscientific method, I expand this idea that theological speculation can bring a different kind of understanding of religion. I then question the assumptions underlying the preference for the scientific approach to the study of religion, asserting that Berger's method of study is an equally valid way of understanding the phenomenon.

I conclude by noting the general lessons that all thinkers and researchers can learn from Berger's example. In my conclusion, I remind the reader of the importance of the problem I tackled in my thesis, and I address the "so what?" question that the reader will ask after finishing my paper. In this case, I discuss the role of assumptions in our search for and interpretation of evidence.

Even though it may seem that students write term papers just to get a grade in a class, I think that writing term papers helps students in a few important ways. First, students practice a method for figuring out what they believe in general about a topic and, specifically, what they want to claim about a topic. People have to know what they believe and why before they can set out to make change. Second, students analyze the assumptions authors use and decide whether or not they agree with those assumptions. Doing this helps students figure out what others believe and why. Knowing that, they are better prepared to create arguments that will convince people to think in a new or different way about a topic.

Peter Berger and the Study of Religion: An Examination of Sociological Method

Philip Park

Introduction: Religion and the Study of Religion

The quest to understand the human experience is not a new one. For millennia, people have questioned the nature of humanity. These questions of human identity have led to speculation regarding the possibility that we exist in some kind of relation to a being or a reality beyond the physical, observable reality. Eventually, such theological speculation has led to groups holding particular beliefs and attitudes about the sacred, giving birth to what we today would name "religion."

Religion (I mean to include all of the world's major religions) has influenced much of human history throughout the world. Clearly, then, studying religion can provide unique insight into how human beings, alone or in groups, make sense of reality. Since the late nineteenth century, religion has become a topic of academic research for scholars from a variety of academic disciplines. And recently the study of religion has become more controversial. At the center of much of this controversy is the method that scholars in academic settings should use to study religion.[1] Some scholars believe that religion should be approached scientifically by examining only what is observable. These scholars are called the functionalists. The substantivists, on the other hand, believe that such a method ignores the "element of the sacred" and the study of religion should acknowledge the unobservable reality at the center of religious thought.[2]

This disagreement raises a critical question regarding the very assumptions that underlie religious studies: Can and should theological speculation (speculation about the unobservable) be part of the academic study of religion, where scholars disagree not only about theological matters but also about what counts as academically respectable scholarship?

Thinking about this disagreement, one does well to consider the thought of American sociologist Peter L. Berger. The number of works he has published on religion is impressive, and the importance of his role in popular and academic thinking on religion cannot be ignored. Berger writes with a mixture of sociological and theological insight. It is this mixture, however, that has attracted criticism from scholars who believe that the study of religion should be limited solely to that which is clearly observable. After discussing two of his earlier books on religion, *The Sacred Canopy* (1967) and *A Rumor of Angels* (1969), I will argue that Berger's method, though exceeding the bounds of scientific study, provides a much needed non-scientific approach to the study of religion, a field typically marked by an exclusive adherence to scientific modes of investigation that can easily preclude a holistic understanding of religion.

The Sacred Canopy and *A Rumor of Angels*: The Limits of Scientific Study

Berger described his personal theological convictions in his earlier *The Precarious Vision* (1961);[3] in *The Sacred Canopy* he states that he aims to "move strictly within the frame of reference of sociological theory." As a result, he acts as a "methodological atheist" and "view[s] religion

Side notes:

From the beginning, I wanted to make it clear that I was making an argument about the assumptions that sociologists of religion hold.

Here is the question that the paper will answer.

This thesis statement is my answer to the question I pose at the end of the preceding paragraph.

as a human projection."[4] Using the functionalist approach to the study of religion, he attempts to remain "value-free" and commits to studying only that which is observable in order so his work can be considered sociology, which is, after all, a social *science*.[5]

Berger begins *The Sacred Canopy* with an analysis of society: "Society is a dialectic phenomenon in that it is a human product, and nothing but a human product, that yet continuously acts back upon its producer."[6] We have created society, and, in turn, society has created us. Berger applies this theory of society as a human-made product to the phenomenon of religion; he theorizes that the creation and maintenance of religion are human efforts as well.[7]

Berger's scientific method here is obvious: he is intent on two things: engaging in "an enterprise of sociological theorizing," one that "bracket[s] the ultimate status of religious definitions of reality,"[8] and avoiding any theological statements or statements based on that which cannot be observed. In so doing, Berger separates observable reality and ultimate reality—that is, a transcendent reality that is beyond human interpretation. He limits the scope of his research to observable reality. Consequently, he admits that he does not, and cannot, assume that there actually exists a being or reality beyond what we can clearly see, as doing so would cause him to cross the boundaries of sociological science.[9]

It is within these boundaries that Berger concludes that all of one's beliefs are dependent on one's social environment. In *A Rumor of Angels,* he argues that sociology allows people to see that society and all that is found within it are constructions made by members of that particular society, a society located in a specific time and geographical location. Everything, from a sociological perspective, seems to be relative to one's society.

If sociology's conclusion that our beliefs are relative to our time and place is indeed true, adherents of religion are bound to be disappointed. Religions claim that their theology tells the one, true story of humanity, a story that lies beyond physical, observable reality. For believers, theology holds the truth about ultimate reality. An exclusively sociological approach, on the other hand, seems to focus solely on the observable reality and also seems to render futile any attempt to speculate about this ultimate reality. After all, how is the one, true story about ultimate reality, if it exists at all, to be known by us if all our ideas are relative to our specific contexts?

Berger answers this question raised by relativity's challenge: ". . . [R]elativizing analysis, in being pushed to its final consequence, bends back upon itself. The relativizers are relativized."[10] What he means is that those who wish to relativize a particular belief because it is contingent upon a society have to realize that their own view that "all is relative" is also a "product . . . of human history, [a] social construction . . . undertaken by human beings."[11] Relativizers, too, cannot claim to know that their view that all our beliefs are relative and that objective truth is unattainable or inexistent is absolutely and irrefutably true. Their claims about relativizing analysis are also influenced by their particular history and geography, and they, too, cannot claim to access truth.

> In this paragraph I was trying to focus attention on the clash of assumptions of the two methods of studying religion. Researchers' assumptions determine their methods.

If Berger remains committed to an exclusively scientific approach based solely on observable evidence, he cannot, as we have seen, make statements about what is theologically true about ultimate reality, an activity outside the boundaries of the scientific method. It is this attempt to understand ultimate reality, however, that fills the very substance of religion, and ignoring this quest leads only to a superficial understanding of a phenomenon based largely on that which is unobservable. As someone engaged in the holistic study of religion, Berger embarks on his own exploratory journey into the territory of theology.[12] In *The Sacred Canopy* Berger engages in what he calls "a conversation between sociology and theology," aiming to continue basing his conclusions on observable data. After examining some of his observations of universal human characteristics, he explores the possibility that these observations imply something about a transcendent reality. In the same way that the mathematical mind produces content that corresponds to a mathematical reality outside the mind, Berger suggests that the "religious projections of man . . . [could correspond] to a reality that is superhuman and supernatural."[13] Berger believes that a study of humanity and its religious projections may lead to knowledge of the ultimate reality that may exist beyond the observable reality to which we have access.

> This sentence summarizes Berger's claim.

Berger suggests that "signals of transcendence" can be found in all human beings, specifically in their desire for order, playfulness, hope, justice, and humor. We have a "propensity for order" and a trust in the order of the universe. We are playful creatures, and, in play, we step out of the "'serious' world in which people suffer and die" and into a world of "beatific immunity." We are hopeful creatures, and our hope often lies in the future. We have a sense of justice, demanding at least that those who deserve damnation receive damnation. Lastly, we have a sense of humor that "reflects the imprisonment of the human spirit in the world" and "recognizes and relativizes" the "comic discrepancy in the human condition."[14] These phenomena of the human experience, although found within " 'natural' reality . . . appear to point beyond that reality," according to Berger.[15]

Criticism and Analysis

> It helps my credibility to describe how others have critiqued Berger's method before I make my own assessment.

Although he bases his conclusions about the supernatural on what he can observe in human experiences, Berger is no longer working from "within the frame of reference of sociological theory." His modest conclusions about the supernatural, including his assumption that such a supernatural reality exists, cannot be verified through observation and thus cannot be called "scientific." Annette Ahern suggests that he wears two hats in this discussion: As a theologian, he holds that "rumors of angels" permeate our reality as "signals of transcendence," while, as a sociologist, he simply describes these phenomena as universal characteristics found in human beings.[16] Regarding his theological speculations, S. D. Gaede states that Berger writes "from the perspective not of scientific disinterest but of one who is religiously curious."[17] Not only do critics note his lack of testable hypotheses and his lack of more observable research, but they also accuse him of imposing his Christian biases on criteria for what constitutes observable data.[18] Consequently, his work has been used more often to build appreciation for religion than to study it.[19]

We must, however, carefully evaluate the criticism Berger's approach has received. Religious studies, which was first named *Religionswissenschaft,* or "science of religion," first presented a more "scientific" approach to religion and a branch of study intentionally differentiated from theology and philosophy of religion,[20] but we must now ask whether such a scientific approach is an adequate way to study religion. Should theology and philosophy of religion continue to be excluded from religious studies? Clearly, both are unique ways to gain a deeper understanding of either religion in general or a specific religion. Even if one does not believe in the validity of Berger's theological position, one walks away from Berger's book more educated on the thought-process affirmed by many religions. Exploring the theological framework of religion results in an understanding of religion that cannot be gained from a scholar's scientific observations.

As Hunter P. Mabry reminds us, "we need . . . a healthy respect for the autonomy of each discipline as a mode of apprehension, and a capacity to recognize the insights provided by each as fragmentary, partial illuminations of areas of reality which cannot be fully comprehended by any single mode of investigation."[21] Each discipline has unique tools for gathering, analyzing, and interpreting data on religion and religious experiences. Scholars from each discipline can bring unique insights into the phenomenon of religion, and through each discipline, our understanding of religion gains depth as well as breadth.[22]

The emphasis on a scientific, mono-disciplinary method, on the other hand, holds the danger of concluding that "religious experience is nothing more than those aspects accessible to and comprehensible through his or her particular discipline," which would "contravene . . . the norms of scientific study."[23] As Berger demonstrates in *A Rumor of Angels,* a strict attempt to investigate only the observable can blind one to other observable data, such as what he sees as signals of transcendence. A so-called observable account of human existence that does not include humanity's "consciousness of something beyond itself" is, according to Berger, simply not faithful to the spirit of a science based on observation.[24] After all, this human consciousness is an observable human impulse even if the "something" is not observable. Berger's approach questions the commonly accepted idea that a scientific account of religion should cancel out human theological speculation.

Here I turn to my evaluation of Berger's method. Given my evaluation of Berger's critics above, the reader shouldn't be surprised that I agree with Berger.

It does not need to be said that the study of religion as Berger proposes it invites controversy. Although this study can provide insight into human religious impulses, Berger's method sets theological truth as a goal, a goal that is rejected by most mainstream academic researchers. Most scholars agree that speculation about ultimate reality cannot rightfully be called an "academic" study of religion.

Once again I want to remind readers of my focus on scholars' assumptions.

This widely accepted view of what can and cannot be studied in the academic setting provides insight into a variety of assumptions held in academia. For instance, many scholars affirm the separation of theology from religious studies based on their theological beliefs. Some hold that a transcendent, unobservable reality does not exist. Consequently no such thing as theology or an objective theological truth exists, either. Others argue that if such a reality does indeed exist, we cannot perceive or understand it. Some scholars believe that theological truth does exist and is accessible to us but that the academic setting is not the proper place for study of it. Berger, clearly, does not share these assumptions. He assumes that there is such an ultimate, theological reality and that it is the task of academic study to pursue it.

Once we realize that this controversy revolves around a set of differing assumptions, we will see that the idea that the scientific mode of investigation is the only or the better way of acquiring knowledge is based on similar assumptions. We must realize that Berger's method not only provides an alternative approach to religious studies but that it, as a means to acquiring knowledge, is not secondary to the scientific approach simply because it is based on a different set of assumptions.

Conclusion

In a culture in which scholars highly value the scientific method, Berger provides a refreshing perspective. His non-scientific approach to the "science of religion" demonstrates that it is possible to learn about religion in other ways, ways that account for a fuller range of human experience. If accounts of religion do not address the human impulses that shape religion, they will offer only a partial understanding of the phenomenon. Berger, realizing the limitations of the scientific approach, explores theological ground in his sociological work and offers a unique and much needed approach to knowledge in religious studies. Though his insights may very well hold theological truth, one does not need to subscribe to Berger's theology to appreciate the benefits of his multidisciplinary approach. His exploration of theology in religious studies, at the very

> In my conclusion I want to extend my thesis to address the larger topic of the purpose of research in the humanities.

least, reminds us that we are creatures who often describe human experience in a spiritual way. And, if academic research in the humanities has left us with anything, it might be the simple truth that in understanding the experiences of others, we come to a better understanding of our own.

Though some scholars may consider Berger's research as non-academic, his scholarship has furthered the perennial quest to understand the human experience. He has been able to provide these new insights only because he was willing to challenge the generally held assumptions in academia. Berger's challenge provides a valuable

> In the end, I want to add a subtle reminder that I'm not just trying to assess scholars' assumptions, but possibly to change my readers' assumptions.

reminder to anyone who attempts to understand human experience: All of us work within a framework of assumptions that shapes the way we interpret human experiences. And, if we are honest in our desire to understand, we will discover that our intellectual search will often require us to examine not only the assumptions that underlie ideas of others but also those that underlie our own.

Notes

1. Charlotte Allen, "Is Nothing Sacred? Casting out the Gods from Religious Studies," *Lingua Franca* (November 1996): 32.
2. Annette Ahern, "Re-enchanting the World: Berger's Sacramental Approach to Religion," *Toronto Journal of Theology* vol. 11, no. 1 (Spring 1995): 24.
3. Peter L. Berger, *The Precarious Vision: A Sociologist Looks at Social Fictions and Christian Faith* (1961; reprint. Westport, CT: Greenwood, 1976), 166.
4. Peter L. Berger, *The Sacred Canopy: Elements of Sociological Theory of Religion* (New York: Doubleday, 1967), 180.
5. Berger, *The Sacred Canopy*, 180.
6. Berger, *The Sacred Canopy*, 3.
7. Paul R. Johnson, "Society, Knowledge, and Religion: The Perspective of Peter Berger," *Perspectives in Religious Studies* 3 (Fall 1976): 299.
8. Berger, *The Sacred Canopy*, 180.
9. Berger, *The Sacred Canopy*, 180.
10. Berger, *A Rumor of Angels*, 47.
11. Berger, *A Rumor of Angels*, 52.
12. Berger, *The Sacred Canopy*, 185.
13. Berger, *A Rumor of Angels*, 53.
14. Berger, *A Rumor of Angels*, 60–79.
15. Berger, *A Rumor of Angels*, 59.
16. Ahern, "Re-enchanting the World," 26.
17. S. D. Gaede, "Excursus: The Problem of Truth," in *Making Sense of Modern Times: Peter L. Berger and the Vision of Interpretive Sociology,* ed. James Davidson Hunter and Stephen C. Ainlay (New York: Routledge and Kegan Paul, 1986): 162.
18. Robert C. Fuller, "Religion and Empiricism in the Works of Peter Berger," *Zygon* vol. 22, no. 4 (December 1987), 507. Robert Wuthnow, "Religion as Sacred Canopy," in *Making Sense of Modern Times: Peter L. Berger and the Vision of Interpretive Sociology,* ed. James Davidson Hunter and Stephen C. Ainlay (New York: Routledge and Kegal Paul, 1986): 139.
19. Wuthnow, "Religion as Sacred Canopy," 139.

20. Annette Ahern, "Towards an Academic Praxis in Religious Studies: Berger's Dual-Citizenship Approach," *Studies in Religion/Sciences Religieuses* vol. 20, no. 3 (Summer 1991): 334.

21. Hunter P. Mabry, "Sociology and Theological Research: Some Assumptions and Issues," *Bangalore Theological Forum* vol. 16 (Sept.–Dec. 1984), 160–1.

22. Mabry, "Sociology and Theological Research," 161.

23. Mabry, "Sociology and Theological Research," 161.

24. Fuller, "Religion and Empiricism," 504.

Reading Responses

1. What is Philip Park's point? Did he convince you? If so, describe the part of his argument that persuaded you. Or, after reading Park's essay, do you disagree with his thesis? On what grounds do you disagree with him?

2. Philip Park focuses on the assumptions that Berger relies on in *The Sacred Canopy* and *The Rumor of Angels* to explain how Berger's research changed. What assumptions does Park rely on in his essay? Which of those assumptions do you agree with? Which do you reject?

3. Park concludes his essay with the claim that "if we are honest in our desire to understand, we will discover that our intellectual search will often require us to examine not only the assumptions that underlie ideas of others but also those that underlie our own." What possible dangers are associated with this kind of intellectual search? Are these dangers worth risking?

PUBLIC WRITING

INTRODUCTION

Daniel Burke writes for The Religion News Service, an organization that provides articles and editorials about religious issues for other news organizations. The RNS describes its mission as "providing intelligent, objective coverage of all religions—Judaism, Christianity, Islam, Asian religions and private spirituality." In 2010 Burke won the prize for Best In-Depth Reporting on Religion from the American Academy of Religion. Kevin Eckstrom is an editor for RNS. In this article, Burke and Eckstrom analyze President Obama's use of civil religion, drawing the reader's attention to their main point: that Obama doesn't just use civil religion, he modernizes it. As is common in journalism, they state their main point in the title of their article. They unfold their argument throughout the rest of the article, requiring a reader to attend to each paragraph to fully understand the complexity of their argument.

Obama Refashions America's Old-Time (Civil) Religion

Daniel Burke and Kevin Eckstrom

Religion News Service
http://www.religionnews.com/index.php?/rnstext/analyzes_president_obamas_inaugural_address_
for_hints_about_what_role_relig/January 20, 2009

WASHINGTON—Seeking to revive a dispirited nation, President Obama on Tuesday (Jan. 20) told Americans to get religion—civil religion.

"We remain a young nation, but in the words of Scripture, the time has come to set aside childish things," Obama said, quoting St. Paul's first letter to the Corinthians, in one of the few explicitly Christian references in his address.

Although at times Obama adopted the cadences of the black church that he called home for 20 years, he borrowed little of its content.

Instead, Obama's inaugural address, like that of previous presidents, drew heavily on what scholars deem America's civil religion: the transcendent ideals laid out in the Declaration of Independence and other foundational documents.

Those ideals are often assumed—but not always said—to be divinely inspired or granted. On Tuesday, Obama seemed to channel the spirit of President John F. Kennedy, who reminded a nation in 1961 that "the rights of man come not from the generosity of the state but from the hand of God."

"The time has come to reaffirm our enduring spirit," Obama said, "to choose our better history; to carry forward that precious gift, that noble idea passed on from generation to generation: the God-given promise that all are equal, all are free, and all deserve a chance to pursue their full measure of happiness."

America's civil religion has been a fixture at inaugural ceremonies since George Washington's, when the peaceful transfer of power at the high altar of American politics takes on an almost sacred air. Obama drew on Washington and other American icons as exemplars of banding together for the common good, a key tenet of civil religion.

"Throughout his speech he is challenging us to be 'We the people,'" said the Rev. Cheryl Townsend Gilkes, professor of African-American studies at Colby College in Maine.

But Obama's unique personal history and the perils of the present moment added new elements to America's old time religion, said Martin E. Marty, the religion scholar and former professor at the University of Chicago Divinity School.

"In talking about civil religion, you make a great deal of the power of the nation to do things," Marty said. On Tuesday, "there was a twist; it wasn't that the nation is perfect . . . but that we have failed to live up to our ideals."

Author and religion scholar Diana Butler Bass said the speech's strain of modesty was a break from the past.

"This is very different from what you would have heard in the civil religion of the 1950s, which was a more jubilant exultation of American rightness, that we're a chosen people," Bass said. "This speech had much more of a 'We're an almost-chosen people.' This is the kind of civil religion that Lincoln is famous for."

The speech was also, she said, a classic example of the liberal Protestant tradition that Obama embraced through the United Church of Christ, a view of "an American future that is based on humility and inclusion rather than triumph and elitism."

Though Obama said American ideals "still light the world," he suggested they've been hidden under a bushel as the government tried to keep its citizens safe from terrorist attacks. American beliefs—particularly tolerance and diversity—are more effective than American bullets in fighting terrorists, Obama said.

"For we know that our patchwork heritage is a strength, not a weakness. We are a nation of Christians and Muslims, Jews and Hindus—and non-believers," he said.

Despite a handful of overt religious references, Obama's nod to "non-believers" reflected the journey of a man whose parents were religious doubters, who didn't find faith until he was an adult, and whose extended family practices diverse religions.

"The fact that he mentioned non-believers leads me to think that he is cognizant of not leaving us out," said Lori Lipman Brown, director of the Secular Coalition of America.

Brown was also heartened at Obama's pledge to "restore science to its rightful place," a veiled reference to criticism that religious ideology trumped research during the Bush administration—especially in the field of bioethics.

In a further break with his predecessor, Obama told "the Muslim world" that "we seek a new way forward, based on mutual interest and mutual respect."

Still, the bulk of Obama's speech was addressed to Americans. The challenges may be new, he said, but the "values on which our success depends . . . are old."

"This is the source of our confidence," the new president said, "the knowledge that God calls on us to shape an uncertain destiny."

Reading Responses

1. Write out Burke and Eckstrom's main point. In what ways did Obama update American civil religion? List the updates that you believe to be improvements.

2. Outline the argument in this article, noting the reasons and the evidence that the authors provide. Which two reasons could benefit from more evidence?

3. List the authors' stated assumptions about civil religion. List the unstated assumptions. Note which assumptions you share with them and which assumptions you do not.

MORE WRITING IN RELIGION AND SOCIETY

INTRODUCTION

Not everyone believes that civil religion is a harmless feature of American culture, and Jay Michaelson, a lawyer and scholar of Judaic thought, would be one of them. Writing on prawfs-blawg, a blog about "a variety of topics related to law and life," Michaelson poses his research question in the title of his post: "Is the Pledge merely Ceremonial Deism?" Michaelson explains his preference for the term "ceremonial deism" over "civil religion" in his post, but it is clear that he is referring to the same civic use of religious terminology that Newdow and Bellah analyze. Partway through his post, Michaelson introduces his reader to a more narrowly focused problem with a second research question: "I wonder if 'under God' is really devoid of religious content after all?" Marshalling reasons and evidence, Michaelson builds support for a thesis that he presents near the conclusion of his essay: "Those words are important to people because they say something, and the something they say is indeed significantly religious."

Is the Pledge Merely Ceremonial Deism?

Jay Michaelson

Posted on February 20, 2008 at 04:35 PM in *Constitutional thoughts | Permalink*

Last week in my law & religion seminar, we went over the *Newdow* case—the infamous 9th circuit case holding that the words "under God" in the Pledge of Allegiance violate the Establishment Clause. The Supreme Court mostly didn't reach the constitutional issue, ruling that Newdow didn't have standing, but Justice O'Connor did present a lengthy concurring opinion concluding that the phrase was part of our country's acceptable "ceremonial deism," like having "In God We Trust" on our coins—a phrase coined by Justice Brennan in 1984.

O'Connor went out of her way to say that the point of ceremonial deism is not that it is *de minimis* [about minimal things], but that it has certain features: history/ubiquity, absence of worship/prayer, absence of reference to a particular religion, and minimal religious content. So, even though "under God" surely flunks the Lemon test, O'Connor's own Endorsement test, and some understandings of the Neutrality principle [all methods to determine appropriate separation of church and state], its status as "ceremonial deism" makes it OK.

Brennan's original formulation, though, is a bit more limited: for him, statements of ceremonial deism are those which "have lost through rote repetition any significant religious content."

Brennan specifically included the Pledge's "under God" as an example of ceremonial deism. But here's my question: given the false allegations about Barack Obama's religion, and his willingness/unwillingness to say the pledge of allegiance, I wonder if "under God" is really devoid of religious content after all? More after the jump.

Ceremonial deism is essentially meant to be a meaningless gesture that's been longstanding and of minimal religious content. Now, "content" isn't the same as "import." A statement may be very low in content but very high in import. But is it really accurate to measure content by number of words and theological propositions? Scholars of religion regularly observe that mere gestures, such as movements of the hand, can have enormous religious content, even without any words at all. "Content" is determined by context and symbol, not just verbiage.

I've been interested for a long time in how changes in culture can lead to changes in constitutional terms. For example, I argued, pre-Lawrence, that changes in cultural understandings of "family" had caused sodomy to become included within the family's "zone of privacy." Now, I wonder if the same process may be afoot. Insofar as the Pledge itself is connected to both religion and nationalism, I wonder if "under God" in the Pledge in fact has significant religious content, as evidenced by the anti-Obama smear, its blending of God and Country, and its disturbing resilience in some circles.

Even the outrage that greeted Newdow itself to me indicates that "under God" is meaningful. Those words are important to people because they say something, and the something they say is indeed significantly religious.

If not saying something means so much, then doesn't saying it mean equally as much?

Reading Responses

1. Write out Michaelson's thesis. Then, organize the reasons and the evidence that support that thesis in a way that makes the most sense to you. How would you have organized the argument in this essay?

2. What is the source of the term "ceremonial deism," according to Michaelson? What reasons might he have for preferring this term to "civil religion"? Which term would you prefer to use? Why?

3. List the assumptions that Michaelson makes about the topic and about his readers.

WRITING ASSIGNMENTS

Assignment 1

Since Bellah wrote his article in 1967, some things have changed and some have remained the same about how Americans invoke civic religion. Your task for this assignment is to select a recent speech given by an American politician on an important occasion—an inauguration, for example, a State of the Union speech, a televised address to the nation, or a eulogy at the funeral for a well-known public official.

Read the speech carefully, noting each instance in which the speaker invokes civic religion. Then analyze the speaker's use of civic religion, noting how it is similar to the uses that Bellah describes. Describe carefully the ways in which you see the speaker using civic religion differently. If the speaker doesn't seem to refer to civic religion much, analyze the rest of the speech carefully. What does the speaker use in place of civic religion? Critique the speaker's use of civic religion or an alternative to civic religion, supporting your critique with sound reasoning and evidence from the speech.

Assignment 2

Chapter 9 (Biology) contains an article written by Marguerite Holloway entitled "The Female Hurt" (pp. 279–285). In that article Holloway details the kinds of sports injuries most common in female athletes and speculates about the reasons that female athletes are more susceptible than male athletes to certain kinds of injuries. Holloway puts some of the blame for these injuries on the assumptions that coaches, doctors, and female athletes make regarding the female body. But Holloway herself bases her claim on assumptions about the nature of athletic training and the importance of athletics, to name just two.

Your task for this assignment is to critique the role of assumptions in Marguerite Holloway's article, paying attention both to the assumptions of female athletes and those who support them and to the assumptions that Holloway makes in her article.

- Note the assumptions that people make about the female body and the effect of these assumptions on the rate of injury and type of injury to female athletes.
- Look carefully for the assumptions that support Holloway's claim. You might find it helpful to write out the most important claims in her article. Then, look at the evidence she uses to support each claim. What assumptions connect the evidence to the claim? Do you agree with these assumptions? Take another look at Holloway's word choices. What words indicate her assumptions?

Assignment 3

When people like Jay Michaelson write a blog post, they usually are thinking about two different audiences: regular readers of the blog and anonymous readers on the Web. In his post, Michaelson uses terms and refers to concepts and court cases that would be familiar to the regular readers of prawfsblawg but unfamiliar to the rest of us. Your task is to rewrite Michaelson's blog entry so that undergraduate students can fully understand his point, reasoning, and evidence. To begin, use a survey to identify the words and concepts that would confuse college students. After researching these words and concepts, revise Michaelson's blog, embedding links to resources that readers can consult for additional information. Create an appendix that reports the results of your survey, identifies each revision that you made, and provides a justification for your revision.

5

SOCIOLOGY: SEARCHING FOR CAUSES OF SOCIAL PROBLEMS

In the comic above, what looks to be an empty ocean is actually full of drama—you just need to know where to look for it.

Human society is full of drama, too, if you know where to look and what to look for. Choose a public place where you can unobtrusively observe couples who appear to be married. Malls, parks, and restaurants are likely places. In a paragraph for each, describe three or four couples, including specifics that you observe.

What evidence makes you believe that the couple is married? Does the couple seem happy together? What is the physical distance between the couple? How affectionate is the couple?

Are they talking together? If so, who does most of the talking? What is the mood of the conversation? At the end of each paragraph, write out a specific question you have about this couple.

PORTABLE RHETORICAL LESSON: LIMITING A RESEARCH TOPIC

Did you find it difficult to write out a different question about each of the couples you observed? You likely felt some frustration because you didn't know the couples well enough to ask specific questions. You may have hesitated to ask a single specific question because you know that marriage is a complicated social relationship. These are the frustrations and worries that sociologists—and all researchers, really—must manage.

To begin to manage the complexity of their research, sociologists have developed methods for narrowing a research topic to a manageable size. The following outline highlights the basic steps.

1. After you identify the general topic of your research, read previous research on the topic to help you identify the problems or questions that deserve further research and the methods that have proven effective for other researchers.

2. Narrow your focus to one aspect of the topic or one specific problem.

3. Develop a theoretical framework—a model that describes the situation, the people involved, and the lens through which you view the situation. A theoretical framework uses precedents from previous scholarship as the foundation for the new framework. By using previous research to help you understand what questions can be answered and are worth answering, the theoretical framework helps to limit the scope of the research questions and hypotheses.

4. Develop one or more hypotheses—possible explanations—that you will test in your research. The hypothesis provides a very clear focus, helping readers to see exactly how the research topic is limited.

5. Develop a research design, using methods to test the hypotheses that have proven effective for other researchers.

6. Assess the research data collected to determine if it does or does not support the hypotheses.

You will notice that these steps drive toward the goal of making a **point** (through refinement of a hypothesis) and work very hard to design **research methods** and collect **evidence** (data) that support the point.

But the special emphasis that propels the steps—and the readings to follow—is the need to limit the scope of the topic. Without limiting the topic, it would be impossible to conduct research in sociology; the variables involved in any human social interactions are far too complex. In the last paragraph of Professor Brandsen's introduction to the first reading, she explains how the reading gets more and more specific about the initial hypothesis. In other words, she shows how sociologists are experts at the **Portable Rhetorical Lesson** of the chapter: limiting a topic. And you will be wise to apply this practice in all your courses.

WRITING IN THE DISCIPLINE

INTRODUCTION

by Cheryl Brandsen, Professor of Sociology

As social scientists, sociologists attempt to research human communities as objectively as possible. To achieve anything like scientific objectivity, sociologists must address two related problems: (1) even seemingly simple human interactions are exceedingly complex, and (2) sociologists' own life experiences affect how they look at human interactions.

Sociologist C. W. Mills argues that if researchers want to understand human behavior and social interaction, they must cultivate a "sociological imagination," a way of thinking about the world that relies on creative thought, careful review of previously published research, and objective scientific practices for their own research. This kind of imagination, says Mills, focuses on the relationship between "private troubles" and "public issues," between what might look like individual, personal problems and the larger structures of society. Sociological imagination helps researchers see how decisions or problems that seem to be solely personal and intimate—unemployment, suicide, or family relationships, for instance—are shaped by larger social, economic, historical, and political forces. And sociological imagination enables researchers to see past cultural stereotypes. When faced with the question from the final reading in this chapter (Why do young women have babies and yet remain unmarried?), for example, cultural stereotypes provide easy answers. But a sociological imagination compels researchers to think more creatively, looking for more complex answers that have greater explanatory power. Those potential answers form hypotheses that can be tested by reliable social science research.

Most people think about divorce, for example, in personal terms. A woman wonders where she "went wrong" or ruminates about her partner's bad habits. To prevent a subsequent divorce, the woman will focus on individual adjustments: "I will work fewer hours," "I will choose more wisely," or "I will manage money more effectively." That nearly 50 percent of marriages end in divorce, however, suggests that divorce might be more than an individual trouble. A sociological imagination pushes sociologists to wonder whether something in society influences the stability of marriages: high rates of unemployment, geographic mobility, changing gender roles and sexual norms, or unrealistic ideals about romantic love.

The authors of "Parenting as a 'Package Deal': Relationships, Fertility, and Nonresident Father Involvement Among Unmarried Parents," are highly respected sociologists (Ronald Mincy is a professor at Columbia University, Kathryn Edin a professor at Harvard, and Laura Tach, at the time of this study, was a graduate student at Harvard). They begin their essay by narrowing their research focus to unmarried couples who have a child together. In the last sentence of the first paragraph (immediately following the Abstract), the researchers narrow their focus even further to the relationship between the father and child after the father's romantic relationship with the child's mother has ended. And they identify a single measureable factor in that relationship: the amount of contact between nonresident fathers (fathers who do not live with the child and mother) and the child.

They conclude their introduction (the last paragraph before the section titled "Background") by presenting hypotheses. Formally defined, a hypothesis is a provisional explanation for a particular phenomenon that can be empirically tested. Informally defined, hypotheses in sociology offer specific answers to the questions that emerge from a sociological imagination. But they are answers that can be tested. Rather than merely accept a cultural stereotype of "deadbeat dad," these authors begin with a previously proven hypothesis: that fathers' involvement with their children lessens after a breakup between parents. This is the "package deal hypothesis"; the "package" is the connection between the relationship between the parents and the fathers' involvement with the children.

The authors then (in the same paragraph) "extend" the established hypothesis to argue that what causes fathers' involvement to lessen after a breakup is more than simply the breakup. Rather, fathers' involvement also depends on whether fathers and mothers move into new romantic relationships and have new children after breaking up. And they restate this hypothesis in the first sentence of the last paragraph of the "Background" section (the restated hypothesis is identified by a marginal note).

In the section entitled "Background," the authors construct the theoretical framework for their study. A useful theoretical framework provides a road map to guide research; more formally, a theoretical framework offers a set of interrelated, logical statements that describe, explain, or predict social events. In sociology, a theoretical framework provides an image of society that guides thinking and research. It includes a summary of previous research on the topic (often called a "literature review") and leads to a clearly defined problem to be investigated. The theoretical framework and the defined problem then shape what research methods are selected.

Regardless of the particular research methods chosen, sociologists work to ensure that the research is reliable, valid, and generalizable. *Reliable* means that the researcher has controlled for personal bias—that there is a high likelihood that other researchers would get the results if they duplicated the study; *valid* means that the results are very likely to represent something true about the social situation; and *generalizable* means that the truth of the results can be applied to situations beyond those of the experiment.

In the "Discussion" section, the authors consider how well their results support and specify their hypothesis. As you read, pay attention to the author's process of narrowing their focus: Step 1: the established "package deal hypothesis" that fathers' involvement with children lessens after a breakup. Step 2: the "extended" hypothesis that fathers' involvement also depends on whether either parent moves into a new relationship and has additional children. Step 3: the finding that mothers' movement into a new relationship and having new children is the most significant factor in lessening fathers' involvement. So the authors arrive at a conclusion that can stand as the starting point, the hypothesis to be extended, in future research.

✓ Reading Tips

Because sociologists achieve objectivity by carefully limiting the focus of their study to a testable hypothesis and by painstakingly describing their research (testing) methods and results, their writing can seem exceedingly complex.

To manage the complexity:

- First, look for the social problem that the authors study. In this article, you find that described in the "Abstract" and again in the "Discussion" section; also note the very last paragraph of the article. Jot down a summary of the problem and keep that handy as you read through the article.

- Next, find the places where the authors limit the topic (for example, the third paragraph after the "abstract"). Be sure that you understand the exact limits of the study.

- Next find the hypothesis that the authors actually test. Look in the section called "The 'Package Deal' and Nonmarital Father Involvement," and follow the marginal comments.

- Try to understand how the findings (look in the first paragraph of the "Discussion" section) do or do not fit in the theoretical framework—the model with which the authors begin their study (again, look for marginal annotations to help identify the relevant information).

Parenting as a "Package Deal": Relationships, Fertility, and Nonresident Father Involvement among Married Parents

Laura Tach, Ronald Mincy, and Kathryn Edin

Demography 47.1 2010

For a more complete description of this study of "fragile families," check out this link: http://www.fragilefamilies.princeton.edu/.

A longitudinal survey is one that takes place over time with the same participants surveyed during each wave of the study.

[Abstract]

Fatherhood has traditionally been viewed as part of a "package deal" in which a father's relationship with his child is contingent on his relationship with the mother. We evaluate the accuracy of this hypothesis in light of the high rates of multiple-partner fertility among unmarried parents using the Fragile Families and Child Wellbeing Study, a recent longitudinal survey of nonmarital births in large cities. We examine whether unmarried mothers' and fathers' subsequent relationship and parenting transitions are associated with declines in fathers' contact with their nonresident biological children. We contend that father involvement drops sharply after relationships between unmarried parents end. Mothers' transitions into new romantic partnerships and new parenting roles are associated with larger declines in involvement than fathers' transitions. Declines in fathers' involvement following a mother's relationship or parenting transition are largest when children are young. We discuss the implications of our results for the well-being of nonmarital children and the quality of nonmarital relationships faced with high levels of relationship instability and multiple-partner fertility.

In the late 1990s, over 80% of nonmarital births in the United States were to couples who were romantically involved. Forty percent of all unmarried parents and over half of urban unmarried parents were living together at the time of the birth (Bumpass and Lu 2000; McLanahan et al. 2003). Even though these parents express a desire to stay together and eventually marry each other, their romantic relationships dissolve rapidly in the first few years after the child's birth. Over 40% of nonmarital relationships end by the child's birthday, and by the time the child is 5 years old, over 60% of parents are no longer romantically involved with each other (Center for Research on Child Wellbeing 2003, 2007). The fragility of nonmarital unions has led to concern about whether fathers will remain in contact with their children after their relationships with mothers end.

There is reason to be skeptical. In the American context, fatherhood has traditionally been viewed as part of a "package deal" (Furstenberg and Cherlin 1991; Townsend 2004) in which fatherhood is contingent on the relationship between the father and the child's mother. In this view, men attempting to father outside the context of a marriage or a coresidential union will have difficulty staying involved with their children. Fatherhood roles may be even more difficult to fulfill if fathers have competing familial obligations, a challenge that is particularly salient for unmarried parents, who have high rates of multiple-partner fertility. Almost 60% of children born to unmarried parents have at least one half-sibling already, despite the fact that their parents are, on average, only in their mid-20s (Carlson and Furstenberg 2006).

In this article, we extend the "package deal" hypothesis, arguing that it predicts not only that fathers' involvement with children will decline after a breakup but also that subsequent transitions into new partner and parenting roles pose significant added barriers to involvement. As the father and mother of a nonmarital child enter into new family-like relationships, they may feel considerable pressure to re-create the "package deal" with the new family, without the interference of prior partners or children from past relationships. Although this may

This is an example of the authors using sociological imagination, seeing a social situation clearly enough to be able to ask reasonable questions about it.

a couple who lives together

notable or important

The "package" is made up of (1) a romantic relationship to a child's mother and (2) a father–child relationship.

The hole in the scholarship that their research will fill.

occur among both married and unmarried parents as they transition from one partner to another, we focus on the latter group, which has received less scholarly attention. And while there are many dimensions of father involvement—including contact, shared activities, communication, emotional closeness, and financial contributions (Hawkins, Amato, and King 2007)—we focus on the amount of contact between father and child here because the level of involvement, rather than financial support (which is often adjudicated by law and collected and disbursed by the state) or the quality and content of involvement, is more closely linked to the concept of the "package deal."

Here the focus of the research is limited to a very specific variable, the amount of contact between father and child.

Background

The image of unwed fathers as uninvolved parents plays a dominant role in public discourse about poverty, family structure, and race. A growing body of evidence from the social sciences, however, suggests that unmarried fathers with young children are usually quite involved. Two panel studies—the National Longitudinal Survey of Youth, which began to follow a sample of youth aged 14–19 in 1979, and the National Survey of Families and Households, a national probability sample of all U.S. households launched in 1981—provided the first nationally representative portraits of unmarried fathers (Lerman 1993; Mott 1990; Seltzer 1991). Mott (1990), for example, found that in the mid-1980s, almost 40% of children under age 4 had contact with their nonresident fathers at least once a week. A number of in-depth qualitative studies have also found that among unmarried fathers, the salience of the father role and engagement in fathering activities is high (Hamer 2001; Sullivan 1993; Waller 2002; Young 2003) and that mothers may serve as gatekeepers, controlling fathers' access to their nonresident children (Classens 2007).

In qualitative research, words, rather than numbers, are used to study social relationships. Qualitative research is used when the problem being investigated is looking at how or why something exists. This contrasts with quantitative research which uses statistical analyses to answer questions.

This body of work also demonstrated that involvement declined quite dramatically as the children got older (Lerman 1993; Seltzer 2000). Additional surveys conducted in the 1990s showed consistent evidence of a downward trend in involvement as the children aged, though the rates differed considerably across the studies (Argys et al. 2007). One study, using adolescents' reports from the National Longitudinal Study of Adolescent Health, found that by the time nonmarital children reach adolescence, their chances of having a regularly involved father are quite low, with only 20% of fathers still involved by the time the children were 15 years old (Argys and Peters 2001).

This decline in father involvement seems surprising given the evidence from the baseline wave of the Fragile Families and Child Wellbeing Study, a representative survey of nonmarital children in large cities that began following families between 1998 and 2000, which found that the vast majority of fathers who had a nonmarital birth were present at the time of the birth and said that they wished to play an active role in their child's life. When the surveyors interviewed the mothers of these children just after the birth, 8 in 10 said the father had been supportive during the pregnancy. Furthermore, nearly all the fathers interviewed said they intended to stay involved (McLanahan et al. 2003).

The degree of father involvement, measured along a variety of dimensions, varies depending on the particular subgroup being examined. Studies that considered all nonresidential children, both marital and non-marital, found lower rates of father involvement with nonmarital children. Father involvement also varies by race and ethnicity: typically, rates for African Americans are higher and rates for Hispanics are lower than for the average American father, all else being equal (Danziger and Radin 1990; Huang 2006; King 1994; King, Harris, and Heard 2004; Mott 1990; Seltzer 1991; but see Seltzer and Bianchi 1988). Additional factors associated with father involvement include parental education (Argys and Peters 2001; Huang 2006; King et al. 2004), father's age (Lerman and Sorenson 2000), earnings (Lerman and Sorensen 2000; Seltzer 1991), work status (Danziger and Radin 1990), child gender (King et al. 2004; Manning and Smock 1999; but see Cooksey and Craig 1998), the presence of additional children, the father's current marital status, the number of years since the father left the home (Argys and Peters 2001), the payment of child support (Seltzer 1991), and the quality of the coparenting relationship (Sobolewski and King 2005; but see Amato and Rezac 1994). Waller and Swisher (2006) focused solely on unmarried fathers and found that a wide array of risk behaviors, such as physical abuse, drug and alcohol use, and incarceration, were associated with lower odds of father–child contact.

In this paragraph the authors list all the factors that have been previously studied before they direct the reader's attention to the ones that they will study.

The "Package Deal" and Nonmarital Father Involvement

Fatherhood has been viewed as a relationship that is not independent of, but largely flows through and is contingent on, the relationship between the father and the child's mother. This explanation is often used to account for the surprisingly low levels of father–child contact and child support payment following a divorce (Furstenberg and Cherlin 1991). To the extent that notions of the "package deal" are still strongly institutionalized within American society, men attempting to father outside the context of a marriage, a coresidential union, or a romantic relationship will have more difficulty staying involved with their children.

On a practical level, fathers must pay additional transaction costs to retain contact with children after a coresidential or romantic partnership ends, such as planning for visitation time, traveling to the mother's house and picking up the child, and having to bargain with the custodial

These are examples of "transaction costs."

parent for access to the child. Never-married fathers' costs may be particularly high because no automatic legal procedure exists for adjudicating conflicts or granting visitation rights to unmarried fathers. Thus, while both formerly married and unmarried couples may enact the "package deal," unmarried fathers may have greater difficulty staying in contact with their children outside of a coresidential union.

The authors use the theoretical model for their hypothesis by noting how their hypothesis relates to the hypothesis in Furstenberg (1995). This shows the relationship between the old "package deal" hypothesis and the new hypothesis being tested in this study. The rest of this paragraph also explains why the research is important.

Following Furstenberg (1995), we extend the application of the "package deal" hypothesis, arguing not only that it predicts declines in involvement after breakup but also that subsequent transitions into new partner and parenting roles pose significant added barriers to involvement. These processes are especially relevant for couples who bear children outside of marriage because such transitions are far more common among them (Graefe and Lichter 2007). The impact of these subsequent transitions is also particularly important in the U.S. context: Andersson (2002) has shown that both married and cohabiting American couples with children are significantly more likely to break up and are far more likely to repartner than comparable couples in other industrialized countries. Unmarried couples in the United States also lack the legal, institutional, and normative supports that unmarried couples in many other industrialized countries enjoy.

Here is a restatement of the authors' hypothesis. It contains two things to be tested: "subsequent relationships" and "subsequent fertility" of father and mothers.

For the large and growing subset of parents who have children outside of marriage and who experience exceptionally high rates of subsequent partner and parenting transitions, we expect that transitions into subsequent relationships, and subsequent fertility within those relationships, are key mechanisms through which nonresidential father involvement declines over time. As fathers move on to subsequent partners and parental roles, the demands inherent in maintaining these new relationships could crowd out obligations to children from prior relationships. Mothers' transitions into subsequent partnerships might also prompt them to play a gatekeeper role, excluding the biological father in favor of the new father figure in the home, especially if the new father figure becomes the biological father of a subsequent child.

Methods . . .

Measurement

A dependent variable is the behavior or attitude that can be explained or predicted by the independent variable. Here the dependent variable is father involvement.

Dependent variables. The main dependent variable in our study is father involvement, measured by two dimensions of father–child contact.[3] Fathers were coded as having *no contact with child* if the mother reported that the father had not seen the child since the previous interview. This measure captures one extreme of father–child contact. We also use a more intensive measure of father involvement, the *number of days in the past month* the father saw the child, given that the father had

The authors tell us the two ways (dimensions) that they will measure the dependent variable.

contact with the child since the previous interview. This is a continuous variable ranging from 0 to 30 days. . . .

> An independent variable is a condition that is relatively stable, understood to be the cause of the relationship between variables.

Independent variables. We use several measures to capture the subsequent relationship characteristics of unmarried mothers and fathers in our sample. We measure the *time since parents stopped coresiding* as an ordinal variable that indexes the number of survey waves the parents have not lived together. For example, in the fourth survey wave, parents were coded as 0 if they still lived together, 1 if they were living together at the third wave but were not living together at the fourth, 2 if they were living together at the second wave, but not in the third or fourth wave, and 3 if they were living together at the first wave but not any of the subsequent waves. Parents who never lived together during the study period (since the child was born) were coded as 4. This indexing was repeated for each of the survey waves.

> Variables can be measured in a number of ways and with varying degrees of precision. When something is an "ordinal variable," it means that there is an order to the possible responses one can make (0 = still living together vs. 4 = never having lived together). This contrasts with nominal variables, which are often thought to have one clear response (e.g., in which state do you live?).

We also measure at each wave whether the *father has a new partner,* the *mother has a new partner,* the *father has subsequent children with a different partner,* and the *mother has subsequent children with a different partner.* At each follow-up survey wave, mothers and fathers were asked whether they were currently involved in a romantic relationship with someone other than the father/mother. Mothers were also asked whether the father was living with or married to another woman at each follow-up survey wave. Each parent was also asked whether s/he had children with someone other than the father/mother, and mothers were asked whether the father had children with someone other than her.

Time-varying controls. The parents' relationship status was categorized as *married, cohabiting, romantically involved,* or *no relationship* based upon the mothers' reports at each wave. Parents' residential status was defined as *living together* if mothers reported they lived together all or most of the time and as *not living together* otherwise. Fathers were coded as *employed* if they reported doing any regular work for pay during the week prior to the interview. Father's *annual earnings* were measured in thousands of dollars, derived from their reports of wages and weeks worked in the past year.

Results

While fathers' behavioral and economic characteristics remain relatively stable across the follow-up survey waves, Table 2 shows that their romantic and cohabiting relationships with mothers quickly dissolve. By the five-year follow-up, about 16% of unmarried mothers were married to the father, about 18% remained together in cohabiting unions, 5% were still romantically involved but did not live together, and over 60% were no longer in a relationship with each other. This does not mean

The first four rows of the table show the characteristics that remain stable over time: father's employment, earnings, prison time, and drug use.

Table 2   Behavioral and Relationship Characteristics After a Nonmarital Birth

Variable	One-Year Follow-up	Three-Year Follow-up	Five-Year Follow-up
All Unmarried Fathers			
Father employed	74	71	76
Father's earnings ($)	19,507	20,669	22,758
Father ever in jail or prison	39	50	53
Father used drugs	10	12	15
Relationship status with biological mother			
Married	11	15	16
Cohabiting	37	26	18
Romantically involved	12	6	5
No relationship	40	53	61
Resident fathers	52	44	36
Nonresident fathers	48	56	65
Nonresident Fathers			
Mother new partner	26	41	51
Married to new partner	9	10	17
Cohabiting with new partner	40	56	69
Father new partner	23	44	51
Married to new partner	13	14	16
Cohabiting with new partner	43	70	60
Mother new child by new partner	2	18	24
Father new child by new partner	3	9	26
Saw child since previous survey	87	73	66
Saw child in past month	63	49	46
Mean number of days father saw child	9.9	8.9	8.7
N	3,243	3,123	3,050

Notes: Weighted by national sampling weights for each survey year. All values are percentages unless otherwise indicated.

that the parents remained single, because transitions out of relationships were followed by rapid transitions into new romantic relationships for both mothers and fathers. Around one year after the child's birth, one quarter of unmarried mothers who did not coreside with the father had new romantic partners. Over half of these new partnerships were cohabiting or marital unions. After five years, about half of unmarried, nonresident parents had a new romantic partner, and over a quarter had a subsequent child with a new partner. Of these new partnerships, 16%–17% were marital unions for both mothers and fathers, and another 60%–69% were cohabiting unions.

Table 2 also details the proportions of nonmarital children who had contact with their biological fathers at one, three, and five years. Both coresidence and involvement rates among unmarried fathers began high but declined throughout the first five years of a child's life. Almost half of nonmarital children resided with their fathers around the time of their first birthday, but this figure declined to only 36% by their fifth birthday. At their first birthday, 63% of nonresident children had seen their fathers in the past month. By the child's third birthday, only half had seen their fathers in the past month. Overall, by the time they reached age 5, nonresident children who had any contact with their fathers (since the prior survey) saw them an average of nine days per month, or about two times per week, on average.

Next, we examine nonresident father involvement at the five-year follow-up by parents' subsequent relationship and fertility statuses. Table 3 shows that mothers' repartnering and subsequent children are strongly associated with lower levels of father involvement. When mothers had no new partners or children, 77% of nonresident fathers had contact with the child in the past year, and 58% in the past month; when mothers had new partners and new children, these percentages decline to 45% and 27%, respectively. In contrast, nonresident fathers' subsequent transitions are not as strongly associated with their involvement. When they had no new partners or children, 71% of fathers had contact with their children since the last survey and 51% had contact in the past month; when they had a new partner and new child, 63% of fathers had contact with their child since the last survey wave, and 40% had contact in the past month. We compared these associations with other factors known to influence father involvement. The lower involvement rates associated with subsequent partners and children for mothers are comparable in magnitude to the lower involvement rates among fathers who have been in jail, have abused drugs, or are unemployed.[6]

. . .

> The authors state their main finding as the concluding sentence of the paragraph.

Table 3   Nonresident Father Involvement by Economic, Behavioral, and Subsequent Relationship Characteristics at the Five-Year Follow-up

Variable	Past Year	Past Month	Number of Days in Past Month	% of Nonresident Fathers
All Nonresident Fathers	66	46	8.7	100
Mother's Subsequent Relationships				
No partner or child	77	58	11.2	45
Partner but no child	67	44	6.5	33
Child but no partner	44	28	7.5	7
Partner and biological child	45	27	5.6	15
Father's Subsequent Relationships				
No partner or child	71	51	10.4	44
Partner but no child	60	41	7.8	30
Child but no partner	75	56	10.5	9
Partner and biological child	63	40	6.6	17
Father's Characteristics				
No drugs in past year	69	50	9.7	80
Drugs in past year	54	30	4.5	20
Never been in jail or prison	69	54	10.4	36
Ever been in jail or prison	64	41	7.6	64
Employed at prior survey wave	70	52	9.6	68
Not employed at prior survey wave	60	32	6.4	32
Earned more than $15,000	65	43	7.9	62
Earned $15,000 or less	68	50	9.9	38

Notes: $N = 2,019$. Figures are weighted by national sampling weights. ~e sample is restricted to couples who were unmarried at child's birth and in which the father was nonresident at the five-year follow-up. Number of days in past month is calculated based on the subsample of fathers who saw their nonresident child in the past year.

Discussion

Our analysis shows that transitions to subsequent partner and parental roles among unmarried parents, especially those of the mother, may be a driving force behind the large declines in father involvement that occur over time. Mothers' subsequent partners and children are strongly associated with increases in the probability that the biological father will have no contact with his child, but the association between fathers' own subsequent partners and children and their involvement is not nearly as large as mothers'. Second, both mothers' and fathers' subsequent romantic partnerships are associated with declines in the intensity of father involvement in the past month, although mothers' subsequent relationships are still nearly twice as strong as fathers'. Changes in a mother's romantic and parental status are strongly related to declines in paternal involvement and are at least as great in magnitude as changes in a father's economic characteristics or other personal characteristics. Changes in a father's status are not predictive of whether the father has contact with the child but are related to the intensity of his involvement, suggesting a "crowding out" effect.

These results are somewhat surprising given that research related to the "package deal" hypothesis has focused primarily on the impact of fathers' subsequent partnerships and parenting roles on ongoing father involvement, even though the theory itself is gender-neutral. Readers should also note the contrast between the small body of work on marriage transitions among divorced *mothers*, which have found only a modest effect, and the rather large associations we report here. It is possible that given the unique constraints and pressures unmarried mothers and fathers face, especially the lack of formal visitation agreements and the much greater frequency of partner transitions and multiple-partner fertility, father involvement is more contingent on cultural norms that regard fatherhood as part of a "package deal."

In all, the evidence points more strongly to the role of mothers "swapping daddies" than it does to the role of fathers "swapping kids." Why might the impacts for mothers' transitions be so large? One possibility is that the sharp difference in the legal context within which divorcing and unmarried fathers must operate matters. Divorcing fathers' custody, financial obligations, and visitation rights are all adjudicated together at the time of the divorce. Conversely, in the nonmarital context, fathers are less frequently involved in the legal process by which child support orders are made and visitation is assigned. Under these circumstances, mothers who wish to "swap daddies" can far more easily do so. A second possibility is that for mothers who are unmarried at the time of their child's birth, subsequent partnerships may be especially

---

Their findings support the "extended" hypothesis that is more specific than the "package deal" hypothesis. The data suggest that father involvement is affected more by mothers' subsequent romantic relationships and children than it is by fathers' subsequent relationships and children.

The authors note that their results are inconsistent with research that forms part of their theoretical framework.

The findings allow the authors to state, in memorable terms, a more specific conclusion than their hypothesis suggested. The hypothesis tested effects of both fathers and mothers; the findings support a more important role for mothers. This finding can in turn become the starting point hypothesis for future research.

fragile (as their past partnerships were) and thus especially vulnerable to the threat of ongoing involvement of a former partner, even if only for the purposes of seeing the child. Third, unmarried mothers who repartner typically do so with men who have more human capital and fewer behavioral problems than did their prior partners (Bzostek, Carlson, and McLanahan 2007; Graefe and Lichter 2007). It is quite possible that unmarried fathers' own very low human capital and high degree of other serious problems make their past partners less likely to cooperate in visitation than would otherwise be the case. Finally, the fact that mothers' transitions are more consequential does not necessarily mean that mothers are primarily responsible for the decline in father involvement. Our results are also consistent with fathers choosing to become less involved when mothers repartner than when they repartner themselves.

The impact of mothers' relationship transitions on intensive father involvement weakens as children get older, however, suggesting that relationship transitions may be less predictive of declines in father involvement after fathers have had sufficient time to cement their role as the primary father figure in their children's lives. The children themselves may also play a greater role in deciding the level of contact, thus limiting the mother's ability to be a gatekeeper. Additionally, qualitative evidence suggests that mothers' new partners do not tend to be active as social fathers unless the child is very young (Nelson and Edin forthcoming).

Because fatherhood is generally enacted in the most meaningful way within the context of a conjugal union, because the fragility of these unions is high, and because repartnering and subsequent childbearing are common, children born to unmarried parents are likely to experience multiple father figures who represent a series of temporary commitments rather than a lifelong obligation. Since stability is critical for child well-being, the shifting cast of fathers and father figures in children's lives is likely to detract from, not add to, their well-being.

sexual relationship

Notes

3. In a comparison of mothers' and fathers' reports of father involvement at the one-year follow-up (when missing data are least for both mothers and fathers), we found that mothers and fathers agreed on reports of yearly contact in 94% of cases for which we had information reported by both the mother and father, and in 91 % of cases for whether the father saw the child in the past month.

6. Of course lack of biological father involvement does not mean that there is no involvement on the part of the asocial father, and we discuss the role of fathers in greater detail at the end of the article.

References

Allison, P. 2001. *Missing Data*. Thousand Oaks, CA: Russell Sage Foundation.

Amato, P. and S. J. Rezac. 1994. "Contact with Nonresident Parents: Interparental Conflict and Children's Behavior." *Journal of Family Issues* 15:191–207.

Amato, P. and J. M. Sobolewski. 2004. "The Effects of Divorce on Fathers and Children: Nonresidential Fathers and Stepfathers." Pp. 341–67 in *The Role of the Father in Child Development*, 4th ed., edited by M. E. Lamb. Hoboken, NJ: John Wiley and Sons.

Andersson, G. 2002. "Children's Experience of Family Disruption and Family Formation: Evidence From 16 FFS Countries." *Demographic Research* 7:343–64.

Argys, L. M. and H. E. Peters. 2001. "Patterns of Nonresident Father Involvement." Pp. 49–78 in *Social Awakenings: Adolescent Behavior as Adulthood Approaches*, edited by R. T. Michael. New York: Russell Sage Foundation.

Argys, L. M., E. Peters, S. Cook, S. Garasky, L. Nepomnyaschy, and E. Sorenson. 2007. "Measuring Contact Between Children and Nonresident Fathers." Pp. 375–98 in *Handbook of Measurement Issues in Family Research*, edited by S. L. Hofferth and L. M. Casper. Mahwah, NJ: Erlbaum.

Bumpass, L. and H.-H. Lu. 2000. "Trends in Cohabitation and Implications for Children's Family Contexts in the United States." *Population Studies* 54:29–41.

Bzostek, S. 2008. "Social Fathers and Child Wellbeing." *Journal of Marriage and Family* 70:950–61.

Bzostek, S., M. J. Carlson, and S. McLanahan. 2007. "Repartnering After a Nonmarital Birth: Does Mother Know Best?" Working Paper #2006-27-FF. Center for Research on Child Wellbeing, Princeton University, Princeton, NJ.

Carlson, M. and F. Furstenberg. 2006. "The Prevalence and Correlates of Multipartnered Fertility Among Urban U.S. Parents." *Journal of Marriage and Family* 68:718–32.

Center for Research on Child Wellbeing. 2003. "Union Formation and Dissolution in Fragile Families." Fragile Families Research Brief No. 14. Princeton University, Princeton, NJ.

———. 2007. "Parents' Relationship Status Five Years After a Non-Marital Birth." Fragile Families Research Brief No. 39. Princeton University.

———. 2008. "Introduction to the Fragile Families Public Use Data." Princeton University, Princeton, NJ.

Cherlin, A. 1978. "Remarriage as an Incomplete Institution." *American Journal of Sociology* 84:634–50.

———. 2004. "The Deinstitutionalization of American Marriage." *Journal of Marriage and Family* 66:848–61.

Claasens, A. 2007. "Gatekeeper Moms and (Un)Involved Dads: What Happens After a Breakup?" Pp. 204–27 in *Unmarried Couples With Children*, edited by P. England and K. Edin. New York: Russell Sage Foundation.

Coleman, M., L. Ganong, and M. Fine. 2000. "Reinvestigating Remarriage: Another Decade of Progress." *Journal of Marriage and the Family* 62:1288–307.

Cooksey, E. C. and P. H. Craig. 1998. "Parenting From a Distance: The Effects of Parent Characteristics on Contact Between Nonresidential Fathers and Their Children." *Demography* 35:187–200.

Furstenberg, F. F. and A. J. Cherlin. 1991. *Divided Families: What Happens to Children When Parents Part*. Cambridge, MA: Harvard University Press.

Graefe, D. R. and D. T. Lichter. 2007. "When Unwed Mothers Marry: The Marital and Cohabiting Partners of Midlife Women." *Journal of Family Issues* 28:595–622.

Halaby, C. N. 2004. "Panel Models in Sociological Research: Theory Into Practice." *Annual Review of Sociology* 30:507–44.

Hamer, J. F. 2001. *What It Means To Be a Daddy: Fatherhood Among Black Men Living Away From Their Children*. New York: Columbia University Press.

Hausman, J. A. 1978. "Specification Tests in Econometrics." *Econometrica* 46:1251–72.

Hawkins, D., P. Amato, and V. King. 2007. "Nonresident Father Involvement and Adolescent Well-being: Father Effects or Child Effects?" *American Sociological Review* 72:990–1010.

Hofferth, S. L. 2006. "Residential Father Family Type and Child Well-being: Investment Versus Selection." *Demography* 43:53–77.

Hofferth, S. L., J. Pleck, J. L. Stueve, S. Bianchi, and L. Sayer. 2002. "The Demography of What Fathers Do." Pp. 63–90 in *Handbook of Father Involvement,* edited by C. S. Tamis-LeMonda and N. Cabrera. Mahwah, NJ: Lawrence Erlbaum Associates.

Huang, C. C. 2006. "Child Support Enforcement and Father Involvement for Children in Never-Married Mother Families." *Fathering* 4:97–111.

Juby, H., J. M. Billette, B. Laplante, and C. Le Bourdais. 2007. "Nonresident Fathers and Children: Parents' New Unions and Frequency of Contact." *Journal of Family Issues* 28:1220–45.

King, V. 1994. "Variation in the Consequences of Nonresident Father Involvement for Children's Wellbeing." *Journal of Marriage and the Family* 56:963–72.

King, V., K. M. Harris, and H. E. Heard. 2004. "Racial and Ethnic Differences in Nonresident Father Involvement." *Journal of Marriage and Family* 66:1–21.

Lerman, R. I. 1993. "A National Prolem of Young Unwed Fathers." Pp. 27–51 in *Young Unwed Fathers: Changing Roles and Emerging Policies,* edited by R. I. Lerman and T. J. Ooms. Philadelphia: Temple University Press.

Lerman, R. I. and E. Sorensen. 2000. "Father Involvement With Their Nonmarital Children: Patterns, Determinants and Effects on Their Earnings." Pp. 137–59 in *Fatherhood: Research, Interventions, and Policies,* edited by H. E. Peters, G. W. Peterson, S. K. Steinmetz, and R. D. Day. New York: The Haworth Press.

Lichter, D. T., Z. Qian, and M. L. Crowley. 2005. "Child Poverty Among Racial Minorities and Immigrants: Explaining Trends and Differentials." *Social Science Quarterly* 86:1037–59.

Manning, W. D. and K. Lamb. 2003. "Adolescent Well-being in Cohabiting, Married, and Single Parent Families." *Journal of Marriage and Family* 65:876–93.

Manning, W. D. and P. J. Smock. 1999. "New Families and Nonresident Father-Child Visitation." *Social Forces* 78:87–116.

———. 2000. "'Swapping' Families: Serial Parenting and Economic Support for Children." *Journal of Marriage and the Family* 62:111–22.

Manning, W. D., S. D. Stewart, and P. J. Smock. 2003. "The Complexities of Fathers' Parenting Responsibilities and Involvement With Nonresident Children." *Journal of Family Issues* 24: 645–67.

McLanahan, S., I. Garfinkel, N. Reichman, J. Teitler, M. Carlson, and C.N. Audigier. 2003. "The Fragile Families and Child Wellbeing Study: Baseline National Report." Center for Research on Child Wellbeing, Princeton University, Princeton, NJ.

Mincy, R. B. 2001. "Who Should Marry Whom? Multiple Partner Fertility Among New Parents." Paper presented at the annual meeting of the Association for Public Policy and Management, Washington, DC.

Mincy, R. B. and C.-C. Huang. 2002. "Determinants of Multiple-Partner Fertility." Paper presented at the annual meeting of the Population Association of America, Atlanta, GA.

Mincy, R. B. and H. Pouncy. 2007. "Baby Fathers and American Family Formation." Essay, *Future of the Black Family Series.* Center for Marriage and Families at the Institute for American Values, New York.

Mott, F. L. 1990. "When Is a Father Really Gone? Paternal-Child Contact in Father-Absent Homes." *Demography* 27:499–517.

Nelson, T. and K. Edin. Forthcoming. *Fragile Fatherhood.* New York: Russell Sage Foundation.

Osborne, C. and S. McLanahan. 2007. "Partnership Instability and Child Wellbeing." *Journal of Marriage and Family* 64:1065–83.

Seltzer, J. A. 1991. "Relationships Between Fathers and Children Who Live Apart: The Father's Role After Separation." *Journal of Marriage and the Family* 53:79–101.

———. 2000. "Child Support and Child Access: The Experiences of Marital and Non-Marital Families." Pp. 69–87 in *Child Support: The Next Frontier,* edited by T. Oldham and M. Melli. Ann Arbor, MI: University of Michigan Press.

Seltzer, J. A. and S. M. Bianchi. 1988. "Children's Contact With Absent Parents." *Journal of Marriage and the Family* 50:663–67.

Sobolewski, J. M. and V. King. 2005. "The Importance of the Coparental Relationship for Nonresident Fathers' Ties to Children." *Journal of Marriage and Family* 67:1196–212.

Stephens, L. S. 1996. "Will Johnny See Daddy This Week? An Empirical Test of Three Theoretical Perspectives of Postdivorce Contact." *Journal of Family Issues* 17:466–94.

Stewart, S. D. 1999. "Nonresident Mothers' and Fathers' Social Contact With Children." *Journal of Marriage and the Family* 61:894–907.

Sullivan, M. L. 1993. "Young Fathers and Parenting in Two Inner City Neighborhoods." Pp. 52–73 in *Young Unwed Fathers: Changing Roles and Emerging Policies.* Philadelphia: Temple University Press.

Townsend, N. W. 2004. *The Package Deal: Marriage, Work, and Fatherhood in Men's Lives.* Philadelphia PA: Temple University Press.

Waller, M. R. 2002. *My Baby's Father: Unwed Parents and Paternal Responsibilities.* Ithaca, NY: Cornell University Press.

Waller, M. R. and R. Swisher. 2006. "Fathers' Risk Factors in Fragile Families: Implications for 'Healthy' Relationships and Father Involvement." *Social Problems* 53:392–420.

Young, A. 2003. *The Minds of Marginalized Black Men: Making Sense of Mobility, Opportunity, and Future Life Chances.* Princeton, NJ: Princeton University Press.

Yuan, A. S. and H. A. Hamilton. 2006. "Stepfather Involvement and Adolescent Wellbeing: Do Mothers and Nonresident Fathers Matter?" *Journal of Family Issues* 27:1191–213.

Reading Responses

1. Review the "Background" section, and list all the prior research findings that shape the authors' hypothesis. Create a visual representation of the relationship between this previous research and the authors' hypothesis.

2. Prior to reading this research, would you have blamed these fathers for not spending much time with their children? Using research described in this study, write a short letter to a nonresident father in which you help him see the factors that affect the time he spends with his child. Decide whether or not you will encourage him to overcome these factors.

3. Describe a study that could follow this one. What factors should the researchers' focus on? Frame your answer as a hypothesis. Sketch out a theoretical framework for your hypothesis, using the research that Tach, Mincy, and Edin present in their essay.

NOTES ON GRAMMAR, STYLE, AND RHETORIC:
NOUN PHRASES

Laura Tach, Ronald Mincy, and Kathryn Edin's "Parenting as a 'Package Deal': Relationships, Fertility, and Nonresident Father Involvement among Unmarried Parents" is a striking mix of sentences that are quite easy to read and those that are more challenging.

Consider some sentences that seem quite easy. Here is one from the first paragraph: "Forty percent of all unmarried parents and over half of urban unmarried parents were living together at the time of the birth" (114). And here is one from later in the article: "By the child's third birthday, only half had seen their fathers in the past month" (120).

Many writing teachers say that such sentences are good examples of the clausal style. That is, they generally use clauses to depict persons existing in a certain state or doing something to someone or something else: some of the parents were living together and only some of the children had seen their fathers in the past month. The core of the meaning is spread across a clause.

These sample sentences contrast to some others in the article. Consider, for example: "Next, we examine nonresident father involvement at the five-year follow-up by parents' subsequent relationship and fertility statuses" (120). This sentence is not markedly longer than the earlier two examples, yet many readers will have to read it more than once to figure out the meaning.

What lies at the heart of the challenge in reading this and similar sentences? Long and densely informative noun phrases, especially noun phrases that contain one or more nominalizations. I'll explain the grammatical terms as I talk about their use.

The main ingredient of a noun phrase is a noun, often preceded by *a, an,* or *the: the involvement.* Such noun phrases can have one or more modifiers before the noun: *the markedly lower involvement.* They can have one or more modifiers after the noun: *the involvement of fathers in parenting activities.* And they can have one or more modifiers both before and after the noun: *the markedly lower involvement of fathers in parenting activities.*

Because writers can include several modifiers both before and after a noun, they can produce phrases that carry a great deal of information. Here is an example from the abstract: "Declines in fathers' involvement following a mother's relationship or parenting transition. . . ." And later in the article we read: "The lower involvement rates associated with subsequent partners and children for mothers . . . ." (120).

Further, since a long noun phrase can appear wherever a single noun can appear (for example, as the subject or the direct object of a sentence), it is possible to construct sentences that are made up almost entirely of noun phrases. Here is a slightly modified version of the first sentence in the Discussion section; in it the subject (underlined) and the direct object (underlined) are each a long noun phrase: *Transitions to subsequent partner and parental roles among unmarried parents may cause the large declines in father involvement that occur over time.*

But there is more to the story of why some sentences in this article can be challenging to understand. Many of the noun phrases contain nominalizations, and most nominalizations pack a lot of information in one word. A nominalization is a noun derived from a verb or an adjective. From the verb *involve,* for example, we have derived the nominalization *involvement.* And from the adjective *salient* we have derived *salience.*

Now consider how writers can use nominalizations to pack up a great deal of information. Without a nominalization, they could describe a situation with a series of sentences: *Sometimes unmarried people have children. In those cases, often the father participates in lots of activities with the children. But sometimes the father and mother of those children decide not to stay together. When that happens, the father and mother can both move on to new relationships. And after that happens, the father frequently does not participate in as many activities with the children.* Or those writers could pack up all this information with nominalizations in a long noun phrase: *the decline in father involvement in parenting activities after a relationship transition.*

For those who are experts in the area of studying fathers' involvement with children born out of wedlock, the noun phrase can actually be economical to use. They don't have to write all those sentences each time they want to write about these ideas; after they present the material with sentences the first time, they can use the noun phrase to refer back to it. However, we often do not write only to experts, and when we do not, we need to remember that if we use such noun phrases as *the decline in father involvement in parenting activities after a relationship transition,* we run the risk of making our readers work too hard to unpack our meaning. And we might even risk looking as if we are trying to show off. Those are risks we should be very cautious about taking.

In Your Own Writing . . .

How do you know when to use long and dense noun phrases and when to avoid them?

- Use long noun phrases when you need a shorthand way of referring to a complex idea. You might want to describe the complex idea first using sentences. After that, you can refer to the complex idea with a noun phrase.
- Use long noun phrases to refer to information that your reader already understands.
- Avoid long noun phrases when your reader is unfamiliar with the subject matter in general or the long complex idea that the noun phrase specifically refers to.
- Avoid long noun phrases when you do not know how well your reader can read. Long noun phrases pose significant challenges for weaker readers.

STUDENT WRITING

INTRODUCTION

by Joy Van Marion, sociology major

The Assignment. In my Introduction to Sociology class, our professor often encouraged us to imagine possible human social relationships. When we conducted our own sociological research, we tested one of those potential relationships with a hypothesis-driven study. Because we were amateur social science researchers, our professor gave us a list of narrow topics with well-established theoretical frameworks. I picked "acceptance of cohabitation" (basically, whether or not people approve of unmarried people in a sexual relationship living together).

The Content. Because I was also taking a political science course that semester, I was doing a lot of thinking about how people identify with a particular political party. I began to wonder if these two aspects of human society related to each other, so I decided to research how students' political views related to their views about cohabitation. This gave me an independent variable (a person's established, chosen political views) and a dependent variable (a person's views on cohabitation). To break these independent and dependent variables down further, I created categories for both variables. For example, I categorized political views as liberal, moderate, and conservative. I categorized reasons to cohabitate as economics, safety, and sex.

From there, I used surveys to gather information from a sample of college students. The survey method was ideal because the surveys didn't take long to fill out, and that left me time to interview students. Once I collected all the student surveys, my professor ran statistical tests through the computer on the data, and I discovered if my hypothesis was right.

Learning to Write in Sociology. Sociologists use the structure of their report to emphasize their objectivity. The first part of my sociology report, the abstract, provided a short summary of the whole project. Then I included my problem statement, which includes my questions and why they are important. In this section, I tried to grab the reader's interest and show why the questions I asked were good ones. Next, in the "Literature Review," I laid out my theoretical framework. I described what I had found in the scholarship on cohabitation and, in particular, how people's political perspectives relate to their views on cohabitation. In this way, I fit my research into a bigger scholarly conversation on the subject.

In "Research Design," I show the reader how I tested my hypothesis—with a survey. A section of my report called "Sampling and Data Collection" describes the characteristics of the people we studied and the strengths and weaknesses of my research design. In the "Data Analysis" (results) section I used tables to show the relationship between my independent variables and dependent variables. For social scientists, tables are like pictures in a story; they present everything at a glance. In my conclusion, I described what I had learned and what my study can offer to other scholars.

[This student essay follows APA guidelines for formatting and documentation.]

The Politics of Cohabitation 1

The Politics of Cohabitation

Joy Van Marion

Abstract

The purpose of this research project is to survey a sample of the student body at a small, Midwestern college to determine their views on cohabitation. Students were given the opportunity to relay personal information such as political identification and opinions on cohabitation. The data were then reviewed and patterns noted. The following paper specifically analyzes survey data regarding students' political associations and their feelings about cohabitation.

The Politics of Cohabitation 2

Problem Statement

Cohabitation is reshaping the structure of family life and society on the whole. Statistics show that this specific relationship is on the rise. In 1970, 523 thousand American couples cohabitated. In 1993 that number rose to 3.5 million (Wilhelm, 1998). Two questions might be asked: "For what reasons do people choose to cohabitate?" and "How do their political views correlate to their willingness to cohabitate?" To answer these questions, researchers must explore the reasons people choose to cohabitate rather than form another relationship such as marriage. Furthermore, they must study the attitudes that members of American society hold toward the social practice of cohabitation. This study attends to possible connections between people's political views and their attitudes toward the practice of cohabitation. By researching the relationship between people's political stances and their acceptance of cohabitation, we may start to better understand people's attitudes toward cohabitation.

Literature Review

Cohabitation is a popular and growing development in social relationships across the United States. Cohabitation in this study specifically refers to a mutual relationship of emotional and/or physical intimacy between two members of the opposite sex who, though not married, share the same residency. This social relationship appeals to heterosexual couples for economic, safety, and physical reasons. Yet cohabitation remains controversial, as evidenced by two articles on this topic that appeared in magazines for the general public.

According to Carin Gorrell, "about half of American couples today live together before marrying" (2000, p. 16). In her article Gorrell describes the relationships of couples who cohabitate prior to marriage and those who do not. Gorrell summarizes a study by Catherine Cohan, Ph.D., to suggest that couples who cohabitate before marriage face more difficulties in marriage than those who don't. According to Cohan's research, cohabitating couples do not problem-solve or communicate as well as other couples (as cited in Gorrell, 2000). Cohan speculates that perhaps the people who choose to cohabit before marriage have weak communication skills prior to cohabitation, and thus their weaker communication skills are not a result of cohabitation.

> The problem statement explains the need or purpose for the study, offering some background context, and sparking interest in the subject.

> I learned the importance of proper citation to verify statistics and give the author credit. Many of the social sciences use the American Psychological Association's formatting method (APA) to cite sources, and that is what was required for this course.

> The literature review explores what other studies have been done on and/or relate to your research subject. This helps you decide where your study fits into the research, what it might verify or disprove that other studies have already looked at, or what it might accomplish that other studies have not yet set out to do. The literature review is therefore the theoretical foundation for my research design.

Cohan also suggests that possibly the lack of commitment in a cohabitating relationship weakens a couple's investment in the relationship and diminishes their attempts to improve their communication patterns (2000). Gorrell's attitude toward cohabitation become clear when she concludes with this statement from Cohan: "There is no evidence that living together before marriage benefits couples" (as cited in Gorrell, 2000, p. 16).

On the other hand, Gunnell argues in favor of cohabitation, claiming that individuals should not be required to limit themselves to marital relationships alone. Furthermore, according to Gunnell, social relationships like cohabitation will evolve to meet society's needs; since social relationships evolve, people should be free to live and love as they like. While Gunnell expresses concern that the children resulting from male/female relationships are cared for in a healthy environment, she argues that all other decisions regarding the characteristics of the relationship should be left to the adults involved (Gunnell, 2000).

These two views appear to suggest a population divided over cohabitation. Lye and Waldron (1997) offer four main hypotheses as to why people hold the beliefs that they do about cohabitating. First, they offer the Consumerism Hypothesis that focuses on people's lifetime goals as a factor that shapes their attitudes about cohabitation. According to this hypothesis, "high aspirations for material goods and living standards contributes to non-traditional family and gender role behavior and attitudes" (p. 201). In other words, people who want to prosper financially would tend to cohabitate and would, as a result, have positive attitudes regarding cohabitation.

Second, Lye and Waldron (1997) describe the Higher Order Needs Hypothesis. This hypothesis focuses on a pattern of human reasoning as the source for people's attitudes toward the social practice of cohabitation. This hypothesis suggests that people's desire for "personal fulfillment, self-actualization and individual autonomy" (p. 201) could cause them to choose a type of relationship (such as cohabitation) that satisfies their sexual needs but does not limit their personal freedom. Thus, the hypothesis predicts that people who focus more intensely on their personal needs and goals are more likely to cohabitate and, in turn, to accept cohabitation as an acceptable (perhaps even preferable) social practice.

Hypotheses mark the research method of many social sciences. It all begins with potential answers to a question about human society.

Next, Lye and Waldron describe the Political Ideology Hypothesis. This hypothesis proposes a correlation between people's political views and their acceptance or rejection of cohabitation as a social practice. The hypothesis suggests that people who hold liberal views about political issues would be inclined to approve of cohabitation. People who hold more conservative views about political issues would be negatively disposed toward this relationship.

Fourth, Lye and Waldron discuss the Social Concerns Hypothesis. This explanation suggests that a combination of "traditional" and "non-traditional" views shape a person's social interactions, and consequently, their attitudes toward cohabitation.

Interestingly, the results of Lye and Waldron's research most closely supported the Political Ideology Hypothesis. Their research seems to suggest that people's political beliefs strongly correlate to their attitudes regarding cohabitation (Lye and Waldron, 1997). Wilhelm (1998) offers supporting data for the relationship between people's political beliefs and their attitudes toward cohabitation. She concludes, "Participation in left-oriented activism strongly affects the likelihood of cohabitation" (p. 310).

For college students in particular, three central factors seem to influence their attitudes toward cohabitation. Knox (1999) outlines these: age, hedonistic sexual values, and interracial dating experiences. He argues that the evidence suggests those students who are older, believe in hedonist practices, and do or would date people of different ethnicities are more likely to enter a cohabitating relationship (Knox, 1999).

In the following report, cohabitation will be studied from the perspective of students enrolled in a small, Midwestern college. The data that were collected for this study are meant to confirm the young adult's attitude toward cohabitation and determine who favors it, who objects to it, and whether the political views of the individual correlates with her or his attitude toward cohabitation.

Hypothesis

There is a significant correlation between an individual's political views and his/her stance on cohabitation. People who hold conservative political views are more likely to disapprove of cohabitation. Persons who have liberal

This section on my hypothesis is where I get to make a statement about what I think the answers to my questions will be, where I put my theory to the test.

political ideologies are more likely to approve of cohabitation. People with "middle-of-the-road" political ideologies are more likely to approve of cohabitation in some circumstances and disapprove of it in others. The independent variable is the political identity of each individual. The dependent variable is the individual's response toward cohabitation. The assumption is that the independent variable affects the dependent variable.

Research Design

Surveys were used to collect data on cohabitation. The advantages of this research method include its time efficiency, cost efficiency, and ability to examine a wide range of subjects. Surveys study a representative sample of the population in a relatively small amount of time (Tischler, 2000). People are asked direct questions and given the opportunity to respond in short answers. However, the answers received from the population are not always accurate. People may not be truthful in their responses if they are uncomfortable with the questions or feel threatened by them. Also, if the respondents misinterpret a question's meaning, their answers may not be accurate reflections of what they really think or believe. Consequently, the results will be skewed. Researchers must recognize the potential for error in a survey (Tischler, 2000).

Sampling and Data Collection

The target for study was the student body of a small, Midwestern college. The sample of subjects drawn from the population at this college included 478 students. Of the 478 respondents, 237 were males and 241 were females. The total number consisted of 143 freshmen, 143 sophomores, 101 juniors, and 91 seniors. Participants ranged from 17 years of age to 24 years of age. The population size was small enough to study carefully and large enough to monitor for results and significant patterns. The surveys were distributed to specific individuals in an attempt to gather data from an equal number of first, second, third, and fourth year students as well as an equal number of male and female students. Though the final sample of students did not match the original outline for the sample, the sample obtained is still valid for study.

Certain limitations of the sampling and data collection did occur. An equal number of first, second, third, and fourth year students were not

---

This is my methods section.

Here I explain some research limitations to help the reader know how to interpret the study's findings.

These explanations help show how the data are skewed. Later, I learned that some student subjects were confused about the definition of cohabitation. This confusion may have affected their answers.

contacted. It is important to note, too, that the actual respondents could only choose between the answers provided for them and may not have been able to provide the fullest explanations. Furthermore, participants may have been confused about the meaning of questions and been unable to provide the most accurate information. Those who answered the questions may have purposely given a false reply if they felt ashamed or were offended by a question. In short, the survey did not reach equal populations of the student body and could not extract the most honest or complete data.

the results section

Cross-tabs are statistical tests.

Data Analysis

The cross-tabs necessary to test this hypothesis address the political views and the social views on cohabitation of 478 college students. In Table 1, the data establish a foundation of political ideologies, distinguishing between liberal, middle-of-the-road, and conservative participants. Tables 2, 3, and 4 show which respondents approved of cohabitation for economic reasons, safety reasons, and the satisfaction of sexual desires. Finally, the data in Tables 2, 3, and 4 also depict the individuals' political views next to their estimation of whether or not there is a chance that they would cohabitate before marriage.

Based on survey data, the 478 respondents are divided into three categories: liberal, middle-of-the-road, and conservative as shown in Table 1.

Table 2 identifies student views on cohabitation for economic reasons. Of the 85 liberal respondents, 76.5% approve of cohabitation for economic

Table 1   Frequency Count Percentage Table

	Frequency	Percent
Liberal	85	17.8
Middle-of-the-road	215	45.0
Conservative	177	36.8
No Response	2	0.4
Total	$n = 478$	100.0

n = number of respondents

Table 2   Cross-Tabs Correlating Political Affiliation with Views on Cohabitation for Economic Reasons

	Yes, I agree with cohabitation for economic reasons	No, I do not agree with cohabitation for economic reasons	Total
Liberal	76.5%	23.5%	100%
Middle-of-the-road	71.5%	28.5%	100%
Conservative	37.5%	62.5%	100%

Looking back, I think I might give a bit more of an explanation about Table 2 by summarizing the test results in words instead of relying on the table alone to illustrate the findings.

reasons and 23.5% disapprove. Of the 214 middle-of-the-road respondents, 71.5% approve of cohabitation and 28.5% disapprove. Of the 174 conservative respondents, 37.5% approved of cohabitation and 62.5% disapproved. The numbers suggest that for economic benefits the liberal students are more approving of cohabitation and the conservatives are less approving.

Regarding cohabitation for security purposes (Table 3), of the 85 liberal respondents, again, 76.5% agree with cohabitation and 23.5% disagree. Of the 214 middle-of-the-road respondents, 70.1% agree and 29.9% disagree. And of the 174 conservative respondents, 39.1% agree while 60.9% disagree. Here, too, there is a decreasing amount of support for cohabitation as the political status of an individual shifts from liberal to conservative.

In response to cohabitation for sexual desires as outlined in Table 4, 8.5% of the 85 liberal respondents approve while 91.5% disapprove. Of the 214 middle-of-the-road respondents, 2.8% approve while 97.2% disapprove. Of

Table 3   Cross-Tabs Correlating Political Affiliation with Views on Cohabitation for Safety Purposes

	Yes, I agree with cohabitation for safety purposes	No, I do not agree with cohabitation for safety purposes	Total
Liberal	76.5%	23.5%	100%
Middle-of-the-road	70.1%	29.9%	100%
Conservative	39.1%	60.9%	100%

Table 4   Cross-Tabs Correlating Political Affiliation with Views on Cohabitation to Satisfy Sexual Desires

	Yes, I agree with cohabitation to satisfy sexual desires	No, I do not agree with cohabitation to satisfy sexual desires	Total
Liberal	8.5%	91.5%	100%
Middle-of-the-road	2.8%	97.2%	100%
Conservative	1.2%	98.8%	100%

the 174 conservative respondents, 1.2% approve and 98.8% disapprove. In this case, too, the liberals were more supportive of cohabitation for sexual purposes than were conservatives.

Finally, respondents were asked to indicate whether there is a chance they might cohabitate before marriage, based on their personal experience. Among liberal students, 63.9% said yes and 36.1% said no. Among middle-of-the-road students, 45.1% of the middle-of-the-road respondents said yes and 54.9% said no. Among conservative students, 19.3% of the conservatives said yes while 80.7% said no.

The results were as expected and the hypothesis made at the beginning of this study is supported. There appears to be a connection between people's political ideals and their views on cohabitation. The liberals strongly favored cohabitation in more circumstances than the conservatives did. Interestingly, the middle-of-the-road respondents were very supportive of cohabitation for economic or safety reasons while they were almost completely disapproving of it for sexual purposes. And overall the liberals were the most likely to cohabitate before marriage, followed by the middle-of-the-road participants, with the conservatives least likely to cohabitate of them all.

The information provided here is valid and reliable for the purposes of a research analysis in an introductory course in sociology. It evaluates a sample of the student body as they understood the questions concerning cohabitation and then reacted from personal opinion. The data are unreliable to the extent that participants may have misinterpreted questions and consequently

I wondered if another table would have helped to clarify these results.

responded incorrectly, intentionally lied, or chosen not to answer at all. The results of this survey cannot be generalized to all college student populations.

Conclusions

In summary, the findings are consistent with the original hypothesis. If these patterns are representative of the college's student body, researchers may begin making predictions about the future social relationships within this local society based on the connections drawn here between the political ideals of students and their views on cohabitation. A greater number of liberals in the community may indicate the potential for a rise in the practice of cohabitation; whereas a greater number of conservatives may suggest the potential for a decline in cohabitating relationships.

On a broader scale, political identification may be taken as an indicator of one's standing on cohabitation. Liberals tend to embrace tolerance of new and developing social relationships that appear appropriate to the present-day culture. If a relationship is financially and physically satisfying, then they tend to approve. Conservatives tend to cling to traditional family structures and reject changes to these relationships. They are strongly tied to their historical and often religious roots, which make little or no room for relationships of cohabitation.

In closing, it is impossible to state from the evidence found here that an individual's political standing will confirm their position on cohabitation. However, the data strongly suggest that there is some association between political ideology and one's stand on cohabiting. The research and findings from this study form a base of empirical evidence on which to build future sociological studies.

Out of the collective knowledge base come creative and resourceful applications.

References

Gorrell, C. (2000, Nov/Dec). Live-in and learn. *Psychology Today,* 33, 16.

Gunnell, B. (2000, Aug 28). "I do"—But not for long, thanks. *New Statesman,* 129, 13.

Knox, D. (1999, Dec). Characteristics of college students who cohabit. *College Student Journal,* 129 (4), 510–12.

Lye, D. N. and Waldron, I. (1997). Attitudes toward cohabitation, family, and gender roles: Relationships to values and political ideology. *Sociological Perspectives,* 40 (2), 199–225.

Tischler, H. L. (2001). *Introduction to sociology* (7th ed.). New York: Harcourt.

Wilhelm, B. (1998, Sept). Changes in cohabitation across cohorts: The influence of political activism. *Social Forces,* 77 (1), 289–313.

Reading Responses

1. Review the research by Lye and Waldron on page 131–132. Prior to reading Van Marion's results, which did you believe to be the most influential factor on people's attitudes toward cohabitation? Did her study change your mind? If not, why not?

2. In her review of literature, Van Marion does more than present all the scholarly research on cohabitation; she builds the theoretical framework for her own study. Analyze how Van Marion builds this framework: What research does she begin with? What research does she end with? And recommend revisions: Which additional topics should she have researched? Which topics could she have eliminated from her review of the literature?

3. Working from Lye and Waldron, Van Marion looks only for a correlation between political affiliation and attitudes toward cohabitation, not for all the causes of students' attitudes toward cohabitation. Using sociological imagination, list possible factors that account for the correlation between students' political affiliation and their attitudes toward cohabitation. Then, rank-order your list from what you suspect to be the most significant to least significant factor.

PUBLIC WRITING

INTRODUCTION

Stephanie Coontz teaches history and women's studies at Evergreen State University. She has appeared before Congress and many television audiences, and she has published several books and many scholarly articles on the history of marriage, global perspectives on marriage, and the nature of modern, Western marriages. In her writing for general audiences (as in this piece, written for the *New York Times*), Coontz encourages her readers to engage in sociological imagination by describing multiple factors that affect personal relationships like happiness in marriage. She does so to encourage her readers to follow the advice she provides in the main point of her article: that couples should invest time into maintaining their romantic relationship, even when they are busy raising children.

Even though she is writing for nonspecialists, Coontz develops a theoretical model from previous scholarship to narrow the focus of her claim. She limits her topic by identifying a cultural stereotype from long ago, describes the effect of parenting on different types of couples, and then focuses on the effects of parenting on one of those types: "collaborative couples."

Till Children Do Us Part
Stephanie Coontz

The New York Times, February 5, 2009

Half a century ago, the conventional wisdom was that having a child was the surest way to build a happy marriage. Women's magazines of that era promised that almost any marital problem could be resolved by embarking on parenthood. Once a child arrives, "we don't worry about this couple any more," an editor at *Better Homes and Gardens* enthused in 1944. "There are three in that family now. . . . Perhaps there is not much more needed in a recipe for happiness."

Over the past two decades, however, many researchers have concluded that three's a crowd when it comes to marital satisfaction. More than 25 separate studies have established that marital quality drops, often quite steeply, after the transition to parenthood. And forget the "empty nest" syndrome: when the children leave home, couples report an increase in marital happiness.

But does the arrival of children doom couples to a less satisfying marriage? Not necessarily. Two researchers at the University of California at Berkeley, Philip and Carolyn Cowan, report in a forthcoming briefing paper for the Council on Contemporary Families that most studies finding a large drop in marital quality after childbirth do not consider the very different routes that couples travel toward parenthood.

Some couples plan the conception and discuss how they want to conduct their relationship after the baby is born. Others disagree about whether or when to conceive, with one partner giving in for the sake of the relationship. And sometimes, both partners are ambivalent.

The Cowans found that the average drop in marital satisfaction was almost entirely accounted for by the couples who slid into being parents, disagreed over it or were ambivalent about it. Couples who planned or equally welcomed the conception were likely to maintain or even increase their marital satisfaction after the child was born.

Marital quality also tends to decline when parents backslide into more traditional gender roles. Once a child arrives, lack of paid parental leave often leads the wife to quit her job and the husband to work more. This produces discontent on both sides. The wife resents her husband's lack of involvement in child care and housework. The husband resents his wife's ingratitude for the long hours he works to support the family.

When the Cowans designed programs to help couples resolve these differences, they had fewer conflicts and higher marital quality. And the children did better socially and academically because their parents were happier.

But keeping a marriage vibrant is a never-ending job. Deciding together to have a child and sharing in child-rearing do not immunize a marriage. Indeed, collaborative couples can face other problems. They often embark on such an intense style of parenting that they end up paying less attention to each other.

Parents today spend much more time with their children than they did 40 years ago. The sociologists Suzanne Bianchi, John Robinson and Melissa Milkie report that married mothers in 2000 spent 20 percent more time with their children than in 1965. Married fathers spent more than twice as much time.

A study by John Sandberg and Sandra Hofferth at the University of Michigan showed that by 1997 children in two-parent families were getting six more hours a week with Mom and four more hours with Dad than in 1981. And these increases occurred even as more mothers entered the labor force.

Couples found some of these extra hours by cutting back on time spent in activities where children were not present—when they were alone as a couple, visiting with friends and kin, or involved in clubs. But in the long run, shortchanging such adult-oriented activities for the sake of the children is not good for a marriage. Indeed, the researcher

Ellen Galinsky has found that most children don't want to spend as much time with their parents as parents assume; they just want their parents to be more relaxed when they are together.

Couples need time alone to renew their relationship. They also need to sustain supportive networks of friends and family. Couples who don't, investing too much in their children and not enough in their marriage, may find that when the demands of child-rearing cease to organize their lives, they cannot recover the relationship that made them want to have children together in the first place.

As the psychologist Joshua Coleman suggests, the airline warning to put on your own oxygen mask before you place one on your child also holds true for marriage.

Reading Responses

1. Describe a family portrayed on a television show or in a movie, paying special attention to how the parents interact with the children and each other. What factors from Coontz's article are evident in the television show?

2. What is the purpose of the final line of Coontz's article? How does that line encourage the reader to engage in sociological imagination? How does that line reinforce Coontz's point?

3. Writers for general audience magazines like *Time, Newsweek,* or the *New Yorker* regularly include references to scholarly research. List the reasons that writers might have for including that research.

MORE WRITING IN SOCIOLOGY

INTRODUCTION

Many people are surprised by the number of poor women who become mothers when they are very young, some as early as 14 or 15. Some policy makers have proposed that fewer young women will get pregnant if these women have access to good sex education and effective birth control. Others seem to blame the girls themselves, pointing to lax morals or the breakdown of the nuclear family. Rather than rely on speculation, two professors of sociology, Kathryn Edin (Harvard Univeristy) and Maria Kefalas (St. Joseph's Univeristy), writing in a journal for sociologists, examine the sociological factors behind the number of poor, young mothers by asking two questions: Why do poor women have children when they are very young? Wouldn't it be wiser for them to wait until marriage to have children?

It might seem that previous research has already answered that last question. In the 1990s social scientists discovered a number of negative outcomes for children raised in mother-only families. Relying in part on these studies, some politicians reformed welfare in 1996 (The Personal Responsibility and Work Opportunity Reconciliation Act) and, even more to the point, politicians authorized nearly two billion dollars in 2003 to encourage welfare recipients to marry.

Edin and Kefalas find it striking that in the midst of these policy discussions the voices of young, unwed mothers—those most affected by poverty and early childbearing—are seldom heard. So they interviewed single mothers from low-income communities in Philadelphia. Edin and Kefalas focus on the answers from one of their interviewees, Jen Burke. Through rich description and Jen's own words, they paint a full picture of Jen's life as a young, poor, single mother. As readers come to understand Jen's life and perspective more fully, they are better able to imagine how Jen's social setting within a larger political and economic context, shapes the complicated choices she makes. Through this informal case study, Edin and Kefalas let readers hear Jen's story for themselves.

Unmarried with Children
Kathryn Edin and Maria Kefalas

Contexts: Understanding People in Their Social Worlds, 2005, 4(2):16–22.

Jen Burke, a white tenth-grade dropout who is 17 years old, lives with her stepmother, her sister, and her 16-month-old son in a cramped but tidy row home in Philadelphia's beleaguered Kensington neighborhood. She is broke, on welfare, and struggling to complete her GED. Wouldn't she and her son have been better off if she had finished high school, found a job, and married her son's father first?

In 1950, when Jen's grandmother came of age, only 1 in 20 American children was born to an unmarried mother. Today, that rate is 1 in 3—and they are usually born to those least likely to be able to support a child on their own. In our book, *Promises I Can Keep: Why Poor Women Put Motherhood Before Marriage,* we discuss the lives of 162 white, African American, and Puerto Rican low-income single mothers living in eight destitute neighborhoods across Philadelphia and its poorest industrial suburb, Camden. We spent five years chatting over kitchen tables and on front stoops, giving mothers like Jen the opportunity to speak to the question so many affluent Americans ask about them: Why do they have children while still young and unmarried when they will face such an uphill struggle to support them?

Romance at Lightning Speed

Jen started having sex with her 20-year-old boyfriend Rick just before her 15th birthday. A month and a half later, she was pregnant. "I didn't want to get pregnant," she claims. "*He* wanted me to get pregnant. As soon as he met me, he wanted to have a kid with me," she explains. Though Jen's college-bound suburban peers would be appalled by such a declaration, on the streets of Jen's neighborhood, it is something of a badge of honor. "All those other girls he was with, he didn't want to have a baby with any of them," Jen boasts. "I asked him, 'Why did you choose me to have a kid when you could have a kid with any one of them?' He was like, 'I want to have a kid with *you*'." Looking back, Jen says she now believes that the reason "he wanted me to have a kid that early is so that I didn't leave him."

In inner-city neighborhoods like Kensington, where child-bearing within marriage has become rare, romantic relationships like Jen and Rick's proceed at lightning speed.

A young man's avowal, "I want to have a baby by you," is often part of the courtship ritual from the beginning. This is more than idle talk, as their first child is typically conceived within a year from the time a couple begins "kicking it." Yet while poor couples' pillow talk often revolves around dreams of shared children, the news of a pregnancy—the first indelible sign of the huge changes to come—puts these still-new relationships into overdrive. Suddenly, the would-be mother begins to scrutinize her mate as never before, wondering whether he can "get himself together"—find a job, settle down, and become a family man—in time. . . .

Most poor, unmarried mothers and fathers readily admit that bearing children while poor and unmarried is not the ideal way to do things. Jen believes the best time to become a mother is "after you're out of school and you got a job, at least, when you're like 21. . . . When you're ready to have kids, you should have everything ready, have your house, have a job, so when that baby comes, the baby can have its own room." Yet given their already limited economic prospects, the poor have little motivation to time their births as precisely as their middle-class counterparts do. The dreams of young people like Jen and Rick center on children at a time of life when their more affluent peers plan for college and careers. Poor girls coming of age in the inner city value children highly, anticipate them eagerly, and believe strongly that they are up to the job of mothering—even in difficult circumstances. Jen, for example, tells us, "People outside the neighborhood, they're like, 'You're 15! You're pregnant?' I'm like, it's not none of their business. I'm gonna be able to take care of my kid. They have nothing to worry about." Jen says she has concluded that "some people . . . are better at having kids at a younger age. . . . I think it's better for some people to have kids younger."

When I Became a Mom

When we asked mothers like Jen what their lives would be like if they had not had children, we expected them to express regret over foregone opportunities for school and careers. Instead, most believe their children "saved" them. They describe their lives as spinning out of control before becoming pregnant—struggles with parents and peers, "wild," risky behavior, depression, and school failure. Jen speaks to this poignantly. "I was just real bad. I hung with a real bad crowd. I was doing pills. I was really depressed. . . . I was drinking. That was before I was pregnant." "I think," she reflects, "if I never had a baby or anything . . . , I would still be doing the things I was doing. I would probably still be doing drugs. I'd probably still be drinking." Jen admits that when she first became pregnant, she was angry that she "couldn't be out no more. Couldn't be out with my friends. Couldn't do nothing." Now, though, she says, "I'm glad I have a son . . . because I would still be doing all that stuff."

Children offer poor youth like Jen a compelling sense of purpose. Jen paints a before-and-after picture of her life that was common among the mothers we interviewed. "Before, I didn't have nobody to take care of. I didn't have nothing left to go home for. . . . Now I have my son to take care of. I have him to go home for. . . . I don't have to go buy weed or drugs with my money. I could buy my son stuff with my money! . . . I have something to look up to now." Children also are a crucial source of relational intimacy, a self-made community of care. After a nasty fight with Rick, Jen recalls, "I was crying.

My son came in the room. He was hugging me. He's 16 months and he was hugging me with his little arms. He was really cute and happy, so I got happy. That's one of the good things. When you're sad, the baby's always gonna be there for you no matter what." Lately she has been thinking a lot about what her life was like back then, before the baby. "I thought about the stuff before I became a mom, what my life was like back then. I used to see pictures of me, and I would hide in every picture. This baby did so much for me. My son did a lot for me. He helped me a lot. I'm thankful that I had my baby."

Around the time of the birth, most unmarried parents claim they plan to get married eventually. Rick did not propose marriage when Jen's first child was born, but when she conceived a second time, at 17, Rick informed his dad, "It's time for me to get married. It's time for me to straighten up. This is the one I wanna be with. I had a baby with her, I'm gonna have another baby with her." Yet despite their intentions, few of these couples actually marry. Indeed, most break up well before their child enters preschool.

I'd Like to Get Married, But . . .

The sharp decline in marriage in impoverished urban areas has led some to charge that the poor have abandoned the marriage norm. Yet we found few who had given up on the idea of marriage. But like their elite counterparts, disadvantaged women set a high financial bar for marriage. For the poor, marriage has become an elusive goal—one they feel ought to be reserved for those who can support a "white picket fence" lifestyle: a mortgage on a modest row home, a car and some furniture, some savings in the bank, and enough money left over to pay for a "decent" wedding. Jen's views on marriage provide a perfect case in point. "If I was gonna get married, I would want to be married like my Aunt Nancy and my Uncle Pat. They live in the mountains. She has a job. My Uncle Pat is a state trooper; he has lots of money. They live in the [Poconos]. It's real nice out there. Her kids go to Catholic school. . . . That's the kind of life I would want to have. If I get married, I would have a life like [theirs]." She adds, "And I would wanna have a big wedding, a real nice wedding."

Unlike the women of their mothers' and grandmothers' generations, young women like Jen are not merely content to rely on a man's earnings. Instead, they insist on being economically "set" in their own right before taking marriage vows. This is partly because they want a partnership of equals, and they believe money buys say-so in a relationship. Jen explains, "I'm not gonna just get into marrying him and not have my own house! Not have a job! I still wanna do a lot of things before I get married. He [already] tells me I can't do nothing. I can't go out. What's gonna happen when I marry him? He's gonna say he owns me!"

Why is Jen, who describes Rick as "the love of my life," so insistent on planning an exit strategy before she is willing to take the vows she firmly believes ought to last "forever"? If love is so sure, why does mistrust seem so palpable and strong? In relationships among poor couples like Jen and Rick, mistrust is often spawned by chronic violence and infidelity, drug and alcohol abuse, criminal activity, and the threat of imprisonment. . . .

Trust has been an enormous issue in Jen's relationship with Rick. "My son was born December 23rd, and [Rick] started cheating on me again . . . in March. . . . " Things finally came to a head when Rick got another girl pregnant. "For a while, I forgave him for everything. Now, I don't forgive him for nothing." Now we begin to understand the source of Jen's hesitancy. "He wants me to marry him, [but] I'm not really sure. . . . If I can't trust him, I can't marry him, 'cause we would get a divorce. If you're gonna get married, you're supposed to be faithful!" she insists. To Jen and her peers, the worst thing that could happen is "to get married just to get divorced." . . .

These Are Cards I Dealt Myself

. . . Jen clearly sees how her life has improved since Rick's dramatic exit from the scene. "That's when I really started [to get better] because I didn't have to worry about what he was doing, didn't have to worry about him cheating on me, all this stuff. [It was] then I realized that I had to do what I had to do to take care of my son. . . . When he was there, I think that my whole life revolved around him, you know, so I always messed up somehow because I was so busy worrying about what he was doing. Like I would leave the [GED] programs I was in just to go home and see what he was doing. My mind was never concentrating." Now, she says, "a lot of people in my family look up to me now, because all my sisters dropped out from school, you know, nobody went back to school. I went back to school, you know? . . . I went back to school, and I plan to go to college, and a lot of people look up to me for that, you know? So that makes me happy . . . because five years ago nobody looked up to me. I was just like everybody else."

Yet the journey has not been easy. "Being a young mom being 15, it's hard, hard, hard, you know." She says, "I have no life. . . . I work from 6:30 in the morning until 5:00 at night I leave here at 5:30 in the morning. I don't get home until about 6:00 at night." Yet she measures her worth as a mother by the fact that she has managed to provide for her son largely on her own. "I don't depend on nobody. I might live with my dad and them, but I don't depend on them, you know." She continues, "There [used to] be days when I'd be so stressed out, like, 'I can't do this!' And I would just cry and cry and cry. . . . Then I look at Colin, and he'll be sleeping, and I'll just look at him and think I don't have no [reason to feel sorry for myself]. The cards I have I've dealt myself so I have to deal with it now. I'm older. I can't change anything. He's my responsibility—he's nobody else's but mine—so I have to deal with that."

Becoming a mother transformed Jen's point of view on just about everything. She says, "I thought hanging on the corner drinking, getting high—I thought that was a good life, and I thought I could live that way for eternity, like sitting out with my friends. But it's not as fun once you have your own kid. . . . I think it changes [you]. I think, 'Would I want Colin to do that? Would I want my son to be like that . . . ?' It was fun to me but it's not fun anymore. Half the people I hung with are either. . . . Some have died from drug overdoses, some are in jail, and some people are just out there living the same life that they always lived, and they don't look really good. They look really bad." In the end, Jen believes, Colin's birth has brought far more good into her life than bad. "I know I could have waited [to have a child], but in a way I think Colin's the best thing that could have happened to me. . . . So I think I had my son for a purpose because I think Colin changed my life. He saved my life, really. My whole life revolves around Colin!"

Promises I Can Keep

There are unique themes in Jen's story—most fathers are only one or two, not five years older than the mothers of their children, and few fathers have as many glaring problems as Rick—but we heard most of these themes repeatedly in the stories of the 161 other poor, single mothers we came to know. Notably, poor women do not reject marriage; they revere it. Indeed, it is the conviction that marriage is forever that makes them think that divorce is worse than having a baby outside of marriage. Their children, far from being liabilities, provide crucial social-psychological resources—a strong sense of purpose and a profound source of intimacy. Jen and the other mothers we came to know are coming of age in an America that is profoundly unequal—where the gap between rich and poor continues to grow. This economic reality has convinced them that they have little to lose and, perhaps, something to gain by a seemingly "ill-timed" birth.

The lesson one draws from stories like Jen's is quite simple: Until poor young women have more access to jobs that lead to financial independence—until there is reason to hope for the rewarding life pathways that their privileged peers pursue—the poor will continue to have children far sooner than most Americans think they should, while still deferring marriage. Marital standards have risen for all Americans, and the poor want the same things that everyone now wants out of marriage. The poor want to marry too, but they insist on marrying well. This, in their view, is the only way to avoid an almost certain divorce. Like Jen, they are simply not willing to make promises they are not sure they can keep.

Reading Responses

1. Did Edin and Kefalas offer you a new way of understanding why young, poor women have children? What surprised you most?

2. Because they use a case study methodology, the authors never state their theoretical framework explicitly. How would you describe their theoretical framework?

3. What in Jen's story most sparked your own curiosity? What aspect of Jen's story would you research in greater depth, if you had the opportunity?

WRITING ASSIGNMENTS

Assignment 1

Your task for this assignment is to create a theoretical framework for a hypothesis about a specific factor affecting marriages in the United States.

To begin, use the readings in this chapter to brainstorm about possible factors. Extend your brainstorming by researching previous scholarship (consult a reference librarian for help) to help you locate a single factor. Do additional research to identify how previous scholars have investigated this factor.

Once you have chosen the factor that you will research, free-write about your personal experience with this factor. Create one list of your own assumptions about this factor, attempting as best you can to identify your biases. Create a second list of common cultural assumptions about this factor.

Now draft a short article in which you present a common cultural assumption about the factor, a hypothesis about that factor, and a theoretical framework of research for your hypothesis.

Assignment 2

Because of the complexity of human relationships, sociologists are careful to detail their theoretical frameworks. But our focus on theoretical framework in this chapter should not imply that researchers in other disciplines do not root their research in theory; it may be that in their published work they do not make those roots as obvious as sociologists do.

Your task for this assignment is to show the theoretical roots in a piece of academic scholarship from religious studies, biotechnology, or nursing.

- "Civil Religion in America" by Robert Bellah (Chapter 4)
- "Feeding the World in the Twenty-first Century" by Gordon Conway and Gary Toenniessen (Chapter 6)
- "A Phenomenologic Study of Chronic Pain" by Sandra P. Thomas (Chapter 7)

To begin, read the piece carefully and describe as specifically as possible what it is that the researcher is curious about. You may find it helpful to formulate this as a research question or a hypothesis. Then, describe for yourself the theoretical frame for this research. You may need to do some careful analysis because the researcher may have left this somewhat or nearly completely unstated. Note the research (if any) that grounds the theoretical frame. Finally, list the conclusions that result from the research as well as the limitations of the research—both those the researcher notes and additional limitations that you note.

In the first part of your report, describe what serves as an equivalent for the sociological imagination—the focus of the researcher's curiosity and the researcher's main point. In the second part of your report, describe the theoretical framework that supports the researcher's point. Then evaluate the researcher's use of that theoretical framework, noting how the researcher helps and hinders the reader's understanding of the main point.

Assignment 3

This assignment requires you to engage your sociological imagination as Joy Van Marion did when she researched attitudes regarding cohabitation. Your task for this assignment is to report on a sociological study that you have conducted, paying special attention to the relationship between your theoretical model and your hypothesis. If your teacher allows it, consider collaborating with a partner on this project.

To begin, propose a list of possible answers to the following question: What sociological factors correspond to a person's ideas about the ideal relationship of parents to children? Once you have isolated one or two factors that you suspect to be especially important, do some library research to build a theoretical model for your study. The most efficient way to conduct this research is to ask for help from a reference librarian.

As you review this research, pay attention to research studies that relate to each other, noting studies that build on other research as well as those that contradict the findings of previous research. As you describe your theoretical model in your research report, be sure to help your reader see these relationships. Cite your sources in APA style.

Choose one of the sociological factors you researched, and draft a hypothesis about the relationship between this factor and people's ideas about ideal parents. Simplify your hypothesis as much as possible, and be sure that you will be able to gather information about your hypothesis through a simple methodology. Design a methodology to test your hypothesis, conduct your study, and analyze the results.

In your report, describe the theoretical model that supports your hypothesis, your methodology, and your results. When you discuss your results, be sure to (1) show the relationship between your study and those that comprise your theoretical model, (2) note the limitations of your study, and (3) describe future research that could provide more information about your hypothesis.

BIOTECHNOLOGY: BUILDING CONSENSUS FOR PROGRESS

When you're hungry for breakfast, the American Egg Board (www.aeb.org) wants you to consider an incredible, edible egg (their trademarked phrase). Cheryl Long and Tabitha Alterman encourage you to eat eggs, too, but in an article in *Mother Earth News,* they warn that some eggs are more incredible than others. Long and Alterman argue that you should avoid eggs from factory farms like those that support the American Egg Board because these farms cruelly restrict the movements of chickens and produce eggs with lower nutritional content (see "Meet Real Free-range Eggs" at motherearthnews.com).

- Go to the American Egg Board site, and watch some of the videos on the Eggs 101 page. List the information that you found most reassuring about egg production. Describe each occasion when they address concerns about the experience of the chickens or the nutritional quality of the eggs that they produce.

- Read Long and Alterman's article and list the information that would persuade you to consider paying more for eggs from free-range hens. How would you describe the way they refer to large-scale egg farmers?

- Can you see any common ground or compromises between the two groups—any goals that they agree on?

PORTABLE RHETORICAL LESSON: PERSUADING WITH BALANCED ARGUMENTS

The preceding exercise requires you to think about food in ways beyond everyday needs: the ethical, scientific, and economic aspects of food production and consumption. You had to weigh competing claims on your morals and your pocketbook, and you had to decide what evidence was most persuasive.

The authors in this chapter face three major challenges that are similar to those you faced in the opening exercise:

1. Their audience is made up of various types of people (scientists, philosophers, politicians, sociologists, and businesspeople); they have different ethical and practical assumptions and agendas, which makes them more open to some approaches to the problems than to others. A person in charge of a country's finances must be persuaded that solutions are affordable; a person who writes about ethics must believe that solutions account for long-term implications for people's health.

2. The authors are talking about highly volatile issues—all the scientific, industrial, and ethical arguments about providing healthy and affordable food. And when the stakes run high, so do emotions.

3. The pressing need to solve problems including food, energy, and health means that stalemate and inaction are not options. They have to find common ground if they hope to move forward toward consensus on solutions that people can enact.

Given those challenges, writers in biotechnology need first to invest in making two kinds of rhetorical choices. First, they make a **point** in the form of what we call an "accommodating thesis," a thesis that will appeal to the various readers who must cooperate to act. Second, they use **research methods and evidence** that their various readers will trust.

To persuade people with varied vested interests to collaborate to solve problems, writers in biotechnology devise balanced arguments—the **Portable Rhetorical Lesson** for this chapter. Balanced arguments aim to keep all the involved parties talking together, involved in the ongoing conversation about problems and solutions. To achieve such balance, biotechnologists practice three particular strategies for building trust and cooperation:

1. Use a moderate tone. They demonstrate respect for those with whom they disagree, they admit the limits of their own claims, they honestly acknowledge their opponents' worthwhile objections, and they imply that effective change will happen only if all sides can find points of agreement. The "Notes on Grammar, Style, and Rhetoric" demonstrates how "hedges" help to convey this moderate tone.

2. Present evidence that everyone respects and understands. Facts, data—gathered through effective scientific methods—provide the best basis for common ground. And the data are presented in forms (tables, graphs, figures) that all readers understand. But authors will lose their audience's ear if they present only the facts that support their proposals. So they offer data that identifies both problems as well as possible effects of solutions—positive, negative, and uncertain.

3. Provide practical solutions. The authors emphasize that their solutions are the best available options—not necessarily perfect, but the best currently available. To argue for the best available solution, authors use data to establish the urgency of the problem, describe possible solutions, and demonstrate the superiority of one solution. A thesis with these features will accommodate both supporters and opponents.

When you write papers for college classes, especially in your first or second year, you write on many different topics. When you are committed to a single topic for only as long as it takes to write one paper, you may tend to build arguments that have strong "end-of-conversation" conclusions. Any one paper could well be the last thing you ever say about the paper's topic. But that experience does not prepare you for the fact that in your professional lives you will likely work on a small number of topics for a long time. To prepare for that reality, imagine yourself in the position of biotechnologists, accommodating yourself to ongoing debates about your topic, offering balanced, reasonable contributions to progress rather than asserting final say.

WRITING IN THE DISCIPLINE

INTRODUCTION

by David Koetje,
Professor of Biology

> People on both sides of the debate are unwittingly collaborating to create a very considerable threat indeed. The threat is that the debate over the pros and cons of genetically modified crops may become so acrimonious that the sides cease speaking to each other altogether. . . . Through our rhetoric, we may erode the foundation of mutual trust apart from which democratic institutions fail.
> *Gary Comstock, "The Threat That Biotechnology Is"*

One surefire way to infuriate your critics is to call their motives into question. Consider this quote from biotechnology proponent Norman Borlaug: "I think the researchers at Cornell who fed Bt corn pollen to monarch butterflies were looking for something that would make them famous and create this big hullabaloo that's resulted."* Put-downs are another conversation buster. In response to a challenge from an environmentalist who was questioning the need for GM crops, one biotechnologist retorted, "Well, I live in the *real* world." Though cheap shots like this may be normal in national politics, they can hardly be considered good persuasive writing because they further entrench existing disagreements rather than encouraging people to work together to solve real-world problems.

"Feeding the World in the Twenty-First Century" addresses widely held concerns about genetically modified (GM) foods and other forms of agricultural biotechnology. This article became an important piece of the history of the GM food debates. The authors, Gordon Conway and Gary Toenniessen, have served, respectively, as the president and the director of the food security program at the Rockefeller Foundation, a philanthropic organization that funds scientific and social research to improve the lives of poor people. The

---

*"Billions Served: Norman Borlaug," interview by Ronald Bailey. *Reason Magazine*, April 2000.

Rockefeller Foundation has funded efforts to advance agricultural science and biotechnology throughout the world. Naturally, Conway and Toenniessen see a lot of promise in biotechnology. Yet their respect for diverse ethical concerns and accurate scientific knowledge makes their writing persuasive for all their readers.

Context and Content of the Argument. Concern about GM crops, which have a gene borrowed from some other species, has spread worldwide. Can GM crops alleviate problems of hunger and death from starvation? Biotechnology proponents claim that GM crops are more resistant to insect infestation, disease, drought, flooding, and pollution. Therefore, they can boost food production, especially in developing countries where soils tend to be poorer. Critics of biotechnologies like genetically modified crops counter that agricultural companies are more likely to benefit more from GM crops than the poor and the hungry.

Conway and Toenniessen published this article in *Nature,* a leading scientific journal headquartered in the U.K. (a country that is deeply opposed to genetically modified crops) and read by scientists and policy analysts worldwide. The authors argue that GM crops help humanity; they "ensure that the world's poorest people do not still go hungry in the twenty-first century." Of course, some readers strongly disagree. But even if they disagree, they may like, for example, the authors' proposal of a partnership between the public sector (universities and international research centers) and the private sector (industry) to ensure that GM technologies are accessible to developing countries.

Conway and Toennicssen strive to make peace by appealing first to proponents, then to critics. First they discuss the benefits of GM crops and validate proponents' passionate advocacy of them; then they validate critics' concerns and admonish the proponents of biotechnology to take these concerns seriously.

Rhetorical Strategies for Balancing Passion, Reason, and Scientific Evidence. Good persuasive writing in bioethics must carefully balance scientific knowledge and ethical considerations. Conway and Toenniessen cite numerous published essays to frame their contributions within the wider conversation. These references point the reader to what has already been written about the topic, but more importantly, they acknowledge the important contributions that others—including critics—are making to the debate. Reference #15 is one such book. Environmentalists praise it for its well-reasoned summary of the ecological risks of GM crops, particularly those with the enhanced fitness traits identified earlier. Conway and Toenniessen refer to these criticisms as "genuine concerns." They also are careful to cite primary sources. Information passed on secondhand by way of a Web site posting, or even published in a review article, is not as reliable as the original source. This general rule applies to all persuasive writing.

Conway and Toenniessen include figures to present scientific data that underscore some of their primary points: the worrisome drop in crop yields in developing countries (Figure 1) and the diversity of biotechnology research in developing countries (Table 1 and Figure 2). But keep in mind that readers may respond to the data in different ways. For example, Figure 1 assumes a type of agricultural production that makes extensive use of high-energy inputs (fertilizers and fuels) to support monocultures (fields devoted to one species). For those who support alternative methods (such as organic farming), these data may underscore their contention that modern production agriculture, and biotechnology by extension, cannot sustain agriculture in developing countries. For a scientifically sophisticated audience, the data represent important talking points.

Finally, note how Conway and Toenniessen maintain the scientific sophistication of their arguments for a very diverse audience. Although most *Nature* readers are scientists, the authors recognize that not every reader will be. So they take care to avoid excessive use of scientific jargon. Most college graduates should understand most of the scientific terms and concepts. That the authors have been considerate of their audience's diversity—both in terms of their familiarity with the science and their ethical value systems—is another earmark of a good persuasive article.

✓ Reading Tips

In some science writing, readers can go to the data in the "Results" section and learn what they need to know. In this thesis-driven essay you need to read the whole text to follow the argument.

- Use the section headings as topic markers. Jot down each heading and sketch out the argument in each section. Determine how the sections fit together.

- Keep a list of the occasions when the authors appeal to people on both sides of the issue. Note the evidence that the authors use to appeal to those in favor of using technology on food production. Note the evidence they use to attract those who are opposed.

Feeding the World in the Twenty-First Century

Gordon Conway and Gary Toenniessen

Nature 1999, 402(suppl): C55–C58

The gains in food production provided by the Green Revolution have reached their ceiling while world population continues to rise. To ensure that the world's poorest people do not still go hungry in the twenty-first century, advances in plant biotechnology must be deployed for their benefit by a strong public-sector agricultural research effort.

This one-paragraph abstract lays out the basic premise of the paper.

The Green Revolution was one of the great technological success stories of the second half of the twentieth century. Because of the introduction of scientifically bred, higher-yielding varieties of rice, wheat and maize beginning in the 1960s, overall food production in the developing countries kept pace with population growth, with both more than doubling. The benefits of the Green Revolution reached many of the world's poorest people. Forty years ago there were a billion people in

Critics disagree strongly with this statement . . .

developing countries who did not get enough to eat, equivalent to 50 per cent of the population of these countries. If this proportion had remained unchanged, the hungry would now number over two billion— more than double the current estimate of around 800 million, or around 20 per cent of the present population of the developing world. Since the 1970s, world food prices have declined in real terms by over 70 per cent. Those who benefit most are the poor, who spend the highest proportion of their family income on food.

The Green Revolution brought benefits too for the industrialized world. The high-yielding varieties of staple crop plants bred by the international agricultural research centres of the CGIAR (the Consultative Group on International Agricultural Research) have been incorporated into the modern varieties grown in the United States and Europe. The additional wheat and rice produced in the United States alone from these improved varieties is estimated to have been worth over $3.4 billion from 1970 to 1993.[1]

Yet today, despite these demonstrable achievements, over 800 million people consume less than 2,000 calories a day, live a life of permanent or intermittent hunger and are chronically undernourished.[2] Most of the hungry are the women and young children of extremely poor families in developing countries. More than 180 million children under five years of age are severely underweight: that is, they are more than two standard deviations below the standard weight for their age. Seventeen million children under five die each year and malnourishment contributes to at least a third of these deaths.

As well as gross undernourishment, lack of protein, vitamins, minerals and other micronutrients in the diet is also widespread.[3] About 100 million children under five suffer from vitamin A deficiency, which can lead to eye damage. Half a million children become partly or totally blind each year, and many subsequently die. Recent research has shown that lack of vitamin A has an even more pervasive effect, weakening the protective barriers to infection put up by the skin, the mucous membranes and the immune system.[4] Iron deficiency is also common, leading to about 400 million women of childbearing age (15–49 years) being afflicted by anaemia. As a result they tend to produce stillborn or underweight children and are more likely to die in childbirth. Anaemia has been identified as a contributing factor in over 20 per cent of all maternal deaths after childbirth in Asia and Africa.

If nothing new is done, the number of the poor and hungry will grow. The populations of most developing countries are increasing rapidly and by the year 2020 there will be an additional 1.5 billion mouths to feed, mostly in the developing world. What is the likelihood that they will be fed?

. . . and this one. However, proponents of agricultural biotechnology typically use this argument to justify their cause.

In other words, 97.7% of kids their age weigh more than these hungry kids.

The authors point this out to set up their argument that biotechnology, which offers tools to address such needs, is essential.

The End of the Green Revolution

The prognosis is not good. As indicated in Fig. 1, there is widespread evidence of decline in the rate of increase of crop yields.[5-7] This slowdown is due to a combination of causes. On the best lands many farmers are now obtaining yields close to those produced on experimental stations, and there has been little or no increase in the maximum possible yields of rice and maize in recent years. A second factor is the cumulative effect of environmental degradation, partly caused by agriculture itself.

Simply exporting more food from the industrialized countries is not a solution. The world already produces more than enough food to feed everyone if the food were equally distributed, but it is not. Market economies are notoriously ineffective in achieving equitable distribution of benefits. There is no reason to believe that the poor who lack access to adequate food today will be any better served by future world markets. Food aid programmes are also no solution, except in cases of specific short-term emergency. They reach only a small portion of those suffering chronic hunger and, if prolonged, create dependency and have a negative impact on local food production.

About 130 million of the poorest 20 percent of people in developing countries live in cities. For them, access to food means cheap food from any source. But 650 million of the poorest live in rural areas where agriculture is the primary economic activity, and as is the case in much of Africa, many live in regions where agricultural potential is low and natural resources are poor.[8] They are distant from markets and have limited purchasing power. For them, access means local production of food that generates employment and income, and is sufficient and dependable enough to meet local needs throughout the year, including years that are unfavourable for agriculture.

All these arguments point to the need for a second Green Revolution, yet one that does not simply reflect the successes, and mistakes, of the first. In effect, we require a 'Doubly Green Revolution', an

---

Supporting data lend scientific credibility to their argument. Note, however, that the root cause of this rate of deceleration is open to speculation.

In this paragraph the authors make these claims to support their contention that biotechnology offers the best solution. Critics may contend that market intervention may offer a better approach.

Cheap food has come to imply "industrial agriculture," which many claim is at the heart of food security problems.

Local food is often touted as a remedy for the economic ills of global industrial agriculture.

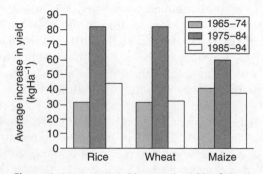

Figure 1 Average annual increase in yields of rice, wheat and maize in developing countries by periods.

agricultural revolution that is both more productive and more 'green' in terms of conserving natural resources and the environment than the first. We believe that this can be achieved by a combination of: ecological approaches to sustainable agriculture; greater participation by farmers in agricultural analysis, design and research; and the application of modern biotechnology directed towards the needs of the poor in developing countries, which is the subject of the rest of this article.

The Price of Biotechnology

The application of advances in plant breeding—including tissue culture, marker-aided selection (which uses DNA technology to detect the transmission of a desired gene to a seedling arising from a cross) and genetic engineering—are going to be essential if farmers' yields and yield ceilings are to be raised, excessive pesticide use reduced, the nutrient value of basic foods increased and farmers on less favoured lands provided with varieties better able to tolerate drought, salinity and lack of soil nutrients.

In the industrialized countries the new life-science companies, notably the big six multinationals—Astra-Zeneca, Aventis, Dow, Dupont, Monsanto and Novartis—dominate the application of biotechnology to agriculture. In 1998, 'genetically modified (GM)' crops, more accurately referred to as transgenic or genetically engineered crops, mostly marketed by these companies or their subsidiaries, were grown on nearly 29 million hectares worldwide (excluding China).[9] That year, 40 percent of all cotton, 35 percent of soya beans and 25 percent of maize grown in the United States were GM varieties.

So far, the great majority of the commercial applications of plant genetic engineering have been for crops with single-gene alterations that confer agronomic benefits such as resistance to pests or to herbicides. These agronomic traits can reduce costs to the farmer by minimizing applications of insecticides and herbicides. However, as with many agricultural inputs, the benefits received by farmers vary from year to year.

Most of the GM crops currently being grown in developing countries are cash crops; Bt cotton, for example, has reportedly been taken up by over a million farmers in China. But despite claims to be 'feeding the world', the big life-science companies have little interest in poor farmers' food crops, because the returns are too low. National governments, the international research centres of the CGIAR, and a variety of western donors are, and will continue to be, the primary supporters of work that produces advances in biotechnology useful to poor farmers. New forms of public–private collaboration could help to ensure that all farmers and consumers benefit from the genetic revolution and, over time, this should increase the number of farmers who can afford to buy new seeds from the private sector.

Those who argue for sustainable agriculture will like these first two points. Conway and Toenniessen are probably hoping this will foster acceptance of their third component.

For many, this stretches the definition of "plant breeding." The authors are no doubt doing this to make a point: there's more to biotechnology than just genetic engineering.

Noting this problem will gain some support among biotechnology's critics.

1 hectare = 10,000 square meters = 2.47 acres

Bt is shorthand for *Bacillis thuringiensis*, a common soil bacterium that produces Bt toxin, which kills caterpillars. It has no effect on humans and is therefore used in organic farming. Biotechnologists have placed the gene for Bt toxin in various crops to deter insect infestations. This may, however, speed insect resistance to Bt toxin.

The cost of accomplishing this will not be insignificant but it should not be excessive. For example, over the past 15 years, the Rockefeller Foundation has funded some US$100 million of rice biotechnology research and trained over 400 scientists from Asia, Africa and Latin America. In several places in Asia there is now a critical mass of talented scientists who are applying the new tools of biotechnology to rice improvement. To date, most of the new varieties are the result of tissue culture and marker-aided selection techniques. For example, scientists at the West Africa Rice Development Association have used anther culture to cross the high-yielding Asian rices with traditional African rices. The result is a new plant type that looks like African rice during its early stages of growth (it is able to shade out weeds, which are the most important constraint on crop production in Africa; . . .) but becomes more like Asian rice as it reaches maturity, thus giving higher yields with few inputs. Marker-aided selection is being used to breed rice containing two or more genes for resistance to the same pathogen, thereby increasing the durability of the resistance, and to accumulate several different genes contributing to drought tolerance.

> Plants can be regenerated from tissues grown in artificial media supplemented with plant growth hormones. Although such plants are typically clones, some can have new useful genetic traits.

> DNA fragments can serve as "markers" to identify plants that have certain genes even before the plant displays the trait associated with that gene. This expedites breeding.

> Anthers are the male parts of a flower.

Potential of Genetic Engineering

For some time to come, tissue culture and marker-aided selection are likely to be the most productive uses of biotechnology for cereal breeding. However, progress is being made in the production of transgenic crops for the developing countries. As in the industrialized countries, the focus has been largely on traits for disease and pest resistance, but genes that confer tolerance of high concentrations of aluminium (found in many tropical soils) have been added by Mexican scientists to rice and maize . . . , and Indian scientists have added two genes to rice which may help the plant tolerate prolonged submergence. There is also the possibility of increasing yield ceilings, through more efficient photosynthesis, for example, or by improved control of water loss from leaves through regulation of stomatal opening and closing.[10]

> That is, submergence under water during floods.

> Stomata are the specialized openings on the surfaces of leaves that allow gas and water exchange with the environment.

In addition to generating new traits that enable the plant to grow better (input traits), which are useful to poor farmers, GM technology can also generate plants with improved nutritional features (output traits) of benefit to poor consumers. One of the most exciting developments so far has been the introduction of genes into rice that result in the production of the vitamin A precursor β-carotene in the rice grain.[11] β-carotene is a pigment required for photosynthesis and is synthesized in the green tissues of all plants, including rice, but is not usually present in non-photosynthetic tissues such as those of seeds. Traditional plant breeding has given us some plants that produce β-carotene in non-photosynthetic tissue, such as the roots of carrots, but despite decades of searching no rice mutants had been

This is a contentious claim. Critics argue that beta-carotene levels are too low and require sufficient body fat for its absorbance via our digestive tract. Conway and Toenniessen should have addressed or acknowledged this issue.

A key implication from Table 1: Biotechnology will positively affect subsistence farming in developing countries.

found that produce β-carotene in the grain, so conventional breeding was not an option. To get the cells of the grain to produce β-carotene, genetic engineers added three genes for key enzymes for β-carotene biosynthesis to the rice genome. The grain of the transgenic rice has a light golden-yellow colour . . . and contains sufficient β-carotene

Table 1 Biotechnology research useful in developing countries

Traits now in greenhouse or field tests	Traits now in laboratory tests
Input traits	*Input traits*
Resistance to insects, nematodes, viruses, bacteria and fungi in crops such as rice, maize, potato, papaya and sweet potato	Drought and salinity tolerance in cereals
	Seedling vigour in rice
Delayed senescence, dwarfing, reduced shade avoidance and early flowering in rice	Enhanced phosphorus and nitrogen uptake in rice and maize
Tolerance of aluminium, submergence, chilling and freezing in cereals	Resistance to the parasitic weed *Striga* in maize, rice and sorghum, to viruses in cassava and banana, and to bacterial blight in cassava
Male sterility/restorer for hybrid seed production in rice, maize, oil-seed rape and wheat	Nematode resistance and resistance to the disease black sigatoka in banana
New plant types for weed control and for increased yield potential in rice	Rice with the alternative C, photosynthetic pathway and the ability to carry out nitrogen fixation
Output traits	*Output traits*
Increased β-carotene in rice and oil-seed rape	Increased β-carotene, delayed post-harvest deterioration and reduced content of toxic cyanides in cassava
Lower phytates in maize and rice to increase bioavailable iron	Increased vitamin E in rice
Modified starch in rice, potato and maize and modified fatty-acid content in oil-seed rape	Apomixis (asexual seed production) in maize, rice, millet and cassava
Increased bioavailable protein, essential amino acids, seed weight and sugar content in maize	Delayed ripening in banana
Lowered lignin content of forage crops	Use of genetically engineered plants such as potato and banana as vehicles for production and delivery of recombinant vaccines to humans
	Improved amino-acid content of forage crops

to meet human vitamin A requirements from rice alone. This 'golden' rice offers an opportunity to complement vitamin A supplementation programmes, particularly in rural areas that are difficult to reach. These same scientists and others have also added genes to rice that increase the grain's nutritionally available iron content by more than threefold.

Over the next decade we are likely to see much greater progress in multiple gene introductions that focus on output traits or on difficult-to-achieve input characteristics (Table 1).

> That the authors are talking about the poor is implied in this comment on potential benefits.

The potential benefits of plant biotechnology are considerable, but are unlikely to be realized unless seeds are provided free or at nominal cost. This will require heavy public investment by national governments and donors, at times in collaboration with the private sector, both in the research and in the subsequent distribution of seed and technical advice. Breeding programmes will also need to include crops such as cassava, upland rice, African maize, sorghum and millet, which are the food staples and provide employment for the 650 million rural poor who need greater stability and reliability of yield as much as increased yield.

The Role of the Public Sector

> In subsequent generations of the crop, these gene technologies would prevent reproduction via seeds or prevent expression of the novel genes. Some are now proposing these technologies as a strategy to reduce genetic pollution from transgenic plants.

None of this will happen through marketing by multinational seed companies, particularly if they decide to deploy gene-protection technologies, commonly referred to as terminator gene technologies, which will mean that farmers cannot save seed from the crop and sow it to get the next crop. In developing countries roughly 1.4 billion farmers still rely on saving seed for their planting materials and many gain access to new varieties through farmer-to-farmer trade. Much of the success of the Green Revolution was due to the true-breeding nature of the higher-yielding rice and wheat varieties.

> Enabling technologies include methods and instruments, some of which are patented.

While terminator technology is clearly designed to prevent rather than encourage such spread of proprietary varieties among poor farmers, some argue that it will do them no harm because they can still use and replant new varieties from the public sector. But if the companies tie up enabling technologies and DNA sequences of important genes with patents, and then use terminator technologies to control the distribution of proprietary seed and restrict its use for further breeding, the public sector will be severely constrained in using biotechnology to meet the needs of the poor.

> Hybrid seed is used extensively in developed countries.

Rather than using the terminator technology to protect their intellectual property in developing countries, it would be better if seed companies focused on producing hybrid seed combined with plant variety protection (PVP) to protect the commercial production of the seed. Hybrid plants do produce viable seed but it is not genetically identical to the original hybrid seed; it may lack some of the desirable characteristics.

Hence, there is still an incentive (for example, increased yield) for farmers to purchase hybrid seed for each planting. However, if such purchase is not possible, farmers can still use a portion of their harvest as seed and obtain a reasonable crop. Such recycling of hybrids is not uncommon in developing countries and is an important element of food security. And with PVP, new varieties can be protected while also becoming a resource that both the private and public sectors can use in further breeding for the benefit of all farmers.

> Plant variety protection is more limited than typical biotechnology patents. It would allow farmers to grow it, but not sell it for seed.

Intellectual Property Rights

Even assuming that terminator technologies are not used, there is cause for concern about the rights of developing countries to use their own genetic resources, the freedom of their plant breeders to use new technologies to develop locally adapted varieties, and the protection of poor farmers from exploitation. In part, these concerns result from the privatization of crop genetic improvement, the rapid expansion of corporate ownership of key technologies and genetic information and materials, and the competitive pressure on these companies to capture world market share as rapidly as possible.

It is only recently that intellectual property rights (IPR) have become an important factor in plant breeding, primarily through the greater use of utility patents. Such patents have stimulated greater investment in crop improvement research in industrialized countries, but they are also creating major problems and potentially significant additional expense for the already financially constrained public-sector breeding programmes that produce seeds for poor farmers.

> Utility patents confer broad rights to patent holders. They might cover, for example, any use of a certain useful gene. University scientists are pursuing these patents too.

The success of the Green Revolution was based on international collaboration which included the free exchange of genetic diversity and information. Most of the "added value" present in modern crops has been accumulated over the centuries by farmers themselves as they selected their best plants as the source of seed for the next planting. These "land races" have traditionally been provided free of charge by developing countries to the world community. The CGIAR centres add value through selective breeding, and the superior varieties they generate are widely distributed without charge, benefiting both developing and developed countries.

> Another appeal from biotechnology's critics: crops are a common heritage that should be freely exchanged.

Patents on biotechnology methods and materials, and even on plant varieties, are complicating and undermining these collaborative relationships. Public-sector research institutions in industrialized countries no longer fully share new information and technology. Rather, they patent and license and have special offices charged with maximizing their financial return from licensing. Commercial production of any genetically engineered crop variety requires dozens of patents and licenses. It is only the big companies that can afford to put together the

> The open exchange of ideas has historically been a critical component of the philosophy of science. This appeal is common among public sector scientists.

IPR portfolios necessary to give them the freedom to operate. And now, under the TRIPS (Trade-Related Aspects of Intellectual Property Rights) agreement of the World Trade Organization, most developing countries are required to put in place their own IPR systems, including IPR for plants. Furthermore, all of this 'ownership' of plant genetic resources is causing developing countries to rethink their policies concerning access to the national biodiversity they control, and new restrictions are likely.

> A key question not adequately addressed here: what does it mean to "own" biodiversity?

So far, international negotiations relevant to agricultural biotechnology and plant genetic resources have not been effectively coordinated. There are inconsistencies, and the interests of poor farmers in developing countries have not been well represented. The days of unencumbered free exchange of plant genetic materials are no doubt over, and agreements and procedures need to be formulated to ensure that public-sector institutions have access to the technological and genetic resources needed to produce improved crop varieties for farmers in developing countries who will not be well served by the for-profit sector. If the big life-science companies wish to find a receptive and growing market in developing countries, they will need to work with the public sector to make sure this happens.

> Here, Conway and Toenniessen are proposing a big change in the way biotechnologists typically think about their enterprise. Following it up with some suggestions in the next paragraph lends practical support.

Some Solutions

While negotiations are underway, there are a number of things that should be done. With little competitive loss, seed companies could agree to use the PVP system (including provisions allowing seed saving and sharing by farmers) in developing countries in cooperation with public plant-breeding agencies, rather than using patents or terminator technologies to protect their varieties.

To speed the development of biotechnology capacity in developing countries, companies that have IPR claims over certain key techniques or materials might agree to license these for use in developing countries at no cost.

We would also like to see an agreement to share the financial rewards from IPR claims on crop varieties or crop traits of distinct national origin, such as South Asian Basmati rice or Thailand's Jasmine rice. The granting of free licenses to use such materials in breeding programmes in the country of origin of the trait might gain the appreciation of developing country researchers and governments.

Finally, the current opposition to GM crops and foods is likely to spread from Europe to the developing countries and maybe even to North America unless there is greater public reassurance. At the heart of the debate about the safety of GM crops and their food derivatives is the issue of relative benefits and risks. The debate is particularly impassioned in Europe. Some of it is motivated by anti-corporate or anti-American

> Risks and benefits are important, but here Conway and Toenniessen are at risk of oversimplifying critics' multifaceted concerns—.

North American biotechnologists typically support the view that GM crops are "substantially equivalent" to their non-GM counterparts and do not need extraordinary testing. This is lumping of a different kind, which critics strongly assail. Conway and Toenniessen imply that GM crops must be considered on a case-by-case basis. Thus, they contend that both camps have adopted the wrong strategy.

sentiment, but underlying the rhetoric are genuine concerns about lack of consumer benefits, about ethics, about the environment and about the potential impact on human health.[12–16]

Much of the opposition tends to lump together the various risks—some real, some imaginary—and to assume there are generic hazards.[17] However, GM organisms are not all the same and each provides different potential benefits to different people and different environmental and health risks. Calls for general moratoria are not appropriate. Each new transgene and each new GM crop containing it needs to be considered in its own right. Well planned field tests are crucial, particularly in the developing countries where the risks of using, or not using, a GM crop may be quite different from those in industrialized countries.

The multinational companies could take a number of specific decisions in this area that would improve acceptance of plant biotechnology in both the developing and the industrialized world. First, consumers have a right to choose whether to eat GM foods or not and although there are serious logistic problems in separating crops all the way from field to retail sale, the agricultural seed industry should come out immediately and strongly in favour of labelling. Second, the industry should disavow use of the terminator technology in developing countries and, third, it should phase out the use of antibiotic-resistance genes as a means of selecting transgenic plants. Alternatives exist and should be used.

These three points will play well with critics, but cause concern among proponents. Clearly, throughout the paper Conway and Toenniessen are relying on their clout among proponents to win their support.

The Rockefeller Foundation and other donors have invested significant sums in helping developing countries put in place biosafety regulations and the facilities necessary for biosafety testing of new crops and foods, but much more needs to be done. The big life-science companies could join forces and establish a fellowship programme for training developing country scientists in crop biotechnology, biosafety, intellectual property rights and international negotiations administered by a neutral fellowship agency.

This claim has far-reaching implications. In this paper they have tried to set the tone by identifying points of discussion from both sides of the debate. If you've been keeping tally, you know that they have placed the ball in the biotechnologists' court. Theirs is primarily a call to heed critics' concerns.

Most important of all, a new way of talking and reaching decisions is required. We believe a global public dialogue is needed which will involve everyone on an equal footing—the seed companies, consumer groups, environmental groups, independent scientists, and representatives of governments, particularly from the developing nations.

Agriculture in the twenty-first century will need to be more productive and less damaging to the environment than agriculture has been in the twentieth. An increased effort is needed to assure that the benefits of agricultural research reach the hundreds of millions of poor farmers who have benefited little from previous research. We believe that biotechnology has significant potential to help meet these objectives but that this potential is threatened by a polarized debate that grows increasingly acrimonious. We need to reverse this trend, to begin working together, to share our various concerns, and to assure the new technologies are applied to agriculture only when this can be done safely and effectively in helping to achieve future food security for our world.

Note added in proof: We commend the Monsanto Company's recent public commitment not to commercialize sterile seed technologies and encourage other companies to follow their lead.

Notes

1. Pardey, P. G. Alston, J. M., Christian, J. E. & Fan, S. *Summary of a Productive Partnership: The Benefits from U.S. Participation in the CGIAR* (International Food Policy Research Institute, Washington DC, 1996).
2. Conway, G. R. *The Doubly Green Revolution: Food for All in the 21st Century* (Penguin Books, London/Cornell University Press, Ithaca NY, 1999).
3. UNICEF. *The State of the World's Children 1998* (Oxford Univ. Press, Oxford/New York, 1998).
4. Somer, A. & West, K. P. *Vitamin A Deficiency: Health, Survival and Vision* (Oxford Univ. Press, New York and Oxford, 1966).
5. Mann, C. C. *Science* 283, 310–314 (1999).
6. Cassman. K. G. *Proc. Natl Acad. Sci. USA* 96, 5952–5959 (1999).
7. Pingali, P. L. & Heisey, P. W. *Cereal Productivity in Developing Countries: Past Trends and Future Prospects.* CIMMYT Economics Paper 99–03 (CIMMYT, Mexico, 1999).
8. Leonard, H. J. in *Environment and the Poor: Development Strategies for a Common Agenda* (ed. Leonard, H. J.) 3–45 (Overseas Development Council, Washington DC, 1989).
9. James, C. *Global Review of Commercialized Transgenic Crops: 1998.* ISAAA Briefs No. 8. (International Service for Acquisition of Agri-biotech Applications, Ithaca NY, 1998).
10. Mann, C. C. *Science* 283, 314–316 (1999).
11. Ye, X. D. et al. *Science* (submitted).
12. The Royal Society of London. *Genetically Modified Plants for Food Use* (The Royal Society, London, 1998).
13. Nuffield Council on Bioethics. *Genetically Modified Crops: The Ethical and Social Issues* (Nuffield Council on Bioethics, London, 1999).
14. UN Food and Agriculture Organization. *Biotechnology and Food Safety.* FAO Food and Nutrition Paper 61. (World Health Organization/FAO, Rome, 1996).
15. Rissler, J. & Mellon, M. *The Ecological Risks of Engineered Crops* (MIT Press, Cambridge MA/London, 1996).
16. May, R. *Genetically Modified Foods: Facts, Worries, Policies and Public Confidence* (http://www.2.dti.gov.uk/ost/ostbusiness/gen.html, 1999).
17. Pretty, J. *The Biochemist* (in the press).

Acknowledgements

We thank M. Lipton, S. Dryden, R. May and colleagues at the Rockefeller Foundation for comments on an earlier draft of this article.

Reading Responses

1. How much did you know about biotechnology before you read Conway and Toenniessen's essay? Did they persuade you that biotechnology is a safe and effective way to combat worldwide poverty? What parts of their essay did you find most convincing? What parts did you find least convincing?

2. On a scale of 1–10 (where 1 = simple and 10 = impossible) where would you plot the difficulty of reading this essay? Note specific places in the text where the authors go out of their way to help readers who know little about biotechnology.

3. In a marginal comment, Professor Koetje notes that Conway and Toenniessen direct most of their recommendations to those in favor of biotechnology solutions to world hunger. Why is this an effective persuasive strategy? How will critics of biotechnology respond to these recommendations?

NOTES ON GRAMMAR, STYLE, AND RHETORIC:
HEDGES IN PERSUASIVE WRITING

A student teacher was introducing a group of high-school seniors to the nature of persuasive writing. As she neared the end of the session, she paused briefly and said, "One last thing—what do you think you should do if you suspect that some readers will have a position opposed to yours? If you have a good idea about what their position is, should you bring it up? Or would you maybe want to soften how you state your position to avoid alienating those readers?"

A young man slouching in a desk responded immediately: "Soften it? You've got to be kidding. If some readers are opposed to your view, you've got to crush them. State your position as if any other view would be stupid." Several of his classmates turned toward him and grinned in agreement.

That teacher would do well in a future class on persuasive writing to show her students Gordon Conway and Gary Toenniessen's "Feeding the World in the Twenty-First Century." For in this persuasive essay, the authors clearly acknowledge that some readers will be opposed to their position. And they express their position in such a way that those opposed to it will probably not get angry or dismissive. In part, Conway and Toenniessen do this work through skillful uses of what linguists call *hedges*.

Hedges are linguistic elements that help us to soften positions, to be somewhat tentative about them, to pull back from expressing them as if we were certain about them. We can hedge with adverbs such as *possibly* and *perhaps*, with modal auxiliary verbs such as *may* and *might*, with main verbs such as *seem* and *suggest*, and with phrases such as *to a certain extent* and *to our knowledge*. In addition, we can hedge clauses that express parts of our position by introducing them with other clauses such as *We believe that*, *We suggest that*, and *It is possible that*.

In "Feeding the World," Conway and Toenniessen use two kinds of hedges at prominent points of their essay. At the end of their opening subsection, they include this sentence, which is the most general statement of their overall position: "We believe that this [having a "Doubly Green Revolution"] can be achieved by a combination of: ecological approaches to sustainable agriculture; greater participation by farmers in agricultural analysis, design and research; and the application of modern biotechnology directed towards the needs of the poor in developing countries, which is the subject of the rest of this article" (155). Note that this statement is introduced with the prominent hedge "We believe that," which Conway and Toenniessen also use to introduce some other clauses near the end of their essay. If you have some doubt about the hedging effect of "We believe that," read the sentence once with the

"We believe that" where it appears in the essay and once with the "We believe that" omitted. You should notice a striking difference in the force of these two sentences.

In the last section of their essay, which carries the modest title "Some Solutions," Conway and Toenniessen do quite a bit of hedging with modal verbs. For instance, here is a controversial claim that is hedged with the modal verb *might:* "To speed the development of biotechnology capacity in developing countries, companies that have IPR [intellectual property rights] claims over certain key techniques or materials might agree to license these for use in developing countries at no cost"(160). In several other sentences in this section, Conway and Toenniessen hedge with the modal verb *could.* Here is one example: "The multinational companies could take a number of specific decisions in this area that would improve acceptance of plant biotechnology in both the developing and the industrialized world" (161).

At this point, you might ask whether such obvious hedges in such prominent positions actually weaken Conway and Toenniessen's argument, making it appear hesitant or wordy. In fact, a hedged passage can be especially persuasive because its reasonable moderation invites readers to respond in kind. Hedges, in other words, can help writers communicate to readers, "We are reasonable people. Why not consider our view seriously?"

Besides, no one can accuse Conway and Toenniessen of being weak in their overall presentation. Indeed, they include many direct statements of what they clearly regard as facts, as when they introduce their final paragraph by writing that "Agriculture in the twenty-first century will need to be more productive and less damaging to the environment than agriculture has been in the twentieth" (161).

In Your Own Writing . . .

- If a claim can be shown to be based on facts, state it directly.
- If a claim cannot clearly be shown to be based on facts or if a claim is controversial, use a strategically placed hedge.
- Where it's especially important that your audience agree with you, use a hedge to create a claim that your audience is more likely to find acceptable.

STUDENT WRITING

INTRODUCTION

by Meghan Sheehan, biotechnology major

The Assignment. What follows is a persuasive paper I wrote for a course titled "Perspectives in Biotechnology." The professor assumed that students had a strong laboratory background and thus could understand the technical terms. Interestingly, though, we also had to have completed prerequisite liberal arts classes before we enrolled in this class. The assignment for this paper asked us to describe a problem associated with biotechnology and provide a solution.

The Content. I chose one of the most troublesome issues in biotechnology—the proper use of genetic testing. Genetic testing, particularly universal genetic testing (that is, testing everyone) raises all sorts of concerns, from worries about private medical information becoming public knowledge to concerns that genetic testing will be used to discriminate against people. I narrowed the focus of my research to the function of genetic testing in the field of medical insurance. I was able to highlight the principal problems associated with the use of genetic testing by medical insurance companies, but providing a solution proved more complicated. Because health care is an issue of public concern that nonetheless involves private companies, I realized that any solution I offered would have political implications. I think that my solution is a good one, but I worry that those who disagree with my political leanings might disagree with my solution, too.

Learning to Write in Biotechnology. When I was writing my essay, I focused on two goals. First, given the controversial nature of my topic, I knew that I could expect both friendly and hostile readers, and I wanted to gain the respect of both. To gain their respect and to encourage them to consider my ideas, I had to respect not only the scholars I cited in my essay, but also my readers, those who disagree with me as well as those who see things my way. I knew that I wouldn't be able to convince every reader, but I hoped that I'd at least be able to make them consider my arguments, instead of angering them and causing them to dismiss my ideas. Additionally, I hoped to revise this essay and publish it in a journal, so reader respect became an absolute necessity. I tried to accomplish this goal primarily by using noninflammatory diction (which was hard) and by not mocking any of the views that I discussed in my essay (also hard, but not as hard as the first part).

The second goal was that my argument had to be practical; I wanted my readers to agree with me because I suggested reasonable solutions. This arose from my personality as much as from the class. We read a number of essays by many different authors for the class, and I disliked the essays that simply named and expounded on a problem without offering suggestions for fixing it. It is well and good to recognize a flaw, but I had no patience (and therefore no respect) for authors who couldn't suggest a way to mend it. Worst of all were the suggestions that were unworkable because they were either too vague or simply impractical. Because of this, I took great pains in my essay to include detailed and practical solutions for the problems I studied.

I kept both of these lessons in mind while I was writing this essay. Too often people are more eager to speak than they are to listen; more eager to win an argument than to find a solution that everyone can live with. By writing to build consensus rather than writing to win, I not only serve as a mediator between opposed groups, I also move us closer to implementing a workable solution rather than continuing an argument. I aimed for a well-reasoned argument that most readers could respect and find thought-provoking.

The Insurance Industry and Adult Preventative Genetic Screening: An Evil Beast Using Awesome Powers for Harm?

Meghan Sheehan

Abstract

In this paper, the issue of genetic screening in the insurance industry is discussed, particularly the practice of predictive screening prior to issuing health and life insurance. Predictive screening raises concerns that

WHAT?!? WHERE IS THE THESIS?!? Not every essay begins with a thesis. Ordering this essay in sections, marked with headings, allows me to describe the problem before I get to my main point—my solution. Without this background information, my audience would be less likely to accept the plan I'm proposing.

I broke my paper into parts, using headings to increase the overall readability of the essay. This section, "Current Issues," provides background information on the problem. The reader needs this information to understand both the nature of the problem and how my solution can fix it.

Depending on your philosophical tradition, you could argue that fairness for society at large is irrelevant. This is an argument I did not think of at the time, so I did not address the point. In general, though, I'm trying to reach out to readers who might otherwise disagree with me by voicing their concerns in a respectful way.

Genetic determinism can mean that your biological fate is caused by your genes and nothing you can do will change this fate.

some clients will not be able to find insurance and that the use of genetic screening raises the risk of genetic determinism. To exemplify these concerns this paper considers attempts by the Association of British Insurers at self-regulation, regulation by the state of Michigan, and one ethicist's call for a system that circumvents the problems associated with genetic screening. Rather than perform genetic screening, the insurance industry should perform as any business would. Since the current insurance system is maladapted to absorb the influx of genetic information and yet insure everyone regardless of genetic condition, this paper presents a new system of insurance more able to handle the claims of *every* individual.

Current Issues in Genetic Screening and Insurance, an Introduction

Currently, outside of reproductive therapies, most genetic screening done on asymptomatic adults is termed predictive or presymptomatic testing. This type of screening is done to judge whether an adult with a familial history of a disease has a genotype conducive to the disease. For example, patients who have a family history of Huntington disease (HD) can have a genetic test performed to determine whether they have the excessive genetic DNA repeat that causes HD long before they show any sort of symptoms of the disease. Again, this type of test is typically performed only on patients who have an established familial history of the disease. Screening of this sort is not currently performed on the population at large.

Many people are concerned, though, that this sort of screening may eventually become a universal prerequisite for receiving health and life insurance.[1] These people worry that if a test reveals a person's genetic disposition towards a disease, especially a chronic disease, that person may face greatly increased insurance premiums or even find herself uninsurable. Along the same lines, some worry that universal predictive screening will produce a class of patients who are deemed genetically superior, from a medical stand point, and who would therefore pay a miniscule premium. In both supposed scenarios, the results of such a screening are unfair: in the first case those patients who have a greatly increased need for insurance would not receive it and in the second society at large does not benefit from the reduced rate of a few "lucky" individuals.

I would argue that we should be concerned about universal predictive screening for another reason—the risk of genetic determinism. If people overly value the results of these tests, they might de-emphasize lifestyle choices that affect the length and quality of their lives. Furthermore, people might presume that if a person is genetically inclined towards a disease he is certain to develop that disease. Socioeconomic and environmental factors play a large role in whether a person actually succumbs to the potential disease. A classic example of other factors determining the onset of disease is the case of diabetes mellitus in genetically identical twins; only one-in-three times do both twins develop diabetes mellitus.[2] Two thirds of the time the second twin (with the exact same genes as the first twin) is able to avoid the disease by changing his exercise regimen and diet. Furthermore, many genetic diseases are not simple monogenic diseases. Therefore, screening for multigenic diseases must account for several factors, both genetic and non-genetic, before it can be fairly concluded, "yes/no, this patient has/does not have a high probability of disease." If an insurance company does not consider all factors, both genetic and non-genetic, when it interprets the results of genetic screening, it may unfairly charge an increased premium throughout the entire life of a person, even if he never develops the disease. The basis of these charges could lie solely in the interpretation of one test showing that he is an increased risk because of his propensity for a disease.

> Monogenic diseases are caused by a single genetic problem.

Addressing These Concerns

These are very valid concerns and both the insurance industry at large and the government have tried to address them. The Association of British Insurers (ABI), a non-government organization which 96% of insurance companies in the United Kingdom are part of, has drafted an extensive code outlining what the member companies may and may not do regarding genetic screening.[3] The guidelines address many topics and specifically state:

> I think my argument would be stronger if I used statistics from an American insurance association. These statistics would appeal more to readers throughout the U.S.

- Applicants must not be asked to undergo a screening in order to obtain insurance.
- If results from a screening are obtained, the insurer must consult a specialist for interpretation of the results.
- The screen must be ruled valid by the ABI genetics board before insurers can use it to cause premium increases.
- Informed, adult consent is required for all types of genetic screening.
- Policyholders are not required to reveal the results of a blood relative's test.
- Insurers must not offer lower than standard premiums on the basis of genetic test results.
- Insurers in the ABI are required to offer a minimum life insurance policy of £100,000 that cannot be affected by a genetic test.
- Each year the insurance company must demonstrate that they are following the Genetics Code set forth by ABI to renew membership status.

In the state of Michigan, citations SB590 and SB593 attempt to address some of the same issues that the ABI regulated in the United Kingdom.

I couldn't find evidence from an American insurance association, but I did find information on the laws pertaining to the state where my professor lives.

Specifically, these laws prohibit health insurers from requiring an asymptomatic applicant or insured person to submit to genetic testing before issuing, renewing or continuing a policy. Additionally, applicants are under no obligation to discuss whether previous testing has been performed, and physicians are prohibited from performing predictive genetic tests without the written, informed consent of the adult subject.[4]

From these examples, we see that both industry associations and government agencies are trying to address the very real concerns discussed above. Especially admirable are the efforts of ABI to ensure that genetic screenings do not unfairly limit a person's access to life insurance and health insurance.

Peterson wrote one of the essays we read for class. I tried to summarize his proposed solution. In retrospect, I think I may have been too brief.

What about industry regulation of insurance in the United States? Will for-profit insurance agencies in corporate America regulate themselves as the ABI does? Already people have complained that some U.S. insurance companies are labeling some people as uninsurable,"[5] especially patients with chronic conditions such as Huntington disease and cystic fibrosis. Would a for-profit industry allow regulation that requires it to insure the "uninsurable"? James Peterson argues that this is unlikely. Furthermore, he calls for an undefined health care system in which all people are guaranteed basic health care.[6] A universal health care system would avoid the potential problems of the current insurance system, and would offer health care to all people, including those who most need the insurance because of their genetic conditions. He does not explain how such a system could be implemented, but he argues that universal, basic health care would ensure that everyone received treatment, regardless of their genes. In Peterson's argument, this concern for the "uninsurable" is the only reason why a system of universal health care is necessary.

I bring up this point here to prepare my audience to see an advantage of my solution—my plan takes into account other considerations in addition to patient need.

Realistically Addressing the Concerns in the United States—A Radical Approach

Is the insurance industry truly evil? Is a universal health care system necessary to ensure that each person, regardless of genetic status, is treated? Should genetic status be a factor, i.e., should genetic screening be required for insurance?

No, the insurance industry is not evil. But insurance companies are in business to make a profit; they exist primarily to make money for shareholders and only secondarily to benefit the insured. If industry companies do not make a profit, they will cease to exist; someone, presumably individuals, will have to pick up the tab for our health expenses. What does this mean for you and me? It means that when I buy health insurance from an agency, I buy a policy from a company that also insures hundreds or thousands of other people. All of us pay a premium to keep our policy active. This money is pooled together, and the company draws from this pool when one of us files a claim. Whatever is leftover in the pool is the company's profit. As a for-profit institution, an insurance company is always looking for ways to maximize the amount of money left in the pool—their profit ratio. Therefore, insurance companies seek to insure low-risk applicants because they are less likely to draw heavily from the pool. People who have no chronic health conditions have fewer regular health expenses, and with few exceptions for unforeseen catastrophic events, their claims take less from the pool than a high-risk applicant who takes out more money, and takes it out more often. To put it very simply, insurance is a business of risk-management—insurance companies seek to minimize their risks to maximize their profits. If they used genetic screening to evaluate potential policyholders, companies could further minimize their risks.

Rather than focusing on universal health care system, we should consider the possibilities for a universal *insurance* system. If we agree that morally and ethically *all* people should have access to affordable health care, we must create a system to make health care affordable. If we agree that businesses have a right to make a profit and that all people deserve affordable healthcare, we must create a system that allows companies to make a profit while still insuring high-risk people. The government can ill-afford to subsidize insurance companies, so we must seek another solution. Extremely large, privately operated insurance companies that operated under a stringent government oversight system and an unheard of profit distribution system could effectively insure all of us, low- and high-risk alike.

Very, very large companies would be necessary, so large that there could be only a few in the entire country. Because insurance companies must be very large to efficiently absorb the costs of high-risk people, there is room in the U.S. for only a few companies. I propose a few companies rather than a monopoly or a government agency because I do not believe that a monopoly would benefit either the insured or the insurance companies. Currently, health insurance is distributed between multiple companies in the United States. For a condition such as Tay-Sachs disease, one in 250 people in the population at large is a carrier while one in 27 people in the Ashkenazi Jew population is a carrier.[7] Imagine one large company with a statistically average percentage of Ashkenazi Jews in their client pool. Only 1 in ~63,000 births will be a child with Tay-Sachs. Now imagine a small company that, through fate of location, insures primarily Ashkenazi Jews. Because 1 in ~800 births will be a child with Tay-Sachs, the company would have an at least 8x larger chance of paying out on Tay-Sachs claims for children of those they insure. Statistically speaking, it does not matter to that smaller company that Tay-Sachs is a rare disease; because they have a

This mysterious person could suffer from a range of diseases—from sickle cell anemia or genetically determined hypertension to diseases like Huntington disease or cystic fibrosis.

Here I link together the two propositions I've carefully established. This lays the groundwork for my proposed solution.

Tay-Sachs is a wasting disease of the neurological system. Babies born with it appear normal at first and seem to develop quite well. Slowly, though, they start to regress, and most die by age five.

comparatively small client pool, statistics simply do not work in their favor. However, if there was a very, very large (i.e., multi-regional) client pool, statistics would be restored to the 1 in ~63,000 births. Additionally, because there would be a large clientele, their pool of money would be quite large. Indeed, the pool would be so large that the payment on large claims would be a smaller percentage and hurt the company much less. Insurance companies with large pools can afford to insure those who are currently "medically uninsurable" because the statistics regarding genetic disorders actually work in their favor—the good news is that most people are not genetically predisposed to catastrophic diseases that require expensive medical treatment.

These large insurance companies should be privately operated because the current system of distributed power and government bureaucracy could not effectively process medical claims. Additionally, for reasons to be discussed below, these companies should be privately operated to ensure that they still turn a profit. Decisions about what is best for the company would still need to be made by the executives within the company to ensure that it remained vital. Additionally, incentives such as profit sharing and bonuses would encourage employees to work efficiently, and these incentives are unheard of from government employers.

The policy decisions of these large companies would require strict governmental oversight to ensure that the veritable monopoly of a few companies does not abuse the people that they serve. The government oversight should also include an independent panel of genetic counselors who interpret the results from genetics tests. In this way, the counselors can avoid the ethical dilemma of trying to serve two contrary masters (the people whose tests they read and the insurance company that employs them). Finally, the government should regulate profit distribution in the companies. Because the companies would operate in near-monopoly conditions, they could potentially make obscene profits. To combat this and to further the cause of benefiting people through advancements in medicine, a large percentage of the profits from the companies (perhaps as large as 50%, although this may not be realistic) should be *donated* to medical research. This would benefit society at large and also the company through more effective, cheaper treatments of their clients in the future.

Returning to the issue that opened this essay—should these companies perform genetic screening? I believe that they should perform genetic screening only for diseases where genetic tendency plays a role equal to other environmental factors and the genetic tendency can be flagged by a simple test. In the spirit of promoting better health for the client and keeping costs for the company down, this kind of testing would allow the company to provide incentives to help clients stay healthy. If, for example, through screening a client is discovered to have the CHD2 gene (the gene that can cause high cholesterol[8]), the insurance company can offer the client a lower premium if she can demonstrate that she lives a healthy lifestyle (through independently administered doctor physical results). In this case, government oversight would ensure two things: (1) the premium rates for those who do and do not live healthy lifestyles and (2) what would count as the minimum physical results for the lower premium. In the end, the first policyholder would benefit from a healthier lifestyle (even if she never developed the disease), the second policyholder would exercise personal autonomy, and the insurance company would benefit from the desire of policyholders to be healthy.

> Here, at the end, is the thesis. The insurance system I describe is the necessary context for this claim. Without the system, my claim is unworkable.

Only this type of universal insurance system offers the necessary controls on universal predictive genetic screening. In this system, selective screening for a few manageable diseases benefits all people. The use of any type of predictive genetic screening outside such an insurance system and government oversight creates the potential for unethical use of this technology.

References

1. "Genetic Testing." Genetics and Public Policy Center. 22 Jan. 2004 http://www.dnapolicy.org/genetics/testing.jhtml.
2. Peterson, James C. *Genetic Turning Points: The Ethics of Human Genetic Intervention.* Grand Rapids: Eerdmans, 2001. p 206–211.
3. Drell, Daniel. "FAQs." *Human Genome News* 9. p 4: nos 1–2. 1998.
4. "Genetic Testing–ABI Code of Practice." Association of British Insurers. 22 Jan. 2004. http://www.abi.org.uk/Display/default.asp?Menu_ID=946&Menu_All=1,946,0&Child_ID=203.
5. "Genetic Information and Health Insurance Enacted State Legislation." National Human Genome Research Institute. 22 Jan. 2004 http://www.genome.gov/page.cfm?pageID=10002338.
6. Peterson. p 210–211.
7. "Tay-Sachs Disease." Jewish Genetic Diseases MazorNet. 22 Jan. 2004 http://www.mazornet.com/genetics/tay-sachs.asp
8. "Gene Responsible for High Cholesterol." *Applied Genetics News.* (2001). Retrieved 22 Jan 2004 http://www.findarticles.com/cf_dls/m0DED/11_21/76142147/p1/article.jhtml

Reading Responses

1. Note three places in her essay where Meghan Sheehan accommodates her audience's prior knowledge and assumptions. For each place, describe the strategy she uses. Find two places where you believe Meghan should have worked harder to reach out to her audience.

2. Sheehan intentionally delays presenting her thesis until the last paragraph of her essay. In what ways does this organization treat the reader respectfully? In what ways might it be disrespectful to the reader? Do you think this is an ethical way to organize the essay? List your reasons.

3. List three adjectives to describe Sheehan's tone in this essay. For each adjective, jot down an example or two from her essay.

PUBLIC WRITING

INTRODUCTION

Different regions of the world have responded differently to the rapid increase in the availability of genetically modified crops. In the United States, for example, although there are many serious opponents, GM crops are common on grocery store shelves. In England, on the other hand, an ethicist at Durham University recently said that asking English people to feed their children GM foods would be like asking them to feed their children anthrax.

South Africa, like many African countries, faces great demand for food production—and thus great pressure to increase production with GM crops. South Africa's Department of Science and Technology has begun a program called "Public Understanding of Biotechnology," which, according to their Web site (www.pub.ac.za/about/aims.php), seeks to "ensure a clear, balanced understanding of the scientific principles, related issues and potential of biotechnology and to stimulate public debate around its applications in society."

The document that follows is a poster created for the "Public Understanding of Biotechnology" campaign. Like the other readings in this chapter, the need for this piece to appeal to an audience of varied opinions and levels of knowledge demands a balanced articulation of the point. In the bottom right corner—the "end" of the document—one finds the main character of the poster saying, "GM is here with its benefits and risks. What choices will you make about using it?" In other words, the main point of the piece is to say that people must make an educated choice about using GM crops, so they must become educated.

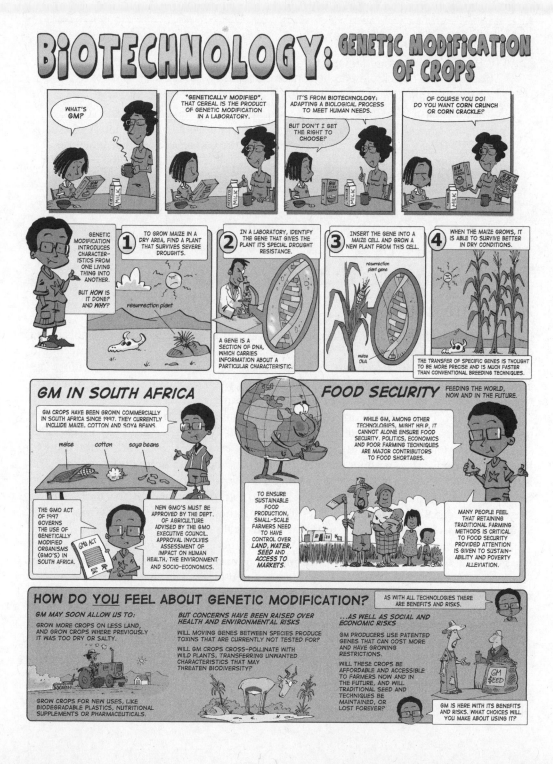

Reading Responses

1. Where does this poster present the arguments of those who support the use of GM crops? Where does it present the concerns of those who oppose GM crops?

2. Who is the audience of this poster? What role does the audience play in the debate over the use of GM crops?

3. Evaluate how this poster conveys information. How would you evaluate the visual appeal? How would you evaluate the amount, the complexity, and the sequence of information presented? Do you see any signs of an attempt to persuade the audience to favor or oppose GM crops?

MORE WRITING IN BIOTECHNOLOGY

INTRODUCTION

In this chapter we have been focusing on how biotechnologists try to create balanced, reasonable arguments. But, of course, we know that the hot-button issues that biotechnologists deal with will cause some heated and biased arguments to surface. "Science and Technology in World Agriculture" is about that very issue, discussing the ways that narratives—stories—can be used to bias or balance an argument.

The author, Pasquale Scandizzo, describes two opposing stories told by people working in biotechnology and agriculture. At one extreme, the "conservative" "conventional" story makes science and technology heroic, always creating newer and better ways for humans to produce food without harming the environment. The alternative, "radical" story is that technology serves big business and that small farmers and the environment are consequently at risk. The World Bank, says Scandizzo, offers the story that balances between these two extremes. In this excerpt we reprint one of the five examples of areas in which the World Bank narrative balances conservative and radical poles.

Scandizzo, who earned a PhD in economics at the University of California, Berkeley, is now a professor at the University of Rome. As an undergraduate he studied agricultural sciences. His knowledge of the World Bank is boosted by the fact that he was an employee of the World Bank for about ten years after he completed his Ph.D.

Science and Technology in World Agriculture: Narratives and Discourses

Pasquale Lucio Scandizzo

AgBioForum 21(1), 2009

Abstract

The narratives characterizing the current debate on world agricultural research tend to be part of a discourse that rationalizes past experience and future tendencies along the lines of extreme recounts of successes and failures. Stories of agricultural development and of accomplishments of research and science in agriculture tend to be organized according to either a conservative or a radical paradigm, which are in sharp contrast with each other and are at the origin of basic disagreements and biased information. For the neutral observer, these contrasting views—to the extent that they seem to concern facts more than opinions—cause disorientation and stress in the form of the well-known phenomenon of cognitive dissonance. Among the international institutions, the World Bank appears to have taken on the responsibility of attenuating such a phenomenon by providing, through its own narratives, stylized truths and balanced interpretations.

Key words: agriculture, research, narratives, discourse, cognitive dissonance, biotechnology, global public goods.

Narratives and Discourses on World Agriculture

According to Abell (2007), ". . . human beings frequently claim to understand events when they manage to formulate a coherent story or narrative explaining how they believe an event was caused or, more often, how the world is causally transformed from one state to another by virtue of human agency/action." The crucial nature of narratives in interpreting reality through story telling, however, goes beyond the search of causal explanations in the absence of strong statistical evidence from recurrent events. . . .

Because of their rhetorical nature, and the fact that they involve characters, plots, and color, narratives provide a more attractive cognitive framework for interpretation and search for meaning than other more descriptive or more quantitative structures of causal explanations.

On the other hand, narratives can be wildly divergent amongst one another in interpretation, meaning, and scope and cause what in psychology is known as *cognitive dissonance*. This condition may give rise to the cognitive stress of entertaining two contradictory ideas simultaneously. In fact, the theory of cognitive dissonance (Aronson, 1969) proposes that one function of narratives may also be used to reduce this dissonance by rationalizing outcomes, modifying beliefs, and justifying differences between reality and self images. . . .

The debate on world agriculture provides an interesting example of contrasting narratives along these lines, as two dominant and conflicting sets of stories confront each other. . . .

For the evolution of world agriculture, the moderate, or conservative narrative tells stories of achievements and hopeful developments with no villain and many heroes. This story is one of uninterrupted scientific progress, continuous increases of yields in the past years, even though, it is admitted, a notable slowdown has progressively occurred as the initial effects of the green revolutions have been gradually consumed and, at the same time, the expected increases from biotechnology have not yet materialized. For example, recounts of the green revolution, how it came about, how it has affected farmers' lives, etc., are common stories consistent with the conservative narrative theme.

A radical, or contrarian, set of narratives elaborates stories along a different theme: while the large farmers have benefited from yield increases, smallholders, whose yields have traditionally been far in excess (from 200 to 1000 times) of those of large farmers, have gained only marginal benefits. . . .

The contrast between the conventional and the contrarian discourse is reminiscent of the opposition between the modernist inclination to attribute scientific discoveries to unqualified social progress and the more problematic attitude of postmodernism toward the nexus between recognizable social progress and the empowerment of the elites. But it may also reflect different power positions of the parties involved, both because, as Foucault (1977, 1980) argues, science and truth are shaped by negotiating power and because discourse operates by rules of exclusion, so that power is assigned to the privileged who can speak and are listened to. . . .

The Ecological Problem

Since the publication in 1962 of Rachel Carson's "Silent Spring," environmental thinking has tended to reject altogether the traditional production paradigm [a pattern or model] governing the application of science to agriculture. The book persuasively argued that agricultural practices may not be sustainable because of their continuous damage to the environment and our health. While sustainability is a slippery concept, it seems clear that present agricultural practices are not sustainable, since they replace natural ecosystems with crop fields and tree farms (with accompanying loss of biodiversity and massive carbon dioxide release) and result in groundwater pollution, soil erosion, aquifer depletion, soil degradation, pesticide pollution, and other environmental stresses. Agricultural research, being guided mainly by the production paradigm, and increasingly dependent on profit-making investments of multinational companies, does not appear to be able to internalize this vision.

According to this line of thought, which represents a narrative directly challenging the story of agricultural research as an environmentally friendly activity, sustainable and multifunctional agriculture should not only be about cheap wholesome food, but also about stewardship of the land, preservation of the resource base, the health of farm workers, the preservation of the small biota [plants and animals] that are rich in biodiversity and are interspersed with fields, the value of rural community, and of the agricultural landscape. These objectives are especially important for climate change, where the capacity to adapt depends critically on the type of agricultural systems implemented.

The paradigm of sustainable systems does appear to be more in line with the increasing need to look at agriculture as a flexible set of opportunities rather than as a growing machinery for production. A wide variety of adaptation options has been proposed, for example, to reduce vulnerability to climate change, to help exploit the opportunities provided by increases in temperature or rainfall, or both. In general, scientists agree that agriculture can adapt to a moderate level of global warming (an increase of about 2.5° Celsius), even though adaptability would be higher for the Northern hemisphere, where climate change may provide opportunities for yield increases. Mendelsohn and Dinar (1999), for example, show that, given that adaptation occurs, increase in the average temperature would benefit US agriculture, even though, at the same time, increases of inter-annual [**year-to-year**] variations would be harmful. For the Southern hemisphere, adaptability would be lower and climate change would be a threat, rather than a potential, albeit limited source of opportunities, since temperatures are already near their maximum tolerable heat level.

The World Bank, in making a major effort to take the lead in suggesting a course of action, intervenes with a soothing message. These problems, it suggests, are a source of only passing and apparent contradictions, because

> . . . tackling climate change requires **leadership, vision, capacity, and resources beyond the development experience to date.** Yet the transformation to a more sustainable development path has already started across the world. This transformation is driven largely by higher energy costs and growing concerns about adequate access to water, land, and mineral resources to support growth and livelihoods. It is facilitated by an increasing value of a healthy and productive environment, and a stronger voice and participation of the civil society. (World Bank, 2008, p. 203)

Clearly, climate change may be creating its own set of economic tales, but the ensuing discourse suggests new boundaries of conceivable knowledge and, as such, may be pointing to a newly established frontier for thought on scientific development. The underlying narrative that the World Bank is developing in order to quench the cognitive dissonance in this regard is clear: climate change is the new prevailing force to reckon with in the field of agricultural development. It is already upon us, so that not only mitigation efforts are necessary, but also adaptation actions are inevitable. Research in agriculture, however, may be inadequate to fulfill the task of offering new choices and new solutions to the problems created by climate change because it has taken an altogether different direction: the pursuit of profit-maximizing micro-agricultural improvements within the single integrated agro-industrial enterprise in a context of thoroughly protectable property rights on innovation. A radical change is thus needed to proceed from narrowly defined, profit-oriented, short-sighted, privately dominated agricultural research to a pursuit of knowledge truly attuned to the planetary adaptation facing humanity and agriculture today. . . .

Conclusions

For agricultural research, the fact that narratives dominate the debate on scope and achievement is somewhat paradoxical, since research is committed to a rigorous methodological approach and is accountable to a scientific community, which should have little propensity to listen to the sirens of the rhetorical discourse. The highly formal nature of the scientific method and the prudence and the caveats that surround all the specific achievements of science, however, may themselves be the source of a peculiar vulnerability, when a comprehensive view of successes and failures, as well as meanings and scope are called for. The discourse about science may thus turn out to be rather un-scientific, involve prejudices, exaggerations, and controversies, and use narratives as the main vehicle of elaboration and understanding. By their very nature, these narratives will tend to dramatize the events and attempt to convey messages that may be considered extreme, either in defense of the status quo or against it.

A provocative way to interpret this state of affairs is provided by the idea that narratives are simply the side effects of technological change and this, in turn, is merely the consequence and not the cause of social change. If this is true, narratives are no more than ways by which social change anticipates and rationalizes technical change, through the predisposition of social machinery capable of engendering the innovations required. Thus, for example, the space race of the 1960s was the consequence of a heightened Cold War, and the narratives on the superiority of one or the other superpower were only part of the process of communicating this conflict to the ordinary citizen. Analogously, the biotechnological revolution, if it is indeed in the making, would be the consequence of a major re-organization of the structure of production, input provision, consumption patterns, and balance between private and public research, which is also already in the making. If this is true, the opposed narratives that are being deployed by different social groups are only the reflection of the conflict between those who feel that they are engendering the change and those who fear that they would be excluded or emarginated by it. The drama and the rhetoric of the competing narratives is due to the fact that this preventive lining up of winners and losers occurs in a transitional situation, where the impending social changes are still unclear and unclearly related to corresponding technological changes.

In this context of uncertainty and dynamic change, widely different interpretations of current events are possible, while the underlying structure of society is shifting in an unpredictable way. Different narratives summarize the attempts at explaining what happens by using a linguistic process formed by plots, heroes and anti-heroes, and, at times, pathos and drama. Because of its standing in the international community as a unique institution with financial, scientific, and moral authority, the World Bank appears to have chosen, alongside its traditional mission as a policy advocate for development, the role to provide comfort and guidance, thereby attenuating the cognitive dissonance arising from highly contradicting stories on themes such as development, research, science, climatic change, and, ultimately, human destiny.

By using . . . the influential World Development Report, . . . the World Bank provides its own set of narratives. These narratives tend to coalesce around the underlying story of the ascent of men throughout the ages by the force of their imagination and concerted efforts, but go much beyond a mere reiteration of this theme. By appealing to a wide repertoire of in-house-researched, stylized truths, they elaborate on the role and the accomplishments of large numbers of unknown and reluctant heroes: the scientists, the innovative farmers, the adapting poor. In the case of science and agriculture, they provide, in a cautious and critical way, much needed policy advice on the future course of agricultural research.

Such policy advice has to be somewhat distilled from the very complex and cautious narratives provided, but it can be summarized as a serious attempt at looking for a balance between the conventional and the radical views. Its main points are three. First, rather than concentrating on marginal innovations for a handful of commercial crops, biotechnological research in agriculture should be directed mainly at seeking a viable alternative to the present energy-intensive modes of production in agriculture. Second, it should take smallholders and local production systems as the main targets for its applications and try to build new varieties less dependent on fertilizer and insecticide inputs—and at the same time, more integrated with, rather than being alternative to—the various cultivation options (rotation, multiple cropping, use of biological pesticide control) of small farmers around the world. Third, because this challenge requires the commitment of large amounts of resources without the prospect of immediate gain, this type of research can only be undertaken by the public sector. Moreover, it can only be undertaken if the international community recognizes this conclusion as the major challenge for development and the reduction of poverty in the years ahead.

References

Abell, P. (2007). Narratives, Bayesian narratives and narrative actions. *Sociologica, 3*(2007), 1–21. Available on the World Wide Web: http://www.sociologica.mulino.it/doi/10.2383/25959.

Aronson, E. (1969). The theory of cognitive dissonance: A current perspective. In L. Berkowitz (Ed.). *Advances in experimental social psychology,* Volume 4, pp. 1–34. New York: Academic Press.

Carson, R. (1962). *Silent Spring.* New York: Houghton Mifflin.

Foucault, M. (1972). *Archeology of knowledge.* New York: Pantheon.

Foucault, M. (1977). *Discipline and punish.* New York: Pantheon.

Foucault, M. (1980). *Two lectures.* In C. Gordon (Ed.), *Power/knowledge: Selected interviews.* New York: Pantheon.

Foucault, M. (2003). *Society must be defended.* New York: Pantheon.

Mendelsohn, R., & Dinar, A. (1999). Climate change, agriculture, and developing countries: Does adaptation matter? *The World Bank Research Observer, 14*(2), 277–293.

World Bank. (2008). *Agriculture for development* (World Development Report). Washington, DC: Author.

Reading Responses

1. How does Scandizzo try to persuade you that the World Bank "intervenes with a soothing message"? Where exactly does Scandizzo try to explain why the World Bank would want to offer a balance between the two sides? Which of Scandizzo's methods of persuasion are least and most effective?

2. Summarize each of the five paragraphs of the "Conclusions" section. Then answer this question: If the World Bank, like those who argue from one of the two extremes about agricultural biotechnology, also uses its own stories, how are the World Bank stories better able to resist listening to what Scandizzo calls the "sirens of rhetorical discourse" than others?

3. Scandizzo argues that people paying attention to the global conversation about agricultural biotechnology suffer from "cognitive dissonance" not just because there are opposing sets of narratives but because both sets rely on "facts" rather than opinion for their evidence. List pieces of factual evidence (from this reading or one of the others in this chapter) that could be used to support either pro- or anti-biotechnology arguments. Can you identify any factual evidence that, depending on how it is "spun," could support either pro or anti arguments?

WRITING ASSIGNMENTS

Assignment 1

Starbucks promotes itself as a socially and environmentally responsible company. The "Responsibility" page on the company Web site (www.starbucks.com) proclaims that "We've always believed that businesses can—and should—have a positive impact on the communities that they serve," and it lists the company's good work across the globe. But Starbucks has received pointed criticism from environmental watchdog organizations like the Organic Consumers Association.

Your task is to draft a Web article for either a global food company like Starbucks or an environmental watchdog organization that describes a difficult environmental issue in a way that builds trust among those who might otherwise think of themselves as adversaries. To complete this assignment, you will have to conduct some research on the environmental issue that has polarized the adversaries. Consult a reference librarian for help with this research.

As you begin drafting, look for common ground: goals, methods, and evidence that the contending groups can agree on. Attempt to describe contentious issues in ways that all groups will accept as fair. Take advantage of strategies for writing on the Web that will help you emphasize ethical—and ultimately effective—arguments about these vital issues.

Assignment 2

Some writing teachers restrict students from writing on topics that have a reputation for dividing people, topics such as abortion, euthanasia, gun control, partisan politics, prayer in public schools, and affirmative action. These teachers claim, rightly so, that people who hold strong opinions on a controversial issue often have a difficult time assessing the validity of evidence, identifying the range of assumptions that people bring to the topic, and treating opposing arguments respectfully.

Your task is to revise an essay or speech that takes a stance on a controversial subject like those listed above so that it better acknowledges the assumptions and concerns of those who might disagree with the author. You might consider selecting a text that takes a position that you oppose. Once you've selected your text, assess how well the author addresses the concerns of those who oppose her stance. Analyze the text for issues like the following:

• What evidence does the author use? Is this evidence that a variety of people will accept?

• How does the author address the assumptions and concerns of those who oppose her?

• In what ways does the author reach out to audience members who disagree with her stance?

As you begin drafting, consider the progression of your argument carefully. What common ground can you start from? How can you address the concerns of those who will oppose point of your piece? What evidence will appeal to these readers?

Assignment 3

New advances in the field of biotechnology have sparked heated debate within the scholarly community and protests from citizens in many countries. One such advance is "Bt corn," so called because it contains *Bacillus thuringiensis* (Bt), a bacterium deadly to the caterpillars that feed on corn plants. People around the world are protesting the effects of Bt corn on the livelihoods of organic farmers, the animals who ingest the corn (and the people who eat those animals), the people who live near the Bt corn fields, and butterfly populations.

Your task is to research the one of the problems associated with Bt corn, to summarize the possible solutions to that problem, and to promote one of these solutions as the best currently available.

As you begin drafting, be sure to carefully assess the research you find, paying close attention to the credibility of the source. Because you likely do not have the expertise to develop your own solution, select a solution from your research and promote that solution in your own work. Be sure to provide citations for the research you use. Following the lead of Conway and Toenniessen, attempt to present the problem in a way that represents fairly the claims of all groups. When you present your preferred solution, emphasize how it addresses the concerns of those who might initially be inclined to disagree with it.

NURSING: OBSERVING TO IMPROVE PRACTICE

The following is a posting on a message board for people who have chronic pain. In it, a person named Braz describes both the physical and social effects of chronic pain:

I am just about at the end of my rope. I am so sick of being in pain, sick of having to plan my life around my med schedule, sick of having people act like I am just using my "pain" to get attention or to get out of doing things and going places. I am sitting here now, have taken my meds and my back is still on fire, left leg and arm needing to be pulled off and I am just sick of it. I did not ask for this and I do not want to be in pain until I die . . . would rather just get it over with and be done with it.

I wake up every morning and swallow a handful of pills just to be able to get the day started, I grit my teeth to get thru those first agonizing hours of the day and then have to swallow handfuls of pills through-out the day to keep the day going, then a handful at night to be able to get what sleep I do get. I am so tired of being told that I am being grumpy . . . DUH . . . if those people could have my arm or leg or back for a rainy weekend I bet my last buck they would be grumpy too.

SO sick of this attitude that we are addicts . . . no one calls a diabetic an addict, or an epileptic one, yet because our problem is physical pain we are treated like shit!! I wish the parts that caused our pain would glow or beep so others would see that we are not being anti-social, we are being held in the grip of the demon pain. . . . Sorry to go on so . . . just not dealing with the pain well tonight.

—*Braz*

- Is Braz reasonable to wish for more sympathy from others? Justify your answer with at least a few reasons. Use the evidence you observe in the Web posting.

- List all the kinds of evidence of chronic pain that others (family members, friends, coworkers, medical personnel) can see in Braz's life. For each kind of evidence, note the expertise that others need to make an accurate observation.

PORTABLE RHETORICAL LESSON: USING PERSONAL OBSERVATION FOR RHETORICAL PURPOSE

Braz's chronic pain demands a specific response from trained medical personnel: a treatment plan. This treatment plan responds to the implied research question: How can we lessen Braz's pain? The **point** of the treatment plan is expressed as a set of recommendations to manage the chronic pain. But how can you recommend treatment without knowing how to understand the symptoms you observe? What would make up the necessary **research methods and evidence** to justify recommending treatment? If you do not have medical training, reading Braz's post may have made you feel a bit helpless. Exactly what in Braz's post tells you something important for diagnosing the source of his pain? If you have suffered chronic pain yourself, or know someone who has, you may have learned to recognize symptoms and make judgments based on some personal observations, but you would not recommend medical treatment.

The exercise with Braz's post implicitly asks: How can a writer use personal observation for a rhetorical purpose (in this case, making recommendations)? And that question takes us to this chapter's **Portable Rhetorical Lesson** on using personal observation. One of the most difficult lessons for writers is learning when—and how—to use observation effectively.

When you wonder whether to include personal observation in a piece of writing, consider two particular points from writing in nursing:

1. "You only see what you know." This piece of advice comes from the "public" reading for this chapter, a book called *Camp Nurse*. The author constantly uses personal observation to evaluate medical crises and treat patients. She can do so only because she has a trained eye—she knows what to look for and how to respond to what she sees. In the reading from *Camp Nurse* you'll see nurses spontaneously running through lists of symptoms and possible causes in the first seconds of observing a patient. Nurses develop expertise through the knowledge they gain in coursework and the experience they gain in supervised clinical work. As a writer, you increase your expertise by increasing your knowledge of the subject matter. Your readers will trust your observations only when they trust your expertise.

2. The importance of process. The readings in this chapter reveal a typical process for nurses: (1) observe symptoms and situations, (2) record observations, (3) assess the observations, (4) seek professional consultation when possible, and (5) map out—and

record—a recommended plan of action. A patient's life can depend on a nurse's ability to translate expertise into a plan of action—a recommendation for treatment. When nurses gather information systematically (note all the specific categories that must be described—and supported with observations—in the "Care Plan" on page 202), they can make effective recommendations. Clarity and reliability are key features of effective recommendations: if patients and other members of a medical team do not understand what the nurse observed or if they do not trust a nurse's expertise, they are not likely to follow through on a nurse's recommendations.

If you wish to use personal observation in your writing, prepare yourself with a well-trained eye and effective processes (for example, assessing the use of your observations by consulting with an expert) for putting your observations to good rhetorical use.

WRITING IN THE DISCIPLINE

INTRODUCTION

by Mary E. Flikkema, Professor of Nursing

As a nurse, writer, and researcher, Dr. Sandra Thomas advocates for those who may not be able to speak for themselves. She desires that health professionals and others will hear the voices of those who are living in chronic pain. Dr. Thomas describes her writing as "giving a voice to the voiceless," a practice consistent with traditions and purposes of nursing research and writing.

The practice of nursing is both an art and a science. It is necessary for nurses to have specific scientific knowledge—in this case, knowledge about the neurological basis of pain sensations, how pain travels through the body, knowledge about pain medications and alternative therapies. The factual, scientific data is part of a much larger picture of holistic care. Holistic care, the art of nursing practice, is the recognition and treatment of human beings as unique individuals with unique lives and health experiences. The art of nursing involves the application of scientific principles in a unique way for each person. The essence of nursing is the art of caring, creatively weaving holistic approaches for each individual person.

Thomas specifies the focus of the study in her abstract, writing that her findings argue against simple or idealized understandings of chronic pain. She hopes to gain insight from those who experience severe pain every day. The content of nursing papers is about interaction with clients, or interaction with health professionals, but the focus is always on improving the health experiences of those seeking care and support.

As nurse writers prepare a document, they begin with a problem or question, an inquiry about a health issue of concern. The nurse writer determines the best method to answer those questions or concerns. For credibility Thomas followed a specific method of research involving a series of carefully controlled steps to gather and report information. She selected a qualitative method of gathering information about individuals' experiences of pain, an examination of peoples' "lived experiences." This involves the process of allowing those experiencing chronic pain to tell their own stories about their lives and experiences. Listening to individuals' experiences provides the person-to-person contact that is the content of the research findings.

Thomas also follows a conventional format in nursing literature, providing an overview of chronic pain and why it is important to write about this topic. She explains the methods used and reports the findings, her interpretation of the findings, and her analysis of the findings.

But Thomas also uses words and images that are almost certain to evoke a response from others, describing how nurses talk about chronic pain sufferers as "difficult, demanding, manipulators and addicts," or the stereotyped "low back loser." Thomas's role is not simply that of the detached, objective observer. She hopes to convey the negativity that characterizes health-care professionals, those who should be the most compassionate, kind, and helpful. She creates these images so that her readers may understand, examine their own behavior, and thus provide more supportive care. The information gathered in person from the interviews of pain sufferers evokes personal response. Thomas makes a good case for the fact that chronic pain sufferers do not have the support they need to cope with chronic pain, and she argues that change must occur in treating those with chronic pain.

In many professions, as well as in community and public life, it is necessary to provide a voice for the voiceless. For the nurse who writes, changing health care for the better is both motive and goal.

✓ Reading Tips

Read this paper from two perspectives:

- as a health-care scientist (looking for concrete, technical knowledge of chronic pain—to develop expertise) and
- as a health-care practitioner (looking for ways to understand patients' experience).

Reading the abstract will give you the first clue that you need to read from both these perspectives, and the rest of the paper will reinforce that need. The section called "Gaps in Our Understanding of Chronic Pain" emphasizes the science background, and the "Findings" section emphasizes the human experience of the study subjects and of the nurses who observed them; that's where your sympathetic response will be called on.

A Phenomenologic Study
of Chronic Pain

Sandra P. Thomas

Western Journal of Nursing Research, 2000, 22(6): 683–705

[Abstract]

Researchers have seldom invited patients with chronic pain to describe their lived experiences. This phenomenologic study involved in-depth interviews with nine women and four men with nonmalignant chronic pain. The essence of participants' experiences was unremitting torment by a force or monster that cannot be tamed. The body was altered and recalcitrant, the life world was shrunken, and the pain set up a barrier that separated them from other people. Time seemed to stop; the future was unfathomable. Findings of this study contribute to the phenomenological literature that explores the human body and its symbolic meanings and call into question the idealized positive depiction of chronic illness that is prominent in contemporary literature.

> This "phenomenologic study" is the type of research that holistically observes "lived experience" of the subjects.

"Pain . . . teaches us how unfree, transitory, and helpless we really are, and how life is essentially capable of becoming an enemy to itself."
—*Buytendijk (1962, p. 27)*

Buytendijk's (1962) words aptly depict the helplessness of individuals with chronic pain, a disabling health problem that affects 75 to 80 million Americans (Matas, 1997). By the time they earn the diagnostic label of chronic pain, these individuals usually have tried to get relief from a variety of self-care measures as well as a host of medical interventions. As they endure the gamut of physical examinations, diagnostic tests, exploratory surgeries, and a bewildering array of remedies, chronic pain patients progressively become more discouraged, weary, and angry. Both patients and caregivers become frustrated with one another when treatments are ineffective and suffering becomes prolonged. The cryptic advice "learn to live with it" is often the final salvo of the health care provider to the departing chronic pain patient. The biomedical approach, with its focus on pathophysiology, does not address the complexity of chronic pain and does not provide adequate guidance for successfully living with it. From the perspective of nursing's holistic philosophy, extant literature has significant limitations, including the tendency to focus on discrete aspects of the chronic pain

> the study of physical illness

experience ("the parts") rather than on its interrelated wholeness. Researchers seldom invite patients to describe their lived experience. A multidisciplinary panel convened at the National Institutes of Health (NIH) in 1995 stated that "qualitative research is needed to help determine patients' experiences with . . . chronic pain" (NIH, 1995, p. 18). In this article, I present the findings of a phenomenologic study designed to "give a voice to the voiceless" (Hutchinson, Wilson, & Wilson, 1994)—the men and women who live daily with chronic pain.

Gaps in Our Understanding of Chronic Pain

The chronic pain literature is voluminous, including studies of its epidemiology and socioeconomic impact as well as its association with anxiety, depression, fatigue, immature defense style, helplessness, locus of control, and substance abuse (Ackerman & Stevens, 1989; Bates & Rankin-Hill, 1994; Covington, 1991; Elton, Hanna, & Treasure, 1994; Latham & Davis, 1994; Skevington, 1983). Notable gaps in our understanding remain nonetheless. Researcher bias is evident in the use of labels such as *immature defense style,* and numerous methodologic problems lessen reader confidence in the conclusions drawn. An excellent summary of these problems may be found in a review of 21 years of research on patients' beliefs, coping strategies, and adjustment to chronic pain (Jensen, Turner, Romano, & Karoly, 1991). Another critical analysis of the literature deplored researchers' heavy reliance on pain clinic samples and failure to use commensurable measures of pain experience (Dworkin, Von Korff, & LeResche, 1992).

Studies that illuminate the nature of interactions between pain patients and their caregivers are particularly relevant to nursing. This literature documents paternalistic staff stoicism (Edwards, 1989); labeling of patients as *difficult, demanding, manipulators,* and *addicts* (Faberhaugh & Strauss, 1977); and adversarial relationships between patients and care providers (McCaffery & Thorpe, 1989). Nurse estimations of patients' pain intensity are often erroneous, especially when they are assessing the chronic patient. For example, in a study of 268 registered nurses, the chronic pain sufferer was negatively stereotyped and judged to have less intense suffering than an individual with acute pain (Taylor, Skelton, & Butcher, 1984). Particularly pejorative views of the chronic low back pain patient were noted, perpetuating the stereotype of the "low back loser."

Although modern analgesic medications may provide episodic relief of the physical pain—at least temporarily—they fail to alleviate the profound suffering of these patients, which often is psychological and spiritual, not just physical. A survey of chronic pain patients who were members of a national self-help organization revealed that 50% of them had considered suicide—a particularly disturbing finding given that this

---

"Qualitative research" in this case is a method of gathering in-depth, holistic information about a topic of interest by interviewing those who are experiencing a particular phenomenon (thus "phenomenologic study").

Note the labels that the author has selected to use based on her review of the literature. These labels arouse the reader's sense of injustice.

Notice again the inflammatory words the author cites to arouse one's recognition of the injustice.

Health-care professionals learn that the definition of pain is "what the person says it is." We are trained to believe what the individuals with pain say about their pain. But the author points out that those with chronic pain may not be believed.

This startling statistic about suicide implies that effective holistic perspective is often lacking in the treatment of chronic pain.

was a select sample of well-educated and financially secure individuals who had actively sought out a group to help them manage their condition (Hitchcock, Ferrell, & McCaffery, 1994). I believe that nurses have a moral obligation to provide more skillful psychosocial care to these patients. According to Price (1996),

> The provision of skillful psychosocial care to patients suffering from chronic illnesses starts with an appreciation of what it is like to live with a chronic condition. . . . Getting inside the experience of such illness may be key to understanding patient motivation, noncompliance with therapy and altered patterns of social engagement. (p. 275)

Research shows that nurses who have personally borne intense pain are more sympathetic to the patient in pain (Holm, Cohen, Dudas, Medema, & Allen, 1989). Qualitative studies that involve in-depth interviewing of patients could permit nurses to vicariously experience the life world of the chronic pain patient.

Although "getting inside the experience" is recommended, few qualitative studies have been conducted. One exception is a British interview study involving a large sample of 75 patients (Seers & Friedli, 1996). Despite its ambitious scope, this study has several significant limitations. The interviews were not audiotaped, and there is a possibility that the researchers' field notes may be subject to selection bias (i.e., tendency to record what the researchers were interested in or wanted to hear). At best, field notes must be regarded as incomplete accounts of participants' subjective experiences. Furthermore, the data-coding scheme was superficial (e.g., psychological state, social activities), and some themes, such as desperation of doctors, were not well supported by the quotations from study participants that the authors cited. In a phenomenological study by Bowman (1991) of 15 individuals with chronic low back pain, data were not plumbed deeply by the researcher; typical themes were varied psychological reactions and related physical symptoms. Although the interpretations were plausible, they were not highly illuminating. Semistructured interviews by Henriksson (1995) with 40 fibromyalgia patients yielded a useful typology of strategies for managing activities of daily living, but the researcher did not attempt to explore the deeper meaning of having continuous muscular pain.

Purpose of Study

Therefore, the purpose of this study was to explore the deeper meaning of what it is like to live with chronic pain, using a qualitative design. The method selected was eidetic (descriptive) phenomenology derived from the Husserlian (1913/1931) tradition, as elucidated by Pollio, Henley, and Thompson (1997). Within phenomenology, particularly within the writing of Merleau-Ponty (1945/1962), the body is viewed as a fundamental

---

Margin notes:

First-person statements like this "I believe" are seldom used in professional health literature. Here the author indicates her strong feelings about the need to understand and attempt to improve the care provided.

Qualitative research (phenomenology) may be considered by some to be "soft" research with no "hard data" to support the findings. Those conducting qualitative research follow specified methods for sampling, data collection, and analysis. Qualitative research provides different, "rich" data, taken directly from those who are experiencing the phenomenon. The author identifies the procedure used in her study, giving others the opportunity to critique her report.

category of human existence. In fact, the world is said to exist only in and through the body. Therefore, phenomenology appeared particularly well suited for the exploration of pain phenomena.

Method

Sample

Thirteen individuals were interviewed for the study. Criteria for participants' inclusion in the study were as follows: willingness to talk about their lived experiences, older than age 18, and nonmalignant chronic pain consistent with the following North American Nursing Diagnosis Association (NANDA) definition: "Chronic pain is an unpleasant sensory and emotional experience arising from actual or potential tissue damage or described in terms of such damage . . . without a predictable end and a duration greater than 6 months" (NANDA, 1996, p. 76). Individuals were recruited for the study via a newspaper article and network sampling. No attempt was made to recruit patients with a particular diagnosis or disease trajectory. As noted by Dworkin et al. (1992, p. 7), "chronic pain conditions at different anatomical sites . . . may share common mechanisms of pain perception and appraisal, pain behavior, and social adaptation to chronic pain." Moreover, variation in experience is considered desirable for phenomenological research because it "enhances the opportunity for the thematic structure of the phenomenon to reveal itself" (Hawthorne, 1988, p. 11).

Ages of the participants ranged from 27 to 79 years. Most were white. Nine were female, and 4 were male. Of the participants, 10 were married, and the remainder were single and/or divorced. Duration of pain ranged from 7 months to 41 years. Back pain was the Number 1 type, although shoulder, arm, neck, hip, leg, jaw, and ear pain were also reported by various participants. Pain was present at multiple sites for many of them.

Procedure

In-depth, nondirective phenomenological interviews, lasting 1 to 2 hours, were conducted with each participant after informed consent was given. Participants were asked to describe what it is like for them to live with chronic pain. Following this initial question, the interviewer sought to elicit richer description and clarification of the narrative. Interviews were audiotaped and transcribed verbatim by a professional transcriptionist who signed a confidentiality pledge. Transcripts of the interviews were analyzed according to the procedure of Pollio et al. (1997), which includes independent examination of the text by the researcher (reading, reflecting, intuiting) and thematizing in an interdisciplinary phenomenology research group in which transcripts are read aloud and discussed: "The group functions in a critical, rather than consensual, capacity" (Pollio et al., 1997, p. 49). Any proffered interpretations must be supported by citation of specific lines of text. . . .

Findings

Chronic pain patients described their experiences as an individualized dialogic process between themselves and their painful condition. Their *Lebenswelt* (life world) was shrunken and their freedom greatly constricted. The pain set up a wall or barrier that separated them from other people. Pain dominated their consciousness, as shown in the following exemplars from the transcripts.

"You can't think about anything else, really." "Pain is king. Pain rules." "The pain just rides on your nerves." "Pain dominates what you can do." "Pain is a monster. All I can say is that it's tormenting." Pain was a formidable opponent with whom they fought daily: "You're drowning and you got that will to fight to get to shore . . . to live with chronic pain is a challenge every day." "I tried to outlast it. I tried to just tough it out. But it was boss." The dyadic nature of the relationship was succinctly captured as follows: "Now it's me and this pain. It's a thing. And you've just got to fight it continuously." Feelings ran the gamut from irritability, anger, helplessness, and frustration to profound depression, despair, and exhaustion. Several participants blamed themselves for causing the original injury. Fear was pervasive: fear of the unknown, further incapacitation, and becoming a burden to the family.

In the following sections, we turn to elucidation of the figural themes—that is, those that stand out most prominently against the existential grounds of body, other people, and time. Participants' narratives included little awareness of the external world, which will soon become evident to the reader.

The Altered, Recalcitrant Body. . . .

Invisibility of Pain

Despite the profound changes in their bodies, study participants ruefully acknowledged that the chronic pain was not readily apparent to other people. Chronic pain was invisible, a "secret disorder" with no outward manifestations. Because their bodies looked healthy in the eyes of others, they were accustomed to hostile glances when they disembarked from vehicles parked in spaces for the handicapped. Some longed for external manifestations of disability that could provide greater societal legitimacy: "You can't look at me and say, 'I guess she has rheumatoid arthritis.' You can't tell by looking." "It's so hard for people to understand if I say I'm in pain because they don't see it; I'm not in a wheelchair or walking with a cane." Ironically, a woman whose

> Qualitative researchers look for similarities in what the study participants say. These are common "figural themes," experiences that several of the participants related to the interviewer(s).

arm was in a sling—who conceivably might have welcomed the device as a badge of legitimacy— actually resented the attention it garnered: "I just want to wear a sign that says, 'Please don't ask.'"

Separation from Other People. . . .

Isolation

Isolation was thematic in all interviews. Dialogue took place between the study participants and their nonhuman tormentor, the pain, more so than with other human beings. Participants described their pain as imprisoning them. For example, they used terms such as locked off, roped off and caged off. Pain had somehow reset their interpersonal parameters, creating separation and distance from the world and other people, even family members. They felt that they no longer had much in common with others and no longer "fit in." Relationships in which they could be honest and authentic were few or nonexistent. Exemplars of the isolation theme included the following: "Pain separates you. It's really hard to be involved with people when you're in pain." "I feel like I'm on this little island all by myself." "My life is pulled in to where I have very little contact with anybody." "I am absolutely alone."

Trust and Mistrust of Physicians

The data indicated that when pain patients do make an effort to leave their solitary "island" to have contact with others, they are most likely to be keeping an appointment with a physician. Clearly, the most prominent others in narratives of pain patients, more significant than family members or friends, were physicians. Despite repeated experiences with doctors who were impersonal, unkind, or even cruel, participants could not abandon a fantasy that there was a caring doctor out there somewhere who could provide relief for them. Therefore, they were willing to entrust their bodies to the Magnetic Resonance Imaging (MRI) machines and scalpels again and again. But their fragile trust of physicians fluctuated, with considerable disillusionment and mistrust evident in some narratives, such as the following. "He didn't even want to listen to what I said. He just wrote out a prescription." "You wonder are they really trying to help or are they just trying to take the money?" "Some of them think females are just a bunch of walking complaints." "I still go to the library and check up on something a doctor has told me. Because I had lost a lot of trust [during the years before lupus was diagnosed]." "In every state we have moved to, I try to get a book telling me those doctors who have had some type of disciplinary action."

The author emphasizes the lack of support from health-care professionals. Recognition of the need for holistic support may help to change treatment.

Lack of Support

Only two chronic pain patients cited anyone to whom they could talk freely about their experience. One mentioned a supportive spouse and the other a sister, but the remainder of the sample did not describe any support persons. Exemplars of nonsupport, such as the following, were common in the data: "My wife wouldn't give me peace if I took a day off." "My ex [husband] couldn't understand." Nurses were virtually invisible in the narratives, a curious omission given the numerous contacts of the patients with both acute care facilities and doctors' offices. One individual spoke briefly about hospital nurses and their poor management of acute pain. Another made a vague statement of admiration for nurses and doctors but described no specific incidents or interactions. No participants mentioned nurses as part of their support system, and none of them were involved in nurse-led support groups.

Moments of Time, Existential Crisis, and Thoughts of Death

The chronicity of these patients' conditions obviously implies a disease process developing and continuing across a span of time. However, the unit of time that was most consequential to study participants was the moment, a diminutive unit but paradoxically also a lengthy, heavy one that does not correspond to customary notions of clock time. The moment contains not only the pain now but also the perceived possibility of an eternity of suffering, taking "pill after pill after pill." The pain was ever present: "I haven't had 2 days pain free in 6 years" "Constant, can't never get comfortable. Can't never rest. Can't do anything." "Wake up with it, go to bed with it, every time I move, something hurts." There is no assurance that the agony of this moment will end; the future is unfathomable. Time seems to stop. Life is on hold, its rhythms disrupted. One participant used the word limbo. Another wondered if he would "ever have a life again."

Hope and Hopelessness

The meaning of life itself was called into question by some study participants. As exemplified in the following transcript segments, participants were confronted with events that had radically revised their expectations: "I was just 25 years old when it happened. I didn't think anything like that could happen to me. . . . I'll probably never be able to carry a child." "What happened to me was quite existential. It made me very aware of my age, very aware of becoming less able, in the process of growing old. Becoming aware and accepting age and dying in all things." Strategies to maintain some hope were described in terms of "holding on" and "hanging on," but exacerbations of the painful condition often shattered tenuous hopes. A rheumatoid arthritis patient related, "I just got this area fixed and now I've got another [painful] area. Is this what it's going to be like forever for me?"

After a cyclical process of seeking the solution or cure for their problems, participants sometimes came to view treatment as futile. In a

The study participants related a fear of trying something new because hopes rise each time they try a different therapy. The continued disappointments may be worse than living with the pain.

world of highly touted medical miracles and dramatic organ transplantations, they expressed bitterness about the lack of a definitive solution to their own distress: "Sometimes I just want to quit taking everything 'cause it doesn't seem like anything's working." "After six surgeries, I am probably no better off than I was to start with." "We can go to the moon, but nobody can find something to change this."

Hopelessness and thoughts of death as liberating were revealed in some interviews. One participant expressed the feelings of many:

> Really don't fear death because one day I won't hurt. . . . On a day where you feel like things are hopeless, you wonder whether you want to go on . . . and whether the quality of your life is enough to keep plugging away.

Another admitted trying to imagine how his suicide could be made to look like an accident or a natural death. Another was acutely aware that a means of liberation from suffering was already available to him: "These pills are very tempting to take more than you're supposed to."

Only 3 participants mentioned any positive aspects of their chronic pain experience. One of these said, "Maybe there's a reason, maybe it's to slow me down [to] look around to see other people are in pain. I'm more and more interested and want to be involved with helping battered women."

Discussion

Here the author interprets her findings in light of other studies and emphasizes differences between the pain experiences and other chronic health concerns. The first paragraph is key in that it contrasts this study's findings with other, more "idealized," descriptions of chronic pain.

Most notably expressed in the powerful metaphors used by study participants, the essence of the chronic pain experience is unremitting torment by a force or monster that cannot be tamed. In contrast to popular pain management parlance, these patients say their pain cannot be managed. Data from this study call into question the idealized positive depiction of chronic illness that is prominent in contemporary literature. Thorne and Paterson (1998), having reviewed 15 years of qualitative research on chronic illness experiences, concluded that the early focus on themes of loss and burden had shifted by the mid-1990s to positive images of normality, courage, and self-transcendence. Patients were increasingly being depicted by researchers as strong, powerful, and competent. But few of my study participants with chronic pain perceived their position as one of strength or described any personal benefit of their suffering. The transformative elements within the chronic illness experience may have been overemphasized in the optimistic literature of the 1990s. On the other hand, there may be substantive differences between chronic pain and other chronic illnesses, precluding their comparison.

The grim, ongoing struggle with chronic pain is a very individual one ("Now it's me and the pain"), although the sufferer longs for a physician rescuer. Physicians are both trusted and mistrusted, with the pendulum swinging toward greater mistrust and alienation after repeated experiences of being unheard and unhealed. Not being listened to by doctors is a well-documented complaint of many types of patients but may be particularly galling to the pain patient. No electrocardiogram can reveal the pattern of the pain; only by talking can the patient describe his or her subjective sensations. But patients interviewed by Miller, Yanoshik, Crabtree, and Reymond (1994) all claimed that their physicians did not listen to them when they tried to describe pain and its impact on their daily lives. When the researchers interviewed the physicians, a different understanding of listening was discovered: It meant hearing words as diagnostic cues, not placing the words into the context of the patients' life world. This communication gap between physician and patient was the strongest theme in Miller et al.'s study and was alluded to by participants in this study as well. It logically follows that chronic pain patients begin to doubt that health professionals can help them. In one recent report, 78% of patients with chronic neuropathic pain resulting from breast cancer treatment declined an offer of free treatment in a pain center because they did not believe that treatment would alleviate the pain. Despite an average of 29 months of living with the pain and a significant decrease in quality of life, the women remained unconvinced that the pain center therapies were efficacious (Carpenter, Sloan, & Andrykowski, 1999).

> Participants' doubts about the effectiveness of treatment lead some to refuse free treatment, believing the treatment for pain would not help. This appeals to readers'—nurses'—sense of professional experience and compassion.

Friedemann and Smith (1997) reported intense family involvement in the lives of their sample of 30 chronic pain patients. Such intense involvement was not evident in this study. However, Friedemann and Smith's interviews were conducted for the specific purpose of obtaining descriptions of family functioning, and the interviews took place after participants had completed a questionnaire about their family's stability and growth. In phenomenological interviewing, if the respondent does not volunteer information, the researcher does not probe. Participants in this study seldom mentioned family members except to deplore their lack of understanding. They concealed their discomfort from family rather than seeking sympathy or assistance. These findings are divergent from literature about the reinforcing "secondary gain" (i.e., attention and solicitude) that chronic pain patients allegedly receive from significant others.

The need to hide pain, a prominent element of study participants' narratives, has been noted by other researchers (e.g., Hitchcock et al., 1994). The culture does not offer a "natural home" for these patients, leaving them on the "amorphous frontier of nonmembership" in society (Hilbert, 1984, p. 375). The concept of internalized stigma, which Phillips (1994) examined in AIDS patients, is perhaps germane to the chronic pain patient as well. Other literature contains concepts and metaphors that are comparable to themes of this study. Existential philosopher Camus once referred to illness as a convent. If one takes his metaphor to mean closed off from the world and deprived of worldly pleasures, it seems relevant to the chronic pain patient. Participants' narratives of pain are consistent with its portrayal by philosopher Hannah Arendt as "a borderline experience between life . . . and death" (as cited in Engelbart & Vrancken, 1984). If there is no one who understands and no place where one fits, is this not a kind of living death?

Findings of this study contribute to the phenomenological literature that explores the human body and its symbolic meanings. In contrast to healthy individuals' relative lack of consciousness of their bodies, the body is the main focus of the chronic pain patient's existence: "Bodily events become the events of the day" (Merleau-Ponty, 1945/1962, p. 85). The life world, in fact, is virtually restricted to the patient's body, as described by Plugge (1967). Themes found in this study may be contrasted with a previous phenomenological study of 16 healthy adults who were interviewed about experiences when they were aware of their bodies (MacGillivray, 1986). One of the three figural themes of the lived body in that study was engagement in the world (i.e., the body as vitality and activity). Vitality involved feeling highly energetic and fully in control of the body while engaging in an absorbing project. For example, a runner spoke of the good feelings of stretching his legs and taking in breaths as he ran. Perhaps because volitional control over the body was largely absent in this sample of pain patients, there were no similar anecdotes of body as an instrument of mastery over the world. Participants' perceptions of their bodies were sharply discrepant from the "socially engaged, skilled bodies" described by Benner (1994, p. xvii) but consistent with MacGillivray's (1986) theme of body as object: "The body 'owns' the person, demands attention, and calls the person back from the world and projects" (as cited in Pollio et al., 1997, p. 79). The chronic pain patient dwells in the world of "I cannot" instead of the world of "I can," like the cancer patients who were studied by Kesselring (1990).

These findings can assist health care providers to understand the chronic pain patient and provide more empathic, supportive care. The psychological pain of being disbelieved and stigmatized is surely as devastating to these patients as their bodily pain, perhaps more so. Therapeutic benefit was obtained by some of the study participants simply by talking to a respectful listener. As one put it, "I believe there has been a release here." Research is needed on nursing interventions that could help chronic patients cope and find meaning in their suffering.

The author summarizes the world in which those with chronic pain live, a world of "I cannot." She has indeed "given a voice to the voiceless" and provided insight for health-care professionals into the needs of those whom they serve.

Note

I am grateful to a number of individuals who assisted with the literature review, interviews, and data analysis for this project: Vicki Slater, Linda Hafley, Karen Heeks, Tracey Martin, Rebecca Ledbetter, Lisa Fleming, and Pam Watson. Linda Dalton transcribed all of the audio-tapes with commendable accuracy. The contributions of my mentor Howard Pollio and the University of Tennessee Phenomenology Research Group have been invaluable. Earlier versions of this article were presented at meetings of the Southern Nursing Research Society, the American Nurses' Association, and the European Health Psychology Society.

References

Ackerman, M., & Stevens, M. (1989). Acute and chronic pain: Pain dimensions and psychological status. *Journal of Clinical Psychology, 45,* 223–228.

Bates, M., & Rankin-Hill, L. (1994). Control, culture, and chronic pain. *Social Science and Medicine, 39,* 629–645.

Benner, P. (1994). Introduction. In P. Benner (Ed.), *Interpretive phenomenology: Embodiment, caring, and ethics in health and illness* (pp. xiii-xxvii). Thousand Oaks, CA: Sage.

Bowman, J. M. (1991). The meaning of chronic low back pain. *American Association of Occupational Health Nursing Journal, 39,* 381–384.

Buytendijk, F. J. J. (1962). *Pain: Its modes and functions.* Chicago: University of Chicago Press.

Carpenter, J. S., Sloan, P., & Andrykowski, M. (1999). Anticipating barriers in pain-management research. *Image: Journal of Nursing Scholarship, 31,* 158.

Covington, E. C. (1991). Depression and chronic fatigue in the patient with chronic pain. *Primary Care, 18,* 341–358.

Dworkin, S. F., Von Korff, M. R., & LeResche, L. (1992). Epidemiological studies of chronic pain: A dynamic-ecologic perspective. *Annals of Behavioral Medicine, 14,* 3–11.

Edwards, R. B. (1989). Pain management and the values of health care providers. In C. S. Hill Jr. & W. S. Fields (Eds.), *Advances in pain research and therapy* (Vol. 11, pp. 101–112). New York: Raven.

Elton, N., Hanna, M., & Treasure, J. (1994). Coping with pain: Some patients suffer more. *British Journal of Psychiatry, 165,* 802–807.

Engelbart, H. J., & Vrancken, M. A. (1984). Chronic pain from the perspective of health: A view based on systems theory. *Social Science and Medicine, 12,* 1383–1392.

Faberhaugh, S. Y., & Strauss, A. (1977). *Politics of pain management.* Reading, MA: Addison-Wesley.

Friedemann, M. L., & Smith, A. A. (1997). A triangulation approach to testing a family instrument. *Western Journal of Nursing Research, 19,* 364–378.

Giorgi, A. (1985). Sketch of a psychological phenomenological method. In A. Giorgi (Ed.), *Phenomenology and psychological research.* Pittsburgh: Duquesne University Press.

Hawthorne, M. C. (1988). The human experience of reparation: A phenomenological investigation. Unpublished doctoral dissertation, University of Tennessee, Knoxville.

Henriksson, C. M. (1995). Living with continuous muscular pain: Patient perspectives. *Scandinavian Journal of Caring Science, 9,* 77–86.

Hilbert, R. (1984). The acultural dimension of chronic pain: Flawed reality construction and the problem of meaning. *Social Problems, 31,* 365–378.

Hitchcock, L., Ferrell, B., & McCaffery, M. (1994). The experience of chronic non-malignant pain. *Journal of Pain and Symptom Management, 9,* 312–318.

Holm, K., Cohen, F., Dudas, S., Medema, P. G., & Allen, B. L. (1989). Effect of personal pain experience on pain assessment. *Image: Journal of Nursing Scholarship,* 21(2), 72–75.

Husserl, E. (1931). *Ideas: General introduction to pure phenomenology* (W. Gibson, Trans.). New York: Collier Books. (Original work published 1913)

Hutchinson, S., Wilson, M., & Wilson, H. (1994). Benefits of participating in research interviews. *Image: Journal of Nursing Scholarship,* 26, 161–164.

Jensen, M. P., Turner, J. A., Romano, J. M., & Karoly, P. (1991). Coping with chronic pain: A critical review of the literature. *Pain,* 47, 249–283.

Kangas, S., Warren, N. A., & Byrne, M. M. (1998). Metaphor: The language of nursing researchers. *Nursing Research,* 47, 190–193.

Kesselring, A. (1990). The experienced body: When taken for-grantedness fails. Unpublished doctoral dissertation. University of California, San Francisco.

Latham, J., & Davis, B. D. (1994). The socioeconomic impact of chronic pain. *Disability and Rehabilitation,* 16, 39–44.

MacGillivray, W. (1986). Ambiguity and embodiment: A phenomenological analysis of the lived body. Unpublished doctoral dissertation, University of Tennessee, Knoxville.

Matas, K. E. (1997). Human patterning and chronic pain. *Nursing Science Quarterly,* 10(2), 88–95.

McCaffery, M., & Thorpe, D. (1989) Differences in perception of pain and the development of adversarial relationships among health care providers. In C. S. Hill & W. S. Fields (Eds.), *Advances in pain research and therapy*, 11, 113–125. New York: Raven.

Merleau-Ponty, M. (1962). *The phenomenology of perception* (C. Smith, Trans.). Boston: Routledge Kegan Paul. (Original work published 1945).

Miller, W. L., Yanoshik, M. K., Crabtree, B. F., & Reymond, W. K. (1994). Patients, family physicians, and pain: Visions from interview narratives. *Clinical Research and Methods,* 26, 179–184.

Munhall, P. L. (1994). *Revisioning phenomenology: Nursing and health science research.* New York: National League for Nursing Press.

National Institutes of Health Technology Assessment Conference Statement. (1995, October 16–18). Integration of behavioral and relaxation approaches into the treatment of chronic pain and insomnia. Bethesda, MD: U.S. Department of Health and Human Services.

North American Nursing Diagnosis Association. (1996). Nursing diagnoses: Definitions and classification 1997–1998. Philadelphia.

Phillips, K. (1994). Testing biobehavioral adaptation in persons living with AIDS using Roy's theory of the person as an adaptive system. Unpublished doctoral dissertation, University of Tennessee, Knoxville.

Plugge, H. (1967). *Der Mensch and sein Leib* (The person and human life). Tubingen: Max Neimeyer.

Pollio, H. R., Henley, T. B., & Thompson, C. J. (1997). *The phenomenology of everyday life.* New York: Cambridge University Press.

Price, B. (1996). Illness careers: The chronic illness experience. *Journal of Advanced Nursing,* 24, 275–279.

Seers, K., & Friedli, K. (1996). The patients' experiences of their chronic non-malignant pain. *Journal of Advanced Nursing,* 24, 1160–1168.

Skevington, S. M. (1983). Chronic pain and depression: Universal or personal helplessness? *Pain,* 15, 309–317.

Taylor, A. G., Skelton, J. A., & Butcher, J. (1984). Duration of pain condition and physical pathology as determinants of nurses' assessments of patients in pain. *Nursing Research,* 33, 4–8.

Thompson, C. J., Locander, W. B., & Pollio, H. R. (1989). Putting consumer experience back into consumer research: The philosophy and method of existential phenomenology. *Journal of Consumer Research,* 16, 133–146.

Thorne, S., & Paterson, B. (1998). Shifting images of chronic illness. *Image: Journal of Nursing Scholarship,* 30, 173–178.

Reading Responses

1. In her article Thomas notes, "Research shows that nurses who have personally borne intense pain are more sympathetic to the patient in pain." Do you believe that readers will be more sympathetic to people with chronic pain after they read the personal experiences Thomas includes in her article? Will her descriptions be enough to change readers' attitudes? Why or why not?

2. Thomas cites other scholarly research as well as the results of her own study. Analyze her use of other research. When does she refer to other studies? What purpose does this research serve in Thomas's essay? What is the relationship between this research and Thomas's own research?

3. What does Thomas want nurses to do differently after reading her article? That is, what is her purpose for writing? Where does she indicate that most clearly? How will the personal experiences in the essay persuade nurses to act differently?

NOTES ON GRAMMAR, STYLE, AND RHETORIC:
APPEALS TO THE GENERAL AND PARTICULAR

Many writing researchers believe that a good way to characterize texts involves determining to what extent those texts appeal to the general or the particular. Taking this approach to "A Phenomenologic Study of Chronic Pain" by Sandra P. Thomas shows it to be an interesting combination of appeals to both the general and the particular.

What do the terms *general* and *particular* mean? To answer this question, it helps to imagine a scale, with the extraordinarily general on one end and the uniquely particular on the other. As you approach the general side of the scale, you focus on generalized people, places, objects, or phenomena. For example, a writer might focus on "thousands of adults suffering from long-term pain arising from multiple causes." As you approach the particular end of the scale, you come ever closer to focusing on one individual person, place, object, or phenomenon. For example, a writer might focus on the stab of arthritic pain Aunt Margaret feels every morning in her left shoulder.

In "A Phenomenologic Study," Thomas focuses on the general by using three closely related kinds of noun phrases. First, she uses many phrases that refer to large groups. Thus we read about "nurses," "study participants," "patients and caregivers," and "men and women who live daily with chronic pain." Second, she uses phrases that refer to types; that is, a singular term represents many individuals or objects of a certain type: "the chronic low back pain patient," "the health care provider," and even "the human body." A closely related kind of phrase refers to characteristics and experiences that many of the subjects in her study have in common: "Isolation," "the chronic pain experience," and "the profound suffering of these patients, which is often psychological and spiritual, not just physical"

(187). All three of these kinds of phrases can appear in a single sentence. For example, in the following sentence, we first find a reference to a generalized experience, then a reference to a group, and finally a reference to a type: "*Therapeutic benefit* was obtained by some of the *study participants* simply by talking to *a respectful listener*" (195, italics added).

Such appeals are accompanied by numerous appeals to the particular. For example, the report includes many exact quotations from individuals. One person says, "I feel like I'm on this little island all by myself" (191). Another complains that "After six surgeries, I am probably no better off than I was to start with" (193). We even learn about some of the patients' relatives, in one case reading about "a supportive spouse" (191).

Sometimes we encounter appeals to both the very general and the uniquely particular in the same sentence. The following example refers to a generalized experience (the "grim, ongoing struggle") and to types ("the sufferer" and "a physician rescuer"), but we also find a quotation from an individual: "The grim, ongoing struggle with chronic pain is a very individual one ('Now it's me and the pain'), although the sufferer longs for a physician rescuer" (193). Further, sometimes we find both kinds of appeals appearing within larger sections of the report. For example, in the first three paragraphs under "Findings," we first see appeals to the general with phrases such as "Chronic pain patients," "their painful condition," and "their freedom" (190). Then we encounter several exact quotations. And after the quotations we move on to generalized traits such as "irritability, anger, helplessness, and frustration . . ." (190). The pattern of appeals in these three paragraphs is the same as the pattern in the report as a whole—first come appeals to the general, then appeals to the particular, and finally some additional appeals to the general.

Why might Thomas have followed this pattern? The answer relates to her overall purpose, which she explains as follows: "I believe that nurses have a moral obligation to provide more skillful psychosocial care to these patients [with chronic pain]" (188). She wants to help nurses see how to "help chronic patients cope and find meaning in their suffering" (195). In other words, she is proposing significant changes in nursing practice. And she lays out the background to and rationale for that proposal with all the appeals to the general. But she also apparently knows that people do not accept significant changes—in medical care and most other endeavors—quickly and easily. If important aspects of nursing practice are to be changed, then nurses themselves will have to feel a sense of urgency about them. As Thomas puts it, nurses will have to get "inside the experience" (188) of long-term pain; they will have to imagine feeling such pain themselves. To help them do that, she includes all the appeals to the particular.

But there is a little more to this story. A respected writer once said that people respond to generalities with their reason and to particulars with their emotions. If he was largely correct, then we can understand even better what Thomas is doing. She uses the appeals to the general to get readers to understand and consider her proposals for changes in nursing. And she uses the appeals to the particular to get readers to feel how desperately each patient in pain needs nurses to care for him or her more sensitively. For the agenda that Thomas is pursuing, her combination of appeals works well.

In Your Own Writing . . .

• Consider how genre and field affect your use of general and particular appeals. Some genres—memoir, for example—do not include a great many appeals to the general. Some fields, such as economic theory, do not include a great many appeals to the uniquely particular.

- When you want readers not just to think about but also to act on a proposal, use appeals to the general to get them thinking and evaluating, but also include appeals to the particular to grip their emotions and move them to action.
- Use general appeals as a way to introduce particular appeals and to follow up appeals to the particular.

STUDENT WRITING

INTRODUCTION

by Curt Gritters, nursing major

The two pieces of student writing in this section each represent a different perspective on nursing.

1. *Care Plan Assignment.* The objective of the assignment was to gather information regarding various aspects of the patient's history and current condition. I then had to use the information to establish goals for this patient's recovery and formulate a plan of care to achieve those goals (see page 203–04 of the care plan). The result was to be a list-style summary of the patient's situation and a fairly precise direction for providing care.

The Content. I had to record both objective and subjective data. Not only do nursing students need to know patients' medical or surgical diagnoses, but they must also consider family concerns or barriers to healing and how the client will take care of himself and return to his usual lifestyle. The care plan shown here describes an 82-year-old man whose recovery from open-heart surgery was complicated by fluid accumulation in his lungs ("pleural effusion"). Because his blood was still "too thin" from anticoagulants, a procedure to remove some of that fluid was postponed (to prevent serious bleeding). Meanwhile, an infection was being treated with antibiotics.

Writing a Care Plan. To write effective care plans, I could not cut and paste portions of interest from the patient's medical record—an easy way out. Many areas in the assignment required a small amount of information, but the patient's medical record was hundreds of pages long. I knew that summarizing in a descriptive yet concise manner was going to be the key. After compiling the lab results, for example, I could write down the ones that were especially important in his current situation.

However, not all of the information I needed was stated explicitly in the medical record. Writing as a nurse required me both to borrow some information gleaned by others and to retrieve much of the subjective or personal data on my own.

2. *Reflection Paper Assignment.* The assignment asked me to step back from the medical record and even from the patient, to analyze legal and ethical concerns, and to make suggestions for improved personalized care.

The Content. A fellow student wrote the reflection paper reproduced here. Her experiences in the operating room (OR) and critical care settings are surprisingly typical. Megan watched an "everyday" (in terms of the OR) back surgery and an "everyday" brain injury case. She wrote about what she saw, identified core virtues of nursing that were either utilized or violated, and suggested improvements.

Writing a Reflection Paper.   A reflection paper starts with general observations and ends by giving specific suggestions for changing the patient's care. The nursing student must be descriptive regarding the situation he or she experienced, analytical and insightful regarding the broader issues involved, and concise in making practical suggestions for improvement in patient care. Writing reflection papers is another way of developing the critical thinking process of a nurse—a way in which nurses examine ethical issues in light of their own practice related to patient's rights (dignity, autonomy, consent, etc.) and the treatment of patients as unique human beings.

Learning to Write in Nursing.   In general nursing writing is . . .

- concise, and writing concisely requires a precise summary. For example, when explaining a heart problem that is directly related to the lungs and kidneys, the nurse must summarize concisely the heart problem, then move on to explain its involvement with the lungs and kidneys. Staying focused and not diverging into unnecessary details is vital when every second counts.

- both technically objective and descriptively subjective: the discipline uniquely stakes claims both in health-care science and patients' individual well-being.

- adaptive because patient conditions are always changing. When conditions change, goals change, and the written records and plans must change as well.

Consequently, good writing assignments for nursing students require them to put critical thinking processes onto paper. Though I realize that much of what I write as a nursing student is not what I will write as a nurse, I know that everything I do on paper now must be done in practice as a nurse. Nurses do not, for example, regularly write reflection papers on their practice, but the thought process that the reflection paper simulates must be continuous in nursing practice.

Nursing writing is a fascinating interplay between professional and personal writing styles. Care plans take the objective, scientific technicalities of health care and apply them to personalize care. Reflection papers complete the cycle by transforming personal and subjective ideas into professional practice—which is again made personal in individual care plans.

Nursing Care Plan
Curt Gritters

Nursing Care Plan: Patient Data

Your Name _____ Date of Care _____

Patient Initials _____ Room Number _____ Gender _____ Age _____

Admission Date _____ Admitting Diagnosis _____

Medical/Surgical Diagnosis (current reason for hospitalization and other potential compounding problems) 1. Cellulitis of L pleural effusion (empyema) 2. . . .	**Family/Significant Other Concerns** 1. Concern re husband's infection 2. . . .
Other health concerns/past medical/surgical history/allergies: MSO$_4$, ASA, CAD, MI in 82, A-fib, L, TKA, ACF, angioplasty × 2	**Financial situation** retired, financially stable, excellent insurance, no concerns
Barriers/cultural considerations (e.g., deaf, indigent, illiterate, etc.) None apparent	**Activity level (why?)** BR c BRP: rest so body can fight infection
Lab tests/diagnostic imaging/procedures (list those completed during the two days you are on the unit and why) Hgb: 10.4, BUN: 32 (azotemia), BNP: 334 (not pathognomic for CHF), INR: 2.8...	
Medications (list those received by the patient during the days you are on the unit and why) 1. Nesteritide: vasodilator/diuretic for acutely decompensated CHF (watch SBP > 90 mmHg and HR) 2. Cefazolin: antibiotic for cellulitis (watch interaction with loop diuretics (Lasix), I/O, BMqd?) . . . 3–14. . . .	

All patient care plans are made in light of the specific information about a patient. An actual data form would contain more technical information than what you see here; this just gives you examples of the contents.

The patient came into the unit after heart surgery and developed some problems that are common to those who undergo heart surgery—congestion in the lungs which makes breathing difficult; the difficulty breathing causes low levels of oxygen to be delivered to the tissues which heal the surgical wound and fight infections. Patients are routinely given drugs to prevent clots from forming, which can lead to strokes or heart attacks. Unfortunately, the drugs also cause the patient to bleed more easily. The patient described in this care plan was being watched for all of the complications that can develop after an extensive surgery such as a CABG (open-heart surgery).

Nursing Care Plan
Current Plan of Care

What is the plan of care and why? _____
Maintain BP while waiting for INR [a blood test
to indicate how long it will take for blood to clot]
to determine whether fluid might be drained
from the lung. Antibiotics until infection is
relieved.

What potential barriers with compliance or
healing do you foresee after discharge?
Compliance will be okay, but obesity, diabetes,
high blood pressure and cholesterol will impair
healing.

What are the most difficult issues/problems
for this patient right now? _____
1. Cellulitis of sternal incision [an infection of
   the chest incision for his heart surgery]
2. Cellulitis of L pleural effusion [lung
   congestion]
3. DOE

How will this data influence your care of this
patient (including teaching)? How will you
approach this patient/family? _____
Pt [patient] very teachable, so encourage
continuing weight loss, watching his diabetes
(diet) → include wife with this teaching,
encourage deep breathing techniques (to flow)
to build R lung and compensate for L; encourage
rest until infection is overcome; praise his
quitting of smoking; good established
relationship and conversational style willl
facilitate encouragement/recommendations.

Nursing Diagnoses (list and prioritize)

1. Impaired gas exchange related to fluid accumulation in lungs as evidenced by ↓'d [decreased]
   lung sounds throughout and dullness upon percussion [indicates fluid in chest]

3. Infection risk for (further) related to inadequate primary defenses (broken skin) chronic disease
   (diabetes, etc), invasive procedures. [surgery]

2. Ineffective breathing pattern related to decreased lung expansion as evidenced by dyspnea
   [difficulty breathing] and lung field auscultation. [lung sounds]

4. Impaired skin integrity related to infection of skin/tissues.

   Risk for imbalanced fluid volume.

Current Plan of Care, continued

Discussion and Reflection on:

Textbook Picture of Patient Diagnosis	Actual Patient Picture/Condition
Discuss the patient's illness/injury including • pathophysiology • common signs/symptoms • expected diagnostic tests and results • usual medical/surgical treatments • usual nursing diagnoses and interventions • reference(s)	Discuss your patient's actual condition including • assessment findings (related to the diagnosis) • diagnostic tests and results • medical/surgical treatments • nursing interventions

Pt has L pleural effusion (empyema). [infected fluid in the lung] This is an accumulation of fluid and pus in the pleural space caused by an infection of surgical wounds of the chest. Often this is manifest by progressive difficulty breathing and decreased mov't of the chest wall on affected side. Dullness to percussion, ↓'d breath sounds over the affected area, fever, night sweats, cough, weight loss.

Diagnostic tests and results: chest x-ray show if effusion is > 250 mL; diagnostic thoracentesis to determine cause/type of fluid; therapeutic thoracentesis to relieve pressure build up from fluid (inserting needle into the lung to drain fluid.)

Tx: therapeutic thoracentesis; drain pleural space via therapeutic thoracentesis or close thoracotomy tube, appropriate antibiotic treatment.

Nursing diagnosis: Impaired gas exchange, ineffective breathing pattern, anxiety.

References: Lewis, Ackley

Pt empyema may be complicated further by his high blood pressure which may force fluid into this space rather than out. Pt did have ↓'d breath sounds over his entire L lung. Pt also had difficulty breathing and cough and dullness upon percussion [tapping on the chest] to L lung field. However he was not running a fever and was actually gaining weight.

A thoracentesis (diagnostic but esp. therapeutic was on hold until his INR dropped into range (so the high Coumadin [a blood thinner] levels did not make him bleed uncontrollably)

Pt was on appropriate antibiotic therapy

Appropriate nursing diagnosis for RK included:
   Impaired gas exchange
   Ineffective breathing pattern
   Excess fluid volume
   Potential for (further) infection

What is the correlation between the textbook pictures and your patient's actual condition? Why?

I think it fits rather well considering the thoracentesis was on hold for his INR to drop.

This part of the "plan of care" is critical because writing about the patient problems allows us to set goals for his recovery and for the health team to evaluate if those goals are met.

Nursing Care Plan
Nursing Process/Teaching Plan

Nursing Diagnosis	Plan/Outcome Criteria	Implementation	Rationale	Evaluation of Outcomes
Impaired gas exchange Related to pleural effusion as evidenced by dyspnea [difficulty breathing], irritability, somnolence [excessive sleepiness], tachycardia.	1. PaO_2 and $PaCO_2$ are maintained within patient's normal range by 9/17. [These indicate the patient's ability to exchange oxygen and carbon dioxide] 2. Normal breath sounds are maintained, and Pt remains free of signs of respiratory distress by 9/18.	1. Monitor SaO_2 for and administer as ordered to SaO_2 levels. 2. Monitor apical radial HR [heart rate] for irregular rhythm, tachy- [too fast], and brachycardia [too slow]. 3. Teach and encourage pursed-lip breathing to improve gas exchange. 4. Position Pt HOB [head of the bed], incline 30 degrees as tolerated.	1. SaO_2 under 90% indicates oxygenation problem. 2. Hypoxia may cause cardiac arrhythmias. 3. Pursed-lip breathing results in increased use of intercostal [between ribs] muscles, increased exercise performance, and ability of Pt to self-manage. 4. Semi-Fowler's [sitting] position allows lung expansion.	1. PaO_2 and $PaCO_2$ in normal range as of 9/17. "Goal met." 2. Breath sounds were improving on left side, but Pt was still experiencing DOE [difficulty breathing with activity]. "Goal partially met."

This plan teaches nursing students various elements that must become normal processes for planning and carrying out patient care.

Teaching—and encouraging—self-care is an important part of a care plan.

The numbers in this chart refer to the four "nursing diagnoses" listed at the bottom of the first page of the "Current Plan of Care."

Reflection Paper: Peri-Operative and Critical Care Experiences

Megan Nyenhuis

the time before and during surgery, and in the recovery room

removal of tissue pressing on nerves in the spine

Nursing students are asked to describe how they see the nurse providing personal as well as technical aspects of care. Reflecting and writing are good ways to organize thoughts and impressions to evaluate them.

Student nurses are taught that an important principle of nursing is patient advocacy. Reflection papers allowed a forum to "recognize reality, search for solutions, and try to transform."

This past week I had the opportunity to have my peri-operative and critical care experiences. During both of these experiences I was able to observe the role of the nurse and identify some ethical issues that exist and virtues necessary in that setting. During my peri-operative experience, I followed a 67-year-old woman through her surgical experience. I first saw her in pre-op where she was with her family, waiting to be taken back to surgery. I then watched her surgery, a lumbar laminectomy. I admit that I did not really enjoy watching the surgery and hearing the surgeon break through some of the bone in her spine, but I made it through and so did my patient. I then followed her into the recovery room where she woke up from the anesthesia, and finally, was transferred to a medical-surgical floor.

This experience allowed me to somewhat understand what patients go through during their surgical experience. It also allowed me to see what the role of the peri-operative nurse is. I saw the pre-op nurse being an educator, communicator, advocator, and comforter. She explained what would happen to the patient, spoke with and listened to the patient to decrease the patient's anxiety, advocated for the patient by making sure everything was in order for the surgery and making sure everything ran smoothly, and comforted the patient by reassuring her and letting her know someone would be with her at all times. The nurse served as advocate in the operating room by being the one to stop the surgeon from cracking jokes about the patient when the patient was starting to wake up.

I was also able to observe an ethical issue in the operating room. After my patient was unconscious from the anesthesia, they moved her into position for the surgery (positioned her on her stomach). She was a bigger lady, so moving her was not the easiest task. However, they really gave little attention to being careful and gentle with the patient. They just flipped her over and pushed her into the right position. Later in the surgery when the patient was just starting to come to, the surgeon make some joke about the patient. I thought that these things were not appropriate actions in the operating room. Just because a patient is unconscious does not mean that the patient should be treated any differently.

Some basic virtues necessary for peri-operative nursing became evident to me as well. The ones that seem most important are courage, empathy, and compassion. Courage is necessary to confront co-workers who are not treating the patient like they should be treated as in the situation described above. Empathy is necessary because many nurses cannot understand what it is like to undergo surgery. The nurse must listen carefully and use therapeutic communication to show that she is trying to understand and that she truly cares for the patient. Compassion is necessary because surgery is a scary thing, and patients need to know that they are cared about and that someone is looking out for them and putting their needs first.

During my critical care experience in the surgical unit, I observed a nurse who was caring for a 64-year-old man who had suffered a traumatic brain injury from a 10–15 feet fall onto cement. He had suffered a left temporal subdural hematoma, rib fractures, left atelectasis, and a mediastinal hematoma. He was unconscious and showed response to very strong stimulus on his arms only. This patient had made little progress since his admission, and doctors were not too hopeful about his prognosis.

> A subdural hematoma is a blood clot on the brain.

> Atelectasis is lung congestion.

> A mediastinal hematoma is a collection of blood around the area of the heart.

An ethical issue was evident during this experience as well. The wife of this patient was understandably very upset and teary-eyed. She came to visit her husband and said things to the nurse like, "When will he wake up? It might take a few weeks, right?" The nurse had told me previously that this patient's prognosis was very poor. However, she felt like it was not her place to give a prognosis especially since the prognosis was still somewhat unknown. But she told me that she also did not want to give false hope to this wife. This situation puts the nurse in a difficult position because she might either overstep her bounds and give the patient's prognosis or give false hope which could be devastating to the family. I thought that this nurse handled the situation well by hugging the wife and reassuring her that they were doing everything they could for the patient.

Virtues that seem especially important in the critical care setting are compassion and empathy. Even if the nurse cannot understand what the patient and family are going through, the nurse can listen and comfort the patient and family and show them that they are cared about.

Reading Responses

1. In reflecting on her experiences shadowing a nurse, Megan Nyenhuis focuses on the interactions that the nurses had with their patients. She does not record the times that the nurses performed clinical tasks like administering medication or recording data. Do you think some nurses would object to this focus? On what grounds? How does Megan's purpose for writing affect the personal experiences she includes in her paper?

2. If you were experiencing severe pain, how important would a nurse's concern be to you? What would be the best way for a nurse to express concern for you?

3. Consider the information that Gritters includes on the patient data sheet. Where does he include emotional or social information? What strategies does he use in writing that must be both technical and abbreviated to showcase the humanness of his patient?

PUBLIC WRITING

INTRODUCTION

Tilda Shalof is a nurse in an intensive care unit in Toronto. She's written two other popular books on being a nurse, including the best-seller, *A Nurse's Story*. In *Camp Nurse*, excerpted here, Shalof tells about several years of nursing at summer camps that her children attended. During those summers she had to respond to a more mixed bag of medical cases than she ever did in the ICU—broken bones, bug bites, a hand almost severed by a meat slicer, self-mutilation, and homesickness. The selection reprinted here recounts the story of one girl—for whom the medical diagnosis and recommendations proved especially challenging.

In the course of the story, Shalof confirms a nurse's need for expertise. In a part of her story not included here, Shalof reports advice that another health-care specialist once gave her: "You only see what you know." In other words, without the training that teaches nurses to know symptoms, they couldn't recognize symptoms *as* symptoms. Shalof's writing also shows a nurse's need for empathy, for professional consultation, and finally, for recognition that humans can sometimes be too complicated to fix.

Camp Nurse: My Adventures at Summer Camp

Tilda Shalof

Kaplan Publishing, New York, 2010

"I sound like a seal," I heard a girl say.

I was in the midst of giving out the evening meds when I heard a strange sound. It was coming from Naomi, an always-smiling, very popular fourteen-year-old who'd never come to the Health Centre for anything before but was now sitting in the waiting room, surrounded by a group of friends while she had fits of coughing. In between bouts of a high-pitched, insistent, squeaky coughing spell, she joked around and giggled. If this had been the ICU and a patient suddenly started coughing like that, I would have placed an oximeter on her finger (an instrument we used to measure a patient's oxygen concentration). Had she been a patient in the ICU, the sudden onset of a harsh cough like this would have garnered her a stat chest x-ray and maybe even a bronchoscopy, which involved a tube placed down into her trachea and lungs, but here, that wasn't necessary—at least not yet. Even without an oximeter, just looking at Naomi's rosy complexion and relaxed manner, I was fairly certain her oxygenation was normal.

I went out into the waiting room. Her friends were joking around with her, making her laugh. "This is not a party," I said, ushering them out.

"I can't breathe!" Naomi said, waving goodbye to her friends. I brought her into the examining room and listened to her chest and heard adequate and equal air entry on both sides, but she was breathing rapidly. "I can't swallow and my chest hurts." Her hands shook. "Is this a heart attack?" Off and on she gave that strange-sounding cough.

"No," I reassured her. "Probably your chest is sore from coughing so much."

Louise [another nurse] examined her thoroughly and then we went aside to speak privately. "I think it's a panic attack," she said. "You were right to throw out the friends. We want to make sure there's no acting up for an audiences' attention. For now, let's try giving her a small dose of sedation."

I gave Naomi a tiny pill under her tongue and let that take effect. After about twenty minutes, we checked on her. She's fallen asleep, and while she slept there was no cough, shakiness or fast breathing. She must have sensed we were standing at the foot of her bed because she startled awake. As soon as she did, the cough and rapid breathing started up again. "I feel like I'm going to pass out," she yelled. I stopped in my tracks. *Someone about to pass out does not have the strength to yell. Someone about to lose consciousness is too weak to speak.*

"My heart is racing," she said, trembling. "It's flip-flopping all around!" Her hands shook violently. She clutched at her chest and took big gulps of air. "I can't breathe."

Her strange cough seemed to be gone but her pulse was racing at 120 beats [normal is 60–80 per minute] per minute and her respiratory rate was also fast at forty-five breaths a minute. I gave her a paper bag to breathe into, to try to retain the carbon dioxide she was losing by hyperventilating.

"My chest hurts," she cried. "I'm going to pass out." Before we could deal with one problem, Naomi had moved on to the next. "The room is spinning. I'm going to faint!" she shouted. I took her blood pressure and it was a robust and normal 132 over 80.

Someone about to faint would have low blood pressure, I thought.

"I feel like I'm losing control of myself," Naomi said. But her words sounded false, like she was repeating lines she'd learned.

"I'm sure it must feel that way," I said quietly. I felt sympathy for her because I could see she genuinely felt upset.

"My feet are numb! They're tingling. I can't feel my feet. They're paralyzed." She suddenly closed her eyes and lay there motionless.

"Naomi?" Look at me! Open your eye," I told her, feeling slightly alarmed.

"I think I just blacked out there for a moment," she said weakly.

But she hadn't lost consciousness. She had been awake and, I was fairly confident, completely aware of everything she was doing. None of this was adding up. I found myself in the situation I've always hated: suspecting a patient was "faking it." It was an especially uncomfortable feeling to doubt a child. I knew Louise was also looking for something deeper by her line of questioning.

"Is something bothering you, Naomi? Are you homesick?

Naomi looked at her fiercely. "I love camp. I've never been homesick, not even for a minute."

"Because, if you are," Louise continued, "that can bring on these kinds of feelings and they can be really scary when you're away from home and missing your family."

"I live for camp." She turned away from us.

Louise and I spoke privately. "I can't find anything wrong," Louise said. "I think it's pure anxiety and nothing physically abnormal, especially since her memory is intact and she can describe her symptoms perfectly . . ." Louise's voice trailed off and I caught her drift: after a true faint, a patient can't recall events immediately prior to losing consciousness. "Let's give her another dose of sedation and watch her closely. If she worsens we'll take her to the hospital," she said, and went to call Naomi's parents.

Just then, Naomi's brother Lorne, an older camper, arrived. He rushed over to her, sat at the edge of her bed, scooped her up into his arms and held her tight. As she clung to him, their two heads of dark, curly hair mixed together like a huge, luxurious wig. . . .

The next morning, Alice told me it had been a quiet night. Naomi had slept and was now smiling and making light of what had happened, even apologizing for worrying us. She was dressed and eager to return to her cabin. Louise examined her and cleared her to return to her cabin. We wrote it off as a weird inexplicable one-off episode and since she was now well and happy again we didn't give it another thought . . . (pp. 236–39).

Late one evening a few days later, I was sitting in my room reading, when a buzz and crackle came over the walkie-talkie. "Is the nurse there?" a counsellor's voice cried out. "Someone's having a seizure!" . . .

When I got [to the cabin] I found Naomi, lying stiffly on the floor beside her bed, her friends and counsellors around her. I knelt down beside her. "Where are you?" I asked. Her eyes were open and I could tell she saw me but she didn't answer. This wasn't a seizure, but something was definitely wrong. "What's your name?" I asked her.

"It's Naomi," someone said. I explained I needed Naomi to answer for herself, because I was testing her level of consciousness, to see how her brain was working.

"What made you think she was having a seizure?" I asked the counselor.

"That's what Naomi told me."

But from what the counsellor described of what she herself had witnessed, Naomi hadn't had convulsions. She was not now in a typical post-seizure state. We brought her to the Health Centre where she immediately began to flail about and breathe rapidly. Again, I gave her a paper bag to breathe into and coached her to slow down. I worried that her hyperventilation could cause her to pass out and might lead to a drop in her carbon dioxide levels so severe that it would disrupt the acid-base balance, or the "Ph," of her blood chemistry. Calcium levels would then be affected, leading to tremors and spasms, a state called tetany. I had seen the condition of "metabolic alkalosis" in my critically ill patients but never in a healthy person.

Again, Lorne, her brother, rushed in. "Naomi! Are you okay?" She stared at him blankly. "Naomi, you're going to be okay," he told her. He turned to Louise. "Is my sister okay?"

"My neck hurts," Naomi mumbled. Louise and I looked at each other grimly. Sudden neck pain was a classic indicator of meningitis, a highly infectious, deadly disease.

"Naomi, touch your chin to your chest," Louise asked her. She couldn't. It was highly unlikely she had meningitis—there were no other signs and she'd probably received the vaccine—but just in case, we closed all the doors and put on masks and gloves to protect ourselves. If it did turn out to be bacterial, or meningococcal, meningitis, it would be life-threatening for her and dangerous for us, as well as everyone at camp who'd come anywhere near her. Anyone exposed to her would have to go on antibiotics.

Naomi's counselor went with her in the ambulance and I followed in my car. In the ER Naomi had a CT scan to examine her brain and lumbar puncture, which involved putting a needle into her spinal column, to obtain fluid to test for meningitis. When these tests were done I went in to visit her. She was now fully conscious, sitting up, giggling, and playing a finger game called Chopsticks with her counselor. It was as if nothing had happened. Again, she apologized for causing us worry.

I knew all the dire things that still had to be ruled out: seizure, a cerebral bleed, a serious disease or a tumour. The ER doctor decided to keep her overnight for close monitoring and more tests. Her counselor slept beside her in a chair, her head resting on the bed, while I headed back to camp . . . (pp. 240–42).

Naomi . . . was not coming back to camp. Her parents drove from their home in Montreal to be with her. Her doctors still couldn't come up with a diagnosis but she was feeling better and kept apologizing for "causing such a fuss and making everyone worry."

"It's bizarre," Louise said, "but I've seen this syndrome before. It's called *la belle indifférence*. It's rare and occurs mostly in adolescent girls, usually well-adjusted, high-achievers like Naomi who have everything going for them. It usually starts with anxiety but quickly spirals out of control, as we saw."

"In between attacks, she was perfectly fine," I said, "even laughing about it."

Louse nodded. "Patients with this syndrome typically make light of their symptoms. The other feature is that each event occurs in front of witnesses and if they fall, they manage to protect themselves, so there's rarely an injury."

"What are her parents like?" Alice asked Louise, who had met them when she'd gone to visit Naomi in the hospital.

"Absolutely lovely. Beside themselves with worry, of course. There was also a younger brother and an older sister and they seemed to be a very close and caring family."

"So, it's hard to understand why . . ." said Alice, her voice trailing off.

We backed off and let it go. We knew and accepted that fact that there weren't always answers. Some medical mysteries never get solved. Many things get better on their own, without our doing, or understanding, anything . . . (pp. 252–53).

Reading Responses

1. Do a Google search for "conversion disorder," a psychological condition that has demanded the attention of health-care professionals for hundreds of years and that Sigmund Freud wrote about as "hysteria." What problems might a nurse face when

the observable symptoms and medical tests all lead to the conclusion that there's nothing physically wrong with a patient, despite severe physical complaints?

2. In what ways does Shalof's knowing her patients personally make her a better caregiver—in what ways a worse caregiver? In what ways does her knowledge make her a better writer?

3. What details tell you the most about Shalof's professional habits? What different kinds of concrete details does she observe? When and how does she record observations? When and how does she consult others for their expertise? How does she make decisions about what to do?

MORE WRITING IN NURSING

INTRODUCTION

"The Man in White" describes the developing profession of "nurse practitioner," or NP. Health-care journalist Lisa Ricciotti followed and talked with an NP on a typical day, and her story later appeared in a journal published for nurses (*Alberta RN*).

Lloyd Tapper is an NP in emergency medicine. In the story, Tapper first appears at the ER nursing station, dressed unlike either a nurse or a doctor; so we begin to learn about the unique role of an NP. We witness Tapper's encounters with patients, observing as he checks up on people he saw the week before, offers advice on how to stop smoking to a man who came to the ER because of a twisted ankle, advises a man with a sore back to get training on proper lifting techniques and prescribes pain meds.

Given that the profession of NP is relatively new, the author of the article seems to hope to show how useful an NP can be and thus to win support and greater pressure from the medical profession to encourage more training and licensing of NPs (the story happens in Canada, but the NP profession is growing in the United States as well). The author defines the NP as a profession that fills gaps in between nurses and doctors, showing readers that an NP has authority to do things that doctors must do (like making referrals to other doctors) and the skill to do things that nurses must do (like helping patients plan for long-term health improvement).

The Man in White
Lisa Ricciotti

Alberta RN January 2009 Volume 65.1 (www.nurses.ab.ca)

"He's the guy in the white shirt," says the receptionist, pointing to the emergency area at Edmonton's Northeast Community Health Centre. That's all the direction needed to find Lloyd Tapper among the bustle of staff moving purposefully around the ER nursing station. For one thing, he's not in a brightly coloured top like the other nurses and he's not in scrubs and a mask like the doctors. In his crisp white dress shirt and black dress pants, Tapper stands out. He also stands out as the province's only nurse practitioner working in an urban emergency department. It's a position that the 38-year-old has held for nearly four years and from day one he's worked to define his role, beginning with a departure from standard medical garb.

"Initially when I introduced the role, I wanted to make sure I had an opportunity to develop it, but not based on any traditional nursing or medical models," says Tapper, "so that the added value of the role could be identified as different, but working in complete collaboration with the entire health-care team."

Nurse practitioners are still relatively new. There are only a few hundred in the entire province—men and women who are stepping beyond the scope of the traditional nursing practice and into areas usually limited to doctors. Tapper is authorized by the College and Association of Registered Nurses of Alberta through the *Health Professions Act* to assess, diagnose, treat and refer patients. Registered nurses work under the Act as well, but are not authorized to diagnose, prescribe or refer patients to medical personnel. "If I am a registered nurse, I cannot call a cardiologist and say I want to refer this patient to your clinic. With my licence, I can pick up a phone and refer that patient to be seen by that service."

For cases beyond his expertise, he consults with, or defers to, attending ER physicians or the appropriate referral service. "If you go to your family doctor and your problem is beyond him, he'll refer you to a specialist or possibly an emergency physician. If it's outside the emergency physician's area, he may also consult with a specialist. At a time when access to health-care services is limited, the focus is on matching the client's concern with the appropriate health-care provider. That's what makes me different." says Tapper. . . .

It's now 8 a.m.—time for the IV therapy clinic, a service Tapper adopted as part of his scope of practice. He personally follows every patient in the clinic to make sure their care is continuous, stable and streamlined. Every Monday he follows up with the patients who have been receiving intravenous antibiotic treatments over the weekend. Depending on the results of their blood work and his hands-on medical examination, Tapper determines whether they can be prescribed oral medication.

Since these patients have had to come to the ward three times a day, all weekend for IV antibiotics, the change is a welcome relief. So is having a scheduled appointment, instead of waiting to see an ER doctor who is rushing between critical cases.

Today, Tapper has three patients to check up on. Blair, 53, came to the emergency room after his leg swelled to three times its normal size and Mike, 44, a paraplegic athlete, is suffering from an infection caused by pressure on his legs from his wheelchair. Tapper sees them individually, greeting each with "Hi, I'm Lloyd. It's very nice to meet you." He discusses their symptoms thoroughly, gives advice, suggesting an update on tetanus shots for Blair and advising Mike to try padding his wheelchair and avoid contact sports in the short term. Both are now well enough for antibiotic pills, but before passing out prescriptions, Tapper discusses their costs and possible side-effects. "My job is about the little things," he says.

Next in line is Brad, 42, who is concerned about numbness in his foot after twisting his ankle. Tapper determines that nothing is broken, recommends ice and ibuprophen and asks whether Brad needs a note to excuse him from work while he rests. Then Tapper leans over and plucks a package of cigarettes from Brad's shirt pocket, exposed as he bent to put on his shoes. "Have you thought about quitting or cutting back?" he asks. "Because if you want to, we can help."

Brad seems surprised, but he listens. He leaves with written instructions on how to ice his ankle and a booklet on how to stop smoking with information on the tobacco reduction clinic that Tapper developed for the Northeast Community Health Centre a year ago. It's an example of how Tapper tries to go that extra mile.

"An emergency nurse practitioner is not about dealing with major trauma situations," says Tapper. "That's more the role of emergency physicians with years of specialized training. What I can offer is health promotion, illness prevention and continuity of care."

Tapper's interactions with his patients reflect that focus. He gives Shawn, a young roofer with a very sore back, instructions on proper icing techniques and a prescription for anti-inflammatories, but also advises him to ask his boss for training on proper lifting techniques. Tapper also suggests Shawn begin wearing a back support. "You only get one back. Look after it," he says.

Between patients, Tapper walks over to the mental health and addictions services clinic, also part of the Northeast Community Health Centre, to make sure counseling sessions have been set up for a woman he treated the week before, a victim of domestic abuse. "I'm there for them, right now or when they're ready. I don't judge. If they let me in, I can help." He recently linked another seriously abused victim with social workers for placement in a safe house. "She's been beaten before," Tapper says. "But it is very difficult for her to leave. The violence is rapidly escalating and if she doesn't her life may be at risk."

Tapper takes the same caring approach wherever he can, using the encounters with his patients as opportunities to provide referrals to ongoing care. That's made easier by the many clinics located within Northeast Community Health Centre, an innovative model of primary health-care services, including a diabetic clinic, a senior's clinic, services for new mothers and a children's asthma clinic.

"He wants to make sure patients don't fall between the cracks," says Carol Yeomans, an emergency nurse who's worked with Tapper for the past four years. "He always tries to link them to whatever they need to get them on track, back on the road to Wellness and responsibility for their health. He takes the extra time that an emergency physician doesn't have."

From an emergency physician's perspective, it's a big benefit to have a nurse with Tapper's training around. "He has the knowledge and he's taken on so much. He can do sutures, IVs, follow-up calls and paperwork. If he wasn't here, there'd be quite a void. We could use a couple of people like him at other hospitals," says Dr. Terry Stetsko.

It's now approaching noon and Tapper has decided to take lunch since it's not too busy—by emergency department standards anyways. This afternoon, he'll see a bit more of everything: sick kids, people with infectious diseases, abdominal pains, breathing problems and maybe this week's cardiac case. Recently, a mother rushed into the department with a newborn who was near death. After being stabilized in the emergency department, the child was transported to intensive care at the Stollery Children's Hospital, eventually making a full recovery. Whatever the day will bring, Tapper feels ready. "Nursing of any kind is a privilege. You have the chance to make an impact on people's lives. When I see a chance to make a difference, I take it. I really love what I do."

Reprinted with permission of *Your Health* magazine. Fall 2008 issue.

Reading Responses

1. What details stand out in your memory about Lloyd Tapper? How do the memorable details help the author to achieve her purposes?

2. How does Tapper identify his role in relationship to nurses and doctors? What particular sentences help to answer that question?

3. Imagine the possibility of being a health-care professional. Why might you want to become a nurse practitioner rather than a nurse or doctor?

WRITING ASSIGNMENTS

Assignment 1

In "A Phenomenologic Study of Chronic Pain," Thomas argues that doctors and nurses tend to dismiss pain because pain does not show up on X-rays, MRIs, blood tests, and other "objective" biomedical tests. To "picture" chronic pain, Thomas interviews thirteen people who are living with chronic pain. She uses quotes from those interviews as her evidence for the nature and significance of chronic pain. In this way, the personal experience of people in chronic pain bears witness to that pain in a way that medical tests often don't.

Your task for this assignment is to picture Thomas's use of personal experience by charting it. You may find it helpful to review Chapter 9, "Biology," for advice on creating effective tables and figures. Reread Thomas's essay, recording each time she uses her observations as evidence. Describe how Thomas presents what she observes: quote, paraphrase, summary, or narrative. How does Thomas introduce the observation to the reader? Does Thomas cluster observations, or does she allow them to stand alone? Once you've collected your data, analyze it. What patterns do you see? How do those patterns shape the reader's experience of Thomas's article? Based on your research and your experiences as a reader of Thomas's article, make recommendations about the use of personal experience evidence in science articles.

As you begin drafting, consider how your own personal experience reading and analyzing Thomas's article can help you explain the results of your study to your reader.

Assignment 2

Chapter 12, "English Education," contains an excerpt from *Bootstraps,* in which Victor Villanueva blends humanities scholarly research with his own experiences. Sandra Thomas, author of "A Phenomenologic Study of Chronic Pain," also blends academic research with personal observations. But she does so in very different ways.

Your task for this assignment is to create a set of recommendations for using personal experience effectively. What are the issues that writers should consider regarding when and how to use personal experience? How does the situation in which they're writing affect their use of personal experience? What purposes do personal experiences serve in academic writing? What kinds of personal experiences are appropriate in academic writing? What are inappropriate? What strategies can writers use to present personal experience? To integrate it in their writing?

As you begin drafting, try to be very clear about the ways that context shapes the answers to the questions above and the means that writers can use to determine the appropriate use of personal experience in a given context.

Assignment 3

College students hear frequent warnings to avoid the "freshman fifteen" (weight gain supposedly experienced by first-year students), but recent research indicates that this warning itself can create trouble for students, especially female students.

Your task is to research and report on the effects of the myth of the "freshman fifteen" by targeting two sources of information: published research on the topic and your observations of college students. A reference librarian can help you locate published research on the topic. To gather observations, create a set of interview questions and then interview five to ten students at your school (you might want to interview only women or only men). Record their answers carefully by taking thorough notes or using a tape recorder.

As you begin drafting, consider the relationship between the kinds of evidence that you collected—how can you present your evidence so that it all works together? Consider, too, the relationship between your evidence and the claims that you make in your report— what kind of evidence will best support a particular claim? If you found particularly compelling evidence, you might direct your report to university administrators who oversee student life and include a set of recommendations in your conclusion.

POLITICAL SCIENCE: BUILDING KNOWLEDGEABLE ARGUMENTS

Where do you draw the line?

Ever heard of Koguryo? Most Americans haven't, but most people in China and South Korea have. Some of the territory that was once ancient Koguryo is now in China; the rest is in North Korea. According to Korean history, Koguryo was one of the three ancient kingdoms of Korea and the site of a famous battle. Thus, modern Koreans claim this ancient region and its history as their own. But China claims it, too. The Chinese *English People's Daily Online* describes Koguryo as "the ancient Koguryo Kingdom of China" and quotes the Chinese scholar Wei Cuncheng: "Koguryo was a regime established by ethnic groups in northern China some 2,000 years ago, representing an important part of Chinese culture."*

But this is ancient history. Why are the Chinese or Koreans passionate about it now? Two reasons: first, tombs in the region are now World Heritage sites. Prestige and tourism dollars are sure to follow. Second, some experts in international politics speculate that China is looking to the future. If North and South Korea ever re-unify, Koreans might claim the ancient Koguryo territory for this new, powerful Korea.

- If you were Korean, what types of evidence could you use to claim Koguryo as a part of your national history? Create a list of at least five different types of evidence, ordering the list from most persuasive type of evidence at the top to least effective evidence at the bottom. You might find it helpful to do an Internet search on the word "Koguryo" to see what kinds of evidence political scientists have used.

*"China's ancient Koguryo Kingdom site added to World heritage List," http://english.peopledaily.com.cn/200407/ 01/eng20040701_148209.html

PORTABLE RHETORICAL LESSON: BUILDING CREDIBILITY AS AN AUTHOR

As you worked through the Koguryo exercise, you did two things that acquainted you with primary rhetorical experiences of writers in political science. First, you conducted **research** to find **evidence.** When writing about international politics, the experts do thorough research, and they cite that research frequently. The first reading in this chapter, for example, contains a staggering 150 citations. Even the student writing in this chapter uses 29 footnotes in an essay of less than 3,000 words—pretty impressive.

Why would you do such thorough research? The second part of your experience in the Koguryo exercise suggests an explanation.

You imagined being a Korean, arguing that part of your ancient land should be restored to you. In that context, your research was deeply important to your personal sense of national pride and patriotism. And if you had the time to carry on through research into publication, what you wrote might help your country make decisions about exerting political pressure or maybe even going to war to regain your land. It is the sense of potential consequences that creates such strong personal commitment—and that makes people who write about international politics deeply aware of the second Key Rhetorical Concept: their role as an **author.**

If you hope to inspire readers to take action because you believe that values such as equality, economic stability, or justice are at stake, your arguments will breathe with passion for the topic. You see that zeal, for example, in some of the language choices of the authors in this chapter. Christopher Layne, in the first reading, describes "democratic peace theory" (which he argues against) as a "myth" in his title and as "wishful thinking" in his conclusion. And James King, the chapter's student writer, takes an impassioned stand, using language such as: "the economic depravity of Israel's Arab population" and "The popular opinion of Jews in Israel regarding their fellow Arab citizens . . . shows an obvious lack of democratic value. . . ."

When writers combine an arsenal of knowledge about their subject with personal commitment to and understanding of the potentially world-changing consequences of international political actions, they achieve this chapter's **Portable Rhetorical Lesson:** a credible authorial voice. You can improve your credibility as an author by

1. Convincing your audience that you know what you're talking about, and
2. Demonstrating that what you're talking about is important.

To achieve those two goals,

1. Do enough research so that you really do know what you're talking about (confident enough even to discuss what your opponents believe), and
2. Write about topics that you really believe are important.

The readings in this chapter provide models that help you to see how you can make use of these rhetorical skills of political scientists in your own writing.

WRITING IN THE DISCIPLINE

INTRODUCTION

by Simona Goi,
Professor of Political Science

Generally speaking, political scientists write to accomplish three goals: to explain why something happened in the past, to predict what might happen in the future, or to influence/change what might happen in the future. Christopher Layne's essay explicitly addresses the first goal, but he does so because he hopes to lead people to see how to accomplish the other two: if we understand why some states chose not to go to war, we might be able to prevent war in the future. This is a source of the passion that drives Layne's research. In this light, we can see that Layne is motivated not just by academic interest, but also by a belief that what he writes can help prevent future wars.

Layne is an international relations theorist who is a professor at Texas A&M. His article reproduced here, one of the truly influential pieces of his distinguished career, is part of the scholarly research on the relationship between a country's type of government and that country's willingness to go to war. Political analysts have noted that democracies do not normally fight other democracies, even though they *do* go to war against nondemocratic states. But *why* won't democracies go to war with other democracies? Are democratic governments inherently more moral than their nondemocratic counterparts, and therefore less likely to use war to accomplish political ends? Or do democratic governments listen more carefully to their citizens who hope to avoid the human and financial costs of a war? One answer to these research questions is "democratic peace theory," the dominant theory regarding the relationships between democratic states. Layne addresses the topic in two ways: first, he summarizes scholarly explanations for why democratic states do not go to war against other democratic states, and then he tests those explanations against an alternative hypothesis that he proposes.

Layne's essay is an excellent example of how political scientists develop complex logical arguments. First, Layne introduces the topic and notes its importance. Democratic peace theory is important, according to Layne, because it shapes American foreign policy in crucial ways: American politicians "who have embraced democratic peace theory see a crucial link between America's security and the spread of democracy" (220). Next he reviews two prominent versions of democratic peace theory, and he introduces a competing theory to explain how nations get along with each other: a theory that he calls "realism." Then, Layne tests democratic peace theory and realism by applying them to case studies of historical events with known outcomes. Using four historical conflicts (only one appears in this abridged version of his essay) as case studies, Layne analyzes how well democratic peace theory and realism each explain the actions of these combating democratic states. Layne concludes that democratic peace theory cannot account for the historical evidence. Instead, realism better explains why these democratic countries avoided war with each other.

When political scientists write, they make good use of the passion that propels them to choose a particular research topic and sustains them through the hard work of collecting and analyzing large amounts of historical and analytical evidence. They write knowing that other scholars, using different evidence or a different method for analyzing the evidence, will likely come to different conclusions. Their various explanations compete with one another. In fact, the same journal issue in which Layne's article appears includes an article entitled "How Liberalism Produces Democratic Peace." It analyzes the same historical period that Layne does, but looks at it from a different perspective and produces different conclusions. But both writers try to convince others to see this topic as they do because they believe that their research will improve the chances for peace in the world.

✓ Reading Tips

Because the writing of political scientists is often long and complex, you'll read more efficiently if you map out the logical progression of ideas. So,

1. List the features of both "democratic peace theory" and "realism."
2. Match those features to the historical events that Layne describes in the Trent affair.
3. Find the three ways that Layne states the point of his essay:
   • Thesis statement (which recognizes that his point is arguable)
   • Hypothesis (which Layne tests by analyzing case studies)
   • Recommendations (which outline ways Layne wants readers to respond)

Compare and combine the different expressions of the point to help you understand what's most important to Layne.

Finally, this essay is very complex. To follow the argument, highlight key ideas, jot down notes in the margins, and refer back to the headings of each section as you read the section. Note how each individual paragraph contributes to the core idea identified by the heading.

> Democratic peace theory is based on the philosophy of Immanuel Kant. The title lets you know that Layne doesn't believe in the theory.

Kant or Cant:
The Myth of the Democratic Peace

Christopher Layne

International Security, 1994 19(2): 5–49

Policymakers who have embraced democratic peace theory[1] see a crucial link between America's security and the spread of democracy, which is viewed as the antidote that will prevent future wars. . . . Because of its theoretical claims and policy implications, the democratic peace theory merits careful examination.[3] In this article, I focus primarily on a critique of the persuasiveness of democratic peace theory's causal logic and ask whether democratic peace theory or realism is a better predictor of international outcomes. I then briefly assess the robustness of democratic peace theory's empirical evidence in light of my conclusions about the strength of its explanatory power.

I begin by reviewing the explanations of the Democratic Peace advanced by democratic peace theorists. There are two strands to the theory's causal logic. One attributes the absence of war between democracies to institutional constraints: the restraining effects of public opinion, or of the checks and balances embedded in a democratic state's domestic political structure. The other posits that it is democratic norms and culture—a shared commitment to the peaceful adjudication of political disputes—that accounts for the absence of war between democratic states. As I demonstrate, the institutional-constraints argument fails to provide a compelling explanation for the absence of war between democracies. Thus, democratic peace theory's explanatory power rests on the persuasiveness of the contention that democratic norms and culture explain why, although democratic states fight with non-democracies, they do not go to war with each other.

This article's centerpiece is a test of the competing explanations of international outcomes offered by democratic peace theory and by realism. This test is based on case studies of four "near misses"—crises where two democratic states almost went to war with each other. These four cases are well-documented instances of democratic great powers going to the brink of war without going over it. As such, they present an opportunity to determine which of the competing hypotheses advanced respectively by democratic peace theory and realism best account for international political outcome. . . .

I conclude that realism is superior to democratic peace theory as a predictor of international outcomes. Indeed, democratic peace theory appears to have extremely little explanatory power in the cases studied. Doubts about the validity of its causal logic suggest that the empirical evidence purporting to support democratic peace theory should also be revisited. Democratic peace theorists contend that the theory is validated by a large number of cases. However, a powerful argument can be made that the universe of cases from which it can be tested is actually quite small. This is a crucial issue, because if the theory's empirical support is based on a small-N universe, this magnifies the importance of possible exceptions to the rule that democracies do not fight each other (for example, World War I, the War between the States, the War of 1812). I conclude by discussing democratic peace theory's troublesome implications for post–Cold War American foreign policy.

The Case for a Democratic Peace: Its Claims and Its Logic

Democratic peace theory does not contend that democratic states are less war-prone than non-democracies; they are not. The theory does,

---

Sidebar notes (left margin):

In the first four paragraphs, Layne summarizes his entire article. Because this is a summary, these paragraphs are difficult to read. Consider rereading these four paragraphs after you finish the entire essay.

Layne states his reason for writing—to test which theory better predicts known, historical outcomes.

In an article as long and complex as this, it is a rhetorical advantage for Layne to be bold and up-front about his point.

A small N means that there are very few cases to study. With too few numbers a statistical study may yield questionable results. So Layne chooses a "case-study" method, looking very closely at a small number of key cases.

however, make two important claims, first, that democracies never (or rarely; there is a good deal of variation about this) go to war with other democracies.[5] As Jack S. Levy observes, the "absence of war between democracies comes as close as anything we have to an empirical law in international relations."[6] Second, when democracies come into conflict with one another, they only rarely threaten to use force, because it is "illegitimate" to do so. Democratic peace theory explicitly holds that it is the very nature of democratic political systems that accounts for the fact that democracies do not fight or threaten other democracies.

> An empirical law is a law that all observable evidence supports—like the law of gravity.

The Causal Logic

> Causal logic refers to the relationship between an event, its causes, and its effects.

Democratic peace theory must explain an anomaly: democracies are no less war-prone than non-democratic states. Yet, while they will readily threaten and fight non-democracies, they do not threaten or fight other democracies. The key challenge for the theory, then, is to identify the special characteristics of democratic states that restrain them from using coercive threats against, or actually going to war with, other democracies. The theory advances two alternative explanations: 1) institutional constraints; and 2) democratic norms and cultures.[8]

There are two major variants of the institutional constraints argument. Michael Doyle, building on Immanuel Kant, explains that democratic governments are reluctant to go to war because they must answer to their citizens.[9] Citizens pay the price for war in blood and treasure; if the price of conflict is high, democratic governments may fall victim to electoral retribution. Moreover, in democratic states, foreign policy decisions carrying the risk of war are debated openly and not made behind closed doors, which means that both the public and policymakers are sensitized to costs of fighting. A second version of the institutional constraints argument focuses on "checks and balances"; it looks at three specific features of a state's domestic political structure: executive selection, political competition, and the pluralism of the foreign policy decision making process.[10] States with executives answerable to a selection body, with institutionalized political competition, and with decision making responsibility spread among multiple institutions or individuals, should be more highly constrained and hence less likely to go to war.

> The U.S. fits this description: the president is elected by the people, we have political parties that compete with each other, and the power of the government is distributed among three branches: the executive, the legislative, and the judicial.

The democratic norms explanation holds that "the *culture, perceptions, and practices* that permit compromise and the peaceful resolution of conflicts without the threat of violence *within countries* come to apply across national boundaries toward other democratic countries."[11] Democratic states assume both that other democracies also subscribe to pacific methods of regulating political competition and resolving disputes, and that others will apply these norms in their external relations with fellow democracies. In other words, democratic states

> In other words, the same things that promote peace within a country will promote peace between that country and others.

develop positive perceptions of other democracies. Consequently, Doyle says, democracies, "which rest on consent, presume foreign republics to be also consensual, just and therefore deserving of accommodation."[12] Relations between democratic states are based on mutual respect rooted in the fact that democracies perceive each other as dovish (that is, negotiation or the status quo are the only possible outcomes in a dispute). This perception, it is argued, is based on a form of learning. Democratic states benefit from cooperative relations with one another and they want to expand their positive interactions. In turn, this desire predisposes them to be responsive to the needs of other democratic states, and ultimately leads to creation of a community of interests. As democracies move towards community, they renounce the option to use (or even to threaten to use) force in their mutual interactions.[13]

The democratic ethos—based on "peaceful competition, persuasion and compromise"—explains the absence of war and war-like threats in relations between democratic states.[14] Conversely, the absence of these norms in relations between democracies and non-democracies, it is said, explains the paradox that democracies do not fight each other even though in general they are as war-prone as non-democracies: "When a democracy comes into conflict with a nondemocracy, it will not expect the nondemocratic state to be restrained by those norms [of mutual respect based on democratic culture]. It may feel obliged to adapt to the harsher norms of international conduct of the latter, lest it be exploited or eliminated by the nondemocratic state that takes advantage of the inherent moderation of democracies."[15] Thus it is a fundamental postulate of democratic peace theory that democracies behave in a qualitatively different manner in their relations with each other than they do in their relations with non-democracies.

The Realist Case: The Same Things Over and Over Again

> In this section, Layne describes realism, an alternative way of explaining how countries get along with each other.

If history is "just one damn thing after another," then for realists international politics is the same damn things over and over again: war, great power security and economic competitions, the rise and fall of great powers, and the formation and dissolution of alliances. International political behavior is characterized by continuity, regularity, and repetition because states are constrained by the international system's unchanging (and probably unchangeable) structure.

The realist paradigm explains why this is so.[16] International politics is an anarchic, self-help realm. "Anarchy," rather than denoting chaos or rampant disorder, refers in international politics to the fact that there is no central authority capable of making and enforcing rules of behavior on the international system's units (states). The absence of a rule-making and enforcing authority means that each unit in the system is responsible for ensuring its own survival and also that each is free to define its own interests and to employ means of its own choice in pursuing them. In this sense, international politics is fundamentally competitive. And it is competitive in a manner that differs crucially from domestic politics in liberal societies, where the losers can accept an adverse outcome because they live to fight another day and can, therefore, ultimately hope to prevail. In international politics, states that come out on the short end of political competition face potentially more extreme outcomes, ranging from constraints on autonomy to occupation to extinction.

> In other words, if a politician loses one battle, she can regroup and try again. If a country loses a battle to another country, it is less likely to remain autonomous.

It is anarchy that gives international politics its distinctive flavor. In an anarchic system, a state's first goal is to survive. To attain security, states engage in both internal and external balancing for the purpose of deterring aggressors, and of defeating them should deterrence fail. In a realist world, cooperation is possible but is hard to sustain in the face of the competitive pressures that are built into the international political system's structure. The imperative of survival in a threatening environment forces states to focus on strategies that maximize their power relative to their rivals. States have powerful incentives both to seek the upper hand over their rivals militarily and to use their edge not only for self-defense but also to take advantage of others. . . .

In the international system, fear and distrust of other states is the normal state of affairs. . . .

Testing Democratic Peace Theory

Institutional constraints do not explain the democratic peace. If democratic public opinion really had the effect ascribed to it, democracies would be peaceful in their relations with all states, whether democratic or not. If citizens and policymakers of a democracy were especially sensitive to the human and material costs of war, that sensitivity should be evident whenever their state is on the verge of war, regardless of whether the adversary is democratic: the lives lost and money spent will be the same. Nor is democratic public opinion, *per se*, an inhibitor of war. For example, in 1898 it was public opinion that impelled the reluctant McKinley administration into war with Spain; in 1914 war was enthusiastically embraced by public opinion in Britain and France. Domestic political structure—"checks and balances"—does not explain the democratic peace either. "This argument," as Morgan and Schwebach state, "does not say anything directly about the war-proneness of democracies," because it focuses on an independent variable—decisional constraints embedded in a state's domestic political structure—that is associated with, but not exclusive to, democracies.

> "Institutional constraints" explanations

> Now Layne takes on the second claim of democratic peace theory: norms and culture.

Because these explanations fall short, the democratic norms and culture explanation must bear the weight of the democratic peace theory's causal logic. It is there we must look to find that "something in the internal makeup of democratic states" that explains the democratic peace.[18]

Democratic peace theory not only predicts a specific outcome—no war between democracies—but also purports to explain why that outcome will occur. It is thus suited to being tested by the case study method, a detailed look at a small number of examples to determine if events unfold and actors act as the theory predicts. The case study method also affords the opportunity to test the competing explanations of international political outcomes offered by democratic peace theory and by realism. To test the robustness of democratic peace theory's causal logic, the focus here is on "near misses," specific cases in which democratic states had both opportunity and reason to fight each other, but did not. . . .

Democratic peace theory, if valid, should account powerfully for the fact that serious crises between democratic states ended in near misses rather than in war. If democratic norms and culture explain the democratic peace, in a near-war crisis, certain indicators of the democratic peace theory should be in evidence: First, public opinion should be strongly pacific. Public opinion is important not because it is an institutional constraint, but because it is an indirect measure of the mutual respect that democracies are said to have for each other. Second, policymaking elites should refrain from making military threats against other democracies and should refrain from making preparations to carry out threats. Democratic peace theorists waffle on this point by suggesting that the absence of war between democracies is more important than the absence of threats. But this sets the threshold of proof too low. Because the crux of the theory is that democracies externalize their internal norms of peaceful dispute resolution, then especially in a crisis, one should not see democracies threatening other democracies. And if threats are made, they should be a last-resort option rather than an early one. Third, democracies should bend over backwards to accommodate each other in a crisis. Ultimata, unbending hard lines, and big-stick diplomacy are the stuff of Realpolitik, not the democratic peace.

A realist explanation of near misses would look at a very different set of indicators. First, realism postulates a ratio of national interest to democratic respect: in a crisis, the more important the interests a democracy perceives to be at stake, the more likely that its policy will be shaped by realist imperatives rather than by democratic norms and culture. When vital interests are on the line, democracies should not be inhibited from using threats, ultimata, and big-stick diplomacy against another democracy. Second, even in a crisis involving democracies, states should be very attentive to strategic concerns, and the relative distribution of military capabilities between them should crucially—perhaps decisively—affect their diplomacy. Third, broader geopolitical

> Social scientists, like natural scientists, always identify their methods for testing their hypotheses.

> "Ultimata" is the plural of "ultimatum"—an all-or-nothing demand that offers no room for negotiation. In "big-stick diplomacy," a country threatens to use its superior military power as a way to coerce another country to do something. *Realpolitik* focuses on self-interest and what is practical over what is moral.

considerations pertaining to a state's position in international politics should, if implicated, account significantly for the crisis's outcome. Key here is what Geoffrey Blainey calls the "fighting waterbirds' dilemma," involving concerns that others watching from the sidelines will take advantage of a state's involvement in war; that war will leave a state weakened and in an inferior relative power position vis-a-vis possible future rivals; and that failure to propitiate the opposing state in a crisis will cause it to ally with one's other adversaries or rivals.[21]

> Because of space limitations, we have included only the first case study.

I have chosen to study four modern historical instances in which democratic great powers almost came to blows: 1) the United States and Great Britain in 1861 ("the Trent affair"); 2) the United States and Great Britain in 1895–96 (the Venezuela crisis); 3) France and Great Britain in 1898 (the Fashoda crisis); and 4) France and Germany in 1923 (the Ruhr crisis).[22]

Anglo-American Crisis I: The *Trent* Affair, 1861

> The Civil War. A rhetorical advantage of the case-study method is that people like to read stories. Beginning this story in the context of what may be America's most captivating story—the Civil War—is smart rhetoric.

In 1861, tensions arising from the War Between the States brought the Union and Britain to the brink of war. The most important causes of Anglo-American friction stemmed from the Northern blockade of Confederate ports and the consequent loss to Britain of the cotton upon which its textile industry depended. The immediate precipitating cause of the Anglo-American crisis, however, was action of the USS *San Jacinto* which, acting without express orders from Washington, intercepted the British mail ship *Trent* on November 8, 1861. The *Trent* was transporting James M. Mason and John Slidell, the Confederacy's commissioners-designate to Great Britain and France; they had boarded the *Trent,* a neutral vessel, in Havana, Cuba, a neutral port. A boarding party from the *San Jacinto,* after searching the *Trent,* placed Mason and Slidell under arrest. The *Trent* was allowed to complete its voyage while the *San Jacinto* transported Mason and Slidell to Fort Warren in Boston harbor, where they were incarcerated.

When word was received in Britain, the public was overcome with war fever. "The first explosion of the Press, on receipt of the news of the *Trent,* had been a terrific one."[28] An American citizen residing in England reported to Secretary of State William H. Seward, "The people are frantic with rage, and were the country polled I fear 999 men out of 1000 would declare for war."[29] From Edinburgh, another American wrote, "I have never seen so intense a feeling of indignation in my life."[30]

The British government was hardly less bellicose than the public and the press. Fortified by legal opinions holding that Mason and Slidell had been removed from the *Trent* in contravention of international law, the Cabinet adopted a hard-line policy that mirrored the public mood. Prime Minister Lord Palmerston's first reaction to the news of the

Trent incident was to write to the Secretary of State for War that, because of Britain's "precarious" relations with the United States, the government reconsider cuts in military expenditures planned to take effect in 1862.[31] At the November 29 Cabinet meeting, Palmerston reportedly began by flinging his hat on the table and declaring to his colleagues, "I don't know whether you are going to stand this, but I'll be damned if I do!"[32]

The Cabinet adopted a dual-track approach towards Washington: London used military threats to coerce the United States into surrendering diplomatically, while on the diplomatic side, Foreign Secretary Lord John Russell drafted a note to the Union government in which, while holding firm to the demand that Mason and Slidell be released, he offered Washington an avenue of graceful retreat by indicating that London would accept, as tantamount to an apology, a declaration that the *San Jacinto* had acted without official sanction. Nevertheless, the note that was actually transmitted to Washington was an ultimatum. Although the British minister in Washington, Lord Lyons, was instructed to present the communication in a fashion calculated to maximize the chances of American compliance, his charge was clear: unless within seven days of receipt the Union government unconditionally accepted Britain's demands, Lyons was to ask for his passports and depart the United States. As Russell wrote to Lyons: "What we want is a plain Yes or a plain No to our very simple demands, and we want that plain Yes or No within seven days of the communication of the despatch."[33]

Although some, notably including Russell, hoped that the crisis could be resolved peacefully, the entire Cabinet recognized that its decision to present an ultimatum to Washington could lead to war. The British believed that there was one hope for peace: that Washington, overawed by Britain's military power and its readiness to go to war, would bow to London's demands rather than resisting them.[34] As the Undersecretary of State for Foreign Affairs stated, "Our only chance of peace is to be found in working on the fears of the Government and people of the United States."[35]

Driven by the belief that Washington would give in only to the threat of force, London's diplomacy was backed up by ostentatious military and naval preparations. Anticipating a possible conflict, the Cabinet embargoed the export to the United States of saltpeter (November 30) and of arms and ammunition (December 4). Underscoring the gravity of the crisis, for only the fourth time in history the Cabinet created a special war committee to oversee strategic planning and war preparations. Urgent steps were taken to reinforce Britain's naval and military contingents in North America. Beginning in mid-December, a hastily organized sealift increased the number of

an ingredient in gunpowder

regular British army troops in Canada from 5,000 to 17,658, and Royal Navy forces in North American waters swelled from 25 to forty warships, with 1,273 guns (compared to just 500 before the crisis).[36] These measures served two purposes: they bolstered London's diplomacy and, in the event diplomacy failed, they positioned Britain to prevail in a conflict.

London employed big-stick diplomacy because it believed that a too-conciliatory policy would simply embolden the Americans to mount increasingly serious challenges to British interests.[37] Moreover, British policymakers believed that England's resolve, credibility, and reputation were at stake internationally, not just in its relations with the United States. The comments of once and future Foreign Secretary Lord Clarendon were typical: a figure . . . we shall cut in the eyes of the world, if we lamely submit to this outrage when all mankind will know that we should unhesitatingly have poured our indignation and our broadsides into any weak nation . . . and what an additional proof it will be of the universal . . . belief that we have two sets of weights and measures to be used according to the power or weakness of our adversary."[38] Thus "the British were prepared to accept the cost of an Anglo-American war . . . rather than sacrifice their prestige as a great power by headlong diplomatic defeat."[39]

London's hard-line policy was fortified by its "general optimism about the ultimate outcome" of an Anglo-American war.[40] Queen Victoria said a war would result in "utter destruction to the North Americans" and Secretary of State for War George Cornewall Lewis said "we shall soon iron the smile out of their face."[41] Palmerston was therefore untroubled by the discomfiture imposed on the Union by London's uncompromising policy. In his view, regardless of whether the crisis was resolved peacefully or resulted in war, Britain's interests would be upheld. He wrote to Queen Victoria:

If the Federal Government comply with the demands it will be honorable to England and humiliating to the United States. If the Federal Government refuse compliance, Great Britain is in a better state than at any former time to inflict a severe blow upon, and to read a lesson to the United States which will not soon be forgotten.[42]

In late 1861, the war against the Confederacy was not going well for Washington and the one major engagement, the first Battle of Manassas, had resulted in a humiliating setback for the Union army. Whipped up by Secretary of State Seward, who was a master at "twisting the lion's tail" for maximum domestic political effect, Northern opinion was hostile in London and resented especially Queen Victoria's May 1861 neutrality proclamation, which Northerners interpreted as *de facto* British recognition of Southern independence. News of the seizure of Mason

in actual fact

and Slidell had a double effect on Northern public opinion. First, it was a tonic for sagging Northern morale. Second, it was seen as a warning to Britain to refrain from interfering with the Union's prosecution of the war against the Confederacy. Thus, although some papers (notably the *New York Times* and the *New York Daily Tribune*) urged that Washington should placate the British, public opinion strongly favored a policy of standing up to London and refusing to release Mason and Slidell.[43] In response to Britain's hard line, "a raging war cry reverberated across the Northern states in America."[44] Charles Francis Adams, Jr., whose father was U.S. minister in London at the time, wrote later of the affair: "I do not remember in the whole course of the half-century's retrospect . . . any occurrence in which the American people were so completely swept off their feet, for the moment losing possession of their senses, as during the weeks which immediately followed the seizure of Mason and Slidell."[45]

The Lincoln administration was aware of the strength of anti-British sentiment among the public and in Congress (indeed, in early December, Congress passed a resolution commending the *San Jacinto's* captain for his action). There is some evidence that in order to placate public opinion, President Lincoln was inclined toward holding on to Mason and Slidell, notwithstanding the obvious risks of doing so.[46] Nevertheless, after first toying with the idea of offering London arbitration in an attempt to avoid the extremes of war or a humiliating climb-down, the United States elected to submit to Britain's demands. Given that Washington "could not back down easily," it is important to understand why it chose to do so.

The United States bowed to London because, already fully occupied militarily trying to subdue the Confederacy, the North could not also afford a simultaneous war with England, which effectively would have brought Britain into the War Between the States on the South's side.[47] This was clearly recognized by the Lincoln administration when the cabinet met for two days at Christmas to decide on the American response to the British note. The cabinet had before it two critical pieces of information. First, Washington had just been informed that France supported London's demands (ending American hopes that Britain would be restrained by its own "waterbird" worries that France would take advantage of an Anglo-American war).[48] Second, Washington had abundant information about the depth of the pro-war sentiment of the British public. . . .

Facing the choice of defying London or surrendering to its demands, Washington was compelled to recognize both that Britain was serious about going to war and that such a war almost certainly would result in the Union's permanent dissolution. During the cabinet discussions, Attorney General Edward Bates suggested that Britain was seeking a war with the United States in order to break the Northern blockade of

Southern cotton ports and he worried that London would recognize the Confederacy. The United States, he said, "cannot afford such a war." He went on to observe, "In such a crisis, with such a civil war upon our hands, we cannot hope for success in a . . . war with England, backed by the assent and countenance of France. We must evade it—with as little damage to our own honor and pride as possible."[51] Secretary of State Seward concurred, stating that it was "no time to be diverted from the cares of the Union into controversies with other powers, even if just causes for them could be found."[52] When the United States realized that Britain's threat to go to war was not a bluff, strategic and national interest considerations—the "waterbird dilemma"—dictated that Washington yield to Britain.

The *Trent* affair's outcome is explained by realism, not democratic peace theory. Contrary to democratic peace theory's expectations, the mutual respect between democracies rooted in democratic norms and culture had no influence on British policy. Believing that vital reputational interests affecting its global strategic posture were at stake, London played diplomatic hardball, employed military threats, and was prepared to go to war if necessary. Both the public and the elites in Britain preferred war to conciliation. Across the Atlantic, public and governmental opinion in the North was equally bellicose. An Anglo-American conflict was avoided only because the Lincoln administration came to understand that diplomatic humiliation was preferable to a war that would have arrayed Britain with the Confederacy and thus probably have secured the South's independence. . . .

Policy Conclusions: Why It Matters

The validity of democratic peace theory is not a mere academic concern. Democratic peace theory has been widely embraced by policymakers and foreign policy analysts alike and it has become a lodestar that guides America's post-Cold War foreign policy. Michael Doyle's 1983 conception of a democratic "zone of peace" is now routinely used in both official and unofficial U.S. foreign policy pronouncements. Following the Cold War, a host of commentators have suggested that the export or promotion of democracy abroad should become the central focus of American's post-Cold War foreign policy.[140] From Haiti to Russia, America's interests and its security have been identified with democracy's success or failure. National Security Adviser Anthony Lake said that America's post-Cold War goal must be to expand the zone of democratic peace and prosperity because, "to the extent democracy and market economics hold sway in other nations, our own nation will be more secure, prosperous and influential."[141]

Those who want to base American foreign policy on the extension of democracy abroad invariably disclaim any intention to embark on a

A guiding star. Layne uses the term to indicate that democratic peace theory directs U.S. foreign policy. He then considers the problems that result from the U.S. using this flawed theory as a guide.

"crusade," and profess to recognize the dangers of allowing policy to be based on excessive ideological zeal."[142] These reassurances are the foreign-policy version of "trust me." Because it links American security to the nature of other states' internal political systems, democratic peace theory's logic inevitably pushes the United States to adopt an interventionist strategic posture. If democracies are peaceful but non-democratic states are "troublemakers" the conclusion is inescapable: the former will be truly secure only when the latter have been transformed into democracies, too.

> That is, following democratic peace theory, the U.S. intervenes in the internal affairs of other countries to press them to adopt a democratic form of government.

Indeed, American statesmen have frequently expressed this view. During World War I, Elihu Root said that, "To be safe democracy must kill its enemy when it can and where it can. The world cannot be half democratic and half autocratic."[143] During the Vietnam War, Secretary of State Dean Rusk claimed that the "United States cannot be secure until the total international environment is ideologically safe." These are not isolated comments; these views reflect the historic American propensity to seek absolute security and to define security primarily in ideological (and economic) terms. The political culture of American foreign policy has long regarded the United States, because of its domestic political system, as a singular nation. As a consequence, American policymakers have been affected by a "deep sense of being alone" and *they* have regarded the United States as "perpetually beleaguered." Consequently, America's foreign and defense policies have been shaped by the belief that the United States must create a favorable ideological climate abroad if its domestic institutions are to survive and flourish. . . ."[145]

> That is, the U.S. must create democracies abroad so that its own democracy will flourish.

Democratic peace theory is dangerous in another respect, as well: it is an integral component of a new (or more correctly, recycled) outlook on international politics. It is now widely believed that the spread of democracy and economic interdependence have effected a "qualitative change" in international politics, and that war and serious security competitions between or among democratic great powers are now impossible.[147] There is therefore, it is said, no need to worry about future great power challenges from states like Japan and Germany, or to worry about the relative distribution of power between the United States and those states, unless Japan or Germany were to slide back into authoritarianism.[148] The reason the United States need not be concerned with the great-power emergence of Japan and Germany is said to be simple: they are democracies and democracies do not fight democracies. . . .

> a change in the nature, character, or degree of something

If American policymakers allow themselves to be mesmerized by democratic peace theory's seductive—but false—vision of the future, the United States will be ill prepared to formulate a grand strategy that will advance its interests in the emerging world of multipolar great power competition. Indeed, as long as the Wilsonian worldview underpins

> A belief typical of President Woodrow Wilson, who thought that the U.S. should promote democracy in other countries and peace among nations.

American foreign policy, policymakers will be blind to the need to have such a grand strategy, because the liberal theory of international politics defines out of existence (except with respect to non-democracies) the very phenomena that are at the core of strategy: war, the formation of power balances, and concerns about the relative distribution of power among the great powers. But in the end, as its most articulate proponents admit, liberal international relations theory is based on hope, not on fact.[150] In the final analysis, the world remains what it always has been: international politics continues to occur in an anarchic, competitive, self-help realm. This reality must be confronted, because it cannot be transcended. Given the stakes, the United States in coming years cannot afford to have either its foreign policy, or the intellectual discourse that underpins that policy, shaped by theoretical approaches that are based on wishful thinking.

Notes

1. I use the term "democratic peace theory" because it is a convenient shorthand term. However, strictly speaking, the claim that democracies do not fight democracies is a proposition, or hypothesis, rather than a theory. Democratic peace "theory" proposes a causal relationship between an independent variable (democratic political structures at the unit level) and the dependent variable (the asserted absence of war between democratic states). However, it is not a true theory because the causal relationship between the independent and dependent variables is neither proven nor, as I demonstrate in this article, adequately explained. See Stephen Van Evera, "Hypotheses, Laws and Theories: A User's Guide," unpub. memo, Department of Political Science, MIT.

3. In this article, I build upon and expand the criticisms of democratic peace theory found in John J. Mearsheimer, "Back to the Future: Instability in Europe After the Cold War," *International Security,* Vol. 15, No. 1 (Summer 1990), pp. 5–56; and Kenneth N. Waltz, "America as Model for the World? A Foreign Policy Perspective," *PS* (December 1991), pp. 667–670.

4. Other cases of crises between democratic great powers that might be studied include Anglo-French relations during the Liberal entente cordiale of 1832–48, Franco-Italian relations during the Late 1880s and early 1890s and, if Wilhelmine Germany is classified as a democracy, the Moroccan crises of 1905–06 and 1911 and the Samoan crises of 1889 and 1899. These cases would support my conclusions. For example, from 1832 to 1843, the Foxite legacy disposed England's Whigs to feel a strong commitment to France based on a shared liberal ideology. Yet Anglo-French relations during this period were marked by intense geopolitical rivalry over Belgium, Spain, and the Near East, and the threat of war was always a factor in the calculations of policymakers in both London and Paris. Foreign Minister Lord Palmerston profoundly distrusted French ambitions and constantly urged that England maintain sufficient naval power to defend its interests against a French challenge. See Kenneth Bourne, *Palmerston: The Early Years, 1784–1841* (New York: Macmillan, 1982), p. 613. Also see Roger Buller, *Palmerston, Guizat and the Collapse of the Entente Cordiale* (London: Athlone Press, 1974); and Sir Charles Webster, *The Foreign Policy Palmerston, Vol. I: 1830–1841, Britain, The Liberal Movement and The Eastern Question* (London: Bell & Sons, 1951). Italy challenged France for Mediterranean ascendancy although the two nations were bound by liberalism, democracy, and a common culture. The two states engaged in a trade war

and came close to a real wax. France apparently was dissuaded from attacking Italy in 1888 when the British Channel Fleet was sent to the Italian naval base of La Spezia. Italy was prevented from attacking France by its military and economic weakness. See C.J. Lowe and F. Marzari, *Italian Foreign Policy, 1870–1940* (London: Routledge & Kegan Paul, 1975), chap. 4; C.J. Lowe, *The Reluctant Imperialists: British Foreign Policy 1879–1902* (London: Routledge & Kegan Paul, 1974), Vol. I, pp. 147–150; John A.C. Conybeare, *Trade Wars: The Theory and Practice of International Commercial Rivalry* (New York: Columbia University Press, 1987), pp. 183–188.

5. Melvin Small and J. David Singer first observed the pattern of democracies not fighting democracies in a 1976 article: Small and Singer, "The War-proneness of Democratic Regimes, 1816–1865," *Jerusalem Journal of International Relations,* Vol. 1, No. 4 (Summer 1976), pp. 50–69. Their finding has been the subject of extensive further empirical testing which has produced a consensus around the propositions stated in the text. See Stuart A. Bremer, "Dangerous Dyads: Conditions Affecting the Likelihood of Interstate War, 1816–1865," *Journal of Conflict Resolution,* Vol. 36, No. 2 (June 1992), pp. 309–441; Steve Chan, "Mirror, Mirror on the Wal . . . Are the Freer Countries More Pacific?" *Journal of Conflict Resolution,* Vol. 28, No. 4 (December 1984), pp. 617–648; Zeev Maoz and Nasrin Abdolali, "Regime and International Conflict," *Journal of Conflict Resolution,* Vol. 33, No. 1 (March 1989), pp. 3–35; R.J. Rummel, "Libertarianism and International Violence," *Journal of Conflict Resolution,* Vol. 27, No. 1 (March 1983), pp. 27–71; Erich Weede, "Democracy and War Involvement," *Journal of Conflict Resolution,* Vol. 28, No. 4 (December 1984), pp. 649–664.

6. Jack S. Levy, "Domestic Politics and War," in. Robert I. Rotberg and Theodore K. Rabb, eds., *The Origin and Prevention of Major Wars* (Cambridge: Cambridge University Press, 1989), p. 88.

7. Russett, *Grasping the Democratic Peace,* p. 33; Michael W. Doyle, "Kant, Liberal Legacies and Foreign Affairs," Part I, *Philosophy and Public Affairs,* Vol. 12, No. 3 (Summer 1983), p. 213.

8. This is the terminology employed by Russett, *Grasping the Democratic Peace;* also see Bruce Russett and Zeev Maoz, "Normative and Structural Causes of Democratic Peace," *American Political Science Review,* Vol. 87, No. 3 (September 1993), pp. 624–638. Russett points out (pp. 40–42) that, although analytically distinct, these two explanations are intertwined.

9. Doyle, "Kant, Liberal Legacies, and Foreign Affairs," pp. 205–235. See also Doyle, "Liberalism and World Politics," *Antedate Political Science Ravine,* Vol. 80, No. 4 (December 198b), pp. 1151–1169; Russett, *Grasping the Democratic Peace,* pp. 38–40.

10. T. Clifton Morgan and Sally N. Campbell, "Domestic Structure, Decisional Constraints and War: So Why Kant Democracies Fight?" *Journal of Conflict Resolution,* Vol. 35, No. 2 (June 1991), pp. 187–211; and T. Clifton Morgan and Valerie L. Schwebach, "Take Two Democracies and Call Me in the Morning: A Prescription for Peace?" *International Interactions.* Vol. 17, No. 4 (Summer 1992), pp. 305–420.

11. Russett, *Grasping the Democratic Peace,* p. 31 (second emphasis added).

12. Doyle, "Kant, Liberal Legacies, and Foreign Affairs," p. 230. It is also argued that the predisposition of democratic states to regard other democracies favorably is reinforced by the fact that liberal democratic states are linked by mutually beneficial ties of economic interdependence. Democracies thus have strong incentives to act towards each other in a manner that enhances cooperation and to refrain from acting in a manner that threatens their stake in mutually beneficial cooperation. Ibid., pp. 230–232; Rummel, "Libertarianism and International Violence,"

pp. 27–28. For the "interdependence promotes peace" argument see Richard Rosecrance, *The Rise of the Trading State* (New York: Basic Books, 1986). In fact, however, for great powers economic interdependence, rather than promoting peace, creates seemingly important interests that may be defended by overseas military commitments. . . .

13. Doyle, "Kant, Liberal Legacies, and Foreign Affairs"; and Harvey Starr, "Democracy and War. Choke, Learning and Security Communities," *Journal of Peace Research,* Vol. 29, No. 2 (1992), pp. 207–213.

14. Maoz and Russett, "A Statistical Artifact?" p. 246.

15. Russett, *Grasping the Democratic Peace,* p. 33.

16. Classic explications of realism are Kenneth N. Waltz, *Theory of International Politics* (Reading, Mass.: Addison-Wesley, 1979) and Hans J. Morgenthau, rev. by Kenneth W. Thompson, *Politics Among Nations: The Struggle for Power and Peace,* 6th ed. (New York: Knopf, 1985).

18. Manz and Russett, "Normative and Structural Causes," p. 624.

21. Geoffrey Blainey, *The Causes of War,* 3rd ed. (South Melbourne: Macmillan Co. of Australia, 1988), pp. 57–67. As the parable goes, while the waterbirds fight over the catch, the fisherman spreads his net.

22. My classification of the United States in 1861 and 1895 and of Germany in 1923 as great powers might be challenged. By the mid-nineteenth century British policy-makers viewed the United States, because of its size, population, wealth, and growing industrial strength (and latent military power), as "a great world power," notwithstanding the fact that it was not an active participant in the European state system. Ephraim Douglass Adams, *Great Britain and the American Civil War* (New York: Russell and Russell, 1924), Vol. I, p. 10. In 1895 the perception of American power had heightened in Britain and in other leading European powers. In 1923, Germany, although substantially disarmed pursuant to Versailles, remained Europe's most economically powerful state. As most statesmen realized, it was, because of its population and industry, a latent continental hegemony. Democratic peace theorists have classified all eight states as having been democracies at the time of their involvement in the crises under discussion. See Doyle, "Kant, Liberal Legacies, and Foreign Affairs," part I, pp. 214–215. Russett, *Grasping the Democratic Peace,* pp. 5–9, briefly discusses the Venezuela and Fashoda crises, but his bibliography has few historical references to these two crises (and related issues), and omits most standard sources.

28. Adams, *Britain and the Civil War,* Vol. I, p. 216.

29. Quoted in Gordon H. Warren, *Fountain of Discontent: The Trent Affair and Freedom of the Seas* (Boston: Northeastern University Press, 1981), p. 105.

30. Quoted in Adams, *Britain and the Civil War,* Vol. I, p. 217.

31. Quoted in Norman B. Ferris, *The Trent Affair: A Diplomatic Crisis* (Knoxville: University of Tennessee Press, 1977), p. 44.

32. Ibid., p. 109; Howard Jones, *Union in Peril: Tice Crisis Over British Intervention in the Civil War* (Chapel Hill: University of North Carolina Press, 1992), pp. 84–85.

33. Quoted in Jones, *Union in Peril,* p. 85.

34. Jenkins, *War for the Union,* p. 214.

35. Quoted in Kenneth Bourne, *Britain and the Balance of Power in North America, 1815–1908* (Berkeley: University of California Press, 1967), p. 219.

36. The figures are from Warren, *Fountain of Discontent,* pp. 130, 136. For an overview of British military and naval activities during the Trent crisis see Kenneth Bourne, "British Preparations for War with the North, 1861–1862," *English Historical Review,* Vol. 76, No. 301 (October 1961), pp. 600–632.

37. Ferris, *Trent Affair,* p. 56; Wilbur Devereux Jones, *The American Problem in British Diplomacy,* 2841–2861 (London: Macmillan, 1974), p. 203. In international

relations theory terms, London's view of Anglo-American relations was based on a deterrence model rather than a spiral model. See Robert Jervis, *Perception and Misperception in International Politics* (Princeton: Princeton University Press, 1976), pp. 58–111. Coexisting uneasily with the positive view of an Anglo-American community was the British image of the United States as a vulgar "mobocracy" that, unless firmly resisted, would pursue a rapacious and bullying foreign policy. Warren, *Fountain of Discontent*, pp. 47–51.

38. Quoted in Bourne, *Balance of Power*, p. 247.

39. Bourne, "British Preparations," p. 631.

40. Bourne, *Balance of Power*, p. 247.

41. Quoted in ibid., pp. 245–246, emphasis in original.

42. Quoted in Jenkins, *War for the Union*, p. 216.

43. Ferris, *Trent Affair*, pp. 111–113.

44. Norman B. Ferris, *Desperate Diplomacy: William H. Seward's Foreign Policy, 1861* (Knoxville: University of Tennessee, 1976), p. 194.

45. Quoted in Adams, *Britain and the Civil War*, Vol. I, p. 218.

46. Warren, *Fountain of Discontent*, pp. 184–185; Adams, *Britain and the Civil War*, p. 231. Howard Jones, however, suggests that Lincoln probably intended to give up Mason and Slidell and that he may have been posturing in order to shift to other members of his cabinet the onus of advancing the argument for surrendering them. Jones, *Union in Peril*, pp. 91–92.

47. Ferris, *Trent Affair*, pp. 177–182; Jenkins, *War for the Union*, pp. 223–226; Warren, *Fountain of Discontent*, pp. 181–182.

48. See Jenkins, *War for the Union*, pp. 225–226.

51. Quoted in ibid., p. 182.

52. Quoted in Jenkins, *War for the Union*, p. 224.

140. See for example Joshua Muravchik, *Exporting Democracy: Fulfilling America's Destiny* (Washington, D.C.: AEI Press, 1991); and Larry Diamond, "Promoting Democracy," *Foreign Policy*, No. 87 (Summer 1992), pp. 25–46.

141. "Remarks of Anthony Lake," Johns Hopkins School of Advanced International Studies, Washington, D.C., September 21, 1993 (Washington, D.C.: National Security Council Press Office).

142. Lake stated that the Clinton administration does not propose to embark on a "democratic crusade." Both Doyle and Russett acknowledge that democratic peace theory could encourage democratic states to pursue aggressive policies toward non-democracies, and both express worry at this. Doyle, "Kant, Liberal Legacies, and Foreign Affairs," part II; Russett, *Grasping the Democratic Peace*, p. 136.

143. Quoted in Russett, *Grasping the Democratic Peace*, p. 33.

145. Lloyd C. Gardner, *A Covenant With Power: America and World Order from Wilson to Reagan* (New York Oxford University Press, 1984), p. 27. For an excellent critique of the notion that America's domestic ideology must be validated by its foreign policy, see Michael H. Hunt, *Ideology and U.S. Foreign Policy* (New Haven: Yale University Press, 1987).

147. Robert Jervis, "The Future of World Politics: Will It Resemble the Past?" *International Security*, Vol. 16, No. 3 (Winter 1991–92), pp. 39–73.

148. For an example of this argument see James M. Goldgeier and Michael McFaul, "A Tale of Two Worlds: Core and Periphery in the Post-Cold War," *International Organization*, Vol 46, No. 3 (Spring 1992), pp. 467–491.

150. Russett, *Grasping the Democratic Peace*, p. 156, argues that, "understanding the sources of democratic peace can have the effect of a self-fulfilling prophecy. Social scientists sometimes create reality as well as analyze it. Insofar as norms do guide behavior, repeating those norms helps to make them effective. *Repeating the norms as descriptive principles can help to make them true.*" (Emphasis added.)

Reading Responses

1. Summarize the central claim of democratic peace theory and the logic that supports it. In other words, what's the chain of reasoning that supports democratic peace theory?

2. Assess Layne's use of the case-study method to test democratic peace theory. Did you find his analysis of the Trent Affair persuasive? Would you have found statistics more effective? What are the limitations of case-study evidence?

3. Near the end of his essay, Layne describes democratic peace theory as "dangerous." What in his article would most persuade you to agree with him—what evidence? What logical reasoning? Why do you think that some readers would respond passionately to this description of democratic peace theory?

Notes on Grammar, Style, and Rhetoric:

Textual Coherence

One striking aspect of the introductory paragraphs of Christopher Layne's "Kant or Cant: The Myth of the Democratic Peace" is that they include several prominent text connectives. Text connectives help show readers how the parts of a text relate to one another, how the overall text is organized, and sometimes how the text relates to its context. Specific examples of text connectives are elements that indicate sequences (*first, in the third place, finally*) as well as those that indicate logical or temporal relationships (*consequently, at the same time*). Other text connectives are reminders about material presented earlier (*as I demonstrated in Chapter Two*) and previews of forthcoming material (*as I will show in the next section*).

In his early paragraphs, Layne uses several statements to preview how his essay will unfold. These preview statements begin already at the end of the first paragraph. There he uses two general statements to give an overview of much of his article. One of these begins with "In this article, I focus primarily on . . . ," and the other begins with "I then briefly assess. . . ."

Then he moves to previews of the specific steps he will take in his essay. At the start of the second paragraph he writes, "I begin by reviewing. . . ." Shortly thereafter he adds, "As I demonstrate. . . ." And then in the third and fourth paragraphs, he adds still other preview statements, introduced as follows: "I deduce . . . ," "Using a process-tracing approach, I examine . . . ," "I conclude . . . ," and finally "I conclude by discussing. . . ."

Because all these preview statements occur within a handful of lines of one another, you might be inclined to ask, "Why does Layne spend so much time telling readers what he is going to do? Why doesn't he just go ahead and start his presentation?" Speculating about how Layne might respond to these questions is instructive. He could, for instance, appeal to aspects of his rhetorical situation and formulate a defense that would include several points.

First, he could note that in the United States we generally place much responsibility on the writer for signaling how texts are organized. Probably all of us, at some point in school, have been advised to use transitions, especially as we begin paragraphs. Our print culture tells us that we should take care to mark the way clearly for readers as they move through our texts. Not all cultures convey this message. In the print culture of some European countries—Germany and Finland, for example—writers are encouraged to let readers discover organizational patterns of texts on their own.

Second, he might note that his essay is long. What is reprinted of Layne's essay in this textbook is only a portion of his overall piece. To make his essay fit within the scope of a chapter in this book, the editors have had to cut several of his case studies. Similarly, Layne's argument is quite complex. He is rejecting a popular view of the democratic peace and offering a different view in its place. To lay out the essence of the view he opposes as well as of the view that he supports involves some careful explaining. In this process he gives the details of several case studies and shows how those details support his view and work against the popular one.

When writers have long and complex presentations, they have good reason to use preview statements to help readers see where they are headed. Similarly, when readers have little knowledge about the writer's subject matter, writers have good reason to use preview statements to keep them from getting lost.

In Your Own Writing . . .

- When your writing is long and complex, consider using preview statements.
- When your topic is new to your reader, consider using preview statements.
- When you write in a new discipline or a new culture, try to determine the level of text connectives that your reader expects.

STUDENT WRITING

INTRODUCTION

by James R. King, political science major

The Assignment. I wrote the following essay as the final project for a political science class on the topic of democracy—theories about democracy as well as political states, worldwide, that follow democratic principles. My professor asked us to write a research paper that analyzed one country's attempts at democratic consolidation. Prior to this project, I had developed an interest in the Arab–Israeli conflict. I was certain that I wanted to write a paper on the status of Arab citizens of Israel, but I was unsure where that would lead.

The Content. Although it may seem obvious, the key to writing a quality political science paper is to become knowledgeable about your topic. When you become aware of the range of opinions that people have about your topic, you can more easily spot the bias of the researcher, and you can better sort out fact from opinion. I had to be well-versed on the subject of Israeli democracy. As I read a number of online and journal articles and books and spoke with my professors, I started to figure out exactly what I wanted to argue. I developed my thesis that because of Israel's heavy emphasis on its Jewish character, it cannot be considered a fully consolidated democracy. As I wrote, I continued to do research, allowing my thesis to evolve, leaving myself open to its possible changes. But, building this initial foundation was essential to the completion of this kind of controversial piece.

Learning to Write about Political Issues. Although writers in all fields must think about the audience for their essays, I think that political scientists—because everyone argues about politics—have to pay especially careful attention to their readers. I decided that I would like to publish this essay to convince people (in addition to my professor) to pay attention to the plight of Israeli-Palestinians, so I kept a secondary audience in mind as I wrote—those potential readers in an academic journal or an online publication.

Appealing to this secondary audience, I knew, would be much more difficult than writing for my professor. In my experience, most people bring strongly held opinions to the issues surrounding Israel and the Middle East; very few people come to an essay on this topic eager to be persuaded. I was aware that regardless of what I said, many of the readers of my paper would not change their views. Therefore, throughout the actual writing process, I chose to focus on the readers who, although perhaps initially uncomfortable with criticism of the state of Israel, might accept my thesis if I provided convincing evidence. I felt that if I could persuade them, then I could certainly convince any readers who were neutral on this issue.

So I set for myself the goal of convincing a slightly biased yet relatively uninformed reader. To reach out to this audience, I relied on three methods most heavily: First, in doing my research, I looked at a wide variety of sources, both in terms of the type of sources (whether a book, academic journal, news source, think tank report, etc.) and especially the political leanings of the author. I knew that it was especially critical that my research not be perceived as (or actually be) biased or one-sided. For example, I cited such well-respected sources as the *New York Times* and the BBC, and I employed quotes and statistics from the former mayor of Jerusalem, a nonpartisan Israeli research institute, and official Israeli government studies.

Second, I sought to incorporate some of the obvious objections to my thesis into the paper. I knew that the uninformed, slightly biased reader would certainly have a number of reservations about my thesis, so I included specific questions readers might have about the paper. By asking—and answering—the imagined audience's questions, I proved that I had thought deeply about the topic and that I had proposed a strong, well-supported thesis, a thesis I hoped they would accept as their own.

Finally, I used a blend of theoretical and factual analysis when I argued for my thesis. The theory helps the reader understand the overall significance of the given idea, while the facts and statistics effectively display the significance. I had to demonstrate that Israel's theory of "ethnic democracy" does not fit the definition of democracy. While certainly some people will disagree with my interpretations of facts, by using statistical evidence, I tried to illuminate tensions within Israeli democracy. After reading this combination of theoretical and factual analysis, my readers ought to have a more complete understanding of the problems facing Arab citizens of Israel and Israeli democracy; as a result, they should be more willing to agree with my thesis.

Being able to argue for an issue that you're passionate about is an important skill for any citizen in a democracy. A single political act, such as declaring war, can affect the lives of millions of people; it is vital that political leaders—and citizens in a democracy—are able to argue effectively about political acts. Perhaps my research will inspire some of my readers to investigate this issue further, or even to take action. Maybe it will inspire you.

Democratic Consolidation in Israel?: The Situation of Arab Citizens of Israel and the Implications for Larger Israeli Democracy

James R. King

In 2003, the Israeli Democracy Institute (IDI), an Israeli non-partisan research institute that analyzes the status of Israeli democracy, presented its Democracy Index to Israeli President Moshe Katsav. The report stated that "Protection of human rights in Israel is poor; there is serious political and economic discrimination against the Arab minority; there is much less freedom of religion than in other democracies; and the socioeconomic inequality indicator is amongst the highest in the sample."[1] Ori Nir, the Washington Bureau Chief for *The Forward,* and former correspondent to *Ha'aretz* newspaper, provided a number of disturbing statistics to a conference sponsored by the Foundation for Middle East Peace and the Middle East Institute:

> I used statistics to convince the reader that Arab-Israelis do not receive equal treatment.

- On a per capita basis, the Government [of Israel] spends two-thirds as much for Arabs as for Jews.
- Most [Israeli government] ministries have less than 5% Arabs on their payroll, and mostly in minor positions. The Ministries of Housing, Transportation, and Trade and Industry all had representation of less than 1% of Arabs in their workforce.
- The budget for the Ministry of Religious Affairs for 2000 only allocated 2.9% of its resources to the non-Jewish sector, although Muslims, Christians, and Druze constituted approximately 20% of the population.
- Between 1975 and 2000, only 0.3% of public construction initiated and subsidized by the Israeli government was for Arabs.
- No Arab community has been created since 1948, except for seven towns created for Bedouins in the Negev, whereas something like 1,000 towns have been created for Israeli Jews.
- Only 30% of Arab communities have an adequate sewage system (approximately 95% of the communities in the Jewish sector do).[2]

Nevertheless, Israel is considered by many Americans to be the only functioning democracy in the Middle East.[3] In a troubled region where democracy has largely failed to develop, this statement certainly has some merit. In the first part of this essay, I will analyze Israeli democracy generally, especially how and why it functions well, despite

It's common in political science writing to describe the organization of the essay first and then introduce the claim.

Rhetoric in political science calls for directly stating the point of your argument—even if it is controversial. Almost any political argument is going to be controversial, so it helps to be humble but straightforward.

I begin with evidence that seems to contradict my thesis.

Bicameral means having two chambers, houses, or branches.

its relatively recent establishment and the difficult circumstances it has faced throughout its brief history. After this important recognition, however, the majority of the essay will examine areas in which Israeli democracy has failed to consolidate. I will contend that Israel, in fact, is not nearly as democratic as is often purported.

This essay will focus primarily on the explicit and inherent Jewish character of the Israeli state and how that affects the minority Arab citizens of Israel, the Israeli-Palestinians.[4] Does the fact that Israel, both as a state and in the beliefs of its Jewish citizens, sees itself ideologically (as well as in law and practice) as an ethnic state, a state for Jews worldwide, necessarily present problems for its non-Jewish citizens? Does Israel's emphasis on its "Jewishness" over its functioning as a democratic state for all its citizens, render it undemocratic, or lacking and in need of democratic transition? Or, is Israel's situation merely the result of unique circumstances? I argue that the Israeli situation is certainly unique, thus requiring different and probably more generous analysis; nonetheless, to better consolidate its democracy, Israel must move from its fundamental and all-pervasive Zionist ideology, one based on security, domination, and ethnic exclusivism, to a post-Zionist statehood that strives for a peaceful, pluralist society that is democratic before it is ethnic.

On the surface and certainly for its Jewish citizens, Israel does sustain a thriving democracy. Israel's bicameral parliament, the Knesset, is comprised of not only two main parties but also a large number of smaller parties, including Arab parties. The current Knesset, elected in 2003, contains eight Arabs, out of 120 total members. All Israeli citizens have voting rights, including women and Israeli-Palestinians.[5] Israeli law guarantees civil liberties for both individuals and groups, including minorities. Certainly, much of Israeli democracy is impressive, especially when one considers Israel's relatively recent establishment (1948) and the instability that results from war with its neighbors and the continued military presence in the Occupied Territories. However, I maintain that many aspects of Israeli government and society, both in structures and attitudes, in fact the very foundation of the state, demonstrate a lack of democratic consolidation. The most obvious manifestation of this failure is the condition of the Israeli-Palestinian, a complicated and under-analyzed situation.

Israeli-Palestinians, representing roughly twenty percent of the total Israeli population, are both Arab-Palestinians and Israeli citizens. They are those Palestinians (or descendents of those) who remained within the post-1948 borders of the newly created state of Israel and were granted Israeli citizenship. Common scholarship tends to view this Israeli-Palestinian minority as parallel to other minority groups in Western liberal democracies. According to this sort of "normal development model,"

Israeli-Palestinians are moving along in a gradual process of development and normalization in Israeli society.[6]

Although there is some validity in this model, it fails to recognize the fundamental and inescapable tension between the values of an *ethnic* state and the principles of a *democratic* one. While democratic process should promote equality by negating the ascendancy of one group or the state's identification with it,[7] Israel, as an ethnic state, "sets its goals with no thought for nationalities other than the dominant group and its members in all sorts of legally-sanctioned ways. The discrimination against other ethnic groups derives from the state's refusal to respond to demands for equality, affiliation, and identification."[8] As opposed to the model of a liberal democracy, where equal citizens compete to collectively determine the "common good,"[9] the commitments of Israeli democracy are first and foremost to its Jewish citizens, even if the policy in question is detrimental to the Arab minority.

Because Israel was founded as a safe haven for Jews worldwide, it became, necessarily, a Jewish state. Beginning in the 1870s, Jews from all over the world immigrated to Israel, with the explicit intention of establishing a Jewish state. After the horrific events of the Holocaust, this immigration project became a priority of the Western states. Finally, in 1948 Israel was founded as a Jewish democracy. From Israel's founding until now, Arabs have been isolated from the project of Israeli statehood; in fact, many within the Palestinian population (and arguably the Palestinians as a collective group) have been unwillingly forced to sacrifice their homes, their land, and their rights for this cause of a Jewish state. Foundational Israeli law, especially the legal definition of the state as the "state of the Jewish people," has also reflected the ethnically exclusive nature of the Israeli state. For example, the Law of Return and the Citizenship Law grant any Jew from anywhere in the world automatic citizenship into the state of Israel, while a Palestinian refugee cannot claim that automatic citizenship.

> In this paragraph the history of Israel seems to support a claim that contradicts my thesis. But I focus on aspects of that history that support my claim.

The current exclusion of Arabs from full democratic participation is rooted in Israel's refusal to acknowledge Arab culture. The former mayor of Jerusalem, Meron Benvenisti, in his book *Sacred Landscape: The Buried History of the Holy Land Since 1948*, argues that Israel established the distinctly Jewish character of the newly established homeland by attempting to disguise its former Arab identity. According to Benvenisti, after 1948 the Jewish state suppressed Arab history by creating a new, Hebrew map of the region. On the map, Israel altered the place names of virtually all Arab villages and geographical features, officially changing them to Hebrew names or to names that were particularly meaningful to Jews. Benvenisti maintains that by changing the long-standing Arabic names, the Jewish state was essentially declaring a war on Arab culture, announcing that it was no longer interested in living side-by-side in a bilingual or bicultural state.[10]

Unfortunately for the Palestinian-Israelis and for Israeli democracy, the unwillingness to integrate the Palestinian population and their culture into the new state certainly continued after Israel's establishment. By appealing almost entirely to this Zionist cultural, religious, and historical heritage, a heritage that Palestinians often associate with war, displacement, and exclusion, modern Israeli symbols such as the national anthem, state flag, and official state holidays[11] have made it painfully clear to Palestinian-Israelis that Israel remains a Jewish state. Eliezer Ben-Rafael and Stephen Sharot, in their book *Ethnicity, Religion, and Class in Israeli Society* recognize the dual nature of the Palestinian-Israeli's situation: "On the one hand, Arabs are granted full citizenship and legal equality. On the other hand, the Jewish-Zionist character of the state has led to the exclusion of Arabs at a number of symbolic and material levels."[12] Ghanem argues that Israel relies on two key policies to maintain this Jewish character. First, the state supports policies that reinforce Jewish superiority in all spheres. Second, the state limits the democratic character of the state and thereby minimizes Arab incorporation. Because this latter policy encourages democracy at some level, it often gives the false appearance of true democracy.[13]

It is obvious, then, that Palestinian-Israelis are isolated from their state in a number of critically important ways, in many cases as a direct result of state intentions to exclude them. Of course, this intentional exclusion results in tangible experiences of discrimination for Palestinian-Israelis. Although a number of areas could be analyzed (remember some of the statistics listed at the beginning of the essay), the remainder of this essay will look to the unequal treatment of Palestinian-Israelis in terms of land expropriation, political involvement, economics, and the popular sentiment of Jewish-Israelis. In these four areas, it will be further demonstrated that Israel has failed to develop the workings of a consolidated democracy.

Founding a Jewish state on a land that was occupied primarily by Palestinians was an extremely formidable task, one that, according to Benvenisti, did not end when the state of Israel was established in 1948. Israel continues to expropriate Arab land for state and Jewish use. Much of the land has been used to enable immigrant Jews (from under the Law of Return and the Citizenship Law) to acquire land in Israel. The Jewish Agency and the Jewish National Fund have largely succeeded in turning much of Israel into state land, or at least land distributed by the state, land that is designed to benefit only Jews. In fact, over 93% of Israeli land is state owned; Arabs own only approximately 3.5% of the land in Israel.[14]

Despite the fact that they constitute roughly twenty percent of the total Israeli population, Palestinian-Israelis are greatly underrepresented in the Israeli government. While Palestinian-Israelis do have full voting rights and some Arabs serve in the Knesset, Arab parties tend to play the permanent role of opposition. A *New York Times* article on Arab involvement in Israeli government states that "No Israeli prime minister has ever given leaders of the Arab parties significant positions of power."[15] This has been a common pattern in Israeli politics. Palestinian-Israelis are systematically excluded from the most important Knesset committees, like Finance, Defense, and Foreign Affairs.[16] Many Israeli government ministries have special departments dealing with matters of the Arab minority, but with a Jewish head.[17]

Amendment 9 to the Basic Law also excludes Arabs from full participation in Israeli government. In January of 2003, Israel's Central Election Committee disqualified two of the most prominent Arab members of the Knesset, Ahmad al-Tibi and Azmi Bisharah, from running in the election. The committee justified their decision based on al-Tibi's and Bisharah's opposition to the existence of a Jewish state (an opposition which is illegal under Amendment 9), and their promotion of an Israeli state for all citizens, regardless of ethnicity. The committee reviewed the candidacy of another controversial figure, Jewish politician Baruch Marzel, because of his open anti-Arab racism; but, amidst assurances that he no longer promoted racist policies (despite his open support for transferring Palestinians out of the West Bank and Gaza), the committee allowed Marzel to run. Eventually, this decision was overturned by the Israeli High Court of Justice.[18] According to a *New York Times* article, however, the message to Palestinian-Israelis was clear: "If you are a Jewish extremist, you can go on the campaign trail. But if you belong to the Arab minority and do not openly toe the government line, you cannot be part of the election game."[19]

The economic situation of Palestinian-Israelis remains quite dire as well, reflecting both their lack of integration into Israeli society and the Israeli government's apathy towards their plight. Statistics provide the best indicator of the difficult economic situation of the Palestinian-Israelis. These statistics were provided by the International Crisis Group, an international advocacy group, in its report entitled "Identity Crisis: Israel and its Arab Citizens"[20]:

- In 2003, some 44.7% of Arab-Israeli families lived in poverty, as opposed to roughly 20% of Israeli Jewish families;[21]
- 27 of the 30 communities in Israel with the highest unemployment rates are Arab, including the top fourteen;[22]
- The average gross hourly income of an Arab wage earner is 60% that of a Jewish counterpart.[23]

According to Sarah Kreimer, co-director of The Center for Jewish-Arab Economic Development, the Israeli Ministry of Education spends nearly twice as much per Jewish child as per Arab child. This has led to an infant mortality in the Arab sector that is nearly double that among Jews.[24]

Certainly, statistics cannot tell the entire story of the current situation of the Palestinian-Israelis. The economic depravity of Israel's Arab population cannot be attributed wholly to government discrimination, as a number of factors have contributed to their poor economic situation. It is clear, however, that the Israeli government has discriminated against this minority group, and it is also clear that this discrimination is supported by a majority of Israel's population. The popular opinion of Jews in Israel regarding their fellow Arab citizens might, in fact, be the most disturbing aspect of Israeli democracy, as it shows an obvious lack of democratic value within the population.

A number of popular opinion surveys have recorded attitudes of Israel's Jewish population toward their fellow Arab-Palestinian citizens. These surveys indicate that a large majority of Jews in Israel emphasize Israel's Jewish identity before and often times against its democratic identity. In a survey conducted in 1995 by Jewish scholar Sammy Smooha of the University of Haifa eighty-five percent of Jews surveyed said that they were opposed to any change to the Israeli state symbols to make them less offensive to the Arab minority, and seventy-four percent believed that the state should manifest great or some preference to Jews over Arab citizens. Ninety-five percent of the Jewish Israelis opposed the idea of Israel as a liberal democratic state in which Arabs can compete freely and live wherever they wish. In fact, fifty-one percent said that the term "Israeli" applies only to Jews and not Arabs.[25] The 2003 Israel Democracy Index revealed that fifty-three percent of Jewish-Israelis are openly against full equality for the Arabs, only thirty-one percent support having Arab parties in the government, and fifty-seven percent agree that Arabs should be encouraged to emigrate.[26] The popular opinions of Israelis indicate that many of the core values of a liberal democracy have failed to take hold, undoubtedly a sign of incomplete democratic consolidation.[27]

In this essay, I have shown how Israeli democracy has largely failed to consolidate in relation to its ethnic minority, the Palestinian-Israelis. In nearly all areas of Israeli society, including land distribution, political participation, the economic sphere, and general attitudes of Israeli's dominant Jewish population, Palestinian-Israelis remain marginalized and discriminated against. However, even if their status in these areas improves, Palestinian-Israelis will remain isolated from their fellow citizens in Israel. Because Israel has established itself in law, symbol, and practice as an inherently and explicitly Jewish state, Palestinian-Israelis will always face the fundamental tension of being Arab and living in a Jewish state.[28] They will remain what Dan Rabinowitz terms a "trapped minority," both Arab and Israeli, accepted by neither world.

To transition to a functioning, fully consolidated democracy, Israel must shift its focus away from its ethnic statehood. In his article, "Israel in Transition from Zionism to Post-Zionism," Herbert C. Kelman argues that Israel must begin to see itself as a state for *all* its citizens, not a state for Jews worldwide. Israel has successfully become a safe haven for persecuted Jews around the world; the Zionist project has largely been completed. Now, he argues, "The primary feature of a post-Zionist state must be to protect and advance the interests and well-being of its citizens, regardless of ethnicity."[29] Israel must regard itself as a democratic state, a state that treats all citizens equally. Only when Israel shifts away from an exclusively Jewish ethnic state to that of a liberal democracy, one that includes both Jews and Arabs, can it be considered a fully transitioned democracy.

Notes

1. "The State of Israeli Democracy," *The Democracy Index*. Israel Democracy Institute. <http://www.idi.org.il/english/article.php?id=1466>. (18 September 2004).
2. Ori Nir, "Israel's Arab Minority," The Foundation for Middle East Peace, Current Analysis, Speech given on April 30, 2003, <http://www.fmep.org/analysis/ori_nir_israels_arab_minority.html>, (25 April 2004).
3. It should be noted that the definition of what states comprise the Middle East is its own topic of debate. Many, for example, would include Turkey and Iran as a part of the Middle East. These states are certainly democratic on a number of levels.
4. "Israeli-Palestinian" is the preferred name for Arabs who are citizens of the state of Israel. They are also known as Arab-Israelis, although this name is not preferred.
5. "Political Parties and Platforms," *Israeli Democracy in Action,* <http://www.israelvotes2003.com/>, (22 April 2004).
6. As'ad Ghanem, *The Palestinian-Arab Minority in Israel, 1948–2000,* (Albany, NY: State University of New York Press, 2001), 5–7.
7. As'ad Ghanem, "State and minority in Israel: the case of ethnic state and the predicament of its minority," *Ethnic and Racial Studies,* Volume 21, No. 3 (May 1998), 429.
8. Ibid., 439.
9. Ghanem, *The Palestinian-Arab Minority in Israel,* 7.
10. Meron Benvenisti, *Sacred Landscape: The Buried History of the Holy Land Since 1948,* (Berkeley, CA: University of California Press, 2000.)
11. Ghanem, "State and Minority in Israel," 432.
12. Eliezer Ben-Rafael and Stephen Sharot, *Ethnicity, religion, and class in Israeli society,* (Cambridge, England: Cambridge University Press, 1991), 233.
13. Ghanem, *The Palestinian-Arab Minority in Israel,* 9.
14. "Identity Crisis: Israel and its Arab Citizens," The International Crisis Group, *ICG Middle East Report,* Number 25 (4 March 2004), <http://www.crisisweb.org//library/documents/middle_east__north_africa/arab_israeli_conflict/25_identity_crisis_israel_arab_citz.pdf>, (26 April 2004), 14.
15. David Newman, "A Decision That Hurts Israeli Democracy," *The New York Times,* January 6, 2003, (A, 21).
16. Ghanem, "State and Minority in Israel," 433.
17. Eliezer Ben-Rafael and Stephen Sharot, 235.
18. "Israeli Arabs urged to vote after disqualifications overruled," *BBC News Online,* 10 January 2003, (8 March 2004).
19. Newman, *New York Times.*

20. The full report can be found at <http://www.crisisweb.org//library/documents/middle_east__north_africa/arab_israeli_conflict/25_identity_crisis_israel_arabcitz.pdf>.

21. From "Identity Crisis: Israel and its Arab Citizens," (Mossawa Center, "Socio-Economic Report on Arab Citizens and Local Councils." <www.mossawacenter.org/eng/reports/summaryeng.htm>).

22. Ibid., (National Security Council, "The Arab Citizens of Israel—Organising Ideas for Addressing the Issue").

23. Ibid., (Central Bureau of Statistics, op. cit.).

24. Sarah Kreimer, The Center for Jewish-Arab Economic Development, <http://www.cjaed.org.il/news_161000_b.html>. (26 April 2004).

25. Ghanem, *The Palestinian-Arab Minority in Israel,* 160–163.

26. "The State of Israeli Democracy."

27. This could also include the public's relative apathy to government corruption, the lack of rule of law in the Occupied Territories, and the frequent undemocratic measures carried out even within Israel, among other things.

28. Mark Tessler and Audra K. Grant, "Israel's Arab Citizens: The Continuing Struggle," *The Annals of the American Academy of Political Science,* Volume 555 (January 1998), 97–113.

29. Herbert C Kelman, "Israel in Transition from Zionism to Post-Zionism," *The Annals of the American Academy of Political and Social Science,* Volume 555 (January 1998), 46–61.

Reading Responses

1. In his introduction, James King notes that he intentionally included objections to his thesis. Review King's essay and list the objections that he includes. Do you have additional objections to King's thesis? What are they?

2. Both Professor Goi and James King emphasize the passion that political scientists bring to their topics. Where in the essay can you detect King's passion for this topic? Is his use of emotion-laden discourse appropriate?

3. What strategies does King use to "map" his argument for his reader? Note the kind of preview statements he uses and record their location. Where in his essay do these most commonly appear?

PUBLIC WRITING

INTRODUCTION

Hassina Sherjan left Afghanistan as a refugee in 1979. She became a successful businessperson, and in 1996 she founded the nonprofit group Aid Afghanistan for Education, which she continues to direct (www.aidafghanistan.net). She first returned to Afghanistan in 1999 and established several girls' schools, which brought her into grave danger with Taliban forces. When the Taliban was defeated, Sherjan returned to Afghanistan to work for the rebuilding of her country.

Sherjan has been frequently interviewed and has published articles on Afghan affairs. Along with her frequent collaborator, Michael O'Hanlon (director of research and a senior foreign policy fellow at the prestigious Washington think-tank, the Brookings Institution), she coauthored the book *Toughing It Out in Afghanistan,* published in 2010.

Sherjan's expertise is thus a product of her decades of work for and personal experience in her home country. The opinion editorial reprinted here, in keeping with the other readings in this chapter, takes up the issues of peace and democracy, asking how Afghanistan can become more democratic when its most educated citizens choose not to participate in elections. Sherjan's piece appeared just two days before the national presidential election that took place in 2009; she was accurate in her prediction of low voter turnout. The election was so tainted with corruption that the U.S. pressured the ruling government to hold a second vote (between Afghan President Karzai, and his closest opponent), but the opponent pulled out of the process before the vote could take place.

Given Hassina Sherjan's lifelong work for social justice and the ongoing political chaos in Afghanistan, it is not surprising that her passion sizzles behind her words about the relationship of peace and democracy.

Apathy Among the Educated
Hassina Sherjan

The New York Times, August 18, 2009

A "fair and transparent election," even if one were possible, would not be enough to set Afghanistan on a path toward stability. Only when democracy is combined with a legitimate process of truth and justice will we achieve peace.

Most educated Afghans, a small but important minority of the population, will not vote because they believe there is no candidate worth voting for. The other day the marketing manager for my company's factory in Kabul told me that he and 10 friends had discussed it and decided not to vote.

"All the development has been done by private companies and nongovernmental groups," he explained. "Government has not done much. We are protesting. They should have created jobs. Youths are suffering. If the youths were busy working, there would be no war or corruption. The candidates say they will fix the roads or create jobs, but how? Talk is cheap."

It's not only the present government that he finds lacking. He pointedly criticized two of President Hamid Karzai's challengers—Ashraf Ghani, a former finance minister, and Abdul Jabar Sabit, a former attorney general. "They say, 'We will bring foreign investors'— but how will they improve security?" he asked. "The election is a mere formality."

Another colleague added: "The candidates talk about donors' funding as if everything is dependent on funding or they won't be able to do it. We have lots of resources in Afghanistan, like gas and oil in Sheberghan Province. These things can put many people to work so we don't have to be dependent on donor's funding, but no one has any solid plan."

Another problem with this "free" election is that the votes of Afghan refugees in Pakistan and Iran will be lost. Five years ago, in our first presidential vote, most Afghans in neighboring countries were able to vote, but this year there is no such mechanism in place. It is unfair to say that there haven't been obvious improvements since 2001. Our currency is stronger. We did not have any real telecommunications system, and there were only the government-controlled TV and radio stations, which were not even functioning. Today we have five phone companies, and around a dozen each of TV and radio stations. Thousands of miles of roads have been built, millions of children are going to school, thousands of Afghans are joining the Army and police forces daily and, most important, we finally have electricity around the clock.

But the big question is why, despite all this development, has the insurgency increased and faith in the government deteriorated?

In part it stems from too much "cosmetic development" and a lack of employment and basic services, like garbage collection. But the main cause is that people lost trust in the government for lack of a proper and transparent justice system. Out of desperation, many young Afghans either leave the country for Iran or Pakistan to seek employment or join the extremists.

Thus, in addition to democracy and accountability, Afghans need a truth and justice process like that of South Africa. Afghan leaders, through all our wars, need to admit their errors and atrocities, and apologize to the Afghan people. War criminals need to withdraw from politics. We also need to protect and empower Afghan women, and prosecute those who have abused and betrayed them.

Afghanistan's collective psyche is scarred, and when emotional traumas are not dealt with properly, they inevitably lead to violence. Even a free and fair election is no substitute for justice.

Reading Responses

1. List the social, economic, and technological advances that Hassina Sherjan describes, and then list the lingering problems she notes. Google Hassina Sherjan to look for evidence of changes since the 2009 election in her more recent writing. How have things changed? How have they stayed the same?

2. Sherjan suggests that Afghanistan needs a "truth and justice process" like that of South Africa. Do the research to learn about South Africa's truth and reconciliation process. Write a short summary of how the process works, the kinds of problems it addresses, and the solutions it provides. Could it work for Afghanistan? Explain your reasoning.

3. Sherjan says that educated Afghanis boycotted the democratic election because they did not trust the candidates. What do you think of their decision to opt out of participating in a democracy? What do they gain and lose? What does the country gain and lose?

MORE WRITING IN POLITICAL SCIENCE

INTRODUCTION

People sometimes say that professors "live in an ivory tower," by which they mean that professors focus on abstract questions and ignore real-world problems. In this brief essay, John Owen (a professor of politics and international relations at the University of Virginia) reviews *Electing to Fight: Why Emerging Democracies Go to War,* a scholarly book published by two well-known political scientists—Edward Mansfield and Jack Snyder. Owen uses his review to persuade his readers not only that *Electing to Fight* is an important book but also that "ivory-tower" research in political science can speak to real-world political problems like U.S. policy in the Middle East.

Owen begins by describing a profound irony: political scientists usually fume that American presidents pay no attention to academic research when they forge foreign policy, but President George W. Bush relied on a prominent theory—democratic peace theory—to justify the war with Iraq, a war that made most academics fume. The problem, according to Owen, is that President Bush, like most politicians, relied on an oversimplified version of democratic peace theory, namely the presumption that democracies go to war less frequently than other forms of government. Applied to the Middle East, the simplified thinking goes like this: if Iraq becomes a democracy it will no longer fight with its neighbors; it will begin to stabilize this politically troubled region. Such thinking is flawed, according to Owen, because it does not pay attention to nuances in what counts as a "democracy," nuances that profoundly affect a democracy's appetite for war. In essence, Owen reminds politicians that "the devil is in the details."

Owen builds his argument that politicians should pay attention to the complexity by describing one in-depth study of democratic peace theory, *Electing to Fight.* Authors Mansfield and Snyder categorize democracies and then examine the war-lust among the different types of democracies. They conclude that "incomplete democracies," countries that have some but not all features of a democracy, are actually more likely to go to war than authoritarian states. Young democracies are also highly likely to instigate war. Because Iraq is both a young and an incomplete democracy, Mansfield and Snyder's research suggests that it will likely retain its appetite for war. Rather than stabilize the region, a democratized Iraq is likely to continue to cause trouble for its neighbors and for the United States.

In this review, Owen does not merely summarize Mansfield and Snyder's book; he uses the book to make his own case. He argues that U.S. presidents should take the time to understand the complexities of political science research before they use it as the basis for going to war.

Iraq and the Democratic Peace: Who Says Democracies Don't Fight?

John M. Owen IV

Foreign Affairs 2005 84(6): 122–7. Review of *Electing to Fight: Why Emerging Democracies Go to War*. By Edward D. Mansfield and Jack Snyder. MIT Press, 2005.

Seldom if ever has the hostility between academics and the U.S. president been so pronounced. Of course, political scientists always seem to complain about the occupant of the White House, and Republicans fare worse than Democrats: Herbert Hoover was called callous, Dwight Eisenhower a dunce, Richard Nixon evil, Ronald Reagan dangerous, and George H.W. Bush out of touch. But professors have consigned George W. Bush to a special circle of their presidential hell. And the White House seems to return the sentiment.

According to the academics, Bush's chief transgressions have had to do with foreign policy, especially the Iraq war—a mess that could have been avoided if only the president and his advisers had paid more attention to those who devote their lives to studying international relations.

The irony of this argument is that few other presidents—certainly none since Woodrow Wilson, a former president of the American Political Science Association, scribbled away in the Oval Office—have tied their foreign policies more explicitly to the work of social science. The defining act of Bush's presidency was grounded in a theory that the political scientist Jack Levy once declared was "as close as anything we have to an empirical law in international relations," namely, that democracies do not fight one another.

The theory, which originated in the work of the eighteenth-century philosopher Immanuel Kant and was refined in the 1970s and 1980s by several researchers working independently, has, since the 1990s, been one of the hottest research areas in international relations. Although some skeptics remain and no one agrees about why exactly it works, most academics now share the belief that democracies have indeed made a separate peace. What is more, much research suggests that they are also unusually likely to sign and honor international agreements and to become economically interdependent.

The administrations of Presidents George H.W. Bush and Bill Clinton made frequent appeals to the theory in public, and it seems to have informed their support for democratization in former communist lands and in Haiti. The current Bush administration, however, has gone much further in its faith in the idea, betting the farm that the theory holds and will help Washington achieve a peaceful, stable, and prosperous Muslim world as, over time, Iraq's neighbors, following Iraq's example, democratize. The United States' real motives for attacking Iraq may have been complex, but "regime change"—the replacement of Saddam Hussein's gruesome tyranny with a democracy—was central to Washington's rhetoric by the time it began bombing Baghdad in March 2003.

Why has a president who set his defining policy around one of political science's crown jewels come in for so much venom from the same academics who endorse the idea? After all, a host of peer-reviewed journal articles have implicitly supported the president's claim that a democratic Iraq would not threaten the United States or Israel, develop weapons of mass destruction, or sponsor terrorism. Are professors simply perpetual critics who refuse to take responsibility for the consequences of their ideas? Or does Bush hatred trump social science?

The Bush administration's desire to break with its predecessors and alter the authoritarian status quo in the Middle East was admirable. But the White House got its science wrong, or at least not completely right: the democratic peace theory does not dictate that the United States can or should remake Iraq into a democracy. In *Electing to Fight: Why Emerging Democracies Go to War,* the veteran political scientists Edward Mansfield and Jack Snyder make two critical points. Not only is turning authoritarian countries into democracies extremely difficult, much more so than the administration seems to have anticipated. The Middle East could also become a much more dangerous place if Washington and the rest of the world settle for a merely semi-democratic regime in Baghdad. Such an Iraq, Mansfield and Snyder imply, would be uncommonly likely to start wars—a bull in the Middle Eastern china shop. Unfortunately, such an Iraq may also be just what we are likely to end up with.

Illiberal Democracies

At first glance, the realists' critique of the Iraq war is easier to understand than that of the democratic peace theorists. Indeed, realism—which holds that a country's type of government has no systematic effects on its foreign policy—is enjoying a revival in Washington these days, precisely because of the war. According to the realists, the best way to have dealt with Saddam would have been not to overthrow him but to use coercive bargaining: to have threatened him with annihilation, for example, if he ever used nuclear weapons.

Even the democratic peace theory, however, does not necessarily prescribe the use of force to transform despotisms such as Iraq into democracies. Indeed, by itself, the argument that democracies do not fight one another does not have any practical implications for the foreign policymaker. It needs an additional or minor premise, such as "the United States can make Iraq into a democracy at an acceptable cost." And it is precisely this minor premise about which the academy has been skeptical. No scholarly consensus exists on how countries become democratic, and the literature is equally murky on the costs to the United States of trying to force them to be free.

This last part of the puzzle is even more complicated than it first appears. Enter Mansfield and Snyder, who have been contributing to the democratic peace debate for a decade. Their thesis, first published in 1995, is that although mature democracies do not fight one another, democratizing states—those in transition from authoritarianism to democracy—do, and are even more prone to war than authoritarian regimes. Now, in *Electing to Fight,* the authors have refined their argument. As they outline in the book, not only are "incomplete democratizing" states—those that develop democratic institutions in the wrong order—unlikely ever to complete the transition to democracy; they are also especially bellicose.

According to Mansfield and Snyder, in countries that have recently started to hold free elections but that lack the proper mechanisms for accountability (institutions such as an independent judiciary, civilian control of the military, and protections for opposition parties and the press), politicians have incentives to pursue policies that make it more likely that their countries will start wars. In such places, politicians know they can mobilize support by demanding territory or other spoils from foreign countries and by nurturing grievances against outsiders. As a result, they push for extraordinarily belligerent policies. Even states that develop democratic institutions in the right order—adopting the rule of law before holding elections—are very aggressive in the early years of their transitions, although they are less so than the first group and more likely to eventually turn into full democracies.

Of course, politicians in mature democracies are also often tempted to use nationalism and xenophobic rhetoric to buttress their domestic power. In such cases, however, they are usually restrained by institutionalized mechanisms of accountability. Knowing that if they lead the country into a military defeat or quagmire they may be punished at the next election, politicians in such states are less likely to advocate a risky war. In democratizing states, by contrast, politicians know that they are insulated from the impact of bad policies: if a war goes badly, for example, they can declare a state of emergency, suspend elections, censor the press, and so on. Politicians in such states also tend to fear their militaries, which often crave foreign enemies and will overthrow civilian governments that do not share their goals. Combined, these factors can make the temptation to attack another state irresistible.

Mansfield and Snyder present both quantitative and case-study support for their theory. Using rigorous statistical methods, the authors show that since 1815, democratizing states have indeed been more prone to start wars than either democracies or authoritarian regimes. Categorizing transitions according to whether they ended in full democracies (as in the U.S. case) or in partial ones (as in Germany in 1871–1938 or Pakistan throughout its history), the authors find that in the early years of democratic transitions, partial democracies—especially those that get their institutions in the wrong order—are indeed significantly more likely to initiate wars. . . . In most of these cases, the authors find what they expect: in these democratizing states, domestic political competition was intense. Politicians, vying for power, appeased domestic hard-liners by resorting to nationalistic appeals that vilified foreigners, and these policies often led to wars that were not in the countries' strategic interests.

Although their argument would have been strengthened by a few comparative studies of democratizing states avoiding war and of full democracies and authoritarian states starting wars, Mansfield and Snyder are persuasive. In part this is because they carefully circumscribe their claims. They acknowledge that some cases are "false positives," that is, wars started by states that have wrongly been classified as democratizing, such as the

Iran–Iraq War, started by Iraq in 1980. They also answer the most likely objections to their argument. Some skeptics, for example, might counter that Mansfield and Snyder get the causality reversed: it is war or the threat of it that prevents states from becoming mature democracies. Others might argue that democratizing states become involved in more wars simply because their internal instability tempts foreign states to attack them—in other words, that democratizers are more sinned against than sinning. Analyzing data from 1816 through 1992, Mansfield and Snyder put paid to these alternative explanations. Bad domestic institutions usually precede wars, rather than vice versa, and democratizing states usually do the attacking. . . .

The authors' conclusions for foreign policy are straightforward. The United States and other international actors should continue to promote democracy, but they must strive to help democratizing states implement reforms in the correct order. In particular, popular elections ought not to precede the building of institutions that will check the baleful incentives for politicians to call for war. Mansfield and Snyder are unsparing toward well-intentioned organizations that have pressured authoritarian governments to rush to elections in the past—often with disastrous consequences. As the authors show, for example, it was organizations such as the World Bank and the National Democratic Institute that pushed Burundi and Rwanda to increase popular sovereignty in the early 1990s—pressure that, as Mansfield and Snyder argue, helped set off a chain of events that led to genocide. Acknowledging their intellectual debt to writers such as Samuel Huntington (particularly his 1968 book *Political Order in Changing Societies*) and Fareed Zakaria, Mansfield and Snyder have written a deeply conservative book. Sounding like Edmund Burke on the French Revolution but substituting statistics and measured prose for rhetorical power, the authors counsel against abruptly empowering people, since premature elections may well usher in domestic upheavals that thrust the state outward against its neighbors.

Back in Baghdad

This brings the conversation back to Iraq, and in particular the notion that the United States can turn it into a democracy at an acceptable cost. In effect, Mansfield and Snyder have raised the estimate of these costs by pointing out one other reason this effort may fail—a reason that few seem to have thought of. Forget for a moment the harrowing possibility of a Sunni-Shiite-Kurdish civil war in Iraq. Set aside the prospect of a Shiite-dominated state aligning itself with Iran, Syria, and Lebanon's Hezbollah. What if, following the departure of U.S. troops, Iraq holds together but as an incomplete democratizer, with broad suffrage but anemic state institutions? Such an Iraq might well treat its own citizens better than the Baathist regime did. Its treatment of its neighbors, however, might be just as bad.

Although Saddam was an unusually bellicose and reckless tyrant, attacking Iran in 1980 and Kuwait in 1990 and engaging in foolish brinkmanship with the United States, as Mansfield and Snyder imply, a democratic Iraq may be no less bellicose and reckless. In the near future, intensely competitive elites there—secularists, leftists, moderates, and both Shiite and Sunni Islamists—could compete for popularity by stirring up nationalism against one or more of Iraq's neighbors. And Iraq lives in a dangerous neighborhood.

Already, Iraqi Shiite parties have been critical of Sunni-dominated Jordan; Iraqi Sunni parties, of Shiite-dominated Iran; and Iraqi Kurdish parties, of Turkey.

One hopes that the White House contemplated this scenario prior to March 2003. Whether it did or not, the possibility must be considered now, by U.S. civilian and military leaders, academics, and U.S. allies who agree with those academics. If Mansfield and Snyder are correct about the bellicose tendencies of young, incompletely democratized states, the stakes of Iraq's transition are higher than most have supposed. . . . The odds may be long that Iraq will ever turn into a mature democracy of the sort envisaged by the Bush administration. But those odds are lengthened by the refusal of those states in Europe and the Middle East that could make a difference actually to do so.

Reading Responses

1. Owen begins his review by focusing his readers' attention on the fact that President George W. Bush relied on democratic peace theory to justify going to war with Iraq. How will his audience likely respond to that claim? How passionate do you expect they will be?

2. How does Owen establish Mansfield and Snyder's credibility? How does he establish his own?

3. Did Owen persuade you? What aspects of his argument did you find persuasive? What aspects did you find less so?

WRITING ASSIGNMENTS

Assignment 1

For his research paper, James King chose a political topic that he already knew and cared about. But his passion for the topic didn't blind him to the strongly argued claims of others. While reading previous research on his topic, King made sure to read what had been written by those who might disagree with his opinions, and he included information from those sources in his essay.

Your task for this assignment is to write a research-based essay on a political topic that you already know something about. Your essay should include a thesis that you really believe in, one you'd be willing (maybe even eager) to defend in public. You might choose to use hypotheses to help you prove your thesis or a set of recommendations to sharpen the point of your thesis. Start brainstorming by creating a list of three topics that you've recently discussed with others. For your own benefit, narrow the scope of each topic as much as possible. So, for example, instead of researching "environmentalism," research "ground water contamination" or even better, "Los Angeles ground water contamination." For each of these topics, use research databases to complete the following lists. Keep track of the sources you find by listing them in a bibliography:

- List the words or search terms that research databases use to describe this topic.
- List the issues that people are currently discussing.
- List the "camps" or groups of people who share opinions about this topic. Be sure to look for a full range of scholarly groups and record their points.
- Note the kind of evidence that authors use: statistics, expert opinions, case studies, scientific experiments, quotes from authorities or authoritative texts, etc.

As you draft, revise your thesis into a point that you believe in, one you can support and defend with scholarly evidence and logic. Be sure to include scholarly research from those who might disagree with your thesis, those who will seem impartial, and those who agree with you. Provide logical reasoning that connects your research to your point. In other words, do everything you can to create a credible voice for yourself—and thereby increase your chances of actually changing your reader's mind.

Assignment 2

In Western countries people with HIV can live almost normal lives, thanks to new anti-retroviral drugs, but that is not the case for the more than 25 million AIDS/HIV-infected people who live in developing countries such as Botswana, Zimbabwe, Haiti, and Thailand. Antiretroviral drugs are rarely available to these people because the drugs are expensive, are complex to administer, and require careful supervision by trained medical personnel. Some have suggested that developing countries forget about trying to treat those infected with HIV/AIDS and, instead, concentrate on preventing new infections. What gets lost in these statistics is the patient—the person suffering the effects of this ravaging disease. The readings in Chapter 7, "Nursing," on the other hand, demonstrate the rhetorical power of personal experience to counter the potentially numbing effect of numeric evidence. When personal experience is not possible—because of geographic or historical distance— examples and case studies can produce a similar rhetorical effect.

Your task is to research the topic of HIV/AIDS in developing countries, looking for both numeric information and information about individuals who suffer the effects of HIV/AIDS. Using both numeric and case study information, write an essay that ends in a set of recommendations. You can start your research with two Web sites that provide reliable information—www.unaids.org (the U.N. Web site for HIV/AIDS) and www.who.int/hiv/en (the World Health Organization Web site for HIV/AIDS). Choose to focus on either a particular developing country or a particular aspect of the HIV/AIDS crisis in developing countries. Decide on the claim you want to make and frame that as the working draft of your thesis.

As you begin drafting, list the likely responses that readers will have to your thesis. Include some of these in your essay and answer these questions or criticisms with evidence and reasoning. Consider the relationship between your working thesis and your recommendations, and revise both to enhance the relationship.

Assignment 3

In Christopher Layne's fourth endnote, he lists political conflicts, other than the Trent conflict, between democracies that also support his claim that realism better predicts historical outcomes than democratic peace theory.

Your task for this assignment is to select one of the political conflicts that Layne lists in his fourth endnote and write a case study of the conflict that emphasizes the features of the conflict that make it good evidence for the value of realism. Consult reference librarians for help finding detailed descriptions of these historical events.

As you begin drafting, consider how you will describe the theory of realism to emphasize the features that your case study will demonstrate. Decide where in your essay you will help the reader make connections between the historical events and how realist theory accounts for them. And think about how you will document the information you include in your essay.

BIOLOGY: DESCRIBING NATURE

The National Center for Catastrophic Injury Research categorizes sports injuries as fatalities, nonfatal but permanently damaging injuries, and serious but not permanent injuries. The spring 2008 report information about injuries sustained by high school female athletes appears in three different forms: words, a table, and graphs. Read the information presented in all three forms, and answer the questions that follow.

Table 7 illustrates high school female catastrophic injuries for the past 26 years—including cheerleading. High school female sports accounted for 112 catastrophic injuries during this time period, and 73 of those injuries were to cheerleaders. Of the

Table 7   High School Female Direct Catastrophic Injuries 1982–83—2007–08

Sport	Fatality	Non-Fatal	Serious	Total
Cheerleading*	2	25	46	73
Gymnastics	0	6	3	9
Track	1	1	6	8
Swimming	0	4	1	5
Basketball	0	1	3	4
Ice Hockey	0	0	2	2
Field Hockey	0	3	0	3
Softball	1	2	1	4
Lacrosse	0	0	1	1
Soccer	0	1	1	2
Volleyball	0	1	0	1
TOTAL	**4**	**44**	**64**	**112**

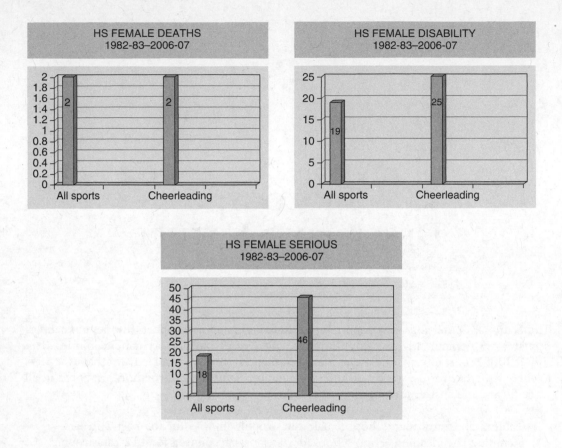

112 injuries, 4 resulted in death, 44 with permanent disability, and 64 were serious injuries with recovery. The 73 cheerleading injuries accounted for two deaths, 25 permanent disability injuries, and 46 serious injuries with recovery. High school cheerleaders accounted for 65.2% of all female sports catastrophic injuries.

- If you were going to make an argument that high school cheerleading is more dangerous than people might imagine, in what form would you present evidence for your argument? List your reasons.

- If you were making an argument to keep cheerleading as a sanctioned sport, what form would you choose for your evidence? List the advantages of the form you have chosen.

- When researchers provide data in table form, like Table 7, they usually include a verbal description like the sentences that precede Table 7. What purposes do the words serve?

PORTABLE RHETORICAL LESSON: USING VISUAL AIDS TO MAKE INFORMATION ACCESSIBLE

What was your first response to the data about catastrophic injuries in women playing high school sports? Were you surprised? Suspicious? What would make you believe the data, even though it might surprise you? Biologists respond to the challenge of suspicious readers by presenting their readers with good data. Readers accept data that has been produced by generally accepted research methods and that demonstrate a very high probability that the results are not due to chance. Consequently, research scientists are always interested in **research methods and evidence.**

Research scientists must also be concerned about **presentation.** To convince readers, scientists must provide a great deal of data, more than they can communicate in words alone. As a result, science writers have developed data-presentation strategies that accomplish two goals: (1) present information clearly so that the reader can read efficiently and (2) emphasize the most important information.

And those challenges from the opening exercise bring us to the chapter's **Portable Rhetorical Lesson:** making information visually accessible. In the introduction to the paper on rugby injuries (the first reading in this chapter), Professor Howell writes, "A scientific paper begins with data." In fact data appear somewhere in the middle of a scientific paper—in a Results section. However, when scientists actually read reports of experimental research, they begin by looking at the data.

And we use the word *looking* intentionally. Scientists have discovered that accessible information almost always appears in some visual form, typically tables and "figures" (a catch-all term for all kinds of images). Our aim in this chapter is to enable you to bring scientists' expertise to your writing tasks—expertise in choosing and creating images that convey information efficiently and that connect the images to the words in the text.

When you are choosing your visuals, remember that you have many options and that each option has its own benefits.

- *Tables* present facts—in columns and rows; they are especially useful for presenting a lot of numbers that can be categorized (into the rows and columns) for comparison.

- *Graphs* (line graphs, bar graphs, pie charts) allow the eye to detect patterns (the bar graphs in this chapter's opening exercise are good examples), and patterns are usually more important for gaining scientific knowledge than are discrete facts.

- *Illustrations* (drawings) can create simplified versions (models) of the natural world's complex systems and processes, revealing patterns in nature.

- *Photographs* are sometimes the best choice: if, for example, you want to explain how a spider can hang upside down from a glass surface, trust an electron microscope photo of the incredibly delicate hairs on a spider's foot.

Furthermore, new technology is constantly improving the presentation options available to scientists and other writers. Consider the advantages, for example, of film and audio in presenting information in electronic formats—rhetorical tools that are becoming increasingly portable.

WRITING IN THE DISCIPLINE

INTRODUCTION

by Elizabeth Howell, Professor of Biology

Imagine that you are the coach of a semiprofessional ice hockey team. Your players train for two months before competing and then play games for eight months while keeping up their training. What information might you need to make decisions about a training program that would minimize injury while maximizing wins? You could rely on your own past experience, anecdotal stories from other coaches, or a more objective source like Tim Gabbett's "Influence of Training and Match Intensity on Injuries in Rugby League." You would then read this paper with the same objectives as scientists—seeking an objective, unbiased answer to a specific research question.

Any scientific paper begins with data that answer the research question. Biologists write papers inside out by first drafting the Results section. In fact, the very first step in writing a paper doesn't involve writing at all. A scientist first designs a study to answer a specific research question; the study then yields data, and the scientist constructs a figure—typically a table or graph—to make the data easy to see and understand. In Gabbett's paper, the specific question at hand is this: How does the intensity and duration of training and play affect the injury rate of rugby players? It doesn't ask whether the players win or lose or if they get stronger as they train and play. Reading this paper explains only injury rates; scientific writing focuses narrowly on a specific research question.

Note also that the data must be quantifiable; that is, you have to be able to measure what you study. If you study the effect of a particular soil additive on plant growth, you will need to measure plant height. If you study the effect of day length on reproductive success of robins, you'll be snooping in nests to count eggs. In this study, the author explains the objective methods he used to measure injury rates, training intensity, and player exertion during matches. The figures (tables and graphs) in the Results section present an accessible summary of those measurements.

Scientists draft the Results section first because the figures represent the complete answer to the specific research question they asked. The figure (or the data it presents) is the reason that the paper exists. A scientific paper with good figures can be accepted for publication even though the text is muddy and poorly written, but even the most elegant, crystal-clear prose can't cover for bad data and confusing figures. That's why scientists write, and read, figures first.

Turn to the graphs in Figure 1 (one of the two central figures of the paper, page 268). They compare the rate of injury to the training duration, intensity, and "load" (duration plus intensity) during a season. On the X axis at the bottom of the graphs we find a spot for each month of the season. We can see at a glance that the training intensity rose over the first three months, then fell until May, and then rose again a bit, finally tapering off at the end of the season. The solid line indicates injury incidence over that same period. By following the line, we can see that as training increased, so did injury. Figure 2, which allows almost instant comparison to Figure 1, *pictures* an increase in injuries that accompanies longer and tougher games.

Having discovered the heart of the paper in the Results, a reader who finds the data potentially useful will read the rest of the paper, all of which supports and contextualizes the data figures. The Introduction provides enough *background* to allow the reader to see how it fits into a larger body of work on the subject. More subtly, by reviewing the history of previous work on the subject, the author *credentials* himself and his study. Gabbett shows his expertise by citing over twenty-five publications (many written by him) in just the first two paragraphs. Most important, the introduction moves from the broader background, to the particular system studied, and finally to the specific question, so it points directly to the results. It is easy to imagine the last sentence of the introduction posed as the central research question: "What is the influence of training and match intensity, duration and load . . . on . . . injury . . . in rugby league players?"

The Methods section describes in great detail the specific techniques used in the study. Any flaw in the methods will cast doubt on the data. (This is the section that nonexperts would be most likely to scan quickly.)

The Discussion both explains and expands on the results. In many ways it mirrors the introduction, except in reverse. Discussions start with the specific findings of a study (as in the first paragraph of Gabbett's Discussion section) and then expand outward, interpreting findings to explain their broader significance.

Once you have finished reading the paper, imagine the author asking the specific question, designing the experiment, collecting the data, generating graphs and tables, then writing the Results, Methods, Discussion, Introduction, and finally the Abstract. Do you see why many scientists write their papers inside-out? It allows them to tie everything into the story: asking an important question, using methods that produce reliable data, and presenting the data figures as the main characters of the story.

✓ Reading Tips

You probably should not read a scientific article straight through, from beginning to end. Instead, read as a scientist would.

- Start by scanning the Abstract.
- Go to the Results section, focusing first on Figures 1 and 2 and the part of the text that explains those figures—the key findings (information) in the paper.
- When you know what the main findings are, scan the Discussion section—to see why the data matter and what might be done to further the research.
- Then scan the Introduction to get the broader context, and scan the Methods only to see how carefully biologists describe methods.
- Throughout the paper, headings and visual aids—and the title assigned to each figure and table—allow you to scan and quickly pick out the information you want, so it's easy to review if you have questions.
- And anytime you need help understanding some of the science, the marginal annotations should clarify things for you. (Remember that the main point is not to learn the science but to learn how scientists think and write to achieve their purpose.)

Influence of Training and Match Intensity on Injuries in Rugby League

Tim J. Gabbett

Journal of Sports Sciences, 2004, 22: 409–17. Accepted 2 October 2003.

[Abstract]

The aim of this study was to examine the influence of perceived intensity, duration and load of matches and training on the incidence of injury in rugby league players. The incidence of injury was prospectively studied in 79 semi-professional rugby league players during the 2001 season. All injuries sustained during matches and training sessions were recorded. Training sessions were conducted from December to September, with matches played from February to September. The intensity of individual training sessions and matches was estimated using a modified rating of perceived exertion scale. Training load was calculated by multiplying the training intensity by the duration of the training session. The match load was calculated by multiplying the match intensity by the time each player participated in the match. Training load increased from December (278.3 [95% confidence interval, CI 262.2 to 294.5] units) to February (385.5 [95% CI 362.4 to 408.5] units), followed by a decline until September (98.4 [95% CI 76.5 to 120.4] units). Match load increased from February (201.0 [95% CI 186.2 to 221.8] units) to September (356.8 [95% CI 302.5 to 411.1] units). More training injuries were sustained in the first half of the season (first vs second: 69.2% vs 30.8%, $P < 0.001$), whereas match injuries occurred more frequently in the latter stages of the season (53.6% vs 46.4%, $P < 0.001$). A significant relationship ($P < 0.05$) was observed between changes in training injury incidence and changes in training intensity ($r = 0.83$), training duration ($r = 0.79$) and training load ($r = 0.86$). In addition, changes in the incidence of match injuries were significantly correlated ($P < 0.05$) with changes in match intensity ($r = 0.74$), match duration ($r = 0.86$) and match load ($r = 0.86$). These findings suggest that as the intensity, duration and load of rugby league training sessions and matches is increased, the incidence of injury is also increased.

Keywords: collision sport, football, performance, rugby league, semi-professional.

Introduction

Rugby league is an international 'collision' sport played by amateurs (Gabbett, 2000a,b), semi-professionals (Gabbett, 2002a,b,c; Courts et al., 2003) and processionals (Gissane et al., 1993; Brewer and Davis,

---

The range of numbers gives the average value and the range that most of the data fell into. CI refers to confidence interval: the researchers are 95% confident that their data falls in this range (confidence is determined by a mathematical formula). In this case, the average training load in December was 278.3 units, but there was a broader range, with the vast majority of loads being between 262.2 and 294.5 units.

P is known as the P-value; it is a measure of the quality of the statistics. These statistical results are quite good.

Scientists include keywords so that their readers can easily search the databases for related studies.

Note that the introduction gives the broader context for the research and the reasons for this particular study.

1995). The game is physically demanding, requiring players to compete in a challenging contest involving frequent bouts of high-intensity activity (e.g. running and passing, sprinting) separated by short bouts of low-intensity activity (e.g. walking, jogging) (Meir et al., 1993). During the course of a match, players are exposed to many physical collisions and tackles (Brewer and Davis, 1995; Gissane et al., 2001a,b). As a result, musculoskeletal injuries are common (Gibbs, 1993; Hodgson-Phillips et al., 1998).

Several researchers interested in rugby league have reported a higher incidence of injury as the playing level is increased (Gissane et al., 1993; Stephenson et al., 1996; Gabbett, 2000a, 2001). These findings have often been attributed to the higher intensity of elite competition (Gissane et al., 1993; Stephenson et al., 1996). It has also been shown that rugby league training injuries occur more frequently in the earlier stages of a season when training intensity and duration are high (Gabbett, 2003), while match injuries increase progressively throughout the course of a season (Gabbett, 2000a, 2003). Collectively, these results suggest that training and match intensity influence injury rates in rugby league players (Gissane et al., 1993; Stephenson et al., 1996; Gabbett, 2000a, 2003). However, no research has quantified the intensity and duration of training sessions and matches for comparison with injury rates over the course of a rugby league season.

The intensity, duration and overall training and match load (i.e. the product of intensity and duration) may impact to differing degrees on injury rates, and therefore warrant individual consideration for injury management throughout the season. The aim of the present study was to examine the influence of training and match intensity, duration and load on the incidence of injury over the course of a season in rugby league players.

Methods

Participants

The incidence, site, nature, cause and severity of training and match injuries were studied prospectively in 79 semi-professional rugby league players over the 2001 season. The season lasted from December 2000 to September 2001 inclusive, with matches played from February 2001 to September 2001 inclusive. All players were registered with the same semi-professional rugby league club, and were competing in the Gold Coast Group 18 senior rugby league competition (New South Wales Country Rugby League, Australia). The players were considered to be 'semi-professional' as they were receiving moderate remuneration to play rugby league, but were also relying on additional employment to generate income. The participants in the present study could be distinguished from amateur players (who do not receive match payments) and professional players (who generate their entire income from their involvement in rugby league) (Gabbett, 2001). The playing roster for the season included 57 players, with the remaining players relegated to the amateur team affiliated with the club. Depending on age and skill, players competed in one of three teams (First Grade, Second Grade or Under 19). The Second Grade and Under 19 teams consisted of a squad of 20 players, while the First Grade team consisted of a squad of 17 players. All participants received a clear explanation of the study, including the risks and benefits involved, and written consent was obtained. The Institutional Review Board for Human Investigation approved all experimental procedures.

> First Grade are the top players.

> Experiments involving human subjects must be approved by a committee of other scientists (including psychologists), and nonscientists to ensure they are safe and worthwhile. A similar board (with a veterinarian) reviews experiments involving other (nonhuman) animals.

Matches

The players participated in 69 matches, which included trial ('friendly'), fixture and finals matches. Trial matches were 60 min in duration. Fixture and finals matches were either 60 min (Under 19), 70 min (Second Grade) or 80 min (First Grade) in duration. One finals match (Second Grade) required 2 × 10-min 'extra-time' periods (i.e. 90 min in duration) because of level scores at the end of regulation time. All matches were played under the unlimited interchange rule.

Training Sessions

> Substitute players can enter the game to replace injured players whenever necessary.

Each player participated in two organized field-training sessions per week. A periodized, game-specific training programme was implemented, with training loads being progressively increased in the preparatory phase of the season (i.e. December to February) and reduced during the competitive phase of the season (i.e. March to September). The duration of training sessions was recorded, with sessions typically lasting between 60 and 100 min. Players participated in a total of 82 training sessions, which included all pre-season and in-season training sessions that corresponded with pre-season, fixture and finals matches. . . .

> This section describes how the intensity of the training and games were quantified. The author measures the intensity of exercise by asking the participants to rate how hard they worked using the Borg Rating of Perceived Exertion.

Results

Site of Injury

> The Results section presents the data in the form of figures, in this case, tables and graphs. Each figure is anchored in the text. The anchor summarizes the important message of the figure, but scientists will find the figure first, look at it and analyze it, and then turn to the textual anchor to see what the author wants to emphasize.

A total of 389 training injuries were recorded, with an overall incidence of injury of 105.9 [95% CI 95.4 to 116.4] per 1000 training hours. More than 35% of the training injuries sustained were to the thigh and calf. Injuries to the ankle and foot (23.9%), knee (12.1%), and thorax and abdomen (12.6%) were less common. Over the course of the season, a total of 948 match injuries were recorded, with an overall incidence of injury of 917.3 [95% CI 857.9 to 976.6] per 1000 playing hours. Approximately 19.0% of the injuries sustained during matches were to the thigh and calf. Injuries to the face (14.2%), knee (13.8%), and arm and hand (12.9%) were less common (Table 1).

Nature of Injury

The types of injuries sustained during training and match-play are shown in Table 2. Muscular injuries (haematomas and strains) were the most common type of training injury (45.2%), while joint injuries (22.6%) and contusions (9.8%) were less common. Muscular injuries were also the most common type of injury sustained during match-play (31.8%), while contusions (20.2%) and abrasions (17.9%) were less common.

Cause of Injury

The causes of injuries sustained during training and match-play are shown in Table 3. Overexertion was the most common cause of training injury (35.2%). The incidence of training injuries sustained while making direct contact with another player (18.8%) or falling and stumbling (13.1%) were less common. Most injuries sustained during matches were the result of tackles (38.2%). In addition, physical collisions with fixed objects (11.8%) and direct contact with another player (22.7%) were also common causes of injury.

Severity of Injury

The majority of training (97.9%) and match (92.9%) injuries were transient, resulting in no loss of playing time. Minor, moderate, and major training injuries were uncommon (Table 4).

> Tables 1–4 give the raw data in great detail; by studying them, you can see exactly what type of injury occurs when in the season, and how severe the injuries are. Note that the tables are not designed to clearly and easily answer his question: Is there a direct relationship between intensity of exertion and rate of injury?

Table 1   Site of Injury

Site of injury	Match injuries			Training injuries		
	Number	Incidence	95% CI	Number	Incidence	95% CI
Thigh and calf	160	174.2	148.7 to 199.6	142	38.6	32.3 to 45.0
Face	135	130.6	108.7 to 152.6	13	3.5	1.6 to 5.5
Arm and hand	122	118.0	97.0 to 139.1	21	5.7	3.3 to 8.2
Knee	131	126.8	105.0 to 148.5	47	12.8	9.1 to 16.5
Shoulder	90	87.1	69.1 to 105.1	13	3.5	1.6 to 5.5
Head and neck	89	86.1	68.3 to 103.9	10	2.7	1.0 to 4.4
Thorax and abdomen	100	96.8	77.8 to 115.7	49	13.3	9.6 to 17.1
Ankle and foot	91	88.1	70.1 to 106.1	93	25.3	20.2 to 30.4
Other	10	9.7	3.6 to 15.8	1	0.3	0.0 to 0.8

Note: Match injuries: incidence expressed per 1000 playing hours. Training injuries: incidence expressed per 1000 training hours. 95% CI = 95% confidence interval.

Table 2   Type of Injury

Type of injury	Match injuries			Training injuries		
	Number	Incidence	95% CI	Number	Incidence	95% CI
Contusions	191	184.8	158.6 to 211.0	38	10.3	7.0 to 13.7
Muscular strains	166	160.6	136.1 to 185.1	160	43.5	36.8 to 50.3
Joint injuries	155	150.0	126.3 to 173.7	88	24.0	18.9 to 29.0
Abrasions	170	164.5	139.8 to 189.2	31	8.4	5.4 to 11.4
Haematomas	135	130.6	108.7 to 152.6	16	4.4	2.2 to 6.5
Lacerations	32	31.0	20.1 to 41.8	4	1.1	0.0 to 2.2
Concussion	36	34.8	23.4 to 46.3	1	0.3	0.0 to 0.8
Fractures and dislocations	18	17.4	9.5 to 25.4	3	0.8	0.0 to 1.7
Unspecified medical conditions	20	19.4	10.8 to 27.9	15	4.1	2.0 to 6.2
Respiratory disorders	14	13.5	6.5 to 20.6	8	2.2	0.7 to 3.7
Blisters	9	8.7	4.7 to 14.4	20	5.4	3.1 to 7.8
Overuse	—	—	—	2	0.5	0.0 to 1.3
Other	2	1.9	0.0 to 4.6	3	0.8	0.0 to 1.7

Note: Match injuries: incidence expressed per 1000 playing hours. Training injuries: incidence expressed per 1000 training hours. 95% CI = 95% confidence interval.

> These are the figures (they appear on page 268) we've been waiting for (or, the ones we should have started with). In clear, direct graphics, Figure 1 demonstrates that as the training intensity and duration (training load) decreases, so does the training injury rate. In Figure 2 we see the match intensity and duration (match load) increases. The visual demonstration of the data offers instant and convincing evidence of how the experimental results add up to useful knowledge.

Month of Injury

The frequencies of injuries sustained during training (x^2 = 121.5, d.f. = 9, $P < 0.001$) and match play (x^2 = 117.3, d.f. = 8, $P < 0.001$) were significantly different throughout different months of the season (Figs. 1, 2). At the beginning of the season (December) the incidence of training injuries was 105.2 [95% CI 55.7 to 154.8] per 1000 training hours. Training injury rates increased progressively from December to February, and then declined through to the end of the season. Expressed relative to training hours, the highest number of training injuries was recorded in February (205.6 [95% CI 162.1 to 249.0] per 1000), near the beginning of the season. When injuries at the beginning and end of the season were compared (by dividing each season in half), more training injuries occurred in the first half of the season (first vs second: 69.2% vs 30.8%; x^2 = 103.9, d.f =1, $P < 0.001$).

At the beginning of the competitive season (February), the incidence of match-play injuries was 935.5 [95% CI 721.9 to 1148.2] per 1000 playing hours. Match injury rates increased from February to

Table 3   Cause of Injury

Cause of injury	Match injuries			Training injuries		
	Number	Incidence	95% CI	Number	Incidence	95% CI
Being tackled	209	202.2	174.8 to 229.7	3	0.8	0.0 to 1.7
While tackling	153	148.0	124.5 to 171.6	2	0.5	0.0 to 1.3
Collision with fixed object	112	108.4	88.2 to 128.5	30	8.2	5.2 to 11.1
Struck by opposition player	159	153.8	130.0 to 177.8	12	3.3	1.4 to 5.1
Overexertion	75	41.6	56.0 to 89.1	137	37.3	31.1 to 43.5
Fall or stumble	66	63.9	48.5 to 79.3	51	13.9	10.1 to 17.7
Collision with player	56	54.2	40.0 to 68.4	51	13.9	10.1 to 17.7
Overuse	19	18.4	10.1 to 26.7	72	19.6	15.1 to 24.1
Temperature-related disorder	1	1.0	0.0 to 2.9	—	—	—
Twisting to pass or accelerate	2	1.9	0.0 to 4.6	—	—	—
Slip or trip	—	—	—	1	0.3	0.0 to 0.8
Scrum collapse or scrum contact	3	2.9	0.0 to 6.1	—	—	—
Struck by ball	2	1.9	0.0 to 4.6	5	1.4	0.2 to 2.5
Other	91	88.1	70.1 to 106.1	25	6.8	4.1 to 9.5

Note: Match injuries: incidence expressed per 1000 playing hours. Training injuries: incidence expressed per 1000 training hours. 95% CI = 95% confidence interval.

Table 4   Severity of Injury

Severity of injury	Match injuries			Training injuries		
	Number	Incidence	95% CI	Number	Incidence	95% CI
Transient	881	852.4	796.1 to 908.8	381	103.7	93.3 to 114.1
Minor	27	26.1	16.3 to 36.0	4	1.1	0.0 to 2.2
Moderate	30	29.0	18.6 to 39.5	4	1.1	0.0 to 2.2
Major	10	9.7	3.6 to 15.8	—	—	—

Note: Match injuries: incidence expressed per 1000 playing hours. Training injuries: incidence expressed per 1000 training hours. 95% CI = 95% confidence interval.

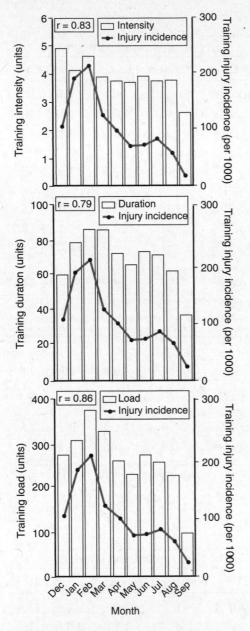

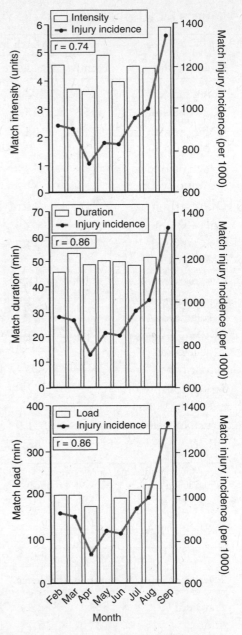

Figure 1 Influence of training intensity, duration and load on the incidence of training injuries in rugby league. Training load calculated from the product of training intensity and training duration. Units for training intensity and training load are reported as arbitrary units.

Figure 2 Influence of match intensity, duration and load on the incidence of match injuries in rugby league. Match load calculated from the product of match intensity and the time each player participated in the match. Units for match intensity and match load are reported as arbitrary units.

September. The highest number of match injuries sustained in a month was 187, recorded in July. Expressed relative to playing hours, the highest number of match injuries was recorded in September (1338.5 [95% CI 058.5 to 1618.51] per 1000), at the end of the season. When injuries at the beginning and end of the season were compared (by dividing each season in half), more injuries sustained during matches occurred in the second half of the season (second vs first: 53.6% vs 46.4%; x^2 = 16.2, d.f. = 1, P <0.001). . . .

Relationship between Incidence of Injury and
Training and Match Intensity, duration and load

A significant relationship (P < 0.05) was observed between changes in the incidence of training injuries and changes in training intensity (r = 0.83), training duration (r = 0.79) and training load (r = 0.86). In addition, changes in the incidence of match-play injuries were significantly correlated (P < 0.05) with changes in match intensity (r = 0.74), match duration (r = 0.86) and match load (r = 0.86).

Discussion

The first paragraph of this section is a nice summary of the results. It says why the study is important and how it's produced knowledge not previously available.

This is the first study to document the intensity and load associated with rugby league training sessions and matches. In addition, the relationships between training and match intensity, duration and load and the incidence of injury in rugby league has not previously been addressed. The findings of the present study demonstrate a significant positive relationship between the incidence of training injuries and the intensity, duration and load of training sessions. In addition, the incidence of match-play injuries was highly correlated with the intensity, duration and load of matches. These findings provide further support for the suggestion that injury rates in rugby league are increased with increased training and playing intensity (Gissane et al., 1993; Stephenson et al., 1996).

The incidence of training injuries was highly correlated with the intensity, duration and load of training despite the implementation of a game-specific, periodized training programme. Periodization refers to the application of sport science principles to training programme design (Bompa, 1983). The application of periodization to team sports such as rugby league is a relatively new concept (Meir, 1994), although its role in preventing unnecessarily high injury rates, and enabling athletes to reach peak performance at an appropriate stage of competition, has been well documented for individual sports (Bompa, 1983). The 38.5% increase in training load from December through to February corresponded with a 95.4% increase in the incidence of injuries sustained during training. These findings suggest that the prescribed increase in training load over the 12-week period (i.e. from December to February) was greater than was tolerable for the musculoskeletal system. Despite the

In other words, the very program designed to get athletes in shape so they don't get injured later in the season is giving them injuries during the training itself, because it is too intense.

significant increase in injury rates in the initial phases of the training programme, the majority of injuries were transient, resulting in no significant loss of match time. In addition, given that all three teams in the present study were successful in reaching the finals series, it could be suggested that the training programme employed was successful in attaining its goal of improving player performance. However, it should be recognized that the relationship between injury incidence and training intensity, duration and load may not be applicable to other rugby league teams who use different training programmes to the present cohort of players.

The finding that injury rates increased with the applied training load raises the question of the appropriate training stimulus required to elicit improvements in physical fitness and performance. While most injuries in the present study were transient, all injuries have the potential to impact on sporting performance (Watson, 1993). It would appear that a given training load designed to elicit improvements in performance will result in a given number of injuries and, as a consequence, will inadvertently lead to some decrement in performance. However, it is unclear if the improvement in performance provided by the training stimulus is adequate to compensate for the potential reduction in performance resulting from injuries sustained while training under that same stimulus. Conversely, a poor preparation, as a result of an inadequate training stimulus, may lead to an excessive increase in match-play injuries. Therefore, the obvious challenge for rugby league conditioning coaches is to develop game-specific programmes that provide an adequate training stimulus to enhance physical fitness and performance, without unduly increasing the incidence of injury.

> One function of the Discussion section is to suggest practical application of the results.

In the present study, the incidence of match-play injuries increased from the beginning to the end of the season. In addition, the incidence of these injuries was significantly correlated with the intensity, duration and load of matches. These findings are to be expected given that the intensity of matches would be expected to increase as a 'finals' series approaches. Furthermore, the lower match intensity and load associated with early season matches most probably reflects the less competitive nature of pre-season trial matches. Rugby league teams devote a significant amount of training time to the development of defensive communication skills and cohesion in attack. It is to be expected that it may take several matches for the development of these team skills to the point where playing performance is enhanced. It is unclear if the injuries sustained in the latter stages of the season impacted significantly on the playing performance of the teams in the present study. While the present study provides important information regarding the influence of match intensity on the incidence of injury, it is equally important to determine the influence of injuries on the playing performance of rugby league players.

> Here the author mentions the limitations of his study. A Discussion section will tell the reader the significance of what was found but also what was not able to be determined. That's a characteristic of scientific ethics.

In the present study, the perceived intensity of training and matches was higher in Under 19 players than First Grade and Second Grade players. This finding may be expected given that Under 19 players have lower physiological capacities than First Grade and Second Grade players (Gabbett, 2002b) and, as a result, any absolute training stimulus would pose a higher relative physiological strain on these players. However, while perceived match intensity was higher in Under 19 players, the overall match load was highest in First Grade players, reflecting the sustained exposure to high-intensity activity for a longer duration in these players. The match injury rates also closely tracked the overall match load, with higher intensity matches resulting in the highest injury rates. These findings are consistent with previous studies that found higher rates of injury as the playing level and match intensity was increased (Gissane et al., 1993; Stephenson et. al., 1996). Although the match intensity and match injury rates of First Grade, Second Grade and Under 19 players were closely related, the training loads and training injury rates of the three teams were inversely related. First Grade players had the lowest perceived training intensity and load, but the highest training injury rates. A high training injury rate in First Grade players may have resulted in a higher number of training stoppages, thereby reducing active training time in these players.

A subjective measurement tool (i.e. RPE scale) was used in the present study to quantify training and match intensity. Although subjective RPE scales have been shown to have good agreement with other objective physiological indicators of intensity (e.g. heart rate, blood lactate concentration) (Foster et al., 1995; Foster, 1997), it is possible that the relationship between training and match intensity and injury incidence may have been different with a different measurement of intensity. Future studies could utilize heart rate, blood lactate concentration or other physiological markers to quantify the relationship between injury incidence and intensity. Alternatively, recent evidence has shown that the speed of matches may influence the incidence of injury in team sport athletes (Norton et al., 2001). The use of video analysis would permit the quantification of training and match speed, thereby providing a more objective estimate of training and match intensity.

In summary, the present study examined the influence of training and match intensity, duration and load on the incidence of injury over the course of a season in rugby league players. The findings suggest that as the intensity, duration and load of rugby league training sessions and matches is increased, the incidence of injury is also increased. Further studies are required to determine the appropriate training stimulus required to enhance the physical fitness and performance of rugby league players, without unduly increasing the incidence of injury.

Margin notes:

In other words, the matches seemed harder for the younger, less experienced players, but in fact the older, better players were working harder during their (more intense) matches.

Researchers often critique their own methods to reveal more limitations of the study. While they did the work, they need to be objective about the strengths and weaknesses of their experiments.

The suggested studies could be done by this researcher or others who are interested in the study.

References

Bompa, T. U. (1983). *Theory and Methodology of Training. The Key to Athletic Performance*. Dubuque, IA: Kendall-Hunt.

Brewer, J. and Davis, J. (1995). Applied physiology of rugby league. *Sports Medicine*, 20, 129–135.

Coutts, A., Reaburn, P. and Aht, G. (2003). Heart rate, blood lactate concentration and estimated energy expenditure in a semi-professional rugby league team during a march: a case study. *Journal of Sports Sciences*, 21, 97, 103.

Dunbar, C. C., Robertson, R.J., Baun, R. et al. (1992). The validity of regulating exercise intensity by ratings of perceived exertion. *Medicine and Science in Sports and Exercise*, 24, 94–99.

Finch, C. F., Valuri, G. and Ozanne-Smith, J. (1999). Injury surveillance during medical coverage of sporting events—development and testing of a standardised data collection form. *Journal of Science and Medicine in Sport*, 2, 42–56.

Foster, C. (1997). Monitoring training in athletes with reference to overtraining syndrome. *Medicine and Science in Sports and Exercise*, 30, 1164–1168.

Foster, C., Hector, L. L., Welsh, R. et al. (1995). Effects of specific versus cross-training on running performance. *European Journal of Applied Physiology*, 70, 367–372.

Foster, C., Florhaug, J. A., Franklin, J. et al. (2001). A new approach to monitoring exercise training. *Journal of Strength and Conditioning Research*, 15, 109–115.

Gabbett, T. J. (2000a). Incidence, site, and nature of injuries in amateur rugby league over three consecutive seasons. *British Journal of Sports Medicine*, 34, 98–103.

Gabbett, T. J. (2000b). Physiological and athropometric characteristics of amateur rugby league players. *British Journal of Sports Medicine*, 34, 303–307.

Gabbett, T. J. (2001). Severity and cost of injuries in amateur rugby league: a case study. *Journal of Sports Sciences*, 19, 311–347.

Gabbett, T. J. (2002a). Influence of physiological characteristics on selection in a semi-professional rugby league team: a case study. *Journal of Sports Sciences*, 20, 399–405.

Gabbett, T. J. (2002b). Physiological characteristics of junior and senior rugby league players. *British Journal of Sports Medicine*, 36, 334–339.

Gabbett, T. J. (2002c). Training injuries in rugby league: an evaluation of skill-based conditioning games. *Journal of Strength and Conditioning Research*, 16, 236–241.

Gabbett, T. J. (2003). Incidence of injury in semi-professional rugby league players. *British Journal of Sports Medicine*, 37, 36–43.

Gibbs, N. (1993). Injuries in professional rugby league. a three-year prospective study of the South Sydney professional rugby league club. *American Journal of Sports Medicine*, 21, 696–700.

Gissane, C., Jennings, D. C. and Standing, P. (1993). Incidence of injury in rugby league football. *Physiotherapy*, 79, 305–310.

Gissane, C., Jennings, D., Jennings, S., White, J. and Kerr, K. (2001a). Physical collisions and injury rates in professional super league rugby. *Cleveland Medical Journal*, 4, 147—155.

Gissane, C., White, J., Kerr, K. and Jennings, D. (2001b). Physical collisions in professional super league: the demands of different player positions. *Cleveland Medical Journal*, 4, 137–146.

Hodgson-Phillips, L., Standen, P.J. and Batt, M. E. (1998). Effects of seasonal change in rugby league on the incidence of injury. *British Journal of Sports Medicine*, 32, 144–148.

Meir, R. (1994). A model for the integration of macrocycle and microcycle structure in professional rugby league. *Strength and Conditioning Coach*, 2, 6–12.

Meir, R., Arthur, D. and Forrest, M. (1993). Time and motion analysis of professional rugby league: a case study. *Strength and Conditioning Coach*, 1, 24–29.

Norton, K., Schwerdt, S. and Large, K. (2001). Evidence for the aetiology of injuries in Australian football. *British Journal of Sports Medicine*, 35, 418–423.

Stephenson, S., Gissane, C. and Jennings, D. (1996). Injury in rugby league: a four year prospective study. *British Journal of Sports Medicine*, 30, 331–334.

Watson, A. S. (1993). Incidence and nature of sports injuries in Ireland: analysis of four types of sport. *American Journal of Sports Medicine*, 21, 137–143.

Reading Responses

1. When you read the Results section, which presentation of data was easiest for you to understand—the written version, the tables, or the graphs? Why?

2. In the Results section, the author presents some data in tables and some in graphs (Figures 1 and 2). Present the information in Table 1 as a bar graph and compare the two: which presentation is more effective? Now create a bar graph for the information in Table 4. Which presentation is more effective? Based on your experience, what factors would you consider when choosing a table or a bar graph for information?

3. Reread the "Nature of Injury" paragraph in the Results section and Table 2. What function do the words fulfill? What function does the table fulfill?

NOTES ON GRAMMAR, STYLE, AND RHETORIC:
PASSIVE VERBS

One significant controversy about scientific prose centers on the question of whether scientists should use verbs in the passive voice. What kind of verbs are these? To begin, they are transitive verbs, verbs that signal the transfer of action from an agent onto some kind of recipient. When transitive verbs appear in the active voice, the agent is expressed as the subject of the sentence, and the recipient is expressed as the direct object:

> *The head trainer* [agent] *classified* [action] *the injury* [recipient].

When these verbs appear in the passive voice, the recipient is expressed in the subject, and the agent is usually expressed after the verb in a prepositional phrase:

> *The injury* [recipient] *was classified* [action] *by the head trainer* [agent].

Sometimes, however, writers choose to delete the reference to the agent:

> *The injury was classified.*

When writers are deciding between the active and the passive voice of a verb, they choose whether to focus on the agent (active voice) or on the recipient (passive voice) of the action.

Writers should be cautious about using passive verbs for several reasons. First, a sentence with a passive verb will typically be longer than the corresponding sentence with an active verb (as in first two of the earlier examples).

Second, passive verbs do not depict actions as directly and energetically as active verbs do:

> Active: *Reckless players sometimes break an arm or a leg.*
> Passive: *An arm or a leg is sometimes broken by reckless players.*

Although both sentences depict the same activity, the passive sentence has a more static quality than does the active sentence.

Third, studies of language processing have shown that a sentence is easier to read when it presents the agent before the action and the action before the recipient. Sentences with passive verbs, you recall, move from the recipient through the action to the agent.

Finally, when writers use passive verbs and omit references to agents, they can mask responsibility:

The toxic chemicals were marketed as environmentally safe.

Who marketed the chemicals? No one can tell. In some cases, then, writers intentionally use passives to avoid revealing who the agents of actions are. And when these actions fall into the realm of the unethical, so does the use of passive verbs.

On the basis of these and related cautionary notes, the current edition of the Council of Science Editors style manual (see page 439 in this book) advises scientists to use active verbs. But why is this advice ignored by so many scientists? And is it possible that you could have good reasons to use some passive verbs in your own scientific writing?

You can take a significant step toward answering these questions by examining the functions of passives in the scientific report on rugby injuries, which contains over sixty verbs in the passive voice. These verbs appear in every major section of the report, but most of them appear in the Methods section. What functions do passive verbs fulfill for the author?

First, he uses passive verbs to present what he views as facts of the world of rugby. For instance, early in the report he writes, "During the course of a match, players are exposed to many physical collisions and tackles . . . " (263). The effect of this sentence is clear: Injuries occur; to whom they occur does not matter, so passive voice is the right choice.

Second, the author writes as if there were no agent at all associated with the activities of conducting and reporting on the study. For example, he uses subject–verb combinations such as these: "The intensity of individual training sessions was estimated," "Training load was calculated," "Injury rates were calculated," "A total of 389 training injuries were recorded" (264), "A subjective measurement tool (i.e., RPE scale) was used" (271), and "Further studies are required" (271). References to the author and experimenter do not occur. In fact, in the entire report the words *I* and *me* never appear. (Quotations not followed by a page reference come from parts of the paper not reproduced here.)

When scientists report on their research and leave out all or almost all references to themselves as the agents, they are usually aiming for at least two effects. For one thing, they hope to keep their readers focused on the scientific objects and processes, an effect that would be difficult to achieve if some sentences included references to agents (as in *We classified almost 400 training injuries*). For another thing, they imply that whatever preparing, experimenting, calculating, and interpreting they do would come out exactly the same way if someone else performed the tasks. The passive voice implies that the study is reproducible. In this way, passive verbs reflect and support the fundamental practices of science.

So . . . the most important style guide for biologists advises the use of active voice, but most publications in biology contain many passive voice constructions. Assume that the debate doesn't continue out of stubbornness; there are good and bad reasons for using passive voice in the sciences. It's clear that you will need to be purposeful in your choices.

In Your Own Writing . . .

- Be alert for passive verbs that mask responsibility for unethical actions. Point them out in what you read, and avoid them in your own writing.
- Determine your reader's attitude toward passive verbs and take that into consideration as you draft.
- Use passive verbs when you want to focus the reader's attention on the action or the recipient of the action rather than on the agent of the action.

STUDENT WRITING

INTRODUCTION

by Cathryn Ghena, exercise science major

The Assignment. Because research is such a vital component of the health sciences, exercise science majors take a course in research methods. The research process, the same used by all health-care scientists, involves asking a question, developing a hypothesis, designing and conducting the experiment, analyzing the data, and, of course, writing the paper. What is then done with this research? In our case, we had the opportunity to present our research in a poster format at the annual conference of the Midwest American College of Sport Medicine. This meant condensing our project on a 4′ × 8′ board and placing it among dozens of other student posters.

The Content. Our results showed a significant increase in mean levels of oxygen consumption, energy expenditure, and heart rate during *Wii* as compared to Mario Tennis. Such results show that interactive video games cause the gamer to work harder than do sedentary video games. However, the values of the interactive *Wii* games were still not intense, not high enough to be considered a replacement for aerobic training.

Learning to Write in Health Sciences. Our research group members were all intrigued by factors influencing childhood obesity. With a bit of questioning and discussion, we formed our research question: Do interactive video games, specifically the *Nintendo Wii*™, cause a greater increase in aerobic exertion than sedentary video games, specifically *Nintendo*™ Mario Tennis, and would such increased levels be comparable to that of aerobic training?

Next we had to design an experiment. We tested ten college-aged males, all regular gamers, enough to gather reliable statistical data. First, we collected base values for each subject, including maximal oxygen consumption (VO_2max), heart rate (HR) and energy expenditure (kcal/min), all of which are good measures of aerobic fitness. While we collected the oxygen consumption data, subjects played an 18-minute round of sedentary tennis doubles on Mario Tennis. After a ten-minute rest, they played an 18-minute round of interactive tennis doubles on the *Wii.*

Once we gathered all the data, we had to figure out how best to share it. First, and maybe most important, is learning to be concise. When doing research, you essentially become an expert on your topic. This makes it easy to ramble on forever. Unfortunately, such detail is rarely necessary or even appreciated, and it's impossible within the limits of a poster project. Having a long paper doesn't mean an automatic "A," nor does it prove your intelligence. At the same time, though, just because your paper is short doesn't mean it's concise; don't sacrifice essential material for the sake of length. To find a balance between these two, determine what material really is essential. Then present that as efficiently as possible, which means using figures.

Another important part of a poster is its visual effect. In a poster session, people literally stand in front of a poster and have to be able to read it from several feet away. It makes sense, then, that generally half of a poster is filled with tables, charts, and photographs of

Oxygen Consumption During Sedentary and Physically Active Video Gaming in College Males

D. Van Dyke, C. Ghena, E. Metzger, K. Kerekes, J. Walton, J. Bergsma, Calvin College, Grand Rapids, MI.

Introduction

A recent study found 85% of students admitted to playing video games regularly, with over 30% of American homes boasting at least one video game system[1]. Traditionally, gaming has been considered a sedentary activity, requiring no gross motor movements. Meanwhile, the percentage of overweight young people has tripled in the last 25 years, and sedentary lifestyles have been linked to a higher risk of CVD, hypertension and Type II Diabetes[2]. In 2006 Nintendo joined the "active" game community when it released its Wii™ system. Nintendo Wii™ uses infrared and gravity sensing components to allow gamers to control play by manipulating a remote controller in a manner which mimics a sport movement. This study examined and compared aerobic strain elicited by the Nintendo Game Club™ and the Nintendo Wii™ to determine if any aerobic training benefit may be derived from either system.

Methods

Subjects: Ten college-age male volunteers (Table 1) were recruited to serve as subjects. All gave written informed consent to participate, and the study was approved by the Institutional Review Board. All Subjects were familiar with both video games used in testing.

Video Games
Sedentary: (SED) Nintendo Game Club™: Mario Tennis™: Doubles
Active: (ACT) Nintendo Wii™: Wii Sports™: Tennis: Doubles

Experimental Design: On the first visit, subjects completed a PAR-Q form and an informed consent before undergoing maximal exercise treadmill testing to determine maximal oxygen consumption ($VO2_{max}$) and heart rate (HR_{max}). The test protocol employed 3-minute stages in an incremental fashion designed to induce fatigue in the 12th minute of exercise. Metabolic measures were made using a Max 1 metabolic cart system. VO_2 was measured throughout, and HR, BP, and RPE were monitored and recorded in the last 10 seconds of each stage. Subjects ran until volitional fatigue. On the second visit, subjects reported to the lab exactly one week later at the same time of day to play two bouts of video games while VO_2, HR, caloric expenditure, and RPE were measured. In each case, the SED game was played first, followed by a 10-minute rest, then the ACT game. Each game was played for 18 minutes.

Statistical Design: Mean values for VO_2, Peak VO_2, calorie expenditure and HR were compared using an ANOVA post-hoc paired *t* test, with significance equal to p=.05.

Table 1. Subject Characteristics

Age	Height (cm)	Weight (kg)	BMI	VO2max (mL·kg–1·min–1)	HRmax (BPM)
21.4	180.4	75	23	44.8	192.8

Results

Mean VO_2 was higher on ACT video game than on SED video game (Figure 1). This difference was significant (p = .05). Mean HR was higher during ACT game play than SED game play (Figure 2). This difference was again significant (p = .05). The ACT game elicited significantly greater keal expenditure than did the SED game (Figure 3) (p = .05). When mean VO2 is expressed as a percent of VO_{2max} values from both ACT and SED systems fail to reach the minimum requirement for aerobic training (Figure 4). Similarly, when mean HR is expressed as a percent of HR_{max} values from both ACT and SED systems fail to reach a minimum requirement for aerobic training (Figure 5). Mean data are expressed in Table 2.

Figure 1

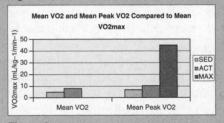

Mean VO2 and Mean Peak VO2 Compared to Mean VO2max

Figure 2

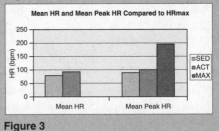

Mean HR and Mean Peak HR Compared to HRmax

Figure 3

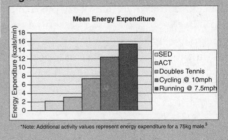

Mean Energy Expenditure

*Note: Additional activity values represent energy expenditure for a 75kg male.[3]

Figure 4

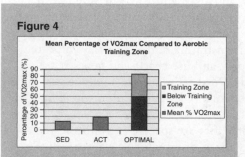

Mean Percentage of VO2max Compared to Aerobic Training Zone

Figure 5

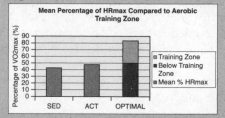

Mean Percentage of HRmax Compared to Aerobic Training Zone

Table 2. Mean Data

	Mean VO2 (mL·kg–1·min–1)	Mean Peak VO2 (mL·kg–1·min–1)	Mean Percent VO2max	Mean HR (bpm)	Mean Peak HR (bpm)	Mean Percent HRmax	Mean kcals/min
SED	4.88	6.51	11.22	80	91	41.57	1.88
ACT	7.6	9.86	17.25	93	102	48.31	2.99

Discussion

While the *Nintendo Wii*™ elicits significantly greater oxygen consumption, calorie expenditure, and heart rate response than the Nintendo Game Club™, these increases are not great enough to provide any aerobic training benefits. The small sample size limits the strength of this study. A larger sample size must be studied to understand the relationship between active games and aerobic training benefits more completely. Additional studies should look at the effect of active games on high BMI and or low VO_{2max} populations, and across varied age groups, particularly in children.

References

1. Schmitt, B. D. (2006). Video Games [Electronic version]. *Clinical Reference Systems, 2006*(2). from General Reference Center Gold
2. TV-Turnoff Network. (2004). *Screened In: How Excessive Screen Time Promotes Obesity.* Washington, D.C.
3. Wilmore, Jack H., and David L. Costill. (2004). *Physiology of Sport and Exercise.* 3rd ed. Hong Kong: Human Kinetics.

Notes on the poster

1. Acronyms and abbreviations: **ACT** = active, stand-up gaming; **BP** = blood pressure; **BMI** = body mass index; **CVD** = cardiovascular disease; **kcal/min** = energy expenditure; **HR** = heart rate; **PAR-Q** = medical history and consent form; **RPE** = rating of perceived exertion, **SED** = sedentary, sit-down gaming; VO_2 **max** = maximal oxygen consumption.

2. Other definitions: **aerobic strain**: amount of oxygen uptake; the harder you're working, the greater your O_2 uptake; **aerobic training zone**: amount of exertion required for aerobic benefit; **Institutional Review Board**: an ethics review board that must grant approval to all research designs that use human or animal subjects.

3. The visual features. **Title**: the large font of the title is a necessary eye-catcher. People at poster sessions often wander around looking for topics of interest; they have to be able to see your topic at a glance. **Graphs and tables**: most of the poster is taken up with figures and tables because they offer the easiest way to quickly see the findings. **Headings**: "Introduction," "Methods," "Results," "Discussion," and "References" are the standard sections of most scientific writing, in posters, published papers, and lab reports.

4. The sections. The **Methods** section includes demographics of the people who participated, what was done, and the statistical design used to analyze the data. The **Results** section summarizes the findings. Notice that all the sentences are short and to the point. The **Discussion** wraps up the poster, in our case, with a one-sentence summary of the results. It also suggests limits of the study and recommendations for further research. Maybe people reading the poster will be intrigued enough to conduct their own study and use ideas or methods from your work.

the research data collection. A health science audience will be able to look at the figures and immediately see the research results. This gets rid of unnecessary reading, saving a lot of time. To aid in this process, you learn that your figures should have features like a title, key, and labeled axes.

A second consideration is the audience. Professionals in health sciences present to either a general audience or an audience of other scientists.

If you write for a general audience, be sure to do a good job breaking everything down. One common barrier is abbreviations like CVD, VO_2max, and BMI. Be sure to explain all abbreviations, no matter how simplistic. This goes hand in hand with the second barrier— complexity. If the audience doesn't understand what they're reading, then they won't get anything out of it. This only makes your paper frustrating and then easily forgotten. Be sure to break all the concepts down, give examples, and use charts and tables.

We presented our poster to fellow specialists. Poster sessions are a unique way of data presentation. Having a day or two at a conference to find the information you're interested in from among thousands of posters can be overwhelming. Using keywords make this possible. In the abstract, there will be different words that are specific to your research topic. The audience can search all the poster abstracts ahead of time for keywords, and they are able to choose what posters to see at the conference. For example, people who searched for VO_2max, aerobic training, or calorie expenditure, might have stumbled on our abstract, which would help them decide whether to go see the poster in person. At the poster presentation interested individuals have the opportunity to ask questions and discuss the research in more detail with the poster's authors. In that situation you can bring out some of your research that you didn't put on the poster.

Overall, writing in the health sciences means learning what's expected of you—having good content and making it really easy and quick to understand.

Reading Responses

1. Write out the sentence that most directly summarizes the main findings of the research. What section was it in? How does that sentence relate to the title of the poster? Revise the title of the poster to emphasize the main findings of the research, rather than the topic of the research.

2. Which of the graphs best supports the findings it reports? Explain your reasons for that choice. List three strategies that the authors could use to emphasize that graph.

3. Study the blocks that are mostly words. What's their function? How do they complement the graphs and tables? Make three revision recommendations to enhance the function of text in this poster.

PUBLIC WRITING

INTRODUCTION

In "The Female Hurt," Maguerite Holloway (contributing editor at *Scientific American*, professor at The Journalism School at Columbia University, and 2009 winner of a Presidential Teaching Award) uses a mixture of illustrations and figures to explain why female athletes have a different rate and pattern of injuries than male athletes. In some ways, the article looks very different than the other articles in this chapter. It begins with a "catchy" title that gives very little specific information, and it also has anatomical drawings that are "artist renderings" of the human body. In other ways, it looks a lot like the other papers in this chapter. The author quotes scientific studies that involve experimental and control subjects, cites specific numbers, and embeds three graphs in the text. The hybrid nature of the paper reflects its intended audience. *Scientific American* articles are written for nonexperts who have a general interest in news-making science.

Keeping in mind the chapter's portable rhetorical lesson, think about the figures in the article. You will notice how clearly and effectively the results are conveyed by the figures. The difference between male and female injury rate and participation in sports is made obvious, at a glance, by the bar graphs.

The figures in this paper share another characteristic with figures in journals published for experts. Although the author of this paper did not collect the data and did not design her paper around her lab work, she still would have started with these figures, as they tell the core of the story. The paper is centered on the following observation: female athletes have a higher rate of ACL injury. This fact (and the graph that conveys it) comprises what amounts to the "results" section: explanations of why the injury rate is higher are equivalent to the introduction and discussion.

The Female Hurt

Marguerite Holloway

Scientific American 2000, 11(3): 32–37.

"I don't want to hear a bunch of thuds," bellows Deborah Saint-Phard from her corner of the basketball court. Several dozen young women and girls, some barefoot, some in jeans and tank tops, some in full athletic regalia, look sheepish. They jump again, trying to keep their knees slightly bent and facing straight forward, trying to make no noise when their feet hit the floor. "I can hear you landing," Saint-Phard nonetheless admonishes, urging them into a softer touchdown. "Control your jump."

Saint-Phard is a doctor with the Women's Sports Medicine Center at the Hospital for Special Surgery in New York City. She and several colleagues have traveled to this gymnasium in Philadelphia for "Hoop City"—a National Collegiate Athletic Association (NCAA) event—to teach young women how to jump safely. Female athletes, particularly those playing basketball, volleyball and soccer, are between five and eight times more likely than men are to injure their anterior cruciate ligament, or ACL, which stabilizes the knee. Some 20,000 high school girls and 10,000 female college students suffer debilitating knee injuries each year, the majority of which are ACL-related, according to the American Orthopedic Society for Sports Medicine. Tearing the ligament can put an athlete out of the game for months, if not forever.

"This is a huge public health problem for women," says Edward M. Wojtys, an orthopedic surgeon at the University of Michigan. "Fourteen- to 18-year-olds are subjected to injuries that many of them will never recover from, that will affect whether they can walk or exercise at 40 and 50." For this reason, physicians are placing new emphasis on teaching female athletes how to jump in such a way that they strengthen their knees and protect their ACLs. "We have to get them when they are young," Saint-Phard says.

Torn ACLs are just one of the medical problems that plague female athletes. Injuries and ailments that occur with higher incidence in women than in men are garnering more attention as women enter sports in record numbers—not only as Olympians and professionals but for fitness and recreation. Today 135,110 women participate in collegiate athletics, according to the NCAA, up from 29,977 in 1972. The number of girls playing high school sports has shot up from 294,015 to 2.5 million in the same time frame. As a result,

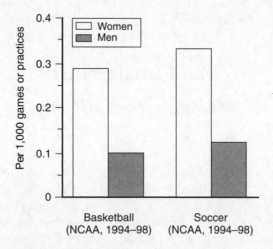

Frequency of ACL injury

Source: "Anterior Cruciate Ligament Injury Patterns" by Elizabeth Arendt et al., *Journal of Athletic Training,* June 1999.

researchers, physicians and coaches are increasingly recognizing that girls and women engaged in sports have some distinct medical concerns.

This makes perfect sense. Women's bodies are shaped differently than men's, and they are influenced by different hormones. They may be at greater risk not only for ACL tears but for other knee problems, as well as for certain shoulder injuries. Women are also uniquely threatened by a condition called the female athlete triad: disordered eating habits, menstrual dysfunction or the loss of their menstrual cycle, and, as a consequence of these two changes, premature and permanent osteoporosis. "We are seeing 25-year-olds with the bones of 70-year-olds," Saint-Phard says.

Although the passage of Title IX legislation in 1972 required that institutions receiving federal funding devote equal resources to men's and women's sports, it has taken a while for the particular needs of female athletes to emerge. As an example, Wojtys points to the ACL: "It took us 15 to 18 years to realize that this problem existed." Women entering sports even a decade and a half after Title IX received less care from coaches and physicians than male athletes did, says Saint-Phard, who competed in the 1988 Olympic shot-put event. When she was in college, she recalls, "the men's teams got a lot more resources and a different level of coaches than the women's teams."

And today even those conditions that are increasingly well recognized as more problematic for women are not fully understood, and their etiology and treatment remain controversial at times. "There is not enough awareness of the differences," says Regina M. Vidaver of the Society for Women's Health Research. For most of the people treating sports injuries, she explains, "their predominant history is with men." . . .

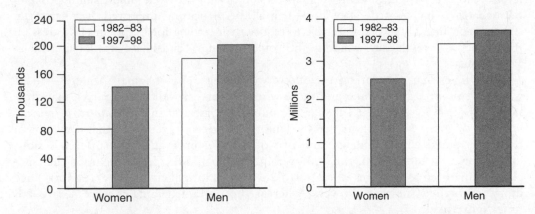

Participation in NCAA Sports   Participation in High School Sports

Sources: National Collegiate Athletic Association Participation Statistics Report, 1982–98; National Federation of State High School Associations Participation Study. Copyright NFHS 2010. Used by permission..

Tearing into ACL Injuries

The most obvious musculoskeletal difference between men and women is the breadth of their hips. Because a woman's pelvis tends to be wider, the muscles that run from the hip down to the knee pull the kneecap (the patella) out to the side more, sometimes causing what is called patellofemoral syndrome—a painful condition that appears to occur more frequently in women. In men, the muscle and bone run more directly vertically, putting less lateral pull on the patella. Some studies also indicate that women's joints and muscles may tend to be more lax than men's; although this adds to greater flexibility, it may mean that female joints and muscles are not necessarily as stable.

Increased laxity and differences in limb alignment may contribute to ACL injuries among female athletes. And yet, even though physicians and coaches first recognized in the 1980s that female athletes were more prone to this injury, there is still no resolution about the cause. "It is an area of controversy," observes Joseph Bosco, an orthopedic surgeon at New York University. . . .

Recent studies indicating that ACL injuries can be prevented by training women to jump differently and to develop their hamstring muscles suggest that inadequate training is at least a large part of the problem. "We train and condition women in the same way that we do the men," says Wojtys, who showed in a 1999 study that women tend not to bend their knees as much as men do when they land a jump, thereby increasing the pressure of the impact on the joints. "They probably need their own training programs."

The Cincinnati Sportsmedicine and Orthopaedic Center focuses on just such an approach. In 1996 Frank R. Noyes and his colleagues there followed 11 high school girl volleyball players who went through Sportsmetrics, a grueling six-week jump-training program the researchers had created. They found that all the participants improved their hamstring strength and that all but one were able to reduce their landing forces, placing less stress on their knees as a result (and achieving the "quiet landing" Saint-Phard was looking for in Philadelphia).

The investigators went on to follow two new groups of female athletes—those who did this strength training and those who did not—as well as a group of male athletes without Sportsmetrics. In an article published last year in the *American Journal of Sports Medicine,* the authors, led by Timothy E. Hewett, reported that only two of the 366 trained female athletes (and two of the 434 male athletes) suffered serious knee injuries, whereas 10 of the 463 untrained women did. They concluded that specially trained female athletes were 1.3 to 2.4 times more likely to have a serious knee injury than the male athletes were, whereas the untrained females were 4.8 to 5.8 times more likely.

The idea that better, or perhaps more, training could have a strong effect on injury rates is supported by work with another set of women: army recruits. According to a recent study by Nicole S. Bell of the Boston University School of Public Health, female recruits were twice as likely to suffer injuries during basic combat training than men were—and two and a half times more likely to have serious injuries. . . .

Noyes is also working to redress another sports medicine imbalance. Historically, men have been more likely than women to have knee surgery. Noyes believes that there are two reasons. First, knee surgery used to be a difficult procedure with often poor outcomes, so it was limited to athletes who really "needed" it—in other words, professional male athletes. Second, there has been a perception among physicians that women would not fare as well during the often painful surgery and recovery. So Noyes and his colleagues decided to examine the responses of both men and women to ACL surgery. They determined that although women took slightly longer to heal, both sexes fared equally well in the long run.

Noyes's work on surgery outcomes and the growing consensus about the importance of neuromuscular control appear to have shifted some attention away from another area of ACL injury investigation: hormonal influences. Researchers have found that the ACL has estrogen and progesterone receptors—target sites that respond to those two hormones. In studies in animals and in vitro, they have discovered that the presence of estrogen decreases the synthesis of collagen fibers, the building blocks of ligaments. It also increases the levels of another hormone, relaxin, which in turn adds to the disorganization of collagen fibers. This change in the ligaments makes the ACL more flexible and, according to the hypothesis, more vulnerable to injury.

This view seems supported by some studies, including one by Wojtys published two years ago in the *American Journal of Sports Medicine*. He and his team questioned 40 women with ACL injuries; the majority of the tears occurred during ovulation, when estrogen levels were highest. Other studies show some increased muscle laxity in ovulating women, but nothing dramatic. . . .

"Estrogen probably has some role," notes Jo A. Hannafin, orthopedic director at the Women's Sports Medicine Center. But, she says, no one is applying the studies' findings to the court—limiting, say, what time of month a player should or should not play. The hormonal result "just reinforces old stereotypes," Bosco adds. "It takes weeks and weeks for the effects [of estrogen] to be seen, so it doesn't make sense. We still strongly encourage women to participate in athletics over the whole month."

Treating the Triad

Estrogen's role in the other major health threat to female athletes is not at all controversial. Exercise or poor eating, or both, can cause an athlete's body to develop an energy deficit, become stressed and lose essential nutrients. Any or all of these changes can cause levels of follicular-stimulating and luteinizing hormones to fall and ovulation to therefore cease. Absent their menstrual cycles, young athletes do not have the requisite estrogen at precisely the time they need the hormone the most to help retain calcium and lay down bone. By the age of 17, nearly all a young woman's bone has been established, explains Melinda M. Manore, a professor of nutrition at Arizona State University. If an athlete's level of estrogen remains low, she can start to lose bone mass at a rapid rate, which can lead to stress fractures and, if the process is not curbed, premature osteoporosis.

The phrase "female athlete triad" was coined in 1992 by participants at an American College of Sports Medicine meeting. Since then, anecdotal reports have indicated that the occurrence of the triad is on the rise. "I think young women are more and more aware of their body size," Manore says. Furthermore, female athletes are especially vulnerable.

Eating disorders—such as obsessive dieting, calorie restriction or aversion to fat (all labeled disordered eating), as well as anorexia and bulimia (the so-called classic eating disorders)—are disproportionately high in girls and women who participate regularly in sports. Averaged across various sports, some 30 percent of these individuals have an eating problem, as opposed to 10 to 15 percent of the general population— although no one knows for sure,

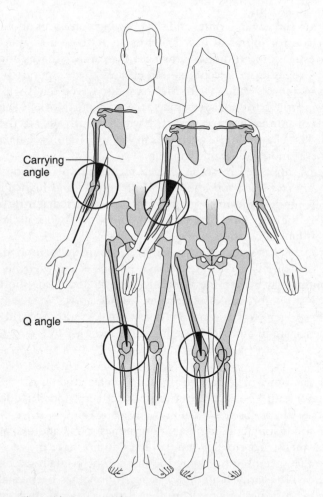

Carrying angle

Q angle

The Inside Story on Injury

The skeletons of women differ from men's most visibly in the width of the pelvis. As a result, women have a wider Q angle (a measure of bone alignment from hip to knee) and carrying angle (from upper to lower arm), which can lead, respectively, to higher rates of knee and elbow or shoulder injuries.

because no large-scale studies on prevalence have been conducted in the U.S. The proportion may be as high as 70 percent in some sports. "High achievers, perfectionists, goal setters, people who are compulsive and determined—those are the things that characterize our best athletes," says Margot Putukian, a team physician at Pennsylvania State University. Those are also the very qualities that often lead people into problem eating.

And athletic culture—particularly for swimmers, runners, skiers, rowers and gymnasts—only continues to reinforce these behaviors and expectations. Many coaches encourage their athletes to lose weight so they can be faster or have less mass to move through acrobatic maneuvers. According to a recent study, female gymnasts weigh 20 pounds less than those in the 1970s did. And many female athletes at all levels see losing their period as a badge of honor.

"They don't see it as a negative," Putukian explains. "They see it as something that happens when you get in shape, a sign that you are training adequately." What they also don't see is what is happening to their bones—until they develop stress fractures. "They fly through their adolescent years with no knowledge of why being too thin is dangerous," Saint-Phard says.

Treating the triad is challenging, and, as Putukian notes, "there is not a lot of great data to tell us what is the best thing." Researchers now recognize that female athletes experiencing these problems need the combined talents of a physician, a nutritionist and, if they have bulimia or anorexia, a psychologist—a multidisciplinary team that most schools and colleges lack. "When you have a kid who has an eating disorder, it is very frustrating," Putukian says. "It is reversible if you catch it early on, irreversible if you don't." She tells her athletes—who are all questioned about their menses and their eating habits during their initial physical—that if they haven't had their period for three months, they are in danger.

Putukian tries to get them on a birth-control pill and works with them to change their eating habits if they have a problem. But although the pill restores some hormonal activity, it does not provide the requisite levels for normal bone development. And hormone replacement therapy, which is used by some physicians, has not been extensively tested in young women. Nevertheless, Putukian notes that athletes may be easier to treat than women in the general population because there is an incentive: competition. "It is an incredible tool," she says. "You can help kids come back." Putukian has refused to let several athletes compete until they got their weight up to healthy levels; their desire to participate drove them to improve their eating habits.

Putukian, Manore and others would like to see young women better educated about the consequences of excessive dieting and amenorrhea. They admit that little can be done about the cultural pressures facing young women—the unrealistic icons of emaciated beauty that destroy many self-images.

But they believe that if girls understand that they may be jeopardizing their freedom to take a simple jog in their 30s without fracturing their osteoporotic hips or leg bones, they will change their behavior.

The investigators hope that athletes will focus on how they feel and how they perform, rather than on how much they weigh. But as with the jump-training program to prevent ACL injuries, there remains a great divide between the medical community's recommendations and the reality of the track or court or gymnasium. Only when those are fully integrated will Title IX have truly fulfilled its promise.

Reading Responses

1. The introduction to the first reading in this chapter indicates that graphics need to be "anchored" in the text. That is, the writers use words to help explain the tables, graphs, figures, etc. Note two places in this article where the author fails to do this and describe how an anchor in the text could make the image more effective.

2. In this article, the author and others make two claims that seem to be contradictory. First, female athletes have been hurt because they have been treated like male athletes. Second, female athletes have been hurt because they have not been treated like male athletes. How have they been treated like males? How have they not? Are these two claims contradictory after all?

3. Compare the introduction to this article to the introduction to "Influence of Training and Match Intensity on Injuries in Rugby League" and to Ghena's introduction to her poster. Which two are most alike? Why do you think these authors chose the rhetorical strategies they used for their introductions?

MORE WRITING IN BIOLOGY

INTRODUCTION

Our purpose for this reading is simple—to show you how an image (in this case an illustration) functions to make communication clear and efficient. Using images in this way probably goes back for as long as humans have been writing and drawing. Famous images come to mind—for example, we all recognize the double-helix model of DNA that James Watson and Francis Crick published in 1953. Without that image, understanding the structure of DNA would be next to impossible.

In the short opening parts of the article printed here, the authors, Manini and Clark (professors at, respectively, the University of Florida and Ohio University), introduce their review essay (a genre that we study in Chapter 11) on a type of exercise. To summarize what researchers at the time knew about "blood flow restricted" exercise, Manini and Clark had to explain how the technique works and its effects on the body. No scientist would imagine trying to convey that kind of information without the use of images.

The illustration in Figure 1, at a glance, shows readers the mechanism of the exercise practice—exactly how it works—and its physiological effects—the use of "up" arrows, for example, indicates four bodily effects that increase under the exercise regime.

By the way, this technique is still highly experimental and potentially very dangerous. The authors report on the available research, but they do not recommend the practice. In fact, they specifically warn, "Considering the limited data regarding the safety and clinical viability of BFR exercise, we must caution against the immediate clinical application of BFR exercise by medical professionals." In other words, they say that doctors should not let their patients use this method even in supervised settings. Please don't try this on your own.

Blood Flow Restricted Exercise and Skeletal Muscle Health

Todd M. Manini and Brian C. Clark

Exercise and Sports Sciences Reviews (2009), 32.2: 78–85

Introduction

The most common method for increasing both muscle mass and strength is through the performance of high intensity resistance exercise, where the American College of Sports Medicine typically recommends that resistance training with loads exceeding 70% of maximal strength be used to induce optimal muscle hypertrophy [enlargement]. These recommendations are based on evidence that has accumulated over the past three decades, indicating that compensatory muscle growth results from mechanical loading of the muscle tissue and occurs in a fasting state and without insulin signaling. Therefore, tension development through either passive or active techniques by itself facilitates protein synthesis and is typically considered a fundamental determinate of skeletal tissue mass (10, 13).

Increasing evidence suggests that hypertrophy also can be induced with low-intensity exercise performed under blood flow restricted (BFR) . . . conditions (1, 21, 29). The observation that BFR exercise at low mechanical loading causes muscle growth seemingly opposes traditionally based programs. Although many questions remain regarding the efficacy, safety, and mechanisms of action of BFR exercise training, scientists are beginning to develop a better understanding of the model. This review aims to present the latest findings regarding BFR exercise and discuss the potential mechanisms of action that seem to be discordant with traditionally based theories of muscle hypertrophy.

Mechanics of Blood Flow Restricted Exercise

The concept of exercise training with BFR has been around for nearly 40 years and was popularized in Japan by Yoshiaki Sato in the mid-1980s. Today, Sato has commercialized his training method in Japan (known as KAATSU training), where it is now relatively common. Although there is no universal way in which the training is used, it uses a relatively simple approach that generally involves placing a narrow compression cuff around an appendicular limb [arm or leg], which is inflated during exercise (Fig. 1). . . . One common feature of most BFR protocols, which may play an important mechanistic role, is that the compressive cuff remains inflated throughout the exercise session, including the rest period. As such, during subsequent sets, the number of repetitions that can be performed is substantially reduced by approximately 30%-50%.

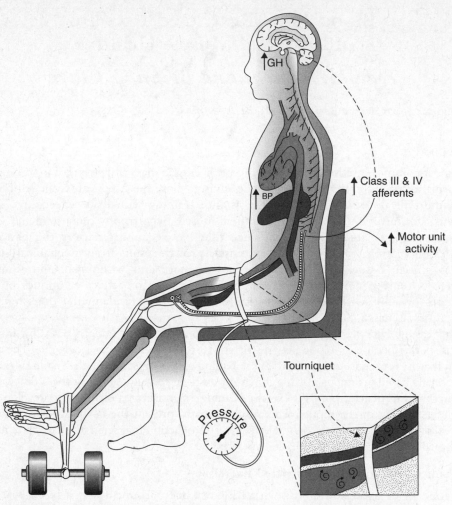

Figure 1 Conceptual model of the physiological responses to blood flow restricted exercise (BFR). GH indicates growth hormone; BP, blood pressure; . . . ["Class III and IV afferents" are nerve fibers that carry messages from the body to the brain; a "motor unit" is a single nerve cell and the muscle fiber it sends messages to, so "motor unit activity" refers to how active, or stimulated, the motor unit is.]

References [cited in excerpt]

Abe, T., Kearns, C. F., Sato, Y. Muscle size and strength are increased following walk training with restricted venous blood flow from the leg muscle, Kaatsu-walk training. *J. Appl. Physiol.* 2006; 100:1460–6.

Goldberg, A. L., Etlinger, J. D., Goldspink, D. F., Jablecki, C. Mechanism of work-induced hypertrophy of skeletal muscle. *Med. Sci. Sports.* 1975; 7: 185–98.

Hornberger, T. A., Esser, K. A. Mecahnotransduction and the regulation of protein synthesis in skeletal muscle. *Proc. Nutr. Soc.* 2004; 63: 331–5.

Ohta, H., Kurosawa, H., Ikeda, H., Iwase, Y., Satou, N., Nakamura, S. Low-load resistance muscular training with moderate restriction of blood flow after anterior cruciate ligament reconstruction. *Acta. Orthop. Scand.* 2003; 74: 62–8.

Reading Responses

1. What is the relationship between the illustration and the text? What parts of the illustration could you not fully understand without reading the text? What does the illustration add to your understanding that the text does not provide? What additional information could the illustration have provided?

2. In the introduction to this reading we mention the double-helix model of DNA. Do some research into the history of science. Describe three other models that have reformed scientific understanding. Were the models described through diagrams, equations, words, or other methods?

3. Think of a process or mechanism that you are studying for one of your classes and draw a diagram to illustrate how the process or mechanism works. Add whatever text is necessary to explain your illustration to a reader.

WRITING ASSIGNMENTS

Assignment 1

So, how much of your athletic ability results from your genetics? Australian researchers have discovered that human muscles contain a protein, alpha-actinin 3, that helps them make fast, strong contractions, like those sprinters use. In some people, a different protein substitutes for alpha-actinin 3; this abnormal protein helps muscles in sustained exercise, such as a marathon. The researchers wondered whether these muscle proteins are present in different ratios in the muscles of different types of athletes, and whether these differences could account for their Olympic success. The researchers presented their data in a paper that can be found at this site: http://www.inmr.com.au/articles/ACTN3AmJHumGenetics.pdf.

The central figure of the paper is presented earlier; just as in the rugby paper, the figure tells most of the story. For you to understand this story, you need to know that in the figure the scientists have nicknamed the normal version of apha-actinin 3 "R" and the abnormal version "X." Humans, like all complex animals and plants, have two versions of every gene. So, a person could have two versions of the normal protein ("RR"), one normal and one abnormal ("RX"), or two abnormal versions ("XX"). The graph measures what percentage of each group has each pattern of genes: RR, RX, and XX. The numbers are represented as the gray, black, or white boxes. (You can ignore the narrow lines. They show the range of high and low values for statistical purposes only.)

Your task for this assignment is to create a verbal explanation of the figure. First, describe the topic a bit so that your reader understands the context for the information that the table and figure provide. Then summarize the data in the figure, drawing your reader's attention to the most important results. Finally, help the reader understand the implications of the results—how does this research affect the reader or others in the world?

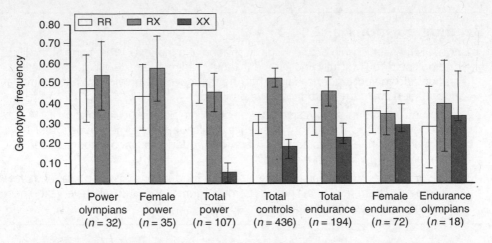

Figure 1 *ACTN3* genotype frequency in controls, elite sprint/power athletes, and endurance athletes. Compared with healthy white controls, there is a marked reduction in the frequency of the *ACTN3 S77*XX genotype (associated with αa-actinin-3 deficiency) in elite white sprint athletes; remarkably, none of the female sprint athletes or sprint athletes who had competed at the Olympic level (25 males and 7 females) were αa-actinin-3 deficient. Conversely, there is a trend toward an increase in the *S77*XX genotype in endurance athletes, although this association reaches statistical significance only in females. Error bars indicate 95% CIs.

As you begin drafting, you'll want to draw the reader's attention to how the pattern of genes in "Total Power" athletes (short-distance runners, swimmers, and cyclists, speed skaters, and judo athletes) differs from those in "Total Endurance" athletes (long-distance runners, swimmers, and cyclists, and cross-country skiers). And you'll want to help the reader understand how the pattern of genes in "Endurance Olympians" and "Power Olympians" differs from the other athletes and from the general population.

Assignment 2

On the Web site for the National Center for Catastrophic Injury Research (http://www.unc .edu/depts/nccsi/) you can find the most recent reports on sports injuries sustained by high school and college players. Each report contains much data, too much for a reader to comprehend at a glance. In marketing, a common way of presenting complex information quickly and effectively is a PowerPoint presentation because you can easily blend visual presentations of information (tables, figures, images) with verbal representations. To create an effective PowerPoint presentation, you must present data effectively so that the audience understands the information and can see the connection between the information and the author's central point.

Your task for this assignment is twofold:

A. Review the most recent NCCSI report and choose a type of athlete and/or type of sport. Create a PowerPoint presentation that supports a claim about catastrophic injuries to these athletes. Use visual and textual presentation to support your claim.

B. In a two-page report, justify your choices, focusing on four questions.

- Why did you choose to use figures to represent certain information?
- Why did you choose text for other information?
- Why did you arrange your figures and text as you did?
- What does your PowerPoint presentation emphasize about the data? What does it de-emphasize?

Assignment 3

Marguerite Holloway ("The Female Hurt") provides a valuable service by using visuals to help professionals interpret the complex biological data produced by scientific experiments. Trainers and coaches are most likely to influence the behavior of female athletes, but they can do so only if they understand the data.

Your task for this assignment is to provide the same kind of service for trainers and coaches of a sport you played as a child. Using research databases that cover biological journals, locate several research articles on your sport. Select one that includes useful information and interpret that information so that trainers, coaches, and athletes can easily understand the data contained in some of the article's tables, graphs, and figures.

As you begin drafting, review the strategies that Holloway uses to help her readers understand complex data and lay out all the options available to you (verbal, visual, design) for displaying information clearly. Think, too, about how you can use options together to achieve a common effect.

MEDIA STUDIES: ANALYZING THE RHETORIC OF IMAGES

It's no news that teenagers rely on cell phones and social networking sites to communicate with each other. Increasingly, children are, too. For example, more than a third of 11-year-olds carried cell phones in 2009, and many participate in social media sites, not only those designed for children but also those that restrict membership to people older than 13. To educate teens about abuse that can occur in digital environments, three nonprofit organizations teamed up to create the "That's not cool" Web site. There, viewers can watch videos, send "call out cards," participate in "talk it out" forums, and find help for reporting abusive behavior.

- Go to the "That's Not Cool" Web site (thatsnotcool.com), and explore the content, paying special attention how the information is visually presented. How would you describe the look of the Web site? What features are especially distinctive?
- Based on your analysis of the Web site, characterize the viewer that this Web site is trying to attract, narrowing your focus to one aspect of the viewer such as age, gender, race, economic class, or sexual orientation. Use evidence from the Web site to justify your characterization.

PORTABLE RHETORICAL LESSON: ANALYZING IMAGES

As you analyzed the "That's not cool" Web site, you immediately saw the many visual features. But then we asked you to explain how the images conveyed meaning. And that's where the exercise gets hard.

When you read things that include images, you first recognize the rhetorical options for visual **presentation.** And you learn better and worse ways to use images in your own writing by seeing how experts put images to work in their writing. Analyzing images is a type of **research** that, when done effectively, yields ideas and information in images, which can function as persuasive **evidence.**

But you cannot take advantage of the rhetorical power of images—as a reader or writer—without analyzing images, the **Portable Rhetorical Lesson** of this chapter.

Much of your response to images is subconscious, embedded in your attitudes to and knowledge of the subjects, your personal taste, and your own experience with photography or other visual arts. Each of those factors can help or hinder your analysis of images. Furthermore, images function in extremely complex ways, many of which are, again, subconscious. So you must analyze images with great caution, humility, and care. Keeping those warnings in mind, here is a beginner's list of things to pay attention to when analyzing an image. We use main categories that we have borrowed from the Van Arragon and Smit introduction to the first reading. As you read the chapter, watch for how these ideas are practiced in each of the readings.

1. Subject matter. What or who is the subject? What is represented by the image?
2. Content. What does the image say about the subject? Does the image trouble you, confuse you, make you defensive, make you angry or happy?

   Do you hear questions coming to mind as you look at the image?

   What details are in the image? Do any details draw attention by seeming out of place? If there are people in the image, what or who are they looking at?
3. Form. What points of interest draw your attention? How does the image accomplish that? Take note of visual elements like line, shape, space—and of principles of design, like rhythm, balance, proportion, and movement. How do features such as light, color, direction, and movement influence your interpretation?
4. Context. What do you know about the history in which the image is set? The politics? Is it intentionally controversial? Does it recall other images, perhaps images from your own experience?

   Can you tell where the image is set? Country? City? A place of particular conflict or peace?

This list is only a starting point. If you want to train yourself to analyze images effectively, there are loads of books and Web sites that can offer guidance, or better yet, take a class in visual rhetoric. But by all means, find some way to prepare yourself to analyze images—doing so is an essential skill for effective reading and writing.

WRITING IN THE DISCIPLINE

INTRODUCTION

by Lisa Van Arragon, Professor
of Art History, and Christopher R. Smit,
Professor of Communication Arts and Sciences

The field of Media Studies originated with the examination of mass communication forms like newspapers and magazines, photography, cinema, radio, and television. The term *mass communication* was coined in reference to mass media forms perceived to have an influence on social and cultural behaviors. Thus early Media Studies writing focused on issues of propaganda, political cohesion, and other media effects. As the field developed, and as communication technologies changed, Media Studies scholars began to turn their attention to how people use media. Contemporary writing in Media Studies considers not only how media communicates but also how audiences are empowered or disempowered by global media systems like the Internet, G3 technology, gaming, and social networking.

The readings in this chapter focus on one of the most common media texts, images, to identify some of the ways in which Media Studies writers go about analyzing the persuasive impact of photographs within a range of contexts. Whether dealing with advertising images, government agency photographs, documents of war, or Google maps, writers must be able to "read" pictures within their historical and cultural frames. This skill in turn allows writers to make analyses and arguments about the images and their relationship to audiences.

At least three common practices are employed by Media Studies writers in addressing images as media forms: reading, interpretation, and evaluation. In reading an image, Media Studies writers attempt to describe what they see for the reader. Although this is a complex process, one that takes a good deal of practice to do well, it nonetheless is essential for both the novice and the professional. Reading an image involves giving intense scrutiny to pictorial evidence within the entire frame, which means taking one's time to sense all the characteristics of the image in question. Close attention must be given to subject matter, content, and form, that is analysis of the internal relationships within the image (line, shape, texture, space, tone, etc.). This is particularly important when the image is a photograph or photography based because these images bear the appearance of reality but are in fact always constructions; unless the constructed qualities of the photograph are carefully identified, audiences tend to trust its objective appearance. Keep in mind that a description does not need to be long to be effective. As Garland-Thomson demonstrates throughout her essay, the keys are brevity and precision. Respect that the image does not ramble on with its rhetorical position by doing the same in your explanation of it.

The second practice, interpretation, connects the first practice of reading the image in its contextual meaning. Marshall McLuhan, an influential media theorist, famously asserted, "The medium is the message." In this short phrase he, among other things, challenged all writers working on image analysis to pay close attention to the "platform" or context in which an image is presented. Indeed, the context dictates a good deal of the meaning of the image itself. The question for the Media Studies writer is, how does context, including political conditions, technology, audiences, ownership, and distribution, dictate codes through which the messages of the image are communicated?

Illustrating the practice of interpretation, Garland-Thomson addresses the historical contexts of photographs taken of people with disabilities. She notes early in the chapter that images of disability themselves mirror the historical condition of being disabled in the Western world, that of being visible and consumable. By doing this, her readers understand that images of people with disabilities are inextricably linked to disability history. In her essay she recognizes different settings for photographs, from freak shows to the fashion industry to political portraiture. She thus interprets the photographs in relationship to the technology, the politics, the reception, and the dissemination of messages about people with disabilities. Note that Garland-Thomson treats context specifically for each image with sound research; making generalizations in the practice of interpretation leads to vague, ineffective conclusions about media communication.

Finally, once an image is read and interpreted, the writer can begin to evaluate how it carries out her argument. Evaluation is a critical analysis enabling the writer to make a link between the rhetorical position of the image and her own rhetorical project. In other words, the practice of evaluation presumes that images have arguments embedded in their formal and contextual qualities. Keep in mind that a writer may study more images than she eventually will incorporate into her essay. The Garland-Thomson essay that follows was only a starting point for a book, *Staring: How We Look* (2009). We can imagine that her research for the essay involved many more images than she was able to incorporate in that earlier, shorter work, images that she later incorporated into the book. The decision to include or not include an image is integral to the process of evaluation.

Although we've discussed the three practices of reading, interpretation, and evaluation as if they are mutually exclusive, in the writing process, all three will often overlap. It is difficult to imagine reading an image without also immediately making interpretations about context, or analyzing its place within an essay. Nonetheless, incorporating all three of these practices ensures that as a writer you preserve the power of the images you are studying and see them as vital elements of mass communication.

✓ Reading Tips

The real challenge of reading this essay is to discover how the words and images work together to convey the argument. Words and images each communicate in different ways, so do not look at the images as if they are simply examples of what the words say, nor can the words simply translate everything the pictures say. You will have to read both forms of communication, keeping both suspended in your attention, and see how they cooperate and complement one another. To do that:

1. Look at the photographs before you start to read (you probably would do that without our instruction). Jot down your first impressions about the people in the pictures and what meaning the pictures convey to you. Make special note of any changes you experienced between your first glance at each picture and your more careful overview of each. What surprises you or makes you do a double-take?

2. As you read the text, the author will periodically refer you to individual photos, but even when she doesn't, keep looking at the photos and connecting them to what Garland-Thompson says with her words.

The Politics of Staring: Visual Rhetorics of Disability in Popular Photography

Rosemarie Garland-Thompson

In *Disability Studies: Enabling the Humanities.* Ed. by Sharon L. Snyder, Brenda Jo Brueggemann, and Rosemarie Garland-Thompson, 2002

The history of disabled people in the Western world is in part the history of being on display, of being visually conspicuous while politically and socially erased. The earliest record of disabled people is of their exhibition as prodigies, monsters, omens from the gods, and indexes of the natural or divine world. From the New Testament to the miracles at Lourdes, the lame, the halt, and the blind provide the spectacle for the story of bodily rehabilitation as spiritual redemption that is so essential to Christianity. From antiquity through modernity, the bodies of disabled people considered to be freaks and monsters have been displayed by the likes of medieval kings and P. T. Barnum for entertainment and profit in courts, street fairs, dime museums, and sideshows.[1] Moreover, medicine has from its beginnings exhibited the disabled body as what Michel Foucault calls the "case," in medical theaters and other clinical settings, in order to pathologize the exceptional and to normalize the ordinary (*Birth of the Clinic* 29). Disabled people have variously been objects of awe, scorn, terror, delight, inspiration, pity, laughter, or fascination—but they have always been stared at.

> The shrine of Our Lady of Lourdes in France has been famous for hundreds of miraculous cures since the late nineteenth century.

Staring at disability choreographs a visual relation between a spectator and a spectacle. A more intense form of looking than glancing, glimpsing, scanning, surveying, gazing, and other forms of casual or uninterested looking, staring registers the perception of difference and gives meaning to impairment by marking it as aberrant. By intensely telescoping looking toward the physical signifier for disability, staring creates an awkward partnership that estranges and discomforts both viewer and viewed. Starers gawk with abandon at the prosthetic hook, the empty sleeve, the scarred flesh, the unfocused eye, the twitching limb, but seldom does looking broaden to envelop the whole body of the person with a disability. Even supposedly invisible disabilities always threaten to disclose some stigma, however subtle, that disrupts the social order by its presence and attenuates the bond between equal members of the human community. Because staring at disability is considered illicit looking, the disabled body is at once the to-be-looked-at and not-to-be-looked-at, further dramatizing the staring encounter by making viewers furtive and the viewed defensive. Staring thus creates disability as a state of absolute difference rather than simply one more

> sign

variation in human form. At the same time, staring constitutes disability identity by manifesting the power relations between the subject positions of disabled and able-bodied.

The rapid flourishing of photography after 1839 provided a new way to stare at disability. In our ocularcentric era, images mediate our desires and the ways we imagine ourselves.[2] Among the myriad, often conflicting, and never indifferent images modernity offers us, the picture of ourselves as disabled is an image fraught with a tangle of anxiety, distance, and identification. As a culture, we are at once obsessed with and intensely conflicted about the disabled body. We fear, deify, disavow, avoid, abstract, revere, conceal, and reconstruct disability—perhaps because it is one of the most universal, fundamental of human experiences. After all, we will all become disabled if we live long enough. Nonetheless, in representing disability in modernity, we have made the familiar seem strange, the human seem inhuman, the pervasive seem exceptional. By the beginning of the twentieth century, for example, public displays of disabled people became inappropriate in the same way that public executions and torture came to be considered offensive. Disabled people were sequestered from public view in institutions and the private sphere as middle-class decorum pronounced it impolite to stare. Photography, however, has enabled the social ritual of staring at disability to persist in an alternate form.

Photographs seem to be transparent windows onto reality that ensnare truth. But like all representations, photographs organize our perceptions, shaping the objects as they depict them by using conventions of presentation that invoke cultural ideas and expectations. Photographs evoke the familiar only to make it seem strange, eliciting a response Alan Trachtenberg describes as "astonishment mingling with recognition" (*Reading* 4). Because disability has such potent cultural resonances, our capitalist democracy has enlisted its imagery to manipulate viewers for a wide range of purposes. Popular photography catapults disability into the public sphere as a highly mediated image shorn from interactions with actual people with disabilities. Photography's immediacy, claim to truth, and wide circulation calcifies the interpretations of disability embedded in the images, at once shaping and registering the public perception of disability.

Photography authorizes staring. Photos are made to be looked at. With the actual disabled body absent, photography stylizes staring, exaggerating and fixing the conventions of display and eliminating the possibility for interaction or spontaneity between viewer and viewed. Photos absolve viewers of responsibility to the objects of their stares at the same time that they permit a more intense form of staring than an actual social interchange might support. Disability photography thus offers the spectator the pleasure of unaccountable, uninhibited,

This simple version of the thesis appears at the end of the introduction. The preceding paragraphs provide necessary context first in the history of disability, then to the history of photography. The thesis thus brings together political issues and the media form that conveys them. It provides a basis from which Garland-Thompson can explore the ways this staring has been employed for different rhetorical strategies.

cements in place

insistent looking. This license to stare becomes a powerful rhetorical device that can be mobilized to manipulate viewers. By exploring some of the purposes to which popular photography's "dialectic of strange and familiar" has been put, I aim here to suggest how modern America imagines disability and disabled people (Trachtenberg, *Reading* 4).[3]

To look at the way we look at disability, I elaborate a taxonomy of four primary visual rhetorics of disability. They are the wondrous, the sentimental, the exotic, and the realistic. This template of visual rhetorics complicates the often restrictive notion of images as being either positive or negative, as communicating either the truth of disability or perpetuating some oppressive stereotype. Thus, I analyze more than evaluate. These visualizations of disabled people act as powerful rhetorical figures that elicit responses or persuade viewers to think or act in certain ways. The wondrous, the sentimental, the exotic, and the realistic converge and inflect one another in individual pictures as well as across all genres of disability photography. These visual rhetorics seldom occur discretely; rather, the photographs blend together in individual photographs. They wax and wane, shift and combine over time as they respond to the purposes for which the photographs are produced. Moreover, these rhetorics constitute part of the context into which all representations of disabled people enter. Not only do these representational modes configure public perception of disability, but all images of disabled people either inadvertently or deliberately summon these visual rhetorics and their accompanying cultural narratives. None of these rhetorical modes operates in the service of actual disabled people, however. Indeed, almost all of them appropriate the disabled body for the purposes of constructing, instructing, or assuring some aspect of a putatively nondisabled viewer.

The first visual rhetoric is the wondrous. The oldest mode of representing disability, the wondrous continues to find a place in modernity's framing of disability. This genre capitalizes on physical differences in order to elicit amazement and admiration. The antecedents of the wondrous disabled figures are the monsters of antiquity, who inspired awe, foretold the future, or bore divine signs, and freaks, who were the celebrities in nineteenth-century dime museums and sideshows (Garland-Thomson, "From Wonder"). The rhetoric of the wondrous springs from a premodern interpretation of disability as either augury or marks of distinction, whether representing good or evil. Oedipus, Teiresias, monsters, giants—even Shakespeare's Richard III—were imposing if ominous disabled figures.

A nineteenth-century example is Charles Tripp, the famous Armless Wonder (fig. 1), pictured eating with his toes in a carte de visite, one of the exceedingly popular photographic portraits commonly sold to augment

---

"dialectic": the connection of two opposing ideas

It is helpful to explain what the essay will accomplish. The author does this here, followed immediately by an explanation of how she will accomplish her goal, pointing toward her final thesis.

A "taxonomy" is a system of classification. In this excerpt, we leave out the section on the "sentimental" rhetoric of disability.

supposedly

visiting card

Figure 1 Surrounded here by the products of his agile feet, the famous nineteenth-century freak show entertainer, Charles Tripp, one of the many "armless wonders," is presented as amazing and yet ordinary.

and promote live appearances. This carefully choreographed portrait includes samples of his calligraphic skills, paper figures he's cut out, as well as the pen and scissors he used to accomplish such remarkable tasks. The silver tea set in the picture refers to other photos of him drinking from a cup with his toes. The composition is a visual résumé documenting Tripp's supposedly amazing accomplishments. The spectacle tries to elicit awe from the viewers, whose sense of their own clumsy toes makes Tripp's feet feat seem wondrous.

Photography introduced into the rhetoric of wonder the illusion of fusing the ordinary with the extraordinary. This picture invites a relation of identification and differentiation between Tripp and his viewer, making him seem simultaneously strange and familiar. Viewers see a typical man engaged in the quotidian acts of writing, eating, or drinking tea, but—to those with arms—he does this in a most extraordinary manner. Only the single detail of eating with feet rather than hands marks this scene as distinctive. Disability operates visually by juxtaposing the singular (therefore strange) mark of impairment in a surrounding context of the expected (therefore familiar). By telescoping the viewer's eye to the mark of impairment, the picture instructs viewers to stare and coaches them to understand impairment as the exception rather than the rule. Orchestrated and provoked by the photo, staring creates a particular relation between the viewer and the viewed that gives meaning to impairment.

Modernity secularized wonder into the stereotype of the supercrip, who amazes and inspires the viewer by performing feats that the nondisabled viewer cannot imagine doing. Contemporary wonder rhetoric emphasizes admiration rather than amazement, in part because bourgeois respectability now deems it inappropriate to delight in staring at disabled people. One example is a recent ad for adventure tours that features a rock climber using a wheelchair. . . . Here the photographic composition literally positions the viewer as looking up in awe at the climber dangling in her wheelchair. By making the disabled figure exceptional rather than ordinary, the wondrous can estrange viewer from viewed and attenuate the correspondence that equality requires.

Sentimentality has inflected the wonder model, producing the convention of the courageous overcomer, contemporary America's favorite figure of disability. Even though armless calligraphers are no longer an acceptable form of middle-class entertainment, photos of disabled people who have adapted tasks to fit their bodies still ask their viewers to feel a sense of wonder. An advertisement for Habitat for Humanity, for example, pictures a disabled volunteer worker building a house (fig. 3). Like Tripp, this man is portrayed as entirely ordinary except for the detail of [his holding the broom without hands], which occupies the center of interest, at once inviting and authorizing the stare. . . . [The photo in Figure 3 replaces one in the original text, by permission of the author.] The picture thus combines the narrative of admiration for overcoming disability with the narrative of empowerment characteristic of a postdisability rights movement consciousness. By making disabled subjects masters of ordinary activities such as climbing rocks, drinking tea, or using hammers, these photos create a visual context that elicits adulation for their accomplishing what the normalized viewer takes to be a superhuman feat. . . .

An effective image analysis not only identifies or describes what is important in the image but also how these elements relate to the thesis. Here the phrase, "this picture invites" reminds readers of the active relationship between the image and the viewer.

The analysis of the second image in this section is much shorter than the previous one because it serves primarily as a comparison to bridge the first and second parts of the essay, reminding the viewer again of the main point of the essay.

Figure 3 This photograph of a volunteer worker for Habitat for Humanity, an organization that builds homes for the needy, utilizes the narrative of overcoming to elicit admiration for working despite having a disability.

The second visual rhetoric is the sentimental. Whereas the wondrous elevates and enlarges, the sentimental diminishes. The sentimental produces the sympathetic victim or helpless sufferer needing protection or succor and invoking pity, inspiration, and frequent contributions. The sentimental disabled figure developed as a part of the larger nineteenth-century bourgeois culture of fine feelings.[4] The pathetic, the impotent, and the suffering confirmed the Victorian bourgeoisie by arousing their finest sentiments. As the increasingly empowered middle class imagined itself capable of capitalizing the world, it began to see itself as responsible for the world as well, a stewardship that launched humanitarian and reform movements to which today's telethons are heir. This discourse of middle-class noblesse oblige operates on a model of paternalism, often trafficking in children and alluding to the cute, the plucky, the long-suffering, and the courageous.

The rhetoric of sentiment found an effective home in the photographic conventions of the poster child of mid-twentieth-century charity campaigns. The 1946 March of Dimes poster child (fig. 4) echoes the spunky cuteness of freak figures such as General Tom Thumb. But where Tom Thumb delighted with his miniature adulthood, this poster

> A featured performer in the Barnum and Bailey circus

Figure 4 The March of Dimes 1946 poster boy appeals to the rhetoric of sentiment, which often employs pathetic, courageous, or cute children to elicit the viewers' sympathy and money.

child breaks hearts as he is propped vulnerably up in a corner of his crib in the before-and-after format. In order to catalyze the adult, to whom the photo addresses itself, this March of Dimes poster presents disability to the middle-class spectator as a problem to solve, an obstacle to eliminate, a challenge to meet. In such appeals, impairment becomes the stigma of suffering, transforming disability into a project that morally enables a nondisabled rescuer. The viewer's dimes, the poster suggests, will literally catapult the unhappy little fellow trapped in braces in his crib into a smiling and spirited tyke, striding with determination and gratitude toward the viewer. Sentimentality makes of disabled people occasions for the viewers' own narratives of progress, improvement, or heroic deliverance and contains disability's threat in the sympathetic, helpless child for whom the viewer is empowered to act. Whereas earlier sentimental literature accentuates suffering to mobilize readers for humanitarian, reform, or religious ends, the poster boy's suffering is only the background to his restoration to normalcy that results from "your dimes." The optimism of cure thus replaces the intensity of sympathy, testifying to an increasing faith in clinical treatment and scientific progress as modernity increasingly medicalizes and rationalizes the body.

The rhetoric of sentiment has migrated from charity to retail in late capitalism's scramble to capture markets. For example, the cover of a 1998 Benetton public relations brochure (fig. 5) distributed in stores employs a chic sentimentality in documenting a school for developmentally disabled children Benetton supports and outfits. This cover girl with both Down syndrome[5] and a stylish Benetton hat fuses sentimental cuteness with high fashion to produce the conviction in the viewer-shopper that Benetton is humanitarian rather than solely commercial. In anticipation of its patron's skepticism, the brochure instructs its viewers that Benetton launched this campaign as social commentary, although people are apt to see it as "cynical advertising." Benetton devotes a whole introductory page to assuring its customers that this brochure is about "the gift of love" (United Colors 3). So while commercial fashion marketing demands a certain sophistication and sleekness that precludes the gushy sentiment of the 1940s poster child, Benetton still assures its viewers of their tolerance and allows them to fantasize rescuing this child from the stigma of being disabled by dressing her smartly and supporting her school.

The third visual rhetoric is the exotic. The rhetoric of sentiment domesticates the disability figure, making it familiar and comforting. In contrast, the visual rhetoric of the exotic presents disabled figures as alien, distant, often sensationalized, eroticized, or entertaining in their difference. The exotic reproduces an ethnographic model of viewing characterized by curiosity or uninvolved objectification and informed by

From the word *ethnography.* An objective study of culture or people groups.

Figure 5 Sentimental cuteness and high fashion come together in this public relations brochure's presentation of a developmentally disabled child in a school supported and outfitted by Benetton clothing stores. Concept: O. Toscani.

the proliferation of popular ethnographic photography that accompanied the era of Western imperialism. For example, nineteenth-century freak photography often transformed disabled people into "wild men" or other exotic "savages," whose impairments were translated into marks of alien ethnicity (Garland-Thomson, "From Wonder" 5). The exotic demedicalizes, fascinates, and seduces with exaggeration, creating a sensationalized, embellished alien.

The introduction of disabled models has exploded the contemporary fashion world in the last several years, returning the rhetoric of the exotic into disability photography. Where the sentimental makes the disabled figure small and vulnerable in order to be rescued by a benevolent agent, the exotic makes the disabled figure large, strange, and unlike the viewer. Ever straining for novelty and capitalizing on titillation, the fashion arm of the advertising world was sure to discover the power of disabled figures to provoke responses from viewers. Advertising has learned that disability sells in two ways. One is by making consumers feel good about buying from a company that is charitable toward the supposedly disadvantaged, which is the Benetton brochure's pitch. The other is to capture the disability market, which is 54 million people and growing fast as the baby boomers age and as their spending power is estimated to reach the trillion-dollar mark in 2000 (J. Williams 29). . . .

> Notice how Garland-Thomson pays attention not only to the photograph, but also the platform on which it was delivered, namely fashion advertising.

Another venue for disability as the exotic is emerging in the high-fashion market, which is always desperate to keep its edge. These advertisements and magazine features present disabled models in a dual attempt to capture a market and to novelize high fashion by introducing bodies that at once depart from and conform to the exhausted image of the high-fashion body. Alexander McQueen, known in England as the bad boy of fashion design, recently collaborated with other designers and the fashion photographer Nick Knight for a shoot called "Accessible," featuring eight disabled models. Knight's shots fold the models' impairments into a context of exoticism that extends to the entire frame, as in the shot of Aimee Mullins, the double-amputee celebrity cover girl, rendered as a kind of high-tech bionic mannequin (fig. 7). No attempt is made to disguise her cosmetic prosthetic legs—so she can pass for nondisabled; rather, the entire photo thematically echoes her prostheses and renders the whole image chic. As a gorgeous amputee, Mullins becomes an embodied contradiction. Her prosthetic legs parody, indeed proudly mock, the very idea of the perfect body that has been the mark of fashion until now, even while the rest of her body conforms precisely to fashion's impossible standards. Rather than conceal, normalize, or erase disability, these photos use the hyperbole and stigma traditionally associated with disability to quench postmodernity's perpetual search for the new and arresting image. These transgressive juxtapositions of disability and high fashion, such as the macho chair user and the athletic . . . Mullins, produce a fresh, attention-grabbing brand of exotic radical chic that redefines disabled identity for the disabled consumer. . . .

This taxonomy of four primary visual rhetorics of disability provides a way to see the way we see disability. These pictures choreograph a social dynamic of looking, suggesting that disability is not simply a natural state of bodily inferiority and inadequacy. Rather, it is

Figure 7 The high-fashion layout of the model, sports star, and double amputee Aimee Mullins emphasizes rather than conceals her prosthetic legs, exploiting the exotic model to make disability seem chic.

a culturally-fabricated narrative of the body, similar to what we understand as the fictions of race and gender. Disability, then, is a system that produces subjects by differentiating and marking bodies. Furthermore, this comparison of bodies legitimates the distribution of resources, status, and power in a biased social and architectural environment. As such, disability has four aspects: first, it is a system for interpreting bodily variations; second, it is a relation between bodies and their environments; third, it is a set of practices that produces both the able-bodied and the disabled; fourth, it is a way of describing the inherent instability of the embodied self. The category of disability exists as a way to exclude the kinds of bodily forms, functions, impairments, changes, or ambiguities that call into question our cultural fantasy of the body as a neutral, compliant instrument of some transcendent will. Moreover, *disability* is a broad term in which cluster ideological categories as varied as sick, deformed, ugly, old, crazy, maimed, afflicted, abnormal, or debilitated—all of which disadvantage people by devaluing bodies that do not conform to cultural standards. Thus disability functions to preserve and validate such privileged designations as beautiful, healthy, normal, fit, competent, intelligent—all of which provide cultural capital to those who can claim such status, who can reside within these subject positions. Thus, the various interactions between bodies and world make disability from the raw material of human variation and precariousness.

All visualizations of disability are mediations that shape the world in which people who have or do not have disabilities inhabit and negotiate together. The point is that all representations have social and political consequences. Understanding how images create or dispel disability as a system of exclusions and prejudices is a move toward the process of dismantling institutional, attitudinal, legislative, economic, and architectural barriers that keep people with disabilities from full participation in society.

> A clear rhetorical move to alert the reader that the final thesis of the argument is about to be presented; note how she avoids using the cliché "in conclusion."

Notes

1. For a historical account of the display of disabled people as monsters and freaks, see Altick; Bogdan; Garland-Thompson, "From Wonder"; and D. Wilson.
2. For an account of the ocularcentric in Western culture, see Barthes; Crary; Debord, and Jay.
3. I am not including medical or artistic photography here, although both genres inform the visual construction of disability. I am limiting this analysis to popular photography, which I take to be the primary register and shaper of public consciousness. For an analysis of images of insanity, see Gilman.
4. For a discussion of the development of middle-class feeling as a form of distinguishing respectability, see Halttunen; for a discussion of how sentimentality uses disabled figures, see Garland-Thompson, "Crippled Little Girls."
5. The term "Down syndrome" is now preferred over "Down's syndrome" by more politicized parents and guardians looking to mark some distance from the English physician John Langdon Down, who first described the syndrome's characteristic features (i.e., they are challenging his "ownership" of Down syndrome). See, for example, Richards.

Works Cited [Including only the works cited in the above excerpt.]

Altick, Richard. *The Shows of London*. Cambridge: Belknap-Harvard UP, 1978.

Barthers, Roland. *Camera Lucida: Reflections on Photography*. Trans. Richard Howard. New York: Hill, 1981.

Bogdan, Robert. *Freak Show: Presenting Human Oddities for Amusement and Profit*. Chicago: U of Chicago P, 1988.

Crary, Jonathan. *Techniques of the Observer: On Vision and Modernity in the Nineteenth Century*. Cambridge: MIT P, 1990.

Debord, Guy. *The Society of the Spectacle*. Detroit: Black, 1983.

Dennett, Andrea Stulman. *Weird and Wonderful: The Dime Museum in America*. New York: New York UP, 1997.

Foucoult, Michel. *The Birth of the Clinic: An Archeology of Medical Perception*. Trans. A. M. Sheridan Smith. New York: Vintage, 1975.

Garland-Thompson, Rosemarie. "Crippled Little Girls and Lame Old Women: Sentimental Spectacles of Sympathy with Rhetorics of Reform in Nineteenth-Century American Women's Writing." *Nineteenth-Century American Women Writers: A Critical Collection*. Ed. Karen Kilcup. New York: Blackwell, 1988. 128–45.

Garland-Thompson, Rosemarie. "From Wonder to Error: A Genealogy of Freak Discourse in Modernity." Garland-Thompson, ed. *Freakery; Cultural Spectacles of the Extraordinary Body*. New York: New York UP, 1996: 1–22.

Gilman, Sander L. *Seeing the Insane*. New York: Wiley; Brunner, 1982.

Halttunen, Karen. "Humanitarianism and the Pornography of Pain in Anglo-American Culture." *American Historical Review* 100 (1995): 303–34.

Jay, Martin. *Downcast Eyes: The Denigration of Vision in Twentieth-Century Thought*. Berkeley: U of California P, 1993.

Richards, Greg. *Growth Charts for Children with Down Syndrome*. 28 Aug. 2001. 29 Aug. 2001 <http:www.growthcharts.com>, under "Terminology."

Trachtenberg, Alan. *Reading American Photographs: Images as History, Mathew Brady to Walker Evans*. New York: Hill, 1989.

United Colors of Bennetton. *The Sunflowers*. Bergamo, It.: Nuovo Instituto Italiana, 1998

Williams, John M. "And Here's the Pitch: Madison Avenue Discoverss the Invisible Consumer." *We Magazine* 3.4 (1999): 28–31.

Wilson, Dudley. *Signs and Portents: Monstrous Births from the Middle Ages to the Enlightenment*. London: Routledge, 1993.

Reading Responses

1. Summarize the basic features of each of the three "visual rhetorics" that are discussed. Explain what makes each different from the others. Explain which is the most common in your experience.

2. Which of the images had the greatest effect on you? Explain why. How did the image's effect on you help you to understand the rhetorical category that Garland-Thompson used the image to exemplify?

3. Identify two of Garland-Thompson's analyses of images that made you see things in the photographs that you had not seen on your own. What did Garland-Thompson reveal? What particular parts of Garland-Thompson's analyses of images serve as a model when you analyze images?

NOTES ON GRAMMAR, STYLE, AND RHETORIC:
FINAL FREE MODIFIERS

In "The Politics of Staring: Visual Rhetorics of Disability in Popular Photography," Rosemarie Garland-Thomson employs a sentence form that we think will be useful in almost all of your writing—the sentence form that includes one or more final free modifiers. Final free modifiers can be made up of several different kinds of elements.

They can be adjectives or adjective phrases:

They stood on the island at night, **alone, lost, afraid to talk.**

They can be present participles (-*ing* forms of verbs used as adjectives) or present participial phrases:

They turned toward the source of the sound, **hoping that someone had discovered they were missing.**

They can be past participles (-*ed* or –*en* forms of verbs used as adjectives) or past participial phrases:

They rushed over to the stranger, **relieved that someone had found them.**

Many people would also include absolute phrases as possibilities, although you have to stretch the meaning of *modifier* somewhat to attach it to absolutes. Absolutes include a noun phrase and a participial phrase:

They exhaled with relief, **their anxiety dissipating rapidly.**

Finally, such modifiers can include a mix of the previously listed elements:

They returned to the ship, **exhausted, uttering words of thanks, their lives restored to normal.**

As Joseph M. Williams puts it in the eighth edition of *Style, Ten Lessons in Clarity and Grace,* free modifiers get their name because they "can both begin and end a sentence" (141). What that means is that there is some freedom in where they appear. Thus you could write either, *They rushed over to the stranger, relieved that someone had found them* or *Relieved that someone had found them, they rushed over to the stranger.*

In her essay Garland-Thomson makes notable use of final free modifiers that come in the form of participles, mainly present participles. Over twenty of her sentences end with a participial phrase, and in one paragraph (the fourth), she uses a final participial phrase in three of her six sentences. Here is an example of a present participial phrase as a final free modifier:

The rhetoric of sentiment domesticates the disability figure, **making it familiar and comforting** (boldface added).

Here is an example of a past participial phrase as a final free modifier:

A nineteenth-century example is Charles Tripp, the famous Armless Wonder . . . , **pictured eating with his toes in a carte de visite, one of the exceedingly popular photographic portraits commonly sold to augment and promote live appearances** (boldface added).

And here is an example with two present participial phrases as final free modifiers:

The rhetoric of the realistic, however, trades in verisimilitude, **regularizing the disabled figure in order to avoid differentiation and arouse identification, often normalizing and sometimes minimizing the visual mark of disability** (boldface added).

Writers of expository and argumentative prose can use final free modifiers to do several different kinds of communicative work. Such modifiers can extend, explain, interpret, reinforce, specify, exemplify, qualify, summarize, or state the implications of the points made before them. In her essay, Garland-Thomson most often uses final free modifiers to add specifications to the points she makes before the free modifiers. Here is an example in which she uses two participial phrases to specify what she means when she writes that "photography stylizes staring":

With the actual disabled body absent, photography stylizes staring, **exaggerating and fixing the conventions of display and eliminating the possibility for interaction or spontaneity between viewer and viewed** (boldface added).

Writers of description and narration also use final free modifiers, often to do kinds of communicative work that are somewhat different from the kinds of work that writers of exposition and argument usually do. Writers of description and narration often use final free modifiers to add details, to thicken the texture, and—because final free modifiers do not come with a verb in a tense—to try to capture the intensity of lots of things happening at virtually the same time. Here, for example, is Katherine Anne Porter ending a sentence with a participial phrase:

> The jockeys sat bowed and relaxed, **moving a little at the waist with the movement of their horses** (boldface added).

And here is Walter Van Tillburg Clark using a long series of participial phrases to describe a bird of prey riding air currents and hunting:

> He could sail for hours, **searching the blanched grasses below him with his telescopic eyes, gaining height against the wind, descending in mile-long, gently declining swoops when he curved and rode back, never beating a wing** (boldface added).

We recommend that you experiment judiciously with some final free modifiers in the various kinds of writing you do. All the writing teachers that we have ever talked to about these stylistic touches say that they see them as among the chief marks of mature prose. They say that, we think, because final free modifiers can provide a pleasant variation in rhythm from that which is associated with one independent clause after another. Further, final free modifiers can encourage engagement by your readers because they invite readers to join you as you appear to be working ideas out. Further still, a final free modifier in a sentence gives you two positions of focus and stress in that sentence, one just before the final free modifier and one at the end of the free modifier. In sum, the final free modifier can be a very important stylistic tool for you, helping you to achieve your particular purposes with your readers, perhaps even encouraging you to extend your ideas further than you thought possible.

In Your Own Writing . . .

- In your writing that is mainly expository or argumentative, consider using some sentences with final free modifiers to perform such tasks as explaining, specifying, or extending your points.
- In your writing that is mainly descriptive or narrative, consider using some sentences with final free modifiers to perform such tasks as adding details and presenting many actions as happening in the same apparent period of time.

STUDENT WRITING

INTRODUCTION

by Katelyn R. Beaty, communication major

The Assignment. In a course on nineteenth- and twentieth-century modernist art, we were assigned a 2,000- to 3,000-word essay that explored an artist or group of artists whose work demonstrated the formal and ideologies themes discussed in class. Such themes included formal abstraction, absurdism, futurism, the aftermath of two world wars, "national" art, and art as a catalyst to challenge dominant political beliefs and create new ones.

The Content. My essay explores the use of photography to bolster public support for the Farm Security Administration's work during the Great Depression. I argue that photography proved an appropriate medium to bolster such support because it played into the "documentary impulse" of the 1930s and did not require the public's initiation into a formal artistic form vocabulary. I also question the objectivity and "real-lifeness" of the FSA's photography by looking at the administration's process for selecting certain photographs over others. I analyze Dorothea Lange's "Migrant Mother," the most famous photograph from the FSA, as well as two other photographs from Lange's portfolio, to demonstrate how the FSA's work was propagandistic. I conclude that "propaganda" need not be a pejorative term, depending on the aims and purposes of the artist, especially if the aims are to reveal social injustice and encourage compassion.

Learning to Write Media Studies. Learning to interpret images in many ways mirrored the process of learning to interpret written communication. Learning each requires decoding symbols to see the landscape of meaning intended by the author. But whereas learning to interpret written communication dominates the Western education system, starting with the alphabet in kindergarten up through annual English courses, learning to interpret images happens only in spurts, in art classes or perhaps a high school photography class. Such classes usually aim to introduce students to formal elements, largely overlooking the symbols of meaning used in contemporary media—film, advertising, Web sites, magazines, music videos, and so on. Clearly the dearth of education in contemporary media disadvantages twenty-first-century students, who need tools to understand and talk about the image-based culture they have grown up in.

I was, thankfully, given such tools in both Communications and Art courses during undergraduate studies. A freshman course called "Visual Culture" introduced the building blocks of contemporary design, showing students how visual elements combine with words to provide symbolic meaning that words alone cannot communicate. We analyzed advertising and print magazines to see how text and image played together, sometimes intentionally creating irony or dissonance to critique the topic at hand. We then created our own text-and-image works using computer programs such as Adobe Illustrator. The course taught that in contemporary media, visual elements are not embellishments added to beautify text, but are essential to the work, at times even supplanting text to convey the author's meaning(s).

Another course, "Visual Rhetoric," also explored the play of text and image in contemporary media, but went a step further by helping us see the recognizable, often powerful cultural symbols that authors use to convey meaning. Often the class examined a print advertisement, Web site, or TV commercial to get at the author's assumptions about human nature, socioeconomics, gender and sexuality, race, commerce, and other fundamental concerns. We learned early on that visual elements in a work are not arbitrary but are chosen to convey the author's intended meaning(s), which makes sense only in the context of a larger symbolic world familiar to the audience. So when I later wrote an essay analyzing government photography during the Great Depression, I kept in mind that the photographs' subjects and formal elements were not happenstance but were chosen to appease a public audience with strong beliefs about family life and poverty.

Finally, a course surveying nineteenth- and twentieth-century modernist movements helped students interpret images that arose out of new symbolic contexts, often abstract and nonrealist. Because many modernist works don't use recognizable forms, they presented a particular challenge for media students; we needed to study the symbolic world the modernists rejected ("picture window" art) to understand what they strove for. Their work demonstrated that media, whether formal or mass market, never emerge from a vacuum but from rich historical contexts or canons, often subverting what came before. Such images also reminded students that sometimes formal elements are *themselves* the author's intended meaning; a large canvas depicting two-tone squares might be what the image is "about." In this way, segments of modernist art might help today's media students re-appreciate basic elements like color, line, and perspective—elements often forgotten or dismissed if they don't convey ideological messages.

My hope is that learning to understand and write about media goes beyond formal analytical exercises, as if finding the "meaning" of a work is all media studies are about. Rather, I hope having such tools helps media students expose works that denigrate the human person and lead to unjust attitudes and systems—and perhaps even create media that undoes such effects.

"Contemplating Things as They Are": Propaganda and the Photography of the Farm Security Administration

Katelyn R. Beaty

A Western art tradition of rendering subjects in a realistic, true-to-vision manner. Also called pictorial art.

A 19th- and 20th-century art tradition that renders subjects in a manner independent of visual references in the physical world.

A label borrowed from political philosopher Karl Marx to describe the economic class that owns property; the middle or upper-middle class. Can be used more broadly to describe an exclusive or elite group.

From Art Nouveau's celebration of idiosyncrasy and craftsmanship, to the Bauhaus's commitment to human-centered architectural design, to even the anti-art Dadaist movement's critique of established culture, nearly all modernist art movements arise from the belief that *art has something to say*—that, at its best, art can change the world. The modernists' obliteration of the "picture window" meant a freedom to go beyond accurately rendering scenes of idyllic beauty to challenge entire cultural and political systems. In place of the picture window, the European and American modernists of the 19th and 20th centuries created new, abstracted form vocabularies to embody their movement's various guiding ideologies. But their move toward abstraction meant that, while they could preserve the integrity of their political convictions, they were perhaps hindered in communicating those convictions to a general, uninitiated audience. Muralist Diego Rivera addressed this problem in his 1932 essay "The Revolutionary Spirit in Modern Art." He criticizes his Russian Communist counterparts for trying to persuade the general public by using what Rivera calls a "bourgeoisie" or "hermetic art, inaccessible except to those who have developed and undergone an elaborate aesthetic preparation" (Harrison 423). Rivera believed that for art to be truly revolutionary, the common citizen must have access to it, geographically and aesthetically.

The photographers of the early 20th-century American realist movement embodied Rivera's vision well, using a recognizable visual vernacular to expose industrialization's effects on urban populations. Ashcan School photographers Jacob Riis and Lewis Hine saw their cameras as instruments of reform that could produce "incontrovertible evidence" for all audiences about poor urban conditions. They became artistic forebears of the renowned Farm Security Administration (FSA) photographers, whose portraits of migrant workers of the 1930s garnered public support for controversial New Deal programs. In this paper, I will argue that the FSA's portfolio proved so effective in exposing suffering because it relied on a hyper-realistic form vocabulary that was accessible to the general public. But I will also examine the "realness" of the FSA files, exploring the issue of propaganda and whether it is justifiable in times of social crisis.

Compared to its European counterpart, the American art tradition has perhaps always been more invested in reality-based form and subject matter. This investment gained new momentum with the Ashcan School's interest in depicting everyday objects and "the man in the street." While many of "The Eight" were interested more in the commonplace than in political revolution, their commitment to depict things as they appeared carried what Arnason calls an "inherent social criticism" (403). The commitment continued into the 1930s with the Social Realist art movement. Painters Raphael Soyer, Isabel Bishop, and Ben Shahn assumed a more aggressive political agenda, detailing the lives of urban working-class people. But while their painting method dignified subjects, it failed to capture the "real-lifeness" of photography. Soyer's 1936 "Office Girls," for example, successfully humanizes his subjects by showing them calm and confident despite the city bustle. But we are left to concentrate more on Soyer's attitude about the subjects, expressed through formal elements, than on the lives of actual women working in New York City. In this and other paintings within social realism, form overshadowed subject.

Photography of the 1930s stripped away such intense focus on form. The 1930s was an era when public demand for "real-life" stories burgeoned and took on a dominant cultural force. Great Depression historian William Stott has aptly named this demand the "documentary impulse," marked by the increasing popularity of movie newsreels, nonfiction writing, news programs, documentary film, and, especially, photojournalism (Finnegan 126; Fleischhauer 27). Magazines such as *Life* and *Look* emerged in the mid-1930s, playing to the demand for photo-based human-interest stories (Ohrn 34). The documentary impulse arose during the search in the U.S. for what Matthew Baigell calls "a people's history"—real stories of everyday people lived out in distinctly

---

An informal group of artists and photographers working in New York City in the 1930s and dedicated to depicting urban life in gritty, realistic detail.

"Form vocabulary": a group of visual symbols that together form a visual "alphabet."

I wanted to offer a basic thesis as a foundation for my argument, but I also wanted to go beyond the basic to make a point about realism and propaganda. So my full thesis does not show up until the end of the paper.

"The Eight" were a loosely affiliated group of artists that organized in 1908; some belonged to the Ashcan School movement.

Social Realism was a worldwide movement of the 1930s whose participants were committed to depicting economic and racial injustice in their particular contexts. Some but not all participants were socialists.

"Office Girls" is one of Soyer's paintings about urban life, it depicts young working women standing in an urban street. Now housed at the Whitney Museum of American Art in NYC.

American contexts (Hill 57). The impulse also marked a shift from a text-based, printed-word culture to one centered on sight and sound (Daniel, ix). But historian Karen Becker Ohrn provides the most comprehensive explanation of the impulse: "The expression of the 1930s was more deeply marked by a search for the roots of the nation's failure and by attempts to bring to light the heroic aspects of those confronting the failure" (29). In other words, the '30s generation turned to documentary media to rebuild truth and meaning during a time of economic crisis and political change.

It was this search for roots that perhaps led the New Deal government to use photography in their efforts to bolster a failing economy. In 1934 President Roosevelt established the Resettlement Administration (RA), led by his assistant secretary of agriculture Rexford Guy Tugwell, to help tenant farmers settle in assumedly better land. The RA's Historical Section was charged with documenting the RA's sociological and economic impact and compiling visual evidence to complement the program's public education campaign. Roy Emerson Stryker, a former teaching assistant of Tugwell's, joined the RA staff to oversee the documenting process. The section's staff—which originally included Arthur Rothstein, Walker Evans, Dorothea Lange, Russell Lee, and painter Ben Shahn—set out to create a record, as complete and unadulterated as possible, of the RA's efforts.

> The name given to a series of broad economic changes initiated by President Franklin D. Roosevelt to bolster the U.S. economy and aid citizens during the Great Depression.

The photographers were sent to troubled areas of the country to document the poor's living conditions and particular challenges. They sent their negatives to Stryker's office in Washington, D.C., where they were added to a vast central file available to publicists and media. The photographers acted as liaisons between the rural population and the government and press, as they witnessed problems firsthand and reported directly to Stryker and other officials. Indeed, Stryker's staff approached their work with a sense of moral obligation. Photography historian Alan Trachtenberg notes that the FSA's commitment to realism was not merely an artistic aim but an entire worldview. "Certainly the documentary photographer is a realist rather than an escapist by the very fact that he accepts his environment," said Stryker. "Realism is defined as a moral stance, a deep respect for human beings" (Fleischhauer 64). On Dorothea Lange's office door hung this Francis Bacon quote: "The contemplation of things *as they are,* without substitution or imposture, without error or confusion, is itself a nobler thing than a whole harvest of inventions" (Curtis 1). This became Lange's creed throughout her career; she believed that to do otherwise would be to "record only one's preconceptions" (Curtis 2).

> Here's the word that signals that I'm taking my argument in a new direction.

A closer look at the section's work, however, reveals that Stryker and his staff *did* record their preconceptions, as they wanted their work not only to record projects but also to record the RA's effectiveness and progress. They believed their photographs could put a tangible human face on "big government" New Deal programs. 20th-century historian Warren Susman noted that New Deal photography benefited from using a visual approach that "*looked* candid, intimate and non-intrusive, even as it promoted the value of forceful, bureaucratic government intervention to shore up a stagnant economy" (Daniel ix). Besides bolstering support for New Deal programs, the RA photographers wanted their work to dispel negative stereotypes of the poor as lazy or deserving of their lot, thus presenting subjects in an intimate and dignifying light. By focusing on individuals' daily trials through a seemingly unbiased medium, the section played directly to the public's documentary impulse. The photographs appeared everywhere from daily newspapers to *Life* and *Look* to congressional reports and museum exhibits, reaching an array of audiences.

Most importantly, however, the RA photographs relied on a stark form vocabulary that did not require foreknowledge of an aesthetic canon. Edward Steichen, director of the Museum of Modern Art's photography department and known for his formalist approach, praised the RA photographs for their truth-telling. "These documents told stories and told them with such simple and blunt directness that they made many a citizen wince," he said. "The question of what stop was used, what lens was used . . . became so completely overshadowed by the story, that even photographers forgot to ask" (Finnegan 152). Even many of NYC's cultural elite were shocked into empathy at the RA portfolio's debut at the 1939 First International Photographic Exposition. The exhibition featured the best work from the RA staff, which had been folded into the FSA, and awoke urbanites to the plight of the "other half." "After the usual diet of the art world—cream puffs, éclairs, and such—the hard, bitter reality of these photographs is the tonic the soul needs," mused art critic Elizabeth McCausland. "For so grim is the truth they present that the vapors of pseudo-intellectual culture are immediately dispelled" (Hurley 134).

But how could Stryker and his staff at once aim to present their subject matter objectively while campaigning for New Deal programs? Here we find perhaps the most controversial dimension of the FSA project: while its staff committed to capturing things *as they were,* they used several alteration methods to document conditions *as they wanted them to appear.* We find, for example, that the photographers were sometimes sent out with Stryker's explicit instructions on what to emphasize and downplay. Such instructions were called "shooting scripts," tailor-made to appeal to specific audiences. In one script, Stryker calls for more pictures of whites and less of blacks, fearing the reaction of a particular newspaper's audience (Finnegan 44). Stryker and FSA officials notoriously insisted that the photographers take more "hard-boiled publicity

---

An approach to art that focuses exclusively on visual elements such as color, line, and shape over against subject. Given the FSA staff's almost sole focus on subjects, Steichen's praise is remarkable.

Farm Service Administration

shots" appropriate for government brochures (Ohrn 97). In the early 1940s, Stryker began calling for more "positive" images; in a 1942 letter he asks for images of "people with a little spirit . . . men, women and children who appear as if they really believed in the United States" (Daniel 4). Photographer John Vachon lamented that the positive images came to "look like [the propaganda] from the Soviet Union" (Daniel 4).

> Vachon here is referring to images of seemingly happy and healthy workers produced by the Communist government. Given the widespread death and suffering under Soviet rule, such images were understood to be deceptive.

While Lange's 1936 "Migrant Mother" portrait has come to embody the entire FSA project, few know of the other images in the series or the alterations Lange made in order to play into public opinion. The second photograph in the series (Fig. 1), for example, shows main subject Florence Thompson in a pitch tent with her four children, one of whom is a teenage girl. Absent is a father or husband, a physical laborer who could work in the fields while the mother watches the children. The setting—a dry, barren landscape lacking people and homes— serves to heighten a sense of the family's own aloneness and barrenness. Even the tent, perhaps the family's most treasured possession, is tattered and ripped. But Lange rejected this image not only because two of the children were smiling, which played down their plight, but also because the teenager's presence might draw public scrutiny about Thompson's age. Another series photo (Fig. 2) shows Thompson with her two youngest children in the tent, surrounded by personal belongings. This time all the faces are somber and forlorn. An empty plate in the

Figure 1 "Migrant Mother: Nipomo, California. March 1936." Dorothea Lange.

Figure 2 "Migrant Mother: Nipomo, California. March 1936." Dorothea Lange.

foreground symbolizes the family's hunger and "proves" their real need to the public. But Lange also rejected this image because she feared the public would sympathize less with migrants who did not pick up their belongings.

"Migrant Mother" (Fig. 3) proved the best image to embody the FSA project because it brought the human element literally front and center. In this photo, Lange strips away any context (surroundings, home items) that might play to public stereotypes about "poor people," instead focusing only on the suffering *person*. Thompson gazes off into an unseen locale, as if she is gazing into the future, and sees only hardship. The trepidation on her face is palpable and easily relatable for anyone, rich or poor, living under the economic strain of the Great Depression. The woman is surrounded by children who depend on her for everything; the baby on her lap physically weighs her down with its need. Again, the theme of familial strife is easily accessible and relatable to the general public. Lange said she also chose it for its reference to the Madonna and Child, imagery powerful and familiar to Lange's audience (Curtis 5).

> An image derived from Christianity of the Virgin Mary with the child Jesus on her lap. A prominent symbol in Western and Eastern art traditions alike.

Figure 3 "Migrant Mother: Nipomo, California. March 1936." Dorothea Lange.
All images taken from the Library of Congress's "Prints and Photographs Reading Room."
http://www.loc.gov/rr/print/list/128_migm.html

Art critics of the 1930s and today are quick to label the FSA enterprise "propagandistic," and in many ways they are correct. Although Stryker refused to label it as such, his efforts were undeniably propagandistic in that they aimed to disseminate information and ideas for the purpose of influencing attitudes and behavior (Carlebach 11). Lange herself was deeply aware of the administration's political aims and had no problem using the term "propaganda," since her personal goals were consistent with the administration's. Given this, one might question whether Lange contradicts her own commitment to Bacon's "contemplation of things as they are." But to do so does not mean to present an objective view of the photograph subject. Even the concept of objectivity, even for photography, has been seriously undermined with the advent of postmodernism. Even though "Migrant Mother" depicts real

A philosophical and cultural shift that rejected values of the previous Enlightenment era. Postmodern thought is marked by (1) a rejection of the ability to know objective truth; (2) an emphasis on personal perspective and context; (3) a suspicion of Western grand narratives; and (4) a new regard for the perspectives of people who lack economic and political power.

people living in truly impoverished living conditions, Lange had to choose her angle, distance, and perspective, and rejected photographs based on what they might communicate to audiences. None of these decisions was arbitrary.

In her 1980 essay "Some Propaganda for Propaganda," art critic Lucy Lippard makes a case for rehabilitating the word, urging artists to begin making "good propaganda . . . what art should be—a provocation, a new way of seeing and thinking about what goes on around us" (Clark 9). Although I will not go as far as saying, as Rivera does, that all art at all times has been propagandistic, like Lippard, I believe that art *should* be propagandistic—it should have something to say, something to contribute to the world. With perpetual global poverty, violence, materialism, and corporate rapacity, how could the post–picture window artist—believed by many of the modernists to fulfill a prophetic role—continue to produce art that doesn't say anything beyond its own creation?

> I left my main point for the end—to surprise readers a little. In my final paragraph, then, I give the most complete version of my thesis.

In the final analysis, an artwork cannot be judged based on whether or not it is propaganda, but instead based on whether it leads to society's betterment or hindrance. Undeniably it seems that the photographic files of the Farm Security Administration led to society's betterment. The FSA photographers became advocates for those who could not advocate for themselves—the countless downtrodden of the Great Depression—and showed what photography could accomplish amid adversity.

Works Cited

Arnason, H. H. and Marla F. Prather. *History of Modern Art,* fourth edition. Upper Saddle River, NJ: Prentice-Hall, 1998.

Carlebach, Michael. "Documentary and Propaganda: The Photographs of the Farm Security Administration." *The Journal of Decorative and Propaganda Arts 8* (Spring 1988): 6–25.

Clark, Toby. *Art and Propaganda in the Twentieth Century.* New York: Calmann & King, 1997.

Curtis, James. *Mind's Eye, Mind's Truth: FSA Photography Reconsidered.* Philadelphia: Temple University Press, 1989.

Daniel, Pete. *Official Images: New Deal Photography.* Washington, D.C.: Smithsonian Institution Press, 1987.

Finnegan, Cara. *Picturing Poverty: Print Culture and FSA Photographs.* Washington, D.C.: Smithsonian Books, 2003.

Fleischhauer, Carl. *Documenting America, 1935–1943.* Berkeley: University of California Press, in association with the Library of Congress, 1988.

Hurley, Jack F. *Portrait of a Decade: Roy Stryker and the Development of Documentary Photography in the Thirties.* Baton Rouge: Louisiana State University Press, 1972.

Ohrn, Karen Becker. *Dorothea Lange and the Documentary Tradition*. Baton Rouge: Louisiana State University Press, 1980.

Rivera, Diego. "The Revolutionary Spirit in Modern Art." *Art in Theory, 1900–2000: An Anthology of Changing Ideas,* new edition. Eds. Charles Harrison and Paul Wood. Oxford: Blackwell Publishing, 2003. 421–424.

Reading Responses

1. Katelyn Beaty starts by announcing her argument at the end of her second paragraph, but she also warns her readers that she will be complicating her thesis. Later in the paper her argument changes directions two more times. Identify those changes. Explain why Beaty's three-step unfolding of her final point does or does not persuade you. Do you believe that a thesis should always be made fully clear at the beginning of a paper? Why or why not?

2. Google the terms *photography* and *propaganda*. List at least five examples of photography being used as propaganda. Summarize the main arguments for and against uses of photography as propaganda.

3. The photo titled "Migrant Mother" (Figure 3) is one of the most famous images in American history. How did Beaty's paper make you consider alternative ways to interpret that image?

PUBLIC WRITING

INTRODUCTION

Susan Sontag (1933–2004) became one of the leading voices in media studies. Her 1977 essay, "On Photography," changed the way we think about photographs, and many other works in her prolific writing career were about photography and the rhetoric of images.

In the essay excerpted here, Sontag makes another major contribution to the theory of how photography works in our lives, including her well-known claim that the trouble with photography is not that "people remember through photographs but that they remember only the photographs," adding, "To remember is, more and more, not to recall a story but to be able to call up a picture."

Sontag was very actively opposed to war; in fact, she chose to live in Sarejevo during the war in Bosnia and Herzegovina, to see it and try to understand it.

Her essay (a long essay from which we excerpt a small portion) begins with a story about British novelist Virginia Woolf, who proposed to a male friend that she and he try an experiment—to look at photos of war together and see if they feel the same thing. That is essentially the experiment that Sontag conducts with her readers.

Looking at War: Photography's View of Devastation and Death

Susan Sontag

The New Yorker, December 9, 2002

In June, 1938, Virginia Woolf published *Three Guineas,* her brave, unwelcomed reflections on the roots of war. Written during the preceding two years, while she and most of her intimates and fellow-writers were rapt by the advancing Fascist insurrection in Spain, the book was couched as a tardy reply to a letter from an eminent lawyer in London who had asked, "How in your opinion are we to prevent war?" Woolf begins by observing tartly that a truthful dialogue between them may not be possible. For though they belong to the same class, "the educated class," a vast gulf separates them: the lawyer is a man and she is a woman. Men make war. Men (most men) like war, or at least they find "some glory, some necessity, some satisfaction in fighting" that women (most women) do not seek or find. What does an educated—that is, privileged, well-off—woman like her know of war? Can her reactions to its horrors be like his?

Woolf proposes they test this "difficulty of communication" by looking at some images of war that the beleaguered Spanish government has been sending out twice a week to sympathizers abroad. Let's see "whether when we look at the same photographs we feel the same things," she writes. "This morning's collection contains the photograph of what might be a man's body, or a woman's; it is so mutilated that it might, on the other hand, be the body of a pig. But those certainly are dead children, and that undoubtedly is the section of a house. A bomb has torn open the side; there is still a bird-cage hanging in what was presumably the sitting room." One can't always make out the subject, so thorough is the ruin of flesh and stone that the photographs depict. "However different the education, the traditions behind us," Woolf says to the lawyer, "we"— and here women are the "we"—and he might well have the same response: "War, you say, is an abomination; a barbarity; war must be stopped at whatever cost. And we echo your words. War is an abomination; a barbarity; war must be stopped." . . .

Central to modern expectations, and modern ethical feeling, is the conviction that war is an aberration, if an unstoppable one. That peace is the norm, if an unattainable one. This, of course, is not the way war has been regarded throughout history. War has been the norm and peace the exception.

Descriptions of the exact fashion in which bodies are injured and killed in combat is a recurring climax in the stories told in the *Iliad.* War is seen as something men do, inveterately, undeterred by the accumulation of suffering it inflicts; to represent war in words or in pictures requires a keen, unflinching detachment. When Leonardo da Vinci gives instructions for a battle painting, his worry is that artists will lack the courage or the imagination to show war in all its ghastliness: "Make the conquered and beaten pale, with brows raised and knit, and the skin above their brows furrowed with pain . . . and the teeth apart as with crying out in lamentation. . . . Make the dead partly or entirely covered with dust . . . and let the blood be seen by its color flowing in a sinuous stream from the corpse to the dust. Others in the death agony grinding their teeth, rolling their eyes, with their fists clenched against their bodies, and the legs distorted." The concern is that the images won't be sufficiently upsetting: not concrete, not detailed enough. . . .

It used to be thought, when candid images were not common, that showing something that needed to be seen, bringing a painful reality closer, was bound to goad viewers to feel—feel more. In a world in which photography is brilliantly at the service of consumerist manipulations, this naive relation to poignant scenes of suffering is much less plausible. Morally alert photographers and ideologues of photography are concerned with the issues of exploitation of sentiment (pity, compassion, indignation) in war photography, and how to avoid rote ways of arousing feeling.

Photographer-witnesses may try to make the spectacular *not* spectacular. But their efforts can never cancel the tradition in which suffering has been understood throughout most of Western history. To feel the pulse of Christian iconography in certain wartime or disaster-time photographs is not a sentimental projection. It would be hard not to discern the lineaments of the Pieta in W. Eugene Smith's picture of a woman in Minamata cradling her deformed, blind, and deaf daughter, or the template of the Descent from the Cross in several of Don McCullin's pictures of dying American soldiers in Vietnam.

The problem is not that people remember through photographs but that they remember only the photographs. This remembering through photographs eclipses other forms of understanding and remembering. The concentration camps—that is, the photographs taken when the camps were liberated, in 1945—are most of what people associate with Nazism and the miseries of the Second World War. Hideous deaths (by genocide, starvation, and epidemic) are most of what people retain of the clutch of iniquities and failures that have taken place in postcolonial Africa.

To remember is, more and more, not to recall a story but to be able to call up a picture. Even a writer as steeped in nineteenth-century and early-modern literary solemnities as W. G. Sebald was moved to seed his lamentation-narratives of lost lives, lost nature, lost cityscapes with photographs. Sebald was not just an elegist; he was a militant elegist. Remembering, he wanted the reader to remember, too.

Harrowing photographs do not inevitably lose their power to shock. But they don't help us much to understand. Narratives can make us understand. Photographs do something else: they haunt us. Consider one of the most unforgettable images of the war in Bosnia, a photograph of which the *New York Times* foreign correspondent John Kifner wrote, "The image is stark, one of the most enduring of the Balkan wars: a Serb militiaman casually kicking a dying Muslim woman in the head. It tells you everything you need to know." But of course it doesn't tell us everything we need to know. . . .

The pictures of Bosnian atrocities were seen soon after they took place. Like pictures from the Vietnam War, such as Ron Haberle's documents of the massacre by a company of American soldiers of some five hundred unarmed civilians in the village of My Lai in March, 1968, they became important in bolstering indignation at this war which had been far from inevitable, far from intractable; and could have been stopped much sooner. Therefore one could feel an obligation to look at these pictures, gruesome as they were, because there was something to be done, right now, about what they depicted. . . .

Could one be mobilized actively to oppose war by an image (or a group of images) . . . ? . . .

Among single antiwar images, the huge photograph that Jeff Wall made in 1992 entitled "Dead Troops Talk (A vision after an ambush of a Red Army Patrol, near Moqor, Afghanistan, winter 1986)" seems to me exemplary in its thoughtfulness, coherence, and passion. The antithesis of a document, the picture, a Cibachrome transparency seven and a half feet high and more than thirteen feet wide and mounted on a light box, shows figures posed in a landscape, a blasted hillside, that was constructed in the artist's studio. Wall, who is Canadian, was never in Afghanistan. The ambush is a made-up event in a conflict he had read about. His imagination of war (he cites Goya as an inspiration) is in the tradition of nineteenth-century history painting and other forms of history-as-spectacle that emerged in the late eighteenth and early nineteenth centuries—just before the invention of the camera—such as tableaux vivants, wax displays, dioramas, and panoramas, which made the past, especially the immediate past, seem astonishingly, disturbingly real.

The figures in Wall's visionary photo-work are "realistic," but, of course, the image is not. Dead soldiers don't talk. Here they do.

Thirteen Russian soldiers in bulky winter uniforms and high boots are scattered about a pocked, blood-splashed pit lined with loose rocks and the litter of war: shell casings, crumpled metal, a boot that holds the lower part of a leg. The soldiers, slaughtered in the Soviet Union's own late folly of a colonial war, were never buried. A few still have their helmets on. The head of one kneeling figure, talking animatedly, foams with his red brain matter. The atmosphere is warm, convivial, fraternal. Some slouch, leaning on an elbow, or sit, chatting, their opened skulls and destroyed hands on view. One man bends over another, who lies on his side in a posture of heavy sleep, perhaps encouraging him to sit up. Three men are horsing around: one with a huge wound in his belly straddles another, who is lying prone, while the third, kneeling, dangles what might be a watch before the laughing man on his stomach. One soldier, helmeted, legless, has turned to a comrade some distance away, an alert smile on his face. Below him are two who don't seem quite up to the resurrection and lie supine, their bloodied heads hanging down the stony incline.

Engulfed by the image, which is so accusatory, one could fantasize that the soldiers might turn and talk to us. But no, no one is looking out of the picture at the viewer. There's no threat of protest. They're not about to yell at us to bring a halt to that abomination which is war. They are not represented as terrifying to others, for among them (far left) sits a white-garbed Afghan scavenger, entirely absorbed in going through somebody's kit bag, of whom they take no note, and entering the picture above them (top right), on the path winding down the slope, are two Afghans, perhaps soldiers themselves, who, it would seem from the Kalashnikovs collected near their feet, have already stripped the dead soldiers of their weapons. These dead are supremely uninterested in the living: in those who took their lives; in witnesses—or in us. Why should they seek our gaze? What would they have to say to us "We"—this "we" is everyone who has never experienced anything like what they went through—don't understand. We don't get it. We truly can't imagine what it was like. We can't imagine how dreadful, how terrifying war is—and how normal it becomes. Can't understand, can't imagine. That's what every soldier, and every journalist and aid worker and independent observer who has put in time under fire and had the luck to elude the death that struck down others nearby, stubbornly feels. And they are right.

"Dead Troops Talk" 1992, Jeff Wall

Reading Responses

1. In the introduction to this essay we suggested that Sontag was conducting an experiment with her audience that was like the experiment that Virginia Woolf conducted with her male friend. Reread the first two paragraphs of Sontag's essay and explain what Woolf believed to be the result of her experiment. Does Sontag offer a conclusion to her experiment? If so what is it?

2. List Sontag's points that support the idea that photography can be a force for good. List her points that photography has only limited effects. Which side of things does she give more weight to?

3. At one point Sontag asks if images could help to make people oppose war. What is her answer to her question? How does she use the Jeff Wall photograph, "Dead Troops Talk," in answering her question? (Google the title to find a larger, color reproduction.)

MORE WRITING IN MEDIA STUDIES

INTRODUCTION

You will not be surprised that, in a chapter devoted to media studies, we ask you to read a Web site. There's no real substitute for the visual experience of navigating through a Web site, scrolling to find images that surprise and arrest your attention, and create strong rhetorical effects. And a Web site about advertising has the additional benefit of asking you to study visual rhetoric that emphatically attempts to persuade.

Since its inception as the "War Advertising Council" in 1941, the Ad Council has helped produce public service announcements (PSAs) that have shaped American culture, giving us, for example, the image of Rosie the Riveter, the slogan "Friends Don't Let Friends Drive Drunk," and the characters of Smokey the Bear and the Crash Test Dummies. Most Americans not only recognize these bits of culture but also can recall the messages that the announcements conveyed.

In 2004 the Ad Council commissioned a report entitled *Public Service Advertising That Changed the World* to provide an overview of the work of the council and, more important, the effect of that work on significant social problems. In particular, the audience of this report was advertising professionals attending an annual conference. It is these professionals (and their bosses) who volunteer to partner with the Ad Council to produce PSAs. The report showcases nine particularly effective campaigns, for example, campaigns on "Pollution Prevention," "Safety Belt Education" (featuring the "Crash Test Dummies"), and "Obesity Prevention."

Because the purpose of the report is to persuade busy professionals to volunteer their services, the report emphasizes an evaluation of the effectiveness of the campaign over reading and interpreting. Because advertising professionals are already expert at analyzing context and form, the report emphasizes subject matter: the significance of the problems that the various campaigns address. The reports draw the reader's attention to the process of targeting a problem, completing background research to help the advertisers target the most effective solution to the problem, and then designing and implementing the PSA campaign. In this way, the Ad Council encourages readers to imagine themselves working as part of a smart, well-informed team of professionals who are working together to improve their world—and using images to achieve that end.

As you enter the Web site, scan the different campaigns to get a sense of what uses of images they have in common and what are unique to each campaign. And don't just get lost in the pictures. The text explains how the images function and will offer many good examples of how to analyze images. Doing these things will help you to answer the Reading Responses that follow.

"Public Service Advertising That Changed a Nation"

The Ad Council and the U.S. Department of Health and Human Services

Directions to the Web site:
You can start at the Ad Council home page: http://www.adcouncil.org/. From there scroll down the left side of the screen to find the "Educational Resources" page and from that page select "Educators" (http://www.adcouncil.org/default.aspx?id=596). On the

"Educators" page, scroll down to a paragraph headed "Available Resources," under which you will find *Public Service Advertising That Changed the World* (in a downloadable pdf format). If for some reason the site changes and that document is no longer available, the Ad Council maintains a "Historic Campaigns" page, which you can get to through the "Educators" page or by Googling "Ad Council: Historic Campaigns."

Reading Responses

1. Which of the nine campaigns did you find most persuasive? Explain how the visual elements of the campaign that you choose contribute to the effectiveness of the message.

2. The text for each campaign reads almost like a story. Choose one of the campaigns and analyze that story. What role in that story do the companies and organizations that contributed to the campaign play? How will the audience for this report likely respond to this portrayal? Who are other important "characters" in that story and what is the relationship to the contributing companies and organizations? What is the persuasive message of these stories for the busy professionals who were its primary audience?

3. Select a campaign description that you find less effective than others. Using the resources available to you, redesign the description, including a plan for both words and visual elements that would improve the appeal of the description for the professionals who are reading the report.

WRITING ASSIGNMENTS

Assignment 1

The Ad Council is one of the three nonprofit organizations that developed the "That's Not Cool" Web site from the chapter opener as an expanded public service announcement. Your task for this assignment is to analyze a public service announcement that is part of an Ad Council campaign. You can locate Ad Council campaigns by going to Adcouncil.org, clicking on Educational Resources, selecting Students, and then selecting a campaign on a topic that interests you. Your professor may direct you to choose a print, radio, television, or web PSA.

To begin your analysis, assess the rhetorical effect of the images, movement, words, music, and text separately. Then consider how these features of the PSA work together to create a message for the viewer. As you begin writing, describe whom you believe to be the intended audience of the PSA and why you think so. Make a claim about the effectiveness of the PSA, providing evidence from the advertisement to support your reasoning.

Assignment 2

If you examine the ergonomic study for Steelcase's Leap Chair in Chapter 13, "Marketing," you might conclude that the creators of that study care more about functionality and less about design. In that report, the words and numbers from a study of employee productivity consistently draw the reader's attention to how the chair functions. But the images that accompany those words and numbers suggest that Steelcase cares about design, too.

Your task for this assignment is to analyze the rhetorical purpose of the words, numbers, and images in that ergonomic study of the Leap Chair. As you begin to analyze the study, pay attention to words, numbers, and images that appear on the same page. What kind of information does each communicate? How do they work together to communicate a point to the reader? Which features of the chair do the words, numbers, and images emphasize? As you begin to draft, consider how you will communicate your method of analyzing to your reader. How much and what kind of evidence will you need to use to convince your reader? How will you present that evidence to your reader?

Assignment 3

After completing the readings in this chapter, you understand that photographs are anything but objective representations of reality. What a photograph "means" is shaped not only by the photographer but also by the viewer. Your task for this assignment is to explain how you view a particular photograph. To begin, select a photograph that has special meaning for you. You can use your own photograph, a photograph from someone you know, or a published photo. Be sure that the photo includes at least one person. Begin by free-writing for a few minutes about the meaning that this photo has for you. You may find it useful to narrate the events before and after the moment captured in the photo or narrate your experience seeing the photo for the first time. Then analyze the photo itself— what features of the photograph make it memorable for you? What meaning do particular features communicate to the viewer? As you begin writing, decide on the best strategy for communicating the meaning that the photograph has for you. How could a narrative, for example, help your reader understand the significance of the moment captured in the photo? Then consider what kind of evidence from the photo itself—or from other sources— will help your reader understand what you see when you view the photo.

CHEMISTRY:
SUMMARIZING RESEARCH

The U.S. Environmental Protection Agency is watching the San Fernando Valley closely because the water in some of its aquifers is contaminated by industrial waste. The EPA required the cities of Los Angeles and Burbank to close wells in the San Fernando watershed and to provide clean water from other, more expensive sources. But over three million people live over those polluted aquifers; should they be afraid of their water? Should you? You may drink bottled water, but the water you use to brush your teeth, take a shower, and wash your dishes probably comes from the tap—and that water probably comes from an aquifer. One of the chief sources of public information about water quality is the EPA Web site (www.epa.gov). Search the site for information regarding water pollution in your area, keeping careful notes on the steps you take and the information you find. Review your experience and answer the following questions:

- List steps you took to get to the information about water quality in your area, including any false steps that you took. Evaluate the site: how well does it provide information that users most need to know?

- If you were to redesign the Web site, what improvements would you suggest to make information more readily available to users?

- Imagine that you have the opportunity to make an appeal to a government agency in your home area that would decide whether to take steps to improve water quality. Summarize the most important information from the site that you will use in your appeal. What additional information would you like to have?

PORTABLE RHETORICAL LESSON: SUMMARIZING TO SHAPE THE FUTURE

As you trekked through the EPA site, you might have been surprised by how much information is available. And you might also have been frustrated that the information comes in so many disconnected pieces. How do you decide what it all means? How do you find out what information is not available—or if anyone is doing research to get the information you need? Through the exercise you experienced the value of summarizing.

The first question you will need to ask yourself when you need to summarize is *why:* What is your particular **purpose** for summarizing? We all summarize to make sense of a complex topic for ourselves; for example, when you read a chapter from a textbook, you may summarize it in your notes so you understand its main ideas. But why summarize for an audience? To answer that question, think of the *effects* that a thoroughly researched and credible summary can have on an audience. A summary makes information more easily available to a reader, and it shapes readers' understanding by choosing the most important pieces and connecting the pieces into patterns.

Because summary emphasizes some information and hides other information, writers who summarize also think carefully about **organization.** In essay-long summaries, the order in which a reader ingests the parts of a summary determines the connections that the reader recognizes. The connections should form a story of what's being summarized—starting in the past, moving into the present, and suggesting a future. The actual work of summarizing is all about sorting—taking loads of information, determining which information is most important, sorting it into sets of like pieces, and then arranging the order of the sets for an audience. It's heavy-duty organizational work.

The scientific review essay, the particular genre that this chapter presents, exists for the purpose of summarizing complicated scientific research and directing the summary to call for future research—or changes in the policies of agencies such as the EPA. You may never have written a review essay; typically it's only an expert in a field that has broad enough knowledge to presume to summarize that field. But when you write an introduction to a research paper, you make the same kind of rhetorical moves that characterize review essays. You summarize enough of what other researchers have said about your topic that you can show the bigger pattern of ideas into which your work fits, and you use those patterns to move your readers toward the new ideas that you have to add.

Think of a review essay as a jigsaw puzzle. Except there's no picture on the box to tell you how the pieces should go together, and all the pieces do not come in one box; they have to be discovered separately. At any point in time, researchers on a given problem have discovered some pieces of the puzzle, but they are still looking for others. A reviewer implicitly says, "Here are the puzzle pieces that we have found so far, this is the picture they seem to be forming, so these are the pieces we need to look for next."

And it's the "what next?" part that gives the review essay its power—and that gives you the chapter's **Portable Rhetorical Lesson:** summarizing to shape the future. For example, when you read the chapter's first essay, you will see that the three-sentence Abstract forms a three-part thesis statement: the first two parts summarize what researchers know from past studies, and the third part states the problem that needs to be solved in the future. When you can use summary—your version of the emerging pattern of a puzzle—to show what's missing, what needs to be learned or done next, you can direct future study and action.

WRITING IN THE DISCIPLINE

INTRODUCTION

by Darla McCarthy, Professor of Chemistry

We all know that the pollution of our environment by toxic chemicals is a serious matter. Several types of cancer and birth defects, as well as increased incidences of miscarriage, infertility, and other physical and developmental maladies, have been linked to exposure to toxic chemicals. Leukemia and prostate cancer, for example, occur more frequently in people who have been exposed to dioxins—by-products of industrial processes such as pulp and paper bleaching, waste incineration, and pesticide manufacturing. Billions of pounds of pesticides, themselves toxic or contaminated with other toxins, are used annually in the United States; hazardous chemicals are accidentally spilled on roadways or fields; and some manufacturers and users of toxic chemicals fail to dispose of them properly. In other words, do not make the mistake of thinking that a highly specialized review in a chemistry journal has no bearing on you.

The review essay reprinted here does not take what you might think is the predictable line on environmental cleanup. Rather, author Martin Alexander (a world-renowned expert in environmental biochemistry and professor at Cornell University) argues that we might be wasting money cleaning some sites that do not pose real threats. His purpose, of course, is scientific, not political. His argument is a summary of the available scientific evidence. (And I hope you will notice how this review essay erases the line between summary and argument.)

Let me step back almost fifty years to place Alexander's work in its historical context. A review essay is, after all, a kind of history of science. Public awareness of the hazards associated with chemical pollutants was raised in the mid-1960s with the publication of *Silent Spring* (a section of which is reprinted in this chapter). In this landmark book, Rachel Carson discussed the decline of the American robin in certain regions of the United States due to its consumption of worms laden with the pesticide DDT, which was used in massive amounts to combat Dutch elm disease. Public attentiveness to chemical pollutants was further heightened in 1978, when Love Canal, a neighborhood in Niagara Falls, New York, was evacuated due to concerns regarding endemic health problems linked to soil and water contamination by toxins that had leaked from a chemical waste disposal site. Because of mounting public pressure, the U.S. Congress passed several laws regulating the production, use, and disposal of hazardous chemicals. They also passed laws that provided funding and regulations for cleaning up, or remediating, contaminated sites.

Since the publication of *Silent Spring,* billions of dollars have been spent to remediate contaminated soil and water. And it is estimated that as many as 350,000 contaminated sites will require clean-up over the next 30 years, at a cost of as much as $250 billion.* With such astronomical costs, there is currently a great deal of interest in developing more efficient, cost-effective methods for remediation. One trend is a move toward more accurate descriptions of contaminated sites.*

---

* *New Report Projects Number, Cost and Nature of Contaminated Site Cleanups in the U.S. Over Next 30 Years.* United States Environmental Protection Agency, 11 Feb. 2005. http://www.epa.gov/superfund/news/30years.htm

This is the point at which Alexander enters the story. Currently, chemists use very rigorous methods for extracting chemical pollutants from soil samples. Then they use chemical analyses to determine the amount of toxin extracted from the soil samples and determine the total amount of toxin contaminating the site. Sites with larger total amounts of contaminants are given higher priority for remediation. Scientists have recently become aware, however, that the total amount of contaminant present at a site is not necessarily a good indicator of the potential danger of that contaminant to the environment—some contaminants become so adsorbed, or stuck, to the soil that the organisms that live on or in the soil are not likely to ingest or absorb the toxin. So, even though there might be a high total amount of contaminant at a site, there may be little danger. Alexander summarizes those scientific findings and argues that they call for improved methods for characterizing contaminated sites.

Alexander, like any author of a scientific review essay, has two main goals: to summarize all the pertinent literature related to his topic, and to suggest an answer to the question "what next?" The most effective way to accomplish these goals is to craft the review as a thesis-based essay in which the main emphasis is placed on data, as if the data inevitably leads to the author's conclusions. We scientists pride ourselves on our objectivity, and the best way to remain objective is to stay focused on the data. To write a review confidently, a scientist must know the material, the research data, thoroughly. Notice that Alexander has seventy-five references in his bibliography. That's actually not much for a review essay—I've read some with more than 300 references!

The author of a review gains additional credibility by showing that he or she has been a participant in the area of science that is under review. Reviewers almost universally refer to their own published work. In other words, one earns the right to review a field of science only through building expertise in the field. Alexander cites his own publications twenty-two times.

With expertise and data in the spotlight, Alexander's review hoped to change both remediation practice and the further study of bioremediation.

✓ Reading Tips

Remember that this review essay is based on a thesis (see the first sentence after the abstract), is data-based, and concludes with a suggested course of action (the sentence just before the "Relevance" section). That means:

- First, that you should read to find the support for a thesis, which is an argument and not a proven fact or set of facts.
- Second, because the paper is data based (and not, for example, driven by emotion or personal appeal), the support for the thesis comes in the facts. Make sure that you judge the effectiveness of the paper by its fair and clear use of scientific data as grounds for the thesis.
- Finally, look for the author's suggestion of what to do next.

Each of these features should be easy for you to find; don't let yourself get bogged down in the technical information. The marginal notes should help you to understand all the science, but if you need to push past some complex chemistry to get the main points and structure of the argument, do so.

Aging, Bioavailability, and Overestimation of Risk from Environmental Pollutants

Martin Alexander

Environmental Science & Technology, 2000, *34*(20): 4259–65

Bioavailability is the ability of a chemical to be ingested or absorbed by living organisms. Bioavailability affects the toxicity of chemicals and affects their potential for biodegradation (degradation by organisms) and/or bioremediation (complete degradation or detoxification by organisms).

Organic chemicals contain carbon.

The traditional method for analyzing polluted soil is to extract, or remove, the pollutant from the soil and then to identify and quantify the pollutant by various chemical procedures. Chemists are always trying to improve their analyses either by increasing the amount of pollutant recovered from the soil in the extraction process or by increasing the sensitivity, or precision, of their chemical procedures.

The toxicological significance is a measure of how changes in the accessibility of chemicals to organisms affects the toxicity of the chemicals to the organisms.

[Abstract]

As they persist, or age, in soil, organic compounds become progressively less available for uptake by organisms, for exerting toxic effects, and for biodegradation and bioremediation by microorganisms. This declining bioavailability is not reflected by currently used methods for the chemical analysis of soils for determining concentrations of organic pollutants. As a result, such methods overestimate exposure, and thus risk, from toxic chemicals in contaminated sites.

The validity of current methods for analyzing soils to assess the risk from organic pollutants has been cast in doubt by recent research. The focus of much of the concern with analytical methods has been increasing the recovery and sensitivity of chemical procedures, and the relevancy of these procedures to living organisms has been largely ignored. However, a primary reason for performing these analyses is to provide information on the exposure of living organisms to, and hence the risk from, these pollutants. The underlying issue is one of bioavailability. . . .

In this review, information will be presented to show that the bioavailability of organic pollutants in soil declines with time and that current analytical methods, because they measure total and not bioavailable concentrations, may overestimate the magnitude of the environmental and societal problem from these pollutants. Both early and recent evidence for these changes in accessibility will be presented, and the toxicological significance of these observations will be considered. The relevance of current analytical methods will then be evaluated. Differences in bioavailability among species, environments, and compounds and the consequent need for new analytical methods will be reviewed. . . .

Many of the organic pollutants in soil were introduced years or sometimes decades ago at a time when industry and the public were not adequately aware of the scope, magnitude, and importance of soil pollution. Even early research, which has largely been forgotten, provided evidence that the availability of certain chemicals that have been in soil for some time is less than freshly added compounds, and hence the term aging (or weathering) was applied to the phenomenon. Although the early findings and their importance have been obscured with the passage of time, awareness now is growing among environmental toxicologists, risk assessors, and regulatory agencies that the total concentration of a toxicant in a contaminated environment frequently overestimates the risk of pollutants to humans, animals, and plants.

Early Evidence

Data showing the time-dependence of changes in bioavailability are now compelling. The early information came from studies of concentrations of pesticides in the field measured for long periods of time and from measurements of toxicity of pesticides to invertebrates and plants.

For example, long-term monitoring of soil revealed that DDT, aldrin and its epoxide (dieldrin), heptachlor and its epoxide, and chlordane disappeared slowly at first, but then the rate of loss fell to such an extent that further loss was either extremely slow or ceased (1). Although the initial disappearance might be partially the result of volatilization or abiotic degradation as well as biodegradation by soil microorganisms, the fact that the disappearance was almost imperceptibly slow after several years indicates that those insecticides had become poorly available to the indigenous microorganisms; otherwise, these biodegradable compounds should have continued to disappear. The results of several long- and short-term monitoring studies are presented in Figure 1, which shows that the period when little or none of the insecticides is available to soil microorganisms may occur either soon or long after the compounds were introduced into the soil. Such results also show that the percentage of the compound that is poorly or no longer bioavailable differs markedly among the several soils and sites that were examined. This failing on the part of the soil microflora cannot be attributed to low winter temperatures, periods of drought, or other adverse conditions because the monitoring often extended for several years and was done in fields or experimental plots where crops were growing. . . .

Recent Evidence

Organic compounds that have aged in the field are less bioavailable, often appreciably so, than the same compounds freshly added to samples of the same soil. In a field treated with DDT 49 years earlier, approximately 30, 12, and 34% of DDT and the DDE and DDD formed from the added insecticide were available for uptake by the earthworm *Eisenia fetida* compared to newly added chemicals, and 28 or 43% of dieldrin applied at the same time was available based on concentration in the worms or percentages assimilated, respectively. Similar reduced bioavailabilities of DDT, DDE, and DDD but not dieldrin were observed in soil from a waste disposal site in which the insecticides had aged for some 30 years (4). Field aging also diminishes the availability to microorganisms of

The heading reminds us that a review essay is partly history of science.

Volatilization is evaporation.

Abiotic degradation is disappearance of a chemical caused by non-biological events such as reaction with oxygen in the air or decomposition initiated by sunlight.

Microflora are populations of microscopic organisms including algae, bacteria, and fungi.

Alexander suggested in the previous section that after a certain aging period pollutants are no longer accessible to microorganisms. If that is true, then we should be able to show experimentally that pollutants are more accessible when they are first applied to soil than they are after they've aged. "Recent Evidence" shows that the accessibility of several pollutants to bacteria and earthworms decreases as the pollutants age in soil.

DDE and DDD are products of the degradation of the infamous pesticide, DDT. Interestingly it is DDE, and not DDT, that is toxic—DDE interferes with the proper incorporation of calcium into eggshells, thus weakening the shells.

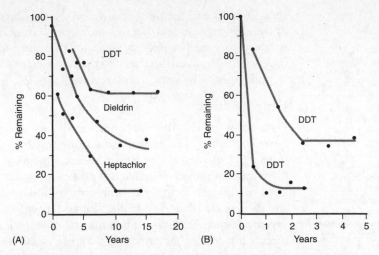

Figure 1 Changes in concentrations of three insecticides in long-term (A) and short-term (B) monitoring of several field sites. Calculated from data of Nash and Woolson and Lichtenslein et al. (1). In other field sites, the monitoring period was not sufficiently long to show the possible existence of a phase with little or no further disappearance of the insecticides.

1,2-dibromoethane that persisted for 3 years (5), simazine applied for 20 consecutive years (6), and polycyclic aromatic hydrocarbons (PAHs) in soils from a closed coking plant (7) and manufactured-gas plant (8).

Laboratory tests confirm the lesser availability to microorganisms of aged than un-aged compounds in highly dissimilar soils (Table 1). The

Table 1 Compounds Shown to Become Less Available for Microbial Degradation as a Result of Aging

Compound	Soil	Aging period (d)	Ref
naphthalene	Colwood loam	365	(73)
naphthalene	Mt. Pleasant silt loam	68	(17)
phenanthrene	Mt. Pleasant silt loam	110	(74)
phenanthrene	16 soils	200	(9)
anthracene	Lima loam	203	(18)
fluoranthene	Lima loam	140	(18)
pyrene	Lima loam	133	(18)
atrazine	Ravenna silt loam	90	(75)
atrazine	16 soils	200	(9)
4-nitrophenol	Lima loam	103	(10)
4-nitrophenol	Edwards much	103	(10)

Tables are excellent tools for summarizing large quantities of data that would otherwise be unwieldy to summarize in words. Here Alexander efficiently summarizes several experiments that illustrate that different compounds in different soil types have different aging periods.

bioavailability to microorganisms decreases with time but reaches a value below which a further decline is no longer detectable. How long it takes to reach that value and the final percentage availability vary among soils and compounds. The process may be complete in days or weeks or may take in excess of 200 days, and the loss in availability may be small or large (9, 10). . . .

Toxicological Significance

Aging is toxicologically significant because the assimilation and acute and chronic toxicity of harmful compounds decline as they persist and become increasingly sequestered with time. Studies with mammals, for example, have shown that less 2,3,7,8-tetrachlorodibenzo-*p*-dioxin (TCDD) was absorbed after it had been in soil for 8 days than after a contact period of 10–15 hours. The number of fruit flies (*D. melanogaster*), house flies (*Musca domestica*), and German cockroaches (*Blatella germanica*) killed by DDT and dieldrin declined markedly with increasing times of residence of these compounds in soil (13). Similar but largely forgotten data were obtained many years earlier by Peterson et al. (14), who found a marked and progressive reduction in toxicity to *D. melanogaster* as DDT persisted for 108 days in soil. An effect of aging on plants has also been noted with three herbicides: napropamide, simazine, and atrazine (3, 6, 15). In each instance, toxicity was less than that anticipated. . . . Aging also reduces the effectiveness of at least some genotoxic compounds in soil. Thus, by means of a solid-phase assay, it has been found that the genotoxicity of the carcinogens benzo(*a*)pyrene and 9,10-dimethyl-1,2-benzanthracene diminished rapidly and to a great extent within a 15-day period, although analysis following vigorous extraction showed only a slight decline in concentration after about 2 months (16). . . .

Nevertheless, a time-dependent decline in bioavailability does not always occur. This may be related to properties of the soil or of the compound. Instances in which bioavailability did not diminish include the biodegradability of simazine (6), the dermal and oral availability of TCDD and dieldrin to rodents (27, 28), and the uptake of DDE by earthworms in one soil (4). Only a small loss in bioavailability of certain compounds in sediments may occur with aging; witness that the rate of microbial dechlorination of polychlorinated biphenyls in Hudson River sediments contaminated for at least 15 years was only about 20% slower than compounds freshly added at 20 ppm (29). In addition, toxic compounds may exist in pockets or in nonaqueous-phase liquids within the soil, and after some physical disturbance, they may be released and become bioavailable. Although such compounds are aged in the sense of time, they have not been sequestered in a fashion to reduce their bioavailability to living organisms.

In the previous two sections, Alexander established that pollutants do indeed become less available for uptake by small organisms over time. In this section Alexander reviews data that show that as pollutants age in soil, their toxicity to larger plants and animals also decreases.

---

acute toxicity: causing an immediate toxic effect such as paralysis or suffocation

---

chronic toxicity: causing long-term effects such as cancer or emphysema

---

Genotoxic compounds modify DNA and thus have potential to alter genes and eventually cause cancer. Here Alexander explains that the ability of certain compounds to modify DNA decreases as the compounds age in soil. He refers to a "solid-phase assay," which is just a fancy way of saying that researchers exposed organisms to genotoxins in the soil—or on a *solid* surface—and then determined if modifications had been made to the organisms' DNA.

Carcinogens are cancer-causing substances.

Incorrect Analytical Methodologies

The widely used protocols of federal and state regulatory agencies rely on analytical methods that entail vigorous extraction of soils and sediments with organic solvents. The aim is to remove all, or as much as possible, of the pollutant from the environmental sample. Each method is carefully evaluated to assess its accuracy, as well as its precision and sensitivity, but the accuracy is interpreted in purely chemical terms. The relevancy of such methods to the toxicity of the compound in the form in which it exists in nature is generally not considered in carrying out risk analyses, except that a default value is sometimes included to relate to the particular environmental matrix. The fact that the compound may become progressively less bioavailable as it persists, even in a single environmental matrix, is not considered in assessing risk. Thus, the regulator is not making use of information that bioavailability may decline with little or no reduction in the concentration as determined by procedures that rely on initial vigorous extractions. Hence, such methods are often not relevant for prediction of potential exposures to, and thus risks from, contaminated soils or sediments.

The evidence is compelling that the quantities recovered by vigorous extraction fail to predict declining bioavailability as compounds persist in soil. For example, despite the marked diminution in effectiveness in killing three species of insects as dieldrin and DDT aged in soil, >90% of the dieldrin and ca. 85% of the DDT could still be recovered by vigorous extraction (13). . . .

If the total concentration at a polluted site is greater than the regulatory level but the bioavailable concentration is below that value, a site that might be slated for expensive cleanup might, instead, be deemed to present an acceptable risk. The public concern about a contaminated location might be allayed by the more meaningful assessment. Moreover, a site that was bioremediated but still contained concentrations of one or more contaminants above the target levels may have indeed been successfully cleaned up, even though conventional analysis suggested that the remediation was inadequate. This is true both of engineered and intrinsic bioremediation, which frequently do not destroy all of the targeted compounds. Because such bioremediation treatments act on the fraction that is bioavailable, to microorganisms at least, the accessibility of the portion that remains may be so low that the site presents little or no risk to higher organisms. . . .

New Assay Methods

The regulator is faced with a major dilemma because the magnitude of reduction in bioavailability resulting from aging is different for a single

---

Here Alexander emphasizes that current methods focus only on chemical analysis—they aim to extract as much pollutant as possible out of the soil to determine the *total* amount of chemical pollutant in the soil. This type of analysis does not account for changes in the bioavailability of pollutants as they age; thus, risks are often overestimated.

Environmental scientists are well aware of the fact that certain chemicals are more accessible to organisms in one type of soil (environmental matrix) than another. So, they account for the differences by including a "correction factor," or "default value."

Here Alexander addresses the key question: If bioavailability changes over time and can't be predicted, how can you predict the risk of exposure? This is his "what next?" question.

Bioassays analyze the effects of pollutants on living organisms, whereas chemical and physical assays simply analyze the amounts and types of pollutants in the soil.

Here is Alexander's proposed answer to the "what next?" question—use mild extraction techniques for chemical assays. Notice that he does not overemphasize his solution; Alexander's purpose in writing the review is to highlight the issue of bioavailability, and not to solve the resulting problems. He does, however, suggest a direction that others could pursue to solve the problem.

In his conclusion, Alexander simply summarizes his review and reminds his audience of why they should be concerned about bioavailability.

compound in different soils, for different compounds in the same soil, and for different periods of time that a compound has remained in soil. How does one predict the degree of exposure and risk from an aged compound? Bioassays are an obvious means of performing assessments, but biological measurements frequently do not have adequate precision for regulatory purposes, and they are time-consuming and expensive. An alternative is a chemical or physical assay, but the results of that assay must correlate well with the results of bioassays. . . .

Several chemical and physical methods have been considered as ways to measure the bioavailability of organic compounds in soil. The results of analyses by such procedures have been correlated with bioavailability to earthworms, springtails, nematodes, and microorganisms (31, 39–43). The observation that the time-dependent decline in bioavailability is accompanied by a time-dependent decline in the quantity of compounds extracted from soil by a mild procedure (9, 10, 31, 44) suggests that a mild-extraction technique might serve as the basis for a surrogate assay for bioavailability. . . .

Relevance

Because exposure to persistent compounds is overestimated by currently used chemical methods, the risk is likewise being overestimated. Inasmuch as aging appears to occur in many and possibly most contaminated soils, the bioavailability of aged chemicals probably is being overestimated very frequently. As a consequence, current approaches to evaluating sites for cleanup sometimes may alarm people in localities where the risk is small. They probably lead to choosing some sites for remediation where little such need exists and thus delay the cleanup of polluted areas where the risk is greater. They also probably result in requirements for cleanup that are unnecessarily stringent and thus lead to expenditure of funds that could be better used to decontaminate additional areas. Therefore, a more widespread recognition of bioavailability of aged compounds is necessary—among scientists, environmental engineers, regulators, and the public at large.

Acknowledgments

Portions of the work were supported by National Institute of Environmental Health Sciences grants ES05950 and ES07052 with partial funding from the U.S. Environmental Protection Agency, U.S. Air Force Office of Scientific Research grant F49620–95–1–0336, the U.S. Department of Agriculture, and GRI. I thank R. C. Loehr, J. W. Gillett, and E. L. Madsen for helpful comments.

Literature Cited

1. Alexander, M. In *Environmentally Acceptable Endpoints in Soil;* Linz, D. G., Nakles, D. V., Eds.; American Academy of Environmental Engineers: Annapolis, MD, 1997; 43–136.

4. Morrison, D. E.; Robertson, B. K.; Alexander, M. *Environ. Sci. Technol.* **2000,** *34,* 709.

5. Steinberg, S. M.; Pignatello, J. J.; Sawhney, B. L. *Environ. Sci. Technol.* **1987,** *21,* 1201.

6. Scribner, S. L.; Benzing, T. R.; Sun, S.; Boyd, S. A. *J. Environ. Qual.* **1992,** *21,* 115.

7. Weissenfels, W. D.; Klewer, H. J.; Langhoff, J. *Appl. Microbiol. Biotechnol.* **1992,** *36,* 689.

8. Erickson, D. C.; Loehr, R. C.; Neuhauser, E. F. *Water Res.* **1993,** *27,* 911.

9. Chung, N.; Alexander, M. *Environ. Sci. Technol.* **1998,** *32,* 855.

10. Hatzinger, P. B.; Alexander, M. *Environ. Sci. Technol.* **1995,** *29,* 537.

13. Robertson, B. K.; Alexander, M. *Environ. Toxicol. Chem.* **1998,** *17,* 1034.

14. Peterson, J. R.; Adams, R. S., Jr.; Cutkomp, L. K. *Soil Sci. Soc. Am. Proc.* **1971,** *35,* 72.

15. Bowmer, K. H. *Aust. J. Soil Res.* **1991,** *29,* 339.

16. Alexander, R. R.; Alexander, M. *Environ. Toxicol. Chem.* **1999,** *18,* 1140.

27. Shu, H.; Teitelbaum, T.; Webb, A. S.; Marple, L.; Brunck, B.; Dei Rossi, D.; Murray, F. J.; Paustenbach, D. *Fundam. Appl. Toxicol.* **1988,** *10,* 335.

28. Midwest Research Institute. *Oral Bioavailability of Soil Associated Aldrin/Dieldrin;* Project 9849-F; Midwest Research Institute: Kansas City, MO, 1991.

29. Abramowicz, D. A.; Brennan, M. J.; Van Dort, H. M.; Gallagher, E. L. *Environ. Sci. Technol.* **1993,** *27,* 1125.

31. Kelsey, J. W.; Kottler, B. D.; Alexander, M. *Environ. Sci. Technol.* **1997,** *31,* 214.

39. Loibner, A. P.; Gartner, M.; Schlegl, M.; Heutzenberger, I.; Braun, R. In *In Situ and On-Site Bioremediation;* Battelle Press: Columbus, OH, 1997; Vol. 5, 617–622.

40. Cornelissen, G.; Van Noort, P. C. M.; Parsons, J. R.; Govers, H. A. J. *Environ. Sci. Technol.* **1997,** *31,* 454.

41. Houx, N. W. H.; Aben, W. J. M. *Sci. Total Environ. Suppl.* **1993,** 387.

42. Ronday, R. *Commun. Soil. Sci. Plant Anal.* **1997,** *28,* 777.

43. Tang, J.; Robertson, B. K.; Alexander, M. *Environ. Sci. Technol.* **1999,** *33,* 4346.

44. Tang, J.; Alexander, M. *Environ. Toxicol. Chem.* **1999,** *18,* 2711.

Reading Responses

1. As Professor McCarthy notes in her introduction, Alexander summarizes a great deal of research in this review essay. How does he join it all together? To answer that question, analyze the structure of three of Alexander's paragraphs (choose paragraphs that include at least four references). For each paragraph, answer these three questions: (1) What seems to be the task of the first sentence? (2) Where in the paragraph do the references appear? (3) Why are these references in this order? Note any similarities you see in the structure of these paragraphs.

2. Alexander's thesis is "that current analytical methods, because they measure total and not bioavailable concentrations, may overestimate the magnitude of the environmental and societal problem from these pollutants." How does this thesis fit with the research he summarizes in his essay? Relying on Alexander's summary of the research, count up the number of studies he cites for two topics: the bioavailability of aging chemicals and the effectiveness of analytical procedures. Compare your

counts with Alexander's thesis, and evaluate Alexander's focus. Does all the research he cites support his thesis? If so, how does it do so? If not, what would you eliminate?

3. Professor McCarthy notes that Alexander is a well-respected scholar on the topic he reviews in this essay. How does his ethos as a respected scholar affect his review essay? As you answer that question, consider how he uses his own research and the other research he cites.

Notes on Grammar, Style, and Rhetoric:
Uses of Old Information in a Critical Review

One illuminating approach to the style of Martin Alexander's "Aging, Bioavailability, and Overestimation of Risk from Environmental Pollutants" is to examine the kinds of information his sentences convey. Most sentences can be divided into two parts, one of which conveys what linguists call old information, the other of which conveys what linguists call new information.

Old information in a sentence is information that readers know on the basis of the particular rhetorical situation, that readers with even minimal experience of the world are aware of, that appears prior to that sentence, or that can be inferred from material leading up to that sentence. For example, certain bits of information become old information after they appear once. Consider the following short text:

> Professor Alexander has written a review essay on toxic chemicals in various kinds of soil. This essay should attract some serious attention.

In the second sentence, "This essay" carries old information because it refers to information mentioned in the first sentence.

New information in a sentence is information that is not obvious from the particular rhetorical situation, that is not known to all people with even minimal experience of the world, that is not mentioned prior to that sentence, or that cannot be inferred from material leading up to that sentence. Consider again the preceding sample text. The words "should attract some serious attention" conveys new information. If these words were blacked out, no one could guess what they are. Therefore, "This essay" makes a connection to earlier material, and "should attract some serious attention" moves the message into new territory. This sentence exemplifies what is true of the old and new information in many sentences: The old information appears early in a relatively short sentence subject, and the new information follows in a longer predicate.

Alexander's sentences use old information in at least three specific ways: (1) by using sentence subjects that package information from fairly extensive prior sections of his essay, (2) by using introductory adverbial clauses to remind readers of information presented earlier, and (3) by including entire sentences that convey only old information.

Consider first Alexander's tactic of using sentence subjects to package old information. One good example of this appears in the section labeled "Recent Evidence." Alexander begins this section with two substantial paragraphs dealing with studies of the bioavailability of organic compounds that have aged in the field. After these two paragraphs, Alexander begins a new sentence and a new paragraph with these words: "These investigations with individual compounds. . . ." This phrase is made up entirely of old information, pointing backward to remind readers of the old information summarized in the two previous paragraphs.

He does similar work with some adverbial clauses that introduce sentences. For example, in the first section of the essay, Alexander writes: "Even early research, which has largely been forgotten, provided evidence that the availability of certain chemicals that have been in soil for some time is less than freshly added chemicals . . ." (332). He then begins the next sentence with an adverbial clause: "Although the early findings and their importance have been obscured with the passage of time . . ." (332–33). This clause conveys mainly old information, referring to the "early research, which has . . . been forgotten. . . ."

Finally, at the end of this essay Alexander includes a short section that he labels "Relevance." The first sentence of this section reads as follows: "Because exposure to persistent compounds is overestimated by currently used chemical methods, the risk is likewise being overestimated" (337). Appearing where it does, this sentence is made up entirely of old information; everything in this sentence has come up earlier in the essay. In fact, most of the information in the section labeled "Relevance" is old. This section summarizes the major claims in Alexander's overall presentation.

You might worry that some readers could find these sentences repetitious, or wonder why anyone should be asked to read a sentence that doesn't add something new.

Because his argument is based on extensive and complex details, Alexander cannot afford to allow his readers to forget all the accumulated information. Readers' memory is critical for the success of the argument, so frequent reminders are necessary. And the upshot of this argument—that we might not have to invest time and money in cleaning up some toxic waste sites—is important and even startling. If he is right in his argument, then we are probably wasting time and money trying to clean up some toxic sites. If he is wrong, the results of following his advice could well be disease, deformity, and death.

In Your Own Writing . . .

- When you revise your writing, pay attention to how you use old and new information.
- Use old information in your sentence subjects to "package" information that you've already provided.
- Include old information in introductory phrases and clauses to contextualize new information.
- Put new information in the predicates of your sentences.
- When you want to help the reader make connections among topics, use entire sentences that include old information. Use entire sentences to help the reader connect new information to the argument you're building.

STUDENT WRITING

INTRODUCTION

by Arianne Folkema, chemistry major

The Assignment. My class was asked to conduct original research (in other words, no one else had previously determined the answers to the questions I was researching) and write a research report. The report was supposed to be similar to a published research report. To justify the validity of the questions I chose to research, my report's introduction had to summarize what was already known about the topic. My introduction also had to define the questions I was trying to answer. That is a lot like a review essay: first summarize what's known, then ask the "what next?" question.

The Content. My report is on the bioremediation of pentachlorophenol (PCP)—the use of live organisms to clean up ("bioremediate") sites contaminated by PCP, a toxic compound that was formerly used as an industrial wood preservative and is now a banned substance. The argument in my introduction follows this outline: (1) PCP is a toxic compound; (2) research has proven that PCP can be degraded by some microbes (bacteria and fungi) occurring naturally in the environment; (3) very little is known about PCP degradation by a microbe called *M. chlorophenolicum* PCP-1; (4) what little is known about PCP degradation by *M. chlorophenolicum* PCP-1 indicates that it degrades PCP in a different manner than do other microbes; (5) it would be beneficial to conduct further research on *M. chlorophenolicum* PCP-1 with the hope of learning if it could be more widely used to bioremediate PCP.

Learning to Write an Introduction to a Scientific Report: Lessons from Review Essays. My first exposure to original laboratory research was certainly a turning point in terms of understanding science in the "real world." I had taken many lab courses, following the protocols written in lab manuals: basic "recipe science" where the outcome is already known. I soon found out this was not the case in independent research, where the purpose is to first look at all the information available on a subject, and from there to figure out where the holes, the missing data, are . . . and to figure out ways to fill in those holes.

An introduction to a scientific report must be confident in its summary, and a scientific writer only gains confidence through thorough research, both in the lab and in published literature. So I began my project at the library. A search engine located abstracts for recently published articles containing information on everything from the metabolism of PCP by bacteria isolated from mushroom compost to observations about the degradation of pesticides by fermented sausages! The abstracts helped me to decide what publications were relevant to my project. My task was to summarize the published data clearly and use it to justify the argument that my research questions were worthwhile.

As I was drafting my paper and thinking about writing style, I took special care to be very specific and concise. One of the best ways for a scientist to be concise is to use figures, and the two figures in my introduction demonstrate the key points of the argument. Figure 1 shows a sequence of chemical changes (a pathway) that is known to break down PCP. Figure 2 shows a pathway with a question mark in the middle. That question mark was the key question for my research: How does the microbe *M. chlorophenolicum* PCP-1 break down PCP? When you see the question mark in the middle of that figure, you know just what my research is after.

When I first started reading professional research reports and reviews, I was amazed at how much research goes on, producing scientific knowledge and guiding scientists to new research. Research in science always leads to more research; scientists create change as part of the unending process of trying to understand the natural world.

Introduction to "Bioremediation of Pentachlorophenol"

Arianne Folkema

Bioremediation is the process of breaking down, or detoxifying, a toxic substance by biological organisms, in this case, the detoxification of the wood preservative, pentachlorophenol, or PCP.

Xenobiotic chemicals are foreign to biological systems, not naturally occurring.

A culture is the growth of bacteria under controlled conditions in a laboratory. The idea here is to grow large quantities of pollutant-degrading bacteria in the lab, and then to spread the bacteria on contaminated soil.

Natural bioremediation is carried out by organisms that are already present at a site prior to contamination.

Artificial bioremediation is carried out by organisms that are added to a site after it has been contaminated.

In situ means at the original site of contamination.

M. chlorophenolicum PCP-1. is the scientific name of a particular strain of bacteria.

Since the beginning of the industrial revolution, many xenobiotic chemicals have been introduced into the environment for a variety of purposes, with little attention paid to their potential long-term effects. The ecological consequences of some of these substances involve substantial damage to both aquatic and terrestrial ecosystems. In today's society, environmental, political, social and regulatory pressures demand that the use of xenobiotics be carefully monitored and that past mistakes be remedied. One technique that holds unique promise is bioremediation—the use of live organisms to clean up contaminated sites. One common technique for bioremediation is the culture of select bacteria that have the ability to break down industrial waste components. These bacteria are then added to contaminated soil.

Pentachlorophenol (PCP) is one example of a xenobiotic compound that can be bioremediated. PCP was initially produced in the 1930s for use as an industrial wood preservative and was mass-produced for this purpose, leading to the production of 45 million pounds in 1983 alone (1). The use of PCP was banned for commercial purposes in 1987 due to its extreme toxicity, which is known to damage the lungs, liver, kidney, gastrointestinal tract, nervous system, and immune system. PCP is currently listed as a priority pollutant by the US Environmental Protection Agency (EPA) (2). Fortunately, in contaminated sites where PCP had previously been used, it has been discovered that there are a number of microbes that have the unique capability to degrade PCP into less toxic substances.

There are numerous reports of the attempted bioremediation of PCP-contaminated sites. One example of natural bioremediation on an actual field site was witnessed in contaminated groundwater near sawmills in Finland, which were reported to contain up to 190mg of chlorophenols, including PCP, per liter of water. Upon study of the site, a variety of chlorophenol-degrading bacteria were isolated and characterized (3). Reports of successful artificial bioremediation (in which cultured bacteria are added to a contaminated site) are scarce, however, due to the compromised survival of bacteria *in situ*. This is illustrated by an attempt to clean up contaminated soils via the introduction of *Mycobacterium chlorophenolicum* PCP-1, a bacterium known to degrade PCP, directly to PCP-contaminated soil. In this field study, PCP degradation was observed to be 5 mg of PCP per kg of soil during the first two weeks after inoculation. However, this was only a slight improvement over the rate of PCP degradation by indigenous bacteria (2). This poor performance is possibly due to the method of inoculation, the soil properties, and/or the presence of toxic contaminants other than PCP in the soil. Additional studies have been carried out in more controlled settings such as bioreactors (vats in which microbes are grown in the presence of the compounds they metabolize), where soil properties and the presence of contaminants are not likely to be an issue. For example, the fungus *Panus tigrinus* was introduced to a mixture of chlorinated phenols at 500mg/L in a 72L bioreactor and was reported to have completely removed the PCP after three weeks (4).

Due to their potential (although often inefficient) bioremediation capabilities, research has been performed on a variety of PCP-degrading microbes. These include *Sphingobium chlorophenolicum* (4), a bacterium, and *Phanerochaete chrysosporium* (5), a fungus, on which thorough research has been done and for which the pathway of PCP degradation is known.

Figure 1 is a schematic diagram showing the chemical structures of PCP and the product of each reaction in the PCP metabolic pathways for *S. chlorophenolicum* and *P. chrysosporium*. Each of the chemical structures after PCP represents an intermediate in the pathway. The important thing to notice here is the minor differences between the structures. In the first reaction, we see that the chlorine atom (Cl) at the bottom of the molecule is removed and replaced by a hydroxyl group (OH). In the second reaction, the chlorine atom on the lower-left side of the molecule is replaced by a hydrogen atom. The last part of the pathway is not well understood, so after the fourth structure two arrows are shown to indicate multiple reactions leading to CO_2 (carbon dioxide).

> Inoculation is the introduction of bacteria to a medium; soil, in this case.

> Indigeneous means living naturally in a particular area.

> During metabolism, organisms break down compounds via a series of reactions to form the final product (often carbon dioxide). The set of reactions, with the accompanying intermediate compounds, is called a metabolic pathway. Figure 1 visualizes this concept.

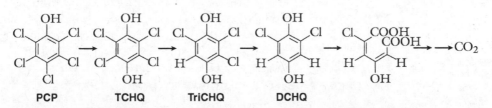

Figure 1 PCP Degradation Pathway for *S. chlorophenolicum* and *P. chrysosporium*.

The PCP degradation pathway for *S. chlorophenolicum* and *P. chrysosporium* is known to proceed through the intermediates TCHQ, TriCHQ, and DCHQ via a series of hydroxylations and reductive dehalogenations. PCP = pentachlorophenol; TCHQ = tetrachlorohydroquinone, TriCHQ = trichlorohydroquinone; DCHQ = dichlorohydroquinone.

When molecules containing chlorine are degraded by microbes, generally only one chlorine atom is removed in each reaction of the pathway. So, when PCP, which contains five chlorines, is degraded, we expect there to be intermediates with four, three, two, and one chlorine atoms. The intermediate containing three chlorines in the PCP metabolic pathway utilized by *M. chlorophenolicum* PCP-1 was not identified in the experiment described here.

Look at the question mark in the third stage of the pathway; that question was the reason for my research. To understand this figure, compare each structure to the one that appears before it in the pathway. Notice that in some reactions Cl is replaced by OH, and in others Cl is replaced by H.

Less research has been conducted on another bacterium with the potential to bioremediate PCP; *Mycobacterium chlorophenolicum* PCP-1. Fewer concrete details are known about its metabolism of PCP, although it is clear that PCP metabolism by *M. chlorophenolicum* PCP-1 differs significantly from PCP metabolism by other organisms. The first step in PCP degradation by *M. chlorophenolicum* PCP-1, is the hydroxylation of PCP to form TCHQ, which is also the case for *S. chlorophenolicum* and *P. chrysosporium* (6). The identity of the second intermediate in PCP degradation by *M. chlorophenolicum* is unknown.

Fig. 2 illustrates that the second reaction in this pathway could involve either the replacement of a chlorine atom (Cl) by a hydrogen atom (H—in the top pathway) or the replacement of a chlorine atom by a hydroxyl group (OH—bottom pathway) (7).

The purpose of my research was to characterize the degradation pathway of PCP by *M. chlorophenolicum* PCP-1: to determine the identity of the second intermediate in the pathway.

The characterization of the metabolic pathway and purification of the enzymes necessary for degradation of PCP is important because it provides information that can be used to further characterize the genes encoding the enzymes involved in PCP degradation. It may then be possible to clone those genes into more robust bacteria capable of growing at more rapid rates and surviving in harsher soil environments. These genetically engineered microbes may ultimately be useful in the improved bioremediation of PCP-contaminated sites.

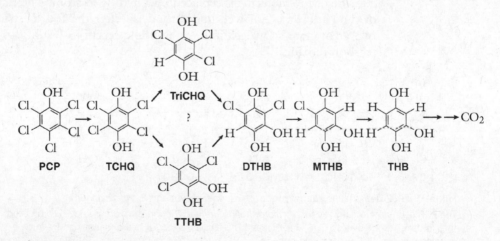

Figure 2   PCP Degradation by *Mycobacterium chlorophenolicum*

The PCP degradation pathway utilized by *M. chlorophenolicum PCP-1* is not completely defined and could either proceed through the intermediate TriCHQ or TTHB. PCP = pentachlorophenol; TCHQ = tetrachlorohydroquinone, TriCHQ = trichlorohydroquinone; TTHB = trichlorotrihydroxybenzene; DTHB = dichlorotrihydroxybenzene; MTHB = monochlorotrihydroxybenzene; THB = trihydroxybenzene.

References

1. *Pentachlorophenol Facts*. PANNA—Pesticide Action Network North America http://www.panna. org/resources/documents/factsPentachlorophenol.dv.html May, 2004.
2. Miethling, R. and U. Karlson. "Accelerated mineralization of pentachlorophenol in soil upon inoculation with *Mycobacterium chlorophenolicum* PCP1 and *Sphingomonas chlorophenolica* RA2." Appl. Environ. Microbiol. **1996,** *62:* 4361–66.
3. Mannisto, M. and M. Tiirola. "Diversity of chlorophenol-degrading bacteria isolated from contaminated boreal groundwater." *Arch. Microbiol.* **1999,** *171:* 189–197.
4. Leontievsky, A. A. and N. M. Myasoedova. "Adaptation of the white-rot basidiomycete *Panus tigrinus* for transformation of high concentrations of chlorophenols." *Appl. Microbiol. Biotechnol.* **2002,** *59:* 599–604.
5. Reddy, G. and M. Gold. "Purification and characterization of glutathione conjugate reductase: A component of the tetrachlorohydroquinone reductive dehalogenase system from *Phanerochaete chrysosporium.*" *Arch. Biochem. Biophys.* **2001,** *391:* 271–77.
6. Apajalahti, J. and M. Salkinoja-Salonen. "Dechlorination and *para*-hydroxylation of polychlorinated phenols by *Rhodococcus chlorophenolicus.*" *J. Bacteriol.* **1987,** *169:* 675–81.
7. Apajalahti, J. and M. Salkinoja-Salonen. "Complete dechlorination of tetrachlrohydroquinone by cell extracts of pentachlorophenol-induced *Rhodococcus chlorophenolicus.*" *J. Bacteriol.* **1987,** *169:* 5125–30.

Reading Responses

1. As Arianne Folkema notes in her introduction, students find themselves in an odd position when they write summaries of research: these are usually written by an expert in a field of research, not a novice. Compare the first three paragraphs of Folkema's essay with the first three paragraphs of Alexander's review (not counting Alexander's Abstract). List the similarities and the differences. For each difference, evaluate if it results from Folkema's status as a novice researcher.

2. Folkema typically includes more information about the research she's summarizing than Alexander does. What additional information does Folkema include? Who might value this information? Why is it/isn't it worth including?

3. If you were a professor of chemistry, would you require students to include a review of literature in their research reports? Provide a set of reasons to support your answer.

PUBLIC WRITING

INTRODUCTION

The publication of Rachel Carson's *Silent Spring* is often credited with launching the environmental movement. Carson, after earning a master's degree in zoology, wrote radio scripts for the U.S. Bureau of Fisheries, later becoming an aquatic biologist and then chief editor of publications for the bureau. She turned to full-time independent writing and, after four years of research for the book, published *Silent Spring* in 1962. Chemical companies tried to prevent its publication, and Carson was threatened with lawsuits and accused of being unprofessional, an "hysterical woman," and a communist. It became, nonetheless, an international bestseller.

Silent Spring begins with a three-page chapter entitled "A Fable for Tomorrow." The chapter's opening sentence, "There once was a town in the heart of America where all life seemed to live in harmony with its surroundings" draws readers into a story of an idyllic town that is beset by unimaginable biological horrors—birds and bees disappear, vegetation withers and dies. Carson concludes the chapter by telling us that no town had suffered all the blight that she visited upon her fictional town but that "every one of these disasters has actually happened somewhere." The final paragraph of the chapter reads, "What has already silenced the voices of spring in countless towns in America? This book is an attempt to explain."

The opening chapter tells us that Carson is offering a natural history—a history of nature assaulted by humans. It is very important to recognize that history is a kind of summary, here enlivened in skin and bone and bark and root. Through this recognition Carson's "review" of the environmental record enriches our sense of the vast usefulness of summary.

There are obvious differences between this piece and a scientific review. It is grounded in thorough research, but the references sit quietly offstage so as not to "burden the text with footnotes," as Carson explains. It is also passionate and personal (note language such as "fantastic," "menace," and "endless problems").

Yet the kinship to a scientific review is evident. The first sixteen chapters of the book summarize the evidence that pesticide use is damaging nature. The last chapter, "The Other Road," answers the "what next?" question. In it she discusses the benefits of biological control over pests, identifying several particular methods, each of which has now been the subject of scientific research. In other words, *Silent Spring* follows the form and purpose of a review essay, and it brought about the field-shaping results that review writers hope for.

Realms of the Soil
Rachel Carson

Chapter 5, *Silent Spring,* 1962

. . . The problem that concerns us here is one that has received little consideration: What happens to these incredibly numerous and vitally necessary inhabitants of the soil **[worms, microbes, and all life forms that inhabit the soil]** when poisonous chemicals are carried down into their world, either introduced directly as soil "sterilants" or borne on the rain that has picked up a lethal contamination as it filters through the leaf canopy of forest and orchard and cropland? Is it reasonable to suppose that we can apply a broadspectrum insecticide to kill the burrowing larval stages of a crop-destroying insect, for example, without also killing the "good" insects whose function may be the essential one of breaking down organic matter? Or can we use a nonspecific fungicide without also killing the fungi that inhabit the roots of many trees in a beneficial association that aids the tree in extracting nutrients from the soil?

The plain truth is that this critically important subject of the ecology of the soil has been largely neglected even by scientists and almost completely ignored by control men. Chemical control of insects seems to have proceeded on the assumption that the soil could and would sustain any amount of insult via the introduction of poisons without striking back. The very nature of the world of the soil has been largely ignored.

From the few studies that have been made, a picture of the impact of pesticides on the soil is slowly emerging. It is not surprising that the studies are not always in agreement, for soil types vary so enormously that what causes damage in one may be innocuous in another. Light sandy soils suffer far more heavily than humus types. Combinations of chemicals seem to do more harm than separate applications. Despite the varying results, enough solid evidence of harm is accumulating to cause apprehension on the part of many scientists.

Under some conditions, the chemical conversions and transformations that lie at the very heart of the living world are affected. Nitrification, which makes atmospheric nitrogen available to plants, is an example. The herbicide 2,4-D causes a temporary interruption of nitrification. In recent experiments in Florida, lindane, heptachlor, and BHC (benzene hexachloride) reduced nitrification after only two weeks in soil; BHC and DDT had significantly detrimental effects a year after treatment. In other experiments BHC, aldrin, lindane, heptachlor, and DDD all prevented nitrogen-fixing bacteria from forming the necessary root nodules on leguminous plants. A curious but beneficial relation between fungi and the roots of higher plants is seriously disrupted.

Sometimes the problem is one of upsetting that delicate balance of populations by which nature accomplishes far-reaching aims. Explosive increases in some kinds of soil organisms have occurred when others have been reduced by insecticides, disturbing the relation of predator to prey. Such changes could easily alter the metabolic activity of the soil and affect its productivity. They could also mean that potentially harmful organisms, formerly held in check, could escape from their natural controls and rise to pest status.

One of the most important things to remember about insecticides in soil is their long persistence, measured not in months but in years. Aldrin has been recovered after four years, both as traces and more abundantly as converted to dieldrin. Enough toxaphene remains in sandy soil ten years after its application to kill termites. Benzene hexachloride persists at least eleven years; heptachlor or a more toxic derived chemical, at least nine. Chlordane has been recovered twelve years after its application, in the amount of 15 per cent of the original quantity.

Seemingly moderate applications of insecticides over a period of years may build up fantastic quantities in soil. Since the chlorinated hydrocarbons are persistent and long-lasting, each application is merely added to the quantity remaining from the previous one. The old legend that "a pound of DDT to the acre is harmless" means nothing if spraying is repeated. Potato soils have been found to contain up to 15 pounds of DDT per acre, corn soils up to 19. A cranberry bog under study contained 34.5 pounds to the acre. Soils from apple orchards seem to reach the peak of contamination, with DDT accumulating at a rate that almost keeps pace with its rate of annual application. Even in a single season, with orchards sprayed four or more times, DDT residues may build up to peaks of 30 to 50 pounds to the acre; under trees, up to 113 pounds.

Arsenic provides a classic case of the virtually permanent poisoning of the soil. Although arsenic as a spray on growing tobacco has been largely replaced by the synthetic organic insecticides since the mid-'40s, *the arsenic content of cigarettes made from American-grown tobacco increased more than 300 per cent* between the years 1932 and 1952. Later studies have revealed increases of as much as 600 per cent. Dr. Henry S. Satterlee, an authority on arsenic toxicology, says that although organic insecticides have been largely substituted for arsenic, the tobacco plants continue to pick up the old poison, for the soils of tobacco plantations are now thoroughly impregnated with residues of a heavy and relatively insoluble poison, arsenate of lead. This will continue to release arsenic in soluble form. The soil of a large proportion of the land planted to tobacco has been subjected to "cumulative and well-nigh permanent poisoning," according to Dr. Satterlee. Tobacco grown in the eastern Mediterranean countries where arsenical insecticides are not used has shown no such increase in arsenic content.

We are therefore confronted with a second problem. We must not only be concerned with what is happening to the soil; we must wonder to what extent insecticides are absorbed from contaminated soils and introduced into plant tissues. Much depends on the type of soil, the crop, and the nature and concentration of the insecticides. Soil high in organic matter releases smaller quantities of poisons than others. Carrots absorb more insecticide than any other crop studied; if the chemical used happens to be lindane, carrots actually accumulate higher concentrations than are present in the soil. In the future it may become necessary to analyze soils for insecticides before planting certain food crops. Otherwise even unsprayed crops may take up enough insecticide merely from the soil to render them unfit for market.

This very sort of contamination has created endless problems for at least one leading manufacturer of baby foods who has been unwilling to buy any fruits or vegetables on which toxic insecticides have been used. The chemical that caused him the most trouble was benzene hexachloride (BHC), which is taken up by the roots and tubers of plants, advertising its presence by a musty taste and odor. Sweet potatoes grown on California fields where BHC had been used two years earlier contained residues and had to be rejected. In one year, in which the firm had contracted in South Carolina for its total requirements of sweet potatoes, so large a proportion of the acreage was found to be contaminated that the company was forced to buy in the open market at a considerable financial loss. Over the years a variety of fruits and vegetables, grown in various states, have had to be rejected. The most stubborn problems were concerned with peanuts. In the southern states peanuts are usually grown in rotation with cotton, on which BHC is extensively used. Peanuts grown later in this soil, pick up considerable amounts of the insecticide. Actually, only a trace is enough to incorporate the telltale musty odor and taste. The chemical penetrates the nuts and cannot be removed. Processing, far from removing the mustiness, sometimes accentuates it. The only course open to a manufacturer determined to exclude BHC residues is to reject all produce treated with the chemical or grown on soils contaminated with it.

Sometimes the menace is to the crop itself—a menace that remains as long as the insecticide contamination is in the soil. Some insecticides affect sensitive plants such as beans, wheat, barley, or rye, retarding root development or depressing growth of seedlings. The experience of the hop growers in Washington and Idaho is an example.

During the spring of 1955 many of these growers undertook a large-scale program to control the strawberry root weevil, whose larvae had become abundant on the roots of the hops. On the advice of agricultural experts and insecticide manufacturers, they chose heptachlor as the control agent. Within a year after the heptachlor was applied, the vines in the treated yards were wilting and dying. In the untreated fields there was no trouble; the damage stopped at the border between treated and untreated fields. The hills were replanted at great expense, but in another year the new roots, too, were found to be dead. Four years later the soil still contained heptachlor, and scientists were unable to predict how long it would remain poisonous, or to recommend any procedure for correcting the condition. The federal Department of Agriculture, which as late as March 1959 found itself in the anomalous position of declaring heptachlor to be acceptable for use on hops in the form of a soil treatment, belatedly withdrew its registration for such use. Meanwhile, the hop growers sought what redress they could in the courts.

As applications of pesticides continue and the virtually indestructible residues continue to build up in the soil, it is almost certain that we are heading for trouble. This was the consensus of a group of specialists who met at Syracuse University in 1960 to discuss the ecology of the soil. These men summed up the hazards of using "such potent and little understood tools" as chemicals and radiation: "A few false moves on the part of man may result in destruction of soil productivity and the arthropods may well take over."

Reading Responses

1. Carson opens the preceding excerpt from her chapter with three questions. Interestingly, each question serves a distinct function in her essay. Describe how each question relates to the rest of the chapter.

2. When Carson discusses particular topics, she describes first old ways of thinking and then new research. Choose one paragraph that contains both old and new information. Analyze the purpose of old information in this paragraph. What "work" does it do?

3. Carson's chapter summarizes previous scientific research just as Alexander's does. But Carson is writing to a general audience, not other experts in the field. Compare Alexander's style with Carson's. What stylistic strategies does Carson use to make her essay more readable?

MORE WRITING IN CHEMISTRY

INTRODUCTION

This reading reviews scientific data regarding the types of exposure, and the consequences of that exposure, caused by the attack on the World Trade Center. The essay is written by a large team of scientists from seven institutions. The intended audience is toxicologists and other scientists who study human exposure to toxins, and, to a lesser extent, physicians who are interested in environmental exposure to toxins. Phillip Landrigan, the lead author of the team, is an award-winning physician and scholar, a regular on TV's *Good Morning America* show, and author of over 500 scientific papers.

This review essay documents the types and amounts of toxins that were released into the atmosphere as a result of the disaster and the observed health consequences of human exposure to those toxins. Most of the scientific data regarding the types and amounts of toxins produced during the disaster has been omitted from this abridged version because it is highly technical and difficult for a nonexpert to follow. We include, however, studies of the health consequences of exposure to those toxins.

The review follows a logical argument: (1) the types and amounts of toxins released as a result of the disaster; (2) the health consequences observed; (3) the consequent need to continue monitoring the health of those exposed to the toxins. In other words, its structure is typical of a review essay, moving from a summary of what has been learned to a projection of what yet needs to be studied.

Health and Environmental Consequences of the World Trade Center Disaster

Philip J. Landrigan, Paul J. Lioy, George Thurston, Gertrud Berkowitz, L. C. Chen, Steven N. Chillrud, Stephen H. Gavett, Panos G. Georgopoulos, Alison S. Geyh, Stephen Levin, Frederica Perera, Stephen M. Rappaport, Christopher Small, and the NIEHS World Trade Center Working Group

Environmental Health Perspectives, 2004, *112*(6): 731–39

[Abstract]

The attack on the World Trade Center (WTC) created an acute environmental disaster of enormous magnitude. This study characterizes the environmental exposures resulting from destruction of the WTC and assesses their effects on health. Methods include ambient air sampling; analyses of outdoor and indoor settled dust; high-altitude imaging and modeling of the atmospheric plume; inhalation studies of WTC dust in mice; and clinical examinations, community surveys, and prospective epidemiologic studies [studies of diseases] of exposed populations. WTC dust was found to consist predominantly (95%) of coarse particles and contained pulverized cement, glass fibers, asbestos, lead, polycyclic aromatic hydrocarbons (PAHs), polychlorinated biphenyls (PCBs), and polychlorinated furans and dioxins [various poisons]. Airborne particulate levels were highest immediately after the attack and declined thereafter. Particulate levels decreased sharply with distance from the WTC. Dust pH was highly alkaline (pH 9.0–11.0). Mice exposed to WTC dust showed only moderate pulmonary inflammation but marked bronchial hyperreactivity. Evaluation of 10,116 firefighters showed exposure-related increases in cough and bronchial hyperreactivity. Evaluation of 183 cleanup workers showed new onset cough (33%), wheeze (18%), and phlegm production (24%). Increased frequency of new onset cough, wheeze, and shortness of breath were also observed in community residents. Follow-up of 182 pregnant women who were either inside or near the WTC on 11 September showed a 2-fold increase in small-for-gestational-age (SGA) infants **[that is, smaller in size than the average human fetus of the same age].** In summary, environmental exposures after the WTC disaster were associated with significant adverse effects on health. The high alkalinity of WTC dust produced bronchial hyperreactivity, persistent cough, and increased risk of asthma. Plausible causes of the observed increase in SGA infants include maternal exposures to PAH and particulates. Future risk of mesothelioma **[cancer of some internal membranes, in this case lung cancer]** may be increased, particularly among workers and volunteers exposed occupationally to asbestos. Continuing follow-up of all exposed populations is required to document the long-term consequences of the disaster. *Key words:* air pollution, airway hyperresponsiveness, asbestos, occupational lung disease, PM2.5, PM10, small for gestational age (SGA).

[Introduction] The destruction of the World Trade Center (WTC) on 11 September 2001 caused the largest acute environmental disaster that ever has befallen New York City (Claudio 2001; Landrigan 2001). The combustion of more than 90,000 L of jet fuel at temperatures above 1,000°C released a dense and intensely toxic atmospheric plume containing soot, metals, volatile organic compounds (VOCs), and hydrochloric acid. The collapse of the towers pulverized cement, glass, and building contents and generated thousands of tons of particulate matter (PM) composed of cement dust, glass fibers, asbestos, lead, polycyclic aromatic hydrocarbons (PAHs), polychlorinated biphenyls (PCBs), organochlorine pesticides, and polychlorinated furans and dioxins (Clark et al. 2003; Lioy et al. 2002; McGee et al. 2003). These materials dispersed over lower Manhattan, Brooklyn, and for miles beyond. They entered nearby office, school, and residential buildings. Much remained at the site to form Ground Zero, a six-story pile of smoking rubble that burned intermittently for more than 3 months.

Populations at greatest risk of exposure included firefighters, police, paramedics, other first responders Prezant et al. 2002; Centers for Disease Control and Prevention (CDC) 2002, and construction workers and volunteers who worked initially in rescue and recovery and then for many months cleared rubble at Ground Zero. Others at potentially elevated risk included workers who cleaned WTC dust from nearby buildings, women who were pregnant on 11 September and succeeding weeks in lower Manhattan and adjacent areas of Brooklyn, and community residents, especially the 3,000 children who resided within 1 km of the towers and the 5,500 who attended school there.

Previous studies have documented the acute traumatic consequences of the attacks on the WTC, most notably the occurrence of 2,726 deaths, including 343 deaths among firefighters and 60 among police officers (CDC 2002). Early clinical and epidemiologic assessments documented a high prevalence of respiratory symptoms, particularly, persistent cough in firefighters and rescue workers exposed to WTC dust (CDC 2002; Prezant et al. 2002). The prevalence of those symptoms was related to intensity and duration of smoke and dust exposure. Studies of the mental health consequences of the disaster have documented a high prevalence of posttraumatic stress disorder (PTSD) (Galea et al. 2002b; Fairbrother et al. 2003) and other psychological sequelae [disease consequences], including increased rates of drug and alcohol abuse (Boscarino et al. 2002; Galea et al. 2002a; Stuber et al. 2002; Vlahov et al. 2002a, 2002b).

In this report we summarize a comprehensive assessment of the impacts on human health and the environment of the chemical contaminants generated by destruction of the WTC. The work was undertaken by a consortium of six research centers supported by the National Institute of Environmental Health Sciences (NIEHS) in collaboration with the New York City Department of Health, the U.S. Environmental Protection Agency (EPA), and the CDC. . . .

Health Risk Assessment

Overview. Health risk assessments by the NIEHS Centers began by identifying populations at high risk of exposure to WTC contaminants and then undertaking clinical and epidemiologic studies within these groups (Landrigan 2001). Future analyses will seek to relate health outcomes data to geocoded information on contaminant levels (McCurdy et al. 2000).

Firefighters. Firefighters were among the most heavily exposed populations. They also suffered the greatest loss of life of all occupational groups. In the first 24 hr after the attack on the WTC, 240 New York City firefighters sought emergency medical treatment; of these, 50 (20.8%) received treatment of acute respiratory symptoms caused by inhalation of airborne smoke and dust (Prezant et al. 2002; Spadafora 2002). Firefighters described walking through dense clouds of dust and smoke in the hours immediately after the attack, in which "the air was thick as soup" (CDC 2002).

Follow-up medical evaluation of 10,116 firefighters was conducted over the 6 months after the attack (Prezant et al. 2002). Persistent cough accompanied by other respiratory symptoms so severe as to require at least 4 weeks' leave of absence, termed "World Trade Center cough," was diagnosed in 332 firefighters (Chen and Thurston 2002; Scanlon 2002). Prevalence of WTC cough was related to intensity of smoke exposure, and occurred in 128 (8%) of 1,636 firefighters with a high level of exposure, in 187 (3%) of 6,958 with moderate exposure, and in 17 (1%) of 1,320 with low-level exposure (Figure 4). Among firefighters without WTC cough, bronchial hyperreactivity was present in 77 (23%) of those with a high level of exposure, and in 26 (8%) of those with moderate exposure (Prezant et al. 2002). One case of eosinophilic pneumonia was diagnosed in a firefighter (Beckett 2002; Rom et al. 2002). Induced sputum analysis of New York City firefighters showed increases in sputum PM [particulate matter: dust, fibers, etc.] levels as well as in neutrophil and eosinophil counts [white blood cell counts]. Those abnormalities were positively correlated with levels of exposure to WTC dust and combustion products, as well as with levels of PAHs in the bodies of firefighters (Edelman et al. 2003).

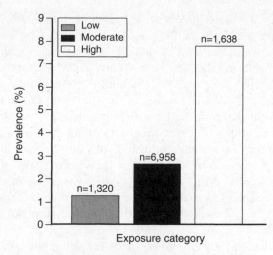

Figure 4 Prevalence of persistent cough in New York City firefighters exposed to smoke and dust from the WTC, September 2001 through March 2002.
Data from Prezant et al. (2002).

Cleanup and Recovery Workers. Many hundreds of workers were involved in clearing rubble and transporting it off-site. To assess the occupational exposures and health status of these workers, many of whom were truck drivers, a team from the Bloomberg School of Public Health at Johns Hopkins University and the Mailman School of Public Health at Columbia University undertook area air monitoring, personal exposure assessment, and health studies.

Air monitoring was conducted in October 2001 and April 2002. It focused on PM, asbestos, and VOCs. Monitoring was conducted across both day and night shifts, 7 days/week. Personal monitoring was conducted for 69 truck drivers. A total of 458 personal and area air samples were collected.

In October 2001, the highest concentrations of total dust were found at the debris pile (median, 1,603 μ_g/m^3 [**micrograms per cubic meter of air**]). Total dust levels on the pile in October were approximately five times higher than at the perimeter. By April 2002, total dust concentrations of the site had become significantly lower and were more uniformly distributed. In October 2001, median personal particulate exposure was 323.7 μ_g/m^3. By April 2002, median exposure had fallen to 137.7 μ_g/m^3. Airborne asbestos concentrations were found to be generally low. The fibers detected were mostly very short. Concentrations of VOCs were generally low. . . .

Among the 183 workers surveyed, a high proportion (32.8%) reported experiencing cough that began after the start of employment at the WTC site; 24.0% reported new onset of phlegm production; and 17.5% reported new onset of wheeze. Approximately half of all workers reported that they had experienced at least one new symptom since they had begun working at the WTC site. . . .

Community Residents. To assess prevalence of new-onset respiratory symptoms after 11 September 2001 among previously healthy persons in lower Manhattan as well as in residents with preexisting asthma, a team from NYU Medical Center in collaboration with the New York State Department of Health and the New York Academy of Medicine conducted a clinical and epidemiologic survey (Reibman et al. 2003). Symptoms were assessed by questionnaire, and pulmonary function was evaluated in a subset of the study population by standard screening spirometry [**a method for determining lung air capacity**].

A total of 2,166 residents of lower Manhattan living within a 1.6-km radius of the WTC were enrolled in this survey and compared with 200 persons living 1.6–8.0 km distant. Spirometry was performed in 52 residents. Preliminary data indicate that previously healthy persons living near Ground Zero had a greater increase in prevalence of respiratory symptoms after 11 September than did more distant residents. These symptoms were predominantly cough, wheeze, and shortness of breath. Symptoms were not associated with abnormal screening spirometry.

Preexisting asthmatic residents in the exposed area also reported a higher prevalence of respiratory symptoms after 11 September. They also reported an increased use of asthma medication relative to controls. . . .

Pregnant Women and their Offspring. Many pregnant women were either working in the WTC or working or residing in the communities of lower Manhattan on 11 September 2001. To assess pregnancy outcomes in these women and impacts on their infants, teams from the Mount Sinai School of Public Health of Columbia University established complementary prospective epidemiologic cohort studies. . . .

Pregnancy Outcomes. In the Mount Sinai cohort, no significant differences were found between the groups in mean gestational age or mean birth weight. There were no significant differences in frequency of preterm births (< 37 weeks of gestation) or in incidence of low birth weight (Table 2) (Berkowitz et al. 2003).

However, the Mount Sinai WTC cohort had a 2-fold increased risk of small-for-gestational-age (SGA) infants, defined as infants with a birth weight below the 10th percentile for gestational age in the nomogram of Brenner et al. (1976) (Table 2). This statistically significant difference was still evident after controlling for relevant covariates and potential confounders, including maternal age, parity, race/ethnicity, sex of the infant, and maternal smoking

Table 2   Pregnancy outcomes in relation to the attack on the WTC, September 2001 through June 2002

	WTC group	Control group	p-Value
No.	187	2,367	—
Mean gestational age (weeks)	39.1	39.0	0.55
Mean birth weight (g)	3,203	3,267	0.14
Frequency of preterm birth (%)	9.9	9.2	0.76
Frequency of low birth weight (%)	8.2	6.8	0.47
Frequency of SGA infants (%)	8.2	3.8	<0.01

Data from Berkowitz et al. (2003).

history. No significant difference in the frequency of SGA infants was observed according to the trimester of pregnancy on 11 September. No associations were evident between symptoms of posttraumatic stress, based on the PTSD Checklist (Schlenger et al. 2002), and frequency of preterm birth, low birth weight, or SGA infants.

Discussion

This report presents the most comprehensive summary to date of the environmental exposures resulting from the attack on the WTC and of their effects on human health. Our main focus was on chemical exposures. Our findings complement earlier reports describing the acute physical consequences of the disaster (CDC 2002; Prezant et al. 2002) and its psychological impacts (Boscarino et al. 2002; Fairbrother et al. 2003; Galea et al. 2002a, 2002b; Stuber et al. 2002; Vlahov et al. 2002a, 2002b).

Our assessments show that exposures to chemical contaminants were not uniform in New York after 11 September (Clark et al. 2003; Lioy et al. 2002; McGee et al. 2003; Offenberg et al. 2003). Instead, there were sharp gradients by time after the attack and by distance from Ground Zero (Table 1). [**Table 1 appears here for the first time because**

Table 1   Sequence of environmental exposures after the attack on the WTC, September through December 2001

Time period	Predominant sources of pollution	Airborne pollutants
First 12 hr after collapse (11 September 2001)	Burning jet fuel	Combustion products: gaseous and particulate
	Fires	Evaporating gases from the collapse of towers
	Collapse of the Twin Towers	Coarse particles
Days 1 and 2	Burning jet fuel	Combustion products: gaseous and particulate
	Resuspension of settled dust/smoke	Gases evaporating from piles
		Resuspended coarse particles
Days 3–13	Smoldering fires	Combustion products: gaseous and particulate
	Resuspension of settled dust/smoke	Coarse particle resuspension
		Diesel exhaust
Day 14 through 20 December 2001	Smoldering fires with occasional flareups	Combustion products: gases and particulates
	Removal of debris by trucks and other heavy equipment	Diesel exhaust

Data from Lioy et al. (2002).

in the published review it was part of a section that we deleted in this abridged version of the essay.] In the first few hours, extremely heavy exposures to high levels of dust and smoke as well as to gaseous products of combustion predominated. This pattern continued for the next 2 days, when there occurred rapid decline of smoke and dust levels and continuing decline in levels of combustion products as jet fuel and flammable building contents were consumed. A large fraction of the outdoor dust was eliminated over the first weekend after the disaster by rain that fell on Friday, 14 September, and by the U.S. EPA's cleanup of the Wall Street area. Over the next several weeks, airborne particulate levels in lower Manhattan continued to decline but rose intermittently at night and when the air was still. Transient increases were noted also when the pile was disturbed and fires flared. Diesel exhaust became an important contaminant with the arrival on site of scores of cranes, heavy trucks, and other construction equipment. For weeks, an acrid cloud hung over lower Manhattan and areas of Brooklyn until the fires were finally extinguished on 20 December.

Asbestos was of great concern to the public in New York City and to government agencies after 11 September. Asbestos, principally chrysotile, was used in the early 1970s in construction of the WTC as fireproofing up to the 40th floor of the North Tower (Nicholson et al. 1971; Reitze et al. 1972). Asbestos was not used beyond that point because of the recognition of its hazard and its replacement in the remainder of the construction with nonasbestiform fireproofing materials. Although some of this asbestos had been removed over the preceding 30 years, hundreds of tons remained on 11 September 2001 and were blasted free. Ambient air samples showed that asbestos exposures were initially elevated but fell to within U.S. EPA standards after the first few days (U.S. EPA 2004). Asbestos was found in settled dust at Ground Zero in concentrations ranging from 0.8 to 3.0% (Lioy et al. 2002). Asbestos was found in dust in nearby apartments, sometimes at higher levels than in the outside environment (Lioy et al. 2002).

Airborne lead levels were elevated in the first days after 11 September, but never highly. There is little indication that ambient air lead exposures posed substantial health risks to the population of lower Manhattan (U.S. EPA 2004).

Airborne dioxin levels were elevated substantially above normal urban background levels in the initial days after 11 September. The U.S. EPA's initial risk analysis suggests that these elevations did not result in a significant elevation in cancer or non-cancer risk (U.S. EPA 2003). Further follow-up of exposed populations will be required to evaluate the accuracy of that assessment.

Risks to health were determined by the timing, duration, and chemical composition of exposures as well as by proximity to Ground Zero. Firefighters, police, and other first responders sustained heaviest initial exposures. Studies of firefighters confirmed the presence of a positive relationship between intensity and duration of exposure and severity of pulmonary effects (Figure 4) (Prezant et al. 2002) as well as of PM levels in sputum. Prolonged exposures occurred among firefighters and other public safety personnel who remained at Ground Zero as well as among construction workers, volunteers, and workers removing rubble (Levin et al. 2002; Lippy 2002). Workers cleaning nearby buildings may also have sustained potentially serious exposures (Malievskaya et al. 2002).

Health data from the study of rubble removal workers confirm that these workers, many of whom worked at Ground Zero for many months, had sustained clinically significant exposures to airborne irritants, resulting in symptoms consistent with upper and lower airway inflammation (Levin et al. 2002). To extend these initial studies, the team at Mount Sinai has initiated the World Trade Center Worker and Volunteer Medical Screening Program. This program, supported by NIOSH, has already examined more than 10,000 workers. These workers will be followed prospectively to assess long-term and delayed effects. . . .

Airborne exposures in the residential and business communities of lower Manhattan beyond Ground Zero were much lower than those sustained by workers (U.S. EPA 2004). Daily average levels of fine particulate pollution in these communities were generally within U.S. EPA limits when averaged over a 24-hr period. Higher short-term peaks were, however, observed especially at night and could have contributed to reported health effects, especially in susceptible populations such as children, the elderly, and persons with respiratory or cardiac disease. Indoor exposures to resuspended dust may have added to total exposures (Lioy et al. 2002). Residents in these communities reported an increased frequency of new-onset pulmonary symptoms (Reibman et al. 2003) but had no abnormalities on pulmonary function testing. These findings are consistent with the observed gradient of exposures. . . .

Important questions about possible future risks to health of persons exposed to contaminants from the WTC remain unanswered:

- Will pulmonary disease persist in workers exposed to dust, especially in those who sustained very heavy exposures in the first days after 11 September and those with prolonged exposures?
- Will an increased incidence of mesothelioma result from exposures to asbestos? All types of asbestos fibers have been shown in laboratory as well as clinical studies to be capable of causing mesothelioma (Nicholson and Landrigan 1996). Pathologic studies have found short chrysotile fibers, the predominant type of fiber in WTC dust, to be the predominant fiber in mesothelioma tissue (Dodson et al. 1991; LeBouffant et al. 1973; Suzuki and Yuen 2002). Mesothelioma has been reported in persons with relatively low-dose, nonoccupational exposure to asbestos (Anderson 1982; Camus et al. 1998; Magnani et al. 2001). The greatest future risk of mesothelioma would appear to exist among first responders who were enveloped in the cloud of dust, other workers employed directly at Ground Zero, and workers employed in cleaning asbestos-laden dust from contaminated buildings. The risk of mesothelioma to residents of lower Manhattan must be considered to be extremely low but may still be elevated above background.
- Will exposure to airborne dioxin in lower Manhattan in the days and weeks after 11 September increase risk of cancer, diabetes, or other chronic disease (Kogevinas 2001)?
- Will the increased frequency of SGA observed in babies born to women who were within or near the WTC on 11 September result in long-term adverse effects on growth or development (Berkowitz et al. 2003)?

Full elucidation of these and other questions concerning the long-term and delayed health effects of exposures resulting from the attack on the WTC will require continuing, prospective, multiyear clinical and epidemiologic follow-up and further refinement of exposure assessments. That work is under way.

References

Beckett WS. 2002. A New York City firefighter overwhelmed by World Trade Center dust. *Am J Respir Crit Care Med* 166:785–6.

Berkowitz GS, Wolff MS, Janevic TM, Holzman IR, Yehuda R, Landrigan PJ. 2003. The World Trade Center disaster and intrauterine growth restriction [Letter]. *JAMA* 290:595–6.

Boscarino JA, Galea S, Ahern J, Resnick H, Vlahov D. 2002. Utilization of mental health services following the September 11th terrorist attacks in Manhattan, New York City. *Int J Emerg Ment Health* 4:143–55.

Brenner WE, Edelman DA, Hendricks CH. 1976. A standard of fetal growth for the United States of America. *Am J Obstet Gynecol* 126:55–64

CDC (Centers for Disease Control and Prevention). 2002. Injuries and illnesses among New York City Fire Department rescue workers after responding to the World Trade Center attacks. *Morbid Mortal Wkly Rep* 51(special issue):1–5.

Chen LC, Thurston G. 2002. World Trade Center cough. *Lancet* 360(suppl):S37–8.

Clark RN, Green RO, Swayze GA, Meeker G, Sutley S, Hoefen TM, et al. 2003. Environmental Studies of the World Trade Center Area after the September 11, 2001 Attack. Available: http://pubs.usgs.gov/of/2001/ofr-01-0429/ [accessed 25 March 2004].

Claudio L. 2001. Environmental aftermath. *Environ Health Perspect* 109:528–36.

Edelman P, Osterloh J, Pirkle J, Caudill SP, Grainger J, Jones R, et al. 2003. Biomonitoring of chemical exposure among New York City firefighters responding to the World Trade Center fire and collapse. *Environ Health Perspect* 111:1906–11.

Fairbrother G, Stuber J, Galea S, Fleischman AR, Pfefferbaum B. 2003. Posttraumatic stress reactions in New York City children after the September 11, 2001, terrorist attacks. *Ambul Pediatrics* 3:304–11.

Galea S, Ahern J, Resnick H, Kilpatrick D, Bucuvalas M, Gold J, et al. 2002a. Psychological sequelae of the September 11 terrorist attacks in New York City. *N Engl J Med* 346:982–7.

Galea S, Resnick H, Ahern J, Gold J, Bucuvalas M, Kilpatrick D, et al. 2002b. Posttraumatic stress disorder in Manhattan, New York City, after the September 11th terrorist attacks. *J Urban Health* 79:340–53.

Landrigan PJ. 2001. Health consequences of the 11 September 2001 attacks [Editorial]. *Environ Health Perspect* 109:A514–15.

Levin S. Herbert R, Skloot G, Szeinuk J, Teirstein A, Fischler D, et al. 2002. Health effects of World Trade Center site workers. *Am J Ind Med* 42:545–7.

Lioy PJ, Weisel CP, Millette JR, Eisenreich S, Vallero D, Offenberg J, et al. 2002. Characterization of the dust/smoke aerosol that settled east of the World Trade Center (WTC) in Lower Manhattan after the collapse of the WTC 11 September 2001. *Environ Health Perspect* 110:703–14.

Lippy BE. 2002. Safety and health of heavy equipment operators at Ground Zero. *Am J Ind Med* 42:539–42.

Malievskaya E, Rosenberg N, Markowitz S. 2002. Assessing the health of immigrant workers near Ground Zero: preliminary results of the World Trade Center Day Laborer Medical Monitoring Project. *Am J Ind Med* 42:548–9.

McGee JK, Chen LC, Cohen MD, Chee GR, Prophete CM, Haykal-Coates N, et al. 2003. Chemical analysis of World Trade Center fine particulate matter for use in toxiciological assessment. *Environ Health Perspect* 111:972–80.

Nicholson WJ, Rohl AN, Ferrand EF. 1971. Asbestos air pollution in New York City. In: *Proceedings of the Second International Clean Air Congress* (Englund HM, Beery WT, eds.) New York: Academic Press, 36–139.

Offenberg JH, Eisenreich SJ, Chen LC, Cohen MD, Chee G, Prophete C, et al. 2003. Persistent organic pollutants in the dusts that settled across lower Manhattan after September 11, 2001. *Environ Sci Technol* 37:502–8.

Prezant DJ, Weiden M, Banauch GI, McGuinness G, Rom WN, Aldrich TK. 2002. Cough and bronchial responsiveness in firefighters at the World Trade Center site. *N Engl J Med* 347:806–15.

Reibman J, Lin S, Matte T, Rogers L, Hoerning A, Hwang S, et al. 2003. Respiratory health of residents near the former World Trade Center: the WTC Residents Respiratory Health Survey [Abstract]. *Am J Respir Crit Care Med* 167:A335.

Reitze WB, Nicholson WJ, Holaday DA, Selikoff IJ. 1972. Application of sprayed inorganic fiber containing asbestos: Occupational health hazards. *Am Ind Hyg Assoc J* 33:178–91.

Rom WN, Weiden M, Garcia R, Yie TA, Vathesatogkit P, Tse DB, et al. 2002. Acute eosinophilic pneumonia in a New York City firefighter exposed to World Trade Center dust. *Am J Respir Crit Care Med* 166:797–800.

Scanlon MD. 2002. World Trade Center cough—a lingering legacy and a cautionary tale. *N Engl J Med* 347:840–2.

Schlenger WE, Caddell JM, Ebert L, Jordan BK, Rourke KM, Wilson D, et al. 2002. Psychological reactions to terrorist attacks: findings from the National Study of Americans' Reactions to September 11. *JAMA* 288:81–88.

Spadafora R. 2002. Firefighter safety and health issues at the Word Trade Center site. *Am J Ind Med* 42:532–38.

Stuber J, Fairbrother G, Galea S, Pfefferbaum B, Wilson-Genderson M, Vlahov D. 2002. Determinants of counseling for children in Manhattan after the September 11 attacks. *Psychiatr Serv* 53:815–22.

U.S. EPA. 2003. Fact Sheet: Release of Reports Related to the World Trade Center Disaster. Exposure and Human Health Evaluation of Airborne Pollution from the World Trade Center Disaster. Toxicological Effects of Fine Particulate Matter Derived from the Destruction of the World Trade Center. Washington, DC: U.S. Environmental Protection Agency.

U.S. EPA. 2004. EPA Response to September 11. Washington, DC: U.S. Environmental Protection Agency. Available: http://www.epa.gov/wtc/ [accessed 25 March 2004].

Vlahov D, Galea S, Frankel D. 2002a. New York City, 2001: reaction and response. *J Urban Health* 79:2–5.

Vlahov D, Galea S, Resnick H, Ahern J, Boscarino JA, Bucuvalas M, et al. 2002b. Increased use of cigarettes, alcohol, and marijuana among Manhattan, New York, residents after the September 11th terrorist attacks. *Am J Epidemiol* 155:988–96.

Reading Responses

1. A scientific review rarely evokes an emotional response from readers, but this review may do exactly that. Who might have an emotional response to this review? What kind of emotions might it call up? What about the review evokes emotion?

2. These researchers review the extensive effects of the WTC attacks on the environment and on human health. Which of these topics receives more attention? Develop a research method that will help you answer that question and apply it to the text. Describe your research method and display your results.

3. This research review is written by scientists for scientists, but the topic is of great concern to all Americans. Create a set of guidelines that could help these authors write about this information for a general audience. What can they keep the same? What must they change?

WRITING ASSIGNMENTS

Assignment 1

It's difficult to find the data to construct a summary of the environmental quality of your neighborhood from the EPA Web site. And yet this information is important for everyone who lives (or is considering living) in your neighborhood.

Your task is to create a summary of the environmental quality of your neighborhood. Consult the EPA's Web site as well as other sources of information: your local EPA office, other local governmental offices (city and state), nongovernmental organizations, and journalists' investigations. Introduce your summary with an overview that describes the general environmental quality for your neighborhood. Include information on several features of environmental quality as well as a list of sources of information on environmental quality in your area.

Assignment 2

Summaries matter. They do more than describe something—they set a path for future action. This is certainly true in the business world. For example, in Chapter 13, "Marketing," you will find a simple ad for a new office chair, but the simplicity is deceptive. The ad relies on summaries of research about the target audience—the people most likely to purchase the chair; and Steelcase, the company that designed the chair, considered this audience from the very beginning.

For this assignment, complete one of the following two tasks involving Scion, the line of cars that Toyota designed and marketed to appeal to the generation of most current college students—the "Millennials." Both require you to speculate about how summary information shaped Toyota's business practice. Before choosing one of these two tasks, search the Internet for summaries of "Millennials" (you can start with the terms "Millennials" and "summary"). List the features of your generation that these summaries identify.

1. Analyze the Toyota Scion's Web site, www.scion.com, looking for ways that the creators of this Web page may have tried to attract your generation. Report on your analysis, being sure to describe features of Millennials you found in the summaries as well as descriptions of specific parts of the Web page that seem to respond to these features of Millennials.

2. Analyze one of the Scion car models, looking for features of the car that designers may have included to appeal to Millennials. Report on your analysis, being sure to describe features of Millennials you found in the summaries as well as descriptions of aspects of the Scion car that seem to respond to these features of Millennials.

Assignment 3

Most academic and professional writers review previous research as part of their own writing. How they do this reviewing differs, though, across different academic disciplines and rhetorical situations. Your task for this assignment is to compare Martin Alexander's review essay with one from another discipline to create a guide for students who have to write summaries in a variety of disciplines. Select an academic discipline that is or might be your major, and ask a professor or a reference librarian for help determining the major scholarly journals in that field.

1. Locate the back issues of one of these journals in the library, and page through them, looking for a review essay. Once you have found an essay that primarily reviews previous research in an area, copy the essay.

2. Read the essay through once so that you understand its scope and the author's argument. Then, analyze how the author crafted the review. How does the author group research on similar topics? What information about the research does the author provide? How does the author arrange the essay? What is the rhetorical effect of that arrangement? What is the author's reason for reviewing this body of research?

3. Determine the most interesting or important points of similarity and contrast between the chemistry review essay and the review essay in your discipline.

As you begin drafting, consider how description and examples from both essays can help you detail the most effective strategies for writing reviews.

ENGLISH EDUCATION:
CHALLENGING CONVENTIONS

In 1987, E. D. Hirsch published *Cultural Literacy, What Every American Needs to Know,* a book that included a list of 5,000 pieces of "basic information" that people need to know to be able to "thrive in the modern world." The book became an instant best-seller—the subject of academic scrutiny, party games, and water-cooler arguments. Some thought that the book offered educational equality, others saw it as tradition-bound elitism, and many thought that instead of focusing on lists of must-know information, educators should focus on how students learn at all.

Here are some items from Hirsch's list.

1939–1945	genocide	Realpolitik
aficionado	Hoover Dam	utilitarianism
Chernobyl	incumbent	vicious circle
the Danube River	prime the pump	xenophobia
fetish	quadratic equation	zero-sum game

- Divide Hirsch's items into three lists: (1) items you know, (2) those that sound familiar but that you couldn't explain, and (3) those you don't know. Do you know more than you don't know?

- Recommend fifteen new items for Hirsch's list. What people, places, events, terms, and brief quotations are now "basic information" that every American should know? How did you pick these?

- What strategies would you use to teach these items to students? Would you require students to memorize information about each item on a list? Would you do something more creative? Explain why you think your teaching strategy would be effective.

PORTABLE RHETORICAL LESSON: CHALLENGING CONVENTIONS PURPOSEFULLY

Most days, you see your teachers doing things that you expect: giving a lecture with Power-Point, explaining answers to a homework assignment, leading a discussion. You can probably remember times, though, when a teacher surprised you. The questions about E. D. Hirsch's *Dictionary of Cultural Literacy* ask you to think about the how you might use traditional or innovative teaching methods. To answer the questions, you probably remembered former teachers, teachers who might be memorable because they tried new methods.

As a writer, when you contemplate using unusual strategies, you need to consider yourself as an **author.** You have to know what your audience thinks and expects of you—your character, personality, values. You should wonder if your persona allows you to experiment with unconventionality. You must trust your ability to come across to readers as creative rather than confusing, or worse, or mistaken. As the student writer in this chapter observes, an author must be sure that readers will recognize breaks with convention as "*choices* rather than *mistakes*." A sentence fragment, for example, could be read either as an effective way to add emphasis or as a grammatical error.

Challenging convention also gets writers thinking about **organization.** A writer can capture and keep a reader's attention by organizing a text so that it surprises and keeps the reader thinking about connections among parts of the writing. Victor Villanueva's writing (the first reading in this chapter) provides a good example.

In some ways, writers are also teachers; they want readers to understand and learn from them. And, like teachers, writers usually communicate by meeting readers' expectations—by following the conventions of a genre. Readers' previous experiences of genres (murder mystery, business memo, lab report, movie review, etc.) tell them what to expect. So it makes sense that writers usually take advantage of readers' expectations and follow conventions. If you fulfill enough of your readers' expectations so that they don't feel confused, you can use unconventionality to pique their curiosity. Using the **Portable Rhetorical Lesson** of this chapter—challenging conventions—catches readers' attention, helps them to remember what they've read, and propels them to mull over ideas long after they finish reading.

Challenging conventions is a powerful rhetorical tool, and you need to use it wisely. In fact, many students shy away from experimenting with conventions because they view it as too risky to their grades. But effective writers upend expectations when they have good reasons for doing so. The readings in this chapter show two different kinds of unconventionality: unconventional *content* and unconventional *form*.

Each of the readings contains unconventional content: new ideas and practices for teaching English. Ideas that create controversy. Each reading also uses minor breaks from formal written conventions. But it is the reading from Villanueva's book that combines the challenge of new ideas with challenges to formal conventions of written English: moving between first- and third-person references to the author, using sentence fragments, arranging the parts so they jump back and forth in time and topic, and so on.

The readings in this chapter show that effective writers use breaks with convention to:

- Call special attention to something—a key problem or question, the author's personal experience, a radical claim
- Jolt readers into alertness and into thinking critically about what they are reading
- Signal readers to expect unconventional ideas

One last note about breaking with convention: a little goes a long way. Most of Villanueva's sentences would escape the red pen of the pickiest of grammarians. He creates no new words or marks of punctuation, his pronouns have clear referents, and his sentences have subjects and verbs. And yet his writing is boldly innovative.

Observing the strong effects of a few breaks with formal conventions teaches you how strongly readers react to the unconventional. And that lesson should help you to decide when unconventionality might work for you.

WRITING IN THE DISCIPLINE

INTRODUCTION

by William J. Vande Kopple, Professor of English

Bootstraps: From an American Academic of Color is a scholarly argument about educational philosophy. It was written for English teachers, published by the National Council of Teachers of English. The author, Victor Villanueva, is a professor of composition and rhetoric at Washington State University and winner of several national awards for his teaching and research. *Bootstraps* was so influential that it is often assigned to students majoring in secondary English education.

Villanueva's final sentences in the section reprinted here capture well his fundamental purpose for writing: "We can do critical literacy. And what better to be critical of than the cultural norms contained in tradition? Start with what students know or have been told they ought to know. Allow and encourage a questioning of the norms. And maybe look to how things might be—and ought to be—changed." In other words, Villanueva aims to move readers to examine the social, economic, and political forces that they have always taken for granted within their culture and to ask how these forces might need to be altered in order to promote justice and equity.

You might be surprised by some aspects of the form of *Bootstraps*. Villanueva calls his book "a postmodern text." If you scan this reading, you will notice abrupt shifts in the organization. For example, Villanueva shifts from one time period to another; at one point readers learn about the autumn of 1984, while shortly thereafter they start reading about 1990. He also includes shifts in subject matter—leaping, for example, from a description of how he learned that he had been replaced as the director of a basic-writing program to some critical examination of E. D. Hirsch's *Cultural Literacy*. Further, Villanueva draws attention to his own experience in education by shifting his references to himself, sometimes referring to himself as "Victor," sometimes "he," and still other times "I"; in other parts of the book, he refers to himself as the "graduate student," the "new Teaching Assistant," "Victor the Curiosity," "Dr. V. the Deadbeat," and "Papi."

Running through the book, however, are five closely related lines of thought. In one line, Villanueva tells the story of his life, describing his successes and failures in teaching. In another line, he introduces readers to educational scholars who have affected his life. In a third line, he discusses theories of the social, economic, and political forces in the United States, especially as these forces affect persons of color. In yet another line, he connects the theoretical discussions to specific aspects of his own life. Finally, he includes several descriptions of classroom practices that he thinks will promote "critical dialogue within a cultural literacy."

I also believe that these pages from *Bootstraps* can help readers examine how they conventionally think about social, economic, and political forces. Too often, we evaluate these forces only in terms of our own experience ("Racism? Sure, when I was a kid there was a lot of trouble. But about half of the families in my neighborhood now are African-American. Racism is probably a thing of the past."). In *Bootstraps* Villanueva alerts us to how social, economic, and political forces actually affect other individuals' lives. Racism, for example, does not mean exactly the same thing for everyone. If we look closely, we will find a mosaic of responses to such forces as racism, materialism, and individualism.

In conveying this general message, Villanueva implicitly asks his readers to think like educators. We should learn humility and fight our tendency to see the entire world only in terms of our own experience. We should be eager to hear how others have been affected by powerful social forces. We should be willing to have our views of powerful social forces become more complex than we usually like them to be. And we should have the courage to evaluate theories about social forces on the basis of both our own and other individuals' experiences.

These emphases are important for everyone, not just for English teachers.

✓ Reading Tips

1. Be prepared to shift your reading speeds when Villanueva shifts his genres between narrative and analysis.
   - Narrative. You can read these sections at story pace. Underline the moments in the story that best illustrate the point Villanueva is making.
   - Analysis of theory. You will have to read these sections more slowly. Find definitions of unfamiliar terms, paraphrase complex ideas, and summarize Villanueva's main point in each analytical paragraph.
2. Find examples that show how the stories and analysis work together to forward the thesis.
3. Analyze challenges to conventions. Each time you notice Villanueva doing something unexpected, add a note in the margin that records:
   - The strategy Villanueva uses to challenge convention
   - The rhetorical purpose for that strategy
   - The way that the strategy helps you to better understand or engage his argument

Of Color, Classes, and Classrooms
Victor Villanueva

In *Bootstraps: From an American Academic of Color,* Urbana: NCTE, 1993.

Villanueva begins this chapter with a long fragment, throwing his readers into the middle of his description of a televised panel discussion. This use of a storyteller's rhetoric makes us feel personally involved from the very first sentence.

Hot, bright, stage lights blaring down on the four teachers and two parents seated in a circle before a TV camera. The six are about to speak on the cable network's public access channel.

Channing is the ring leader. He is a big man, large, round face with a shock of rumpled gray hair, a large belly pressing on a gray vest, not the rotund of the sedentary, but the large of the powerlifter. He is big, blustery, and brilliant: a polymath, well-versed in everything it seems, another who had traveled the class system: a childhood of unusual affluence, son of a government ambassador, an adulthood of unusual poverty.

There is Jolinda. She is lovely, thin, with shoulder-length auburn hair, sparse make-up. She has a quick, critical mind—decisive, un-flinching. A long-time interracial marriage and a racially mixed child to raise keeps her decidedly active politically, a hard-working Democrat for Jesse Jackson's Rainbow Coalition, a hard-working advocate for her children's school.

David Zank, goatee, beret, an administrator and a teacher at Jolinda's and Channing's and Victor's children's school. He administers an alternative public school. It's an elementary school, one not divided into traditional grades, though the students tend to group themselves into the younger, the older, the middle kids. It's a school that attracts children from all of the city's classes and races. Instead of a set curriculum, children decide on projects of interest, the teachers providing all that is necessary to carry out the projects: the mechanics, say, of building an airplane, lessons on aerodynamics, on the history of experiments in flight, and so on, though this ideal isn't always reached. Discipline is handled through "forum": students, teachers, and parents in a circle to discuss injustices. Injustices, not rules—there are no rules, really, but infringements on what is generally held to be socially acceptable behavior. Anyone can call for a forum. Issues are discussed. The school is democracy in action, not the usual contradiction of an authoritarian structure preaching democracy. Zank is an instrumental part of that school.

There are also two teachers from one of the more traditional public schools in the area. Their names are now forgotten, our being together limited to that one show. Channing had found them. Silver gray hair on both, off the neck, tastefully curled atop heads, the look of professional coiffeurs. They have stylish glasses, pleasant faces. Both are part of this discussion before the camera because they are upset by recent changes in their curriculum, changes imposed from above, from higher administration.

Villanueva lists some of his identities in the third person—as if he is joining his readers in observing himself from a distance.

And there is Victor, graduate student, parent.

Channing opens the discussion. At issue is a new curriculum the city has purchased from a major publishing house. It's a computerized package. Depending on how they perform on a standardized pretest, students are presented with a series of hierarchically ordered mastery tests. Versions of a mastery test are taken and retaken until a certain score is attained; then students are directed to the next test, which is taken, retaken again, until a certain score is reached; then onto the next, and so on. The guarantee of the package is that there will be a city-wide improvement on national standardized scores, a guarantee that will be made good, no doubt. But the teachers protest that all curricular decisions are thereby taken from them, that they will be able to do nothing but teach to tests.

Zank's school has annually refused to administer standardized tests on the grounds that even though they measure nothing but the ability to take tests they are too easily read as matters of intellectual ability by the students themselves. He tells the teachers to do the same as his school's teachers—refuse to take part. The teachers say that though they agree with Zank on principle, they cannot afford to jeopardize their jobs. They would not have the support of their principal, would not enjoy the support of Zank's teachers. Jolinda argues that their jobs are the education of children—matters of public responsibility more than personal security. Again, there is agreement on principle, but personal security is not confined to any one individual; there are families to care for. Victor suggests not teaching to the tests, but teaching test-taking. His life would have been easier, perhaps, if he had understood standardized test-taking and knew not to take what they actually measure (test-taking) seriously. Zank nods, saying "Paulo Freire kind of stuff."

Victor had never heard of Paulo Freire before Zank's comment. He reads *Pedagogy of the Oppressed*. The things written there make sense. He sees what has been working in his children's school: children believing in their humanity, willing and able to take social responsibility, even at the age of six. He sees the problem he has had with the school, despite being pleased in the main: "laissez-faire." Here's Freire:

After growing up in a poor family in Brazil, at a time when the ruling class oppressed the poor, Paulo Freire (1921–1997) was exiled. After his years in exile, he returned to Brazil to become Secretary of Education in Brazil's largest school district. His radical pedagogy, which calls for teachers and students to examine cultural practices to expose, critique, and change oppressive situations, has been adopted by numerous North American educators.

I cannot leave the students by themselves because I am trying to be a liberating educator. Laissez-faire! I cannot fall into laissez-faire. On the other hand, I cannot be authoritarian. I have to be radically democratic and responsible and directive. *Not* directive of the *students,* but directive of the process, the liberating teacher is not doing something to the students but with the students. (Shor and Freire 46)

To be "laissez-faire" is to interfere in the affairs of others as little as possible.

Students cannot be left to their own devices totally, yet they cannot be handed everything.

Fall 1984. Victor is placed in charge of the English department's basic-writing program. He is the best candidate for the job in a number of ways; his fields are rhetoric and composition; he is doing research that focuses on basic writing; he is of color in a program replete with students of color; and he is willing, as were the directors of the program before him, to undertake the job at teaching-assistant pay. Administration denies the color aspect. Tokenism, stereotyping—sensitive issues.

He institutes a Freire-like dimension to the curriculum. He does away with the focus on sentence-combining, adopts the autobiography of Carolina Maria deJesus, *Child of the Dark,* the story of a woman from the *favelas* of Brazil, where Freire had spent his adolescence, the likely nurturing ground for his pedagogy. Her diary presents a view from the eyes of a barely literate woman, her political awareness and the contradictions she embodies, her understanding of social stratification, and her desire for what she believes she cannot have, the social stigma she suffers in having to provide for her children by collecting trash, and the pride she nevertheless feels, the way she is labeled a Marxist by a local politician when she complains about her living conditions in a system she somehow believes in. It's the story of an American of color and of poverty set in Brazil. It is a story that the basic-writing students might well understand. And, because she is barely literate, the writing is such that the students can be critical of her language use, can gain confidence in their own abilities with literacy.

The basic-writing teachers seem to enjoy teaching the book. But the political is downplayed. Discussions turn on the cultural: "Tell me 'bout the ghetto and I'll tell you 'bout the 'burbs." Students enjoy the dialogue. But there seems to be no dialectic, no sustained probing into the conditions that relegate certain peoples to the ghettos and others to the 'burbs in disproportionate numbers. In some sense, this is a minor problem, outweighed by the students' being heard at all.

Still there are problems, not with the material but with the relations between students and teachers, the kinds of problems discussed by Lisa Delpit. Students are being graded on their courage more than on how others at a university or elsewhere might regard their writing. Disgruntled students complain that they have been lied to, that they thought they really were "A" or "B" writers, only to find that others consider them barely literate. Irate professors say that the university is no place for remedial courses. Victor convinces the higher administration that the basic-writing program is a cultural education, not remediation. The program survives, eventually acquiring a regular, permanent administrator.

But while Victor was still there, there were still the disgruntled and the irate to contend with. He prepares a memo that quotes Louis Faraq'an, a naive move. The memo notes that Faraq'an defines black power as the ability for black people to come to the table with their own food. The point is to have teachers stop proffering academic charity, no matter how well intentioned. Victor knew the pain of charity.

If an organization were to engage in "tokenism," it would offer just enough opportunities to minorities so that it would avoid criticism and perhaps even look good.

Favela is a term used commonly in Brazil to describe slums.

Lisa Delpit grew up on the "wrong side of the tracks" in Baton Rouge, LA, where she was among the first African Americans to integrate the Catholic schools. She has devoted her life to challenging the educational system. She argues that linguistic and cultural standards must be taught to African Americans and other minorities to empower these oppressed groups. Rather than just teaching to one cultural norm, though, Delpit says that teachers need to take a critical approach to the dominant culture, while also recognizing and drawing on the cultural strengths that all of their students bring to the classroom.

Louis Farrakhan (born 1933) currently serves as a leading Muslim thinker and teacher. He organizes groups for the political empowerment of black people in the U.S. and around the world.

He goes on a job interview. He returns to find a memo announcing his replacement for the coming academic year. He had not been consulted. The rationale was that he would surely get a job. But he remembered the teachers' argument in that television show. He had gone too far.

There must be a way to go about doing our jobs in some traditional sense and meeting some of the potential inherent in our jobs, the potential for social change, without inordinately risking those jobs. Utopianism within pragmatism; tradition and change.

When I think of tradition, I think of the literary critic turned compositionist, turned social critic—E. D. Hirsch. His *Cultural Literacy* is simplistic and politically dangerous, say his critics in English studies (e.g., Bizzell, Johnson, and Scholes). There is surely the sense that he's suggesting a return to halcyon days that never were, surely not wondrous bygone days for people of color, surely not for the poor. Hirsch is among those who believe that "multilingualism is contrary to our traditions and extremely unrealistic" (93). More myth than history. It is this mythic nostalgia that permeates his book that causes him to be read as advocating teaching a literary canon. He denies it (xiv). He says that he is advocating a national-cultural set of common assumptions to be learned through an understanding of national-cultural allusions, his list of "what literate Americans know," a list, he points out, containing relatively few references to literary works (146–215; xiv). But he apparently senses the superficiality, backing up his theory with references to broad reading (109, 23). What, then, to read? Seems like we're back to a canon.

And that canon has historically favored one gender and one race. That this is the case, says Hirsch, is an accident of history (106). He seems not to regard how that particular accident has had a high casualty count over time. And it keeps recurring—like the same fender-bender with the same car at the same intersection—time and again. But Hirsch does go on to argue that national-cultural allusions are subject to change, that as more women and people of color become literate, they will affect the norms. And there is something to this. There are more women in the canon nowadays, more people of color. But the changes are not proportionate to the accomplishments or the potentials of women or people of color, surely. And those who enter the canon tend to be those who are politically safe. We read Langston Hughes's "Theme for English B" more often than Hughes's more angry "The Negro Speaks of Rivers." We read Martin Luther King, Jr. but little of W. E. B. DuBois, Richard Rodriguez instead of Ernesto Galarza, Emily Dickinson more often than Virginia Woolf (see Aiken; West "Canon Formation"). Hirsch's hopes are for better test scores and for greater access to the middle class, not for making the class system more equitable.

For all that, there *is* something to cultural literacy. One has to know how to be heard if one is to be heard. Those who rail the loudest against

A professor and educational theorist, E. D. Hirsch (born 1928) is perhaps best known for his *Cultural Literacy: What Every American Needs to Know.* He's been accused of elitism for arguing that there is a single cultural literacy every student ought to learn.

Arguments about a canon, a list of books that everyone should read, have been very common in discussions of literature in the last several decades.

Note how Villanueva here—and elsewhere—strives to give opposing arguments the credit they deserve.

A "polemic" is a controversial argument, and "dialectic" is argument through an exchange of opposing ideas, so the point is that students should stretch themselves to see things from opposing points of view.

Antonio Gramsci (1891–1937). Villanueva refers to Gramsci's belief that the ruling ideology or culture must be resisted by alternative cultural perspectives, an ideal that has been embraced by many educators and political theorists.

"Ideological" means based on a fixed system of beliefs

Stanley Aronowitz is a proponent of radical social change, protesting the corporate nature of many educational institutions.

Henry Giroux is a leading critical theorist who has adopted Freire's notion of education as a process of uncovering political and cultural ideologies that will lead students and teachers to social activism. Here Villanueva shifts from the theoretical to the personal and familial.

"Tradition and change for changes in traditions" forms a key to Villanueva's argument: we need to recognize both the need for change and the fact of traditions. Only when we accept tradition and change can we achieve the long-term changes that will create future traditions.

cultural literacy can afford to. They already have it. How, then, to exploit it without being subsumed by it?

Critical literacy, like that espoused by Paulo Freire and others, will lead to change, we're told. And I agree with that too. But what are the students to be critical of? How do they come to know what to be critical of? Why not cultural literacy, the national culture? Play out the polemic; develop the dialectic.

One theorist who has seen the necessity for both the cultural and the critical is Antonio Gramsci. His theories will provide the focus of the next chapter. For now, it's enough just to mention that he was an advocate of teaching a national culture, of teaching the classics, of something that sounds a lot like cultural literacy. Yet Gramsci also added that the classics and the national-cultural should be taught in such a way as to expose what he called the folkloristic, the commonly accepted ways of the world, the things too often accepted as if they are a part of nature—in short, the ideological. This suggests to me that it is possible to provide what's needed for the commonly accepted notions of success but with a critical dimension that might foster social action among teachers and among students. This is what sociologist Stanley Aronowitz and educational theorist Henry Giroux call "the language of possibility" (138–62). This is likely what Freire alludes to when he writes of pedagogy that pits permanence with change (Pedagogy 72). I prefer "tradition" to "permanence," given Hirsch's observation that traditions can and do change. Tradition and change for changes in traditions.

In a way, the graduate course on classical rhetoric I teach lends itself best to Gramsci's ideas. We read Plato, Aristotle, Cicero, Quintilian, and others. And we discuss and write about the ways in which some of the things they espoused are still with us—things like censorship for children's better good; things like the only meaningful language should be on abstractions rather than concretes. Plato and the rhetoric of the constitution. We find the first-century idea of proper oratorical arrangement and discover the basis for the five-paragraph theme. We find Cicero writing of writing as a mode of learning and Quintilian writing of peer-group work. We look at how the ancients are still with us and question the degree to which they ought to be. Students gather something of a classical education, a matter of some prestige, and they develop a critical perspective.

Something of the same ideas can be adapted for undergraduates, secondary students, elementary students.

1990, Flagstaff: Victor and Carol's younger children attend the public school. The school district has adopted a literacy package from a major publishing house that explicitly discourages individual instruction. All the children perform their drills in unison, do their reading together—everybody, every time, getting 100 percent on everything.

This isn't a matter of collaboration. Just recitation. No talking to neighbors seated ten inches away; no looking at neighbors. The books contain color: drawings of kids with nappy hair or slant eyes, not caricatures, done respectfully; yet there is a single cultural norm being advanced—force-fed cultural literacy.

More than hints at racism start to crop up at home. The brown-skinned, curly haired five-year-old daughter asks whether an Indian woman (the largest number of people who are of color in the community) would care for a human baby if she found one. A human baby! Another daughter, seven at the time, considerably more immersed in this literacy package than the kindergartner, mentions in passing that she doesn't care for black people. She doesn't know any. And she fails to see her own sister's features, forgets the pictures of her aunt, on whom the West African comes out clearly.

Victor and Carol don't blame the school completely. Market forces have them living in a predominately white community, making for little exposure to the kind of cultural complexity Victor and Carol's older children had known in Seattle or that Victor had known as a child in New York. But even if the school was not completely to blame for the hints at racism Victor and Carol would now have to counter, there remained the school's blind acceptance of a reductive notion of cultural literacy, a presentation that did nothing to expose and glory in difference as well as similarity.

Home schooling becomes the only short-term (and economically viable) alternative. Victor and Carol expose the national-cultural, but with an eye to multiplicity. The seven-year-old reads Cinderella, for instance. But she doesn't just stop with the Disney version. She reads translations of the Grimm Brothers' version, Poirot's seventeenth-century French version, an older Italian version, an ancient Chinese version. They're readily available. Discussion concerns how different people, with different ways and living in different times, can see some of the same things differently. She writes her own Cinderella story, which inevitably includes characters and situations from her own life. Spelling comes from the words she's trying to use in her own writing. It has a context. Grammar comes from trying to make her stories sound like she wants them to.

Other subjects take a similar tact. For history and geography, for example, she reads stories of dragons from China and dragons of the middle ages and dragons of C. S. Lewis and even dragons of Homer. She writes dragon stories.

Oral proficiency more or less takes care of itself; no need to impose doggedly the standard dialect. Victor's dialect changed without his being overtly conscious of it. The Spanish accent that Sister Rhea Marie had long ago warned his parents about disappeared, as did much of the black dialect he had acquired on the block. The more he became

C. S. Lewis (1898–1963) is perhaps best known today for his *Chronicles of Narnia*.

exposed to written discourse, the more his speaking came to reflect that exposure. And exposure to different worldviews, even if written in one standard dialect, provided the critical perspective. Reading aloud would help hone speaking skills in the prestige dialect.

I take the Cinderella idea to high school and college. The only real difference in the high school and the college is that I have the college students look up and report on literary critics who write about fairy tales. They read people like Bruno Bettelheim, who comes up with crazy interpretations of Cinderella as going through Freudian puberty rites, or others who write about fairy tales and archetypes, or Plato and his notion that fairy tales should be used to indoctrinate children into proper attitudes about life and the gods. I have the students do research about the historical or cultural conditions which existed at the time and place of the various versions. They become exposed to academics and academic discourse using a kind of literature they know intimately. They feel comfortable being critical of the great authorities. With the junior high and high school kids I've visited on short stints, I have provided the histories and selected the critical analyses; otherwise, the assignments have been the same.

Students resist being critical of fairy tales. They want to say that fairy tales are simply diversions for children. And this is okay as a jumping-off point for discussion. Resistance is a good thing, an assertion of authority, an opening for dialogue (see Giroux). So it tends that through the dialogue some begin to question what else might be contained in those simple diversions. A student writes about Rosie the Riveter during World War Two, women not just entering male-dominated jobs, like business and medicine, but performing "man's work," physical labor—and doing well. Then she wonders at Disney's Cinderella, which promotes the house wench whose only hope for the future is to marry well. She wonders if Disney's version didn't help put Rosie's daughters "back in their place." Another writes about the Chinese version, about foot binding as a way to keep women in their place. She wonders if having Cinderella wear glass is a kind of modern foot binding. Another notices how Red Riding Hood's stories become more and more sexual as they approach the Victorian era. Another student: Is Jack and the Beanstalk a promotion of laissez-faire economics, get rich however you can? Is Robin Hood a proto-socialist? Students look at fairy tales and children's stories, and, in looking, begin to question the obvious and the natural, begin to question ideology.

Another way we look at ideology is by using Roland Barthes's little book *Mythologies*. The book contains a series of articles Barthes had written for a popular French magazine in the 1950s. Here, again, the idea works for high school and for college. The college students are asked to read and work with the theoretical essay at the end of the book,

Bruno Bettelheim (1903–1990) was a developmental psychologist who taught at the University of Chicago from 1944–1973 and who directed the Orthogenic School for children with emotional problems.

Roland Barthes (1915–1980) was a French structuralist-turned-poststructuralist critic who saw a text as "a fabric of quotations, resulting from a thousand sources of cultures." His book *Mythologies* (1957) contains 54 short pieces that demonstrate the presence of ideology and power structures in a variety of cultural situations.

where Barthes explains semiology. Others get the idea without the thick theoretical language. But I want to introduce the college students to the esoteric language of "pure" theory. They resist—vehemently. There was outright mutiny in one class.

But, generally, they do tend to respond well to the essays. In one essay, for example, Barthes explains the popularity of professional wrestling as a spectacle, as containing the elements of ancient Greek plays. Students get the notion of the spectacle. One student writes about how wrestling in the 1990s exploits stereotypes, exploits and promotes existing prejudices. A videotape of contemporary wrestling backs him up. In terms of ideological mythologies, another student, a retired policeman, writes about TV ads to help the hungry as maintaining the myth of American prosperity. The poor and hungry children are in Latin America or in Africa, never dying of hunger and disease in America's cardboard shacks. A sophisticated literary theory is introduced—traditional academic discourse—and critical questioning arises—a possibility for change.

The basic idea is to present the cultural in such a way as to have students question worldviews, become critical. Action presupposes a need for action. Questioning what is commonly accepted makes clear the need for action. Among the things that are commonly accepted is the canon.

Literature can be set up so as to create a dialectic between differing worldviews, between the national-cultural and the critical. Students read Hemingway, for example, as male, white, middle-class as they come, skeptical, perhaps, but no radical. Then they read Buchi Emecheta's *Double Yoke*—the story of a black African woman trying to get through different value systems, cultures, different ways of viewing the world, her struggles at gaining a college degree. Men and women are at issue, black and white; the tribal ways that the main character, Nko, was raised with against the modern Western ways of the university. White students confronting the college community, women, African American students, American Indian students—all have a portion of Nko's pains, and, since the story takes place far away, the defense of bigotries does not come up immediately, as it often does in more explicitly African American or Latino or American Indian literature (though it is good to have these prejudices present themselves). Nko and Hemingway's Nick Adams handle things differently, confront different obstacles. Ideologies peep out of the classroom discussions (which usually begin with moral questions: Nick's sense of responsibility, Nko's integrity). What is it about where the characters come from that causes them to behave and believe in different ways? We can look at Steinbeck and Ayn Rand, Rodriguez and Galarza, Louis L'Amour and Leslie Marmon Silko. Students sometimes shock themselves with their own prejudice—anti-color *and* anti-white.

> Here Villanueva uses the passive voice to describe this pedagogy: he avoids attributing the success of the class to the teacher, the students, or the texts. He reinforces his belief that collaborative critical engagement produces both greater understanding and the potential for change.

The students write about how they too must confront conflicts, and about the sources of those conflicts. These aren't always explained in grand cultural terms, but the cultural is always present, often coming out in discussions. They write autobiographies (or narratives if culturally uncomfortable with the autobiographic). The things they are to write about concern their own experiences, experiences that are tied to the things they are reading. Toward the end of the semester they are asked to downplay the autobiographical elements but keep them in mind. The autobiographical is an important assessment tool, even essential—always there, really. "[A]ll writing, in many different ways, is autobiographical," says Donald Murray, even "academic writing, writing to instruct, textbook writing" (67; 73). But outside the English classroom the autobiographical, the narrative, is not usually appreciated (Spellmeyer). So we look at how the personal is impersonally imparted in writing, still looking to different worldviews espoused in standard written form. We look at Booker T. Washington and W. E. B. DuBois, then find out about their backgrounds, how two African Americans living in the same time can come to polar viewpoints. Or we look at Martin Luther King, Jr. and Malcolm X. In a sense, the strategy is not much different from that proposed by David Bartholomae and Anthony Petrosky: an investing of the personal into what is read and an investigation into how what is read appears, its presentation. The difference is in the introduction of difference within convention. Throughout, there are the culturally literate and the critical, both in what they read and in what they write.

Some students—even a lot, even those who come from poor minority backgrounds—reject the critical views. This is to be expected. People are not turned around overnight. Floyd, back in Kansas City, showed that. But the goal is not necessarily to have students relinquish national-cultural myths. The goal is to expose them to differences and similarities within the literacy conventions they have to contend with, to know the traditional norms while also appraising them, looking at the norms critically. It's a directed process, not propaganda.

All of this is to say that it is possible to have our educational cake and eat it too. It is possible to do our jobs as others define them: provide *haute couture,* "high literacy," literacy skills, standardized-test-ready cultural literacy. And it is possible to do our jobs as we believe they ought to be done: with students recognizing that education should carry social responsibility. We can do critical literacy. And what better to be critical of than the cultural norms contained in tradition? Start with what students know or have been told they ought to know. Allow and encourage a questioning of the norms. And maybe look to how things might be—and ought to be—changed.

David Bartholomae and Anthony Petrosky both teach at the University of Pittsburgh. Villanueva refers to Petrosky and Bartholomae's pedagogy that combines personal experience with critical inquiry, a pedagogy made especially evident in their *Ways of Reading* (sixth edition, 2002).

Villanueva had met Floyd earlier in his life, when he had conducted some ethnographic research in the Midwest. In Villanueva's words, Floyd tried "to promote a Freire-like pedagogy in a school designed exclusively for students who had been locked out of the public schools, mainly by the court system."

Geoff argues that to be intelligent, it's
not always important to be good in
academics only.

I agree with Kim because a student
may be interested in some other areas
rather than the studies only

Susan Bordo

this view's main proponents, "Age of Internet".

In sum, then, the issue is whether a child be allowed to have the access to internet or not.

My own view is that modern world is the world of internet, and it is a really helpful technology for everyone. Though I concede that one should not remain stuck to the internet for the whole day, I still maintain that, if used properly, and appropri its very beneficial. For example, a student can get the help from internet for his online studied projects and assignments. Although some might object that one should not use the internet, I would supply that internet accessibility is a good way to

In recent discussions of use of internet
in Today's world, a controversial issue
has been whether it's usage is beneficial
for students or not. On the one hand
some argue that internet helps a lot
in the field of studies. From this
perspective, it is good to use the internet.
On the other hand, however, others argue
that the internet is ruining their child's
life as their child remain Gifted in
front of computers, playing games on
internet, without paying attention To
his studies. In the words of various
speciallists, it

improve oneself in the academic field.
The issue is important because by a
child became addicted to internet, it's
difficult for him to leave it's usage,
so, a time limit should be there to
use the internet.

Claim

• Many persons believe that one who is
so intelligent in doing various things in
life, may be unable to apply that
intelligence to to academic work.

Works Cited

Aiken, Susan Hardy. "Women and the Question of Canonicity." *College English* 48 (1986): 288–301.

Aranowitz, Stanley, and Henry Giroux. *Education Under Seige: The Conservative, Liberal, and Radical Debate Over Schooling.* South Hadley, MA: Bergin and Garvey, 1985.

Barthes, Roland. *Mythologies.* Trans. Annette Lavers. London: Hill and Wang, 1972.

Bartholomae, David, and Anthony Petrosky. *Facts, Artifacts, and Counterfacts: A Theory and Method for a Reading and Writing Course.* Upper Montclair, NJ: Boynton/Cook, 1986.

DeJesus, Carolina Marie. *Child of the Dark: The Diary of Carolina Marie deJesus.* Trans. David S. Clair. New York: E.P. Dutton, 1962.

Delpit, Lisa D. "The Silenced Dialogue: Power and Pedagogy in Educating Other People's Children." *Harvard Educational Review* 58 (1988): 280–98.

Emecheta, Buchi. *Double Yoke.* New York: Braziller, 1982.

Freire, Paulo. *Pedagogy of the Oppressed.* Trans. Myra Bergman Ramos. New York: Herder and Herder, 1970.

Giroux, Henry. *Theory and Resistance in Education: A Pedagogy for the Opposition.* London: Heinemann, 1983.

Hirsch, E. D., Jr. *Cultural Literacy: What Every American Needs to Know.* Boston: Houghton Mifflin, 1987.

Murray, Donald M. "All Writing is Autobiography." *College Composition and Communication* 42 (1991): 66–74.

Shor, Ira, and Paulo Freire. *A Pedagogy for Liberation: Dialogues on Transforming Education.* South Hadley, MA: Bergin & Harvey, 1987.

Spellmeyer, Kurt. "Foucault and the Freshman Writer: Considering the Self in Discourse." *College English* 51 (1989): 715–29.

West, Cornel. "Minority Discourse and the Pitfalls of Canon Formation." *Yale Journal of Criticism* 1:1 (1987): 193–201.

Reading Responses

1. Villanueva begins this chapter by describing two events from his life: his appearance on a TV show and his directing of a basic writing program at a state university. Do you think he's described things even-handedly? List the people who come off looking good in Villanueva's description. List those who come off looking bad. For each person you've listed describe how he/she views the purpose of education. How does Villanueva use autobiography to make his argument?

2. List the goals that Villanueva has for education—that is, catalog the ways Villanueva hopes education will shape students. What goals do you have for your education? How closely do they match Villanueva's?

3. Consider the "interruptions" in Villanueva's writing—those surprising shifts in content, structure, and style. List three shifts that you found to be effective and the reasons they were effective. List three that you found to be ineffective and the reasons they were ineffective.

NOTES ON GRAMMAR, STYLE, AND RHETORIC:
SENTENCE FRAGMENTS AND SPECIAL EFFECTS

In *Bootstraps* Villanueva regularly violates conventions of formal, academic writing. Here we focus on his willingness to go against the convention that forbids the use of sentence fragments.

What is a sentence fragment? The sixth edition of *The Longman Handbook for Writers and Readers* states that a sentence fragment is "[a] cluster of words punctuated as a sentence but lacking a crucial element that enables it to stand alone as a sentence . . ." (578). The *Longman Handbook* goes on to give examples of various kinds of sentence fragments:

- A fragment because it lacks a subject: "Yet also needs to establish a family counseling program" (578).
- A fragment because it lacks a verb: "The new policy to determine scholarship size on the basis of grades rather than on the basis of need" (579).
- A fragment because it begins with a subordinating word and lacks an independent clause: "Although they also consider most criticism of the test overblown" (580).
- A fragment because it includes an example and lacks an independent clause: "For example, knowledge of computer-aided design" (581).

You must take care never to leave unintentional fragments in your writing, especially your formal writing. If you leave unintentional fragments in such writing, readers might not take your ideas seriously. In fact, since the convention forbidding fragments is so strong, readers might start to question your ability to write.

But it is a fact that skilled writers sometimes use intentional fragments for special effects, even in formal writing. In the reading selection from *Bootstraps* Villanueva uses about a dozen fragments. And he uses them to try to achieve several kinds of effects. Here is a sampling:

1. At one point he uses a fragment to mark one of his abrupt shifts in topics: "Fall 1984" (368).
2. At another point he uses a fragment to make a biting comment about one of E. D. Hirsch's positions: "More myth than history" (369).
3. At the very beginning of the selection he uses a fragment to throw readers into the middle of a scene he will describe: "Hot, bright, stage lights blaring down on the four teachers and two parents seated in a circle before a TV camera" (366).
4. And in an anecdote about his family, he uses a fragment to add emphasis and drama to his reaction to a racist comment his five-year-old daughter had made: "A human baby!" (371). The use of fragments for special emphasis or drama is the most common use of intentional fragments. And this use is particularly interesting because it probably exemplifies something that Villanueva tries to accomplish throughout his book: facilitating "the reader's participation in creating the text" (quoted from a later chapter). That is, a fragment leaves room for a reader to fill in the missing parts, to help in creating the meaning and thus feel an emotional connection to the story.

In Your Own Writing . . .

- Assess your relationship with your reader and consider the context of your writing before you decide to use sentence fragments to make a point.
- Edit your final work carefully to ensure that it contains only the sentence fragments that you've used intentionally.
- Be sure that you know what you are trying to achieve with a sentence fragment and that a sentence fragment is the best way to achieve that effect.
- Check that the sentence fragment does not overly confuse the reader.
- Be sure that your reader will think that the effect justifies breaking the convention forbidding fragments.

STUDENT WRITING

INTRODUCTION

by Cherilyn Dudley, English education major

The Assignment. During my student teaching semester I taught in a remedial reading class for first- and second-year students at an inner-city high school with a lot of ethnic diversity. For the seminar we took while student teaching, we had to read Victor Villanueva's book *Bootstraps* and write an essay in which we critiqued Villanueva's perspectives on education. After writing the critique, we wrote a lesson plan (I wrote mine for my remedial reading class) that embodied our philosophy in light of Villanueva's ideas.

The Content. I feel strongly that education should raise awareness about social issues and that students should be enabled and encouraged to take action in these areas. So in my critique I focused on how and when students should be encouraged to think critically about the world around them. I also discussed the importance of writing style. Villanueva's unusual method of writing is one way to communicate a passion for social justice, but there are other media through which students may feel more comfortable voicing their opinions and beliefs: art, poetry, music, narrative, nonfiction essay, journalism, etc.

The lesson plan, "Debatable Civil Rights," was the second part of my assignment. My goal was to encourage students to think critically about society and to realize that things are not as equal as they might seem. I also wanted them to explore some civil rights Web sites so that they would become familiar with the many organizations that tackle social inequalities in our society and so they could see the many ways in which they can bring about change in their communities.

Learning to Write in English Education. As an English education major, most of the books I've read and papers I've written have consistently followed the Standard English requirements that my professors so highly esteem. For this reason, reading *Bootstraps* was an unusual experience. Were I to write a paper for an English professor in the style of Villanueva, I know I would get much corrective feedback: sentence fragments underlined, misplaced or missing punctuation circled, and innumerable remarks about fluidity and continuity. Many English professors would either not accept Villanueva-style writing from their students, or they would give it a bad grade.

I wonder about two things: (1) the writing I have done as an English education student and (2) the challenges and benefits of stepping outside those standard writing forms. To be honest, aside from an occasional introduction in which I tried to be creative, I have intentionally adhered to the conventions of academic English. Although I had some creative writing assignments in high school, only once did I take the chance to exercise such creativity in college. The professor of my English class gave us the option to write an essay in the same voice as that of the author we had read. Because the author had poured out his soul in his writing, I decided to be equally honest and vulnerable. Turning in the paper, I was terrified; I had not held back at all and had no idea how the professor would respond. When I got the paper back, I saw that the professor had made a few structural and stylistic notes and had given me an A–. But what really horrified me was the lack of comments about *what* I had written. Just like Villanueva, I had used the medium of an experimental style to communicate something that was very important to me. Although the professor had helpful things to say about my style, I felt as though the style was just a means to convey the most important part of the essay: my thoughts, beliefs, and experiences. I was satisfied with the grade, but I couldn't help feeling uncomfortable about knowing that my professor had scrutinized my deepest feelings—especially since I had no idea what his response to them had been.

I believe that Villanueva's style of writing makes people nervous because it is so genuine. Villanueva is passionate about what he writes because he has experienced it himself. These experiences shape not only the educational philosophy he recommends but also the practical suggestions he makes for teachers. Most students avoid this kind of genuine expression for several reasons: (1) we aren't passionate about every single topic we write about, (2) our life experiences don't always connect to the topics we're writing about, and (3) we don't have the same authority or confidence as Villanueva. He makes it clear that he has read and understands complex philosophies. And as an influential scholar in the field of English education, readers accept his unconventional choices as *choices* rather than as *mistakes*. He has gained enough academic respect to put unconventionality to good use. In a classroom, only one person has the final say about our writing—the professor. If the professor doesn't buy into our forms of individualistic expression, then our own grades are at stake. So most students shy away from this option and continue to adhere to Standard English expectations.

Who Cares?: Analysis and Application of Victor Villanueva's *Bootstraps*

Cherilyn Dudley

Some of the most frequently asked questions in high school include "Why does this matter?" and "Why should I care?" And many teachers can't give convincing answers. Because of these common student frustrations about a useless education, I decided to teach a unit in my student teaching classroom about the history of civil rights and the value of social action. I introduced these topics through biographies of liberation movement leaders like Martin Luther King Jr., César Chávez, Malcolm X, Fannie Lou Hamer, and Nelson Mandela.

> A unit is a set of lesson plans on a particular topic or theme.

On the first day of the unit, I asked students to complete a survey of their attitudes regarding civil rights. Students quickly completed the sheet on their own, and once we began sharing perspectives, the class erupted into debate. I hadn't expected students to respond so strongly to the statements on the sheet, but the school has a diverse student body, and many felt that their civil rights had been violated at one time or another. As we further examined and discussed civil rights in class, students moved from feeling angry to making specific plans to safeguard their rights. What I experienced as a student teacher convinces me that Victor Villanueva is right to promote the challenging of social norms as a goal for education. Through individual assignments as well as larger decisions about curriculum, teachers should strive to implement Villanueva's ideas about critical cultural literacy. At each stage of education, we must encourage children to analyze how they see the world, to understand that different people perceive the world in different ways, to discuss sources and effects of these worldviews, and to put what they've learned into practice as actively engaged citizens.

As my experience proves, questioning norms and traditions can lead to controversy, so it is important that teachers consider when and how to encourage such questioning. In this endeavor, we can find guidance from child psychologist Jean Piaget. Piaget claims that children go through three main cognitive stages during the elementary and high school years. From the time they begin to talk until the age of seven, children are in a "preoperational" stage of development. During this stage, they perceive everything as "here and now" and nicely fitting what they believe about the world. Although the egocentrism of infancy influences the early years of this stage, it is during this time that young children should be exposed to the idea that not everyone lives as they do. Villanueva describes how he accomplished this in his own family: his daughters read international versions of fairy tales and identified the similarities and differences among them. Teachers can accommodate this stage in the classroom by introducing literature and art from a variety of cultures, bringing in speakers or going on fieldtrips that showcase different ways of life, and teaching cultural units in which teachers and students affirm and celebrate cultural differences. Through mere exposure to diversity, young children will begin to realize that there is more than one way of seeing the world and that not everyone thinks the way they do.

Between first grade and early adolescence, children transition into the "concrete operational" stage of development. During this time, they develop critical thought processes and begin to make rational judgments about concrete and abstract ideas. Using the preoperational observations they made in their younger years, students in later elementary and junior high school should learn to critique world literature, politics, history, and other subject matters. As the educational focus shifts from telling to asking, students can discuss why our society does things the way it does. Under the teacher's guidance, students can begin to formulate ideas and perspectives about what literature might reveal about cultures, both foreign and familiar. In junior high, students should be exposed to literature that raises questions and concerns about

Although this essay is a "critique," I agree with most of the philosophies Villanueva advocates. Therefore, I analyze the *Bootstraps* excerpt by extending the application of his ideas and discussing practical ways to use his philosophies in the classroom.

Education is a field in which the rhetoric of experience can carry weight in an argument.

Although the next few paragraphs are mostly about the application of Villanueva's ideas, I occasionally reference specifics from his book so my reader doesn't think I'm getting too far away from the assignment to critique *Bootstraps*.

In my mind, critical thought processes include weighing the positives and negatives of something and making a judgment about its value.

society. Students can begin to make connections between other cultures and their own as they wonder why their government and society operate as they do. Through this stage of critical analysis, students begin to define who they are and what they believe, and as they begin to make judgments about their own culture, they will learn to see it in a more objective light.

During adolescence, young adults apply the critical thinking of the concrete operational stage to an active "formal operational" stage of development. In this stage, they learn to use hypothetical and deductive reasoning to make conclusions about society and suggest solutions to problems in the world around them. In high school classrooms, teachers can foster this type of thinking through interdisciplinary studies. When students bring history and politics into their English classes, they can examine different models of cultures and societies in literature, comparing these structures to those found around the world. Students can research and debate social equality, economic opportunity, political infrastructure, and other aspects of life as they begin to articulate their own worldviews. Reading books such as *Lord of the Flies, The Jungle, Utopia, Animal Farm,* and other culturally, socially, and politically critical literature will nurture students' own critical consciousness. And making connections between books such as these and current events—i.e., newspaper or magazine articles—will turn the inevitable high school question "Who cares?" back to the students: Do *they* care enough about their world to express their ideas publicly and to act on them? As adolescents prepare to establish lives separate from their parents and enter the workforce, they must become confident enough to express unconventional opinions and disagree with mainstream society. This isn't an easy mindset for teachers to teach or for students to learn. Even in his college classes, Villanueva has to encourage students to become comfortable "being critical of the great authorities" (98). Rather than accepting everything the way it is, Villanueva advocates an education that encourages questioning, engagement, and reflection. Piaget agrees, and so do I.

By making a general statement that applies both to the application I've discussed as well as to Villanueva himself, I shift the focus back to *Bootstraps* after the discussion about applying his ideas.

Unconventional critical thoughts are often best represented by experimental, unconventional ways of communication. In *Bootstraps,* Villanueva defies Standard English grammatical and syntactical rules as he aims to convey not only knowledge and philosophies, but also emotionally-charged experiences and perceptions of the world. As students develop their own philosophies and perceptions, they must discover how to best express themselves genuinely. Taking a non-traditional approach to communication can be intimidating, but so is holding culturally critical viewpoints. Villanueva chooses to express himself through a varied narrative writing style, but students might choose a different medium to convey their thoughts: poetry, journalism, research essays, or even art or music. The important decision is not necessarily *how* an individual's beliefs are communicated, but rather *that* they are communicated in a genuine and effective manner.

Although there are many benefits and strengths of authentic, unique self-expression, there are also draw-backs. Writing is only powerful when it meets the needs of its audience. Readers who want to learn about the demographics of education for minorities or the poor would seek statistics, charts, or clear organizational structure of most research articles. And Villanueva's unconventional style might encourage these readers to dismiss *Bootstraps* as unscholarly. On the other hand, Villanueva's descriptive, emotive writing style is more effective for readers who want to learn about someone's experiences with education and perspectives on educational philosophy. As students decide how to best express their developing worldviews, they must keep this tension in mind.

> Every good argument should include a counterargument, and this paper is no different. In this paragraph I point out legitimate disadvantages of Villanueva's experimental style, while also sending a cautionary message to students: they need to be discerning about how, when, and with whom to use unique, creative forms of expression.

As students discover what issues to be critical of and what stylistic means they should use to communicate those concerns, they need to make the personal decision about how this criticism should affect their life and learning. Students should learn to put their convictions into action as they find ways to get involved in their communities. Teachers should encourage students to seek out information resources and organizations that challenge them to go beyond classroom learning. Through such venues, students can live out their ideals and discover that they can influence the world around them. And as long as students find a way to get involved that matches their talents and interests, they will continue to be active in those areas even after the school year ends.

> As this critique touches on many different aspects of Villanueva's philosophy and style, the concluding paragraph is meant to summarize and bring cohesion to the different areas of the paper's focus.

Although some may perceive Villanueva's ideals of educating for cultural criticism as radical or threatening to the classroom teacher's authority, I believe that evoking a critical consciousness in students is the most powerful and effective method of educating. Students too often feel that they can get away with passively regurgitating facts in the classroom. Quite often, they don't "care" about what is being taught; they think their voice doesn't matter because they are not as educated as the teacher or lack a position of authority. However, their experiences and perceptions about the world can and should be articulated and shared. Students need to know that each of them has something valuable to contribute to the world. And while they must be stylistically aware of how to effectively communicate their worldviews, they must also find a method of communication that accurately conveys their individuality. Whether they express themselves through art or music, narrative or non-fiction, conventional Standard English or experimental Villanueva-style reflection, when students critique and question the world around them, their critical thought will often lead to active promotion of positive, much needed changes in society.

Lesson Plan: Debatable Civil Rights

Cherilyn Dudley

Objectives:

> The objectives help the teacher, as well as anyone else who looks at the lesson plan, identify the main goals of the class period. Through them, the teacher articulates what he or she wants the students to learn.

1. Students will become familiar with the three main rights listed in the Declaration of Independence.
2. Students will be able to formulate definitions of words based on their nature and function.
3. Students will be able to examine and critique their own as well as one another's perspectives on the enactment of civil rights today both in society and in politics.
4. Students will be able to identify and articulate ways they can participate in promoting social justice and equality in today's society.

Materials:

> You don't want to be standing in front of 30 expectant students before you realize you've forgotten the hand-outs and overheads you need for your lesson! The Materials section ensures that you'll be well-prepared for class.

Overhead with opening sentence of Declaration of Independence
Anticipation Guide: *Get it Right!*

Methods:

Introduction (10 minutes)

> The Methods section describes the specific activities a teacher will do in class. It includes how the material will be introduced, how it will be developed as it is further explained, and how the class will be concluded.

1. Students will share what they know about the Declaration of Independence and the three rights it lists in its introduction.
2. Teacher will put up Declaration of Independence, and a student will read the first sentence aloud to the class:

   "We hold these truths to be self-evident, that all men are created equal, that they are endowed by their Creator with certain unalienable Rights, that among these are Life, Liberty and the pursuit of Happiness."

3. Hand out Anticipation Guide; Students will write their own definitions for the three rights (Life, Liberty, pursuit of Happiness).
4. Student definitions for each of these rights will be listed on the board.

> Anticipation Guides are a type of introductory activity designed to pique student interest in a subject before it is studied more in-depth.

Development (40 minutes)

5. Students will read the Anticipation Guide statements and mark whether they agree or disagree.
6. The teacher will ask students to review the definitions they came up with for "Life, Liberty, and pursuit of Happiness." Class will discuss

what makes a definition a "good definition": how to make it specific, yet broad enough so it doesn't exclude anything. Students will revise at least one of their personal definitions of the three rights to make it stronger and more effective.

7. Students will share the conclusions they reached for each of the Anticipation Guide statements, as well as justification for these differing conclusions. The class will debate statements that were more controversial.

| During the Conclusion of a lesson, class material is reviewed and the teacher gives the assignment. |

Conclusion (5 minutes)

8. Class will review the Declaration of Independence sentence, and the teacher will reiterate how even in today's society, rights that may seem to be quite straight-forward and simple are not always valued and preserved.

9. Students will be assigned to use the Internet to research a specific area of Civil Rights that interests them (women's rights, minority rights, economic rights, etc.). They must write a journal describing (1) a recent event in today's news that demonstrates either respect or disrespect for others' rights, (2) how they think the rights listed in the Declaration of Independence were, or could have been, justly applied in that situation, according to their definition of those rights, and (3) what they can do to influence and/or promote the continued goal of equality (students may reference website suggestions for getting involved).

Assignment:

Journal, which will be discussed in class the next day

Assessment:

Class participation with Anticipation Guide and debate Journal

| It's amazing how students can pretend they're listening but never actually hear a thing. Prompting them to list the three rights is an easy way to make sure they specifically note which three we're talking about. Defining them gives them some ownership over the material and encourages them to think about the rights more in-depth. |

["Anticipation Guide"]
Get it Right!

What rights does the Declaration of Independence say everyone should have? List them here, and write your own definition of what each right means:

1.
2.
3.

> I intentionally designed this activity to create some controversy and disagreement about civil rights so students would recognize the ongoing debate that occurs over this issue. Numbers 2–5 are the most controversial, and student responses will be influenced by their individual beliefs and experiences. Number 5 encourages students to think critically about their own society and its practices.

Based on what you know and believe about Civil Rights, circle AGREE or DISAGREE next to each statement. Be prepared to justify your decisions, and remember there is no one right answer!

1. AGREE   DISAGREE   Regardless of ethnicity, religion, political preference, gender, or social class, all people should have access to the same rights.

2. AGREE   DISAGREE   U.S. citizens should have more rights in the U.S. than people who are not U.S. citizens.

3. AGREE   DISAGREE   Illegal immigrants should not be given any of the rights that U.S. citizens possess.

4. AGREE   DISAGREE   Even if they are U.S. citizens, convicted criminals should not have the same rights as other citizens.

5. AGREE   DISAGREE   It is the duty of the U.S. to make sure other countries provide their citizens with the same rights as those we enjoy in our country.

6. AGREE   DISAGREE   Regardless of ethnicity, religion, political preference, gender, or social class, all people *do* have access to the same rights in our society today.

Reading Responses

1. How does Dudley's reading of *Bootstraps* compare with yours? Do you think that she has been critical enough of Villanueva in her "critique"? Why or why not?

2. Review Dudley's essay, noting each time she describes her personal experience. How do her descriptions compare with Villanueva's?

3. Consider what Dudley asks her students to reveal on the "Get It Right!" survey. Do you think that some students might be uncomfortable with this activity? Is it necessary for teachers to make students uncomfortable? What do they accomplish by doing so? What do they risk?

PUBLIC WRITING

INTRODUCTION

At several points in *Bootstraps*, Villanueva refers to E. D. Hirsch's *Cultural Literacy, What Every American Needs to Know* (1987). Now retired, Hirsch was a Professor of English at the University of Virginia when he published *Cultural Literacy*, and he had developed a reputation as an influential literary critic and theorist on the teaching of writing. His work on education includes *The Schools We Need and Why We Don't Have Them* (1996) and *The Knowledge Deficit* (2006). And his influence can be connected to a focus on "core knowledge" that is a feature of the No Child Left Behind act.

Cultural Literacy quickly became a topic of conversation among educators and noneducators alike. It is easy to imagine why it touched off such interest and conflict.

Here we reproduce a short article that Hirsch uses as part of the introduction to a different book, *The New Dictionary of Cultural Literacy*, Third Edition (2002). The dictionary lists the specific facts that Hirsch and his collaborators think people in our culture should know. In this introductory essay, Hirsch offers an abbreviated version of his famous argument for promoting cultural literacy through teaching common knowledge. Hirsch reasons that because we learn by associating something new with something we already know, learning requires "a knowledge of shared, taken-for-granted information."

Compared to Villanueva, Hirsch sounds like a thorough traditionalist. But does the larger project, the dictionary that this piece introduces, play with convention? Have you read any other books for your college courses that are made up of lists of facts—places, people, dates, slang words and phrases—that a culturally literate person should know?

The Theory Behind the Dictionary: Cultural Literacy and Education

E. D. Hirsch Jr.

From the Introduction to *The New Dictionary of Cultural Literacy*, Third Edition (2002)

The conceptions that underlie this dictionary are outlined in my book *Cultural Literacy*, published in 1987. But in fact, the dictionary project was begun before I thought of writing a separate book, and the book itself was first conceived merely as a technical explanation of the ideas that led us to undertake the dictionary. . . . So here, in brief compass, is why this project was undertaken, and why we hope it will help improve American public education and public discourse. . . .

The novelty that my book introduced into this discussion is its argument that true literacy depends on a knowledge of the *specific* information that is taken for granted in our public discourse. My emphasis on background information makes my book an attack on all formal and technical approaches to teaching language arts. Reading and writing are not simply acts of decoding and encoding but rather acts of communication. The literal words we speak and read and write are just the tip of the iceberg in communication. An active understanding of the written word requires far more than the ability to call out words from a page or the possession of basic vocabulary, syntax, grammar, and inferencing techniques. We have learned that successful reading also requires a knowledge of shared, taken-for-granted information that is not set down on the page.

To grasp the practical importance of that point for our entire education system, we need to ask a fundamental question. Why is high national literacy the key to educational progress in all domains of learning, even in mathematics and natural sciences? We have long known that there is a high correlation between students' reading ability and their ability to learn new material in diverse fields. That sounds vaguely reasonable, even obvious, but why *exactly* should it be the case? Let's try to understand the not-so-obvious reason for the high correlation between reading ability and learning ability.

The true measure of reading ability is the ease and accuracy with which a person can understand *diverse* kinds of writing. All standardized tests of reading ability include samples from several different subject matters. But why isn't one long sample just as effective a test as several short ones? Well, if reading ability were a purely generalizable skill, one long sample would be an adequate diagnostic test. But in fact, reading ability is not a generalizable skill. If a young boy knows a lot about snakes but very little about lakes, he will make a good score on a passage about snakes, but a less good score on a passage about lakes. So to get a fairly accurate picture of his overall reading ability, we have to sample how he does on a variety of subjects.

But notice that this variability in a person's performance shows us something of utmost importance about reading ability. To have a good *general* reading ability, you need to know about a lot of things. If you know about lakes and snakes, and rakes and cakes, you will have a higher reading ability than if you just know about snakes. Aha! you might say, that simply means you will read better if you have a broad vocabulary. That is true. But remember what it means to have a broad vocabulary. Knowing a lot of words means knowing a lot of things. Words refer to things. Language arts are also knowledge arts.

We have now taken a first step in understanding the correlation between reading ability and learning ability. We have established that high reading ability is a multiplex skill that requires knowledge in a wide range of subjects. It turns out that the same is true of learning ability. A basic axiom of learning is that the easiest way to learn something new is to associate it with something we already know. Much of the art of teaching is the art of associating what kids need to learn with what they already know. The process of learning often works as metaphor does, yoking old ideas together to make something new. In the nineteenth century, when people wanted to describe the new transportation technology that went *chug-chug-chug,* they called the engine an "iron horse" and the rail system the "track way" (if they were Dutch) or "rail way" (if they were English) or "iron way" (if they were French, German, or Italian) or "narrow iron lane" (if they were Greek). All of these metaphors successfully conveyed a new concept by combining old concepts. . . .

It should now be clear why reading ability and learning ability are so closely allied. They both depend on a diversity of prior knowledge. You can easily read a range of new texts if you already know a lot; so too you can easily learn a broad range of knowledge if you already know a lot. It should not surprise us, therefore, that back in the 1950s the College Board found out that the best predictor of how well students would perform in school was their performance on a general knowledge test. "Reading, writing and arithmetic" and the general ability to learn new things all show a high correlation with broad background knowledge.

I must ask your indulgence to take another step along the path I am leading you. Reading and learning ability depend on something more definite than broad, unspecified knowledge. To a significant degree, learning and reading depend on *specific* broad knowledge. The reason for this goes back to my earlier point that reading is not just a technical skill but also an act of communication. When somebody is reading with understanding, communication is taking place between writer and reader. Conversely, if communication isn't taking place, the reader isn't accurately understanding what he or she is reading. Successful communication depends on understanding both the text's literal meanings and its implied meanings. These all-important implied meanings can only be constructed out of specific knowledge shared between writer and reader. Let me give a very brief example of why this is so. Here are the beginning words of a school textbook on chemistry:

> You are beginning your study of chemistry at a time when growing numbers of people are concerned about the declining quality of life. Chemistry can help you gain a deeper and more satisfying understanding of our environment than you have now. If you are curious and wish to know more about natural processes, minerals of the earth, water and solutions, and gases of the atmosphere, the activities in chemistry beckon to you.

That's it. As a child, I'm supposed to know before reading the passage that chemistry has to do with minerals, water, and solutions, that numbers of people are concerned about the quality of life, that quality of life has something to do with water and solutions. Understanding that passage will be easy if I already know what "chemistry," "solution," and "declining quality of life" are supposed to signify. . . .

Therefore, learning depends on communication, and effective communication depends on shared background knowledge. The optimal way to fulfill this requirement of communication is simply to insure that readers and writers, students and teachers do in fact share a broad range of specific knowledge. This makes good communication possible, which in turn makes effective learning possible, and also enables a society to work. In short, we have come round to the point of my book. An important key to solving the twin problems of learning and literacy is to attain the broadly shared background knowledge I have called "cultural literacy." My book argues that the content of this literate background knowledge is not a mystery, and that it can be taught systematically to all our students. The book further claims that if we do impart this content, we can achieve the universal literacy that is a necessary foundation for further educational, economic, and social improvements. No active reading researcher—that is to say, no one who is thoroughly conversant with the empirical data in cognitive research—has challenged this analysis. . . .

Publishers and schools need to direct their energies to enhancing the effectiveness with which core literate content is presented. They should not try to overhaul the entire content of literate culture, which cannot successfully be done in any case. Professional linguists have often remarked on the inherent conservatism of literacy. Some of its elements do not change at all. Spelling, for example is extraordinarily conservative, because so many people have learned the traditional forms, and so many books have recorded them, that successful spelling reform would require orthographical thought-police. This linguistic inertia induced by print and mass education also extends to other contents of literate culture.

But the conservatism of literate culture is far from total. New elements are constantly coming in, and the old ones falling out of use. Americans have successfully pressed for cultural reforms, including greater representation of women, minorities, and non-Western cultures. In addition, literate culture must keep up with historical and technical change. Yet the materials of literate culture that are recent introductions constitute about a fifth of its total. The disputed territory of literate culture is much smaller still—about 4 percent. Thus, 96 percent of literate culture is undisputed territory, and most striking of all, *80 percent of literate culture has been in use for more than a hundred years!*

Such cultural conservatism is fortunate and useful for the purposes of national communication. It enables grandparents to communicate with grandchildren, southerners with midwesterners, whites with blacks, Asians with Latinos, and Republicans with Democrats—no matter where they were educated. If each local school system imparts the traditional reference points of literate culture, then everybody is able to communicate with strangers. That is a good definition of literacy: the ability to communicate effectively with strangers. We help people in the underclass rise economically by teaching them how to communicate effectively beyond a narrow social sphere, and that can only be accomplished by teaching them shared, traditional literate culture. Thus the inherent conservatism of literacy leads to an unavoidable paradox: the social goals of liberalism *require* educational conservatism. We only make social and economic progress by teaching everyone to read and communicate, which means teaching myths and facts that are predominantly traditional.

Those who evade this inherent conservatism of literacy in the name of multicultural antielitism are in effect elitists of an extreme sort. Traditionally educated themselves, and highly literate, these self-appointed protectors of minority cultures have advised schools to pursue a course that has condemned minorities to illiteracy. The disadvantaged students for whom antielitist solicitude is expressed are the very ones who suffer when we fail to introduce traditional literate culture into the earliest grades. . . .

The real test of any educational idea is its usefulness. We hope this dictionary will be a useful tool. We also hope and expect that no one will be willing to stop with cultural literacy as a final educational aim. Cultural literacy is a necessary but not sufficient attainment of an educated person. Cultural literacy is shallow; true education is deep. But our analysis of reading and learning suggests the paradox that broad, shallow knowledge is the best route to deep knowledge. Because broad knowledge enables us to read and learn effectively, it is the best guarantee that we will continue to read, and read and learn, and deepen our knowledge. True literacy has always opened doors—not just to deep knowledge and economic success, but also to other people and other cultures.

Reading Responses

1. Describe times when teachers have pressed you to learn background information. How did you respond? When have you felt the need for this knowledge? When have you resisted learning this kind of information? Why did you resist?

2. Review Hirsch's argument, looking for places where he breaks with convention. Describe two places where Hirsch breaks convention and what effect each has on the reader.

3. Summarize Hirsch's argument about the conservatism of literate culture, paying special attention to the advantages Hirsch describes. What disadvantages can you imagine?

MORE WRITING IN ENGLISH EDUCATION

INTRODUCTION

James Paul Gee has won widespread attention and acclaim for his work on literacy, which includes how we "read" visual and verbal messages in complex contexts. He is a professor in the College of Education at Arizona State University.

It is very common to read reports on the effect of playing video games on a student's performance in school. Conventional thinking focuses on the negative effects of video games on students. In his book *What Video Games Have to Teach Us about Learning and Literacy*, Gee challenges those conventional ideas. He announces his challenge to the thinking that video gaming is bad in his very first sentence: "I want to talk about video games—yes, even violent video games—and say some positive things about them."

In this excerpt from the book, Gee analyzes what teachers can learn about reading from the ways that gamers use manuals and online help sites. Additional ways that Gee challenges convention in his writing are the following: using short, simple sentences; including information in multiple parentheses, addressing readers directly with "you."

Situated Meaning and Learning: What Should You Do After You Have Destroyed the Global Conspiracy?

James Paul Gee

From *What Video Games Have to Teach Us about Learning and Literacy,* Palgrave Macmillan, 2nd ed., 2007

. . . Games often come with manuals. They also sometimes come with a booklet, written as a diary, or notes, or otherwise set as part of the virtual world of the game, that gives the back story or background information for that virtual world. For example, *American McGee's Alice,* a game where Alice has gone insane and returned to a nightmarish Wonderland, comes with a booklet entitled "Rutledge Private Clinic and Asylum Casebook," which contains Alice's physician's daily notes on her treatment.

For most games, publishers offer highly colorful and detailed strategy guides that tell players all about the game (its characters, maps and geography of the world, weapons, enemies, objects to be found, fruitful strategies to follow, etc.). Such guides also give a complete walkthrough for the game. A number of Internet sites offer (usually free) a variety of different walkthroughs ("faqs") written by players themselves. These sites also offer hints from players and "cheats" for the games. (Cheats are ways to manipulate the game's programming to do things like give yourself extra life or more ammunition.)

These texts are all integrated into the appreciative systems associated with the affinity groups connected to video games. Different players and groups have different views about whether, when, and how to use these texts. For example, consider walkthroughs on a site like gamefaqs.com. These documents often run to 70 or more single-spaced pages and are written according to a tight set of rules about what they should contain and look like (including a list of each date on which the walkthrough was revised). Some players shun walkthroughs entirely, though they may write them. Others argue that walkthroughs can and should be used, but only to get a hint when one is thoroughly stuck. Indeed, the writers of the walkthroughs themselves often recommend that players use them this way. (Imagine producing a 70-page, single-spaced document and advising people to look at it only when they are stuck.)

Of course, if children had walkthroughs in school when they studied things like science, we would call it "cheating" (let alone if they had "cheat codes"). But, then, imagine what a science classroom would look like where learners wrote extensive walkthroughs according to strict norms and debated when and how to use them, debates that became part and parcel of the learners' growing appreciative systems about what it means to "do science (well)." And, indeed, in a sense, real scientists do have walkthroughs. They know (through talk with others and through texts) the case histories of how relevant related discoveries in their field were made. They also have opinions about how closely one should consult or follow these histories.

It is now a piece of folk wisdom that "young people" don't read things like manuals but just start playing games, often looking at the manual or other guides later. Yet I would argue that these young people are using print in the way it should be used when people actually understand what they read in a useful and situated way. Baby boomers—perhaps too influenced by traditional schooling—often try to do otherwise to their regret and frustration, when they insist on reading a manual before they have any embodied understanding of what the manual is about (i.e., the game).

The problem with the texts associated with video games—the instruction booklets, walkthroughs, and strategy guides—is that they do not make a lot of sense unless one has already experienced and lived in the game world for a while. Of course, this lack of lucidity can be made up for if the player has read similar texts before, but at some point these texts originally made sense because the player had an embodied world of experience with games in terms of which to situate and spell out their meanings. . . .

When I give talks on video games to teachers, I often show them a manual or strategy guide and ask them how much they understand. Very often they are frustrated. They have no experience in which to situate the words and phrases of the texts. All they get is verbal information, which they understand at some literal level, but which does not really hang together. They cannot visualize this verbal information in any way that makes sense or makes them want to read on. I tell them that that is how their students feel when confronted with a text or textbook in science or some other academic area if they have had no experiences in terms of which they can situate the meanings of the words and phrases. It's all "just words," words the "good" students can repeat on tests and the "bad" ones can't.

When you have played a video game for a while, something magical happens to the texts associated with it. All of a sudden they seem lucid and clear and readable. You can't even recall how confusing they seemed in the, first place. At that point, players can use the text in a great variety of ways for different purposes. For instance, they can look up details that enhance their play. Or such guides can fill out players' knowledge of the places, creatures, and things in the virtual world in which they are living. Players can troubleshoot problems they are having in the game, with the game, or with their computer. They can get hints or compare their play to how others have done.

Let me take the booklet that comes with *Deus Ex* as an example of what I mean by saying that texts associated with video games are not lucid unless and until one has some embodied game experience in which to "cash out" the meanings of the text. The book contains 20 small pages, printed in double columns on each page. In these pages, there are 199 bolded references that represent headings and subheadings. One small randomly chosen stretch of headings and subheadings that appears at the end of page five and the beginning of page six says: *Passive Readouts, Damage Monitor, Active Augmentation and Device Icons, Items-at-Hand, Information Screens, Note, Inventory, Inventory Management, Stacks, Nanokey ring, Ammunition*. Each of these 199 headings and subheadings is followed by text that gives information relevant to the topic and relates it to other information throughout the booklet. In addition, the booklet assigns 53 keys on the computer keyboard to some function in the game, and these 53 keys are mentioned 82 times in relation to the information contained in the 199 headings and subheadings. So, although small, the booklet is packed with relatively technical information.

Here is a typical piece of language from this booklet:

Your internal nano-processors keep a very detailed record of your condition, equipment and recent history. You can access this data at any time during play by hitting Fl to get to the Inventory screen or F2 to get to the Goals/Notes screen. Once you have accessed your information screens, you can move between the screens by clicking on the tabs at the top of the screen. You can map other information screens to hotkeys using Settings, Keyboard/Mouse.

This makes perfect sense at a literal level, but that just goes to show how worthless the literal level is. When you understand this sort of passage at only a literal level, you have only an illusion of understanding, one that quickly disappears as you try to relate this information to the hundreds of other important details in the booklet. First of all, this passage means nothing real to you if you have no situated idea about what "nano-processors," "condition," "equipment," "history," "Fl," Inventory screen," "F2," "Goals/Notes screen" (and, of course, "Goals" and "Notes"), "information screens," "clicking," "tabs," "map," "hotkeys," and "Settings, Keyboard/Mouse" mean in and for playing games like *Deus Ex*.

Second, though you know literally what each sentence means, together they raise a plethora of questions if you have no situated understandings of this game or games like it. For instance: Is the same data (condition, equipment, and history) on both the Inventory screen and the Goals/Notes screen? If so, why is it on two different screens? If not, which type of information is on which screen and why? The fact that I can move between the screens by clicking on the tabs (but what do these tabs look like; will I recognize them?) suggests that some of this information is on one screen and some on the other. But, then, is my "condition" part of my Inventory or my Goals/Notes—it doesn't seem to be either, but, then, what is my "condition" anyway? If I can map other information screens (and what are these?) to hotkeys using "Setting, Keyboard/Mouse," does this mean there is no other way to access them? How will I access them in the first place to assign them to my own chosen hotkeys? Can I click between them and the Inventory screen and the Goals/Notes screens by pressing on "tabs"? And so on—20 pages is beginning to seem like a lot; remember, there are 199 different headings under which information like this is given.

Of course, all these terms and questions can be defined and answered if you closely check and cross-check information over and over again through the little booklet. You can constantly turn the pages backward and forward. But once you have one set of links relating various items and actions in mind, another drops out just as you need it and you're back to turning pages. Is the booklet poorly written? Not at all. It is written just as well or as poorly as—just like, in fact—any of a myriad of school-based texts in the content areas. It is, outside the practices in the semiotic domain from which it comes, just as meaningless, no matter how much one could garner literal meanings from it with which to verbally repeat things or pass tests.

When I first read this booklet before playing *Deus Ex* (and having played only one other shooter game, a very different one), I was sorely tempted to put the game on a shelf and forget about it. I was simply overwhelmed with details, questions, and confusions. When I started the game, I kept trying to look up stuff. But I understood none of it well enough to find things easily without searching for the same information over and over again. In the end, you just have to actively play the game and explore and try everything. Then, at last, the booklet makes good sense, but by then you don't need it all that much. . . .

There is much discussion these days about how many children fail in school—especially children from poor homes—because they have not been taught phonics well or correctly in their early years. But the truth of the matter is that a great many more children fail in school because, while they can decode print, they cannot handle the progressively more complex demands school language makes on them as they move up in the grades and on to high school.

School requires, in respect to both oral and written language, forms or styles of language that are different from and, in some respects, more complex than everyday oral language used in informal face-to-face conversations. The forms of language used in texts and discussions in science, math, social studies classes, and other content areas go by the general name of "academic language," though different varieties of academic language are associated with different content areas in school.

Academic language, like the language in the *Deus Ex* booklet, is not really lucid or meaningful if one has no embodied experiences within which to situate its meanings in specific ways. For example, consider this academic-language quote from a high school science textbook:

> The destruction of a land surface by the combined effects of abrasion and removal
> of weathered material by transporting agents is called erosion . . . The production
> of rock waste by mechanical processes and chemical changes is called weathering.

Again, one can certainly understand this at some literal word-byword, sentence-by-sentence way. However, this is not "everyday" language. No one speaks this way at home around the table or at a bar having drinks with friends. But this language is filled with all the same problems the language of the *Deus Ex* booklet held for me when I had not lived through any experiences in terms of which I could situate its meanings. Without embodied experiences with which to cash out its meanings, all the above academic text will do—as the *Deus Ex* booklet did to me initially—is fill one with questions, confusion, and, perhaps, anger.

For example: I have no idea what the difference is between "abrasion" and "removal of weathered material by transporting agents," which I would have thought was one form of abrasion. What's a "transporting agent"? What's a "mechanical process"? I am not really clear on the difference between "mechanical processes," especially in regard to weather, and "chemical changes." And what chemicals are we talking about here—stuff in rain?

Since the first sentence is about "erosion" and the second about "weathering," I suppose these two things are connected in some important way—but how? They must be two forms of "destruction of a land surface," given that this is the subject of the first sentence. But, then, I would have thought that producing "rock waste" was a way of building, not just destroying, land, since rock waste eventually turns into dirt (doesn't it?) and thus, I would have supposed, eventually into potentially fertile land. But this is a geology text, and they don't care about fertile land (or do they?). The word "land" here has a different range of possible situated meanings than I am familiar with.

Of course, I can turn the pages of the book back and forth clarifying all these points. After all, these two sentences are meant to be definitions—not of the words "erosion" and "weathering" in everyday terms but in specialist terms in a particular semiotic domain. And, of course, I do need to know that they *are* definitions, and I may not even know that if I have had little experience of specialists trying to define terms in explicit and operational ways so as to lessen the sort of ambiguity and vagueness that is more typical of everyday talk. Since they are definitions, they are linked and cross-linked to a myriad of other terms, descriptions, and explanations throughout the book, and I can follow this tangled trail across the pages, back and forth, losing bits of the connections just as I need them and page turning yet again.

However, once I have experienced the sorts of embodied images, actions, and tasks that engage geologists—including their ways of talking and debating, their reasons for doing so, their interests, norms, and values—then the text is lucid and useful. Confusion, frustration, and anger disappear. Given such understanding, everybody would pass the test and we couldn't fail half the class and reward a small set of "winners"—people who can repeat back verbal details they remember well when they don't fully understand them in any practical way.

In the end, my claim is that people have situated meanings for words when they can associate these words with images, actions, experiences, or dialogue in a real or imagined world. Otherwise they have, at best, only verbal meanings (words for words, as in a dictionary). Situated meanings lead to real understanding and the ability to apply what one knows in action. Verbal meanings **do not** (though they do sometimes lead to the ability to pass paper and pencil tests). This is why so many school children, even ones who are good at school, can pass tests but still cannot apply their knowledge to real problem solving.

More Learning Principles

Let me conclude this discussion by listing further learning principles that our discussion of learning and thinking in video games in this chapter has implicated. Once again, in this list, I intend each principle to be relevant both to learning in video games and learning in content areas in classrooms. . . .

17. **Situated Meaning Principle** The meanings of signs (words, actions, objects, artifacts, symbols, texts, etc.) are situated in embodied experience. Meanings are not general or decontextulized. Whatever generality meanings come to have is discovered bottom up via embodied experiences.

18. **Text Principle** Texts are not understood purely verbally (i.e., only in terms of the definitions of the words in the text and their text-internal relationships to each other) but are understood in terms of embodied experiences. Learners move back and forth between texts and embodied experiences. More purely verbal understanding (reading texts apart from embodied action) comes only when learners have had enough embodied experience in the domain and ample experiences with similar texts.

Reading Responses

1. Do you play video games? If you do not, interview a college student to answer the following questions. Describe the effect that playing video games has had on your performance in school. What have been the positive effects? What have been the negative effects? Have the positive effects outweighed the negative ones?

2. Which of Gee's challenges to convention is most risky? What is he risking? How significant is the risk?

3. Gee suggests that providing students with "walkthroughs" as they study science might be considered "cheating." Make a brief argument that providing this kind of help in school would be cheating. Provide reasons and examples to support your claim.

WRITING ASSIGNMENTS

Assignment 1

Your task is to take on the role of student teacher and create two different lesson plans for teaching high school students about one of the new terms you recommended for Hirsch's list. One plan should replicate the kind of education you experienced in high school classes that used conventional teaching methods. The other plan should include features that challenge conventional teaching practice. To begin, free-write about your opinions of modern high schoolers: What do they take for granted? What do you as a teacher need to wake them up to? How can you break conventions to help them understand in a new way?

As you begin drafting, use Dudley's lesson plan as a template for your own, including all the features that she has in hers. Record your thoughts and emotional responses as you create the two lesson plans: Which was easiest to craft? Which do you expect to be more effective? Which best enacts what you believe should be the goals of a high school education? Consider how you might use your experience in introducing your lesson plans or comparing them.

Assignment 2

In the years immediately after September 11, 2001, most college students could vividly describe their experiences on that day because they had been teenagers on that day. They had understood the gravity of the horrible scenes that were playing out on their television and computer screens. You are likely to have been a child in 2001, and to remember much less. In a few years, college students will know September 11, 2001, as only one more date in history.

Your task for this assignment is to describe American life—during, or soon after September 11, 2001—in a way that will help future students understand what happened and why those events were important. Be sure to combine personal experience and academic research in ways that help the reader engage your main point in the essay.

To begin, free-write about your memories of September 11, 2001, including as many details as possible. Interview others, family members if possible, about their own memories of that time in American history, and—if possible—about their memories of how you experienced that time. Do some research about September 11 and the time following that event, paying attention to how people and governments responded to those events. Consider researching your hometown and local events rather than events in distant cities.

As you begin drafting, consider what you want your reader to understand about September 11. Begin with a working idea of your main point that you will refine as you draft.

Experiment with ways you could use unconventional form, style, organization, evidence, and so on to encourage your reader to engage with your main point.

Assignment 3

For almost a decade, the U.S. educational system has been shaped by the "No Child Left Behind" act (known by the acronyms NCLB or ESEA for Elementary and Secondary Education Act). This federal law requires school districts to test students regularly to determine what they're learning and how well they're learning it. The U.S. Department of Education maintains a Web site that provides data on how students in individual school systems have performed on standardized tests and advice for teachers and parents (http://www.ed.gov/nclb/landing.jhtml?src=pbt). Not surprisingly, it describes the NCLB act in positive terms. An Internet search combining the phrases "No Child Left Behind" and "NCTE," the acronym for the National Council of Teachers of English, produces fewer than one thousand hits, but among those is NCTE's critique of the NCLB act as well as descriptions of the effects of the NCLB act from English teachers across the country.

Your tasks for this assignment are three:

1. Free-write about your experience taking standardized tests in school, including as many specific details as possible. How often did you take standardized tests? Was there a routine to test-taking days? How did you feel as you took the test? How did you and others react to your performance on the tests? How did your teachers seem to view the test? If you did not take standardized tests in school, describe who assessed your academic work, how they did so, and how you and your parents responded to that assessment.

2. Read about the NCLB (now ESEA) act on the Department of Education Web site and on other reputable Web sites such as NCTE's. Keep track of the Web sites you visit, jotting notes for yourself about the author of the Web site, the author's attitude about the NCLB act, and any information you find interesting. Free-write about your opinion of the NCLB act—overall, is it a good law or a bad one? What effects does it have on education in the United States? Which of these effects are positive? Which are negative?

3. Write a thesis-based essay in which you support your claim about the NCLB act. Develop and support your claim as Victor Villanueva does, by blending your autobiographical experience and your research. Expand your earlier autobiographical descriptions with vivid, effective specifics. Be sure to note the source of your research support. If you have good reason to do so, consider breaking conventions that readers associate with a thesis-based academic essay, conventions related to organization, type and presentation of evidence, logical structure, and grammar. Be prepared to justify your choices.

13

MARKETING:
MOTIVATING ACTION

Do you have a preference when it comes to choosing a sandwich shop for lunch? If so, how did your preference develop? Do you have logical reasons for your preference?

Check out the Web sites for Subway (www.subway.com) and Quiznos (www.quiznos.com) (Web sites change frequently; if you open these two sites and find that they're very similar, find another sandwich or fast food site to compare.) List the different groups of people that each company targets, and then rank-order your list from the group that gets the most attention to the group that gets the least.

- Compare your lists—which groups do both Web sites target?
- Which groups seem more important on one Web site than the other? What kind of information (if any) does this tell you about the sandwich company?
- Would a Web site analysis like this alter your sandwich-shop preference? How could a sandwich shop use their Web site to earn or keep your loyalty?

PORTABLE RHETORICAL LESSON:
USING "ALL AVAILABLE MEANS" OF PERSUASION

What were your first impressions when you opened each of the two sandwich shop Web sites? At each site you encountered many different kinds of rhetorical tools: Words, sounds, shapes, movements, and colors directed you to links that held the information you wanted. The exercise should have reminded you of at least two rhetorical lessons. First, we wanted to draw your attention to a concrete example of something we talked about in Chapter 1: Aristotle's classical definition of rhetoric as the art of discovering "all available means" of persuasion. So we hoped that the exercise would remind you that the number of "available means" is vast. The number of elements that work to communicate—about something as simple as a sandwich shop—is astonishing.

Second, although the designers of these Web sites used a barrage of different means of persuasion to catch your attention, not all of them worked equally well. Some may have been more distracting than appealing. So the second lesson from the exercise, and the first rhetorical principle you would have to wrestle with if you were writing in marketing is to decide your **purpose.**

Marketing is more complex than advertising. Although it's true that professionals in marketing focus on customers, they also must communicate clearly with "partner" audiences: employees, stockholders, investors, suppliers, consultants. In effect, marketing professionals use writing to persuade people to "buy into" a company's mission or business goals. The goal of the marketing division of a major company is to align all communication so that what the consumer sees in an advertisement matches what the employees of a company believe about their product. The Quiznos Web site, for example, appeals to customers and should feel familiar to employees, too (many retailers now call a store's employees the "cast," to reinforce the sense that everyone is part of the same show). And look at the title of the marketing plan that is the first reading: *One Common Purpose*. The need to create a unified vision for a company is the primary goal of the marketing team, and they can only accomplish that if they are dead certain about their purpose.

With a clear sense of purpose, a marketing team also makes careful choices about **presentation.** Writers in marketing make deliberate choices in verbal style (key words and metaphors, for example, unify each reading in this chapter) and their visual style (quickly flip through the chapter to get a sense of how different the readings *look* than the readings in most of the earlier chapters).

Furthermore, remember that the verbal and visual choices that you see in this chapter were originally accompanied by PowerPoint presentations, with sounds, colors, and animation. Here's the key point: the **Portable Rhetorical Lesson** of this chapter is to use all available means of persuasion, but the opening exercise teaches you that *the number of means of persuasion is constantly growing*. The technology of the digital age expands your means of persuasion to the limits of imagination. When you were in grade school you probably learned to import pictures into papers that you composed on a computer; now you may be able to create Web sites almost as sophisticated as those you search for; 3-D is just around the corner for home users; the possibilities of virtual gaming will eventually be at the fingertips of very writer. Imagine what you'll have to do to keep up.

So, in this the last chapter of this book, the portable rhetorical lesson carries the larger message that if you hope to adapt effectively to every writing situation, you will have to keep up-to-date on the available means of persuasion. You will sometimes have to go beyond words on paper or screen, beyond images, beyond animation and music. The ultimate portable lesson of this book is that you should, through the rest of your life, habitually "read" widely; carry away lessons from everything that you read; adapt and change so that you can use writing—in media that humans haven't yet imagined—to persuade others and to make a difference.

WRITING IN THE DISCIPLINE

INTRODUCTION

by Robert Eames, Professor of Business

In January of 2001, three very different companies found themselves in similar situations. All three were preparing for major changes. Bissell, a family-owned company known for its floor sweepers and deep cleaning carpet scrubbers, was contemplating a major move into the vacuum cleaner market, where it was virtually unknown. Apple Computers, the computer maker known for its Macintosh and iMac computers, had just launched iTunes 1.0 and was beginning to develop its own digital music players. Steelcase, the world's leading designer and manufacturer of office furniture, was weathering an unprecedented downturn in demand in their industry, which threatened their leadership position. A few short years later, Bissell was the number one brand in the entire floor care category. The iPod not only grew to dominate sales in the digital music player category—to most consumers it *was* the category. And Steelcase had enjoyed a major sales resurgence. Other than phenomenal sales success in their respective markets, what did Bissell, Apple, and Steelcase have in common? They all knew their customers well and communicated that knowledge throughout their companies. That is, they all had effective marketing plans.

Writing effectively in marketing requires finding and filling needs. Great marketers thoroughly understand their customers. In fact, great marketers are obsessed with learning anything and everything about their customers, including their wants and needs—and aligning customers' needs with company objectives.

To write successfully for a business audience, a writer must be able to answer several questions, including:

> Who is the primary audience?
>
> What do they already know?
>
> What do I want the audience to do?
>
> What is necessary to get them to do what I want them to do?

The companies then respond to the answers to these questions with effective rhetorical choices.

One Common Purpose (OCP), written for Steelcase, Inc., is a good example of a marketing document that answers these questions well and thus expresses the key elements of a business plan. As the global market leader in the early stage of what would become a severe and prolonged industry downturn, Steelcase needed to improve their product offering *and* cut costs to improve profitability and maintain their leadership position. Written as a confidential internal company document, *OCP's* initial audience consisted of the executive management team. The document was also intended for use by management throughout the company in divisions such as finance, marketing, engineering, design, operations, and administration.

The writers of *OCP* wanted the executive team and the entire organization to understand, approve, and execute the plan. The goal was to persuade employees in each part of the company not only to accept the plan but also to act on it. Like most good plans, *OCP* does three things that help create change: it provides *context, direction,* and *motivation.* These three functions are the *what,* the content, of the plan.

The *how* of the plan, or the strategies the writers used to perform these functions, is also critical. *OCP,* for example, makes extensive use of graphic images that represent key ideas of the plan. Take note of the graphics; they show how well the writers knew their audience, which is very visually oriented because of the design-driven nature of the furniture industry. The plan also demonstrates the sophisticated understanding of how the audiences process information and learn. The graphics help to create metaphors (images that evoke comparisons to related ideas). Although the power of metaphors has long been appreciated by writers, scientists and marketers using brain scanning technology have recently learned that 95 percent of our thoughts, emotions, and learning occur unconsciously in metaphors. Good business writers know the metaphors that will resonate with their audience.

Now let's look at ways that the *what* (context, direction, and motivation) is communicated by the *how* (the rhetorical strategies). Good marketing plans provide readers with *context*—a clear picture of the current market situation—usually in the form of a situation analysis. These analyses tend to be very direct and economically written. Sentence fragments, tables, and bullet points are commonly used to summarize a great deal of analytical work that needs to be efficiently presented for a busy executive audience. In *OCP,* "The Big Picture" and the "Three-Year Business Plan" sections provide this context, using metaphors to establish the critical importance of product development. Important metaphors include (1) the intersection of Wall Street and Main Street, (2) the progressive graphics showing the growth in Steelcase's market from office furniture to a much larger "AFT" (combined architecture, furniture, and technology), and (3) the product "platforms" (the common rules for all products so that they coordinate across divisions). These metaphors then carry into the last section of *OCP,* the specific studio plans for architecture, furniture, and technology (the studio plans are not included here). The metaphors also increase the sense of unity and significance among employees who actually develop and launch products by connecting their work to the broader context of organizational goals and strategies.

OCP provides *direction* for Steelcase. "The Big Picture" and "Three-year Business Plan" sections provide a road map of strategies and tactics built around the four P's of marketing: Product, Price, Place, and Promotion. This helps management communicate, implement, and control strategies by clarifying employee's specific roles and responsibilities. Look at the drawings that indicate forward and upward direction.

Plans also provide *motivation.* For new companies or new parts of existing companies, plans might motivate investors by demonstrating just how well the management team knows the market. For an established company like Steelcase, marketers create plans not only to increase organizational alignment and commitment to a new strategic direction, but also to make decisions to allocate scarce resources to the best opportunities. The graphics in *OCP* target internal audiences in order to get and keep people on the same page. When people feel both a sense of need and a sense that they are part of a coordinated team, they gain motivation.

The various pieces of *OCP* are integrated, coordinated, and directionally aligned. That's good marketing and good writing.

✓ Reading Tips

You need active eyes to read this chapter. Its writers use multiple rhetorical strategies at the same time. So as you read each page and each section, think about its purpose. To identify the purpose of each part:

- Consider how the words and images support, complement, and clarify one another; use the connections among the various "means of persuasion" to help you figure out the purpose of the plan.

- Pay attention to where you are in the structure of the document, and figure out the particular purpose of the "Big Picture" and the "Three-year Business Plan" (each part serves a different function in setting up the later, more detailed parts of the plan that are not reprinted here).

- Look for patterns and repetitions (for example, there are lots of images of various intersected and integrated parts—the "Main St./Wall St." image you see on the first page and the "AFT" plan—are metaphors that control the overall message).

- Imagine the various engineering, financial, manufacturing, and marketing groups that the plan must unify, and look for the features that you think would appeal to all the groups and the features that apply to particular groups.

One
Common Purpose

Three-year Business Plan
Marketing and Product Development

December 21, 2001

Company Confidential

The Big Picture

If we were to do a balance sheet on the assets which support the delivery of product, and hence the delivery of value to our customers… the vast majority could be linked to products and therefore product development.

Because product development touches everything the business does – both today and tomorrow – there are few processes or outputs of any corporation that possess the same strategic importance. The results of product development here at Steelcase have a direct impact on our competitiveness and future profitability.

Product development is the future of any manufacturing company. What a company develops today will determine its revenue stream tomorrow. In essence, today's product development results are the first look at the company's financial future.

The company with the most competitive product wins on Main Street.

The company with the most profitable product wins on Wall Street.

Success is winning on both.

One reason for the simplicity of image and theme on this page is that this business plan has to appeal to a wide range of professionals in the company. It also has to unify all those people around a single message.

The Big Picture

Different No Longer

Historically, architecture, furniture and technology have been considered different from each other... separate and distinct elements. They were subject to *different* development disciplines and cared for by *different* professions; they required *different* purchasing methods.

Our research and experience, however, indicate that when architecture, furniture and technology are synchronized to the business objectives of the organization, people are more productive. And workplace synergy permits people and organizations to work better.

So it's time to help our customers switch focus... from the differences among architecture, furniture and technology, to their similarities and interrelationships and the value this can mean to their organizations.

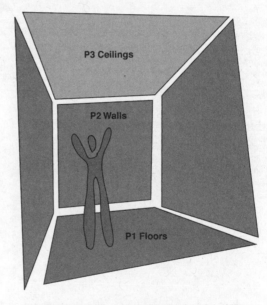

The harmonious integration of the three planes within the shell of a building.

Steelcase Inc. · December 2001 · Company Confidential

The plan offers the image, in the graphic, of integrated planes to counter the old "differences."

The Big Picture

AFT: Leveraging the Strengths of All Three

Architecture... the structural elements. Floors, walls, and ceilings, along with panels and post and beam, create and define the physical boundaries of the workplace – the elements of greater permanence. They determine individual and group work areas, create various levels of acoustical and visual privacy, and provide larger surface areas for information persistence.

To synchronize with furniture and technology... architectural elements require common dimensions and simple interfaces; they need to give users planning flexibility to relocate elements as needs change.

Furniture... the movable elements that exist within the three planes. Desks, tables, storage, and seating, along with panels and post and beam, set the tone for the environment, making the workplace more stimulating, more personal, and ultimately more productive. They help people work – individually and in groups – by providing the support and comfort needed to create and manage knowledge.

To synchronize with architecture and technology... furniture needs to be conveniently mobile and flexible.

Technology... is divided in two broad areas: appliances and infrastructure.

Appliances are tools: cell phones, Palm Pilots, notebooks, modems, Websigns, etc. Appliances often start out as stand-alone devices, but if they have broad appeal, they seek entree into the infrastructure.

Infrastructure is the delivery system that carries technology to every nook-and-cranny in the workplace; it crisscrosses the organization, distributing power, lighting, voice and data. Organizations depend on infrastructure to provide convenient access for communication and information sharing.

To synchronize with architecture and furniture... technology must accommodate emerging appliances and adapt to constant change.

Reframing the market opportunity from furniture to the combination of architecture, furniture, and technology (AFT) was essential to gain support for the plan. The drawings portray the expanded opportunities: the top drawing shows the architecture, the second adds furniture, and the third adds technology. These graphics were also used in PowerPoint presentations.

The Big Picture

AFT Benefits

Why Customers Care

The workplace that seamlessly integrates architecture, furniture and technology enables people to focus on their work, connect with one another in meaningful ways, and share the knowledge and experience that ultimately ensures an organization's success. In addition, this integrated workplace helps "future-proof" the customer's investment.

Why Steelcase Cares

The effective implementation of AFT in the marketplace can uniquely differentiate Steelcase from our competitors. In addition, it can help us focus our investments on integrated solutions and develop new revenue opportunities for Steelcase and our dealers. It also allows us to continue building our brand.

Existing Building. The Steelcase University Learning Center demonstrates the harmonious integration of architecture, furniture and technology within existing real estate.

New Construction. The Patterson Building is an excellent example of supporting users through a higher level of integration of architecture, furniture and technology in new construction.

Steelcase Inc. • December 2001 • Company Confidential

The buildings pictured in these photos are well known to Steelcase employees. They evoke images of expanded market opportunities, reinforcing the benefits of the plan.

The Big Picture

AFT: The Future and the Present

The idea of tying architecture, furniture and technology together is not unique to Steelcase. A number of our competitors, in fact, are laying claim to the same strategy. Our product development, therefore, must focus both on "catching up" to our competitors with more desirable features at lower price points, while providing innovative solutions that leap over competitive positions.

At a practical level, as well, we need to keep an eye on improving profit margins across the board to meet corporate targets.

While our current product offerings, development activities, and promotional tactics are intended to lay the foundation for establishing Steelcase as the market leader, we face critical challenges in the areas of product integration, pricing, communications, and dealer capabilities.

The volume of needed development demands that we develop products faster than we ever have before. Quicker teamwork and faster decision-making are essential.

It is also imperative that we effectively educate and energize our channel. The strength of Steelcase dealerships, aided by a well-trained Steelcase sales force can enable Steelcase to become the undeniable market leader in the AFT market.

Steelcase Inc. • December 2001 • Company Confidential

The plan recognizes challenges and risks and outlines them here. The frankness about potential trouble helps build team unity and motivation.

The Big Picture	Steelcase North America

Great Design Innovation Isn't Enough

Is it possible to have a successful business in which our products are designed separate and apart from manufacturing considerations? We don't think so.

First, design and innovation are not one in the same. Innovation is the commercial application of unique knowledge and skill that satisfies customers, thereby turning a profit.

So a truly innovative product solution is one in which both the customer and the producer are delighted with the results: the customer receives high value; and the producer receives good margins, sustains a competitive advantage, and thwarts competitive efforts to undermine investment.

In the interest of getting the most out of both design and manufacturing, we propose to have both disciplines work together under two imperatives:

> Design firms get paid to design stuff; that's how they make their money. Manufacturing firms get paid to make stuff; that's how they make their money.
>
> We need to do both.

1. Kit-of-Parts

Since we expect that customers will continue to ask for the ability to blend elements of one product line with another, we will implement a product strategy that moves away from discrete product lines to groups of product components that are systemically compatible with one another:

- To achieve greater flexibility to meet performance, visual, lifecycle-cost requirements
- To provide customers with exactly what they value
- To help migrate customers to the future, while leveraging their large installed base
- To support AFT strategy with Kit-of-Parts compatibility in the development of all architecture, furniture, and technology products

		Value	Performance	Premium
Architecture	Walls	□	○	
	Panels	□	○	△
Furniture	Large Case Storage	□	○	△
	Small Case Storage	□	○	△△
	Desking	□	○	△
	Alternative Systems	□	○	
Seating	Primary Work Chairs	□	○	△△
	Support Chairs	□	○○	△△
	Alternative Postures	□	○	
Wood	Systems	□	○○	△
	Seating	□	○	△△
	Casegoods	□		△
Technology	Power	□	○	△△
	Network Connectivity	□	○	△
	Access Floors	□	○○	△△
	Lighting Alliance	□		

> This section of the plan introduces the key initiatives: the integrated "Kit-of-Parts" and the "Product Platforms." They set the stage for the studio plans that follow.

The Big Picture

Great Design Innovation Isn't Enough *(continued)*

2. Product Platforms

Gone are the days when new Steelcase product lines are developed around their own proprietary dimensions, interfaces and aesthetics. Our new product strategy will require that all new products adhere to the guidelines of foundational Steelcase platforms that:

1. Establish a small number of "rules" that permit broad design interpretation and materials diversity
2. Adhere to manufacturing criteria established in collaboration with manufacturing norms

Conforming to platform guidelines, will allow us to:

- Develop innovative product components that are systemically compatible with one another
- Employ internal tools for cost-effective manufacturing, warehousing, and distribution of our products
- Utilize common platform construction across product types, increasing flexibility and customization options
- Offer increased product compatibility across all Steelcase Inc. brands
- Simplify customer options
- Realize substantial cost savings through manufacturing efficiencies, which can be passed along to customers or result in higher profit margins for select products

Plan the Work. Work the Plan.

The studios are aligned.

As we move forward, securing alignment against this plan throughout the company will enable us all to achieve our desired goal: To maintain and grow our industry leadership position and market share with substantially improved profitability.

We look forward to you joining us on this journey.

> Note the point of the last statement in "The Big Picture" section: join us on this journey.

Three-year Business Plan

Steelcase North America

Strategic Intent

Market leadership means expanding the total opportunity

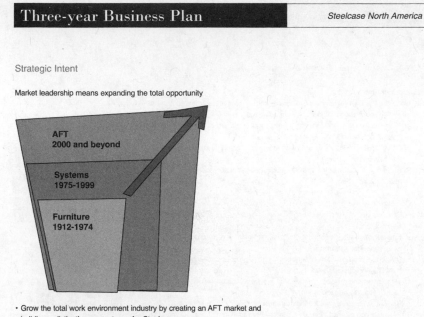

AFT
2000 and beyond

Systems
1975-1999

Furniture
1912-1974

- Grow the total work environment industry by creating an AFT market and building a distinctive competency for Steelcase
- The products in this market will be differentiated by their unique, user-centered design and holistic integration of architecture, furniture and technology
- The success of these products will be the result of their design aesthetic, functional fit, and the "experience" users associate with them
- As a result of their perceived value add, these products will be able to command premium prices and result in an overall more profitable product portfolio for Steelcase

Steelcase Inc. • December 2001 • Company Confidential

As *OCP* moves from "The Big Picture" to the "Three-year Business Plan," it uses a graphic that connects expanded market opportunities to company evolution, creating employee alignment and motivation.

Three-year Business Plan

Steelcase North America

Market Trends
(As identified by ACRD Research and Steelcase North American Situation Analysis)

Recognizing and understanding market trends reveal business opportunities.

People
- Increasingly diverse workplace encompasses four generations
- Expectations of bosses and workers changed
- Hierarchies replaced by networks
- Ideas equal value, capital
- Privacy, acoustical, social, environmental needs unmet

Process
- Shift in favor of knowledge workers
- Network importance blurring corporate boundaries
- Increase in distributed team-based work, remote collaboration

Space
- Declining building size, office space per worker
- New construction less expensive than renovation
- Hoteling, shared spaces reduce cost per person
- People working anywhere, anytime
- Largest expenditures on sustainable architecture: lighting, HVAC, energy

Technology
- New products, markets created by technology
- Work processes, patterns impacted by technology
- Efficiency improved through alternative e-business value chain
- Old and new technology co-exist

Steelcase Inc. • December 2001 • Company Confidential

Note that there is not a single complete sentence on this page. Writing effective phrases—that communicate complete thoughts—is a critical skill in business writing.

Three-year Business Plan
Steelcase North America

Driving Goals

Solidify and enhance the Steelcase position as the world's leading provider of effective work environments through:

User-Centered Design Innovation
Matching user needs with invention to develop commercially viable and innovative products

Portfolio Migration
Balancing short-term profitability while migrating customers to profitable Kit-of-Parts solutions

Profitability
Meeting and exceeding targeted corporate goals

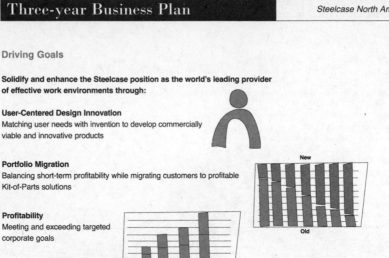

Overriding Strategies

Key activities of the product lifecycle process that are driven by Marketing and Product Development.

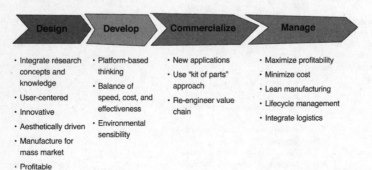

Design	Develop	Commercialize	Manage
· Integrate research concepts and knowledge	· Platform-based thinking	· New applications	· Maximize profitability
· User-centered	· Balance of speed, cost, and effectiveness	· Use "kit of parts" approach	· Minimize cost
· Innovative		· Re-engineer value chain	· Lean manufacturing
· Aesthetically driven	· Environmental sensibility		· Lifecycle management
· Manufacture for mass market			· Integrate logistics
· Profitable			

Steelcase Inc. · December 2001 · Company Confidential

The stylized graphic of a person—"the user"— picked up on a major strategic theme of user-centered design. The image was used extensively in written communications and PowerPoint slides.

Three-year Business Plan

Steelcase North America

Critical Success Factors

We will succeed *only* **if Steelcase:**

Aligns on product goals at all levels of the organization

Improves the accuracy and reliability of the cost reporting system

Implements product strategies with discipline and accountability

Implements "Lean Manufacturing" to improve profitability

Educates about and aligns to the AFT market:

- Streamlines the entire value chain to maximize continuity, simplicity, cost effectiveness for AFT implementation
- Enters the sales process much earlier to effectively execute AFT
- Becomes the supplier of choice within the dealer network

Commercializes AFT with the same single-minded focus as systems in the 1980s (furniture and IOWT)

Measurements of Success

We will develop measurement targets against these criteria:

User-centered Design Innovation

- Number of icon products and product design awards
- Measured market perception
- Number of patent applications
- Recognition for environmental sensitivity
- Reaching lean manufacturing targets

Portfolio Migration

- Meeting new product sales targets
- Measured transition in applications from hierarchical/universal to community-based

Profitability

Meeting financial results targets as measured by:

- Sales
- Gross Profit
- EVA

True performance means understanding the vision and flawlessly implementing against it. The following studio plans outline how this will be accomplished.

Reading Responses

1. Because *One Common Purpose* is a document written primarily for audiences within the company, it talks about customers in the third person. Review *One Common Purpose* and record all the references to customers. Then consider the data you collected—what do your data indicate about Steelcase's relationship with its customers?

2. In his introduction, Professor Eames notes that the authors of *One Common Purpose* paid careful attention to the metaphors they used throughout the document. Track the occurrences of the metaphor of forward movement throughout the document, paying attention to its presence in both the text and the graphics.

3. The phrase *One Common Purpose* takes on multiple meanings throughout the document. List the different meanings that *One Common Purpose* has and, for each meaning, list the rhetorical means that the authors use to communicate that meaning.

NOTES ON GRAMMAR, STYLE, AND RHETORIC:
THE LANGUAGE OF MOTIVATION

One Common Purpose, the Steelcase document that serves as the primary reading selection for this chapter, is a three-year business plan for marketing and product development. You might expect it to be charts, figures, diagrams, financial statements—dry business writing. You might not suspect that the piece would carry personal force. You would be wrong. *One Common Purpose* does indeed express powerful personal force and offers some significant rhetorical lessons. In fact, reading this document is like doing a case study of the essence of interpersonal motivation.

In order to motivate their coworkers, what strategies do the writers of the document use? First, they sound prominent notes of unity; they stress that they and all other Steelcase employees are part of the same team, are in this endeavor together. This strategy shows itself already in the title, *One Common Purpose.* And not too long after the title page the emphasis on being or becoming a team comes out again, this time when the writers emphasize that they "look forward to you [their coworkers] joining us on this journey" (409). Beyond this, throughout the document the writers stress that for their proposed plan to succeed, they will have to secure "alignment against this plan throughout the company . . ." (409), not just on certain levels or in particular divisions of the company. We can see the emphasis on unity perhaps most clearly through the pronouns that often appear in this piece—the plan is full of first-person plural pronouns such as *we* and *our.* Some of these, of course, stand in for referents to the writers of the document. But what is more important is that many of them stand in for referents to all Steelcase employees. We can identify both antecedents that give meaning to first-person pronouns in the following two sentences: "Is it possible to have a successful business in which our [all employees'] products are designed separate and apart from manufacturing considerations? We [the writers] don't think so" (408).

The writers' second key motivational strategy is to lay out clear and specific goals for the future of the company. They state their overarching goal as follows: "To maintain and grow our industry leadership position and market share with substantially improved profitability" (409). As the plan goes into greater detail, this overarching goal develops into additional, more specific, goals.

Interestingly, these more specific goals usually appear in one of two forms. Many goals are expressed as infinitives (the base form of the verb plus *to,* as in *to plan*). In the section dealing with product strategy, for instance, one goal is "To achieve greater flexibility to meet performance, visual, lifecycle-cost requirements" (408). Other goals appear as statements with future-tense verbs. For example, we read that "The success of these products will be the result of their design aesthetic . . ." (410). Even when the verb in a sentence is not in the future tense, it is clear that these writers are trying to get everyone in the company to focus on the future: "In essence, today's product development results are the first look at the company's financial future" (403).

However, it is also clear from this plan that it will not necessarily be easy for the company to achieve its goals for the future. We can sense this from the notes of urgency that the writers sound. To stress the urgency of the situation that the company faces, these writers use several closely related expressions such as "is critical for," "will require," "we need to," and "we must." Why this tone of urgency? To put it simply, there were some strong challenges to the company's leading position in the office-furniture business. Many of these challenges were posed by their competitors. In fact, the writers warn, "We will succeed only if. . . ." They follow the "if" with a line of action plans signaled by active verbs: "aligns," "improves," "implements," "educates." The company, it is clear, had to respond to these challenges quickly and wisely.

In Your Own Writing . . .

When you need to motivate others in a group to help you accomplish something, employ the strategies of interpersonal motivation:

• Address those you wish to motivate as if they are working with you on the same team.
• Lay out clear and specific goals.
• Use sentence fragments to offer sharply focused reminders of key concepts.
• Use appropriate linguistic markers of urgency to highlight the challenges that you face.

STUDENT WRITING

INTRODUCTION

by Sarah Steen, business major

The Assignment. The assignment to write a marketing plan for a real organization hit me like a slap in the face. Welcome to the real world! Invariably, all my other business writing assignments had been the typical, formulaic, often dry—and dreaded—"reflection papers." I had been expressing my thoughts and feelings about business without ever getting my hands dirty with the real thing. So I was up for a new challenge, but my first reaction was one of anxiety: "Wait a minute! No one has ever taught me how to write a marketing plan!"

The Content. But I had to start somewhere. I sat down at my computer with the assignment from my professor, a sample marketing plan from a textbook, some hot chocolate, and . . . a blank Word document. I had no idea where to begin. I frantically tried to think of important marketing concepts that might pertain to the task at hand, until I realized that it all came down to the first lesson I ever learned in marketing: it's all about the customer.

Two other students and I had been assigned to work with a nonprofit organization called Safe Haven (it helps women who are suffering from abuse). It became clear, then, that their employees and their Board of Directors were our customers. The marketing plan we were creating for Safe Haven was the final piece of our group project that would tie together almost one hundred hours of our background research.

At the beginning of the project we spoke with the executive director, who shared with us her big dreams for the way our project could fit in with the larger mission of Safe Haven. She told us that they would soon be hiring a new staff member who would follow up on our findings by creating a new church liaison program. My group members and I were excited to see how important our research would be to this organization's future, but we also hoped that we could do this project justice.

Learning to Write in Marketing. As we began the project, we thought it was important to get to know our customers by spending time at their office. After a tour and introductions, we settled into a conference room to pore over their computer files and handwritten records of the past 14 years. After several visits we had all gained an appreciation for their work and what was before us, and each of us felt drawn to pursue different avenues of our marketing project.

Even though I now understood my customer, I still wasn't out of the woods when it came time to write the marketing plan. I fretfully reminded myself that I still didn't know how to write real business documents. My mind drifted: what *had* I learned to write? I had learned how to write informative essays: now I would show my customer that I understood their situation from an inside perspective. I had learned how to write persuasive essays: now I would persuade my customer that because I understood their situation and performed countless hours analyzing their data, I could offer the organization worthwhile suggestions. With these things in mind, I began to write. I tried to picture the executive director cocking her head and asking at certain points along the way, "How do you know that?" I rephrased things and expanded the explanations, trying to show her our line of thinking.

I finally worked out a draft and showed it to my professor. He was pleased with the content, but, as he pointed out, it was almost entirely long paragraphs, and businesspeople apparently have no patience for such things. Those reflection papers I wrote never asked me to consider how I felt about sentence fragments, but that was my next challenge: to find lists, key words, and main ideas in my plan and make them pop with effective formatting, bullets, and sentence fragments. Unlike my initial writing struggles, this process was much more intuitive. Often I just remembered the words and phrases we used most often in our group meetings. "Geography," for example, turned out to be a key in our plan; there had been missed opportunities. For example, there were geographical locations from which a lot of Safe Haven clients came, but not many donors in those areas were giving money to Safe Haven. I figured that just as a professor will put a term on a test if he mentions it three days in a row, Safe Haven would want to understand the ideas our group kept coming back to day after day. It took some time to create a parallel structure for my lists and to make my paragraphs more concise, but I noticed that at a glance the entire document seemed a lot more accessible by the time I was finished.

The most rewarding part of the entire composition process was when we finally presented the marketing plan and accompanying research to the executive director. Her face was glowing, and we were taken aback by her gratefulness and determination to take action on our plan that very day. At that moment I realized that I had accomplished what I set out to do from that first day at the computer—satisfy my customer.

Safe Haven Marketing Campaign
Sarah Steen

Executive Summary

The direction of this marketing plan and accompanying project is focused specifically on one of the seven goals presented in Safe Haven's Strategic Plan: "to expand and continue to cultivate consistent revenue sources." The specific focus is to find ways to increase financial support from churches.

Our team accomplished this by:

- **segmenting** Kane County by geographical locations and church groups;
- **identifying** segments that have high giving potential; and
- **targeting** churches in these segments in order to initiate and strengthen relationships.

We found several trends:

1. Several zip codes in Kane County have a high average disposable income, yet churches in these areas give relatively small amounts to Safe Haven.
2. Clients come from a variety of Grand Falls suburbs in Kane County, yet Safe Haven has not made contacts with churches in all of these areas.
3. Several denominations have no contact with Safe Haven or do not currently support the organization, even though there are a significant number of Safe Haven clients that identify with that denomination.

Specific zip codes, denominations, computations, and other information can be found in the Recommendations section of this marketing plan and in the appendix.

Based on these findings, our team suggests the following goals:

- Make five "Raise Hope" presentations in each of the targeted denominations and zip codes within the next twelve months
- Expect an average increase in giving of $1000 by each of these churches and their members
- Establish commitments and identify a liaison with five of these churches within the next 18 months
- Expect an average increase in giving of $5000 by each of these churches

---

Sidebar notes:

An "executive summary" serves its audience in ways similar to an "abstract." As you might expect from a business document, it identifies itself by its audience: executives.

The organizations that sought the help of my marketing class were those who need help but didn't have great financial resources. So my class worked with several not-for-profit organizations, many of which were "faith based."

subgroups of major religions

In this largest section of the report we provide *context*, a key in marketing. By explaining the history and mission and summarizing market opportunities, we also suggest *direction* and *motivation*, the other two keys in marketing.

Situation Analysis

Safe Haven exists to provide both shelter and non-residential services for abused women and their children. They are also dedicated to raising awareness of domestic violence within the community. Safe Haven is founded on the basic principle that through charitable love they might begin to renew the human spirit and build a stronger community by ending the cycle of domestic abuse.

Safe Haven is located in Grand Falls, but their services extend to all of Kane County and beyond. It was founded in 1990 by six churches located in the heart of Grand Falls. The growth of the organization since its inception is remarkable:

Then: 1990

6 supporting churches

Yearly budget: $35,000

One shelter

Now: 2004

285 churches in contact database

Yearly budget: $447,000

Multi-faceted services.

Safe Haven is able to help more than 400 women and children per year through their Harbor House and Protective Helper programs. In order to continue serving families in both these and their Lift Hope program, Safe Haven seeks volunteer, financial, and spiritual support from both individuals and church communities.

It is clear that church support has increased since Safe Haven first began:

Then: 1990

6 supporting churches

all in one denomination

Now: 2004

285 churches in contact database

25+ denominations

The preceding growth is an encouragement to Safe Haven's effort to reach a greater cross-section of its geographical location. However, there is still need to strengthen current contacts and develop new ones:

• Only 91 of the 285 churches in the database (32%) have supported Safe Haven financially
• 70% of financial support received from churches has been from within the denomination of the founding churches

Market Summary

The overarching market important to all aspects of Safe Haven is Kane County. Within Kane County, Safe Haven has three sub-markets: the client market, the awareness market, and the support market. The market most relevant to this marketing plan is the support market.

Client Market

This includes abused women and their children who need shelter, legal advocacy, counseling, and support because they presently are in an abusive relationship or as they recover from one.

Awareness Market

This includes everyone, because Safe Haven believes that everyone needs to know the realities of domestic abuse and what can be done to stop it and prevent it, including the ways that Safe Haven can help.

Support Market

Safe Haven believes that it benefits from the time, spiritual support, and financial support of people through many different outlets:

- **Individually**
- Through their **place of work**
- Through a **foundation** that they support
- Through their **church**

Of these sources, the support of churches is especially critical to the success of Safe Haven. Safe Haven has the opportunity to partner with churches in addressing the issues of domestic violence. Together they can affirm the dignity and worth of every person and offer healing and support. Over the years Safe Haven has learned that the more church members who get involved with their ministry, the more people from that same congregation who will get the help that they need.

> Here's another example of how we combine direction and motivation.

This project will focus its efforts on churches, clients, and programs in Kane County, where the core of Safe Haven's activity takes place. However, Johnstown will also be included in our data because it is a geographically significant area to Safe Haven's work. It is on the border of Kane and Otswega Counties and many of the Protective Helper clients from Johnstown go to churches in Kane County. Safe Haven has reached people and churches in Grand Falls and all surrounding counties, but due to time constraints on the project it is most important to focus on clients and churches closest to the point of service.

Kane County Demographics

Within the zip codes in Kane County and Johnstown, from which Safe Haven has made church contacts with or has drawn clients, the demographic data is as follows:*

- The total population of the **27** zip codes is **610,077**
- The total number of households in the **27** zip codes is **237,026**

*Source: United States Zip Code Directory: http://www.zip-codes.com/zip_code_directory.asp

- The average house value is **$120,397.39**
- The average income per household is **$48,697.32**
- The total population based on ethnicity is:
  - White: **512,988**
  - Black: **51,530**
  - Hispanic: **40,843**

Market Needs

Within the **client** market, victims of domestic abuse need to know that they are not alone and that help is available to them. They need to be aware of the services Safe Haven provides and how to access these services.

Within the **support** market, churches and individuals need to know that Safe Haven provides an important service to the greater Grand Falls area and is a worthy recipient of their financial support. Because churches are a major source of funds for Safe Haven services, they need to know that Safe Haven is run by individuals who recognize the importance of faith-based service.

Also within the support market it is important that Safe Haven provides other ways for people to contribute to its work beyond gift-giving. Safe Haven must establish opportunities, and people in the support market must be empowered to contribute. The desire to get involved is already there, but there must be opportunities for this value exchange to take place.

Within the **awareness** market it is important for all people to understand the issues surrounding domestic violence. They also need to understand what Safe Haven has to offer any victim of domestic violence. In this way, people will be able to recognize domestic violence in their lives or the lives of their friends or family and refer them to the help that they need.

Because domestic violence is a taboo issue, it is sometimes difficult to address and discuss. Safe Haven needs to provide safe avenues for people to talk openly about domestic violence. Safe Haven has several measures already in place that may be further developed, including women's restroom flyers and other advertising campaigns, Lift Hope presentations, Domestic Violence Orientations, and the annual Faith Breakfasts.

> Of course we could not provide direction without showing trends. Trend analysis is essential for marketing plans.

Market Trends

By comparing the amount of money a church gives to its involvement in Safe Haven's programs the following market trends may be inferred:

- Churches that send representatives to the annual Faith Breakfasts increase their giving by an average of 200%
- Churches that host Lift Hope presentations increase giving by an average of 90%

By reviewing the Lift Hope program evaluations and speaking with presenters the following trends are also evident:

- Response to presentations is overwhelmingly positive and appreciative
- Attendees wish to talk further about issues surrounding domestic violence with both representatives of Safe Haven and other members of their congregation
- One or more attendees approach the presenter to share their own story of domestic abuse

By examining these trends it is clear that Safe Haven's goal should be to set up more presentations and to increase the attendance at each presentation. These presentations are meant to raise awareness, but it is clear that they are also a way for victims to begin the process of getting the help that they need.

Market Growth

Since Safe Haven began its Protective Helper program, the number of clients has increased steadily. However, the number of clients in 2002 and 2003 remained about the same, perhaps because the ministry reached its current carrying capacity.

People have become more aware of Safe Haven through the distribution of their clergy packets, through flyers in women's restrooms, and through the many presentations and orientations they host throughout Grand Falls.

However, because most of Safe Haven's contacts are within the denomination of the founding churches, this denomination's share of support has been growing while other denominations remain under-contacted and under-utilized. The six founding churches represent 54% of Safe Haven's church donations, and giving from all churches in the same denomination as the founding churches represents 70%.

Even though Safe Haven was begun by the founding churches, over the years Safe Haven has received an increasing amount of support from other churches and other denominations. A great example of this is Church A which has raised more than $130,000 for Safe Haven. It would be incredibly beneficial for Safe Haven to identify a few other churches like this outside the founding denomination. Like Church A, the large congregational sizes of churches like Church B, Church C, Church D, and even Church E present great potential for giving.

It is difficult to analyze the growth of church giving because our data is limited to amount of contribution to date. However, data per year is available for Faith Breakfast attendance. From this we see that an increased number of people from multiple denominations have been attending and supporting Safe Haven through this annual event.

Not only have people from different denominations been coming to the Faith Breakfasts, overall attendance has also been on the rise. It is interesting to note, however, that after not holding a 2002 Faith Breakfast, attendance at the 2003 breakfast was down a small amount. It is important for this to remain an annual event in order to keep up the enthusiasm and momentum for supporting Safe Haven.

SWOT Analysis

> A SWOT analysis is perhaps the most common feature of marketing plans—or any strategic planning.

Strengths

- 14 years of **experience** in the geographical area
- **Faith-basis** that complements the work of churches and other religious organizations
- Well-organized **methods** of raising awareness including presentations and published materials
- Basic, committed **financial support**

Weaknesses

- Small **size** of the organization with only one point of service for the entire client base
- An unspoken **taboo** that may prevent social discussion of domestic violence
- **Unfamiliarity** with denominations other than the founding denomination
- Various unorganized, missing **data**
- No history of **marketing goals**, targets, or segments

Opportunities

- Greater **awareness** due to recent publicized cases of domestic violence
- Increasingly **diverse attendance** at Faith Breakfasts
- New **staff person** to coordinate Church Liaison Program
- Large, untapped **giving potential** among Safe Haven's church contacts

Threats

- **Perception** that as Safe Haven expands it becomes too commercial and anonymity may be compromised
- **Economic downturn** that creates less disposable income
- Limit of future **growth** without increased financial support
- **Incorrect perception** that Safe Haven promotes divorce
- **Competition** between charities for donations

Alternative Providers

Safe Haven is one of the few domestic violence abuse and prevention shelter organizations in Grand Falls. The other social service agencies in the area include the YWCA and Catholic Social Services. Although these three organizations are complementary to one another, Safe Haven occupies a unique position as the only one of the three that uses a faith-based approach to all of their services.

Services Offered

Harbor House can offer short-term, emergency shelter for a maximum of 4 women and 11 children by providing a safe house and retreat. Services include: housing for victims and their children, crisis intervention, information and referrals, legal advocacy, housing and job assistance, childcare, individual counseling and support groups, a caring and professional staff, as well as a listening ear.

Protective Helper, Safe Haven's non-residential program, employs certified therapists and family advocates who offer professional, confidential services to abused women and their children. Services include: education-based support groups, therapy-based support groups, individual counseling, case management, legal advocacy, information and resources, the "I Feel Better Now" Children's Workshop Series, a resource library, and continued support for former residents of Ramoth House.

Lift Hope is the education part of Safe Haven and is organized around four specific goals:

- Raising awareness and informing
- Gaining church support
- Educating the public through presentations
- Partnering with local churches and organizations to develop and nurture relationships of time, energy, and resources

Recommendations

Here we get the focus of our plan; it's all about helping the customers see what they can do to create positive change.

In order to meet Safe Haven's second goal, "to expand and continue to cultivate consistent revenue sources," our team began by segmenting Kane County **geographically** by zip code and also **denominationally.** By studying these segments we have discovered several areas of high potential but low share:

- The following zip codes in Kane County comprise areas of high disposable income, yet the churches in these areas give relatively small amounts to Safe Haven:

59544: Wilbur	59505: NE Grand Falls
59548: Kanewood	59509: Wilsonville
59341: Rockford	59321: Comston Park

- The following suburbs of Grand Falls are home to a relatively high number of clients, yet Safe Haven has few or no contacts with churches in these areas:

- 59544: Wilbur   8 clients   0 churches
- 59321: Comston Park   16 clients   0 churches
- 59341: Rockford   14 clients   5 churches

- The following denominations have a relatively high number of Safe Haven clients who identify with one of their churches yet none of the churches currently support Safe Haven financially: Baptist, Assemblies of God, Bible, Seventh-Day Adventist, Pentecostal, Wesleyan

We suggest that Safe Haven target churches in any of the preceding areas or denominations. It is especially noteworthy that all three areas with high client and low church concentrations are also areas of high disposable income. The appendix of this marketing plan includes contact information for many churches that meet one or more of these criteria.

> These possible goals put some flesh on the recommendations; they allow the customer to imagine specific actions and results.

Potential Goals

- Make five Raise Hope presentations in each of the targeted denominations and zip codes within the next twelve months
- Expect an average increase in giving of $1000 by each of these churches and their members
- Establish covenant commitments and identify a liaison with five of these churches within the next 18 months
- Expect an average increase in giving of $5000 by each of these churches

Reading Responses

1. Compare the information in the executive summary with the information contained in the rest of the marketing plan. What information would you have added to the executive summary? What information would you eliminate?

2. In her introduction, Sarah Steen notes that when she revised her first draft of the marketing plan, she shortened long paragraphs. But her marketing plan still contains many more words than the Steelcase *One Common Purpose*. Take one section of the Safe Haven report and condense it, using all the rhetorical strategies available to you.

3. If you consider the metaphors Safe Haven uses for its services, you'll quickly notice that they emphasize refuge and protection—appealing ideas to victims of domestic violence. Create a series of graphics that link the different sections to each other and that link the different sections to the central theme of Safe Haven.

PUBLIC WRITING

INTRODUCTION

There are few more public kinds of writing than an advertisement. The ad reprinted here accompanies the first and last readings in this chapter, so we need not say anything more about the context of this particular product, which is part of the *One Common Purpose* business plan.

Of special interest here is the strategy of gaining readers' attention with the loud, colloquial word choices and then letting readers' eyes drift down to the small-font detail that refers to the finding (as you'll see reported more fully in the last reading in the chapter) that the Leap Chair increases productivity by 17.8 percent.

Leap Chair Advertisement

The problem isn't
that your employees are
sitting on their butts.

It's that their butts are
in the wrong chair.

©2003 Steelcase Inc.

Steelcase work environments can yield real business results.
In a recent study, our Leap® Chair—with ergonomic training—
increased productivity by 17.8%. Details at steelcase.com/results.

Steelcase   Do what you do better.™

Reading Responses

1. Analyze the different uses of language, fonts, kinds of information—all the "means of persuasion" that the ad uses. How do various elements work individually? How do they work in harmony? Is there anything you would change about the ad? If so, explain why.

2. Using information, ideas, or graphics from the final reading in the chapter or the first reading, *One Common Purpose,* design your own advertisement for the Leap Chair.

3. This ad makes prominent use of simple black and white. List all the possible messages that this use of black and white gives to the reader.

MORE WRITING IN MARKETING

INTRODUCTION

Sometimes the best way to sell something is by letting someone else sell it for you. Think, for example, of the number of times you've heard that a health or personal care product has been recommended by a group of doctors or dentists. Third-party credibility is often a great way to position the value of a product or service in the mind of a marketplace that is constantly being bombarded with claims of new and improved features. This was definitely the case when Steelcase launched their new Leap Chair in 2002. What would persuade purchasing agents in corporate America to buy this chair over the many other well-designed chairs on the market? The answer had to be based in cold hard facts: what could Leap do that would make it worth the money?

Steelcase commissioned a research study (coordinated by independent agencies and conducted by independent scientists) to investigate the impact of the Leap Chair on the productivity of office workers. The report concluded that the combination of the advanced ergonomic features of the chair and proper office ergonomics training resulted in a significant increase in productivity.

Steelcase knows that businesspeople don't really enjoy reading scientific papers and dry, statistics-laden research reports. But the research was important, and Steelcase used the information to position the Leap Chair as a productivity-improving work tool in the minds of their target customers. They did this by using the statistic of greatest interest to the market—a 17.8% increase in productivity—as the headline in the report and as the basis for an advertising campaign designed to increase sales of the chair. Steelcase connected a benefit the customer cares about (worker productivity) to the features of the Leap Chair through the report, which combines elements of a scientific research report with elements found in promotional brochures (visual design and graphic content). Notice how the headlines and subheads in the report actually deal with objections commonly found in the sales process. For example, when the report calculates the payback of the cost of the chair at less than ten working days, it diminishes the price of the chair. These rhetorical devices combine to create a readable and effective claim that a high quality ergonomic office chair can increase worker productivity and improve business results. The launch of this chair proved to be one of the most successful in the company's history.

In a year-long study of over 200 participants, people who received the Leap chair and office ergonomics training achieved a 17.8% increase in productivity.

Steelcase

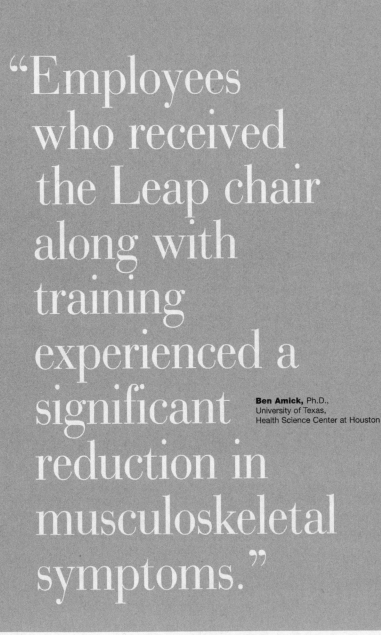

"Employees who received the Leap chair along with training experienced a significant reduction in musculoskeletal symptoms."

Ben Amick, Ph.D.,
University of Texas,
Health Science Center at Houston

As the number of knowledge workers grows worldwide, so does the need to design ergonomic programs that improve the health and productivity of these workers. So what creates a healthy, inspiring office that helps people do their best work—an ergonomic chair, a keyboard support, a window view, good lighting, great tasting coffee?

It's not the coffee.

Objectives

Many studies analyze the effectiveness of ergonomic programs, but since they look at overall changes to the office, they don't readily identify which changes actually led to reduced symptoms and injuries.

Leap® seating technology was designed based on extensive research of the human body and how to support it. The Leap chair had been proven, in biomechanic laboratory tests[1], to provide exceptional fit, movement, and support. The goal of this study was to test the measurable effects of the Leap chair and office ergonomics training on employees' well-being and productivity in a "real world" setting.

The Study Team
Academic and research institutes in the U.S. and Canada participated in conducting the study and analyzing the results, including the University of Texas Health Science Center at Houston, W.E. Upjohn Institute for Employment Research, and other partners.

The research was coordinated by Health and Work Outcomes, an independent health research and consulting company.

The study looked at three things:

• What is the real health benefit of an ergonomic program?

• Can an ergonomic program lead to increased worker productivity?

• How quickly can an increase in productivity yield a return on investment for the company?

"This study was one of the most comprehensive scientific efforts to link an ergonomic product and training to health, employee productivity, and return on investment for a corporation," said Ben Amick, Ph.D., University of Texas, Health Science Center at Houston.

"This study was designed to assess how well a highly adjustable chair and office ergonomics training could affect ergonomic knowledge, postural behavior, health and productivity." – Ben Amick

2

1 Michigan State University, "An Evaluation of Postural Motions, Chair Motions, and Contact in Four Office Chairs" 1999

One year + over 200 participants = one in-depth study.

Study Design

Two companies participated in the study, and hundreds of employees volunteered as test subjects. The results from the first company—tracking 200 knowledge workers for one year—are complete. By the time the entire study is complete, over 450 individuals will have participated.

For the first company, over 200 volunteers were selected from a state agency that collects sales taxes. In order to qualify, each participant had to spend at least six hours a day sitting in their chair, and at least four of those hours working on a computer.

Data was collected in two areas, over a one year period:
(see side-bar for detail)

A. Health Status   B. Productivity

Volunteers were divided into three study groups:

Control group | A group that received ergonomic training | A group that received ergonomic training and the Leap chair

Received office ergonomic training <u>after</u> the study was completed.

Received 90-minute office ergonomic training and learned how to adjust their existing chair.

Received 90-minute office ergonomic training and learned how to adjust their new Leap chair.

A. Health Status Measures

Researchers created a baseline measure (the "before" measure) by collecting data prior to the ergonomic program. After the ergonomic program began, data was collected at two, six, and twelve months. During each data collection period, participants completed short symptom surveys three times a day for one week to rate pain in different parts of the body. They also completed a longer Work Environment and Health Questionnaire to rate overall pain and discomfort.

B. Productivity Measures

One of the most significant aspects of this study was that the productivity data was objective (amount of sales tax collected per worker in the first company), rather than a subjective performance measure. The agency provided data for revenue collected and hours worked for the eleven months prior to the ergonomic program (the "before" measure), and for the twelve months following the ergonomic program.

"The Leap chair-with-training group experienced a significant reduction in symptom growth over the course of the work day, compared to both the training-only group and the control group." — Ben Amick

3

Feeling good makes good business sense.

Study Results*

The Leap chair-with-training group showed significant improvements in both health status and productivity.

Health Status Results

The employees who received a Leap chair and ergonomic training reported significantly lower pain and discomfort in their symptom surveys and in their Work Environment and Health Questionnaires. Their overall musculoskeletal symptoms were lower than the other two groups. But that's not all. Researchers made another interesting finding.

You can normally expect people to feel more discomfort at the end of a day of sitting, compared to how they felt in the morning. For both the control group and the training-only group, the data showed this was certainly true. However, for the people receiving a Leap chair, any discomfort at the end of the day was only a slight increase compared to the morning. So not only were the people who received a Leap chair more comfortable overall, they were comfortable for longer.

Productivity Results

The study results also showed an increase in productivity. After one year, the Leap chair-with-training group achieved a 17.8% increase in productivity. This number reflects the increase in taxes collected per hour worked, which was an average increase of $6,250 collected per month, per employee. "In contrast," reported Kelly DeRango, the researcher who led the productivity portion of the study, "the training-only and the control group did not show any significant increase in productivity."

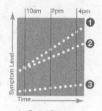

Musculoskeletal Symptom Growth Over Time

1 = Control Group
2 = Training-Only Group
3 = Leap+Training Group

> " The productivity benefits shown by the Leap chair-with-training group were quite large compared with the program's costs. In contrast, the training-only group did not show any statistically significant changes in productivity." – Kelly DeRango

4

* Individual customer results may vary from those shown in this study.

Study Results
continued

Comparing the cost of the Leap chair to the increase in productivity, this study determined that the Leap chair paid for itself in less than ten working days.

The Leap chair's design includes several unique features that can contribute to improved well-being and productivity.

Live Back™
The Leap chair's back changes shape to support the entire spine. This can reduce the chance of lower back sag and a hunched posture, which weakens disc walls, stresses back ligaments and causes deterioration of the spine.

Upper and Lower Back Controls
Upper back force control enables users to set the amount of "push back" that they desire as they recline, regardless of their body size. Lower back firmness control enables users to set a constant amount of firmness to maintain their lower back's natural curve.

Height, Width, and Pivot Arms
Arms telescope, pivot and adjust up and down so users can find a natural position that comfortably supports the wrists, forearms, shoulders and neck.

Natural Glide System™
Seat glides forward so users can recline without leaving their Vision and Reach Zone, so they stay oriented to their work. This encourages more varied postures so there's less static load on the spine.

Seat Edge Angle Control
Enables people to ease pressure on thighs and widen the angle between legs and torso without feeling like they're sliding out of their chair. Plus, shorter people gain nearly two inches of seat height.

Adjustable Seat Depth
People don't fit neatly into three average sizes. Leg and torso lengths can vary independent of a person's overall height. Adjustable seat depth accommodates different body shapes for long-term comfort.

Leap Chair-With-Training Group's Productivity Increase

17.8%

In this study, individuals who received office ergonomic training and sat in Leap chairs increased average productivity by 17.8% after a year.

"Most importantly, the findings of this study suggest that companies may benefit by improving the seating of their office workers in conjunction with a training program in office ergonomic practices," said Kelly DeRango. "Based on the findings of this study, we believe it can make good business sense for companies to provide Leap chairs to their employees." As this study continues, the results from the second company will provide additional data to researchers on the effects of the Leap chair and office ergonomic training.

Resources

Ben Amick, Ph.D., University of Texas, Health Science Center at Houston

Dr. Amick is an internationally recognized leader in building healthy workplaces and developing new outcome-based measures of people's ability to enjoy their life and work. He received his Ph.D. from The Johns Hopkins University in 1986. From 1992 to 1999, Ben served as a research scientist at The Health Institute at Boston's New England Medical Center, world-renowned for its research on health outcomes. He was also a faculty member at both the Harvard School of Public Health and Tufts School of Medicine. Ben has also worked in the private sector as an ergonomics consultant and in management consulting with The Hay Group.

Currently, Ben is an Associate Professor at the University of Texas Health Science Center at Houston, School of Public Health. www.benamick.com

Kelly DeRango, Ph.D., W.E. Upjohn Institute for Employment Research

Dr. DeRango is a research fellow at the W.E. Upjohn Institute for Employment Research. As an economist with the Upjohn Institute, Kelly is responsible for data analysis, instrument design, and program evaluation for projects sponsored by The Department of Labor, The Social Security Administration, and Health and Work Outcomes. He also researches urban labor markets and the effects of racial discrimination on housing and labor markets. Kelly received a Ph.D. in economics from the University of Wisconsin Madison in 2000. He earned an MBA from the University of Michigan in 1992, where he received a Ford Scholarship.

Credits

The University of Texas Health Science Center at Houston
7000 Fannin, Suite 1200
Houston, Texas 77030
Tel: 713.500.4472
www.uth.tmc.edu

W.E. Upjohn Institute for Employment Research
300 South Westnedge Avenue
Kalamazoo, Michigan 49007
Tel. 269.343.5541
Fax: 269.343.3308
www.upjohninst.org

Health and Work Outcomes
47 Rossmore Road
Brunswick, Maine 04011
Tel: 207.729.4929
www.healthandwork.com

References

Amick III, Benjamin C; Robertson, Michelle M; Bazzani, Lianna; Rooney, Ted; Moore, Anne; Harrist, Ron. "Effects of an Office Ergonomic Intervention on Musculoskeletal Symptoms." Published in the December 15, 2003 issue of SPINE Journal.

DeRango, Kelly; Amick III, Benjamin C; Robertson, Michelle M; Rooney, Ted; Moore, Anne; Bazzani, Lianna. "The Productivity Consequences of Two Ergonomic Interventions." Upjohn Institute Staff Working Paper No. WP03-95, May 2003, available at: www.upjohninst.org.

If you would like further information, please call 1.888.783.3522.

Reading Responses

1. What about the Leap Chair report was most appealing to you? Can you imagine using any of its rhetorical strategies in your own writing—even for classes that are not in business? If you think that there are useful strategies but you don't believe you could use them in your writing, explain why you believe that.

2. Compare this research report with one other scientific report in this book (there are examples in Chapters 5, 7, and 9). What features do the two have in common? Do you think that there are any features from the Leap Chair report that might improve the traditional scientific report? What might prevent traditional scientific publications from using those features?

3. What are the parts of the Leap Chair report that are most in harmony with the company business plan, *One Common Purpose?* Do you see the chair fitting into the larger vision for an integrated marketing plan? How?

WRITING ASSIGNMENTS

Assignment 1

The fact that Americans are gaining weight at an unprecedented rate has caught the attention of most food retailers, including those who plan the menus at school cafeterias. Healthier food costs more, in general, than food laden with fat, sugar, and salt, but school dieticians are nevertheless beginning to offer more healthy eating options. Of course, a key issue for school dieticians is figuring out how to make those healthy options appeal to kids!

Your task is to write a marketing plan for improving the nutritional value of the food offered at one of the food venues on your campus. Your instructor might require you to write as if you were going to present your plan to the appropriate university officials, and your instructor may ask you to work in a group for this assignment. First you should analyze the food options available to students on your campus and target one that seems potentially problematic. Then you should do some background research so that you understand the current and prospective customers for this food venue. What features or services do the customers value? What kinds of healthier alternatives would they accept? What factors will affect their choice to purchase and consume healthier food? Using the SWOT method (strengths, weaknesses, opportunities, and threats) that Sarah Steen and her teammates used, organize the results of your analysis, and determine a set of recommendations.

As you begin drafting, think carefully about the audience for your marketing plan—officials at your university. What are their goals? How can your marketing plan help them achieve those goals? What vital information does your marketing plan offer them? Then consider all the rhetorical strategies at your disposal. Which ones will help you communicate clearly, efficiently, and effectively?

Assignment 2

Academic research targets important issues like the rates at which athletes receive injuries (as described in the biology chapter), or the reasons that governments do and do not go to war with each other (as described in the political science chapter). These research reports are complex and often difficult to read; readers must bring a great deal of expertise, background knowledge, and patience to the task. As a result, most people don't regularly read reports like these. But the information that these reports contain can have a positive effect on how trainers prepare their athletes or how politicians negotiate with leaders of other countries.

Your task is to translate the information presented in an academic research report like those mentioned in the preceding paragraph into a form that will appeal to those who can put the information to good use. Begin by asking a professor in your discipline, your major (or possible major), for a few academic reports that contain findings that Americans should be aware of. As you begin drafting, determine the central message you want to convey to your readers—an overarching theme or metaphor that helps your readers understand the importance of the information that you are presenting. Then consider what rhetorical strategies you can use to provide the three key elements of a good marketing plan that Professor Eames describes in his introduction: context, direction, and motivation.

Assignment 3

In marketing, as in many other fields, professionals rely on their presentation skills to communicate effectively and persuasively. Even as new employees, business professionals are expected to be able to create PowerPoint presentations that demonstrate the writer's ability to manage multiple rhetorical tools simultaneously. How do new professionals develop these skills? Like Sarah Steen, they learn the basics as students; throughout their careers, they develop their skills by watching others make presentations and noting what works . . . and what doesn't.

Your task for this assignment is threefold: (1) Search for information on "best practices" for creating business presentations. You may find it easiest to consult a reference librarian to help you do the research you will need to complete for this assignment. (2) Create a presentation that communicates those best practices to marketing students, like Sarah Steen, who are trying to solve real-world problems with marketing solutions. (3) Provide a description of the rhetorical choices that you made, including decisions about the information to present, the skills and needs of your audience, and the rhetorical strategies you used to communicate with your audience.

As you begin drafting, think carefully about the students who will read what you write. What tasks do they face? What information are they likely to know already? What additional information do they need to know? How can you present the information so that it is succinct and yet complete enough that they can use it in their work? How will you capture and keep their attention? How can you use metaphors and other rhetorical strategies to convince students to trust you and to put your recommendations to use?

APPENDIX

CITING SOURCES AND AVOIDING PLAGIARISM

CITING AND DOCUMENTING SOURCES

Definitions

Though the terms *citation* and *documentation* are often used as synonyms, we find it helpful to distinguish them.

- To cite sources means that you identify for readers everything that appears in your writing (ideas, facts, images, whatever) that comes from a source.

- To document sources is to provide readers with the information (the "documentation") that tells readers how and where they can find the source.

- A source, or "reference," is anything you have read, heard, or seen—anything that you did not create on your own.

Realities

It's necessary for you to understand that:

- Citing and documenting sources is expected in academic writing and in most professional writing. If you do not cite and document your sources, you may face harsh penalties.

- Citing and documenting requires following a very detailed set of rules. Following these rules demonstrates: (1) your ability to attend to detail, (2) your trustworthiness, and (3) your ability to be a part of a particular group of readers and writers.

- Different disciplines follow different sets of citation and documentation rules, which are explained in "style guides" (also called "style manuals"). There are over two hundred style guides that control documentation formats in academic disciplines, but only a handful of different guides are very widely used. Additionally, most large companies have a "house style" guide to ensure consistency across company documents. Therefore, the styles that you see in what you read may not conform exactly to any of the popular style guides.

- Style manuals and house style guides are updated regularly, particularly for citing and documenting digital media and online documents. In short, you must follow the rules, the rules differ from one discipline to another, and the rules are always changing.

To work efficiently, you need to be thinking about citation and documentation at the very beginning of your research project. As soon as you receive an assignment, find out what style guide the professor in your course expects you to use, and consult that style guide before you start taking notes on your research *and* while you are writing. You don't want to have to go back and search for information you forgot to write down when you had your source in hand or on your computer screen. Even if you use a computer-based "citation generator," you must feed in the correct information to get a correct citation. Pearson (the publisher of this textbook) offers guides to documentation on its MyCompLab Web site (http://www.mycomplab.com). The prominent style guides— CMS, APA, MLA, CSE (see the descriptions that follow)—also maintain their own Web sites, and you can find dozens of other sources that offer more and less detailed summaries of the main style guides.

Common Parts

Despite the very complex rules and differences among style guides, all citation and documentation styles contain two parts:

1. In-text citations. Whenever you include material from a source, you must—at that point in your text—identify (cite) the source. Cite all material that you reference, summarize, paraphrase, quote, or include. When, you use a quotation in the middle of a paragraph, for example, you must use some method to cite the source of the quote at that point rather than at the end of the paragraph. Each style manual has a system for in-text citations. Use the particular system for the style manual that you are following.

2. Documentation of sources. Somewhere in your document you must supply all the information that a reader would need to easily find the source you cited. Authors include this information in a variety of ways, depending on the style manual that

they are following: footnotes, a list of endnotes, a bibliography (a list of all important sources on the topic), or a works cited list (a list of the sources that you used in your writing). The information that authors typically provide includes items such as the author's name, title of source, date of publication, page numbers, journal name/publisher, and Web address.

Popular Style Guides

Check to ensure that you are using the most up-to-date version of the style guide that you are following. Here is a brief description of the most commonly used style guides:

CMS. *Chicago Manual of Style* is the granddaddy of style guides, having first appeared in 1906. It is used by more disciplines than other manuals, offering guidelines for writing in both the sciences and humanities. You are most likely to use the CMS for classes in philosophy, history, and religion, but it's not uncommon in many other social science and humanities courses.

APA. *Publication Manual of the American Psychological Association.* The APA guide has grown dramatically in its influence over the past few decades (and has similarly increased in length). It is almost certainly the guide you will use in your social science courses, but you may also use it for courses in disciplines such as nursing, physical therapy, or education.

MLA (Modern Language Association). *MLA Style Manual and Guide to Scholarly Publishing.* The MLA guide has, for several decades, been *the* style manual used in English and foreign language studies. It may well have been the style guide you were taught in your writing classes because it is what most English teachers know best.

CSE (Council of Science Editors). *Scientific Style and Format: The CSE Manual for Authors, Editors, and Publishers.* Until 2000 the CSE was called the Council of Biology Editors, and many composition textbooks still describe the "CBE" style. The change in name reflects an attempt to influence the natural sciences, which have had a history of being resistant to a single style guide. In fact, your teachers in the natural sciences may never mention the CSE style guide, but in science writing you will probably use one of the options explained in the CSE guide. On the other hand, because one option in the CSE (CSE allows three different citation-documentation methods) is very similar to APA style, some science teachers will allow you to use the more readily available APA style manual.

Most of these guides offer more than one option for citation and documentation style, and the options from one guide can be very similar to those from another guide, so it's not always easy to identify what guide a published paper has used.

Basic Types of Citation and Documentation Styles

Both citation styles and documentation styles appear in three most common forms. (Notes: 1. Sources *cited* in the upper row of examples are *documented* in the lower row. 2. The examples are taken form readings in this book, but the formats are sometimes changed from what appears in the text to match current versions of style guides. 3. The single example of each basic type of documentation shows you the variety among the different guides; it does not show you the dozens of different models for documenting books, journal articles, Web sites, broadcast speeches, etc.)

In-Text Citations	Type 1. *Numbers,* in superscript (called "notes" in CMS, or the "citation sequence" method in CSE). The numbered citations in the text match the numbers of the references list at the end of a document.	Type 2. *Author and date,* in parentheses (the "author-date" or "name-year" method, described in APA, CMS, and CSE)	Type 3. *Author and page number,* in parentheses (MLA style)
Examples	Israeli Palestinians are moving along in a gradual process of development and normalization in Israeli society.[6]	This literature documents paternalistic staff stoicism (Edwards, 1989).	That this is the case is an accident of history (Hirsch 106).
Documentation of References	Type 1. *A numbered list of references and comments,* corresponding to the sequence of numbered citations in the text (called a "References" list in CMS and CSE; "Notes" or "Bibliography" in CMS)	Type 2. *Alphabetized list of authors' names* (called a "References" list in APA style; also used in CMS and CSE)	Type 3. *Alphabetized list of authors' names,* (called "Works Cited" in MLA)
Examples	**Notes** 6. As'ad Ghanem. *The Palestinian-Arab Minority in Israel, 1948-2000.* (Albany, NY: State University of New York Press, 2001), 5–7.	**References** Edwards, R. B. (1989). Pain management and the values of health care providers. In C. S. Hill Jr. & W. S. Fields (Eds.), *Advances in pain research and therapy, 11,* 101–112. New York: Raven.	**Works Cited** Hirsch, E.D., Jr. *Cultural Literacy: What Every American Needs to Know.* Boston: Houghton Mifflin, 1987. Print.

AVOIDING PLAGIARISM

When we first think about plagiarism, we think of the obvious cases of theft: the politician who presents someone else's speech as if it were an original, or the student who buys a paper from an online "paper mill." Offering someone else's work as one's own is both foolish and immoral. If you plagiarize in that intentional, obvious way, you know what you are doing, and you will live with the risks and consequences.

But we focus your attention on those times when you may be unsure about whether you should provide a citation and documentation—the situations in which you might plagiarize unintentionally.

Try a thought experiment (a portable rhetorical lessoned practiced by philosophers and physicists). Imagine that you must stand on a stage and read aloud every paper that you write, and sitting next to you on the stage are the authors of every book, article, Web site, TV program, etc. that you have encountered in your research. And each of those authors has a perfect memory. When you start reading your paper, you quote a phrase from one of your sources, but you don't cite the source, so the author raises her hand and says, "That was my phrase that you just quoted." And the audience knows that you are have just plagiarized, cheated.

You continue, now facing a suspicious audience. You summarize some ideas from an author without giving him credit; he raises his hand and scolds you. You show a PowerPoint slide with a chart that summarizes some main ideas on your topic—all general knowledge, but you took the organization of the chart from another source that you read; you do not cite that source, and the author points out your plagiarism. Every time you present words, ideas, patterns of thought, and so on that you have found in someone else's work, without citing that person, the author speaks up and exposes you.

Computer technology gives your teachers something like the perfect memory of the authors in the thought experiment. While some teachers have access to plagiarism-detection software, even a simple Google search can expose your borrowing, whether or not you intended to borrow.

The purpose of our thought experiment is not to frighten you, but rather to show you the rhetorical effectiveness of thorough citation. Imagine that when you *do* cite the authors in your audience, you draw them into a partnership of ideas; you present yourself as a member of their learning community, and you create trust among yourself, your teacher, and the rest of the audience.

In that sense plagiarism is a failure to join in a conversation of readers and writers, a failure to take your place in the ongoing learning of a culture. Understanding that context may help you to understand why your teachers, people who have dedicated their lives to learning, so detest plagiarism.

CREDITS

Alexander, Martin, from "Aging, Bioavailability, and Overestimation of Risk from Environmental Pollutants" by Martin Alexander in *Environmental Science and Technology*, 2000, 34(20): 4259–62, 4264–65. Reprinted with permission of the American Chemical Society.

Bellah, Robert, "Civil Religion in America" from *Daedalus*, 96:1, Winter 1967, pp. 1–21. Copyright © 1967 by the American Academy of Arts and Sciences. Used by permission of MIT Press.

Burke, Daniel and Kevin Eckstrom, "Obama Refashions America's Old-Time (Civil) Religion" by Daniel Burke and Kevin Eckstrom, from Religion News Service, January 20, 2009. Copyright © 2010 Religion News Service. Used by permission.

Carson, Rachel, excerpt from "Realms of the Soil" from *Silent Spring* by Rachel Carson. Copyright © 1962 by Rachel L. Carson, renewed 1990 by Roger Christie. Reprinted by permission of Houghton Mifflin Harcourt Company. All rights reserved.

Conway, Gordon and Gary Toenniessen, "Feeding the world in the twenty-first century" by Gordon Conway and Gary Toenniessen from *Nature*, December 2, 1999, supplement to Vol. 402, Issue 6761, pp. C55–C58. Reprinted by permission of Macmillan Publishing Ltd.

Coontz, Stephanie, "Till Children Do Us Part" by Stephanie Coontz from *The New York Times,* © February 5, 2005 The New York Times. All rights reserved. Used by permission and protected by the Copyright Laws of the United States. The printing, copying, redistribution, or retransmission of the Material without express written permission is prohibited.

Edin, Kathryn and Maria Kefalas from "Unmarried with Children" by Kathryn Edin and Maria Kefalas from *Contexts: Understanding People in Their Social Worlds,* 2005, 4(2): 16–22. Reprinted by permission of University of California Press.

Gabbett, Tim J., from "Influence of training and match intensity on injuries in rugby league" by Tim J. Gabbett from *Journal of Sports Science,* 2004, 22: 409–17. Reprinted by permission of Taylor and Francis Group.

Garland-Thomson, Rosemarie, from "The Politics of Staring" by Rosemarie Garland-Thomson in *Disability Studies: Enabling the Humanities,* Sharon L. Snyder, Brenda Jo Brueggemann, and Rosemarie Garland-Thomson, eds. 2002, Modern Language Association. Reprinted by permission of the Modern Language Association.

Gee, James Paul, from *What Video Games Have to Teach Us about Learning and Literacy, Second Edition,* by James Paul Gee. Copyright © 2007 Palgrave Macmillan. Reproduced with permission of Palgrave Macmillan.

Hagy, Jessica, Two sketches from blog on www.thisisindexed.com Used by permission of Jessica Hagy.

Holloway, Marguerite, reprinted with permission from "The Female Hurt" by Marguerite Holloway in *Scientific American* 11 (3), May 2000. Copyright © 2000 Scientific American, a division of Nature America, Inc. All rights reserved.

Jolliffe, David A. and Allison Harl, from "Studying the 'Reading Transition' from High School to College: What Are Our Students Reading and Why" by David A. Jolliffe and Allison Harl in "College English," Vol. 70, No. 6, July 2008. Copyright © 2008 by the National Council of Teachers of English. Reprinted with permission.

Layne, Christopher, "Kant or Cant: The Myth of Democratic Peace" from *International Security,* 19:2, Fall 1994, pp. 5–49. Copyright © 1994 by the President and Fellows of Harvard College and the Massachusetts Institute of Technology. Used by permission of MIT Press.

Manini, Todd M. and Brian C. Clark "Blood Flow Restricted Exercise and Skeletal Muscle Health" by Todd M. Manini and Brian C. Clark from "Exercise and Sport Sciences Reviews," 2009, Vol. 37, No. 2, pp. 78, 79, 85. Used by permission of Wolters Kluwer.

Michaelson, Jay, "Is the Pledge Merely Ceremonial Deism?" by Jay Michaelson from Prawfsblawg.blogs.com, February 20, 2008. Reprinted by permission of the author.

Mueller, Dr. Frederick O. Table 7: High School Female Direct Catastrophic Injuries; Graph: HS Female Deaths; Graph: HS Female Disability; and Graph: HS Female Serious. Used by permission of Dr. Frederick O. Mueller.

National Council of Teachers of English, "Of Color, Classes, and Classrooms" from *Bookstraps: From an American Academic of Color.* Copyright © 1993 by the National Council of Teachers of English. Reprinted with permission.

National Federation of State High School Associations Participation Study, "Participation in High School Sports" from the National Federation of State High School Associations Participation Study. Copyright NFHS 2010. Used by permission.

Photo Credits

INDEX